FUNDAMENTALS of MANAGEMENT

FUNDAMENTALS of MANAGEMENT

Core Concepts and Applications

Ricky W. Griffin
Texas A & M University

HOUGHTON MIFFLIN COMPANY
Boston New York

For my sisters, Donna and Cathy

Sponsoring Editor: Jennifer B. Speer
Senior Associate Editor: Susan M. Kahn
Project Editor: Elizabeth Gale Napolitano
Senior Production/Design Coordinator: Carol Merrigan
Editorial Assistants: Tami Forman, Joy Park
Senior Manufacturing Coordinator: Marie Barnes
Marketing Manager: Michael B. Mercier

Cover Design: Len Massiglia
Cover Image: Al Held, PUTU, 1989, Crown Point Press

Part Opener Photo Credits: Part I: Jonathan Blair/National Geographic; inset photo: Michael Newman/Photo Edit; Part II: Will & Deni McIntyre/Tony Stone Images; inset photo: Walter Hodges/Tony Stone Images; Part III: Marc Romanelli/The Image Bank; inset photo: Bob Daemmrich/Stock, Boston, Inc.; Part IV: Lee E. Day/Black Star; inset photo: Terry Husebye; Part V: Wayne Eastep/Tony Stone Images; inset photo: Charles Gupton/Tony Stone Images.

Photo Credits: Chapter 1: p. 10: Susan Van Etten; p. 20: Portnoy/Black Star; Chapter 2: p. 38: Doris DeWitt/Tony Stone Images; p. 39: Courtesy of Lockheed Martin; p. 43: NBA Photos; p. 47 (left): © 1994 David Reed, *Material World,* Godalming, England, Hodson Family; p. 47 (right): © 1994 Louis Psihoyos, *Material World,* Burrel, Albania, Cakoni Family; (credits continued on page 453)

Printed in the U. S. A.

Library of Congress Catalog Card Number: 96-76906

Student Edition ISBN: 0-395-80066-8

Examination Copy ISBN: 0-395-84382-0

123456789-VH-00-99-98-97

BRIEF CONTENTS

CONTENTS

Chapter 2 The Environment of Management

PART III ORGANIZING 141

Chapter 8 Managing Human Resources 198

PART IV LEADING 228

PART V CONTROLLING 364

Chapter 14 Managing the Control Process 366

Chapter 15 Managing for Total Quality 392

PREFACE

CURRENT TRENDS CALLING FOR A NEW FUNDAMENTALS TEXT

Over the last four decades, literally hundreds of books have been written for basic management courses. As the body of material comprising the theory, research, and practice of management has grown and expanded, textbook authors have continued to mirror this expansion of material in their books. Writers have felt that it is important to continue to add new material pertinent to traditional topics, like planning and organizing, while simultaneously adding coverage of new and emerging topics, such as diversity and total quality management. As a by-product of this trend, our textbooks have grown longer and longer, making it difficult to cover all the material in one course.

Another emerging trend in management education is a new focus on teaching in a broader context. That is, increasingly the principles of management course is being taught with less emphasis on theory alone and more on application of concepts. Teaching how to successfully apply management concepts often involves focusing more on skills development and the human side of the organization. This trend requires that textbooks cover theoretical concepts within a flexible framework that allows instructors to make use of interactive tools such as case studies, exercises, and projects.

This text represents a synthesis of these trends toward a more manageable and practical approach. By combining concise text discussion, standard pedagogical tools, lively and current content, an emphasis on organizational behavior coverage, and exciting skills development materials, *Fundamentals of Management* provides what I think is the answer to the call for a new approach to management education. This book provides almost infinite flexibility, a solid foundation of knowledge-based material, and an action-oriented learning dimension that is unique in the field.

ORGANIZATION OF THE BOOK

Most management instructors today like to organize their course around the traditional management functions of planning, organizing, leading, and controlling. *Fundamentals of Management* uses these functions as its organizing framework. The book consists of five parts, with fifteen chapters and two appendices.

Part I provides an introduction to management consisting of two chapters. Chapter 1 provides a basic overview of the management process in organizations, while Chapter 2 introduces students to the environment of management.

Part II covers the first basic management function, planning. In Chapter 3, we introduce the fundamental concepts of planning and discuss strategic management. Managerial decision making is the topic of Chapter 4. Finally, in Chapter 5 we cover entrepreneurship and the management of new ventures.

The second basic management function, organizing, is the subject of Part III. In Chapter 6 the fundamental concepts of organization structure and design are introduced and discussed. Chapter 7 discusses organization change and innovation. Chapter 8 is devoted to human resource management.

Many instructors and managers believe that the third basic management function, leading, is especially important in contemporary organizations. Thus, in Part IV we devote five full chapters to this management function. Basic concepts and processes associated with individual behavior are introduced and discussed in Chapter 9. Employee motivation is the subject of Chapter 10. Chapter 11 discusses leadership and influence processes in organizations. Communication in organizations is the topic of Chapter 12. Finally, the management of groups and teams is covered in Chapter 13.

The fourth management function, controlling, is the subject of Part V. Chapter 14 introduces the fundamental concepts and issues associated with the management of the control process. A special area of control today, managing for total quality, is discussed in Chapter 15.

Finally, two appendices provide coverage of managerial careers and important tools for planning and management.

SKILLS-FOCUSED PEDAGOGICAL FEATURES

With this text I have been able to address new dimensions of management education without creating a text that is unwieldy in length. Specifically, each chapter in this book is followed by a new and exciting set of features organized into a ***Skills Development Portfolio***. The resources in this Portfolio were created to bring an active and behavioral orientation to management education by requiring students to solve problems, make decisions, respond to situations, and work in groups. In short, these materials simulate many of the day-to-day challenges and opportunities faced by real managers.

Each Portfolio contains two different *Building Management Skills* exercises organized around the set of basic management skills introduced in Chapter 1 of the text. Another feature in the Portfolio is entitled *You Make the Call*. This feature follows a real company and its managers through a series of situations corresponding to chapter content (the names in this feature have been altered to protect the identity of the actual business and managers that are described). Each Portfolio also includes a *Skills Self-Assessment Instrument* that helps readers learn something about their own approach to management. Finally, an *Experiential Exercise* in each portfolio provides additional action-oriented learning opportunities, usually in a group setting.

In addition to the Skills Development Portfolio, every chapter includes important standard pedagogy: learning objective, chapter outline, opening incident, boldface key terms, summary of key points, questions for review, questions for analysis, and an end-of-chapter case with questions.

A COMPLETE AND EFFECTIVE TEACHING PACKAGE

In addition to the text itself, instructors have available to them an array of support materials that will facilitate instruction and education.

- *Instructor's Resource Manual* (David D. Van Fleet, Arizona State University West, Ella W. Van Fleet, Professional Business Associates). This resource includes suggested class schedules, detailed teaching notes for each chapter of the text, and video guide teaching notes. The teaching notes for each chapter include: chapter summary; learning objectives; detailed chapter lecture outline, including opening incident summary, highlighted key terms, teaching tips, group exercise ideas, discussion starters, and references to the transparencies; responses to review, analysis, and case questions; and information to help facilitate the materials in the *Skills Development Portfolio*.

- *Test Bank* (David D. Van Fleet, Arizona State University West, Ella W. Van Fleet, Professional Business Associates). With over 2,000 test items, the Test Bank includes true/false, multiple-choice, completion, matching, and essay questions. Each question is identified by learning objective, page references, and question type (knowledge, understanding, or application).

- *Computerized Test Bank* (Windows). This electronic version of the printed Test Bank allows instructors to edit, add, and select questions or to generate randomly selected tests.

- *Transparencies*. Approximately 80 full-color transparencies illustrate major topics in the text. Two types of transparencies are included: highlights of key figures from the text, and additional images that can be used to enhance lecture presentation.

- *PowerPoint Slides*. These visually appealing and engaging slides, developed by the author, illustrate text content with outlines, charts, exhibits, and artwork, and they allow instructors to lecture directly from the slides. Where PowerPoint software is available, instructors can edit the slide program to include their own illustrations or notes, and they can print out the slides to use as class handouts.

- *Videos*. A professionally developed video program corresponds to each of the five parts of the text. The Video Guide provides suggested uses, teaching objectives, an overview, issues for discussion, and a skills perspective section for each segment.

ACKNOWLEDGMENTS

I would like to acknowledge the many contributions that others have made to this book. My faculty colleagues at Texas A&M University and my secretary, Phyllis Washburn, have contributed enormously to both this book and to my thinking about management education. At Houghton Mifflin, an outstanding team of professionals including Jennifer Speer, Susan Kahn, Mike Mercier, Tony Grima, and Liz Napolitano have also made more contributions to this book than I could even begin to list. A special thanks is also due the many reviewers who helped shape the content and form of the material in this book. While any and all errors are of course my own responsibility, thanks to Patricia Gaudette (Pine Manor College), Andrew Hoh (Creighton University), Mary Jane Saxton (University of Colorado at Denver), Pamela Smith (SUNY College of Agriculture & Technology—Morrisville), Steven Sommer (University of Nebraska), and Nancy E. Stetson (College of Marin), for their help. My wife, Glenda, and our children, Dustin and Ashley, are, of course, due the greatest thanks. Their love, care, interest, and enthusiasm help sustain me in all that I do.

I would like to invite your feedback on this book. If you have any questions, suggestions, or issues to discuss, please feel free to contact me. The most efficient way to reach me is through e-mail. My address is GRIFFIN@TAMVM1.TAMU.EDU.

R. W. G.

FUNDAMENTALS of MANAGEMENT

What could the people in these two images possibly have in common? The Pakistani women are sorting apricots for shipment to customers in foreign markets, and the people in aprons are discussing how to improve customer service at The Home Depot. In short, each group is involved in managing a business enterprise through effective customer service.

PART

I

An Introduction to Management

CHAPTER

Understanding the Manager's Job

OBJECTIVES

After studying this chapter, you should be able to:

- *Define management, describe the kinds of managers found in organizations, and identify and briefly explain the four basic management functions.*
- *Justify the importance of history and theory to management and explain the evolution of management thought.*
- *Discuss contemporary management issues and challenges.*

OUTLINE

An Introduction to Management
- Kinds of Managers
- Basic Management Functions
- Fundamental Managerial Skills
- The Science and the Art of Management

The Evolution of Management
- The Importance of Theory and History
- The Historical Context of Management
- The Classical Management Perspective
- The Behavioral Management Perspective
- The Quantitative Management Perspective

Contemporary Management Theory
- The Systems Perspective
- The Contingency Perspective
- Emerging Contemporary Management Challenges

ONE OF THE most widely read business publications in the world, *Fortune* magazine, recently suggested that Herbert Kelleher may be the best CEO in the United States. Kelleher runs Southwest Airlines Co., the only major U.S. airline to remain consistently profitable. Indeed, the U.S. Department of Transportation recently concluded that Southwest has become the dominant carrier in the nation's busiest air travel markets and is the primary force behind change throughout the entire industry. Kelleher himself launched the airline in 1971, in Dallas.

"I feel that you have to be with your employees through all their difficulties, that you have to be interested in them personally. They may be disappointed in their country. Even their family might not be working out the way they wish it would. But I want them to know that Southwest will always be there for them."

Today the company has annual revenues approaching $2 billion, little debt, and steadily growing profits. Southwest has 199 aircraft serving 46 cities in 21 states and has prospered by offering low fares and flying only short routes. Southwest offers 83 flights between Dallas and Houston every business day, some with fares as low as $39. No flight is longer than two hours, and many are less than one hour.

An important part of Southwest's success is its ability to control costs. Southwest flies no international routes, serves no meals on any of its flights, subscribes to no computerized reservation systems, and refuses to transfer passenger baggage to other airlines. Because Southwest flies only Boeing 737s, maintenance and training procedures are much simpler (and cheaper) than at other companies. Because of its low fares, Southwest cannot afford to let its planes sit idle or to spend money on frills. Many airlines take an hour to clean and reboard between flights—Southwest can generally do it in less than twenty minutes.

In an industry long plagued by labor problems, Kelleher is affectionately known by his employees as "Uncle Herbie." One of Kelleher's policies is that no employee will be laid off, even when times get tough. His concern and commitment to his employees have been repaid many times over. For example, as fuel prices increased during the Persian Gulf crisis, more than one-third of Southwest's employees took voluntary pay cuts to help the airline buy fuel. Wages at Southwest are only about industry average, but employees quickly become immersed in the Southwest culture, and most seem willing to put extra time, effort, and energy into their jobs.[1] ●

Source of Quotation: Herb Kelleher, quoted in *Fortune*, May 2, 1994, p. 50.

This book is about managers, like Herb Kelleher, and the work they do. In Chapter 1, we introduce the nature of management, its dimensions, and its challenges. We explain the concepts of management and managers, discuss the management process, and summarize the origins of contemporary management thought. We conclude by introducing critical contemporary challenges and issues.

AN INTRODUCTION TO MANAGEMENT

• **management**
A set of functions directed at the efficient and effective utilization of resources in the pursuit of organizational goals

• **efficient**
Using resources wisely and in a cost-effective manner

• **effective**
Making the right decisions and successfully implementing them

Management is a set of functions directed at the efficient and effective utilization of resources in the pursuit of organizational goals. By **efficient**, we mean using resources wisely and in a cost-effective manner. By **effective**, we mean making the right decisions and successfully implementing them. In general, successful organizations are both efficient and effective.[2]

Today's managers face a variety of interesting and challenging situations. The average executive works 60 hours a week, has enormous demands placed on his or her time, and faces increased complexities posed by globalization, domestic competition, government regulation, and shareholder pressure.[3] The task is further complicated by rapid change, unexpected disruptions, and both minor and major crises. The manager's job is unpredictable and fraught with challenges, but it is also filled with opportunities to make a difference.

Kinds of Managers

There are many different kinds of managers. Figure 1.1 indicates how managers within an organization can be differentiated by level and area.

• **top managers**
Make up the relatively small group of executives who manage the overall organization

Levels of Management One way to differentiate among managers is by their level in the organization. **Top managers** make up the relatively small group of executives who manage the overall organization. Titles found in this group include president, vice president, and chief executive officer (CEO). Thus, Herb Kelleher is a top manager. An organization's top managers establish its goals, overall strategy, and operating policies. They also officially represent the organization to the external environment by meeting with government officials, executives of other organizations, and so forth. Top managers make decisions about such activities as acquiring other companies, investing in research and development, entering or abandoning various markets, and building new plants and office facilities.[4]

• **middle managers**
Primarily responsible for implementing the policies and plans developed by top management and for supervising and coordinating the activities of lower-level managers

Middle managers comprise the largest group of managers in most organizations. Common middle-management titles include plant manager, operations manager, and division head. Libby Sartain, Southwest Airlines' Director of Employee Benefits and Compensation, is a middle manager. **Middle managers** are primarily responsible for implementing the policies and plans developed by top management and for supervising and coordinating the activities of lower-level managers.[5] Plant managers, for example, handle inventory management, quality control, equipment failures, and minor union problems. They also coordinate the work of supervisors within the plant.

FIGURE 1.1 Kinds of Managers by Level and Area

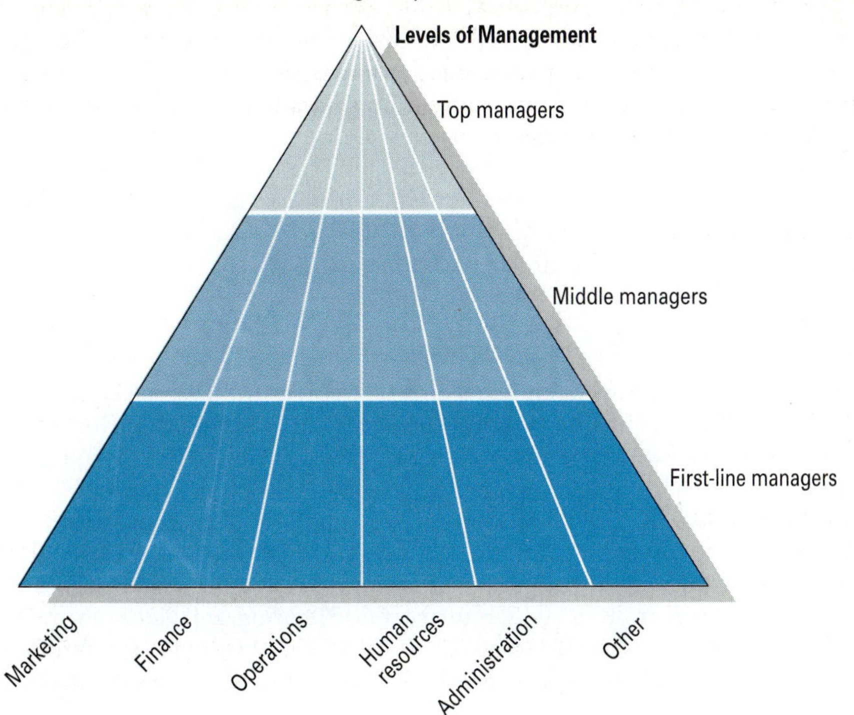

Organizations generally have three levels of management, represented by top managers, middle managers, and first-line managers. Regardless of level, managers are also usually associated with a specific area within the organization, such as marketing, finance, operations, human resources, administration, or some other area.

First-line managers supervise and coordinate the activities of operating employees. Common titles for first-line managers are foreman, supervisor, and office manager. Debbie Henderson, a flight services manager for Southwest Airlines, is a first-line manager. She flies several trips a day, handles preflight instructions, oversees the flight attendants on each flight, and deals with any passenger complaints that may arise on one of her flights. These positions are often the first ones held by employees who enter management from the ranks of operating personnel. In contrast to top and middle managers, first-line managers typically spend a large proportion of their time supervising the work of subordinates.[6]

- **first-line managers** Supervise and coordinate the activities of operating employees

Areas of Management Regardless of their level, managers may work in various areas within an organization. *Marketing managers* work in areas related to the marketing function—getting consumers and clients to buy the organization's products or services (be they Ford automobiles, *Newsweek* magazines, Associated Press news reports, or flights on Southwest Airlines). These areas include new product development, promotion, and distribution. *Financial managers* deal primarily with an organization's financial resources. They are responsible for activities such as accounting, cash management, and investments.

Operations managers are concerned with creating and managing the systems that create an organization's products and services. Typical responsibilities of operations managers include production control, inventory control, quality control, plant layout, and site selection. *Human resource managers* are responsible for hiring and developing employees. They are typically involved in human resource planning, recruiting and selecting employees, training and development, designing compensation and benefit systems, formulating performance appraisal systems, and discharging low-performing and problem employees. *General managers* are not associated with any particular management specialty. Probably the best example of a general management position is that of a hospital or clinic administrator. General managers tend to have some basic familiarity with all functional areas of management rather than specialized training in any one area.

Basic Management Functions

Regardless of level or area, management involves the four basic functions of planning and decision making, organizing, leading, and controlling. This book is organized around these basic functions, as illustrated in Figure 1.2.

- **planning**
Setting an organization's goals and deciding how best to achieve them

- **decision making**
Part of the planning process that involves selecting a course of action from a set of alternatives

Planning and Decision Making In its simplest form, **planning** means setting an organization's goals and deciding how best to achieve them. **Decision making**, a part of the planning process, involves selecting a course of action from a set of alternatives. Planning and decision making help maintain managerial effectiveness by serving as guides for future activities. Part II of this book is devoted to planning and decision making.

Management involves four basic activities—planning and decision making, organizing, leading, and controlling. Most managers engage in more than one activity at the same time.

FIGURE 1.2 The Management Process

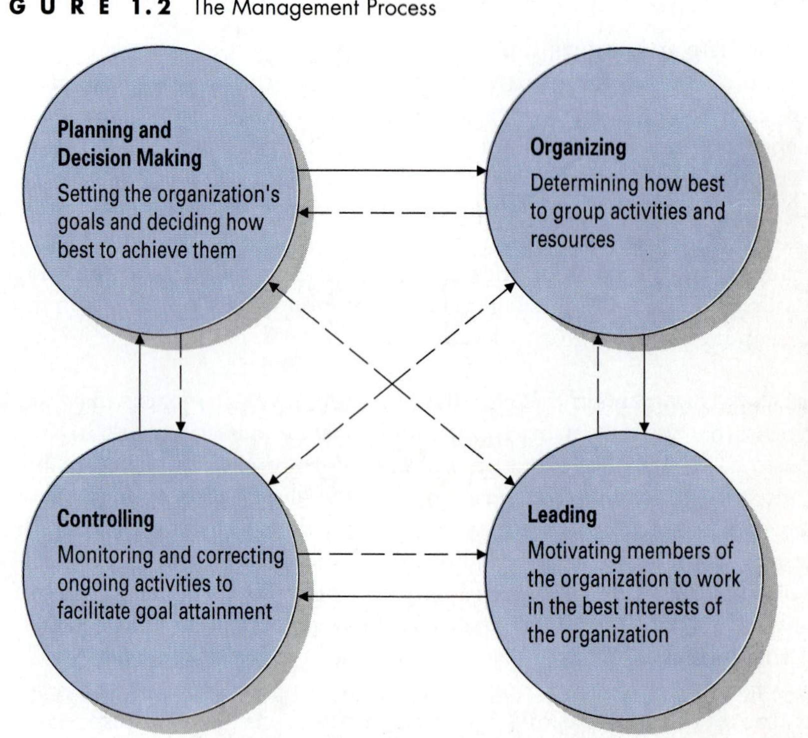

Organizing Once a manager has set goals and developed a workable plan, the next management function is to organize people and groups to carry out the plan. Specifically, **organizing** involves determining how activities and resources are to be grouped. While some people equate this function with the creation of an organization chart, we will see in Part III of this book it is actually much more.

- **organizing**
Grouping activities and resources in a logical fashion

Leading The third basic managerial function is leading. Some people consider leading to be both the most important and the most challenging of all managerial activities. **Leading** is the set of processes used to get people to work together to advance the interests of the organization. For example, most experts credit Herb Kelleher's leadership abilities as perhaps the key ingredient to his success at Southwest. We cover the leading function in detail in Part IV.

- **leading**
The set of processes used to get members of the organization to work together to further the interests of the organization

Controlling The final phase of the management process is **controlling**, or monitoring the organization's progress toward its goals. As the organization moves toward its goals, managers must monitor progress to insure that the organization is performing in such a way as to arrive at its "destination" at the appointed time. Part V of the book is devoted to controlling.

- **controlling**
Monitoring organizational progress toward goal attainment

Fundamental Managerial Skills

To carry out these management functions properly, managers rely on a number of specific skills. The most important managerial skills include technical, interpersonal, conceptual, diagnostic, communication, decision-making, and time-management skills.[7]

Technical Skills **Technical skills** are the skills necessary to accomplish or understand the specific kind of work being done in an organization. For example, David Packard and Bill Hewlett understand the inner workings of their company, Hewlett-Packard Co., because they were trained as engineers. Project engineers, physicians, and accountants all have the technical skills necessary for their respective professions. Technical skills are especially important for first-line managers. These managers spend much of their time training subordinates and answering questions about work-related problems. They must know how to perform the tasks assigned to those they supervise if they are to be effective managers.

- **technical skills**
Necessary to accomplish or understand tasks relevant to the organization

Interpersonal Skills Managers spend considerable time interacting with people both inside and outside the organization. For obvious reasons, then, the manager also needs **interpersonal skills**—the ability to understand and motivate individuals and groups. As a manager climbs the organizational ladder, she must be able to get along with subordinates, peers, and those at higher levels of the organization. Because of the multitude of roles a manager must fulfill, she must also be able to work with suppliers, customers, investors, and others outside of the organization. One reason for Herb Kelleher's success at Southwest Airlines is his ability to motivate his employees and to inspire their loyalty and devotion to his vision for the firm.

- **interpersonal skills**
The ability to understand and motivate both individuals and groups

- **conceptual skills** The manager's ability to think in the abstract

Conceptual Skills **Conceptual skills** depend on the manager's ability to think in the abstract. Managers need the mental capacity to understand the overall workings of the organization and its environment, to grasp how all the parts of the organization fit together, and to view the organization in a holistic manner. This allows them to think strategically, to see the "big picture," and to make broad-based decisions that serve the overall organization.

- **diagnostic skills** A manager's ability to visualize the most appropriate response to a situation

Diagnostic Skills Successful managers also possess **diagnostic skills**, or skills that enable a manager to visualize the most appropriate response to a situation. A physician diagnoses a patient's illness by analyzing symptoms and determining their probable cause. Similarly, a manager can diagnose and analyze a problem in the organization by studying its symptoms and then developing a solution.

- **communication skills** A manager's abilities both to effectively convey ideas and information to others and to effectively receive ideas and information from others

Communication Skills **Communication skills** refer to the manager's abilities both to effectively convey ideas and information to others and to effectively receive ideas and information from others. These skills enable a manager to convey ideas to subordinates whereby they know what is expected of them, to coordinate work with peers and colleagues so that they work well together, and to keep higher-level managers informed about what is happening. In addition, communication skills help the manager listen to what others say and understand the real meaning behind letters, reports, and other written communication.

- **decision-making skills** A manager's ability to recognize and define problems and opportunities and to select an appropriate course of action for each

Decision-Making Skills Successful managers also possess strong decision-making skills. **Decision-making skills** include the manager's ability to correctly recognize and define problems and opportunities and to then select an appropriate course of action to solve problems and capitalize on opportunities. Decision-making skills play a critical role in virtually every phase of a manager's work. We explore decision making in more detail in Chapter 4.

- **time-management skills** A manager's ability to prioritize work, to work efficiently, and to delegate appropriately

Time-Management Skills Finally, effective managers have good time-management skills. **Time-management skills** refer to the manager's ability to prioritize work, to work efficiently, and to delegate appropriately. As already noted, managers face many different pressures and challenges. It is too easy for a manager to get bogged down doing work that can easily be postponed or delegated to others. When this happens, unfortunately, more pressing and higher-priority work may get neglected.

The Science and the Art of Management

Given the myriad skills and complexity inherent in the manager's job, a reasonable question relates to whether management is a science, or if it is more of an art. In fact, effective management is a blend of both science and art. Successful executives recognize the importance of combining both the science and the art of management as they practice their craft.[8]

The Science of Management Many management problems and issues can be approached in ways that are rational, logical, objective, and systematic.

Managers can gather data, facts, and objective information. They can use quantitative models and decision-making techniques to arrive at "correct" decisions. And they need to take such a systematic approach to solving problems whenever possible, especially when they are dealing with relatively routine and straightforward issues. Whenever Southwest Airlines considers entering a new market, its managers look closely at current air traffic in that market, existing competitors and fare structures, and other objective details as they formulate their plans. Technical, diagnostic, and time-management skills are especially important when practicing the science of management.

The Art of Management Even though they may try to be scientific as much as possible, managers must often make decisions and solve problems on the basis of intuition, experience, instinct, and personal insights. Relying heavily on conceptual, interpersonal, and communication skills, for example, a manager may have to decide between multiple courses of action that look equally attractive. Solving unusual and nonroutine problems almost certainly requires an element of intuition and personal insight.

THE EVOLUTION OF MANAGEMENT

Most managers today recognize the importance of history. Knowing the origins of their organization and the kinds of practices that have led to success—or caused failures—can be an indispensable tool to managing the contemporary organization. Thus, in the next section we trace the history of management thought. We then move forward to the present day by introducing contemporary management issues and challenges.

The Importance of Theory and History

Some people question the value of history and theory. Their arguments are usually based on the assumptions that history has no relevance to contemporary society and that theory is abstract and of no practical use. In reality, however, both theory and history are important to all managers today.

A theory is simply a conceptual framework for organizing knowledge and providing a blueprint for action. While some theories may seem abstract and irrelevant, they can also be very simple and practical. Management theories, used to build organizations and guide them toward their goals, are grounded in reality.[9] For example, Andrew Grove, CEO of Intel Corporation, has developed his own operating theory of organizations. The basis of his theory is that organizations need to become more agile and responsive to their environment. Grove has implemented his theory at the company and transformed Intel into just such a company. As a direct result of Grove's keen understanding of his business and his ability to implement his operating theory, Intel has become the world's largest manufacturer of semiconductors.[10]

An awareness and understanding of important historical developments are also important to contemporary managers.[11] Understanding the historical

No one knows the origins of Stonehenge, a mysterious circle of huge stones rising from Salisbury Plain in England. But one fact that is known is that whoever built the ancient monument must have relied heavily on a variety of management tools and techniques. For example, the stones were probably cut over 300 miles away, in Wales, and transported to Salisbury Plain. This enormous feat alone would have required careful planning and coordination and the united efforts of hundreds of laborers.

context of management provides a sense of heritage and can help managers avoid the mistakes of others. Most courses in U.S. history devote time to business and economic developments in this country, including the Industrial Revolution, the early labor movement, and the Great Depression, and to such captains of U.S. industry as Cornelius Vanderbilt (railroads), John D. Rockefeller (oil), and Andrew Carnegie (steel). The contributions of those and other industrialists left a profound imprint on contemporary culture.[12] Managers at Wells Fargo & Company still clearly recognize the value of history. For example, the company maintains an extensive archival library of its old banking documents and records and even employs a full-time corporate historian. As part of their orientation and training, new managers at Wells Fargo take courses to acquaint them with the bank's history.[13]

The Historical Context of Management

The practice of management can be traced back thousands of years. The Egyptians used the management functions of planning, organizing, and controlling when they constructed the great pyramids. Alexander the Great employed a staff organization to coordinate activities during his military campaigns. The Roman Empire developed a well-defined organizational structure that greatly facilitated communication and control.[14]

Even though there are these scattered illustrations of management throughout recorded history, the serious study of management did not begin to develop until the nineteenth century. Robert Owen (1771–1858), a British industrialist and reformer, was one of the first managers to recognize the importance of an organization's human resources. Whereas Owen was primarily interested in employee welfare, Charles Babbage (1792–1871), an English mathematician, focused his attention on efficiencies of production.[15] Babbage placed great faith in the division of labor and advocated the application of mathematics to problems such as the efficient use of facilities and materials.

The Classical Management Perspective

The **classical management perspective** emerged during the early years of this century. These ideas represent the first well-developed framework of management. Their emergence was a natural outgrowth of both the pioneering earlier works just noted and the evolution of large-scale business and management practices. The classical management perspective includes two different approaches to management: scientific management and administrative management.

- **the classical management perspective**
Consists of two distinct branches—scientific management and administrative management

Scientific Management Productivity emerged as a serious business problem during the first few years of the 20th century. Business was expanding and capital was readily available, but labor was in short supply. Hence, managers began to search for ways to use existing labor more efficiently. In response to this need, experts began to focus on ways to improve the performance of individual workers. Their work led to the development of **scientific management**. Some of the earliest advocates of scientific management included Frederick W. Taylor (1856–1915), Frank Gilbreth (1868–1924), and Lillian Gilbreth (1878–1972).[16]

- **scientific management**
Concerned with improving the performance of individual workers

One of Taylor's first jobs was as a foreman at the Midvale Steel Company in Philadelphia. At Midvale he observed what he called **soldiering**—employees deliberately working at a pace slower than their capabilities. Taylor studied and timed each element of the steelworkers' jobs. He determined what each worker should be producing, and then he designed the most efficient way of doing each part of the overall task. Next he implemented a piecework pay system. Rather than paying all employees the same wage, he began increasing the pay of each worker who met and exceeded the target level of output set for his or her job.

- **soldiering**
Employees deliberately working at a slow pace

After Taylor left Midvale, he worked as a consultant for several companies, including Simonds Rolling Machine Company and Bethlehem Steel. At Simonds he studied and redesigned jobs, introduced rest periods to reduce fatigue, and implemented a piecework pay system. The results were higher quality and quantity of output and improved morale. At Bethlehem Steel, Taylor studied efficient ways of loading and unloading rail cars and applied his conclusions with equally impressive results. During these experiences, he formulated the basic ideas that he called scientific management. Figure 1.3 illustrates the basic steps Taylor suggested. He believed that managers who followed his guidelines would improve the efficiency of their workers.[17]

Frederick Taylor developed this system of scientific management, which he believed would lead to a more efficient and productive workforce. Bethlehem Steel was among the first organizations to profit from scientific management and still practices some parts of it today.

FIGURE 1.3 Steps in Scientific Management

1 Develop a science for each element of the job to replace old rule-of-thumb methods → **2** Scientifically select employees and then train them to do the job as described in step **1** → **3** Supervise employees to make sure they follow the prescribed methods for performing their jobs → **4** Continue to plan the work, but use workers to actually get the work done

Taylor's work had a major impact on U.S. industry. By applying his principles, many organizations achieved major gains in efficiency. He was not without his detractors, however. Labor argued that scientific management was just a device to get more work from each employee and to reduce the total number of workers needed by a firm. There was a congressional investigation into Taylor's ideas, and evidence suggests that he falsified some of his findings.[18] Nevertheless, Taylor's work left a lasting imprint on American business.[19]

Frank and Lillian Gilbreth, contemporaries of Taylor, were a husband-and-wife team of industrial engineers. One of Frank Gilbreth's most interesting contributions was to the craft of bricklaying. After studying bricklayers at work, he developed several procedures for doing the job more efficiently. For example, he specified standard materials and techniques, including the positioning of the bricklayer, the bricks, and the mortar at different levels. The results of these changes were a reduction from eighteen separate physical movements to five and an increase in output of about 200 percent. Lillian Gilbreth made equally important contributions to several different areas of work, helped shape the field of industrial psychology, and made substantive contributions to the field of personnel management. Working individually and together, the Gilbreths developed numerous techniques and strategies for eliminating inefficiency. They applied many of their ideas to their family. Their experiences in raising twelve children are documented in the book and movie *Cheaper by the Dozen*.

● **administrative management**
Focuses on managing the total organization

Administrative Management Whereas scientific management deals with the jobs of individual employees, **administrative management** focuses on managing the total organization. The primary contributors to administrative management included Henri Fayol (1841–1925), Lyndall Urwick (1891–1983), and Max Weber (1864–1920).

Henri Fayol was administrative management's most articulate spokesperson. A French industrialist, Fayol was unknown to American managers and scholars until his most important work, *General and Industrial Management,* was translated into English in 1930.[20] Drawing on his own managerial experience, he attempted to systematize the practice of management to provide guidance and direction to other managers. For example, Fayol was the first to identify the specific managerial functions of planning, organizing, leading, and controlling. He believed that these functions accurately reflect the core of the management process. Most contemporary management books still use this framework, and practicing managers agree that these functions are a critical part of their jobs.

After a career as a British army officer, Lyndall Urwick became a noted management theorist and consultant. He integrated scientific management with the work of Fayol and other administrative management theorists. He also advanced modern thinking about the functions of planning, organizing, and controlling and developed a list of guidelines for improving managerial effectiveness. Urwick is noted not so much for his own contributions as for his synthesis and integration of the work of others.

Although Max Weber lived and worked at the same time as Fayol and Taylor, his contributions were not recognized until some years had passed. Weber was a German sociologist, and his most important work was not translated into English until 1947.[21] Weber's work on bureaucracy laid the foundation for contemporary organization theory, discussed in detail in Chapter 6. The concept of bureaucracy, as we discuss later, is based on a rational set of guidelines for structuring organizations in the most efficient manner.

Assessment of the Classical Perspective The classical perspective deserves credit for focusing serious attention on the importance of effective management. Many of the concepts developed during this era, such as job specialization, time and motion studies, and scientific methods are still used today. On the other hand, these early theorists often took a simplistic view of management and failed to understand the human element of organizations.

The Behavioral Management Perspective

Early advocates of the classical perspective essentially viewed organizations and jobs from a mechanistic point of view: that is, they essentially sought to conceptualize organizations as machines and workers as cogs within those machines. Even though some early writers recognized the role of individuals, their focus tended to be on how managers could control and standardize the behavior of their employees. In contrast, the **behavioral management perspective** placed much more emphasis on individual attitudes and behaviors and on group processes and recognized the importance of behavioral processes in the workplace.

• **the behavioral management perspective** Emphasizes individual attitudes and behaviors and group processes

The behavioral management perspective was stimulated by a number of writers and theoretical movements. One of those movements was industrial psychology, the practice of applying psychological concepts to industrial settings. Hugo Munsterberg (1863–1916), a noted German psychologist, is recognized as the father of industrial psychology.[22] He suggested that psychologists could make valuable contributions to managers in the areas of employee selection and motivation. Industrial psychology is still a major course of study at many colleges and universities.

Another early advocate of the behavioral approach to management was Mary Parker Follett.[23] Follett worked during the scientific management era, but quickly came to recognize the human element in the workplace. Indeed, her work clearly anticipated the behavioral management perspective and she appreciated the need to understand the role of behavior in organizations. Her specific interests were in adult education and vocational guidance. Follett believed that organizations should become more democratic in accommodating employees and managers.

The Hawthorne Studies While Munsterberg and Follett made major contributions to the development of the behavioral approach to management, its primary catalyst was a series of studies conducted near Chicago at Western Electric's Hawthorne plant between 1927 and 1932. The research, originally sponsored by General Electric Co., was conducted by Elton Mayo and his associates.[24] The first study involved manipulating illumination for one group of workers and comparing their subsequent productivity with the productivity of another group whose illumination was not changed. Surprisingly, when illumination was increased for the experimental group, productivity went up in both groups. Productivity continued to increase in both groups, even when the lighting for the experimental group was decreased. Not until the lighting was reduced to the level of moonlight did productivity begin to decline (and General Electric withdrew its sponsorship).

Another experiment established a piecework incentive pay plan for a group of nine men assembling terminal banks for telephone exchanges. Scientific management would have predicted that each man would try to maximize his pay by producing as many units as possible. Mayo and his associates, however, found that the group itself informally established an acceptable level of output for its members. Workers who overproduced were branded "rate busters," and underproducers were labeled "chiselers." To be accepted by the group, workers produced at the accepted level. As they approached this acceptable level of output, workers slacked off to avoid overproducing.

Other studies, including an interview program involving several thousand workers, led Mayo and his associates to conclude that human behavior was much more important in the workplace than previously had been believed. In the lighting experiment, for example, the results were attributed to the fact that both groups received special attention and sympathetic supervision for perhaps the first time. The incentive pay plans did not work because wage incentives were less important to the individual workers than was social acceptance in determining output. In short, individual and social processes played a major role in shaping worker attitudes and behavior.[25]

• **human relations movement**
Argued that workers respond primarily to the social context of the workplace

Human Relations The **human relations movement**, which grew from the Hawthorne studies and was a popular approach to management for many years, proposed that workers respond primarily to the social context of the workplace, including social conditioning, group norms, and interpersonal dynamics. A basic assumption of the human relations movement was that the manager's concern for workers would lead to increased satisfaction, which would, in turn, result in improved performance.[26] Two writers who helped advance the human relations movement were Abraham Maslow and Douglas McGregor.

In 1943, Maslow advanced a theory suggesting that people are motivated by a hierarchy of needs, including monetary incentives and social acceptance.[27] Maslow's hierarchy, perhaps the best known human relations theory, is described in detail in Chapter 10. Meanwhile, Douglas McGregor's Theory X and Theory Y model best represents the essence of the human relations movement (see Table 1.1).[28] According to McGregor, Theory X and Theory Y reflect two extreme belief sets that different managers have about their workers. **Theory X** is a relatively negative view of workers and is consistent with the views of scientific management. **Theory Y** is more positive and represents the assumptions that human relations advocates make. In McGregor's view, Theory Y was a more appropriate philosophy for managers to adhere to. Both Maslow and McGregor notably influenced the thinking of many practicing managers.

• **Theory X**
A pessimistic and negative view of workers

• **Theory Y**
Represents the assumptions that human relations advocates make

Contemporary Behavioral Science in Management Munsterberg, Mayo, Maslow, McGregor, and others have made valuable contributions to man-

TABLE 1.1 Theory X and Theory Y

Theory X Assumptions	1. People do not like work and try to avoid it. 2. People do not like work, so managers have to control, direct, coerce, and threaten employees to get them to work toward organizational goals. 3. People prefer to be directed, to avoid responsibility, and to want security; they have little ambition.
Theory Y Assumptions	1. People do not naturally dislike work; work is a natural part of their lives. 2. People are internally motivated to reach objectives to which they are committed. 3. People are committed to goals to the degree that they receive personal rewards when they reach their objectives. 4. People will both seek and accept responsibility under favorable conditions. 5. People have the capacity to be innovative in solving organizational problems. 6. People are bright, but under most organizational conditions their potentials are under-utilized.

Source: Douglas McGregor, *The Human Side of Enterprise*, pp. 33–34, 47–48, © 1960, reproduced with the permission of The McGraw-Hill Companies.

Douglas McGregor developed Theory X and Theory Y. He argued that Theory X best represented the views of scientific management and Theory Y represented the human relations approach. He believed that Theory Y was the best philosophy for all managers.

agement. Contemporary theorists, however, have noted that many assertions of the human relationists were simplistic and inadequate descriptions of work behavior. Current behavioral perspectives on management, known as **organizational behavior**, acknowledge that human behavior in organizations is much more complex than the human relationists realized. The field of organizational behavior draws from a broad, interdisciplinary base of psychology, sociology, anthropology, economics, and medicine.

organizational behavior A current behavioral perspective that focuses on complex behavior in organizations from interdisciplinary and holistic viewpoints

Organizational behavior takes a holistic view of behavior and addresses individual, group, and organization processes.[29] These processes are significant elements in contemporary management theory. Important topics in this field include job satisfaction, stress, motivation, leadership, group dynamics, organizational politics, interpersonal conflict, and the structure and design of organizations.[30] A contingency orientation also characterizes the field (discussed more fully later in this chapter). Our discussions of organizing (Chapters 6–8) and leading (Chapters 9–13) are heavily influenced by organizational behavior.

Assessment of the Behavioral Perspective The primary contributions relate to ways in which this approach has changed managerial thinking. Managers are now more likely to recognize the importance of behavioral processes and to view employees as valuable resources rather than mere tools. On the other hand, organizational behavior is still very imprecise in its ability to predict behavior, and it is not always accepted or understood by practicing managers. Hence, the contributions of the behavioral school have yet to be fully realized.

The Quantitative Management Perspective

• **the quantitative management perspective** Applies quantitative techniques to management

Of the three major schools of management thought, the quantitative perspective is the newest. The classical approach was born in the early years of this century, and the behavioral approach began to emerge in the 1920s and 1930s. The **quantitative management perspective** was not fully developed until World War II. During the war, managers, government officials, and scientists were brought together in England and the United States to help the military deploy its resources more efficiently and effectively. These experts took some of the mathematical approaches to management developed decades earlier by Taylor and Gantt and applied them to logistical problems during the war.[31] Decisions regarding troop, equipment, and submarine deployment were all solvable through mathematical analysis.

After the war, many businesses began to use the same techniques for deploying employees, choosing plant locations, and planning warehouses. Basically, then, this perspective is concerned with applying quantitative techniques to management. More specifically, quantitative management focuses on decision making, economic effectiveness, mathematical models, and the use of computers. There are two branches of the quantitative approach: management science and operations management.

• **management science** Focuses specifically on the development of mathematical models

Management Science The term *management science* appears to be related to scientific management, the approach developed by Taylor and others early in this century. But the two have little in common and should not be confused. **Management science** focuses specifically on the development of mathematical models. A mathematical model is a simplified representation of a system, process, or relationship.

At its most basic level, management science focuses on models, equations, and similar representations of reality. For example, managers at Detroit Edison use mathematical models to determine how best to route repair crews during blackouts. The Bank of New England uses models to figure out how many tellers need to be on duty at each location at various times throughout the day. In recent years, paralleling the advent of the personal computer, management science techniques have become more sophisticated. For example, automobile manufacturers Daimler-Benz and Chrysler use realistic computer simulations to study collision damage to cars. This gives the manufacturers more precise information and avoids the costs of "crashing" so many test cars.

• **operations management** Concerned with helping the organization more efficiently produce its products or services

Operations Management Operations management is somewhat less mathematical and statistically sophisticated than management science and can be applied more directly to managerial situations. Indeed, we can think of **operations management** as a form of applied management science. Operations management techniques are generally concerned with helping the organization produce its products or services more efficiently and can be applied to a wide range of problems.[32]

For example, Rubbermaid and The Home Depot each use operations management techniques to manage their inventories. (Inventory management is concerned with specific inventory problems such as balancing carrying costs and ordering costs and determining the optimal order quantity.) Linear programming (which involves computing simultaneous solutions to a set of linear equations) helps United Airlines plan its flight schedules, Consolidated Freightways develop its shipping routes, and General Instrument Corporation plan what instruments to produce at various times. Other operations management techniques include queuing theory, break-even analysis, and simulation. All of these techniques and procedures apply directly to operations, but they are also helpful in such areas as finance, marketing, and human resource management.

Assessment of the Quantitative Management Perspective Like the other management perspectives, the quantitative perspective has made important contributions and has certain limitations. It has provided managers with an abundance of decision-making tools and techniques and has increased understanding of overall organizational processes. It has been particularly useful in the areas of planning and controlling. On the other hand, mathematical models cannot fully account for individual behaviors and attitudes. Some believe that the time needed to develop competence in quantitative techniques retards the development of other managerial skills. Finally, mathematical models typically require a set of assumptions that may not be realistic.

CONTEMPORARY MANAGEMENT THEORY

It is important to recognize that the classical, behavioral, and quantitative approaches to management are not necessarily contradictory or mutually exclusive. Even though very different assumptions and predictions are made by each of the three perspectives, each can also complement the others. Indeed, a complete understanding of management requires an appreciation of all three perspectives. In addition, contemporary management theory based on systems and contingency perspectives builds from these earlier perspectives in a variety of ways.

The Systems Perspective

The systems perspective is one important contemporary management theory. A **system** is an interrelated set of elements functioning as a whole.[33] As shown in Figure 1.4, by viewing an organization as a system, we can identify four basic elements: inputs, transformation processes, outputs, and feedback. First, inputs are the material, human, financial, and information resources the organization gets from its environment. Next, through technological and managerial processes, these are transformed into outputs. Outputs include products, services, or both (tangible and intangible); profits, losses, or both (even not-for-profit organizations must operate within their budgets); employee behaviors; and information. Finally, the environment reacts to these outputs and provides feedback to the system.

● **system**
An interrelated set of elements functioning as a whole

By viewing organizations as systems, managers can better understand the importance of their environment and the level of interdependence among subsystems within the organization. They must also understand how their decisions affect and are affected by other subsystems within the organization.

FIGURE 1.4 The Systems Perspective of Organizations

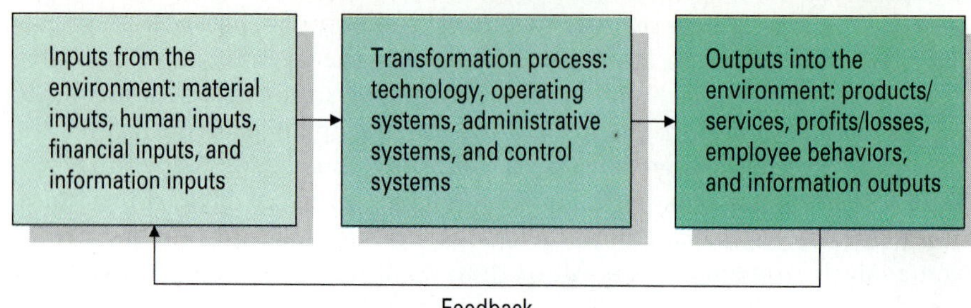

- **open systems** Interact with their environment
- **closed systems** Do not interact with their environment
- **subsystem** A system within another system
- **synergy** Two subsystems working together to produce more than the total of what they might produce working alone
- **entropy** A normal process leading to system decline

Thinking of organizations as systems provides us with a variety of important viewpoints on organizations. These include the concepts of open systems, subsystems, synergy, and entropy. **Open systems** are systems that interact with their environment, whereas **closed systems** do not. All organizations are open systems but sometimes make the mistake of ignoring their environment. U.S. automobile manufacturers lost market share to Japanese imports in part because they failed to recognize Toyota, Nissan, and Honda as competitors.

The systems perspective also stresses the importance of **subsystems**—systems within a broader system. For example, the marketing, production, and finance functions within Mattel are systems in their own right but are also subsystems within the overall organization. Because they are interdependent, a change in one subsystem can affect other subsystems as well. If the production department at Mattel lowers the quality of the toys being made (by buying lower-quality materials, for example), the effects are felt in finance (improved cash flow in the short run owing to lower costs) and marketing (decreased sales in the long run because of customer dissatisfaction). Managers must therefore remember that although organizational subsystems can be managed with some degree of autonomy, their interdependence should not be overlooked.

Synergy suggests that organizational units (or subsystems) may often be more successful working together than working alone. Disney, for example, benefits greatly from synergy. The company's movies, theme parks, television programs, and merchandise licensing programs all benefit one another. Children who enjoy a Disney movie, such as *The Hunchback of Notre Dame,* want to go to Disney World to see the Hunchback show there and buy stuffed toys of the film's characters. In Europe today, banks and insurance companies are linking up in an effort to market a wide array of financial products that each would have trouble selling on its own.[34] Synergy is an important concept for managers because it emphasizes the importance of working together in a cooperative and coordinated fashion.

Finally, **entropy** is a normal process that leads to system decline. When an organization does not monitor feedback from its environment and make appropriate adjustments, it may fail. For example, Studebaker, W. T. Grant, and Penn Central Railroad were once among the largest businesses in the

United States. Each went bankrupt because it failed to revitalize itself and keep pace with changes in its environment. A primary objective of management, from a systems perspective, is to continually re-energize the organization to avoid entropy.

The Contingency Perspective

Another recent noteworthy addition to management thinking is the contingency perspective. The classical, behavioral, and quantitative approaches are considered **universal perspectives** because they try to identify the "one best way" to manage organizations. The **contingency perspective**, in contrast, suggests that universal theories cannot be applied to organizations because each organization is unique. Instead, the contingency perspective suggests that appropriate managerial behavior in a given situation depends on, or is contingent on, unique elements in that situation.[35] Stated differently, effective managerial behavior in one situation cannot always be generalized to other situations. Recall, for example, that Frederick Taylor assumed that all workers would generate the highest possible level of output to maximize their own personal economic gain. We can imagine some people being motivated primarily by money—but we can just as easily imagine other people being motivated by the desire for leisure time, status, social acceptance, or any combination of these (as Mayo found at the Hawthorne plant).

- **universal perspective** An attempt to identify the one best way to do something
- **contingency perspective** Suggests that appropriate managerial behavior in a given situation depends on, or is contingent on, a wide variety of elements

A few years ago Continental Airlines hired Hollis Harris, a respected and successful executive at Delta Air Lines, to become its CEO. At the time, Delta was very profitable and had its costs under control. Continental, however, was losing money and its costs were not being controlled. Harris tried to manage at Continental just as he had at Delta, with relatively little concern for costs. As a result, he failed to rescue the airline from bankruptcy and was forced to resign. He made the mistake of not recognizing that he needed to manage Continental differently because it was in a different situation.

Emerging Contemporary Management Challenges

The Globalization of Business One major emerging contemporary challenge faced by all managers today is international business. No longer can any organization—regardless of its size, vitality, or industry—ignore the globalization of business. Ford competes with Nissan and Volkswagen, Timex with Seiko, and Exxon with British Petroleum. Small retailers carry merchandise from around the globe. Businesses from just about any country can borrow funds from lenders in New York, Tokyo, or London. We integrate international issues throughout this book.

Quality and Productivity Another area of interest to emerge in recent years has been quality, productivity, and their interrelationship. As they attempt to understand why Japanese and German firms have been so successful, U.S. companies have discovered that their foreign counterparts have an edge in quality. As a result, U.S. firms have developed renewed interest in how they can enhance the quality of their products and services. As a part of this discovery process, U.S. managers have also learned that many of their foreign competitors are producing higher-quality products with

International management is a growing priority for all businesses, large and small. Although Coca-Cola has long been sold around the world, the firm has recently been expanding into international markets even more aggressively. Because the U.S. soft drink market is not growing very fast, and because domestic competition is so fierce, Coke has realized that its best opportunities for expansion are in foreign markets, especially developing markets with growth potential. For example, Coke has recently started to expand its operations in Hanoi (shown here) and in Moscow.

fewer resources. Hence, managers have become more and more interested in how to increase the productivity of American workers.[36]

Ethics and Social Responsibility Although ethical scandals in business are not really new, media attention focused on them in recent years has increased public sensitivity about them. Many organizations today are taking steps to enhance the ethical standards of their managers and to avoid legal or public sentiment problems. Social responsibility and environmentalism are important related issues.

Workforce Diversity Still another set of issues that managers today must confront involves workforce diversity. A wide variety of factors—globalization, an aging population, an influx of workers into new career and occupational tracks—have created workforces that are much more heterogeneous than at any time in history. Managers in every organization are finding that they must learn to be more sensitive to the needs, perceptions, and aspirations of many different kinds of workers.

Change Managers also face more change today than ever before. The requirements, demands, and expectations placed on those managers and their organizations are greater than in the past, as is the complexity of the environment within which they must compete. While in the past managers may have seen change as something that had to be addressed periodically, it has now become a fact of everyday life for everyone in the business world.[37]

Empowerment Finally, managers today are also dealing with issues associated with empowerment—efforts to more fully take advantage of the organization's human resources by giving everyone more information and control over how they perform their jobs. Various techniques and methods for empowerment range from participation in decision making to the use of integrated work teams.

SUMMARY OF KEY POINTS

Management is a set of functions directed at the efficient and effective utilization of resources in the pursuit of organizational goals. Managers can be differentiated by level and by area. By level, we can identify top, middle, and first-line managers. Kinds of managers by area include marketing, financial, operations, human resources, general, and specialized managers.

The basic functions that comprise the management process are planning and decision making, organizing, leading, and controlling. Effective managers also tend to have technical, interpersonal, conceptual, diagnostic, communication, decision-making, and time-management skills. The effective practice of management requires a synthesis of science and art; that is, a blend of rational objectivity and intuitive insight.

Theories are important as organizers of knowledge and as road maps for action. Understanding the historical context and precursors of management and organizations provides a sense of heritage and can also help managers avoid repeating the mistakes of others. Evidence suggests that interest in management dates back thousands of years, but a scientific approach to management has emerged only in the last hundred years.

The classical management perspective had two major branches: scientific management and administrative management. Scientific management was concerned with improving efficiency and work methods for individual workers. Administrative management was more concerned with how organizations themselves should be structured and arranged for efficient operations. Both branches paid little attention to the role of the worker.

The behavioral management perspective, characterized by a concern for individual and group behavior, emerged primarily as a result of the Hawthorne studies. The human relations movement recognized the importance and potential of behavioral processes in organizations but made many overly simplistic assumptions about those processes. Organizational behavior, a more realistic outgrowth of the behavioral perspective, is of interest to many contemporary managers.

The quantitative management perspective and its two components, management science and operations management, attempt to apply quantitative techniques to decision making and problem solving. These areas are also of considerable importance to contemporary managers. Their contributions have been facilitated by the tremendous increase in the use of personal computers and integrated information networks.

Two relatively recent additions to management theory, the systems and contingency perspectives, appear to have great potential both as approaches to management and as frameworks for integrating the other perspectives. Challenges facing managers today include the globalization of business, the importance of quality and productivity, ownership issues, ethics and social responsibility, workforce diversity, change, and empowerment.

QUESTIONS FOR REVIEW

1. What are the four basic functions that comprise the management process?
2. Identify different kinds of managers by both level and area in the organization.
3. Identify the different skills of managers. Give an example of each.
4. Briefly summarize the classical and behavioral management perspectives and identify the most important contributors to each.
5. Describe the contingency perspective and outline its usefulness to the study and practice of management.

QUESTIONS FOR ANALYSIS

1. The text notes that management is both a science and an art. Is one of these more important than the other? Under what types of circumstances might one ingredient be more important than the other?
2. Recall a recent group project or task in which you have participated. Explain how each of the four basic management functions was performed.
3. Some people argue that CEOs in the United States are paid too much. Find out the pay for a CEO and discuss whether you think he or she is overpaid.

4. Explain how a manager can use tools and techniques from each of the major management perspectives in a complementary fashion.
5. Which of the contemporary management challenges do you think will have the greatest impact on you and your career? Which will have the least?

CASE STUDY

The Woman At the Top

Warnaco is not exactly a household word, at least not in the same way that AT&T, IBM, Ford, GM, and Exxon are. But with total sales of nearly $600 million, Warnaco Inc. is one of the largest businesses in the country and has become firmly entrenched in the *Fortune* 500. Warnaco's business is manufacturing and selling apparel, especially intimate apparel. Some of its brands and products include Warner's, Olga, Valentino, Scaasi, Ungaro, Bob Mackie, and Blanche. Warnaco also makes menswear, including Christian Dior, Hathaway, Chaps by Ralph Lauren, Golden Bear by Jack Nicklaus, Puritan, and Valentino accessories. In 1992 Warnaco became a *Fortune* 500 company, the only one headed by a woman at that time. That woman was Linda Wachner.

Wachner became CEO of Warnaco after helping a group of investors capture the company in a bitter, hostile takeover in 1986. She immediately replaced most top managers and energized employees throughout the firm. She quickly cut Warnaco's debt by 40 percent and nearly doubled its operating cash, largely by cutting weak divisions (women's apparel, for example) and combining those that remained into only two divisions (intimate apparel and menswear). After restoring the firm's financial health, Wachner took the company public (that is, she changed it from a privately owned company into a company whose stock can be bought and sold by the general public). Further, she accomplished all of this during the late 1980s when many department stores and other retailers were going bankrupt and consumer spending for apparel was dropping.

Wachner attributes her success as a manager to three main guidelines. The first is keeping in close touch with customers' tastes, wants, and needs—clearly vitally important in the apparel field. The second is keeping on top of the business itself. For Wachner, this involves keeping up with technology, distribution channels, store layouts, problems, and the like so that there are no surprises in running the organization. Her third guideline is carefully monitoring the cash flow. She constantly checks both costs and revenues to ensure solid profits for the organization as well as to identify both opportunities and problems in time to take advantage of or solve them.

Wachner is known to be a tough boss and has been criticized for pushing profits so hard that occasionally people get treated roughly. She is blunt and to the point. Further, she can get angry with fellow managers if they seem to be talking too much about problems and not enough about solutions. She believes that she tries not to hurt people and admits that criticisms of her still hurt. *Fortune* recently named her one of the toughest bosses in the United States. Her meetings frequently start as early as 5:00 AM, and she has been known to run evening meetings to as late as midnight. She expects results and is willing to put in the hours necessary to obtain them.

By most indications, Wachner's efforts are paying off handsomely. Warnaco's sales, profits, and stock prices are all strong and rising. Wachner has also increased the value of stockholder equity and seen her own personal stake in the firm mushroom to $72 million. In a highly competitive environment, she has led her firm to a lofty position, and she seems determined to keep it there. Wachner clearly knows how to manage.

Case Questions

1. Which management functions can you identify in Wachner's handling of Warnaco?
2. What managerial skills do you think contribute most to Wachner's success?
3. How would an understanding of Warnaco's past help a new manager function more effectively in the organization?

References: "Lingerie Firm's CEO Steers a Turnaround," *USA Today,* August 4, 1994, pp. 1B, 2B; Brian Dumaine, "America's Toughest Bosses," *Fortune,* October 18, 1993, pp. 37–50; Gary Hoover, Alta Campbell, and Patrick J. Spain (Eds.), *Hoover's Handbook of American Business: Profiles of Over 500 Major U.S. Corporations* (Austin, Tex.: The Reference Press, 1993), pp. 228 and 526–527; Susan Caminiti, "America's Most Successful Businesswoman," *Fortune,* June 15, 1992, pp. 102–107; "Her Own Shop," *Business Week,* June 8, 1992, p. 81; and Maggie Mahar, "The Measure of Success," *Working Woman,* May 1, 1992, pp. 70–87.

SKILLS • DEVELOPMENT • PORTFOLIO

BUILDING EFFECTIVE TECHNICAL SKILLS

Exercise Overview

Technical skills refer to the manager's abilities to accomplish or understand work done in an organization. Today more and more managers realize that having the technical ability to use the Internet is an important part of communication, decision making, and other facets of their work. This exercise introduces you to the Internet and provides some practice in using it.

Exercise Background

The so-called information highway, or the Internet, refers to an interconnected network of information and information-based resources using computers and computer systems. While electronic mail was perhaps the first widespread application of the Internet, increasingly popular applications are based on home pages and search engines.

A *home page* is a file (or set of files) created by an individual, business, or other entity. It contains whatever information its creator chooses to include. For example, a company might create a home page that includes its logo, address and telephone number, information about its products and services, and so forth. An individual seeking employment might create a home page that includes a résumé and a statement of career interests. Home pages are indexed by key words chosen by their creators.

A *search engine* is a system through which an Internet user can search for home pages according to their indexed key words. For example, suppose an individual is interested in knowing more about art collecting. Key words that might logically be linked to home pages related to this interest include *art, artists, galleries,* and *framing.* A search engine will take these key words and provide a listing of all home pages that are indexed to them. The user can then browse those pages to see what information they contain. Popular search engines include Yahoo, Lycos, and Webcrawler.

Exercise Task

1. Visit your computer center and learn how to get access to the Internet.

2. Using whichever search engine your computer center supports, conduct a search for three or four general management-related terms (e.g., *management, organization, business*).

3. Select a more specific management term and search for two or three specific topics. (If you cannot think of any terms, scan the margin notes in this book.)

4. Select three or four companies and search for their home pages.

BUILDING EFFECTIVE DIAGNOSTIC SKILLS

Exercise Overview

Diagnostic skills are those that enable a manager to visualize the most appropriate response to a situation. This exercise will encourage you to apply your diagnostic skills to a real business problem to assess the possible consequences of different courses of action.

Exercise Background

For some time now, college textbook publishers have been struggling with a significant problem. The subject matter that comprises a particular field, such as management, chemistry, or history, continues to increase in size, scope, and complexity. Thus, authors feel compelled to add more and more information to new editions of their textbooks. Publishers have also sought to increase the visual sophistication of their texts by adding more color and photographs. At the same time, some instructors find it increasingly difficult to cover the material in longer textbooks. Moreover, longer and more attractive textbooks cost more to produce, resulting in higher selling prices to students.

Publishers have considered a variety of options to confront this situation. One option is to work with authors to produce briefer and more economical books (such as this one). Another option is to cut back on the complimentary supplements that publishers provide to instructors (such as videos and color transparencies) as a way of lowering the overall cost of producing a textbook with all its peripherals. Another option is to eliminate traditional publishing altogether and provide educational resources via CD-ROM, the Internet, or other new media.

Confounding the situation, of course, is cost. Profit margins in the publishing industry are such that managers feel the need to be cautious and conservative. That is, they cannot do everything, and they must not risk alienating their users by taking too radical a step. Remember, too, that publishers must consider the concerns of three different sets of customers: the instructors who make adoption decisions, the bookstores that buy educational materials for resale (at a retail markup), and the students who buy the books for classroom use and then often resell them to the bookstore.

Exercise Task

With this background in mind, respond to the following:

1. Discuss the pros and cons of each option currently being considered by textbook publishers.

2. Identify the likely consequences of each option.

3. What other alternatives should publishers in the industry consider?

4. What specific recommendations regarding this set of issues would you make to an executive in a publishing company?

YOU MAKE THE CALL

Mark Spenser owns and manages Sunset Landscape Services, a nursery, landscape, and lawn-care business located in Central City, Texas. Mark moved to Central City in 1970 to attend the state university located there. After receiving his degree in horticulture, Mark decided to remain in Central City and start his own business. He spent three years as assistant manager at a small nursery located in a neighboring town, and then launched Sunset Landscape Services in 1978.

Mark's timing could not have been better. Beginning in the late 1970s, Central City enjoyed a dramatic increase in population and economic growth, fueled primarily by unprecedented expansion and growth at the university. Over the course of the next ten years, Central City grew from a population of less than 70,000 to over 120,000. Surrounding communities also grew as several major new businesses moved into the area.

Mark anticipated the real estate boom through an analysis of state demographics and population trends and through conversations with local leaders who were, for the first time, actively attempting to attract new businesses to the area. He realized that there were only two small local nurseries in operation. He predicted that an increase in housing construction would fuel demand for both initial landscaping services by building contractors and follow-up nursery sales as home owners began to establish their lawns and flower beds.

As do most new businesses, SLS struggled a bit at first. Mark did a good job of planning how his business would be run and setting up an efficient organization. He also did an excellent job of hiring employees and getting them to work hard. He had a more difficult time, however, keeping his costs in line with his income and ordering new plants at the most efficient times. Finally, he took a couple of business courses at the university and learned how to manage better the various parts of his business. Today, SLS is a thriving business that is well respected throughout the community.

Discussion Questions

1. What kind of manager is Mark Spenser?

2. Can you identify examples of management functions and management skills in this case?

3. What emerging contemporary management challenges might be most relevant for Mark Spenser and Sunset Landscape Services? Why?

SKILLS SELF-ASSESSMENT INSTRUMENT

Self-Awareness

Introduction: Self-awareness is an important skill for effective management. This assessment is designed to help you evaluate your level of self-awareness.

Instructions: Please respond to the following statements by writing a number from the following rating scale in the column. Your answers should reflect your attitudes and behavior as they are *now,* not as you would *like* them to be. Be honest. This instrument is designed to help you discover how self-aware you are so that you can tailor your learning to your specific needs.

Rating Scale

6 Strongly agree	**3** Slightly disagree
5 Agree	**2** Disagree
4 Slightly agree	**1** Strongly disagree

_____ **1.** I seek information about my strengths and weaknesses from others as a basis for self-improvement.

_____ **2.** When I receive negative feedback about myself from others, I do not get angry or defensive.

_____ **3.** In order to improve, I am willing to be self-disclosing to others (i.e., to share my beliefs and feelings).

_____ **4.** I am very much aware of my personal style of gathering information and making decisions about it.

_____ **5.** I am very much aware of my own interpersonal needs when it comes to forming relationships with other people.

_____ **6.** I have a good sense of how I cope with situations that are ambiguous and uncertain.

_____ **7.** I have a well-developed set of personal standards and principles that guide my behavior.

_____ **8.** I feel very much in charge of what happens to me, good and bad.

_____ **9.** I seldom, if ever, feel angry, depressed, or anxious without knowing why.

_____ **10.** I am conscious of the areas in which conflict and friction most frequently arise in my interactions with others.

_____ **11.** I have a close relationship with at least one other person in which I can share personal information and personal feelings.

For interpretation, turn to page 447.

Source: Adapted from *Developing Management Skills,* Second Edition, by David A. Whetten and Kim S. Cameron, pp. 38–39. Copyright © 1991 by HarperCollins Publishers, Inc. Reprinted by permission of Addison-Wesley Educational Publishers, Inc.

EXPERIENTIAL EXERCISE

Johari Window

Purpose: This exercise has two purposes: to encourage you to analyze yourself more accurately, and to start you working on small group cohesiveness. This exercise encourages you to share data about yourself and then to assimilate and process feedback. Small groups are typically more trusting and work better together, and you will be able to see this after this exercise has been completed. The Johari Window is a particularly good model for understanding the perceptual process in interpersonal relationships.

This skill builder focuses on the *human resources model.* It will help you develop your *mentor role.* One of the skills of a mentor is self-awareness.

Introduction: Each individual has four sets of personality characteristics. One set, which includes such characteristics as working hard, the individual is well aware of and so are others. A second set is unknown to the individual but obvious to others. For example, in a working situation a peer might observe that your jumping in to get the group moving off dead center is appropriate. At other times, you jump in when the group is not really finished, and you seem to interrupt. A third set is known to the individual but not others. These are situations that you have elected not to share, perhaps because of a lack of trust. Finally, there is a fourth set, which is not known to the individual or to others, such as why you are uncomfortable at office parties.

Instructions: Look at the Johari window on page 26. In quadrant #1 list three things that you know about yourself and that you think others know. List three things in quadrant #3 that others do not know about you. Finally, in quadrant #2, list three things that you did not know about yourself last semester that you learned from others.

Sources: Adapted from Joseph Luft, *Group Processes: An Introduction to Group Dynamics* (Palo Alto, Ca.: Mayfield Publishing Co., 1970), pp. 10–11, and William C. Morris and Marshall Sashkin, *Organizational Behavior in Action* (St. Paul, Minn.: West Publishing Co., 1976), p. 56.

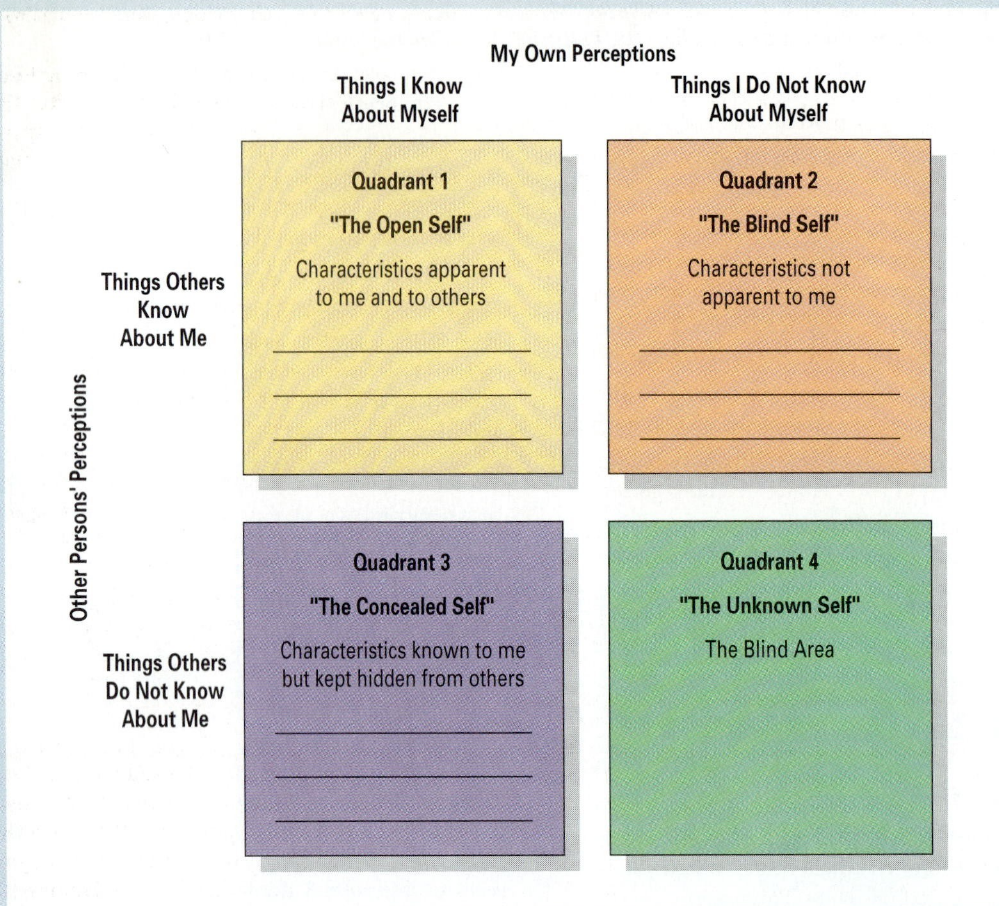

CHAPTER NOTES

1. Kenneth Labich, "Is Herb Kelleher America's Best CEO?" *Fortune*, May 2, 1994, pp. 44–52; "Hit 'em Hardest with the Mostest," *Forbes*, September 16, 1991, pp. 48–51; and "No-Frills Firm Flies Aginst the Ordinary," *USA Today*, August 24, 1989, pp. B1, B2.
2. Fred Luthans, "Successful vs. Effective Real Managers," *The Academy of Management Executive*, May 1988, pp. 127–132.
3. Alex Taylor III, "How a Top Boss Manages His Day," *Fortune*, June 19, 1989, pp. 95–100.
4. See Patricia Sellers, "Does the CEO Really Matter?" *Fortune*, April 22, 1991, pp. 80–94; Charles M. Farkas and Suzy Wetlauter, "The Ways Chief Executive Officers Lead," *Harvard Business Review*, May–June 1996, pp. 110–122.
5. Rosemary Stewart, "Middle Managers: Their Jobs and Behaviors," in Jay W. Lorsch (Ed.), *Handbook of Organizational Behavior* (Englewood Cliffs, N.J.: Prentice-Hall, 1987), pp. 385–391.
6. Steven Kerr, Kenneth D. Hill, and Laurie Broedling, "The First-Line Supervisor: Phasing Out or Here to Stay?" *Academy of Management Review*, January 1986, pp. 103–117; and Leonard A. Schlesinger and Janice A. Klein, "The First-Line Supervisor: Past, Present, and Future," in Lorsch (Ed.), *Handbook of Organizational Behavior*, pp. 358–369.
7. Robert L. Katz, "The Skills of an Effective Administrator," *Harvard Business Review*, September–October 1974, pp. 90–102.
8. Gary Hamel and C. K. Prahalad, "Competing for the Future," *Harvard Business Review*, July–August 1994, pp. 122–128.

9. Peter F. Drucker, "The Theory of the Business," *Harvard Business Review*, September–October 1994, pp. 95–104.

10. "Can Andy Grove Practice What He Preaches?" *Business Week*, March 16, 1987, pp. 68–69; "Intel to Motorola: Race Ya," *Business Week*, March 13, 1989, p. 42; Patrick J. Spain and James R. Talbot (Eds.), *Hoover's Handbook of American Business 1996* (Austin, Tex.: The Reference Press, 1995), pp. 776–777.

11. "Why Business History?" *Audacity*, Fall 1992, pp. 7–15. See also Alan L. Wilkins and Nigel J. Bristow, "For Successful Organization Culture, Honor Your Past," *The Academy of Management Executive*, August 1987, pp. 221–227.

12. Daniel Wren, *The Evolution of Management Theory*, 4th ed. (New York: Wiley, 1994); and Page Smith, *The Rise of Industrial America* (New York: McGraw-Hill, 1984).

13. Alan M. Kantrow (Ed.), "Why History Matters to Managers," *Harvard Business Review*, January–February 1986, pp. 81–88.

14. Wren, *The Evolution of Management Theory*.

15. Charles Babbage, *On the Economy of Machinery and Manufactures* (London: Charles Knight, 1832).

16. Wren, *The Evolution of Management Theory*.

17. Frederick W. Taylor, *Principles of Scientific Management* (New York: Harper and Brothers, 1911).

18. Charles D. Wrege and Amedeo G. Perroni, "Taylor's Pig-Tale: A Historical Analysis of Frederick W. Taylor's Pig-Iron Experiment," *Academy of Management Journal*, March 1974, pp. 6–27; and Charles D. Wrege and Ann Marie Stoka, "Cooke Creates a Classic: The Story Behind Taylor's Principles of Scientific Management," *Academy of Management Review*, October 1978, pp. 736–749.

19. Edwin A. Locke, "The Ideas of Frederick W. Taylor: An Evaluation," *Academy of Management Review*, January 1982, pp. 14–20. See also Stephen J. Carroll and Dennis J. Gillen, "Are the Classical Management Functions Useful in Describing Managerial Work?" *Academy of Management Review*, January 1987, pp. 38–51.

20. Henri Fayol, *General and Industrial Management*, trans. J. A. Coubrough (Geneva: International Management Institute, 1930).

21. Max Weber, *Theory of Social and Economic Organizations*, trans. T. Parsons (New York: Free Press, 1947); and Richard M. Weis, "Weber on Bureaucracy: Management Consultant or Political Theorist?" *Academy of Management Review*, April 1983, pp. 242–248.

22. Hugo Munsterberg, *Psychology and Industrial Efficiency* (Boston: Houghton Mifflin, 1913).

23. Wren, *The Evolution of Management Theory*, pp. 255–264.

24. Elton Mayo, *The Human Problems of an Industrial Civilization* (New York: Macmillan, 1933); and Fritz J. Roethlisberger and William J. Dickson, *Management and the Worker* (Cambridge, Mass.: Harvard University Press, 1939).

25. For a recent commentary on the Hawthorne studies, see Lyle Yorks and David A. Whitsett, "Hawthorne, Topeka, and the Issue of Science versus Advocacy in Organizational Behavior," *Academy of Management Review*, January 1985, pp. 21–30.

26. Barry M. Staw, "Organizational Psychology and the Pursuit of the Happy/Productive Worker," *California Management Review*, Summer 1986, pp. 40–53.

27. Abraham Maslow, "A Theory of Human Motivation," *Psychological Review*, July 1943, pp. 370–396.

28. Douglas McGregor, *The Human Side of Enterprise* (New York: McGraw-Hill, 1960).

29. Paul R. Lawrence, "Historical Development of Organizational Behavior," in Jay W. Lorsch (Ed.), *Handbook of Organizational Behavior* (Englewood Cliffs, N.J.: Prentice-Hall, 1987), pp. 1–9. See also Larry L. Cummings, "Toward Organizational Behavior," *Academy of Management Review*, January 1978, pp. 90–98.

30. See Gregory Moorhead and Ricky W. Griffin, *Organizational Behavior*, 4th ed. (Boston: Houghton Mifflin, 1995) for a recent review of current developments in the field of organizational behavior.

31. Wren, *The Evolution of Management Theory*, Chapter 21.

32. For a recent review of operations management, see Everett E. Adam, Jr., and Ronald J. Ebert, *Production and Operations Management: Concepts, Models, and Behavior*, 5th ed. (Englewood Cliffs, N.J.: Prentice-Hall, 1993).

33. For more information on systems theory in general, see Ludwig von Bertalanffy, C. G. Hempel, R. E. Bass, and H. Jonas, "General Systems Theory: A New Approach to Unity of Science," I–VI *Human Biology*, Vol. 23, 1951, pp. 302–361. For systems theory as applied to organizations, see Fremont E. Kast and James E. Rosenzweig, "General Systems Theory: Applications for Organizations and Management," *Academy of Management Journal*, December 1972, pp. 447–465. For a recent update, see Donde P. Ashmos and George P. Huber, "The Systems Paradigm in Organization Theory: Correcting the Record and Suggesting the Future," *Academy of Management Review*, October 1987, pp. 607–621.

34. "European Banks, Insurance Firms Search for Synergies," *The Wall Street Journal*, April 26, 1989, p. A10.

35. Fremont E. Kast and James E. Rosenzweig, *Contingency Views of Organization and Management* (Chicago: Science Research Associates, 1973).

36. See Tom Peters, "Restoring American Competitiveness: Looking for New Models of Organizations," *The Academy of Management Executive*, May 1988, pp. 103–109.

37. "Leaders of Corporate Change," *Fortune*, December 14, 1992, pp. 104–114.

CHAPTER

2

The Environment of Management

OBJECTIVES

After studying this chapter, you should be able to:

- *Discuss the environment of organizations and identify the components of the general, task, and internal environments.*
- *Describe the ethical and social environment of management, including individual ethics and social responsibility.*
- *Describe the international environment of management, including recent trends, levels of internationalization, and related contextual issues.*
- *Discuss the importance and determinants of an organization's culture and how the culture can be managed.*

OUTLINE

OPENING INCIDENT

SCHWINN. LIKE KITES and tree houses, this venerable bicycle was once synonymous with growing up. During the 1950s and early 1960s, just about every kid in the United States wanted a big Schwinn bike for Christmas or a birthday—complete with handlebar streamers, fat balloon tires, saddlebags, and a big gaudy tank in front.

Schwinn Bicycle Co. was founded in 1895 by a German immigrant named Ignaz Schwinn. After his death, his descendants continued to run the company, which eventually became the largest bicycle manufacturer in the United States. In the 1960s, Schwinn controlled 25 percent of the U.S. domestic market and was selling several million bikes a year.

> **"When they were asked who were their competition, they said, 'We don't have competition. We're Schwinn.'"**

But then things started to turn sour. In the 1980s managers at Schwinn made two critical mistakes. First, they switched to overseas suppliers for many of their bicycle parts. Unfortunately, Schwinn did not adequately investigate its new suppliers, and it was unprepared for the avalanche of quality and delivery problems that ensued. The second mistake that Schwinn made was deciding that mountain bikes were just a fad. Schwinn managers had always assumed that the firm was invincible and did not really need to worry about what their competitors were doing.

As the 1980s drew to a close, Schwinn began to falter. On one front, Huffy Corp. and Murray took advantage of Schwinn's delivery and quality snags to make major inroads in the low-end discount sales market (Wal-Mart Stores and Kmart Corp.). Meanwhile, newcomers like Trek, Giant, and Specialized established major positions in the mountain bike market, which proved to be anything but a fad: Mountain bikes today account for two-thirds of all new bikes sold.

By the early 1990s, Schwinn was on the verge of bankruptcy. In January 1993, however, Scott USA (a ski-equipment manufacturer) and a private investor group called Zell/Chilmark Fund bought Schwinn. Scott's management focused first on getting quality back to industry standards and then on developing a new line of mountain bikes. Next they doubled the firm's advertising budget and met with major distributors to convince them that Schwinn was back. So far, their approach appears to be working. Schwinn returned to profitability in 1994 and gained back some its market share.

Schwinn has also tried to alter its image a bit in the eyes of the bicycle world and to send a message to its employees. For example, the firm has become a major sponsor of the mountain bike racing tour. It also shifted its corporate headquarters from Chicago to Boulder, Colorado, the center of the mountain biking sport. Schwinn has also adopted a new corporate slogan—"Established 1895. Re-established 1994."[1] ●

Source of Quotation: Tom Stendahl, Scott Sports Group CEO, quoted in *Business Week*, August 23, 1993, p. 79.

Managers at Schwinn made mistakes that are all too common in the business world—they lost contact with their customers, failed to recognize that their competitive environment was changing, and misjudged international suppliers. Their production and delivery problems, combined with their failure to enter the mountain-bike market on a timely basis, almost drove the firm out of business. Fortunately, a new management team seems to have turned things around and Schwinn is once again becoming a major force in the bicycle market.

Managers must have a deep understanding and appreciation of the environment in which they and their organizations function. This chapter is devoted to the environment of management. We first describe the general, task, and internal environments of organizations. Next, we discuss two special parts of the environment: the ethical and social environment and the international environment. We conclude by discussing the organization's culture, another key environmental force.

THE ORGANIZATION'S ENVIRONMENT

The organization's external environment consists of two different sets of forces. The general environment is the set of broad dimensions and forces in an organization's surroundings that create its overall context. The task environment consists of specific organizations or groups that affect the organization. In addition, organizations also have an internal environment.

The General Environment

The general environment consists of several basic dimensions, including economic, technological, and political-legal dimensions. These dimensions embody conditions and events that have the potential to influence the organization in important ways. Two other important parts of the general environment, social and international, are discussed separately later in this chapter.

• **economic dimension** The overall health of the economic system in which the organization operates

The Economic Dimension The **economic dimension** of an organization's general environment is the overall health of the economic system in which the organization operates.[2] Particularly important economic factors for business are inflation, interest rates, and unemployment, all of which affect demand for different products. During times of inflation, for example, a company pays more for resources and must raise its prices to cover the higher costs. When interest rates are high, consumers are less willing to borrow money and the company itself must pay more when it borrows. When unemployment is high, the company is able to be very selective about whom it hires, but consumer buying may decline because fewer people are working.

• **technological dimension** The methods available for converting resources into products or services

The Technological Dimension The **technological dimension** of the general environment refers to the methods available for converting resources into products or services. Although technology is applied within the organization, the forms and availability of that technology come from the general environment. Computer-assisted manufacturing and design techniques, for example, allow McDonnell Douglas Corp. to simulate the three miles of hydraulic tubing that run through a DC-10. The results include decreased warehouse needs, higher-quality tube fittings, fewer employees, and major time savings.[3] New innovations in robotics and other manufacturing techniques also have implications for managers.

The Political-Legal Dimension The **political-legal dimension** of the general environment refers to government regulation of business and the relationship between business and government. It is important for three basic reasons. First, the legal system partially defines what an organization can and cannot do. Although the United States is basically a free market economy, there is still significant regulation of business activity.[4] Second, probusiness or antibusiness sentiment, in government influences business activity. For example, during periods of probusiness sentiment, firms find it easier to compete and have fewer concerns about antitrust issues. On the other hand, during a period of antibusiness sentiment, firms may find their competitive strategies more restricted and have fewer opportunities for mergers and acquisitions because of antitrust concerns. Finally, political stability has ramifications for planning. No company wants to set up shop in another country unless trade relationships with that country are relatively well defined and stable. Hence, U.S. firms are more likely to do business with England, Mexico, and Canada than with Iran and El Salvador. Similar issues are also relevant to assessments of local and state governments. A change in the mayor's or the governor's position can affect many organizations, especially small firms that do business in only one location and are susceptible to deed and zoning restrictions, property and school taxes, and the like.

• **political-legal dimension** The government regulation of business and the general relationship between business and government

The Task Environment

Because the impact of the general environment is often vague, imprecise, and long-term, most organizations tend to focus their attention on their task environment. While it is also quite complex, the task environment provides useful information more readily than does the general environment because the manager can identify environmental factors of specific interest to the organization rather than having to deal with the more abstract dimensions of the general environment. Figure 2.1 depicts the task environment of Ford Motor Company. As shown, this environment consists of five dimensions.

Competitors An organization's **competitors** are other organizations that compete with it for resources. The most obvious resources that competitors vie for are customer dollars. Reebok, Adidas, and Nike are competitors, as are A&P, Safeway, and Kroger. But competition also occurs between substitute products. Thus, Chrysler competes with Yamaha (motorcycles) and Schwinn (bicycles) for your transportation dollars, and The

• **competitors** Organizations that compete for resources

FIGURE 2.1 Ford's Task Environment

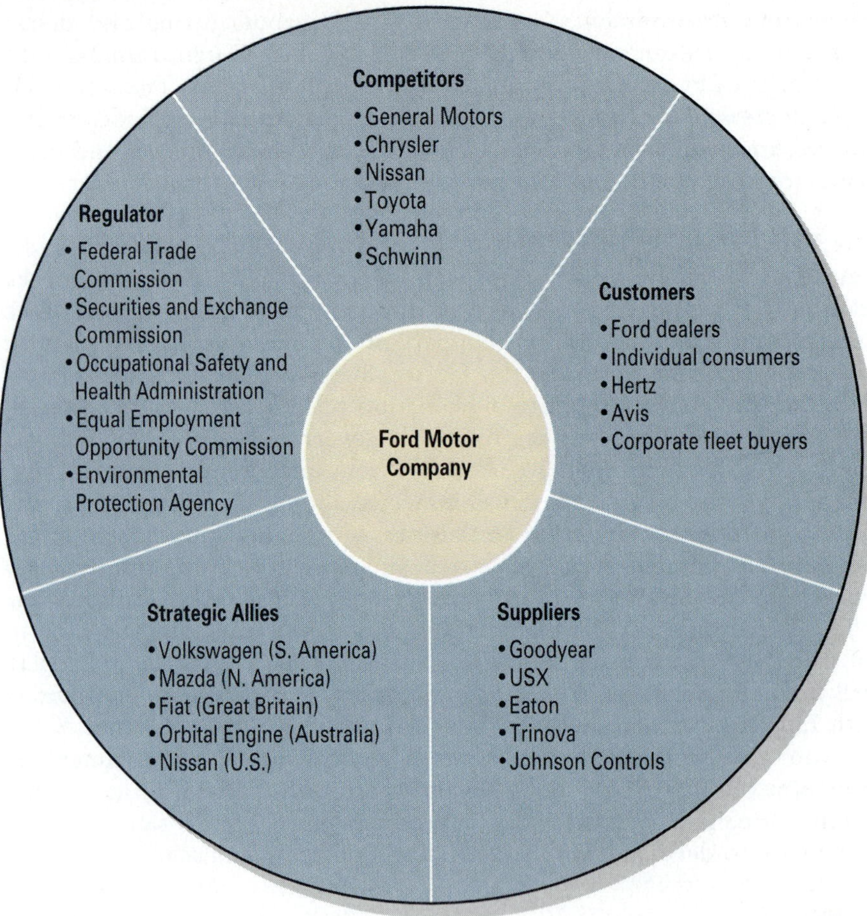

Walt Disney Company, Club Med, and Carnival Cruise Lines compete for your vacation dollars. Nor is competition limited to business firms. Universities compete with trade schools, the military, other universities, and the external labor market to attract good students, while art galleries compete with each other to attract the best exhibits.[5] Organizations may also compete for different kinds of resources besides consumer dollars. For example, two totally unrelated organizations may compete to acquire a loan from a bank that has only limited funds to lend. In a large city, the police and fire departments may compete for the same tax dollars. And businesses also compete for quality labor, technological breakthroughs and patents, and scarce raw materials.

Fortunately for managers, information about competitors is often quite easily obtained. Kmart can monitor Wal-Mart's prices by reading its newspaper advertisements, for example, or by sending someone to a store to inspect price tags. Similarly, Hilton can monitor Marriott's hotel management practices by having some of its own managers check in at Marriott hotels as guests and observe how Marriott does things. Firms can also buy their competitors' products to learn more about their technology, assembly methods, and so forth. This practice, called *benchmarking*, has become an important tool in quality improvements programs in recent years.[6] (We discuss benchmarking in more detail in Chapter 15.) Other kinds of information, however, may be more difficult to obtain. Ongoing research activities, new product developments, and future advertising campaigns, for example, are often closely guarded secrets.[7]

Customers A second dimension of the task environment consists of customers. **Customers** are whoever pays money to acquire an organization's products or services. In many cases, however, the chain of customer transactions is not as straightforward as it might seem. As consumers, for example, we do not buy a bottle of Coke from Coca-Cola. We may buy it from Safeway or 7-Eleven, which bought it from an independent bottler, which bought the syrup and the right to use the name from Coca-Cola. Customers also need not be individuals. Schools, hospitals, government agencies, wholesalers, retailers, and manufacturers are just a few of the many kinds of organizations that may be major customers of other organizations. Common sources of information about customers include market research, surveys, consumer panels, and reports from sales representatives.

• **customers**
Whoever pays money to acquire an organization's products or services

Dealing with customers has become increasingly complex in recent years. New products and services, new methods of marketing, and more discriminating customers have all added uncertainty to how businesses relate to their customers. Many firms have found it necessary to focus their advertising on specific consumer groups or regions. General Foods Corporation, for example, has found it necessary to promote its Maxwell House coffee differently in different regions of the country, even though doing so costs two or three times what a single national advertising campaign would cost.[8] Pressures from consumer groups about packaging and related issues also complicate the lives of managers.

Suppliers **Suppliers** are organizations that provide resources for other organizations. Disney World buys soft-drink syrup from Coca-Cola, monorails from Daewoo, food from Sara Lee and Smucker, and paper products from Mead. Suppliers for manufacturers such as Corning and Ford include the suppliers of raw materials as well as firms that sell machinery and other equipment. Another kind of supplier provides the capital needed to operate the organization. Banks and federal lending agencies are both suppliers of capital for businesses. Other suppliers, including public and private employment agencies such as Kelly Services and college placement offices, provide human resources for the organization. Still other suppliers furnish the organization's managers with the information they need to function effectively. Many companies subscribe to periodicals such as *The Wall Street Journal, Fortune,* and *Business Week* to help their managers keep abreast of news. Market research firms are used by some companies. And some firms specialize in developing economic forecasts and keeping managers informed about pending legislation.

• **suppliers**
Organizations that provide resources for other organizations

Common wisdom used to be that a business should try to avoid depending exclusively on particular suppliers. A firm that buys all of a certain resource from one supplier may be crippled if the supplier goes out of business or is faced with a strike. Using more than one supplier can also help maintain a competitive relationship between those suppliers, keeping costs down.[9] In recent times, however, some businesses have come to recognize that building especially strong relationships with a smaller set of suppliers can also pay off. Honda picked Donnelly Corp. to make all the mirrors for its U.S.-manufactured cars. Honda chose Donnelly because it learned enough about the firm to know that Donnelly did high-quality work and that its corporate culture and values were consistent with Honda's. Recognizing the value of Honda as a customer, Donnelly built an entirely new plant to make the mirrors. And all this was accomplished with only a handshake. Motorola goes even further, providing its key suppliers with access to its own renowned quality training program and evaluating the performance of each supplier as a way of helping that firm boost its own quality.[10]

• **regulators**
Units that have the potential to control, regulate, or otherwise influence the organization's policies and practices

• **regulatory agencies**
Created by the government to regulate business activities

Regulators **Regulators** are units in the task environment that have the potential to control, regulate, or influence an organization's policies and practices. There are two important kinds of regulators. The first, **regulatory agencies**, are created by the government to protect the public from certain business practices or to protect organizations from one another. Powerful federal regulatory agencies include the Environmental Protection Agency (EPA), the Occupational Safety and Health Administration (OSHA), the Securities and Exchange Commission (SEC), the Food and Drug Administration (FDA), and the Equal Employment Opportunity Commission (EEOC).

Many of these agencies play important roles in protecting the rights of individuals. The FDA, for example, helps ensure that the food we eat is free from contaminants. The costs a firm incurs in complying with government regulations may be substantial, but these costs are usually passed on to the customer. Even so, many organizations complain that there is too much regulation at the present time. One study found that forty-eight major companies spent $2.6 billion in one year—over and above normal environmental protection, employee safety, and similar costs—because of stringent government regulations. On the basis of these findings, the extra costs of government regulations for all businesses have been estimated at more than $100 billion per year.[11] Obviously, the impact of regulatory agencies on organizations is considerable.

Although federal regulators get a lot of publicity, the effect of state and local agencies is also important. California has more stringent automobile emission requirements than those established by the EPA. For example, that state has mandated that automobile companies that sell cars in California must include an electric car model in their product mix no later than 1997. Not-for-profit organizations must also deal with regulatory agencies. Most states, for example, have coordinating boards that regulate the operation of colleges and universities.

• **interest group**
Formed by its own individual members to attempt to influence business

The other basic form of regulator is the **interest group**. An interest group is organized by its members to attempt to influence organizations.

Prominent interest groups include the National Organization for Women (NOW), Mothers Against Drunk Drivers (MADD), the National Rifle Association (NRA), the League of Women Voters, the Sierra Club, Ralph Nader's Center for the Study of Responsive Law, Consumers Union, and industry self-regulation groups like the Council of Better Business Bureaus. Although interest groups lack the official power of government agencies, they can exert considerable influence by using the media to call attention to their positions. MADD, for example, puts considerable pressure on alcoholic-beverage producers (to put warning labels on their products), automobile companies (to make it more difficult for intoxicated people to start their cars), local governments (to stiffen drinking ordinances), and bars and restaurants (to refuse to sell alcohol to people who are drinking too much).

Strategic Allies A final dimension of the task environment is **strategic allies**—two or more companies that work together in joint ventures or other partnerships. As shown in Figure 2.1, Ford has a number of strategic allies, including Volkswagen (to make cars in South America) and Nissan (to make vans in the United States). Ford and Mazda Motor Corporations also jointly make the Probe automobile. Alliances such as these have been around for a long time, but they became popular in the 1980s and are now increasing at a rate of around 22 percent per year.[12] IBM used to shun strategic alliances but now has seventy-five active partnerships around the globe.[13] And recall that Schwinn's new life is the result of a strategic alliance.

• **strategic allies**
Two or more organizations working together in a joint venture or similar arrangement

Strategic alliances help companies get from other companies the expertise they may lack. They also help spread risk. Managers must be careful, however, not to give away sensitive competitive information. For example, when Unisys Corp. entered into a strategic alliance with Hitachi, Ltd., a Japanese computer maker, it found that it had to divulge valuable trade secrets to make the partnership work. Strategic alliances, however, need not always involve business. Texas A&M University and the University of Texas, for example, often work together to secure government grants. And some churches sponsor joint missionary projects.

The Internal Environment

Organizations also have an internal environment that consists of their owners, board of directors, employees, and culture (we discuss culture later in a separate section).

Owners The **owners** of a business are, of course, the people who have a legal property right to that business. Owners can be a single individual who establishes and runs a small business, partners who jointly own the business, individual investors who buy stock in a corporation, or other organizations. The Ford family still controls a large block of stock in Ford Motor Company, although a significant share is also available for sale to other investors. Individuals who own and manage their own businesses are clearly a part of the organization's internal environment. But increasingly, so too are corporate stockholders. Until recently, stockholders of major

• **owner**
Whoever can claim property rights on an organization

corporations were generally happy to sit on the sidelines and let top management run their organizations. Lately, however, more and more of them are taking active roles in influencing the management of companies they hold stock in. This is especially true of owners who hold large blocks of stock. For example, a few years ago Time Warner Inc. announced that it was going to issue new stock to reduce its debt. Current stockholders were to be given first option on buying the stock, but its price was not going to be known at the time options had to be exercised. Several large stockholders complained and some threatened lawsuits. Time Warner eventually backed down and cancelled its plans.[14]

Another group increasingly exerting influence is the managers of large corporate pension funds. These enormous funds control 50 percent of the shares traded on the New York Stock Exchange and 65 percent of *Standard & Poor's 500* stocks. AT&T's pension fund, for example, exceeds $35 billion. Because pension funds are growing at twice the rate of the U.S. gross national product (GNP), it follows that their managers will have even more power in the future.[15] And given the increased power wielded by owners (and the increased willingness to use that power), some fear that managers are sacrificing long-term corporate effectiveness for the sake of short-term results. For example, managers at Carnation Company were afraid to increase advertising costs too much for fear of attracting the attention of institutional investors. As a result, sales declined. After Nestlé SA took over and loosened the purse strings, sales took off again.[16] Thus managers are finding that they are having to be considerably more concerned about owners now than in the past.

Board of Directors Not every organization has a board of directors. Corporations, of course, are required to have them, but nonincorporated businesses and many nonbusiness organizations are not. Most universities, however, do have a board of regents, and most other large organizations, such as hospitals and charities, have a board of trustees that serves essentially the same purpose. A corporate board of directors is elected by the stockholders and is charged with overseeing the general management of the firm to ensure that it is being run in a way that best serves the stockholders' interests.[17] Some directors, called inside directors, are also full-time employees of the firm holding top-management jobs. Outside directors, in contrast, are elected to the board for a specific purpose—to assist with financial management, legal issues, and so forth—but are not full-time employees of the organization. Ford Motor Company has eight board members who also work for the firm, and another seven who work for other companies. Among the latter are the CEOs of Coca-Cola, Seagram, and several other firms. The board plays a major role in helping set corporate strategy and seeing that it is implemented properly. The board also reviews all important decisions made by top management and determines compensation for top managers.

Employees An organization's employees are also a major element of its internal environment. When managers and employees embrace the same values and have the same goals, everyone wins. When managers and employees work toward different ends, however, or when conflict and hostility pervade the organization, everyone suffers.[18] Many of the issues that we discuss in Part IV, Leading, are aimed at enhancing interpersonal relationships in the organization. Of particular interest to managers today is the changing nature of U.S. workers. The workforce of tomorrow will have more women, Hispanics, blacks, and older people than the workforce of today. The worker of tomorrow is also expected to want more job ownership—either partial ownership in the company or at least more say in how the job is performed.[19]

The employees of many organizations are organized into labor unions. The National Labor Relations Act of 1935 requires organizations to recognize and bargain with a union if that union has been legally established by the organization's employees. Presently, around 23 percent of the U.S. labor force is represented by unions. Some large firms such as Ford, Exxon, and General Motors have to deal with several different unions. Even when an organization's labor force is not unionized, its managers do not ignore unions. For example, Kmart, J. P. Stevens, Honda of America, and Delta Air Lines, Inc., all actively seek to avoid unionization. And even though people think primarily of blue-collar workers as union members, many government employees, teachers, and other white-collar workers are also represented by unions.

THE ETHICAL AND SOCIAL ENVIRONMENT OF MANAGEMENT

The ethical and social environment has become an especially important area for managers in the last few years. In this section we first explore the concept of individual ethics and then describe social responsibility.

Individual Ethics in Organizations

Ethics are an individual's personal beliefs about whether a behavior, action, or decision is right or wrong.[20] It is important to note that ethics are relative, not absolute; although **ethical behavior** is in the eye of the beholder, it usually refers to behavior that conforms to generally accepted social norms. **Unethical behavior**, then, is behavior that does not conform to generally accepted social norms.

- **ethics**
An individual's personal beliefs regarding what is right and wrong or good and bad

- **ethical behavior**
Behavior that conforms to generally accepted social norms

- **unethical behavior**
Behavior that does not conform to generally accepted social norms

- **managerial ethics**
Standards of behavior that guide individual managers in their work

Managerial Ethics **Managerial ethics** are the standards of behavior that guide individual managers in their work.[21] Ethical or unethical actions by particular managers do not occur in a vacuum, however.[22] Indeed, they most often occur in an organizational context that is conducive to them. Actions of peer managers and top managers, as well as the organization's culture, all contribute to the ethical context of the organization.

The starting point in understanding the ethical context of management is the individual's own ethical standards. Some people, for example, would risk personal embarrassment or lose their job before they would do something unethical. Other people are much more easily swayed by the unethical behavior they see around them and other situational factors, and they may be willing to commit major crimes to further their own careers or to reap financial gain. Organizational practices may strongly influence the ethical standards of employees. Some organizations openly permit unethical business practices as long as they are in the best interests of the firm.

If a manager becomes aware of an unethical practice and allows it to continue, he has contributed to the organizational culture that says such activity is permitted. For example, when the CEO of Beech-Nut discovered that his firm was using additives in its apple juice, advertised as 100 percent pure, he decided to try to cover up the deception until the remaining juice could be disposed of. Many employees participated in his plan. When the cover-up was finally discovered, the company suffered grave damages to its reputation and had to pay several million dollars in fines. In addition, the CEO was sentenced to a jail term.[23]

Managing Ethical Behavior Spurred partially by the recent spate of ethical scandals and partially from a sense of enhanced corporate consciousness about the importance of ethical and unethical behaviors, many organizations have reemphasized ethical behavior on the part of employees.[24] This emphasis takes many forms, but any effort to enhance ethical behavior must begin with top management. It is this group that establishes the organization's culture and defines what will and will not be acceptable behavior. Some companies have also started offering employees training in how to cope with ethical dilemmas. At Boeing, for example, line managers lead training sessions for other employees, and the company also has an ethics committee that reports directly to the board of directors. The training sessions involve discussions of different ethical dilemmas that employees might face and how managers might handle those dilemmas. Xerox and

The government plays an active role in social responsibility in the United States. Public transit providers are now designing new buses using alternative energy sources to help meet federal regulations. As indicated by its graphics, this bus in Chicago is powered by natural gas. Of course, the transportation providers also benefit from the positive public image conveyed by the design of the bus.

McDonnell Douglas have also established ethics training programs for their managers.[25]

Organizations are also going to greater lengths to formalize their ethical standards. Some, such as General Mills and Johnson & Johnson, have prepared guidelines that detail how employees are to treat suppliers, customers, competitors, and other constituents. Others, such as Whirlpool Corporation and Hewlett-Packard, have developed formal **codes of ethics**—written statements of the values and ethical standards that guide a firm's actions. Figure 2.2 shows the code of ethics used at Lockheed Martin.

codes of ethics Formal, written statements of the values and ethical standards that guide a firm's actions

Social Responsibility and Organizations

As we have seen, ethics relates to individuals. Organizations themselves do not have ethics, but they do relate to their environment in ways that often involve ethical dilemmas and decisions. **Social responsibility** is the set of obligations an organization has to protect and enhance the society in which it functions.[26] On the surface, there would seem to be little disagreement about the need for organizations to be socially responsible. In truth, though, there are several convincing arguments used by those who oppose these wider interpretations of social responsibility.[27] Some of the more

social responsibility The set of obligations an organization has to protect and enhance the societal context in which it functions

FIGURE 2.2 The Lockheed Martin Code of Ethics

Our Vision

- *Our vision is for Lockheed Martin to be recognized as the world's premier systems engineering and technology enterprise*
- *Our mission is to build on our aerospace heritage to meet the needs of our customers with high-quality products and services*
- *And in so doing, produce superior returns for our shareholders and foster growth and achievement for our employees*

Overarching Principles

In realizing our vision, we will adhere to the highest standards of ethical conduct in everything we do. We will achieve mission success for our customers, create opportunity for our employees, provide strong returns for our shareholders, and serve the communities where we live and work. Our actions are guided by certain unifying principles:

Ethical conduct in dealing with our colleagues, customers, shareholders, suppliers and the public, providing the basis for earned trust

Mission success as we carry out our responsibility to achieve superior performance and to provide our customers the quality products and services they have a right to expect

Technological leadership in all disciplines that contribute to fulfilling our vision

Financial strength and profitability to meet the expectations of our shareholders and enable us to aggressively pursue new business opportunities

Competitiveness through attention to cost, efficiency and continuous improvement

Fair treatment and candid communication with the diverse work force from whom our enterprise derives its strength

Decisiveness and responsiveness in addressing our internal and external challenges

Active, responsible citizenship to the nation and the communities in which we live and work

Lockheed Martin S² Strategy: Strength with Speed

Leverage technology breadth, employee talent, corporate scale, global market access and financial strength
- *Invest in our people; realize corporate-wide synergies*
- *Focus technology and investments on true market differentiators*
- *Capitalize on corporate resources as targeted competitive advantage*

Improve competitiveness, profitability and agility
- *Drive costs down at all levels — reduce cycle times*
- *Embrace commercial practices wherever beneficial*
- *Foster change-oriented, high-performance environment*

Grow leadership positions in core businesses
- *Focus on superior people, technology, performance and affordability*
- *Continuously improve mission success and customer satisfaction*
- *Benefit from industry consolidation opportunities*

Expand into related domestic and international growth markets
- *Apply premier technology base to meet emerging market needs*
- *Capitalize on international presence with broader products and services*
- *Adopt innovative approaches for profitable market penetration*

Consistently deliver superior shareholder value growth

LOCKHEED MARTIN

salient arguments on both sides of this contemporary debate are summarized in Figure 2.3.

Arguments for Social Responsibility People who argue in favor of social responsibility claim that because organizations create many of the problems that need to be addressed—such as air and water pollution and resource depletion—they should play a major role in solving them. They also argue that because corporations are legally defined entities with most of the same privileges as private citizens, businesses should not try to avoid their obligations as citizens. Advocates of social responsibility point out that while governmental organizations have stretched their budgets to the limit, many large businesses often have surplus revenues that could potentially be used to help solve social problems. For example, IBM routinely donates surplus computers to schools.

Arguments Against Social Responsibility Some people argue that social responsibility undermines the U.S. economy by detracting from the basic mission of business: to earn profits for owners. For example, money that Chevron or General Electric contributes to social causes or charities is money that could otherwise be distributed to owners as a dividend. Another objection to deepening the social responsibility of businesses points out that corporations already wield enormous power and that pushing them to be more active in social programs gives them even more power.

Another argument against social responsibility is that it increases the potential for a conflict of interest. For example, a baby formula manufacturer would face such a conflict if it became too involved in a welfare mother's program. Further, critics argue that organizations lack the expertise to un-

FIGURE 2.3 Arguments for and Against Social Responsibility

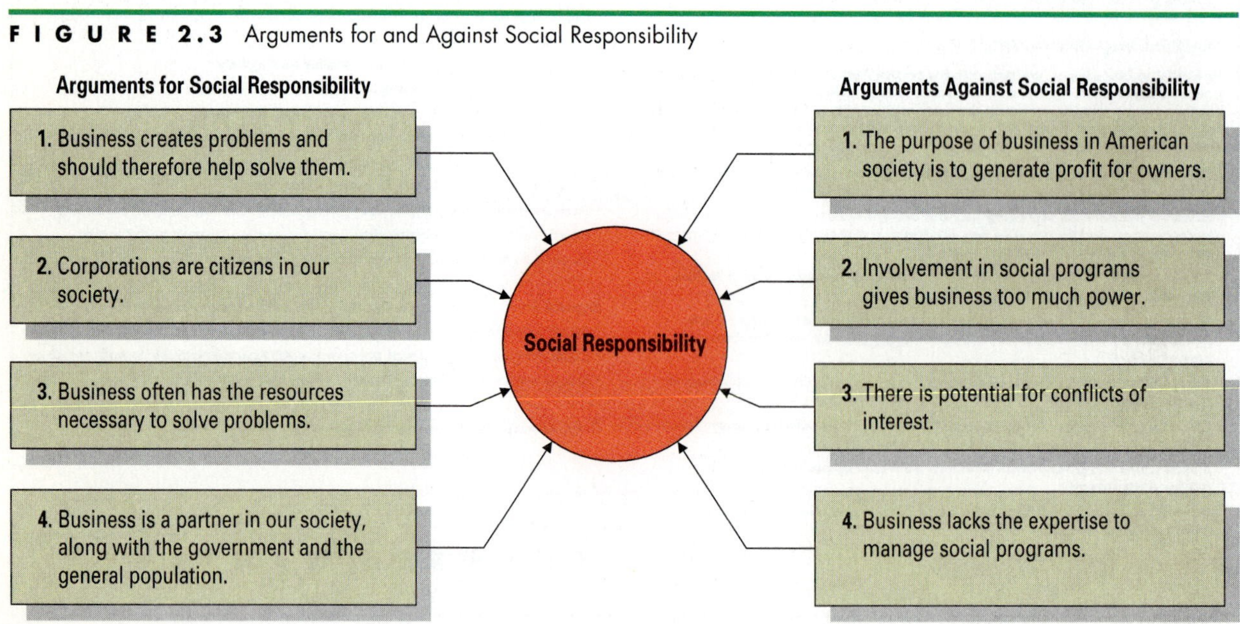

derstand how to assess and make decisions about worthy social programs. How can a company truly know which cause or program is most deserving of its support? People who ask these questions also see an alarming trend on the part of organizations to tie products to social causes. This practice began when American Express Company pledged to donate one cent to the Statue of Liberty restoration project each time one of its credit cards was used. Critics fear that this practice will enable companies to exert too much influence over the charitable causes with which they become associated and that charities will begin to function merely as marketing agents to help the firms sell their products.[28]

Managing Social Responsibility

The demands for social responsibility placed on contemporary organizations by an increasingly sophisticated and educated public are probably stronger than ever. As we have seen, there are pitfalls for managers who fail to adhere to high ethical standards and for companies that try to circumvent their legal obligations. Organizations therefore need to fashion an approach to social responsibility the way they develop any other business strategy; that is, they should view social responsibility as a major challenge that requires careful planning, decision making, consideration, and evaluation. They may accomplish this through both formal and informal dimensions of managing social responsibility.[29]

Formal Organizational Dimensions Some formal dimensions of managing social responsibility are legal compliance, ethical compliance, and philanthropic giving.[30]

Legal compliance is the extent to which the organization conforms to local, state, federal, and international laws. The task of managing legal compliance is generally assigned to the appropriate functional managers. For example, the organization's top human resource executive is generally responsible for ensuring compliance with regulations concerning recruiting, selection, pay, and so forth. Likewise, the top finance executive generally oversees compliance with securities and banking regulations. The organization's legal department is also likely to contribute to this effort by providing general oversight and answering queries from managers about the appropriate interpretation of laws and regulations.

• **legal compliance** The extent to which an organization complies with local, state, federal, and international laws

Ethical compliance is the extent to which the members of the organization follow basic ethical (and legal) standards of behavior. We noted earlier that organizations have started doing more in this area—providing training in ethics and developing guidelines and codes of conduct, for example. These activities serve as vehicles for enhancing ethical compliance. Many organizations also establish formal ethics committees, which may be asked to review proposals for new projects, help evaluate new hiring strategies, or assess a new environmental protection plan. They might also serve as a peer review panel to evaluate alleged ethical misconduct by an employee.[31]

• **ethical compliance** The extent to which an organization and its members follow basic ethical standards of behavior

Finally, **philanthropic giving** is the awarding of funds or other gifts, for example, to charities or other social programs. Dayton-Hudson, for example, routinely gives 5 percent of its taxable income to charity and

• **philanthropic giving** Awarding funds or other gifts to charities or worthy causes

social programs. Giving across national boundaries has also become more common. For example, Alcoa recently gave $112,000 to a small town in Brazil to build a sewage treatment plant. And Japanese firms such as Sony and Mitsubishi have started making contributions to a number of social programs in the United States.[32]

Informal Organizational Dimensions In addition to these formal dimensions for managing social responsibility, there are also informal ones. Two of the more effective ways to clarify the organization's approach are to provide appropriate leadership and culture and to allow for whistle blowing.

Leadership practices and organization culture can go a long way toward defining the social responsibility stance an organization and its members will adopt. For example, Johnson & Johnson executives for years provided a consistent message to employees that customers, employees, communities where the company did business, and shareholders were all important—primarily in that order. Thus when packages of poisoned Tylenol showed up on store shelves in the 1980s, Johnson & Johnson employees didn't need to wait for orders from headquarters to know what to do: They immediately pulled all the packages from shelves before any more customers could buy them.[33] By contrast, the message sent to Beech-Nut employees by the actions of their top managers communicated much less regard for social responsibility.

• **whistle blowing**
The disclosing by an employee of illegal or unethical conduct on the part of others within the organization

Whistle blowing is the disclosure by an employee of illegal or unethical conduct on the part of others within the organization. How an organization responds to this practice often indicates its stance toward social responsibility.[34] Whistle blowers may have to proceed through a number of channels to be heard, and may even get fired for their efforts. Many organizations, however, welcome their contributions. A person who observes questionable behavior typically reports the incident to his or her boss at first. If nothing is done, the whistle blower may then inform higher-level managers or an ethics committee if one exists. Eventually, the person may have to go to a regulatory agency or even the media to be heard.[35] The apple juice scandal at Beech-Nut, for example, started with a whistle blower. A manager in the firm's R&D department began to suspect that its apple juice was not "100% pure." His boss, however, was unsympathetic, and when the manager went to the president of the company, he too turned a deaf ear. Eventually, the manager took his message to the media, which publicized the incident. This eventually led to a criminal investigation.

THE INTERNATIONAL ENVIRONMENT OF MANAGEMENT

Another important competitive issue for managers today is the international environment. After describing recent trends in international business, we examine levels of internationalization and the international context of business.

Trends in International Business

International business is a growing trend in virtually every industry. Even the sports world is getting in the act. For example, the NFL has played exhibition games in Japan, England, and Mexico. Baseball has long been a popular sport in Japan, soccer's World Cup was recently hosted by the United States, and basketball is a national pastime in Italy. The NBA sponsors this local tournament in Paris to help promote the game's growth in France.

In the years immediately following World War II, the United States was by far the dominant economic force in the world because most of the industrialized countries in Europe and Japan had been devastated during the war. Businesses in those war-torn regions had no choice but to rebuild from scratch. Although it took many years for these countries to recover, they eventually did so, and their economic systems were subsequently poised for growth. During the same era, U.S. companies grew complacent. Increased population spurred by the baby boom and increased affluence resulting from the postwar economic boom greatly raised the average person's standard of living and expectations. The U.S. public continually wanted new and better products and services. Many U.S. companies profited greatly from this pattern but most were also perhaps guilty of taking it for granted.

U.S. firms are no longer isolated from global competition or markets.[36] Consider, for example, that the volume of international trade increased more than 2,500 percent from 1960 to 1993. Foreign investment in the United States by foreign firms was more than $42 billion in 1993 alone, and U.S. firms invested more than $36 billion in foreign markets. In 1960, seventy of the world's one hundred largest firms were American. This figure dropped to 64 in 1970, to 45 in 1985, and to 32 in 1994.[37] Clearly, U.S. dominance of the global economy is a thing of the past.

U.S. firms are also finding that international operations are an increasingly important element of their sales and profits. For example, in 1993 Exxon Corporation realized 79 percent of its revenues and 78 percent of its profits abroad. For Avon, these percentages were 59 percent and 62 percent, respectively.[38] From any perspective, then, it is clear that we live in a truly global economy. The days when U.S. firms could safely ignore the rest of the world and concentrate only on the U.S. market are gone forever. Now these firms must be concerned both with the competitive situations they face in foreign markets and with how foreign companies are competing in the United States.[39]

Levels of International Business Activity

Firms can choose from a variety of levels of international business activity as they seek to gain competitive advantage in foreign markets. The most basic levels are exporting, licensing, strategic alliances, and direct investment. Table 2.1 summarizes the advantages and disadvantages of each.

- **exporting**
Making a product in one country and selling it in another

- **licensing**
An arrangement whereby one company allows another company to use its brand name, trademark, technology, patent, copyright, or other assets in exchange for a royalty based on sales

Exporting **Exporting** is usually the first type of international business in which a firm gets involved. **Exporting** occurs when a firm makes a product in one country and then sells it in another. For example, firms in the United States routinely export grain to the Soviet Union, gas turbines to Saudi Arabia, locomotives to Indonesia, blue jeans to Great Britain, and diapers to Italy. Boeing is the largest exporter in the United States.

Licensing **Licensing** is an arrangement whereby a firm allows another company to use its brand name, trademark, technology, patent, copyright,

When organizations decide to increase their level of internationalization, there are several strategies that they can adopt. Each strategy is a matter of degree, as opposed to being a discrete and mutually exclusive category. And each has unique advantages and disadvantages that must be considered.

TABLE 2.1 Advantages and Disadvantages of Different Approaches to Internationalization

Approach to Internationalization	Advantages	Disadvantages
Exporting	1. Small cash outlay 2. Little risk 3. No adaptation necessary	1. Tariffs and taxes 2. High transportation costs 3. Government restrictions
Licensing	1. Increased profitability 2. Extended profitability	1. Inflexibility 2. Helps competitors
Strategic alliance/ Joint ventures	1. Quick market entry 2. Access to materials and technology	1. Shared ownership (limits control and profits)
Direct investment	1. Enhances control 2. Existing infrastructure	1. Complexity 2. Greater economic and political risk 3. Greater uncertainty

or other assets. In return, the licensee pays a royalty, usually based on sales. For example, Kirin Brewery, Japan's largest producer of beer, wanted to expand its international operations but feared that the time involved in shipping it from Japan would cause the beer to lose its freshness. Thus, it has entered into a number of licensing arrangements with breweries in other markets. These brewers make beer according to strict guidelines provided by the Japanese firm, and then package and market it as Kirin Beer. They then pay a royalty back to Kirin for each case sold. Molson produces Kirin in Canada under such an agreement, while the Charles Wells brewery does the same in England.[40]

● **strategic alliance**
A cooperative arrangement between two or more firms for mutual benefit

● **joint venture**
A special type of strategic alliance in which the partners share in the ownership of an operation on an equity basis

● **direct investment**
When a firm headquartered in one country builds or purchases operating facilities or subsidiaries in a foreign country

Strategic Alliances We noted earlier the role of **strategic alliances**. Indeed, most such alliances today involve international partners.[41] A **joint venture** is a special type of strategic alliance in which the partners actually share ownership of a new enterprise. General Mills and Nestlé recently formed a new company called Cereal Partners Worldwide. The purpose of CPW is to produce and market cereals. General Mills supplies the technology and proven formulas, and Nestlé provides its international distribution network. The two partners share equally in the new enterprise.[42]

Direct Investment **Direct investment** occurs when a firm headquartered in one country builds or purchases operating facilities or subsidiaries in a foreign country. Kodak recently made a direct investment when it built a new research laboratory in Japan. Similarly, Ford's plants in Germany and Unilever's distribution centers in the United States represent direct investments. At the present time, many Asian firms are investing heavily in Europe.[43]

A major reason many firms make direct investments is to capitalize on lower labor costs. That is, the goal is often to transfer production to locations where labor is cheap. Japanese businesses have moved much of their production to Thailand because labor costs are much lower there than in Japan. Many U.S. firms are using maquiladoras for the same purpose. **Maquiladoras** are light assembly plants built in northern Mexico close to the U.S. border. The plants are given tax breaks by the Mexican government, and the prevailing wage rates are relatively low.[44]

• **maquiladoras**
Light assembly plants built in northern Mexico close to the U.S. border that are given special tax breaks by the Mexican government

The Context of International Business

Managers involved in international business must also be aware of three major areas of concern: controls on international business, the existence of economic communities, and cultural variations across national boundaries.[45]

Controls on International Trade In some instances, the government of a country may decide that foreign competition is hurting domestic trade. To protect domestic business, such governments may enact barriers to international trade.

A **tariff** is a tax collected on goods shipped across national boundaries. Tariffs can be collected by the exporting country, the countries through which goods pass, and the importing country. Import tariffs, which are the most common, can be levied to protect domestic companies by increasing the cost of foreign goods. Japan charges U.S. tobacco producers a tariff on cigarettes imported into Japan as a way to keep their prices higher than the prices charged by domestic firms. Tariffs can also be levied, usually by less developed countries, to raise money for the government.

• **tariff**
A tax collected on goods shipped across national boundaries

Quotas are the most common form of trade restriction. A quota is a limit on the number or value of goods that can be traded. The quota amount is typically designed to ensure that domestic competitors will be able to maintain a certain market share. Honda is allowed to import 425,000 autos each year into the United States. This quota is one reason Honda opened manufacturing facilities here. The quota applies to cars imported into the United States, but the company can produce as many other cars within our borders as it wants, as they are not considered imports.

• **quotas**
Limits on the number or value of goods that can be traded

Export restraint agreements are designed to convince other governments to voluntarily limit the volume or value of goods exported to a particular country. They are, in effect, export quotas. Japanese steel producers voluntarily limit the amount of steel they send to the United States each year.

• **export restraint agreements**
Accords reached by governments in which countries voluntarily limit the volume or value of goods they export to and import from one another

"Buy national" legislation gives preference to domestic producers through content or price restrictions. Several countries have this type of legislation. Brazil requires that Brazilian companies purchase only Brazilian-made computers. The United States requires that the Department of Defense purchase only military uniforms manufactured in the United States, even though the price of foreign uniforms would be half as much. Mexico requires that 50 percent of the parts of cars sold in Mexico be manufactured in Mexico.

Economic Communities Just as government policies can either increase or decrease the political risk facing international managers, trade relations between countries can either help or hinder international business. Relations dictated by quotas, tariffs, and so forth can hurt international trade. There is currently a strong movement around the world to reduce many of these barriers. This movement takes its most obvious form in international economic communities.

- **economic community** A set of countries that agree to reduce or eliminate trade barriers among member nations
- **European Union (EU)** The first and most important international market system
- **North American Free Trade Agreement (NAFTA)** An agreement between the United States, Canada, and Mexico to promote trade with one another

An international **economic community** is a set of countries that agree to markedly reduce or eliminate trade barriers among member nations. The first—and in many ways still the most important—of these economic communities is the **European Union** (**EU**). Figure 2.4 illustrates the member nations of the EU. Similarly, the recent **North American Free Trade Agreement** (**NAFTA**) represents perhaps the first step toward creating an economic system between Canada, Mexico, and the United States. Such economic systems make it easier for member states to conduct business with one another, but may make it more difficult for nonmember states to compete.

National Culture Another challenge for the international manager is the cultural environment and how it affects business. Cultural values and beliefs are often unspoken; they may even be taken for granted by those who live

F I G U R E 2.4 The European Union

Within the structure of the global economy there is considerable variation in wealth and standards of living between mature market economies and developing economies. For example, the family on the left, from England, clearly has an abundance of material possessions. On the other hand, the family on the right, from Albania, has far fewer possessions.

in a particular country. Cultural factors do not necessarily cause problems for managers when the cultures of two countries are similar. Difficulties can arise, however, when there is little overlap between the home culture of a manager and the culture of the country in which business is to be conducted. For example, most U.S. managers find the culture and traditions of England familiar. The people of both countries speak the same language and share strong historical roots, and there is a history of strong commerce between the two countries. When U.S. managers begin operations in Japan or the People's Republic of China, however, most of those commonalities disappear.[46]

Cultural differences between countries can have a direct impact on business practice. For example, the religion of Islam teaches that people should not make a living by exploiting the misfortune of others and that making interest payments is immoral. This means that in Saudi Arabia there are no businesses that provide auto-towing services to tow stalled cars to the garage (because that would be capitalizing on misfortune), and in the Sudan banks cannot pay or charge interest. Given these cultural and religious constraints, those two businesses—automobile towing and banking—don't seem to hold great promise for international managers in those particular countries.

Some cultural differences between countries can be even more subtle and yet have a major impact on business activities. In the United States, for example, most managers clearly agree about the value of time. Most U.S. managers schedule their activities very tightly and then adhere to their schedules. Other cultures don't put such a premium on time. In the Middle East, managers do not like to set appointments, and they rarely keep appointments set too far into the future. U.S. managers interacting with managers from the Middle East might misinterpret the late arrival of a potential business partner as a negotiation ploy or an insult, when it is rather a simple reflection of different views of time and its value.

Language itself can be an important factor. Beyond the obvious and clear barriers posed by people who speak different languages, subtle differences in meaning can also play a major role. For example, Imperial Oil of Canada markets gasoline under the brand name Esso. When the firm tried to sell its gasoline in Japan, it learned that Esso means "stalled car" in Japanese. The Chevrolet Nova was not selling well in Latin America and General Motors executives couldn't understand why until it was brought to their attention that, in Spanish, *no va* means "it doesn't go." The color green is used extensively in Moslem countries, but it signifies death in some other countries. The color associated with femininity in the United States is pink, but in many other countries yellow is the most feminine color.

THE ORGANIZATION'S CULTURE

• **culture**
The set of values that helps an organization's members understand what it stands for, how it does things, and what it considers important

The **culture** of an organization is the set of values that helps its members understand what the organization stands for, how it does things, and what it considers important. Culture is an amorphous concept that defies objective measurement or observation. Nevertheless, because it is the foundation of the organization's internal environment, it plays a major role in shaping managerial behavior.[47]

The Importance of Culture

Several years ago, executives at Levi Strauss felt that the company had outgrown its sixty-eight-year-old building. Even though everyone enjoyed its casual and relaxed atmosphere, more space was needed. So Levi Strauss moved into a modern office building in downtown San Francisco, where its new headquarters spread over twelve floors in a skyscraper. It quickly became apparent that the change was affecting the corporate culture—and that people did not like it. Executives felt isolated, and other managers missed the informal chance meetings in the halls. Within just a few years, Strauss moved out of the skyscraper and back into a building that fosters informality. For example, there is an adjacent park area where employees converge for lunchtime conversation. Clearly, Levi Strauss has a culture that is important to everyone who works there.[48]

Culture determines the "feel" of the organization. The stereotypic image of the IBM executive is someone wearing a white shirt and dark suit. Even though IBM has recently moved to more casual attire, the stereotype still lingers. In contrast, Texas Instruments likes to talk about its "shirt-sleeve" culture, in which ties are avoided and few managers ever wear jackets. Of course, the same culture is not necessarily found throughout an entire organization. For example, the sales and marketing department may have a culture quite different from that of the operations and manufacturing department. Regardless of its nature, however, culture is a powerful force in organizations, one that can shape the firm's overall effectiveness and long-term success. Companies that can develop and maintain a strong culture, such as Hewlett-Packard and Procter & Gamble, tend to be more effective than companies that have trouble developing and maintaining a strong culture.[49]

Determinants of Culture

Where does organizational culture come from? Typically it develops and blossoms over a long period of time. Its starting point is often the organization's founder. For example, James Cash Penney believed in treating employees and customers with respect and dignity. Employees at JC Penney are still called associates rather than employees (to reflect partnership), and customer satisfaction is of paramount importance. The impact of Sam Walton, Ross Perot, and Walt Disney is still felt in the organizations they founded. As an organization grows, its culture is modified, shaped, and refined by symbols, stories, heroes, slogans, and ceremonies. For example, a key value at Hewlett-Packard is the avoidance of bank debt. A popular story still told at the company involves a new project being considered for several years. All objective criteria indicated that HP should incur bank debt to finance it, yet Bill Hewlett and David Packard rejected it out of hand simply because "HP avoids bank debt." This story, involving two corporate heroes and based on a slogan, dictates corporate culture today.[50]

Corporate success and shared experiences also shape culture. For example, Hallmark Cards has a strong culture derived from its years of success in the greeting-card industry. Employees speak of the Hallmark family and care deeply about the company; many of them have worked at the company for years. At Navistar International, in contrast, the culture is quite weak, the management team changes rapidly, and few people sense any direction or purpose in the company. The differences in culture at Hallmark and Navistar are in part attributable to past successes and shared experiences.

Managing Organizational Culture

How can managers deal with culture, given its clear importance but intangible nature? The key is for the manager to understand the current culture and then decide if it should be maintained or changed.[51] By understanding the organization's current culture, managers can take appropriate actions. At Hewlett-Packard, the values represented by "the HP way" still exist. Moreover, they guide and direct most important activities undertaken by the firm. Culture can also be maintained by rewarding and promoting people whose behaviors are consistent with the existing culture and by articulating the culture through slogans, ceremonies, and so forth.

To change culture, managers must have a clear idea of what they want to create. As noted in our opening case, Schwinn's new motto—"Established

1895. Re-established 1994"—represents an effort to create a new culture that better reflects today's competitive environment in the bicycle market. One major way to shape culture is to bring outsiders into important managerial positions. The choice of a new CEO from outside the organization is often a clear signal that things will be changing. Adopting new slogans, telling new stories, staging new ceremonies, and breaking with tradition can also alter culture. Culture can also be changed by methods discussed in Chapter 7.

SUMMARY OF KEY POINTS

The general environment of an organization is composed of the nonspecific elements of the organization's surroundings that might affect its activities—economic, technological, political-legal, social, and international dimensions. The task environment consists of specific dimensions of the organization's surroundings that are very likely to influence the organization. It consists of five elements: competitors, customers, suppliers, regulators, and strategic allies. The internal environment consists of the organization's owners, board of directors, employees, and culture.

Ethics are an individual's personal beliefs about what constitutes right and wrong behavior. The ethical context of organizations consists of each manager's individual ethics and messages sent by organizational practices. Organizations use leadership, culture, training, codes, and guidelines to help them manage ethical behavior.

Social responsibility is the set of obligations an organization has to protect and enhance the society in which it functions. There are strong arguments both for and against social responsibility. Organizations use three types of activities to formally manage social responsibility: legal compliance, ethical compliance, and philanthropic giving. Leadership, culture, and allowing for whistle blowing are informal means for managing social responsibility.

International business is also a major part of the environment of management. Recent trends have shown a dramatic increase in the level of international business. Firms may compete internationally via exporting, licensing, strategic alliances, and direct investment. Controls on international trade, the existence of economic communities, and national culture are important issues that must be considered.

Culture is an especially important environmental concern for organizations. Managers must understand that culture is an important determinant of how well their organization will perform. Culture can be determined and managed in a number of different ways.

QUESTIONS FOR REVIEW

1. What is an organization's task environment? What are the major dimensions of that environment?
2. What are the components that comprise an organization's internal environment?
3. Summarize the arguments for and against social responsibility.
4. What are the basic levels of international business activity that can be identified?
5. What is organizational culture? Why is it important?

QUESTIONS FOR ANALYSIS

1. Can you think of dimensions of the task environment that are not discussed in the text? Indicate their connection to those that are discussed.
2. Identify examples of people or groups who may be part of both the internal and the external environment of an organization.
3. Can an action be ethical but illegal? Unethical but legal?
4. Describe how international business activity affects your day-to-day activities.
5. Does your college or university have a culture? How would you describe it to an outsider?

CASE STUDY

Emerson Enjoys Its Environment

Emerson Electric Co. was founded in 1890 in St. Louis by brothers who made electric motors. Their first product was a fan. Later they put the motors in player pianos, hair dryers, sewing machines, water pumps, and air-circulating systems. During World War II, Emerson was highly successful in adapting its motors for military use. However, Emerson became so dependent on its military business that, after the war, it lost so much business it almost went bankrupt.

In 1954 Wallace Persons became president and Emerson has been successful ever since. Persons decentralized the company and bought twenty-two other companies between 1957 and 1973 to convert Emerson into an aggregation of electric and electrical companies. He moved factories from St. Louis to the deep rural South, where labor costs were low and the company's anti-union stance was acceptable. That practice was continued by his successor, Charles F. Knight, who also moved companies offshore (to countries other than the U.S.) in a continuing quest for lower labor costs.

Emerson is often cited as one of the U.S. companies that compete best. CEO Knight is repeatedly named to "best manager" lists, although he is just as often named to "toughest bosses" lists. Terms and phrases used to describe Emerson and its management style are "an aggressive machine," "they rule by plans and budgets," "relentless," and "demanding"—these capture the organizational culture. The primary goal in any given year is to better the record of the previous year, especially in terms of profits. The second goal is to be number one in market share in each product line. In 1989 Emerson claimed that nearly 90 percent of its products were, indeed, number one in their markets (up from 76 percent in 1978). Emerson has had few price increases since the mid-1980s. This means that Emerson's sales revenues have not substantially gone up for six or so years, but its profits have—by almost 50 percent during that time!

Even with this enviable record, however, Knight was concerned. Early in 1993 he had a group of top executives tell him that he needed to create an environment that supported revenue growth as well as profit margins. Knight noticed that the forecasts from Emerson's meticulous planning process suggested that further gains from cost cutting would be marginal so growth was indeed the way to go.

To ensure that this tough, demanding organizational environment does not lead to disgruntled workers, Knight has each employee complete a questionnaire every two years. If as many as one-third of a plant's employees seem dissatisfied with something, management must come up with a plan to correct it. This concern for workers has paid off because the firm has an extremely loyal workforce.

Emerson's strategy for responding to its changing environment, then, involves developing new products, integrating the various parts of the company better, and expanding to overseas markets. Each of these goals is a sizable challenge, but Knight believes that each is achievable and, with the clear objective of profit growth, that each will be achieved over the next five to ten years. And joint ventures and expanding into markets in India, China, Singapore, and Eastern Europe are well under way.

Case Questions

1. Describe Emerson's external environment. What implications does that have for the company? Why?
2. Describe Emerson's internal environment. How does that contribute to and detract from the company's performance? Why?
3. How do the social and international environments apply to Emerson?

References: "It Ain't Broke, but Fix It Anyway," *Forbes*, August 1, 1994, pp. 56–60; Charles F. Knight, "Emerson Electric: Consistent Profits, Consistently," *Harvard Business Review*, January 1, 1992, pp. 57–70; Gary Hoover, Alta Campbell, and Patrick J. Spain (Eds.), *Hoover's Handbook of American Business 1994* (Austin, Tex.: The Reference Press, 1993), pp. 475–476; Milton Moskowitz, Robert Levering, and Michael Katz, *Everybody's Business* (New York: Doubleday, 1990), pp. 451–453; and Bill Saporito, "Companies That Compete Best," *Fortune*, May 22, 1989, pp. 36–38.

SKILLS • DEVELOPMENT • PORTFOLIO

BUILDING EFFECTIVE COMMUNICATION SKILLS

Exercise Overview

Communication skills refer to the manager's abilities both to effectively convey ideas and information to others and to effectively receive ideas and information from others. As noted in the chapter, international business has grown dramatically in recent times. This exercise will help sensitize you to some of the issues and complexities involved in communication in international business.

Exercise Background

More and more businesses today have various operations scattered around the globe. Of course, managers in these far-flung locations must periodically communicate with one another.

Assume that you have just been hired as a communications consultant by a small but rapidly growing international business. The owner of the business is frustrated because managers in different locations are having trouble maintaining contact with one another. This has led to several mistakes and missed opportunities.

The business has operations in New York, Paris, Munich, Tokyo, Hong Kong, and Rio de Janeiro. Your task is to determine how to improve interorganizational communication in the business.

Exercise Task

1. Look at a map and find the various locations where the business has operations. You may also need to do some research into each location.

2. Develop a list of every communication problem that managers in each city may face when attempting to communicate with the others.

3. Identify one or more ways managers could overcome each of these problems.

BUILDING EFFECTIVE TIME MANAGEMENT SKILLS

Exercise Overview

Time management skills refer to the manager's ability to prioritize work, to work efficiently, and to delegate appropriately. This exercise will provide you with an opportunity to relate time management issues to environmental pressures and opportunities.

Exercise Background

As discussed in the chapter, managers and organizations must be sensitive to a variety of environmental dimensions and forces reflected in the general, task, and internal environments. The general environment consists of the economic, technological, and political-legal dimensions. The task environment consists of competitors, customers, suppliers, regulators, and strategic allies. The internal environment consists of owners, the board of directors, and employees. In addition, the ethical and social environment, as well as the international environment, are also important.

The problem managers face is that time is a finite resource. There are only so many hours in a day and only so many things that can be done in a given period of time. Thus, managers must constantly make choices about how they spend their time. Clearly, they should try to use their time wisely and direct it at the more important challenges and opportunities they face. Spending time on a trivial issue while an important issue gets neglected is a mistake.

Time management experts often suggest that managers begin each day by making a list of what they need to accomplish that day. After the list is compiled, the manager then is advised to sort these daily tasks into three groups: those that must be addressed that day, those that should be addressed that day but which could be postponed if necessary, and those that can easily be postponed. The manager then is advised to perform the tasks in order of priority.

Exercise Task

With the background information above as context, do the following:

1. Write across the top of a sheet of paper the three priority levels noted above.

2. Write down the left side of the same sheet of paper the various elements and dimensions of the task and internal environments of business.

3. At the intersection of each row and column, think of an appropriate example that a manager might face. For example, think of a high-priority, a moderate-priority, and a low-priority situation involving a customer.

4. Form a small group with two or three classmates and share the examples each of you developed.

YOU MAKE THE CALL

As Sunset Landscape Services grew and prospered, Mark Spenser led his firm to occupy a unique niche in the local business community. He also had to make a number of difficult choices, however, having recently entered a complex new business arena. He knew that the booming local and regional economy was a strong contributor to his success, but he was smart enough to know that he could not rely on economic growth alone to fuel his business.

Mark recognized immediately that it was necessary to establish and maintain good relationships with various constituents. Thus, he worked hard to develop close relationships with various suppliers and his local banker. He made sure that he demonstrated his loyalty to them, and this paid off in a variety of ways. For example, when SLS hit a tight spot in 1985, his suppliers extended him extra credit and his banker provided him with a short-term loan for working capital.

He also paid close attention to his competitors. In addition to the two local nurseries already in business in Central City, he often checked the prices and product lines at the nursery at the nearby Wal-Mart store and the local grocery store, which also carried plants and plant supplies. Mark also found it necessary to deal with various inspectors from the U.S. Department of Agriculture, and even had his taxes audited one year. He also put a premium on customer service in his business, treating every customer with respect and insisting that each of his employees do the same.

One of the more difficult issues Mark faced from the very beginning, however, has been a bit more personal in nature. Within the first few months of opening, he was called on to make contributions to the local United Way campaign and to support little league baseball, community soccer, Girl Scouts and Boy Scouts, and other similar programs. While he believed that each of these programs was worthwhile, he found it necessary to say no, simply because he could not afford it. As his business grew, however, Mark increasingly found it possible to say yes, and today supports a number of local social programs and activities.

One of Mark's most recent ventures grew out of the passage of the North American Free Trade Agreement. Because Central City has a mild climate, some local residents like to use cactus plants in their landscaping. While some cactus plants can be obtained from domestic suppliers, Mark determined that he could obtain a wider variety of plants at a lower cost from suppliers based in northern Mexico. On the other hand, he also found that trying to import plants across the border was not as easy as he had anticipated.

Discussion Questions

1. What elements of the general and task environments are reflected in this case?

2. How might a manager with limited rescources go about deciding which social programs to support?

3. What are the advantages and disadvantages to Sunset Landscape Services of exploring avenues for doing business in Mexico?

SKILLS SELF-ASSESSMENT INSTRUMENT

Global Awareness

Introduction: As we have noted, the environment of business is becoming more global. The following assessment is designed to help you understand your readiness to respond to managing in a global context.

Instructions: You will agree with some of the following statements and disagree with others. In some cases, you may find it difficult to make a decision, but you should force a choice. Record your answers next to each statement according to the following scale:

4 Strongly agree	**2** Somewhat disagree
3 Somewhat agree	**1** Strongly disagree

_____ **1.** Some areas of Switzerland are very much like Italy.

_____ **2.** Although aspects of behavior such as motivation and attitudes within organizational settings remain quite diverse across cultures, organizations themselves appear to be increasingly similar in terms of design and technology.

_____ **3.** Spain, France, Japan, Singapore, Mexico, Brazil, and Indonesia have cultures with a strong orientation toward authority.

_____ **4.** Japan and Austria define male-female roles more rigidly and value qualities like forcefulness and achievement more than Norway, Sweden, Denmark, and Finland.

_____ **5.** Some areas of Switzerland are very much like France.

_____ **6.** Australia, Great Britain, the Netherlands, Canada, and New Zealand have cultures that view people first as individuals and place a priority on their own interests and values, whereas Colombia, Pakistan, Taiwan, Peru, Singapore, Mexico, Greece, and Hong Kong have cultures in which the good of the group or society is considered the priority.

_____ **7.** The United States, Israel, Austria, Denmark, Ireland, Norway, Germany, and New Zealand have cultures with a low orientation toward authority.

_____ **8.** The same manager may behave differently in different cultural settings.

_____ **9.** Denmark, Canada, Norway, Singapore, Hong Kong, and Australia have cultures in which employees tolerate a high degree of uncertainty, but such levels of uncertainty are not well tolerated in Israel, Austria, Japan, Italy, Argentina, Peru, France, and Belgium.

_____ **10.** Some areas of Switzerland are very much like Germany.

For interpretation, turn to page 447.

EXPERIENTIAL EXERCISE

Ethics of Employee Appraisal

Purpose: Many management activities occur within an ethical context. The appraisal of employees' performance is one of those activities that can raise ethical issues. This skill builder focuses on the *human resources model.* It will help you develop the *mentor role* of the human resources model. One of the skills of the mentor is the ability to develop subordinates.

Introduction: Much attention has been given in recent years to ethics in business, yet one area often overlooked is ethical issues when hiring or appraising employees. Marian Kellogg developed a list of principles to keep in mind when recruiting or appraising.

How to Keep Your Appraisals Ethical: A Manager's Checklist

1. Don't appraise without knowing why the appraisal is required.

2. Appraise on the basis of **representative** information.

3. Appraise on the basis of **sufficient** information.

4. Appraise on the basis of **relevant** information.

5. Be honest in your assessment of all the facts you obtain.

6. Don't write one thing and say another.

7. In offering an appraisal, make it plain that this is only your personal opinion of the facts as you see them.

8. Pass appraisal information along only to those who have good reason to know it.

9. Don't imply the existence of an appraisal that hasn't been made.

10. Don't accept another's appraisal without knowing the basis on which it was made.

Instructions: Read each incident individually and decide which of the ten rules is violated, marking the appropriate number on the right. In some cases, more than one rule is violated. In your group go over each case and come to a consensus on which rules are violated.

Incidents:

1. Steve Wilson has applied for a transfer to Department O., headed by Marianne Kilbourn. As part of her fact finding, Marianne reads through the written evaluation, which is glowing, and then asks Steve's boss, Bill Hammond, for information on Steve's performance. Bill starts complaining about Steve because his last project was not up to par, but does not mention Steve's wife has been seriously ill for two months. Marianne then decides not to accept Steve's transfer.
Rule violation # ______

2. Maury Nanner is a sales manager who is having lunch with several executives. One of them, Harvey Gant, asks him what he thinks of his subordinate George Williams, and Nanner gives a lengthy evaluation.
Rule violation # ______

3. Phillip Randall is working on six-month evaluations of his subordinates. He decides to rate Elisa Donner less-than-average on initiative because he thinks she spends too much time, energy, and money making herself look attractive. He thinks it distracts the male employees.
Rule violation # ______

4. Paul Trendant has received an application from an outstanding candidate, Jim Fischer. However, Paul decides not to hire Jim because he heard from someone that Jim only moved to town because his wife got a good job here. Trendant thinks Jim will quit whenever his wife gets transferred.
Rule violation #______

5. Susan Forman is on the fast track and tries to make herself look good to her boss, Peter Everly. This morning she has a meeting with Pete to discuss which person to promote. Just before the meeting, Pete's golf buddy, Harold, a coworker of Susan's, tells Susan that Alice, Jerry, and Joe are favored by Pete. Susan had felt Darlene was the strongest candidate, but she goes into the meeting with Pete and suggests Alice, Jerry, and Joe as top candidates.
Rule violation #______

6. Sandy is a new supervisor for seven people. After several months Sandy is certain that Linda is marginally competent and frequently cannot produce any useful work. Looking over past appraisals Sandy sees all of Linda's evaluations were positive, and she is told that Linda "has problems" and not to be "too hard on her." Realizing this is not healthy, Sandy begins documenting Linda's inadequate performance. Several supervisors hint that she should "lighten up because we don't want Linda to feel hurt."
Rule violation #______

Source: Marian S. Kellogg, *What to Do About Performance Appraisal,* AMACOM, a division of the American Management Association, New York, 1975; Marian S. Kellogg, *Personnel,* July–August 1965, American Management Association, New York; Dorothy Marcic, *Organizational Behavior: Experiences and Cases,* 3rd ed. (West Publishing Company, 1992).

CHAPTER NOTES

1. "Pump, Pump, Pump at Schwinn," *Business Week*, August 23, 1993, p. 79; John Kukoda, "Birth of a Bike," *Bicycling*, April 1990, pp. 160–165; and "The End of a Long Road for Schwinn?" *Newsweek*, October 19, 1992, p. 52
2. See John Huey, "Waking Up to the New Economy," *Fortune*, June 27, 1994, pp. 36–46 for an overview of how current economic conditions affect business. See also Jay B. Barney and William G. Ouchi (Eds.), *Organizational Economics* (San Francisco: Jossey-Bass, 1986) for a detailed analysis of linkages between economics and organizations.
3. Robert H. Hayes and Ramchandran Jaikumar, "Manufacturing's Crisis: New Technologies, Obsolete Organizations," *Harvard Business Review*, September–October 1988, pp. 77–85.
4. "Regulation Rises Again," *Business Week*, June 26, 1989, pp. 58–59.
5. Paul Krugman, "Competitiveness: Does it Matter?" *Fortune*, March 7, 1994, pp. 109–115.
6. Jeremy Main, "How to Steal the Best Ideas Around," *Fortune,* October 19, 1992, pp. 102–106.
7. See Ian C. MacMillan, "Controlling Competitive Dynamics by Taking Strategic Initiative," *The Academy of*

Management Executive, May 1988, pp. 111–118, for an interesting view of influencing competitors.

8. "National Firms Find That Selling to Local Tastes Is Costly, Complex," *The Wall Street Journal*, July 9, 1987, p. 17. See also Regis McKenna, "Marketing in an Age of Diversity," *Harvard Business Review*, September–October 1988, pp. 88–95.
9. Susan Helper, "How Much Has Really Changed Between U.S. Automakers and Their Suppliers?" *Sloan Management Review*, Summer 1991, pp. 15–28.
10. Myron Magnet, "The New Golden Rule of Business," *Fortune*, February 21, 1994, pp. 60–64.
11. "Many Businesses Blame Governmental Policies for Productivity Lag," *The Wall Street Journal*, October 28, 1980, pp. 1, 22.
12. "More Competitors Turn to Cooperation," *The Wall Street Journal*, June 23, 1989, p. B1.
13. Jeremy Main, "The Winning Organization," *Fortune*, September 26, 1988, pp. 50–60; update by IBM Corporate Public Relations Office, October 1994.
14. "Time Warner Feels the Force of Stockholder Power," *Business Week*, July 21, 1991, pp. 58–59.
15. Rob Norton, "Who Owns This Company, Anyhow?" *Fortune*, July 29, 1991, pp. 131–142.
16. John J. Curran, "Companies That Rob the Future," *Fortune*, July 4, 1988, pp. 84–89.
17. Idalene F. Kesner, "Directors' Characteristics and Committee Membership: An Investigation of Type, Occupation, Tenure, and Gender," *Academy of Management Journal*, March 1988, pp. 66–84; and Jeffrey Kerr and Richard A. Bettis, "Boards of Directors, Top Management Compensation, and Shareholder Returns," *Academy of Management Journal*, December 1987, pp. 645–664.
18. Marsha Sinetar, "Building Trust into Corporate Relationships," *Organizational Dynamics*, Winter 1988, pp. 73–79.
19. Louis Richman, "The New Worker Elite," *Fortune*, August 22, 1994, pp. 56–66.
20. See Thomas M. Garrett and Richard J. Klonoski, *Business Ethics*, 3rd ed. (Englewood Cliffs, N.J.: Prentice-Hall, 1990) for a review of the different meanings of the word *ethics*.
21. Thomas Donaldson and Thomas W. Dunfee, "Toward a Unified Conception of Business Ethics: An Integrative Social Contracts Theory," *Academy of Management Review*, Vol. 19, No. 2, 1994, pp. 252–284.
22. Linda Klebe Trevino, "Ethical Decision Making in Organizations: A Person-Situation Interactionist Model," *Academy of Management Review*, July 1986, pp. 601–617; and Bart Victor and John B. Cullen, "The Organizational Bases of Ethical Work Climates," *Administrative Science Quarterly*, Vol. 33, 1988, pp. 101–125.
23. "What Led Beech-Nut Down the Road to Disgrace," *Business Week*, February 22, 1988, pp. 124–128.
24. Alan Richter and Cynthia Barnum, "When Values Clash," *HR Magazine*, September 1994, pp. 42–45.
25. "Businesses Are Signing Up for Ethics 101," *Business Week*, February 15, 1988, pp. 56–57; "Ethics on the Job: Companies Alert Employees to Potential Dilemmas," *The Wall Street Journal*, July 14, 1986, p. 17.
26. Jerry W. Anderson, Jr., "Social Responsibility and the Corporation," *Business Horizons*, July–August 1986, pp. 22–27.
27. For discussions of this debate, see Abby Brown, "Is Ethics Good Business?" *Personnel Administrator*, February 1987, pp. 67–74; Jean B. McGuire, Alison Sundgren, and Thomas Schneeweis, "Corporate Social Responsibility and Firm Financial Performance," *Academy of Management Journal*, December 1988, pp. 854–872; "Business Ethics for Sale," *Newsweek*, May 9, 1988, p. 56; Kenneth E. Aupperle, Archie B. Carroll, and John D. Hatfield, "An Empirical Examination of the Relationship Between Corporate Social Responsibility and Profitability," *Academy of Management Journal*, June 1985, pp. 446–563; and Margaret A. Stroup, Ralph L. Neubert, and Jerry W. Anderson, Jr., "Doing Good, Doing Better: Two Views of Social Responsibility," *Business Horizons*, March–April 1987, pp. 22–25.
28. "Doing Well by Doing Good," *Business Week*, December 5, 1988, pp. 53–37.
29. Steven L. Wartick and Philip L. Cochran, "The Evolution of the Corporate Social Performance Model," *Academy of Management Review*, October 1985, pp. 758–769; Jerry W. Anderson, Jr., "Social Responsibility and the Corporation," *Business Horizons*, July–August 1986, pp. 22–27.
30. Anderson, "Social Responsibility and the Corporation."
31. Lynn Sharp Paine, "Managing for Organizational Integrity," *Harvard Business Review*, March–April 1994, pp. 106–115.
32. "Charity Doesn't Begin at Home Anymore," *Business Week*, February 25, 1991, p. 91.
33. "Unfuzzing Ethics for Managers," *Fortune*, November 23, 1987, pp. 229–234.
34. Marcia P. Miceli and Janet P. Near, "Whistleblowing: Reaping the Benefits," *The Academy of Management Executive*, Vol. 8, No. 3, 1994, pp. 65–74.
35. Janelle Brinker Dozier and Marcia P. Miceli, "Potential Predictors of Whistle-Blowing: A Prosocial Behavior Perspective," *Academy of Management Review*, October 1985, pp. 823–836; Janet P. Near and Marcia P. Miceli, "Retaliation Against Whistle Blowers: Predictors and Effects," *Journal of Applied Psychology*, February 1986, pp. 137–145.
36. Philip M. Rosenzweig and Jitendra V. Singh, "Organizational Environments and the Multinational Enter-

prise," *Academy of Management Review*, April 1991, pp. 340–661.

37. "The *Fortune* Global 500," *Fortune*, July 25, 1994, pp. 144–145.

38. Gary Hoover, Alta Campbell, and Patrick J. Spain (Eds.), *Hoover's Handbook of American Business 1994* (Austin, Tex.: The Reference Press, 1993), pp. 228–229, 486–487.

39. Alan Farnham, "Global—Or Just Globaloney?" *Fortune*, June 27, 1994, pp. 97–100.

40. "Creating a Worldwide Yen for Japanese Beer," *Financial Times*, October 7, 1994, p. 20.

41. Kenichi Ohmae, "The Global Logic of Strategic Alliances," *Harvard Business Review*, March–April 1989, pp. 143–154.

42. Jeremy Main, "Making Global Alliances Work," *Fortune*, December 17, 1990, pp. 121–126.

43. "Asian Tigers Are on the Prowl in Europe," *The Wall Street Journal*, October 26, 1994, p. A17.

44. "The Magnet of Growth in Mexico's North," *Business Week*, June 6, 1988, pp. 48–50; and "Will the New Maquiladoras Build a Better Mañana?" *Business Week*, November 14, 1988, pp. 102–106.

45. Ricky Griffin and Michael Pustay, *International Business* (Reading, Mass.: Addison-Wesley, 1996).

46. "Firms Address Workers' Cultural Variety," *The Wall Street Journal*, February 10, 1989, p. B1.

47. Terrence E. Deal and Allan A. Kennedy, *Corporate Cultures: The Rights and Rituals of Corporate Life* (Reading, Mass.: Addison-Wesley, 1982); see also Benjamin Schneider, Arthur P. Brief, and Richard A. Guzzo, "Creating a Climate and Culture for Sustainable Organizational Change," *Organizational Dynamics,* Spring 1996, pp. 7–19.

48. Gurney Breckenfield, "The Odyssey of Levi Strauss," *Fortune*, March 22, 1982, pp. 110–124. See also "Levi Strauss . . . at $3 Billion Plus," *Daily News Record*, October 10, 1988, p. 44.

49. Jay B. Barney, "Organizational Culture: Can It Be a Source of Sustained Competitive Advantage?" *Academy of Management Review*, July 1986, pp. 656–665.

50. "Hewlett-Packard's Whip-Crackers," *Fortune*, February 13, 1989, pp. 58–59.

51. Benjamin Schneider, Sarah K. Gunnarson, and Kathryn Niles-Jolly, "Creating the Climate and Culture for Success," *Organizational Dynamics*, Summer 1994, pp. 17–29.

Like the tugs guiding this cargo ship through the Panama Canal, managers must make decisions and develop strategies for steering their organizations through an ever-changing, competitive landscape. Even on a local level, managers make decisions, plan, and promote entrepreneurship in their quest for improved organizational performance.

PART

Planning

C H A P T E R

Planning and Strategic Management

OBJECTIVES

After studying this chapter, you should be able to:

- *Summarize the planning process and describe organizational goals.*
- *Discuss the components of strategy and types of strategic alternatives.*
- *Describe how to use SWOT analysis in formulating strategy.*
- *Identify and describe various alternative approaches to business-level strategy formulation.*
- *Identify and describe various alternative approaches to corporate-level strategy formulation.*
- *Discuss how tactical plans are developed and executed.*
- *Describe the basic types of operational plans used by organizations and discuss contingency planning.*

OUTLINE

OPENING INCIDENT

ONE OF THE great paradoxes of business today is that sometimes managers can confidently decide what they and their organization need to do and be exactly right. At other times, however, they can just as confidently decide what to do and then be wrong. Starbucks Corporation provides a good example of each situation.

"If we are going to build a 100-story skyscraper, we have to build a foundation strong enough to sustain 100 stories. I believe in the adage: Hire people smarter than you are and get out of their way."

Starbucks was started in Seattle in 1971 by three coffee afficionados. Their primary business at the time was buying premium coffee beans, roasting them, and then selling the coffee by the pound. The business performed modestly well, soon growing to nine stores, all in the Seattle area. The three partners sold Starbucks to a former employee, Howard Schultz, in 1987. Schultz promptly reoriented the business away from bulk coffee and increasingly emphasized retail coffee sales through the firm's coffee bars. Today Starbucks is not only the largest coffee importer and roaster of specialty beans, but also the largest specialty coffee bean retailer in the United States. Schultz refuses to franchise, fearing a loss of control and potential deterioration of quality.

Schultz recently announced a goal of opening one hundred new stores every year for the next decade. He also plans international expansion and recently entered into a new joint venture with PepsiCo. The venture calls for the firm to develop a new bottled coffee that will be packaged under the Starbucks' label and distributed through Pepsi's softdrink network. This approach worked well for a similar venture between Pepsi and Lipton Tea a few years ago, so Starbucks management feels confident that its new entry will also be successful.

Interestingly, however, for a firm that has changed the way Americans drink coffee and shown an almost uncanny sense of the coffee market, even Starbucks occasionally makes a mistake. In preparation for its first New York store in 1994, Starbucks managers spent months studying and surveying the coffee drinking tastes of New Yorkers. Their confident conclusion was that New Yorkers preferred drip coffees over the more exotic espresso-style coffees that were Starbucks' mainstays in the west.

Accordingly, Starbucks' first New York store opened with more drip coffeemakers and fewer espresso machines than in their other stores. What happened? The drip coffees were ignored and the line for espresso went out the door and down the block. Thus a hasty renovation was necessary within the first month of operation to provide more espresso and less drip coffee. And today, that store still sells far more espresso than drip coffee.[1] ●

Source of Quotation: Howard Schultz, Starbucks CEO, quoted in *Business Week*, October 24, 1994, p. 78.

Starbucks initially floundered because its owners did not have the right goals or an effective strategy for the business. When Howard Schultz took over, however, he set new goals and formulated a new strategy. Because of the nature of that strategy and the firm's environment, Starbucks took off and has grown to become a major business. One of the keys to the firm's success, therefore, has been effective planning.

This chapter is the first of three that explores the planning process in more detail. We begin by discussing the nature of planning and organizational goals. We then examine strategic management, including its components and alternatives, and describe the kinds of analyses needed for firms to formulate their strategies. Next we examine how organizations formulate business and corporate strategies. Finally, we discuss how strategies are implemented via tactical and operational planning.

PLANNING AND ORGANIZATIONAL GOALS

The planning process can be thought of as a generic activity. All organizations engage in planning activities, but no two organizations plan in exactly the same fashion. Figure 3.1 is a general representation of the planning process that many organizations attempt to follow.[2] But although most firms follow this general framework, each also has its own nuances and variations.

As Figure 3.1 shows, all planning occurs within an environmental context. With this context as a foundation, managers first establish the organization's mission. The mission outlines the organization's purpose, premises, values,

The planning process takes place within an environmental context. Managers must develop a complete and thorough understanding of this context to determine the organization's mission and develop its strategic, tactical, and operational goals and plans.

FIGURE 3.1 The Planning Process

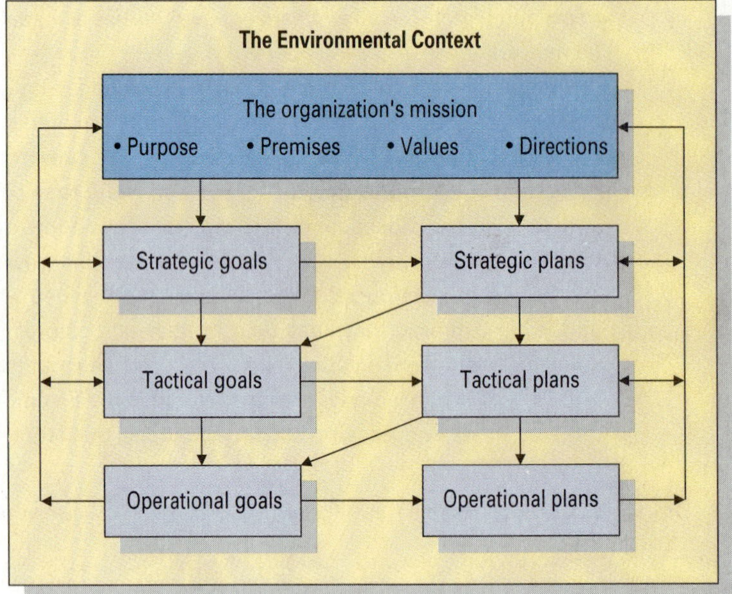

and directions. Flowing from the mission are parallel streams of goals and plans. Directly following the mission are strategic goals. These goals and the mission help determine strategic plans. Strategic goals and plans are primary inputs for developing tactical goals. Tactical goals and the original strategic plans help shape tactical plans. Tactical plans, in turn, combine with the tactical goals to shape operational goals. These goals and the appropriate tactical plans determine operational plans. Finally, goals and plans at each level can also be used as input for future activities at all levels.

Organizational Goals

Goals are critical to organizational effectiveness and they serve a number of purposes in the planning process. There are several different kinds of goals.

Purposes of Goals Goals serve four important purposes.[3] First, they provide guidance and a unified direction for people in the organization. The goal set for Starbucks of opening one hundred stores per year helps everyone in the firm recognize the strong emphasis on growth and expansion that is driving the firm. Second, goal-setting practices strongly affect other aspects of planning. The success of Starbucks demonstrates how setting goals and developing plans to reach them are complementary activities. Third, goals can serve as a source of motivation to employees of the organization. Goals that are specific and moderately difficult can motivate people to work harder, especially if attaining the goal is likely to result in rewards.[4] Managers at Starbucks see the firm's growth goals as a hurdle to reach, but, based on recent experience, are likely to see this hurdle as something they can surpass. Finally, goals provide an effective mechanism for evaluation and control. This means that performance in the future can be assessed in terms of how successfully today's goals are accomplished. Thus, if managers at Starbucks do not meet their growth goals, attention can be focused on how to meet them in the future.

Kinds of Goals Organizations establish many different kinds of goals. As noted earlier, the four basic levels of goals are the mission and strategic, tactical, and operational goals. An organization's **mission** is a statement of its "fundamental, unique purpose that sets a business apart from other firms of its type and identifies the scope of the business's operations in product and market terms."[5] **Strategic goals** are goals set by and for top management of the organization and focus on broad, general issues. **Tactical goals** are set by and for middle managers. Their focus is on how to operationalize actions necessary to achieve the strategic goals. **Operational goals** are set by and for lower-level managers. Their concern is with shorter-term issues associated with the tactical goals. (Some people use the words *objectives* and *goals* interchangeably.)

● **mission**
A statement of an organization's fundamental purpose

● **strategic goals**
Goals set by and for top management of the organization

● **tactical goals**
Goals set by and for middle managers of the organization

● **operational goals**
Goals set by and for lower-level managers of the organization

Kinds of Plans

Organizations establish many different kinds of plans. At a general level, these include strategic, tactical, and operational plans.

● **strategic plan**
A general plan outlining decisions of resource allocation, priorities, and action steps necessary to reach strategic goals

Strategic Plans Strategic plans are the plans developed to achieve strategic goals. More precisely, a **strategic plan** is a general plan outlining decisions of resource allocation, priorities, and action steps necessary to reach strategic goals.[6] These plans are set by the board of directors and top management, generally have an extended time horizon, and address questions of scope, resource deployment, competitive advantage, and synergy. We discuss strategic plans in the next major section.

● **tactical plan**
A plan aimed at achieving tactical goals, developed to implement parts of a strategic plan

Tactical Plans A **tactical plan**, aimed at achieving tactical goals, is developed to implement specific parts of a strategic plan. Tactical plans typically involve upper and middle management, have a somewhat shorter time horizon than strategic plans, and have a more specific and concrete focus. Thus tactical plans are concerned more with actually getting things done than with deciding what to do. We describe tactical planning after the discussion of strategic planning.

● **operational plan**
A plan aimed at carrying out tactical plans to achieve operational goals

Operational Plans An **operational plan** focuses on carrying out tactical plans to achieve operational goals. Developed by middle and lower-level managers, operational plans have a short-term focus and are relatively narrow in scope. Each one deals with a fairly small set of activities. We discuss operational plans in the last section of this chapter.

THE NATURE OF STRATEGIC MANAGEMENT

● **strategy**
A comprehensive plan for accomplishing an organization's goals

● **strategic management**
A way of approaching business opportunities and challenges; a comprehensive and ongoing management process aimed at formulating and implementing effective strategies

A **strategy** is a comprehensive plan for accomplishing an organization's goals. **Strategic management**, in turn, is a way of approaching business opportunities and challenges—it is a comprehensive and ongoing management process aimed at formulating and implementing effective strategies.[7]

The Components of Strategy

● **distinctive competence**
An organizational strength possessed by only a small number of competing firms

In general, a well-conceived strategy addresses three areas: distinctive competence, scope, and resource deployment. A **distinctive competence** is something the organization does exceptionally well. The Limited, a large clothing chain, stresses its distinctive competence of speed in moving inventory. It tracks consumer preferences daily with point-of-sale computers, electronically transmits orders to suppliers in Hong Kong, charters 747s to fly products to the United States, and has products in stores forty-eight hours later. Since other retailers take weeks or sometimes months to accomplish the same things, The Limited relies on this distinctive competence to stay ahead of its competition.[8]

● **scope**
The part of a strategy that specifies the range of markets in which an organization will compete

The **scope** of a strategy specifies the range of markets in which an organization will compete. Hershey Foods has essentially restricted its scope to the confectionery business, with a few related activities in other food-processing areas such as pasta. In contrast, its biggest competitor, Mars, has adopted a broader scope by competing in the pet-food business and the

Strategic management is one of the most vital keys to the success of any enterprise. Michael Giles was thinking strategically when he became aware that millions of people in the black townships of South Africa lacked many basic services that many people take for granted. Using a grant from the U.S. government, Giles has launched a chain of laundromats throughout South Africa.

electronics industry, among others. Some organizations, called *conglomerates*, compete in dozens or even hundreds of markets.[9]

A strategy should also include an outline of the organization's projected **resource deployment**—how it will distribute its resources across the areas in which it competes. Disney, for example, is currently using some of the profits it generates from successful movies and theme park operations to fund new start-up businesses in book publishing and music recording.

resource deployment How an organization distributes its resources across the areas in which it competes

Types of Strategic Alternatives

Most businesses today also develop strategies at two distinct levels: business strategies and corporate strategies. These levels of strategy provide a rich combination of strategic alternatives for organizations. **Business-level strategy** is the set of strategic alternatives from which an organization chooses as it conducts business in a particular industry or a particular market. Such alternatives help the organization focus its competitive efforts for each industry or market in a targeted and focused manner. For example, Quaker Oats has one business strategy for its cereal business, another for its pet-food business, and yet another for its beverage operations (Gatorade and Snapple).

Corporate-level strategy is the set of strategic alternatives from which an organization chooses as it manages its operations simultaneously across several industries and several markets.[10] As we will see later, most larger companies today compete in a variety of industries and markets. Thus, while they develop business-level strategies for each industry or market, they also develop an overall strategy that helps define the mix of industries

business-level strategy The set of strategic alternatives from which an organization chooses as it conducts business in a particular industry or market

corporate-level strategy The set of strategic alternatives from which an organization chooses as it manages its operations simultaneously across several industries and several markets

and markets that are of interest to the firm. Quaker Oats, for example, has made the corporate-level decision to operate businesses in the cereal, pet-food, and beverage industries, but not in the retail or electronics industries.

A distinction should be drawn between strategy formulation and strategy implementation. **Strategy formulation** is the set of processes involved in creating or determining the strategies of the organization, while **strategy implementation** is the set of methods by which strategies are executed within the organization. The primary distinction is along the lines of content versus process: the formulation stage determines what the strategy is, and the implementation stage focuses on how the strategy will be achieved.

● **strategy formulation** The set of processes involved in creating or determining the strategies of the organization; it focuses on the content of strategies

● **strategy implementation** The set of methods by which strategies are executed within the organization; it focuses on the processes through which strategies are achieved

USING SWOT ANALYSIS TO FORMULATE STRATEGY

The starting point in formulating strategy is usually SWOT analysis. **SWOT** is an acronym that stands for Strengths, Weaknesses, Opportunities, and Threats. As shown in Figure 3.2, SWOT analysis is a very careful evaluation of an organization's internal strengths and weaknesses and of its environmental opportunities and threats. In SWOT analysis, the best strate-

● **SWOT** An acronym that stands for Strengths, Weaknesses, Opportunities, and Threats

FIGURE 3.2 Using SWOT Analysis to Formulate Strategy

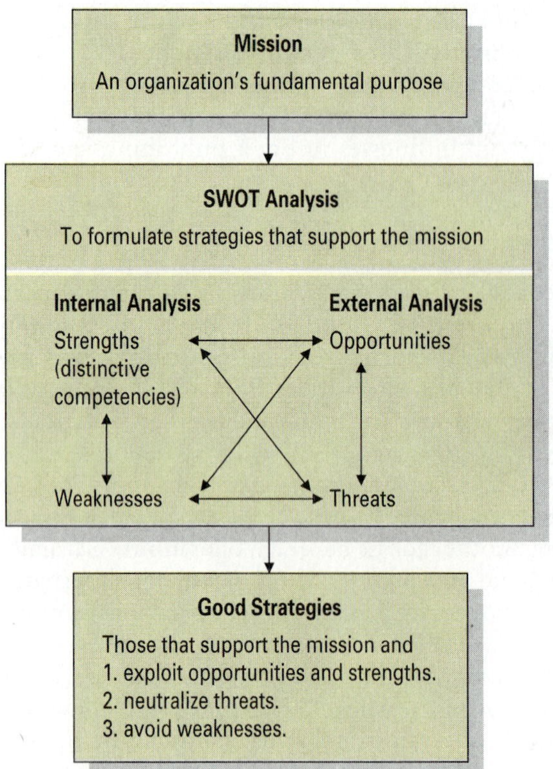

SWOT analysis is one of the most important steps in formulating strategy. Using the organization's mission as a context, managers assess internal strengths (distinctive competencies) and weaknesses and external opportunities and threats. The goal is to then develop good strategies that exploit opportunities and strengths, neutralize threats, and avoid weaknesses.

gies accomplish an organization's mission by (1) exploiting an organization's opportunities and strengths while (2) neutralizing its threats and (3) avoiding (or correcting) its weaknesses.

Evaluating an Organization's Strengths

Organizational strengths are skills and capabilities that enable an organization to conceive and implement its strategies. Different strategies call for different skills and capabilities. For example, Matsushita Electric has demonstrated strengths in manufacturing and selling consumer electronics under the brand name Panasonic. However, Matsushita's strength in electronics does not ensure success if the firm expands into insurance, swimming-pool manufacture, or retail. Different strategies such as these require different organizational strengths.

● **organizational strengths** Skills and capabilities that enable an organization to conceive and implement its strategies

A distinctive competence is a strength possessed by only a small number of competing firms. Distinctive competencies are rare among a set of competitors. George Lucas' well-known company, Industrial Light and Magic (ILM), for example, has brought the cinematic art of special effects to new heights. Some of ILM's special effects can be produced by no other organization; these rare special effects are thus ILM's distinctive competencies. Organizations that exploit their distinctive competencies often obtain a competitive advantage and attain above-normal economic performance.[11]

Evaluating an Organization's Weaknesses

Organizational weaknesses are skills and capabilities that do not enable an organization to choose and implement strategies that support its mission. An organization has essentially two ways of addressing weaknesses. First, it may need to make investments to obtain the strengths required to implement strategies that support its mission. Second, it may need to modify its mission so that it can be accomplished with the skills and capabilities that the organization already possesses.

● **organizational weaknesses** Skills and capabilities that do not enable an organization to choose and implement strategies that support its mission

In practice, organizations have a difficult time focusing on weaknesses, in part because organization members are often reluctant to admit that they may not possess all the skills and capabilities needed. Evaluating weaknesses also calls into question the judgment of the managers who chose the organization's mission in the first place and who failed to invest in the skills and capabilities needed to accomplish it. Organizations that fail to either recognize or overcome their weaknesses are likely to suffer from competitive disadvantages. An organization has a competitive disadvantage when it is not implementing valuable strategies that are being implemented by competing organizations. Organizations with a competitive disadvantage can expect to attain below-average levels of performance.

Evaluating an Organization's Opportunities and Threats

Whereas evaluating strengths and weaknesses focuses attention on the internal workings of an organization, evaluating opportunities and threats requires analysis of an organization's environment. **Organizational opportunities**

● **organizational opportunities** Areas in the environment that, if exploited, may generate high performance

Evaluating an organization's opportunities and threats is an important part of strategy formulation. A few years ago managers at Bausch & Lomb recognized that the billions of people in China represented a vast untapped market for contact lenses. The firm took early and aggressive steps to position itself in the Chinese market (opening a factory, for example, and teaching opticians to fit lenses). Today, Bausch & Lomb dominates the market in China.

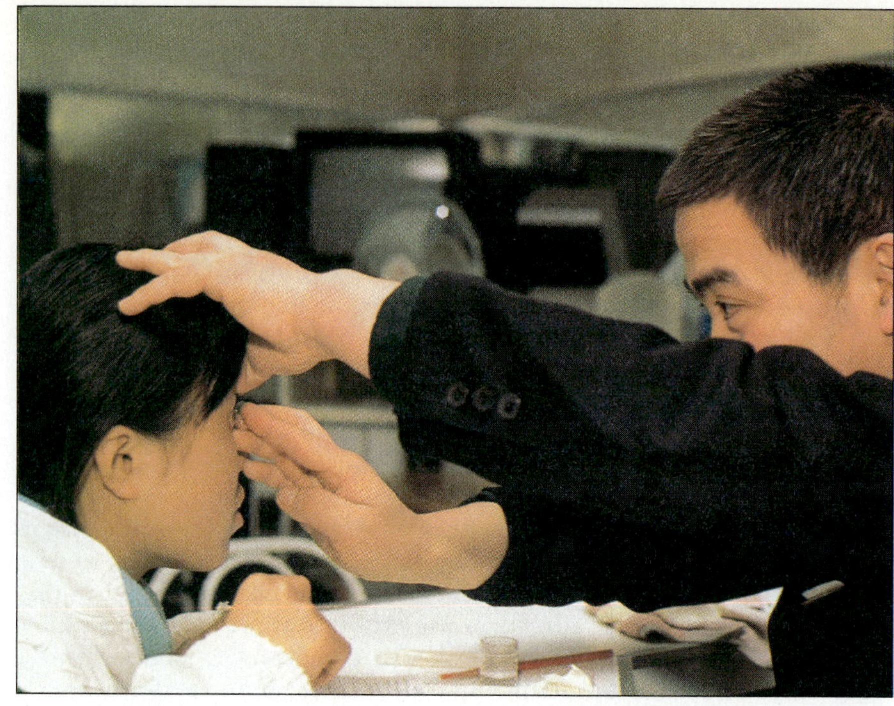

● **organizational threats** Areas in the environment that make it difficult for an organization to achieve high performance

are areas that may generate higher performance. **Organizational threats** are areas that make it difficult for an organization to perform at a high level.

FORMULATING BUSINESS-LEVEL STRATEGIES

A number of frameworks have been developed for identifying the major strategic alternatives that organizations should consider when choosing their business-level strategies. Two important classification schemes are Porter's generic strategies and strategies based on the product life cycle.

Porter's Generic Strategies

● **differentiation strategy** The strategy pursued by an organization that seeks to distinguish itself from competitors through the quality of its products or services

According to Michael Porter, a prominent strategy researcher, organizations may pursue a differentiation, overall cost leadership, or focus strategy at the business level.[12] An organization that pursues a **differentiation strategy** seeks to distinguish itself from competitors through the quality of its products or services. Firms that successfully implement a differentiation strategy are able to charge more because customers are willing to pay more to obtain the extra value they perceive. Rolex, for example, pursues a differentiation strategy. Rolex watches are handmade of gold and stainless steel and are subjected to strenuous tests of quality and reliability. The firm's reputation enables it to charge thousands of dollars for its watches. Other firms that use differentiation strategies include Mercedes-Benz, Nikon, Cross, and Hewlett-Packard.

An organization implementing an **overall cost leadership strategy** attempts to gain a competitive advantage by reducing its costs below the costs of competing firms. By keeping costs low, the organization is able to sell its products at low prices and still make a profit. Timex uses an overall cost leadership strategy. For decades, this firm has specialized in manufacturing relatively simple, low-cost watches for the mass market. The price of Timex watches, starting around $29.95, is low because of the company's efficient, high-volume manufacturing capacity. Other firms that implement overall cost leadership strategies include Hyundai, Kodak, Bic, and Texas Instruments.

- **overall cost leadership strategy** The strategy implemented by an organization that attempts to gain a competitive advantage by reducing its costs below the costs of competing firms

A firm pursuing a **focus strategy** concentrates on a specific regional market, product line, or group of buyers. This strategy may have either a differentiation focus, whereby the firm differentiates its products in the focus market, or an overall cost leadership focus, whereby the firm manufactures and sells its products at low cost in the focus market. In the watch industry, Longines follows a focus differentiation strategy by selling highly jeweled watches to wealthy female consumers. Fiat follows a focus cost leadership strategy by selling its automobiles only in Italy and in selected regions of Europe; Alpha Romeo uses focus differentiation to sell its high-performance cars in these same markets. Fisher Price uses focus differentiation to sell electronic calculators with large, brightly colored buttons to the parents of preschoolers.

- **focus strategy** The strategy pursued by an organization that concentrates on a specific regional market, product line, or group of buyers

Strategies Based on the Product Life Cycle

The **product life cycle** is a model that shows how sales volume changes over the life of products. An understanding of the four stages in the product life cycle helps managers recognize that strategies need to evolve over time. As Figure 3.3 shows, the cycle begins when a new product or technology is first introduced. In this **introduction stage**, demand may be

- **product life cycle** A model that portrays how sales volume for products changes over the life of products

- **introduction stage** The stage in the product life cycle in which demand may be so high that it outpaces the firm's ability to supply that product

FIGURE 3.3 The Product Life Cycle

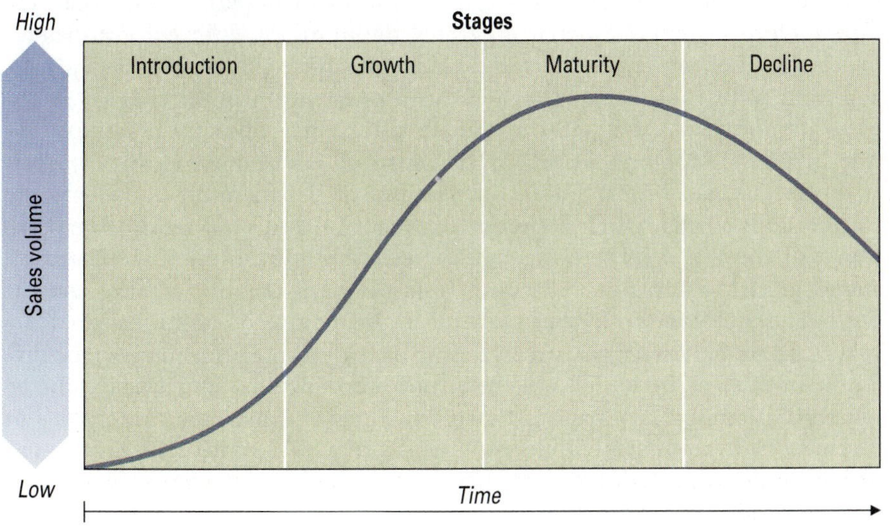

Managers can use the framework of the product life cycle—introduction, growth, maturity, and decline—to plot strategy. For example, management may decide on a differentiation strategy for a product in the introduction stage and a prospector approach for a product in the growth stage. By understanding this cycle and where a particular product falls within it, managers can develop more effective strategies for extending product life.

very high and may even outpace the firm's ability to supply the product. At this stage, managers need to focus their efforts on "getting product out the door" without sacrificing quality, managing growth by hiring new employees, and managing inventories and cash flow.

● **growth stage**
The stage in the product life cycle in which more firms begin to produce the product and sales continue to grow

During the **growth stage**, more firms begin producing the product, and sales continue to grow. Key management issues include ensuring quality and delivery and beginning to differentiate an organization's product from competitors' products. Entry into the industry during the growth stage may threaten an organization's competitive advantage; thus strategies to slow the entry of competitors are important.

● **mature stage**
The stage in the product life cycle in which overall demand growth begins to slow down and the number of new firms producing the product begins to decline

After a period of growth, products enter a third phase. During this **mature stage**, overall demand growth for a product begins to slow down and the number of new firms producing the product begins to decline. The number of established firms producing the product may also begin to decline. This period of maturity is key if an organization is to survive in the long run. Product differentiation concerns are still important during this stage, but keeping costs low and beginning the search for new products or services are also important strategic considerations.

● **decline stage**
The stage in the product life cycle in which demand decreases, the number of organizations producing the product drops, and total sales drop

In the **decline stage**, demand for the product decreases, the number of organizations producing the product drops, and total sales drop. The decline in demand is often due to the fact that all those who might have an interest in purchasing a particular product have already done so. Organizations that failed to anticipate the decline stage in earlier stages of the life cycle may go out of business. Those that differentiated their product, kept their costs low, or developed new products or services may do well during this stage.

FORMULATING CORPORATE-LEVEL STRATEGIES

● **strategic business unit (SBU)**
A single business or set of businesses within a larger organization

Most large organizations are engaged in several businesses, industries, and markets. Each business or set of businesses within such an organization is frequently referred to as a **strategic business unit (SBU)**. An organization such as General Electric operates hundreds of different businesses, making and selling products as diverse as jet engines, nuclear power plants, and light bulbs. GE organizes these businesses into around twenty SBUs. Even organizations that sell only one product may operate in several distinct markets. McDonald's sells only fast food, but it competes in markets as diverse as the United States, Europe, Russia, Japan, and South Korea.

● **diversification**
Refers to the number of different businesses in which an organization is engaged and the extent to which these businesses are related to one another

Decisions about which businesses, industries, and markets an organization will enter, and how to manage these different businesses, are based on an organization's corporate strategy. The most important strategic issue at the corporate level concerns the extent and nature of organizational diversification. **Diversification** is a term that describes the number of different businesses in which an organization is engaged and the extent to which these businesses are related to one another. There are three types of diversification strategies: single-product strategy, related diversification, and unrelated diversification.[13]

Single-Product Strategy

An organization that pursues a **single-product strategy** manufactures just one product or service and sells it in a single geographic market. The WD-40 Company, for example, manufactures only a single product, WD-40 spray lubricant, and sells it in just one market, North America. WD-40 has considered broadening its market to Europe and Asia, but it continues to center all manufacturing, sales, and marketing efforts on one product.

single-product strategy The strategy pursued by an organization that manufactures just one product or service and sells it in a single geographic market

The single-product strategy has one major strength and one major weakness. By concentrating its efforts so completely on one product and market, a firm is likely to be very successful in manufacturing and marketing that product. Because it has staked its survival on a single product, the organization works very hard to make sure the product is a success. On the other hand, if the product is not accepted by the market or is replaced by a new product, the firm will suffer. This happened to slide-rule manufacturers when electronic calculators became widely available and to companies that manufactured only black-and-white televisions when color televisions became available.

Related Diversification

Given the disadvantage of the single-product strategy, most larger businesses today operate in several different businesses, industries, or markets. If the businesses are somehow linked, that organization is implementing a strategy of **related diversification**. Approximately 490 of the 500 largest organizations in the United States implement related diversification.

related diversification The strategy pursued by an organization that operates in several businesses that are somehow linked with one another

Pursuing a strategy of related diversification has three primary advantages. First, it reduces an organization's dependence on any one of its business activities and thus reduces economic risk. Even if one or two of a firm's businesses lose money, the organization as a whole may still survive because the healthy businesses will generate enough cash to support the others.[14] At The Limited, sales declines at Lerner's, one of The Limited's businesses, may be offset by sales increases at Victoria's Secret, another of The Limited's businesses.

Second, by managing several businesses at the same time, an organization can reduce the overhead costs associated with managing any one business. In other words, if the normal administrative costs required to operate any business, such as legal services and accounting, can be spread over a large number of businesses, then the overhead costs *per business* will be lower than they would be if each business had to absorb all costs itself. Thus the overhead costs of businesses in a related diversified firm are usually lower than those of similar businesses that are not part of a larger corporation.[15]

Third, related diversification allows an organization to exploit its strengths and capabilities in more than one business. When organizations do this successfully, they capitalize on synergies, which are complementary effects that exist among their businesses. **Synergy** exists among a set of businesses when the businesses' economic value together is greater than their economic value separately. Disney has been very skilled at creating and exploiting synergies. Its recent hit movie *The Lion King* earned almost

synergy Exists among a set of businesses when their economic value together is greater than their economic value separately

$300 million in box-office revenues. In addition, Disney earned hundreds of millions more from the sales of licensed Lion King toys, clothing, and video games. *The Lion King* stage show at Disney World attracts more guests to the park, and the video earned millions more for the firm.

Unrelated Diversification

unrelated diversification Strategy pursued by an organization that operates several businesses that are not related to one another

Firms that implement a strategy of **unrelated diversification** operate multiple businesses that are not related to one another. Unrelated diversification was a very popular strategy in the 1960s and early 1970s. During this time, several conglomerates like ITT and Transamerica grew by acquiring literally hundreds of other organizations and then running these numerous businesses as independent entities. Even if there are important potential synergies between their different businesses, organizations implementing a strategy of unrelated diversification do not attempt to exploit them.

In theory, unrelated diversification has two advantages. First, a business that uses this strategy should have stable performance over time. During any given period, if some businesses owned by the organization are in a cycle of decline, others may be in a cycle of growth. Unrelated diversification is also thought to have resource allocation advantages. Every year, when a corporation allocates capital, people, and other resources among its various businesses, it must evaluate information about the future of those businesses so that it can place its resources where they have the highest return potential. Given that it owns the businesses in question and thus has full access to information about the future of those businesses, a firm implementing unrelated diversification should be able to allocate capital to maximize corporate performance.

Despite these presumed advantages, research suggests that unrelated diversification usually does not lead to high performance. First, corporate-level managers in such a company usually do not know enough about the unrelated businesses to provide helpful strategic guidance or to allocate capital appropriately. To make strategic decisions, managers must have complete and subtle understanding of a business and its environment. Since corporate managers often have difficulty fully evaluating the economic importance of investments for all the businesses under their wing, they tend to concentrate only on a business's current performance. This narrow attention at the expense of broader planning eventually hobbles the entire organization.

Second, because organizations that implement unrelated diversification fail to exploit important synergies, they are at a competitive disadvantage compared to organizations that use related diversification. Universal Studios has been at a competitive disadvantage relative to Disney because its theme parks, movie studios, and licensing divisions are less integrated and therefore achieve less synergy.

For these reasons, almost all organizations have abandoned unrelated diversification as a corporate-level strategy. ITT and Transamerica have sold off numerous businesses and now concentrate on a core set of related businesses and markets. Large corporations that have not concentrated on a core set of businesses eventually have been acquired by other companies and then broken up. Research suggests that these organizations are actually worth more when broken up into smaller pieces than they are when joined.[16]

Managing Diversification

However an organization implements diversification, it must monitor and manage its strategy. **Portfolio management techniques** are methods that diversified organizations use to make decisions about what businesses to engage in and how to manage these multiple businesses in order to maximize corporate performance.[17] Two important portfolio management techniques are the BCG matrix and the GE Business Screen.

portfolio management techniques
Methods that diversified organizations use to determine which businesses to engage in and how to manage these businesses to maximize corporate performance

BCG Matrix The BCG (for Boston Consulting Group) matrix provides a framework for evaluating the relative performance of businesses in which a diversified organization operates. It also prescribes the preferred distribution of cash and other resources among these businesses.[18] The **BCG matrix** uses two factors to evaluate an organization's set of businesses: the growth rate of a particular market and the organization's share of that market. The matrix suggests that fast-growing markets in which an organization has the highest market share are more attractive business opportunities than slow-growing markets in which an organization has small market share. Dividing market growth and market share into two categories (low and high) creates the simple matrix shown in Figure 3.4.

BCG matrix
Evaluates businesses relative to the growth rate of their market and the organization's share of the market

The matrix classifies the types of businesses that a diversified organization can engage in as dogs, cash cows, question marks, and stars. **Dogs** are businesses that have a very small share of a market that is not expected to grow. Since these businesses do not hold much economic promise, the BCG matrix suggests that organizations either should not invest in them or should consider selling them as soon as possible. **Cash cows** are businesses that have a large share of a market that is not expected to grow substantially. These businesses characteristically generate high profits that the organization should use to support question marks and stars. (Cash cows are "milked" for cash to support businesses in markets that have greater growth potential.) **Question marks** are businesses that have only a small share of a quickly growing market. The future performance of these businesses is uncertain. A question mark that is able to capture increasing amounts of this growing market may be very profitable. On the other hand, a question mark unable to keep up with market growth is likely to have low profits. The BCG matrix suggests that organizations should carefully invest in question marks. If their performance does not live up to expectations, question marks should be reclassified as dogs and divested. **Stars** are businesses that have the largest share of a rapidly growing market. Cash generated by cash cows should be invested in stars to ensure their pre-eminent position.

dogs
Businesses that have a very small share of a market that is not expected to grow

cash cows
Businesses that have a large share of a market that is not expected to grow substantially

question marks
Businesses that have only a small share of a quickly growing market

stars
Businesses that have the largest share of a rapidly growing market

GE Business Screen In response to the narrow focus of the BCG matrix, General Electric (GE) developed the **GE Business Screen**—a portfolio

GE Business Screen
Evaluates businesses along two dimensions: industry attractiveness and competitive position; in general, the more attractive the industry and the more competitive the position, the more an organization should invest in a business

The BCG matrix helps managers develop a better understanding of how different strategic business units contribute to the overall organization. By assessing each SBU on the basis of its market growth rate and relative market share, managers can make decisions about whether to commit further financial resources to the SBU or to sell or liquidate it.

FIGURE 3.4 The BCG Matrix

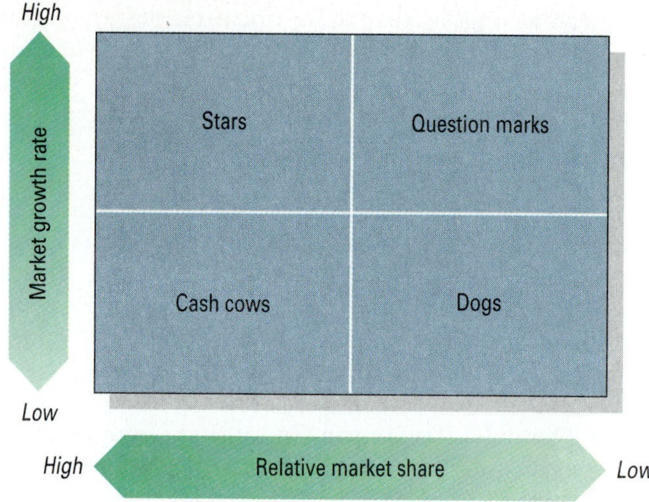

Source: *Perspectives,* No. 66, "The Product Portfolio." Adapted by permission from The Boston Consulting Group, Inc., 1970.

management technique that can also be represented in the form of a matrix. Rather than focusing solely on market growth and market share, however, the GE Business Screen considers industry attractiveness and competitive position. These two factors are divided into three categories to make the nine-cell matrix shown in Figure 3.5.[19]

As Figure 3.5 shows, both market growth and market share appear in a broad list of factors that determine the overall attractiveness of an industry and the overall quality of a firm's competitive position. Other determinants of an industry's attractiveness (in addition to market growth) include market size, capital requirements, and competitive intensity. In general, the greater the market growth, the larger the market, the smaller the capital requirements, and the less the competitive intensity, the more attractive an industry will be. Other determinants of an organization's competitive position in an industry (besides market share) include technological know-how, product quality, service network, price competitiveness, and operating costs. In general, businesses with large market share, technological know-how, high product quality, a quality service network, competitive prices, and low operating costs are in a favorable competitive position.

Think of the GE Business Screen as a way of applying SWOT analysis to the implementation and management of a diversification strategy. The determinants of industry attractiveness are similar to the environmental opportunities and threats in SWOT analysis, and the determinants of competitive position are similar to organizational strengths and weaknesses. By conducting this type of SWOT analysis across several businesses, a diversified organization can decide how to invest its resources to maximize corporate performance.

FIGURE 3.5 The GE Business Screen

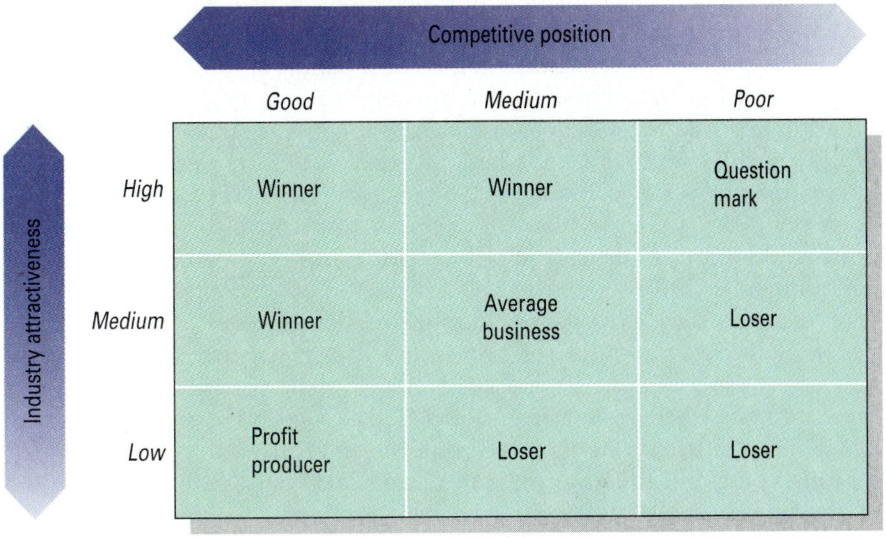

Industry attractiveness \ Competitive position	Good	Medium	Poor
High	Winner	Winner	Question mark
Medium	Winner	Average business	Loser
Low	Profit producer	Loser	Loser

Competitive position

1. Market share
2. Technological know-how
3. Product quality
4. Service network
5. Price competitiveness
6. Operating costs

Industry attractiveness

1. Market growth
2. Market size
3. Capital requirements
4. Competitive intensity

Source: Reprinted by permission from page 32 of *Strategy Formulation: Analytical Concepts* by C.W. Hofer and D. Schendel. Copyright © 1978 by West Publishing Company. All rights reserved.

The GE Business Screen is a more sophisticated approach to portfolio management. As shown here, several different factors combine to determine a business's competitive position and the attractiveness of its industry. These two dimensions, in turn, can be used to classify businesses as winners, question marks, average businesses, losers, or profit producers. Such a classification enables managers to more effectively allocate the organization's resources across various business opportunities.

In general, organizations should invest in winners and in question marks (where industry attractiveness and competitive position are both favorable), maintain the market position of average businesses and profit producers (where industry attractiveness and competitive position are average), and sell losers.

TACTICAL PLANNING

As we noted earlier, tactical plans are developed to implement specific parts of a strategic plan. You have probably heard the saying about "winning the battle but losing the war." A tactical plan is to a battle what strategy is to a war: an organized sequence of steps designed to execute strategic plans. Strategy focuses on resources, environment, and mission, whereas tactics deal primarily with people and action.[20]

Developing Tactical Plans

Although effective tactical planning depends on many factors that vary from one situation to another, some basic guidelines can be identified. First, the manager needs to recognize that tactical planning must address a number of tactical goals derived from a broader strategic goal.[21] An occasional situation may call for a stand-alone tactical plan, but most of the time tactical plans flow from and must be consistent with a strategic plan.

For example, when Roberto Goizueta became CEO of Coca-Cola, he developed a strategic plan for carrying the firm into the twenty-first century. As part of developing the plan, Goizueta identified a critical environmental threat—considerable unrest and uncertainty among the independent bottlers who packaged and distributed Coca-Cola's products. To simultaneously counter this threat and strengthen the company's position, Coca-Cola bought several large independent bottlers and combined them into one new organization called Coca-Cola Enterprises. Selling half of the new company's stock reaped millions in profits while still effectively keeping control of the enterprise in Coca-Cola's hands. Thus the creation of the new business was a tactical plan developed to contribute to the achievement of an overarching strategic goal.[22]

Second, although strategies are often stated in general terms, tactics must deal more with specific resource and time issues. A strategy can call for being number one in a particular market or industry, but a tactical plan must specify precisely what activities will be undertaken to achieve that goal.[23] Consider the Coca-Cola example again. Another element of its strategic plan involves increased worldwide market share. To facilitate additional sales in Europe, managers developed tactical plans for building a new plant in the south of France to make soft-drink concentrate and for building another canning plant in Dunkirk. Building these plants represents a concrete action involving measurable resources (i.e., funds to build the plants) and a clear time horizon (i.e., a target date for completion).[24]

Finally, tactical planning requires the use of human resources. Managers involved in tactical planning spend a great deal of time working with other people. They must be in a position to receive information from others in and outside the organization, process that information in the most effective way, and then pass it on to others who might make use of it. Coca-Cola executives have been intensively involved in planning the new plants, setting up the new bottling venture noted above, and exploring a joint venture with Cadbury Schweppes in the United Kingdom. Each activity has required considerable time and effort from dozens of managers. One manager, for example, crossed the Atlantic twelve times while negotiating the Cadbury deal.

Executing Tactical Plans

Regardless of how well a tactical plan may be formulated, its ultimate success depends on the way it is carried out. Successful implementation, in turn, depends on the astute use of resources, effective decision making, and insightful steps to ensure that the right things are done at the right time and in the right ways. A manager can have an absolutely brilliant idea, but it can fail if not properly executed.

Proper execution depends on a number of important factors. First the manager needs to evaluate every possible course of action in light of the goal it is intended to reach. Next he or she needs to make sure each decision maker has the information and resources necessary to get the job done. Vertical and horizontal communication and integration of activities must be present to minimize conflict or inconsistent activities. And finally, the manager must monitor ongoing activities derived from the plan to make sure that they are achieving the desired results. This monitoring typically takes place within the context of the organization's ongoing control systems.

OPERATIONAL PLANNING

Another critical element in effective organizational planning is the development and implementation of operational plans. Operational plans are derived from tactical plans and are aimed at achieving operational goals. Thus operational plans tend to be narrowly focused, have relatively short time horizons, and involve lower-level managers. The two most basic forms of operational plans, and specific types of each, are summarized in Table 3.1. Contingency plans are also important.

Single-Use Plans

A **single-use plan** is developed to carry out a course of action that is not likely to be repeated in the future. The two most common forms of single-use plans are programs and projects.

- **single-use plan** Developed to carry out a course of action that is not likely to be repeated in the future

Programs A **program** is a single-use plan for a large set of activities. It might consist of identifying procedures for introducing a new product line, opening a new facility, or changing the organization's mission. A few years ago Black & Decker bought General Electric's small-appliance business. The deal involved the largest brand-name switch in history, with a total of 150 products being converted from GE to the Black & Decker label. Each product was carefully studied, redesigned, and reintroduced with an extended warranty. A total of 140 steps were used for each product. It took three years to convert all 150 products over to Black & Decker. The total conversion of the product line was a program.

- **program** A single-use plan for a large set of activities

Projects A **project** is similar to a program but is generally of less scope and complexity. A project may be a part of a broader program, or it may be a self-contained single-use plan. For Black & Decker, the conversion of each of the 150 products was a separate project in its own right. Each product had its own manager, its own schedule, and so forth. Projects are also

- **project** A single-use plan of less scope and complexity than a program

Organizations develop various operational plans to help achieve operational goals. In general, there are two types of single-use plans and three types of standing plans.

TABLE 3.1 Types of Operational Plans

Plan	Description
Single-use plan	Developed to carry out a course of action not likely to be carried out in the future
Program	Single-use plan for a large set of activities
Project	Single-use plan of less scope and complexity than a program
Standing plan	Developed for activities that recur regularly over a period of time
Policy	Standing plan specifying the organization's general response to a designated problem or situation
Standard operating procedure	Standing plan outlining steps to be followed in particular circumstances
Rules and regulations	Standing plans describing exactly how specific activities are to be carried out

used to introduce a new product within an existing product line or to add a new benefit option to an existing salary package.

Standing Plans

● **standing plan**
Developed for activities that recur regularly over a period of time

Whereas single-use plans are used for nonrecurring situations, a **standing plan** is used for activities that recur regularly over a period of time. Standing plans can greatly enhance efficiency by routinizing decision making. Policies, standard operating procedures, and rules and regulations are three kinds of standing plans.[25]

● **policy**
A standing plan that specifies the organization's general response to a designated problem or situation

Policies As a general guide for action, a policy is the most general form of standing plan. A **policy** specifies the organization's general response to a designated problem or situation. For example, McDonald's has a policy that it will not grant a franchise to an individual who already owns another fast-food restaurant. Similarly, Starbucks' stance regarding franchising represents a policy. Likewise, a university admissions office might establish a policy that admission will be granted only to those applicants who have a minimum SAT score of 1,000 and a ranking in the top quarter of their high-school class. Admissions officers may routinely deny admission to applicants who fail to reach these minimums. A policy is also likely to describe how exceptions are to be handled. The university's policy statement, for example, might create an admissions appeals committee to evaluate applicants who do not meet minimum requirements but may warrant special consideration.

Standard Operating Procedures Another type of standing plan is the **standard operating procedure (SOP)**. A SOP is more specific than a policy in that it outlines the steps to be followed in particular circumstances. The admissions clerk at the university, for example, might be told that when an application is received, he or she should (1) set up a file for the applicant; (2) add test-score records, transcripts, and letters of reference to the file as they are received; and (3) give the file to the appropriate admissions director when it is complete. Gallo Vineyards in California has a 300-page manual of standard operating procedures. This planning manual is credited for making Gallo one of the most efficient wine operations in the United States.[26] McDonald's has SOPs explaining exactly how Big Macs are to be cooked, how long they can stay in the warming rack, and so forth.

● **standard operating procedure (SOP)**
A standing plan that outlines the steps to be followed in a particular circumstance

Rules and Regulations The narrowest of the standing plans, **rules and regulations** describe exactly how specific activities are to be carried out. Rather than guiding decision making, rules and regulations actually take the place of decision making in various situations. Each McDonald's restaurant has a rule prohibiting customers from using its telephones, for example. The university admissions office might have a rule stipulating that if an applicant's file is not complete two months prior to the beginning of a semester, the student cannot be admitted until the next semester. Of course, in most organizations a manager at a higher level can suspend or bend the rules. If the high-school transcript of the daughter of a prominent university alumnus and donor arrives a few days late, the director of admissions would probably waive the two-month rule. Rules and regulations can become a problem if they become excessive or if they are enforced too rigidly.

● **rules and regulations**
Standing plans that describe exactly how specific activities are to be carried out

Rules and regulations and SOPs are similar in many ways. They are both relatively narrow in scope, and each can serve as a substitute for decision making. An SOP typically describes a sequence of activities, however, whereas rules and regulations focus on one activity. Recall our examples: the admissions-desk SOP consisted of three activities, whereas the two-month rule related to one activity only. In an industrial setting, the SOP for orienting a new employee could involve enrolling the person in various benefit options, introducing him or her to coworkers and supervisors, and providing a tour of the facilities. A pertinent rule for the new employee might involve when to come to work each day.

Contingency Planning

● **contingency planning**
The determination of alternative courses of action to be taken if an intended plan is unexpectedly disrupted or rendered inappropriate

Another important type of planning is the development of contingency plans. **Contingency planning** is the determination of alternative courses of action to be taken if an intended plan of action is unexpectedly disrupted or rendered inappropriate.[27] Consider, for example, Starbucks' plans for building one hundred new stores a year. Howard Schultz realizes that a shift in the economy might call for a different rate of expansion. Therefore, he likely has two contingency plans based on extreme positive or negative economic shifts. First, if the economy begins to expand beyond some specific level (contingency event), then the rate of the company's growth will increase from one hundred to a higher number of new stores per year (contingency plan). Second, if inflation increases substantially or the economy experiences a downturn, the expansion rate may drop from one hundred to seventy-five new stores per year. Starbucks therefore would have specified two crucial contingencies (economic expansion or inflation in the economy outside the tolerable range) and two alternative plans (increased or decreased growth of the organization).

The mechanics of contingency planning are shown in Figure 3.6. In relation to an organization's other plans, contingency planning comes into play at four action points. At action point 1, the basic plans of the organization are developed. These may include strategic, tactical, and operational plans. As part of this development process, managers usually consider various contingency events. Some management groups even assign someone the role of devil's advocate to ask "But what if . . ." about each course of action. A variety of contingencies is usually considered.

At action point 2, the plan that has been chosen is put into effect. The most important contingency events are also defined. Only the events that are likely to occur and whose effects would have a substantial impact on the organization are used in the contingency-planning process. Next, at action point 3, the company specifies certain indicators or signs that might suggest that a contingency event is about to take place. A bank might decide that a 2 percent drop in interest rates should be considered a contingency event. An indicator might be two consecutive months with a drop of .5 percent in each. As indicators of contingency events are being defined, the contingency plans themselves should also be developed. Possible contingency

Most organizations develop contingency plans. These plans specify alternative courses of action to be taken if an intended plan is unexpectedly disrupted or rendered inappropriate.

FIGURE 3.6 Contingency Planning

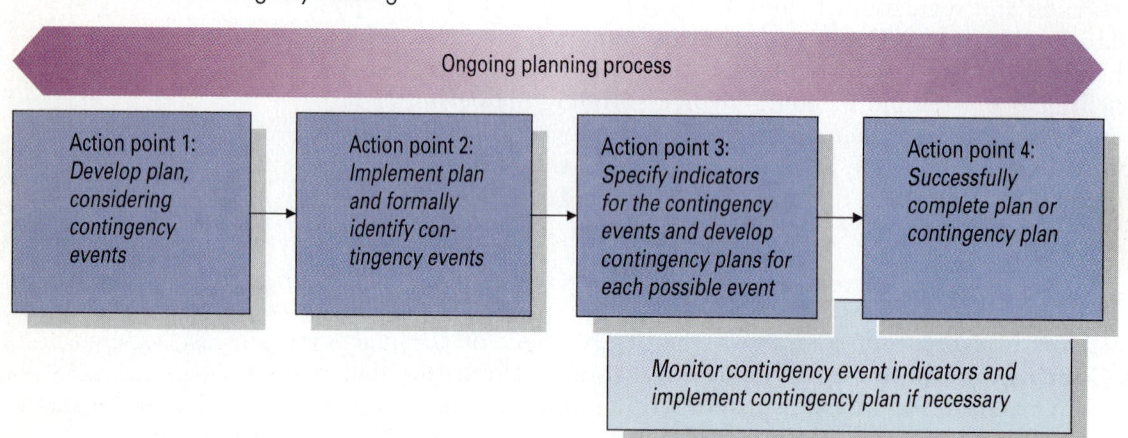

plans for various situations might include delaying plant construction, developing a new manufacturing process, and cutting prices.

After this stage, the managers of the organization monitor the indicators identified at action point 3. If the situation dictates, a contingency plan may be implemented. Otherwise the primary plan of action continues in force. Finally, action point 4 marks the successful completion of either the original or a contingency plan.

Contingency planning is becoming increasingly important for most organizations and especially for those operating in particularly complex or dynamic environments. Few managers have such an accurate view of the future that they can anticipate and plan for everything. Contingency planning is a useful technique for helping managers cope with uncertainty and change.[28]

SUMMARY OF KEY POINTS

The planning process is the first basic managerial function that organizations must address. With an understanding of the environmental context, managers develop a number of different types of goals and plans. Organizations establish several different kinds of goals which serve a variety of purposes. The major types of plans are strategic, tactical, and operational plans.

Strategy is a comprehensive plan for accomplishing the organization's mission. Strategic management is a comprehensive and ongoing process aimed at formulating and implementing effective strategies. Effective strategies address three organizational issues: distinctive competence, scope, and resource deployment. Most large companies have both business-level and corporate-level strategies.

SWOT analysis considers an organization's strengths, weaknesses, opportunities, and threats. Using SWOT analysis, an organization chooses strategies that support its mission and (1) exploit its opportunities and strengths, (2) neutralize its threats, and (3) avoid its weaknesses.

A business-level strategy is the plan an organization uses to conduct business in a particular industry or market. Porter suggests that businesses may formulate a differentiation strategy, a cost leadership strategy, or a focus strategy at this level. Business-level strategies may also take into account the stages in the product life cycle.

A corporate-level strategy is the plan an organization uses to manage its operations across several businesses. A firm that does not diversify is implementing a single-product strategy. An organization pursues a strategy of related diversification when it operates a set of related businesses. An organization pursues a strategy of unrelated diversification when it operates a set of unrelated businesses. Organizations manage diversification through portfolio management techniques. The BCG matrix classifies an organization's diversified businesses as dogs, cash cows, question marks, or stars according to market share and market growth rate. The GE Business Screen classifies businesses as winners, losers, question marks, average businesses, or profit producers according to industry attractiveness and competitive position.

After plans have been developed, the manager must address how they will be achieved. This often involves tactical and operational plans. Tactical plans are at the middle of the organization and have an intermediate time horizon and moderate scope. Tactical plans are developed to implement specific parts of a strategic plan. They must flow from strategy, deal with specific resource and time issues, and commit human resources. It is also important that tactical plans be effectively executed.

Operational plans are at the lower levels of the organization, have a shorter time horizon, and are narrower in scope. Operational plans are derived from a tactical plan and are aimed at achieving one or more operational goals. Two major types of operational plans are single-use and standing plans. Single-use plans are designed to carry out a course of action that is not likely to be repeated in the future. Programs and projects are examples of single-use plans. Standing plans are designed to carry out a course of action that is likely to be repeated several times. Policies, standard operating procedures, and rules and regulations are all standing plans. Contingency planning is also an important type of operational planning.

QUESTIONS FOR REVIEW

1. Describe the nature of organizational goals. Be certain to include both the purposes and kinds of goals.
2. What are the two main types of strategic alternatives available to an organization?
3. List and describe Porter's generic strategies.
4. What is the difference between a single-product strategy, a related diversification strategy, and an unrelated diversification strategy?
5. What is tactical planning? What is operational planning? What are the similarities and differences between them?

QUESTIONS FOR ANALYSIS

1. Suppose that an organization does not have any distinctive competencies. If the organization is able to acquire some distinctive competencies, how long are these strengths likely to remain distinctive competencies? Why?
2. Suppose that an organization moves from a single-product strategy to a strategy of related diversification. How might the organization use SWOT analysis to select attributes of its current business to serve as bases of relatedness among its newly acquired businesses?
3. For decades now, Ivory Soap has advertised that it is 99 percent pure. Ivory has refused to add deodorants, facial creams, or colors to its soap. It also packages its soap in plain paper wrappers—no foil or fancy printing. Is Ivory implementing a product differentiation, low cost, focus strategy, or some combination of these? Explain your answer.
4. Which kind of plan—tactical or operational—should an organization develop first? Why? Does the order of development really make a difference as long as plans of both types are made?
5. Think of examples of each type of operational plan you have used at work, in school, or even in your personal life.

CASE STUDY

Heineken

Commercial brewing has long been an important business in the Netherlands. Indeed, two breweries there date back to the thirteenth century. Currently there are twenty breweries in the Netherlands, and Heineken N. V. owns four of them—Heineken, Amstel, Brand, and De Ridder.

Heineken is the number-one imported beer in terms of sales revenue in the U.S. market, and it is sold in more countries than any other beer. It recently moved from third to second place in terms of beer sales in the world (behind Anheuser-Busch Companies but now ahead of Miller Brewing Company). Although Europe and the Americas comprise a large proportion of its sales, it exports to more than 160 countries, and it is expanding its international operations.

The typical Heineken expansion move involves first exporting its brands to a particular country to establish a brand image and to test the market. Then, if the market appears promising, it licenses its brands to a local brewer. Finally, as that relationship develops and if sales continue to be strong, it will obtain partial ownership or enter into a joint venture with the local firm. This keeps the local brands relatively low-priced while allowing the Heineken brand to be a higher-priced, premium brand.

Heineken maintains the quality of its brands by carefully controlling the use of its special yeast, Heineken-A. Twice a month shipments of that yeast are sent to each of the breweries that make Heineken around the world. Careful quality control and premium pricing have been Heineken's strategy for success in the global marketplace.

Despite its success, international competition remains fierce and is increasing. When Czechoslovakia was one country, Anheuser-Busch began negotiations with the Czechoslovakian government-owned brewery, Budvar (the brewer of the original Budweiser beer). Heineken countered by opening negotiations with Pilsner Urquell, another major Czechoslovakian brewery. Miller obtained a 20 percent interest in Canada's Molson Breweries and Miller's parent company, Philip Morris, bought into Femsa, the Mexican brewery that makes Dos Equis.

Heineken, on the other hand, bought a controlling interest in Komaromi Sorgyar, a Hungarian brewer, to strengthen its position in Eastern Europe. In addition, it acquired breweries in France, Greece, Italy, Spain, and Ireland. By 1994 numerous plans were underway to strengthen its U.S. position through a new advertising campaign, an expansion of Amstel Light, and the possibility of a new brand.

Rumors that Heineken was to be a takeover target for Philip Morris in late 1992 proved false as Heineken had no interest in selling. It trimmed its workforce, closed or sold out-of-date breweries, and installed a new computerized system so that wholesalers in the Netherlands could use personal computers to place orders directly with the company. By doing all of these things, Heineken has been able to maintain the premium image for its products without incurring premium costs in their manufacture. Heineken has also expanded its beverage line. It acquired several distilleries to establish a presence in the wine and spirits business. And it entered the soft-drink market, including becoming the distributor for Pepsi-Cola in the Netherlands.

Case Questions

1. Describe Heineken's business strategy.
2. Describe Heineken's corporate strategy.
3. Based on the information presented in the case, perform a SWOT analysis and develop recommendations for Heineken's managers regarding strategies for the future.

References: "Heineken's Battle to Stay Top Bottle," *Business Week*, August 1, 1994, pp. 60–62; "Making Haste Slowly," *Forbes*, November 9, 1992, pp. 44–45; Gary Hoover, Alta Campbell, Alan Chai, and Patrick J. Spain (Eds.), *Hoover's Handbook of World Business 1993* (Austin, Tex.: The Reference Press, 1993), p. 203; Nico van Dijk, "Dutch Beer: The World's Safest Drink?" *Europe*, September 1992, pp. 22–23; and Brett Duval Fromson, "Cheers to Heineken," *Fortune*, November 19, 1990, pp. 172–175.

SKILLS • DEVELOPMENT • PORTFOLIO

BUILDING EFFECTIVE DECISION-MAKING SKILLS

Exercise Overview

As noted in the chapter, many organizations use SWOT analysis as part of the process of strategy formulation. This exercise will help you better understand how managers obtain the information they need to perform such an analysis and use it as a framework for making decisions.

Exercise Background

SWOT is an acronym for **S**trengths, **W**eaknesses, **O**pportunities, and **T**hreats. Good strategies are those that exploit an organization's opportunities and strengths while neutralizing threats and avoiding or correcting weaknesses.

Assume that you have just been hired to run a medium-size manufacturing company. The firm has been manufacturing electric motors, circuit breakers, and similar electronic components for industrial use. In recent years, the firm's financial performance has gradually eroded. You have been hired to turn things around.

Meetings with both current and former top managers of the firm have led you to believe that a new strategy is needed. In earlier times the firm was successful in part because its products were of top quality. This allowed the company to charge premium prices for them. Recently, however, various cost-cutting measures have resulted in a decrease in quality. Moreover, competition has also increased. As a result, your firm no longer has a reputation for top-quality products, but your manufacturing costs are still relatively high. The next thing you want to do is to conduct a SWOT analysis.

Exercise Task

Using the situation just described as background, do the following:

1. List the sources you will use to obtain information about the firm's strengths, weaknesses, opportunities, and threats.

2. Rate each source in terms of its probable reliability.

3. Rate each source in terms of how easy or difficult it will be to access.

4. How confident should you be in making decisions based on the information obtained?

BUILDING EFFECTIVE CONCEPTUAL SKILLS

Exercise Overview

Conceptual skills refer to the manager's ability to think in the abstract. This exercise gives you some experience in using your conceptual skills on real business opportunities and potential.

Exercise Background

Many successful managers have at one time or another had an idea for using an existing product for new purposes or in new markets. For example, Arm & Hammer Baking Soda (a food product used in cooking) is now also widely used to absorb odors in refrigerators. Commercials advise consumers simply to open a box of Arm & Hammer and place it in their refrigerator. This has led to a big increase in sales of the baking soda.

In other situations, managers have extended product life cycles by taking them into new markets. The most common example today involves products that are becoming obsolete in more industrialized countries and introducing them in less industrialized countries.

Exercise Task

Apply your conceptual skills by doing each of the following:

1. Make a list of ten simple products that have relatively straightforward purposes (e.g., a pencil, which is used for writing).

2. Next, try to identify two or three alternative uses for each product (e.g., a pencil can be used as a splint for a broken finger in an emergency).

3. Evaluate the market potential for each alternative product use as high, moderate, or low (e.g., the market potential for pencils as splints is low).

4. Form small groups of two or three members and pool your ideas. Have each group choose two or three ideas and present them to the class.

YOU MAKE THE CALL

When Mark Spenser first launched Sunset Landscape Services, he knew it was important to establish goals for his business. His first goal, of course, was survival. After the urgency of business start-up eased, however, he then found it useful to establish a clear and unambiguous set of business goals stressing the value of high-quality customer service and consistent business growth. Looking back today, Mark believes that these goals have served him well on two important occasions.

By 1984, SLS was on reasonably secure financial footing, and Mark decided to expand his business. The firm initially consisted of two related but distinct businesses. One business was a retail nursery selling plants, pots, baskets, plant food, gardening supplies, and so forth. Mark's wife, Cynthia, managed this part of the operation. The other business was the actual landscape operation, which Mark himself managed. This business provided such services as planning new lawns and landscaping for local builders and owners of new homes. Mark also drew plans for decks and patios, and worked with a local swimming-pool builder to jointly design and install pools and accompanying landscaping.

Mark then decided to expand his business into lawn-care services. This operation would handle routine mowing and related lawn-maintenance services for homeowners. He launched this new business in 1985. The initial start-up operation took a little longer than expected, however, and he ran into a financial crunch. Support from his suppliers and banker helped weather the storms, so that within a year the new business was running on a profitable basis. Today, this business is as important to the overall operation as were the first two businesses.

The other time that Mark's goals were critical to his success was in 1990. A regional nursery chain, Lion Gardens, opened a store in Central City. Because of Lion's size, it was able to buy in bulk and sell at a discount. Mark knew that Lion's prices would be lower than his, and he worried that he would lose customers to Lion. He initially considered cutting his own prices to meet those of Lion, but then realized that if he did so he would not be able to provide the same level of customer support that he currently offered. For example, many customers sought advice on what kinds of plants would work best in different locations, how to best care for those plants, and so forth.

Mark eventually decided to not worry about Lion's prices. He realized that people who were only interested in price could already buy their plants at a discount at Wal-Mart, for example. Thus, he continued to stress quality customer service with reasonable prices. He was gratified to observe that, although his business took a bit of a hit during the first few months that Lion was open, his customers soon returned.

Discussion Questions

1. How important have goals been to Sunset Landscape Services?

2. What business strategy is SLS using? What corporate strategy is SLS using?

3. What business opportunities might Mark Spenser consider next?

SKILLS SELF-ASSESSMENT INSTRUMENT

Are You a Good Planner?

Introduction: Planning is an important skill for managers. The following assessment is designed to help you understand your planning skills.

Instructions: Answer either *yes* or *no* to each of the following eight questions.

	Yes	No
1. My personal objectives are clearly spelled out in writing.	______	______
2. Most of my days are hectic and disorderly.	______	______
3. I seldom make any snap decisions and usually study a problem carefully before acting.	______	______
4. I keep a desk calendar or appointment book as an aid.	______	______
5. I make use of "action" and "deferred action" files.	______	______
6. I generally establish starting dates and deadlines for all my projects.	______	______
7. I often ask others for advice.	______	______
8. I believe that all problems have to be solved immediately.	______	______

For interpretation, turn to page 447.

EXPERIENTIAL EXERCISE

The SWOT Analysis

Purpose: SWOT analysis provides the manager with a cognitive model of the organization and its environmental forces. By developing this ability, the manager builds both process knowledge and a conceptual skill. This skill builder focuses on the *administrative management model.* It will help you develop the *coordinator role* of the administrative management model. One of the skills of the coordinator is the ability to plan.

Introduction: This exercise helps you understand the complex interrelationships between environmental opportunities and threats and organizational strengths and weaknesses.

Instructions:

Step 1: Study the exhibit below, Strategy Formulation at Marriott, and the text materials concerning the matching of organizations with environments.

Step 2: The instructor will divide the class into small groups. Each group will conduct a SWOT (strengths, weaknesses, opportunities, threats) analysis for Marriott and prepare group responses to the discussion questions. Marriott has been successful in its hotel and food services businesses but less than successful in its cruise ship, travel agency, and theme park businesses.

Strategy formulation is facilitated by a SWOT analysis. First the organization should study its internal operations in order to identify its strengths and weaknesses. Next the organization should scan the environment in order to identify existing and future opportunities and threats. Then the organization should identify the relationships that exist among the strengths, weaknesses, opportunities, and threats. Finally, major business strategies usually result from matching an organization's strengths with appropriate opportunities or from matching threats with weaknesses. To facilitate the environmental analysis in search of opportunities and threats, it is helpful to break the environment down into its major components—international, economic, political-legal, sociocultural, and technological.

Step 3: One representative from each group may be asked to report on the group's SWOT analysis and to report the group's responses to the discussion questions.

Discussion Questions

1. What was the most difficult part of the SWOT analysis?

2. Why do most firms not develop major strategies for matches between threats and strengths?

3. Under what conditions might a firm develop a major strategy around a match between an opportunity and a weakness?

Source: From *Exercises in Management,* 5th ed., by Gene E. Burton. Copyright © 1996 by Houghton Mifflin Co. Reprinted by permission of the publisher.

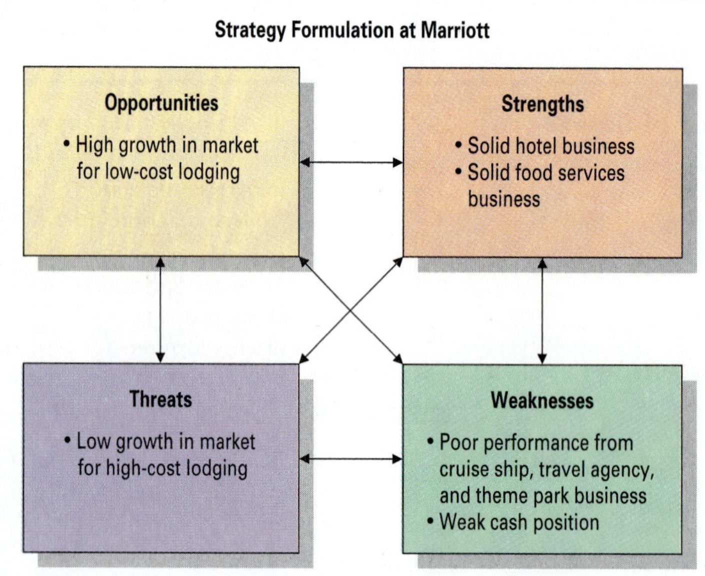

Source: Ricky Griffin, *Management,* 4th ed., © 1993 by Houghton Mifflin Company, p. 180.

Marriott SWOT Analysis Sheet

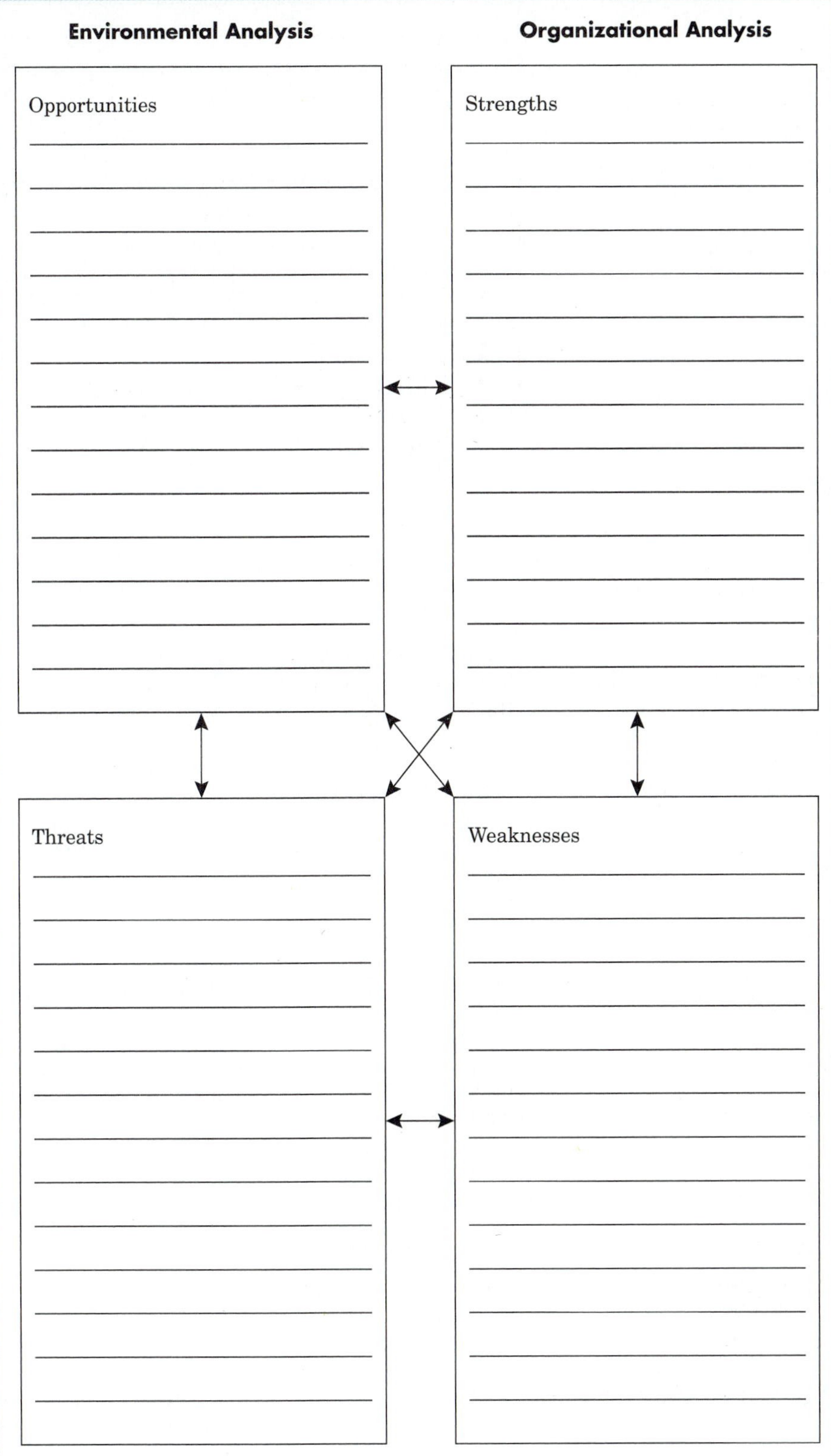

Relationships Between Opportunities and Strengths

1. ______________________
2. ______________________
3. ______________________

Relationships Between Opportunities and Weaknesses

1. ______________________
2. ______________________
3. ______________________

Relationships Between Threats and Strengths

1. ______________________
2. ______________________
3. ______________________

Relationships Between Threats and Weaknesses

1. ______________________
2. ______________________
3. ______________________

Major Strategies Matching Opportunities with Strengths

1. ______________________
2. ______________________
3. ______________________
4. ______________________

Major Strategies Matching Threats with Weaknesses

1. ______________________
2. ______________________
3. ______________________
4. ______________________

CHAPTER NOTES

1. "The Starbucks Enterprise Shifts into Warp Speed," *Business Week*, October 24, 1994, pp. 76–79; Patrick Spain and James Talbot (Eds.), *Hoover's Handbook of Emerging Companies 1996* (Austin, Tex.: The Reference Press, 1995), p. 276.
2. This framework is inspired by numerous sources: George Steiner, *Top Management Planning* (New York: Macmillan, 1969); John E. Dittrich, *The General Manager and Strategy Formulation* (New York: Wiley, 1988); Henry Mintzberg, "Crafting Strategy," *Harvard Business Review*, July–August 1987, pp. 66–75; Michael E. Porter, *Competitive Strategy* (New York: Free Press, 1985); and Charles W. L. Hill and Gareth R. Jones, *Strategic Management: An Integrated Approach,* 3rd ed. (Boston: Houghton Mifflin, 1995).
3. Max D. Richards, *Setting Strategic Goals and Objectives*, 2nd ed. (St. Paul, Minn.: West, 1986).
4. Shawn Tully, "Why to Go for Stretch Targets," *Fortune*, November 14, 1994, pp. 145–158.
5. John A. Pearce II and Fred David, "Corporate Mission Statements: The Bottom Line," *The Academy of Management Executive*, May 1987, p. 109.
6. See Hill and Jones, *Strategic Management*.
7. For early discussions of strategic management, see Kenneth Andrews, *The Concept of Corporate Strategy,* rev. ed. (Homewood, Ill.: Dow Jones-Irwin, 1980); Igor Ansoff, *Corporate Strategy* (New York: McGraw-Hill, 1965); and E. P. Learned, C. R. Christensen, K. R. Andrews, and W. D. Guth, *Business Policy* (Homewood, Ill.: Irwin, 1969).
8. Steve Caminiti, "Can The Limited Fix Itself?" *Fortune*, October 17, 1994, pp. 161–172.
9. Bill Saporite, "The Eclipse of Mars," *Fortune*, November 28, 1994, pp. 82–92.
10. For a discussion of this distinction, see Hill and Jones, *Strategic Management*.
11. Jay Barney, "Firm Resources and Sustained Competitive Advantage," *Journal of Management,* 1991, pp. 99–120.
12. Porter, *Competitive Strategy*.
13. Alfred Chandler, *Strategy and Structure: Chapters in the History of the American Industrial Enterprise* (Cambridge, Mass.: MIT Press, 1962); Richard Rumelt, *Strategy, Structure, and Economic Performance* (Cambridge, Mass.: Division of Research, Graduate School of Business Administration, Harvard University, 1974); and Oliver Williamson, *Markets and Hierarchies* (New York: Free Press, 1975).
14. See Chandler, *Strategy and Structure,* and Yakov Amihud and Baruch Lev, "Risk Reduction as a Managerial Motive for Conglomerate Mergers," *Bell Journal of Economics,* 1981, pp. 605–617.
15. Chandler, *Strategy and Structure*; Williamson, *Markets and Hierarchies*.
16. See Jay B. Barney and William G. Ouchi, *Organizational Economics* (San Francisco: Jossey-Bass, 1986), for a discussion of the limitations of unrelated diversification.
17. Michael Lubatkin and Sayan Chatterjee, "Extending Modern Portfolio Theory into the Domain of Corpo-

rate Diversification: Does It Apply?" *Academy of Management Journal*, Vol. 37, No. 1, 1994, pp. 109–136.

18. See Barry Hedley, "A Fundamental Approach to Strategy Development," *Long Range Planning,* December 1976, pp. 2–11, and Bruce Henderson, "The Experience Curve—Reviewed. IV: The Growth Share Matrix of the Product Portfolio," *Perspectives,* no. 135 (Boston: Boston Consulting Group, 1973).

19. Michael G. Allen, "Diagramming GE's Planning for What's WATT," in Robert J. Allio and Malcolm W. Pennington (Eds.), *Corporate Planning: Techniques and Applications* (New York: AMACOM, 1979). Limits of this approach are discussed in R. A. Bettis and W. K. Hall, "The Business Portfolio Approach: Where It Falls Down in Practice," *Long Range Planning,* 1983, pp. 95–105.

20. James Brian Quinn, Henry Mintzberg, and Robert M. James, *The Strategy Process* (Englewood Cliffs, N.J.: Prentice-Hall, 1988).

21. Vasudevan Ramanujam and N. Venkatraman, "Planning System Characteristics and Planning Effectiveness," *Strategic Management Journal*, Vol. 8, 1987, pp. 453–468.

22. Gary Hector, "Yes, You *Can* Manage Long Term," *Fortune*, November 21, 1988, pp. 64–76; John Huey, "The World's Best Brand," *Fortune,* May 31,1993, pp. 44–54.

23. Henry Mintzberg, "Crafting Strategy," *Harvard Business Review*, July–August 1987, pp. 66–75.

24. Huey, "The World's Best Brand."

25. Thomas L. Wheelon and J. David Hunger, *Strategic Management and Business Policy*, 5th ed. (Reading, Mass.: Addison-Wesley, 1995).

26. Jaclyn Fierman, "How Gallo Crushes the Competition," *Fortune*, September 1, 1986, pp. 23–31.

27. K. A. Froot, D. S. Scharfstein, and J. C. Stein, "A Framework for Risk Management," *Harvard Business Review*, November–December 1994, pp. 91–102.

28. See Donald C. Hambrick and David Lei, "Toward an Empirical Prioritization of Contingency Variables for Business Strategy," *Academy of Management Journal*, December 1985, pp. 763–788.

CHAPTER

Managerial Decision Making

4

OBJECTIVES

After studying this chapter, you should be able to:

- *Define decision making and discuss types of decisions and decision-making conditions.*
- *Discuss rational perspectives on decision making, including the steps in decision making.*
- *Describe the behavioral nature of decision making.*
- *Discuss group decision making, including the advantages and disadvantages of group decision making and how it can be more effectively managed.*

OUTLINE

IN 1958, AN undergraduate business major and member of the track team at the University of Oregon complained to his coach about the lack of a good American running shoe. The German firm Adidas ruled the market then, and the student believed that considerable opportunity existed for new entrants into the market. In 1968, he and his coach decided to start their own firm. The student was Philip Knight, and the new company was Nike.

For the first several years, Nike struggled for recognition and market opportunity. In the mid-1980s, however, Nike took off. Fueled by spokesperson Michael Jordan, a barrage of new products (like pump basketball shoes and cross trainers), the "Just Do It" slogan, and a boom in aerobics exercise programs, Nike experienced tremendous growth and left rivals like Adidas and Reebok in its dust. From the beginning, Knight has served as CEO of the firm; he is also its largest shareholder.

"The days when a few decision makers can get together in the hall are over."

During those heady days of phenomenal growth, Knight left the day-to-day management of his firm to its president, Richard Donahue. Donahue, in turn, kept most of the decision-making power for himself. He often made major decisions with little or no input from others. As long as the firm was growing at an exponential rate, this system never caused much concern.

By the mid-1990s, however, the aerobics boom was stalling, and the tastes of young consumers were turning away from athletic shoes and toward hiking-style outdoor boots. As a result, Nike also stalled, and management seemed to lack any clear idea of how to get things moving again.

Finally, Knight decided that the firm needed to recapture the entrepreneurial style that had launched its initial success. He eased Donahue into retirement and installed Thomas Clarke, then a vice president, as president. Clarke was known as an excellent communicator who believed in shared responsibility. Clarke's mandate was to launch a number of new initiatives to jumpstart the firm's growth.

One of Clarke's first steps was to call a series of meetings with every group of managers in the firm. He told them that decision making at Nike was going to change. He argued that the old, centralized approach to doing business had served Nike well in the past but that a new, decentralized approach to making decisions was now needed. He concluded by saying that he expected every manager in the firm to exercise increased control in making the decisions affecting that individual's area of responsibility. It's too soon to know how well the new approach is working, but Phil Knight himself seems genuinely excited about Nike's future prospects.[1]

Source of Quotation: Thomas Clarke, Nike president, quoted in *Business Week*, April 18, 1994, p. 86.

Executives at Nike exemplify two extreme views of how managers in organizations make decisions. In earlier days at Nike, most decisions were made by managers at the top of the firm, with little collaboration or participation of lower-level managers. Now, however, decision-making authority is spread throughout the firm, and more managers than ever before are expected to participate in the decision-making process.

Some experts believe that decision making is the most basic and fundamental of all managerial activities.[2] Thus we discuss it here in the context of the first management function, planning. Keep in mind, however, that although decision making is perhaps most closely linked to the planning function, it is also part of organizing, leading, and controlling. We begin our discussion by exploring the nature of decision making. We then describe rational perspectives on decision making. Behavioral aspects of decision making are then introduced and described. We conclude with a discussion of group decision making.

THE NATURE OF DECISION MAKING

Managers at BMW recently made the decision to build a new manufacturing plant in South Carolina at a cost of over $600 million. At about the same time, the manager at the BMW dealership in Bryan, Texas, made a decision to sponsor a local youth soccer team for $150. Each of these examples includes a decision, but the decisions differ in many ways. Thus as a starting point in understanding decision making, we must first explore its meaning as well as the types of decisions and conditions under which decisions are made.[3]

Decision Making Defined

• **decision making**
The act of choosing one alternative from among a set of alternatives

• **decision-making process**
Recognizing and defining the nature of a decision situation, identifying alternatives, choosing the "best" alternative, and putting it into practice

Decision making can refer either to a specific act or to a general process. **Decision making** per se is the act of choosing one alternative from among a set of alternatives. The decision-making process, however, is much more than this. One step of the process, for example, is that the person making the decision must recognize that a decision is necessary and identify the set of feasible alternatives before selecting one. Hence, the **decision-making process** includes recognizing and defining the nature of a decision situation, identifying alternatives, choosing the "best" alternative, and putting it into practice.[4]

The word "best" implies effectiveness. Effective decision making requires that the decision maker understand the situation driving the decision. Most people would consider an effective decision to be one that optimizes some set of factors such as profits, sales, employee welfare, and market share. In some situations, though, an effective decision may be one that minimizes loss, expenses, or employee turnover. It may even mean selecting the best method for going out of business, laying off employees, or terminating a contract.

We should also note that managers make decisions about both problems and opportunities. For example, making decisions about how to cut costs by 10 percent reflects a problem—an undesired situation that requires a solution. But decisions are also necessary in situations of opportunity. Learning that the firm is earning higher-than-projected profits, for example, requires a decision. Should the extra funds be used to increase shareholder dividends, reinvested in current operations, or used to expand into new markets?

Of course, it may take a long time before a manager can know if the right decision was made. For example, Jack Welch, CEO of General Electric, took an enormous gamble a few years ago by trading his company's consumer-electronics business to Thomson, a French company, for its medical-equipment business. At the time of the exchange, GE held 23 percent of the U.S. color-television market and 17 percent of the U.S. VCR market. Moreover, it was the only serious consumer-electronics business left in the United States, and it was generating enormous profits. Welch, however, believed the medical-equipment business held even more promise for growth and profits. Analysts believe that the "winner" of the exchange will not be known until at least the turn of the century.[5]

Types of Decisions

Managers must make many different types of decisions. In general, however, most decisions fall into one of two categories: programmed and nonprogrammed.[6] A **programmed decision** is one that is fairly structured or recurs with some frequency (or both). For example, suppose a manager of a distribution center knows from experience that she needs to keep a

• **programmed decision** A decision that is fairly structured or recurs with some frequency (or both)

Nonprogrammed decisions are unstructured and nonroutine decisions. When an earthquake cut power at Santa Monica's Saint John's Hospital, these nurses had to make several nonprogrammed decisions. They fought valiantly to save several infants whose lives depended on various electronic life-support systems. The nurses had to quickly assess the condition of each infant and then decide how best to provide life support without electric power.

thirty-day supply of a particular item on hand. She can then establish a system whereby the appropriate quantity is automatically reordered whenever the inventory drops below the thirty-day requirement. Likewise, the Bryan BMW dealer has made a decision that he will sponsor a youth soccer team each year. Thus when the soccer club president calls, the dealer already knows what he will do. Many decisions regarding basic operating systems and procedures and standard organizational transactions are of this variety and therefore can be programmed.

nonprogrammed decision
A decision that is relatively unstructured; occurs much less often than a programmed decision

Nonprogrammed decisions, on the other hand, are relatively unstructured and occur much less often. Consider GE's decision to exchange businesses with Thomson and BMW's decision to build a new plant: no business makes decisions like those on a regular basis. Managers faced with such decisions must treat each one as unique, investing enormous amounts of time, energy, and resources into exploring the situation from all perspectives. Intuition and experience are major factors in nonprogrammed decisions. Most of the decisions made by top managers involving strategy (including mergers, acquisitions, and takeovers) and organization design are nonprogrammed. So are decisions about new facilities, new products, labor contracts, and legal issues.

Decision-Making Conditions

Just as there are different kinds of decisions, there are also different conditions under which decisions must be made. Jack Welch at GE has no guarantees that the new medical-equipment business will be successful, whereas he had a pretty clear picture of how the electronics business was doing. Managers sometimes have an almost perfect understanding of conditions surrounding a decision, but at other times they have few clues about those conditions. In general, the circumstances that exist for the decision maker are conditions of certainty, risk, or uncertainty.[7] These conditions are represented in Figure 4.1.

Decision Making Under Certainty When the decision maker knows with reasonable certainty what the alternatives are and what conditions are

FIGURE 4.1 Decision-Making Conditions

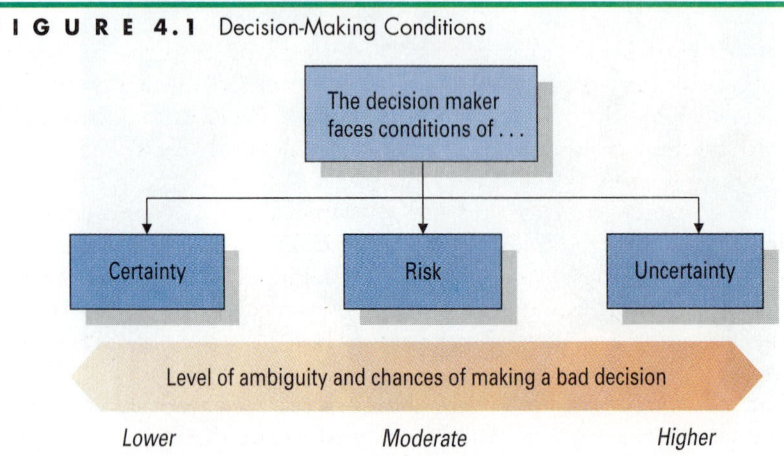

Most major decisions in organizations today are made under a state of uncertainty. Managers making decisions in these circumstances must be sure to learn as much as possible about the situation and approach the decision from a logical and rational perspective.

associated with each alternative, a **state of certainty** exists. Suppose, for example, that Singapore Airlines needs to buy five new jumbo jets. The decision is from whom to buy them. Singapore has only three choices: Boeing, McDonnell Douglas, and Airbus. Each has a proven product and will specify prices and delivery dates. The airline thus knows the alternative conditions associated with each. There is little ambiguity and relatively low chance of making a bad decision.

• **state of certainty**
When the decision maker knows with reasonable certainty what the alternatives are and what conditions are associated with each alternative

Few organizational decisions are made under conditions of true certainty.[8] The complexity and turbulence of the contemporary business world make such situations rare. Even the airplane purchase decision we just considered has less certainty than it appears. The aircraft companies may not be able to guarantee delivery dates so they may write cost-increase or inflation clauses into contracts. Thus the airline may not be truly certain of the conditions surrounding each alternative.

Decision Making Under Risk A more common decision-making condition is a state of risk. Under a **state of risk**, the availability of each alternative and its potential payoffs and costs are all associated with probability estimates.[9] Suppose, for example, that a labor contract negotiator for a company receives a "final" offer from the union right before a strike deadline. The negotiator has two alternatives: to accept or to reject the offer. The risk centers on whether or not the union representatives are bluffing. If the company negotiator accepts the offer, she avoids a strike but commits to a costly labor contract. If she rejects the contract, she may get a more favorable contract if the union is bluffing; she may provoke a strike if it is not.

• **state of risk**
A condition in which the availability of each alternative and its potential payoffs and costs are all associated with probability estimates

On the basis of past experiences, relevant information, the advice of others, and her own intuition, she may believe that there is a 75 percent chance that the union is bluffing and a 25 percent chance that it will back up its threats. Thus she can base a calculated decision on the two alternatives (accept or reject the contract demands) and the probable consequences of each. When making decisions under a state of risk, managers must accurately determine the probabilities associated with each alternative. For example, if the union negotiators are committed to a strike if their demands are not met, and the company negotiator rejects their demands because she guesses they will not strike, her miscalculation will prove costly. As indicated in Figure 4.1, decision making under conditions of risk is accompanied by moderate ambiguity and chances of a bad decision.[10]

Decision Making Under Uncertainty Most major decision making in contemporary organizations is done under a **state of uncertainty**. The decision maker does not know all the alternatives, the risks associated with each, or the likely consequences of each alternative.[11] This uncertainty stems from the complexity and dynamism of contemporary organizations and their environments. Consider, for example, the first decision Nike's Philip Knight made regarding footware. He could have decided to use existing sneaker technology to reduce risk and avoid uncertainty. But he also saw that he then would have fewer competitive advantages over Adidas, the dominant firm in the market at the time. Thus, he based his shoes on a new waffle-type design that gave them another unique feature to highlight. But this choice carried with it considerable uncertainty because Knight had no idea how it would be received in the market.

• **state of uncertainty**
A condition in which the decision maker does not know all the alternatives, the risks associated with each, or the consequences each alternative is likely to have

Indeed, many of the decisions already discussed—BMW's decision to build a new plant and GE's decision to get out of consumer electronics—were made under conditions of uncertainty. To make effective decisions in these circumstances, managers must acquire as much relevant information as possible and approach the situation from a logical and rational perspective. Intuition, judgment, and experience always play major roles in the decision-making process under conditions of uncertainty. Even so, uncertainty is the most ambiguous condition for managers and the one most prone to error.

RATIONAL PERSPECTIVES ON DECISION MAKING

● **classical decision model** A prescriptive approach to decision making that tells managers how they should make decisions. It assumes managers are logical and rational and that their decisions will be in the best interests of the organization

● **steps in rational decision making** Recognize and define the decision situation; identify appropriate alternatives; evaluate each alternative in terms of its feasibility, satisfactoriness, and consequences; select the best alternative; implement the chosen alternative; follow up and evaluate the results of the chosen alternative

The classical model of decision making assumes that managers are rational and logical. It attempts to prescribe how managers should approach decision situations.

Most managers like to think of themselves as rational decision makers. And indeed, many experts argue that managers should try to be as rational as possible in making decisions.[12]

The Classical Model of Decision Making

The **classical decision model** is a prescriptive approach that tells managers how they should make decisions. It rests on the assumptions that managers are logical and rational and that they make decisions that are in the best interests of the organization. Figure 4.2 shows how the classical model views the decision-making process: (1) Decision makers have complete information about the decision situation and possible alternatives. (2) They can effectively eliminate uncertainty to achieve a decision condition of certainty. (3) They evaluate all aspects of the decision situation logically and rationally. As we will see later, these conditions rarely, if ever, actually exist.

Steps in Rational Decision Making

A manager who really wants to approach a decision rationally and logically should try to follow the steps listed in Table 4.1. These in **steps in rational decision making** help keep the decision maker focused on facts and logic and help guard against inappropriate assumptions and pitfalls.

Recognizing and Defining the Decision Situation The first step in rational decision making is recognizing that a decision is necessary—that is, there must be some stimulus or spark to initiate the process.[13] For many

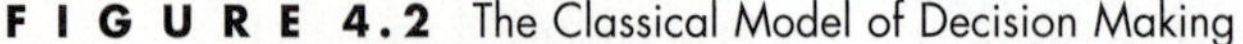

FIGURE 4.2 The Classical Model of Decision Making

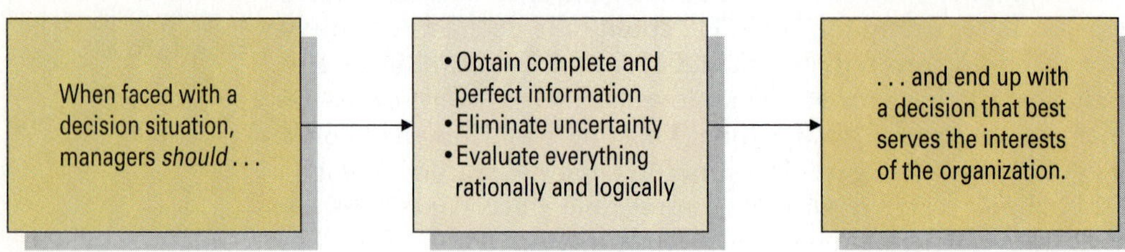

TABLE 4.1 Steps in the Rational Decision-Making Process

Step	Detail	Example
1. Recognizing and defining the situation	Some stimulus indicates that a decision must be made. The stimulus may be positive or negative.	A plant manager sees that employee turnover has increased by 5 percent.
2. Identifying alternatives	Both obvious and creative alternatives are desired. In general, the more important the decision, the more alternatives should be generated.	The plant manager can increase wages, increase benefits, or change hiring standards.
3. Evaluating alternatives	Each alternative is evaluated to determine its feasibility, its satisfactoriness, and its consequences.	Increasing benefits may not be feasible. Increasing wages and changing hiring standards may satisfy all conditions.
4. Selecting the best alternative	Consider all situational factors, and choose the alternative that best fits the manager's situation.	Changing hiring standards will take an extended period of time to cut turnover, so increasing wages is the best alternative.
5. Implementing the chosen alternative	The chosen alternative is implemented into the organizational system.	The plant manager may need permission of corporate headquarters. The human resource department establishes a new wage structure.
6. Follow-up and evaluation	At some time in the future, the manager should ascertain the extent to which the alternative chosen in step 4 and implemented in step 5 has worked.	The plant manager notes that, six months later, turnover dropped to its previous level.

decisions and problem situations, the stimulus may occur without any prior warning. When equipment malfunctions, the manager must decide whether to repair or replace it. Or when a major crisis erupts, such as an explosion or fire, the manager must quickly decide how to deal with it. As already noted, the stimulus for a decision may be either positive or negative. A manager who must decide how to invest surplus funds, for example, faces a positive decision situation. A negative financial stimulus could involve having to trim budgets because of cost overruns.[14]

Although the presumptions of the classical decision model rarely exist, managers can approach decision making with rationality. By following the steps of rational decision making, managers ensure that they are learning as much as possible about the decision situation and its alternatives.

Inherent in problem recognition is the need to define precisely what the problem is. The manager must develop a complete understanding of the problem, its causes, and its relationship to other factors. This understanding comes from careful analysis and thoughtful consideration of the situation. Consider the recent problem faced by Olin Pool Products. Even though Olin controlled half the market for chlorine-based pool-treatment systems, its profits were slipping and it was rapidly losing market share to new competitors. These indicators provided clear evidence to General Manager Doug Cahill that something needed to be done. He went on to define the problem as a need to restore profitability and regain lost market share.[15]

Identifying Alternatives Once the decision situation has been recognized and defined, the second step is to identify alternative courses of action that might be effective. It is generally useful to develop both obvious, standard alternatives and creative, innovative alternatives.[16] In general, the more important the decision, the more attention is directed to developing alternatives. If the decision involves a multimillion-dollar relocation, a great deal of time and expertise will be devoted to identifying the best locations—JC Penney Company spent two years searching before selecting the Dallas–Fort Worth area for its new corporate headquarters. If the problem is to choose a color for the company softball-team uniforms, less time and expertise will be brought to bear.

Although managers should seek creative solutions, they must also recognize that various constraints often limit their alternatives. Common constraints include legal restrictions, moral and ethical norms, authority constraints (constraints imposed by the power and authority of the manager), available technology, economic considerations, and unofficial social norms. Greg Cahill at Olin identified several alternatives that might help his firm: seek a bigger firm to take control of Olin and inject new resources, buy one or more competitors to increase Olin's own size, maintain the status quo and hope that competitors stub their toes, or overhaul the organization in order to become more competitive.

Evaluating Alternatives The third step in the decision-making process is evaluating each of the alternatives.[17] Figure 4.3 suggests a decision tree that can be used to judge different alternatives. The figure suggests that each alternative be evaluated in terms of its feasibility, its satisfactoriness, and its consequences. The first question to ask is whether an alternative is feasible. Is it within the realm of probability and practicality? For a small, struggling firm, an alternative requiring a huge financial outlay is probably out of the question. Other alternatives may not be feasible because of legal barriers. And limited human, material, and information resources may make other alternatives impractical.

When an alternative has passed the test of feasibility, it next must be examined to see how well it will satisfy the conditions of the decision situation. For example, a manager searching for ways to double production capacity might consider purchasing an existing plant from another company. If closer examination reveals that the new plant would increase production capacity by only 35 percent, this alternative may not be satisfactory. Finally, when an alternative has proven both feasible and satisfactory, its probable consequences still must be assessed. To what extent will a particular alternative influence other parts of the organization? What financial and nonfinancial costs will be associated with such influences? For example, a plan to boost sales by cutting prices may disrupt cash flows, require a new advertising program, and alter the behavior of sales representatives because it requires a different commission structure. The manager, then, must put "price tags" on the consequences of each alternative. Even an alternative that is both feasible and satisfactory must be eliminated if its consequences are too expensive for the total system. Cahill decided that being taken over would cause too great a loss of autonomy (consequences not affordable), that buying a competitor was too expensive (not feasible), and that doing nothing would not solve the problem (not satisfactory).

FIGURE 4.3 Evaluating Alternatives in the Decision-Making Process

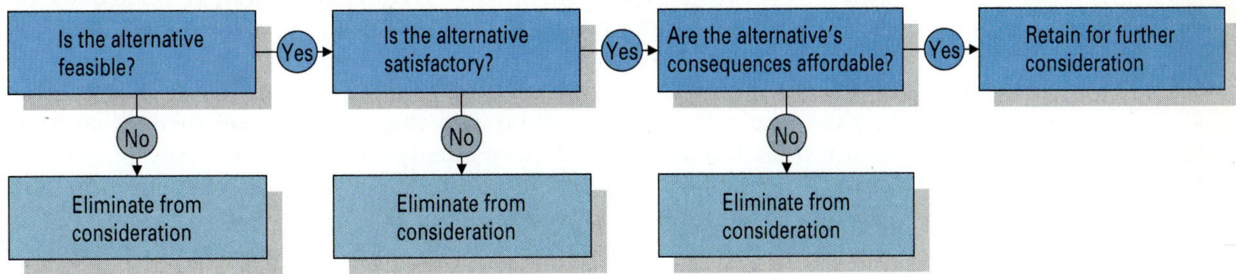

Selecting an Alternative Even though many alternatives fail to pass the triple tests of feasibility, satisfactoriness, and affordable consequences, two or more alternatives may remain. Choosing the best of these is the real crux of decision making. One approach is to choose the alternative with the highest combined level of feasibility, satisfactoriness, and affordable consequences. Even though most situations do not lend themselves to objective, mathematical analysis, the manager can often develop subjective estimates and weights for choosing an alternative.

Managers must thoroughly evaluate all of the alternatives, which increases the chances that the alternative finally chosen will be successful. Failure to evaluate an alternative's feasibility, satisfactoriness, and consequences can lead to a wrong decision.

Optimization is also a frequent goal. Because a decision is likely to affect several individuals or subunits, any feasible alternative will probably not maximize all of the relevant goals. Suppose the manager of the Kansas City Royals needs to select a starting center fielder for the next baseball season. Bill might hit .350 but not be able to catch a fly ball; Joe might hit only .175 but be outstanding in the field; and Sam might hit .290 and be a solid but not outstanding fielder. The manager would probably select Sam because of the optimal balance of hitting and fielding. Decision makers should remember that it may be possible to find multiple acceptable alternatives—it may not be necessary to select just one alternative and reject all the others. For example, the Royals' manager might decide that Sam will start each game, Bill will be retained as a pinch hitter, and Joe will be retained as a defensive substitute. In many hiring decisions, the candidates remaining after evaluation are ranked. If the top candidate rejects the offer, it may be automatically extended to the number-two candidate, and, if necessary, to the remaining candidates in order. Olin Pool Products selected the alternative of overhauling the organization to become more competitive.

Implementing the Chosen Alternative After an alternative has been selected, the manager must put it into effect. In some decision situations, implementation may be fairly easy; in others, it will be more difficult. In the case of an acquisition, for example, managers must decide how to integrate all the activities of the new business, including purchasing, human resource practices, and distribution, into an ongoing organizational framework. When American Telephone & Telegraph Co. (AT&T) acquired NCR Corp., it took months to consolidate NCR's operations into existing systems. Operational plans, discussed in Chapter 3, are useful in implementing alternatives.

Managers must also consider people's resistance to change when implementing decisions. The reasons for such resistance include insecurity, inconvenience, and fear of the unknown. When Penney's decided to move from New York to Texas, many employees resigned rather than relocate. Managers should anticipate potential resistance at various stages of the implementation process. (Resistance to change is covered in Chapter 7.) Managers should also recognize that, even when all alternatives have been evaluated as precisely as possible and the consequences of each alternative weighed, unanticipated consequences are still likely. Any number of situations—such as unexpected cost increases, a less-than-perfect fit with existing organizational subsystems, or unpredicted effects on cash flow or operating expenses—could develop after the implementation process has begun. Greg Cahill eliminated several levels of management at Olin, combined fourteen departments into eight, gave new authority to every manager, and empowered employees to take greater control over their work.

Following Up and Evaluating the Results The final step in the decision-making process requires that managers evaluate the effectiveness of their decision—that is, that they make sure that the chosen alternative has served its original purpose. If an implemented alternative appears not to be working, the manager can respond in several ways. Another previously identified alternative (the second or third choice) could be adopted. Or the manager might recognize that the situation was not correctly defined to start with and begin the process all over again. Finally, the manager might decide that the original alternative is in fact appropriate but has not yet had time to work or should be implemented in a different way.

Failure to evaluate decision effectiveness may have serious consequences. The Pentagon spent $1.8 billion and eight years developing the Sergeant York anti-aircraft gun. From the beginning, tests revealed major problems with the weapon system, but not until it was in its final stages, when it was demonstrated to be completely ineffective, was the project scrapped.[18] In a classic case of poor decision making, managers at Coca-Cola decided to change the formula for the soft drink. Consumer response was extremely negative. In contrast to the Pentagon, however, Coca-Cola immediately reacted: it reintroduced the old formula within three months as Coca-Cola Classic. Had managers stubbornly stuck with their decision and failed to evaluate its effectiveness, the results would have been disastrous. Greg Cahill's decisions at Olin are paying big dividends—the firm's profits are back up and most of the market share it recently lost has been regained as well.

BEHAVIORAL ASPECTS OF DECISION MAKING

If all decision situations were approached as logically as described in the previous section, more decisions would prove to be successful. Yet, decisions are often made with little consideration for logic and rationality. Kepner-Tregoe, a Princeton-based consulting firm, estimates that American companies use rational decision-making techniques less than 20 percent of the time.[19] And even when organizations try to be logical, they sometimes fail. For example, managers at Coca-Cola decided to change Coke's formula after four years of extensive marketing research, taste tests, and rational deliberation—but the decision was still wrong. On the other hand, sometimes when a decision is made with little regard for logic, it can still turn out to be correct. A key ingredient in how these forces work is the behavioral aspect of decision making.[20] The administrative model better reflects these subjective considerations. Other behavioral aspects include political forces, intuition and escalation of commitment, risk propensity, and ethics.

The Administrative Model of Decision Making

Herbert A. Simon was one of the first people to recognize that decisions are not always made with rationality and logic.[21] Simon was subsequently awarded the Nobel Prize in economics. Rather than prescribing how decisions should be made, his view of decision making, now called the **administrative model**, describes how decisions often actually are made. As illustrated in Figure 4.4, the model holds that managers (1) have incomplete and imperfect information, (2) are constrained by bounded rationality, and (3) tend to satisfice when making decisions.

administrative model A decision-making model that argues that decision makers (1) have incomplete and imperfect information, (2) are constrained by bounded rationality, and (3) tend to satisfice when making decisions

Bounded rationality suggests that decision makers are limited by their values and unconscious reflexes, skills, and habits. They are also limited by less-than-complete information and knowledge. Bounded rationality partially explains how U.S. auto executives allowed Japanese automakers to become so strong in the United States. For years, executives at GM, Ford, and Chrysler compared their companies' performance only to one another and ignored foreign imports. The foreign "threat" wasn't acknowledged until the domestic auto market had been changed forever. If managers had seen things more clearly from the beginning, they might have been better able to thwart foreign competitors. Essentially, then, the concept of bounded rationality suggests that although people try to be rational decision makers, their rationality has limits.

bounded rationality A concept that suggests that decision makers are limited by their values and unconscious reflexes, skills, and habits

satisficing The tendency to search for alternatives only until one is found that meets some minimum standard of sufficiency

Another important part of the administrative model is **satisficing**. This concept suggests that rather than conducting an exhaustive search for the best possible alternative, decision makers tend to search only until they identify an alternative that meets some minimum standard of sufficiency. A manager looking for a site for a new plant, for example, may select the first site she finds that meets basic requirements for transportation, utilities, and price, even though further search might yield a better location. People satisfice for a variety of reasons. Managers may simply be unwilling to ignore their own motives (such as reluctance to spend time making a decision) and therefore may not be able to continue searching after a minimally acceptable

The administrative model is based on behavioral processes that affect how managers make decisions. Rather than prescribing how decisions should be made, it focuses more on describing how they are made.

FIGURE 4.4 The Administrative Model of Decision Making

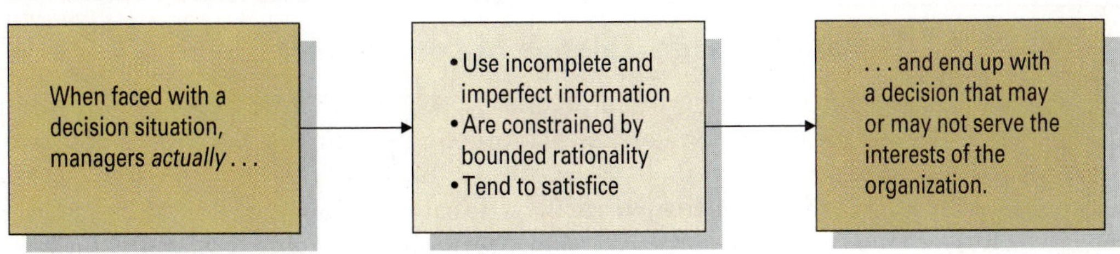

alternative is identified. The decision maker may be unable to weigh and evaluate large numbers of alternatives and criteria. Also, subjective and personal considerations often interfere with decision situations.

Because of the inherent imperfection of information, bounded rationality, and satisficing, the decisions made by a manager may or may not actually be in the best interests of the organization. A manager may choose a particular location for the new plant because it offers the lowest price and best availability of utilities and transportation. Or she may choose the location because it's in a community in which she wants to live.

In summary, then, the classical and administrative models paint quite different pictures of decision making. Which is more correct? Actually, each can be used to better understand how managers make decisions. The classical model is prescriptive: it explains how managers can at least attempt to be more rational and logical in their approach to decisions. The administrative model can be used by managers to develop a better understanding of their inherent biases and limitations.[22] In the following sections, we describe more fully other behavioral forces that can influence decisions.

Political Forces in Decision Making

• **coalition**
An informal alliance of individuals or groups formed to achieve a common goal

Political forces are another major element that contribute to the behavioral nature of decision making. Organizational politics is covered in Chapter 11, but one major element of politics, coalitions, is especially relevant to decision making. A **coalition** is an informal alliance of individuals or groups formed to achieve a common goal. This common goal is often a preferred decision alternative. For example, coalitions of stockholders frequently band together to force a board of directors to make a certain decision.

Coalitions led to the formation of Unisys Corporation, a large computer firm. Sperry was once one of America's computer giants, but a series of poor decisions put the company on the edge of bankruptcy. Two key executives waged battle for three years over what to do. One wanted to get out of the computer business altogether, and the other wanted to stay in. Finally, the manager who wanted to remain in the computer business, Joseph Kroger, garnered enough support to earn promotion to the corporation's presidency. The other manager, Vincent McLean, took early retirement. Shortly thereafter, Sperry agreed to be acquired by Burroughs Wellcome Co. The resulting combined company is called Unisys.[23]

Coalitions can have either positive or negative effects. They can help astute managers get the organization on a path toward effectiveness and profitability, or they can strangle well-conceived strategies and decisions. Managers must recognize when to use coalitions, how to assess whether coalitions are acting in the best interests of the organization, and how to constrain their dysfunctional effects.

Intuition and Escalation of Commitment

• **intuition**
An innate belief about something without conscious consideration

Two other important decision processes that go beyond logic and rationality are intuition and escalation of commitment to a chosen course of action.

Intuition **Intuition** is an innate belief about something without conscious consideration. Managers sometimes decide to do something because it "feels right" or they have a hunch. This feeling is usually not arbitrary, however. Rather, it is based on years of experience and practice in making decisions in similar situations. An inner sense may help managers make an occasional decision without going through a full-blown rational sequence of steps. Liz Claiborne and three partners founded Liz Claiborne Inc. to design and sell clothes for working women. Conventional wisdom at the time suggested that they needed to build plants to make the clothing and develop a traveling salesforce to market it. Pure intuition, however, told them not to follow this "wisdom." They subcontracted production to other makers instead of building plants, and they sold their clothes only to large department and specialty store buyers willing to travel to New York. The result? Very low overhead and annual sales of more than $1 billion.[24] Of course, all managers, but most especially inexperienced ones, should be careful not to rely too heavily on intuition. If rationality and logic are continually flouted for what "feels right," the odds are that disaster will strike one day.

Intuition is a behavioral process that can play an important role in the decision-making process. When Lisa Frankenberg arrived in Prague, her intuition told her that the city's booming business sector would support an English-language newspaper. She and a partner started the business-oriented *Prague Post,* which now has a circulation of 15,000.

Escalation of Commitment Another important behavioral process that influences decision making is **escalation of commitment** to a chosen course of action. In particular, decision makers sometimes make decisions and then become so committed to the course of action suggested by that decision that they stay with it even when it appears to have been wrong.[25] For example, when people buy stock in a company, they sometimes refuse to sell it even after repeated drops in price. They choose a course of action—buying the stock in anticipation of making a profit—and then stay with it even in the face of increasing losses.

escalation of commitment A decision maker's staying with a decision even when it appears to be wrong

A few years ago IBM decided to develop a new operating system to replace what was then the industry standard, DOS. DOS had been jointly developed several years earlier by IBM and MicroSoft Corporations. IBM recognized that DOS was becoming outdated and that Microsoft was developing its own new system called Windows. IBM countered with a system called OS/2. Windows went on to become the most successful software product in history, garnering over 75 percent of the market, while OS/2 became only a minor player in the market. But in 1995, as Microsoft was introducing a new version of its Windows system, called Windows 95, IBM similarly announced a new version of OS/2. Many experts, however, predicted that the new OS/2 would meet the same fate as its predecessor.[26]

Thus decision makers must walk a fine line. On the one hand, they must guard against sticking with an incorrect decision too long. To do so can bring about financial decline. On the other hand, they should not bail out of a seemingly incorrect decision too soon, as did Adidas. Adidas once dominated the market for professional athletic shoes. It subsequently entered the market for amateur sports shoes and did well there also. But managers interpreted a sales slowdown as a sign that the boom in athletic shoes was over. They thought that they had made the wrong decision and ordered drastic cutbacks. The market took off again with Nike at the head of the pack, and Adidas never recovered.[27]

Risk Propensity and Decision Making

risk propensity The extent to which a decision maker is willing to gamble in making a decision

The behavioral element of **risk propensity** is the extent to which a decision maker is willing to gamble when making a decision.[28] Some managers are cautious about every decision they make. They try to adhere to the rational model and are extremely conservative in what they do. Such managers are more likely to avoid mistakes, and they infrequently make decisions that lead to big losses. Other managers are much more aggressive in making decisions and are more willing to take risks. They rely heavily on intuition, reach decisions quickly, and often risk big investments on their decisions. As in gambling, these managers are more likely than their conservative counterparts to achieve big successes with their decisions; they are also more likely to incur greater losses. The organization's culture is a prime ingredient in fostering different levels of risk propensity.

Ethics and Decision Making

As we introduced in Chapter 2, individual ethics are personal beliefs about right and wrong behavior. Ethics are clearly related to decision making in a number of ways.[29] For example, suppose after careful analysis a manager realizes that her company could save money by closing her department and subcontracting with a supplier for the same services. But to recommend this course of action would result in the loss of several jobs, including her own. Her own ethical standards will clearly shape how she proceeds. Indeed, each component of managerial ethics (relationships of the firm to its employees, of employees to the firm, and of the firm to other economic agents) involves a wide variety of decisions, all of which are likely to have an ethical component. A manager must remember, then, that just as behavioral processes such as politics and risk propensity affect the decisions she makes, so too do her ethical beliefs.

GROUP DECISION MAKING IN ORGANIZATIONS

In more and more organizations today, important decisions are made by groups rather than individuals. Examples include the executive committee of Rockwell International, product design teams at Texas Instruments Incorporated, and marketing planning groups at General Foods. Managers can typically choose whether to have individuals or groups make a particular decision. Thus it's important to know about forms of group decision making and their advantages and disadvantages.[30]

Forms of Group Decision Making

The most common methods of group decision making are interacting groups, Delphi groups, and nominal groups.

• **interacting group**
A decision-making group in which members openly discuss, argue about, and agree on the best alternative

Interacting Groups An **interacting group** is the most common form of group decision making. The format is simple—either an existing or a newly designated group is asked to make a decision. Existing groups might be functional departments, regular work groups, or standing committees. Newly designated groups can be ad hoc committees, task forces, or work teams. The group members talk among themselves, argue, agree, argue some more, form internal coalitions, and so forth. Finally, after some period of deliberation, a decision is made. An advantage of this method is that the interaction between people often sparks new ideas and promotes understanding. A major disadvantage, though, is that political processes can play too big a role.

Delphi Groups A **Delphi group** is sometimes used for achieving a consensus of expert opinion. Developed by the Rand Corporation, the Delphi procedure solicits input from a panel of experts who contribute individually. Their opinions are combined and, in effect, averaged. Assume, for example, that the problem is to establish an expected date for a major technological breakthrough in converting coal into usable energy. The first step in using the Delphi procedure is to obtain the cooperation of a panel of experts. For this situation, experts might include various research scientists, university researchers, and executives in a relevant energy industry. At first, the experts are asked to anonymously predict a time frame for the expected breakthrough. The persons coordinating the Delphi group collect the responses, average them, and ask the experts for another prediction. In this round, the experts who provided unusual or extreme predictions may be asked to justify them. These explanations may then be relayed to the other experts. When the predictions stabilize, the average prediction is taken to represent the decision of the "group" of experts. The time, expense, and logistics of the Delphi technique rule out its use for routine, everyday decisions, but it has been successfully used for forecasting technological breakthroughs at Boeing, market potential for new products at General Motors, research and development patterns at Eli Lilly, and future economic conditions by the U.S. government.[31]

• **Delphi group**
A form of group decision making in which a group is used to achieve a consensus of expert opinion

Nominal Groups Another useful group decision-making technique occasionally used is the **nominal group**. Unlike the Delphi method, where group members do not see one another, nominal group members are brought together. The members form a group in name only, however; they do not talk to one another freely like the members of interacting groups. Nominal groups are used most often to generate creative and innovative alternatives or ideas. To begin, the manager assembles a group of knowledgeable people and outlines the problem to them. The group members are then asked to individually write down as many alternatives as they can think of. The members then take turns stating their ideas, which are recorded on a flip chart or blackboard at the front of the room. Discussion is limited to simple clarification. After all alternatives have been listed, more open discussion takes place. Group members then vote, usually by rank-ordering the various alternatives. The highest-ranking alternative represents the decision of the group. Of course, the manager in charge may retain the authority to accept or reject the group decision.

• **nominal group**
A structured technique used to generate creative and innovative alternatives or ideas

Advantages of Group Decision Making

The advantages and disadvantages of group decision making relative to individual decision making are summarized in Table 4.2. One advantage of group decision making is simply that more information is available in a group setting—as suggested by the old axiom "Two heads are better than one." A group represents a variety of education, experience, and perspective. Partly

To increase the chances that a group's decision will be successful, managers must learn how to manage the process of group decision making. Westinghouse, FedEx, and IBM are increasingly using groups in the decision-making process.

TABLE 4.2 Advantages and Disadvantages of Group Decision Making

Advantages	Disadvantages
1. More information and knowledge are available.	1. The process takes longer, so it is costlier.
2. More alternatives are likely to be generated.	2. Compromise decisions resulting from indecisiveness may emerge.
3. More acceptance of the final decision is likely.	3. One person may dominate the group.
4. Enhanced communication of the decision may result.	4. Groupthink may occur.
5. Better decisions generally emerge.	

as a result of this increased information, groups typically can identify and evaluate more alternatives than can one person.[32] The people involved in a group decision understand the logic and rationale behind it, are more likely to accept it, and are equipped to communicate the decision to their work groups or departments. Finally, research evidence suggests that groups may make better decisions than individuals.[33]

Disadvantages of Group Decision Making

Perhaps the biggest drawback of group decision making is the additional time and, hence, the greater expense entailed. The increased time stems from interaction and discussion among group members. If a given manager's time is worth $50 an hour, and if the manager spends two hours making a decision, the decision costs the organization $100. For the same decision, a group of five managers might require three hours of time. At the same $50-an-hour rate, the decision costs the organization $750. Assuming the group decision is better, the additional expense may be justified, but the fact remains that group decision making is more costly.

Group decisions may also represent undesirable compromises.[34] For example, hiring a compromise top manager may be a bad decision in the long run because he or she may not be able to respond adequately to various subunits in the organization. Sometimes one individual dominates the group process to the point where others cannot make a full contribution. This dominance may stem from a desire for power or from a naturally dominant personality. The problem is that what appears to emerge as a group decision may actually be the decision of one person.

groupthink
A situation that occurs when a group's desire for consensus and cohesiveness overwhelms its desire to reach the best possible decision

Finally, a group may succumb to a phenomenon known as groupthink. **Groupthink** occurs when the group's desire for consensus and cohesiveness overwhelms its desire to reach the best possible decisions.[35] Under the influence of groupthink, the group may arrive at decisions that are not in the best interest of either the group or the organization but rather avoid conflict among group members. One of the clearest examples of groupthink that has been documented involved the space shuttle *Challenger* disaster. As NASA was preparing to launch the shuttle, numerous problems and questions arose. At each step of the way, however, decision makers argued that there was no reason to delay and that everything would be fine. Shortly after the launch on January 28, 1986, the shuttle exploded, killing all seven crew members.

Managing Group Decision-Making Processes

Managers can do several things to help promote the effectiveness of group decision making. One is simply being aware of the pros and cons of having a group make a decision. Time and cost can be managed by setting a deadline by which the decision must be made final. Dominance can be at least partially avoided if a special group is formed just to make the decision. An astute manager, for example, should know who in the organization may try to dominate a group and can either avoid putting that person in the group or put several strong-willed people together.

To avoid groupthink, each member of the group should critically evaluate all alternatives. So that members present divergent viewpoints, the leader should not make his or her own position known too early. At least one member of the group should be assigned the role of devil's advocate. And, after reaching a preliminary decision, the group should hold a follow-up meeting wherein divergent viewpoints can be raised again if any group members wish to do so.[36] Gould Paper Company, Inc., used these methods by assigning managers to two different teams. The teams then spent an entire day in a structured debate presenting the pros and cons of each side of an issue to ensure the best possible decision. These procedures are similar to those practiced at Sun Microsystems.

SUMMARY OF KEY POINTS

Decisions are an integral part of all managerial activities, but they are perhaps most central to the planning process. Decision making is the act of choosing one alternative from among a set of alternatives. The decision-making process includes recognizing and defining the nature of a decision situation, identifying alternatives, choosing the "best" alternative, and putting it into practice. Two common types of decisions are programmed and nonprogrammed. Decisions may be made under states of certainty, risk, or uncertainty.

Rational perspectives on decision making rest on the classical model. This model assumes that managers have complete information and that they will behave rationally. The primary steps in rational decision making are (1) recognizing and defining the situation, (2) identifying alternatives, (3) evaluating alternatives, (4) selecting the best alternative, (5) implementing the chosen alternative, and (6) following up and evaluating the effectiveness of the alternative after it is implemented.

Behavioral aspects of decision making rely on the administrative model. This model recognizes that managers will have incomplete information and that they will not always behave rationally. The administrative model also recognizes the concepts of bounded rationality and satisficing. Political activities by coalitions, managerial intuition, and the tendency to become increasingly committed to a chosen course of action are all important. Risk propensity is also an important behavioral perspective on decision making. Finally, ethics also affect how managers make decisions.

To help enhance decision-making effectiveness, managers often use interacting, Delphi, or nominal groups. Group decision making in general has several advantages as well as disadvantages relative to individual decision making. Managers can adopt a number of strategies to help groups make better decisions.

QUESTIONS FOR REVIEW

1. Describe the nature of decision making.
2. Identify and discuss the conditions under which most decisions are made.
3. What are the main features of the classical model of the decision-making process? What are the main features of the administrative model?
4. What are the steps in rational decision making? Which step do you think is the most difficult to carry out? Why?
5. Describe the behavioral nature of decision making. Be certain to provide some detail about political forces, risk propensity, ethics, and commitment in your description.

QUESTIONS FOR ANALYSIS

1. Was your decision about what college or university to attend a rational decision? Did you go through each step in rational decision making? If not, why not?
2. Can any decision be purely rational, or are all decisions at least partially behavioral in nature? Defend your answer against alternatives.
3. Think of an example for each decision-making condition. Then think of how conditions might change to alter the condition for each decision.
4. Is satisficing always a bad thing? Under what conditions might it be desirable?
5. Under what conditions would you expect group decision making to be preferable to individual decision making, and vice versa? Why?

CASE STUDY

Is Quaker Quaking?

The Quaker Oats Company began with a merger of seven millers in the late 1800s, although it didn't adopt its name until 1901. It dominated the oats market early on and has never lost that domination. Quaker diversified its product line into animal feed and some grocery items and, in 1911, bought Aunt Jemima pancake flour. During the early part of this century, then, Quaker concentrated on production and marketing and grew to be one of the larger corporations in the United States with two of the oldest brand symbols in America.

Beginning in the 1960s Quaker management decided to pursue diversification as a strategy for growth and profits. Quaker purchased Burry Biscuit Company, the leading supplier of Girl Scout cookies, in 1962. In 1969 it bought Fisher-Price toys (and sold it in 1991); a Chicago pizza restaurant, Celeste; and a San Francisco crepe restaurant, Magic Pan (which it also later sold). In 1972 it acquired Needlecraft Corporation of America and again sold it later. In 1983, Quaker bought Stokely-Van Camp with its top brand of pork and beans and its sports beverage, Gatorade.

Quaker then decided to focus its acquisitions on food companies. In 1986 it purchased the Golden Grain Macaroni Company, makers of Rice-a-Roni and Noodle-Roni brand products. That same year Quaker purchased Anderson, Clayton & Company, producers of dog-food products, including Gaines Burgers and Gravy Train. Quaker became number one in hot cereals, pork and beans, and sports beverages and number two in dog food.

Quaker Oats sports beverage Gatorade had more than 85 percent of the market in 1993, but competition from new entrants such as PepsiCo's All Sport and Coke's PowerAde was increasing fast. The Gatorade unit decided to become a more aggressive marketer—introducing promotions and improving its distribution network. In addition, Gatorade introduced its SunBolt, a chilled breakfast beverage that came on the market during the summer of 1994. Quaker also began to work with Sunkist to produce a powdered beverage targeted at U.S. Club stores, and it bought Snapple.

In 1994 Quaker decided to begin a restructuring effort. It combined its in-house promotion, package design, and media services divisions. About three hundred persons were let go and another fifty vacant positions were not filled, a far cry from the thousands laid off by many other companies as a result of downsizing.

One reason for this small impact from restructuring may well be the human resource policies and practices used by Quaker. Quaker offers employees several childcare services and benefits such as work flexibility to recruit and retain the best personnel it can. Those benefits grew out of an employee-developed benefits program. Fifteen persons representing as many varying demographics of its employees as possible were assembled as The Flex Team. They ranked one hundred proposed benefits and met with coworkers to check their rankings. The plan was communicated to Quaker personnel in small group meetings and a print campaign. This high-involvement approach enabled Quaker to identify problems with the plan and ensured its enthusiastic acceptance by workers.

Case Questions

1. What kinds of decisions are described in this case? How would you classify them in terms outlined in the chapter?
2. Are the problems and solutions in this case unique to the food-products industry or could they be found in other products and situations?
3. What role might group decision making play in a firm like Quaker?

References: "Gatorade Is Starting to Pant," *Business Week*, April 18, 1994, p. 98; Eric Sfiligoj, "Ace of Clubs," *Beverage World*, April 1994, p. 70; Joyce E. Santora, "Employee Team Designs Flexible Benefits Program," *Personnel Journal*, April 1994, pp. 30–39; Jim Kirk, "Gatorade Stirs Morning Drink," *Brandweek*, May 23, 1994, p. 6; "Opportunities Lost," *Forbes*, July 20, 1992, pp. 70–76; Milton Moskowitz, Robert Levering, and Michael Katz, *Everybody's Business* (New York: Doubleday, 1990), pp. 20–22; and "Quaker Oats Takeover Talk Goes Flat," *USA Today*, January 17, 1995, p. 3B.

SKILLS • DEVELOPMENT • PORTFOLIO

BUILDING EFFECTIVE COMMUNICATION SKILLS

Exercise Overview

Decision making and communication are highly interrelated. This exercise will give you insights into some of those interrelations.

Exercise Background

Identify a decision that you will need to make sometime in the near future. If you work in a managerial position, you might select a real problem or issue to address, for example, the selection or termination of an employee, the allocation of pay raises, or the selection of someone for a promotion.

If you do not work in a managerial position, you might instead select an upcoming decision related to your academic work. Examples include what major to select, whether to attend summer school or to work, which job to select, and whether to live on or off campus next year. Be sure to select a decision that has not yet been made.

Exercise Task

Using the decision selected above, do each of the following:

1. On a sheet of paper, list the kinds of information that you will most likely use in making your decision. Beside each one, make notes as to where you can obtain the information, in what form the information will be presented, the reliability of the information, and other relevant characteristics of the information.

2. Next, assume that you have used the information obtained above and have made the decision (it might be helpful at this point to select a hypothetical decision and choice to frame your answers). On the other side of the paper, list the various communication consequences that come with your decision. For example, if your choice involves an academic major, you may need to inform your adviser and your family. List as many consequences as you can. Beside each one, make notes as to how you would communicate with each party, the timeliness of your communication, and any other factors that seem to be relevant.

3. What behavioral forces might play a role in your decision?

BUILDING EFFECTIVE INTERPERSONAL SKILLS

Exercise Overview

Interpersonal skills refer to the manager's ability to understand and motivate individuals and groups. This exercise will allow you to practice your interpersonal skills in a role-playing exercise.

Exercise Background

You supervise a group of six employees who work in an indoor facility in a relatively isolated location. The company you work for has recently adopted an ambiguous policy regarding smoking. Essentially, the policy states that all company work sites are to be smoke free, unless the employees at a specific site choose differently, in which case the decision is at the discretion of the site supervisor.

Four members of the work group you supervise are smokers. They have come to you with the argument that since they constitute the majority that they should be allowed to smoke at work. The other two members of the group, both nonsmokers, have heard about this and have also discussed the situation with you. They argue that the health-related consequences of secondary smoke should outweigh the preferences of the majority.

To compound the problem further, your boss wrote the new policy and is quite defensive about it—numerous individuals have already criticized the policy. You know that your boss will get very angry with you if you too raise concerns about the policy. Finally, you are personally indifferent about the issue. You do not smoke yourself, but your spouse does. Secondary smoke does not bother you, and you do not have strong opinions about it. Still, you have to make a decision about what to do. You see that your options are to (1) mandate a smoke-free environment, (2) allow smoking in the facility, or (3) ask your boss to clarify the policy.

Exercise Task

Based on the background presented above, do the following:

1. Assume that you have chosen option 1. Write down an outline that you will use to announce your decision to the four smokers.

2. Assume that you have chosen option 2. Write down an outline that you will use to announce your decision to the two nonsmokers.

3. Assume that you have chosen option 3. Write down an outline that you will use when you meet with your boss.

4. Are there other alternatives?

5. Which option would you choose if you were actually the group supervisor?

YOU MAKE THE CALL

In 1992, Cynthia Spenser made an important decision that had a major effect on Sunset Landscape Services. Around the same time that SLS was built, a local developer had built a small shopping complex adjacent to the Spensers' site. This complex had an elegant ambiance and was named The Arbor. Its retail tenants included an interior decorator, a gourmet coffee shop, an upscale toy store, a bookstore, and a clothing store.

For years there had been considerable synergy between The Arbor and Sunset Landscape Services. The two establishments shared a parking lot, for example, and many customers could be observed strolling back and forth between SLS and The Arbor. Indeed, many people assumed that the two were actually one business.

The developer who had originally built The Arbor retired in 1992 and put the property on the market. The Spensers initially were quite concerned by this event. They feared that a new owner might revamp the shopping complex and alter the tenant mix in some way that might be to their disadvantage. Mark joked that it might be turned into a tattoo parlor or a video emporium.

But the Spensers soon decided that their fears were groundless. The current tenants of The Arbor all had long-term leases, and the property was in a location that would not work as well for other kinds of businesses. Mark put his concerns aside and went back to work on a big landscaping project. Cynthia, however, continued to think about the property.

She soon realized that she wanted to buy The Arbor herself. Aside from helping to protect the business interests of Sunset Landscape Services, she recognized that The Arbor was an attractive investment. Its cash flow was strong and the tenant base solid. And whenever a tenant had left, the current owner had been able to attract a replacement with little difficulty.

Cynthia also felt that The Arbor had additional possibilities. For example, the property behind the shopping complex was vacant, so the retail center could easily be expanded. Moreover, Cynthia was excited about the possibility of running her own business, rather than essentially managing one of Mark's businesses. Although she was the co-owner of SLS and obviously had considerable control over the nursery, the business itself had been conceptualized and planned by Mark. Cynthia also felt constrained by the overall landscape services environment. The Arbor, she realized, would represent something that she could put her own stamp on. The more she thought about it, the more she realized that she had made the decision to buy The Arbor.

Discussion Questions

1. What perspectives on decision making are reflected in this case?

2. What role have various behavioral processes played in Cynthia's decision?

3. What challenges and hurdles does Cynthia face?

SKILLS SELF-ASSESSMENT INSTRUMENT

Decision-Making Styles

Introduction: Decision making is clearly important. However, individuals differ in their decision-making style, or the way that they approach decisions. The following assessment is designed to help you understand your decision-making style.

Instructions: Respond to the following statements by indicating the extent to which they describe you. Circle the response that best represents your self-evaluation.

1. Overall, I'm ______ to act.
a. quick **b.** moderately fast **c.** slow

2. I spend ______ amount of time making important decisions as/than I do making less important ones.
a. about the same **b.** a greater **c.** a much greater

3. When making decisions, I ______ go with my first thought.
a. usually **b.** occasionally **c.** rarely

4. When making a decision, I'm ______ concerned about making errors.
a. rarely **b.** occasionally **c.** often

5. When making decisions, I ______ recheck my work more than once.
a. rarely **b.** occasionally **c.** usually

6. When making decisions, I gather ______ information.
a. little **b.** some **c.** lots of

7. When making decisions, I consider ______ alternatives.
a. few **b.** some **c.** lots of

8. I usually make decisions ______ before the deadline.
a. way **b.** somewhat **c.** just

9. After making a decision, I ______ look for other alternatives, wishing I had waited.
a. rarely **b.** occasionally **c.** usually

10. I ______ regret having made a decision.
a. rarely **b.** occasionally **c.** often

For interpretation, turn to page 447.

Source: Adapted from Lussier, Robert N., *Supervision: A Skill-Building Approach,* Second Edition, pp. 122–123. Copyright 1994 by Richard D. Irwin, Inc. Used with permission.

EXPERIENTIAL EXERCISE

Programmed and Nonprogrammed Decision Making

Purpose: This exercise will allow you to make decisions and help you understand the difference between programmed and nonprogrammed decisions. You will also learn how decision making by an individual differs from decision making by a group.

Introduction: You will be asked to make decisions both individually and as a member of a group.

Instructions: Following is a list of typical organizational decisions. Your task is to determine whether they are programmed or nonprogrammed. Number your paper, and write P for programmed or N for nonprogrammed next to each number.

Next, your instructor will divide the class into groups of four to seven. All groups should have approximately the same number of members. Your task as a group is to make the decisions that you just made as individuals. In arriving at your decisions, do not use techniques such as voting or negotiating ("OK, I'll give in on this one if you'll give in on that one"). The group should discuss the difference between programmed and nonprogrammed decisions and each decision situation until all members at least partly agree with the decision.

Decision List

1. Hiring a specialist for the research staff in a highly technical field

2. Assigning workers to daily tasks

3. Determining the size of the dividend to be paid to shareholders in the ninth consecutive year of strong earnings growth

4. Deciding whether to officially excuse an employee's absence for medical reasons

5. Selecting the location for another branch of a 150-branch bank in a large city

6. Approving the appointment of a new law-school graduate to the corporate legal staff

7. Making the annual assignment of graduate assistants to the faculty

8. Approving the request of an employee to attend a local seminar in his or her special area of expertise

9. Selecting the appropriate outlets for print advertisements for a new college textbook

10. Determining the location for a new fast-food restaurant in a small but growing town on the major interstate highway between two very large metropolitan areas

Follow-Up Questions

1. To what extent did group members disagree about which decisions were programmed and which were nonprogrammed?

2. What primary factors did the group discuss in making each decision?

3. Were there any differences between the members' individual lists and the group lists? If so, discuss the reasons for the differences.

Source: From *Organizational Behavior,* Fourth Edition, by Gregory Moorhead and Ricky Griffin. Copyright © 1995 by Houghton Mifflin Company. Reprinted by permission.

CHAPTER NOTES

1. "Can Nike Just Do It?" Business Week, April 18, 1994, pp. 86–90; "Nike's Management Races to Remake Company's Image, The Wall Street Journal, September 14, 1994, p. B4; "The Soul of a New Nike," Business Week, June 17, 1996, pp. 70–72; Kenneth Labich, "Nike vs. Reebok," Fortune, September 18, 1995, pp. 90–106.
2. Richard Priem, "Executive Judgment, Organizational Congruence, and Firm Performance," *Organization Science*, August 1994, pp. 421–432.
3. Paul Nutt, "The Formulation Processes and Tactics Used in Organizational Decision Making," *Organization Science*, May 1993, pp. 226–240.
4. For recent reviews of decision making, see E. Frank Harrison, *The Managerial Decision Making Process*, 3rd ed. (Boston: Houghton Mifflin, 1987)
5. Charles R. Day, Jr., "Industry's Gutsiest Decisions of 1987," *Industry Week*, February 15, 1988, pp. 33–39; and Stratford P. Sherman, "Inside the Mind of Jack Welsh," *Fortune*, March 27, 1989, pp. 38–50.
6. George P. Huber, *Managerial Decision Making* (Glenview, Ill.: Scott, Foresman, 1980).
7. Huber, *Managerial Decision Making*. See also David W. Miller and Martin K. Starr, *The Structure of Human Decisions* (Englewood Cliffs, N.J.: Prentice-Hall, 1976); and Alvar Elbing, *Behavioral Decisions in Organizations*, 2nd ed. (Glenview, Ill: Scott, Foresman, 1978).
8. Huber, *Managerial Decision Making*.
9. See Avi Fiegenbaum and Howard Thomas, "Attitudes Toward Risk and the Risk-Return Paradox: Prospect Theory Explanations," *Academy of Management Journal*, March 1988, pp. 85–106; Jitendra V. Singh, "Performance, Slack, and Risk Taking in Organizational Decision Making," *Academy of Management Journal*, September 1986, pp. 562–585; and James G. March and Zur Shapira, "Managerial Perspectives on Risk and Risk Taking," *Management Science*, November 1987, pp. 1404–1418.
10. Kenneth Froot, David Scharfstein, and Jeremy Stein, "A Framework for Risk Management," *Harvard Business Review*, November–December 1994, pp. 91–99.
11. See Richard M. Cyert and Morris H. DeGroot, "The Maximization Process Under Uncertainty," in Patrick D. Larkey and Lee S. Sproull (Eds.), *Information*

Processing in Organizations (Greenwich, Conn.: JAI Press, 1984), pp. 47–61.

12. Glen Whyte, "Decision Failures: Why They Occur and How to Prevent Them," *The Academy of Management Executive*, August 1991, pp. 23–31.

13. See R. T. Lenz and Jack L. Engledow, "Environmental Analysis Units and Strategic Decision Making: A Field Study of Selected 'Leading-Edge' Corporations," *Strategic Management Journal*, Vol. 7, 1986, pp. 69–89, for a recent analysis of how decision situations are recognized.

14. William Q. Judge and Alex Miller, "Antecedents and Outcomes of Decision Speed in Different Environmental Contexts," *Academy of Management Journal*, June 1991, pp. 449–463.

15. Thomas Stewart, "How to Lead a Revolution," *Fortune*, November 28, 1994, pp. 48–61.

16. See Charles A. O'Reilly III, "The Use of Information in Organizational Decision Making: A Model and Some Propositions," in Larry L. Cummings and Barry M. Staw (Eds.), *Research in Organizational Behavior*, Vol. 5 (Greenwich, Conn.: JAI Press, 1983), pp. 103–139.

17. Carol Saunders and Jack William Jones, "Temporal Sequences in Information Acquisition for Decision Making: A Focus on Source and Medium," *Academy of Management Review*, January 1990, pp. 29–46.

18. Kenneth Labich, "Coups and Catastrophes," *Fortune*, December 23, 1985, p. 125.

19. "The Wisdom of Solomon," *Newsweek*, August 17, 1987, pp. 62–63.

20. Elbing, *Behavioral Decisions in Organizations*.

21. Herbert A. Simon, *Administrative Behavior* (New York: Free Press, 1945). Simon's ideas have been recently refined and updated in Herbert A. Simon, *Administrative Behavior*, 3rd ed. (New York: Free Press, 1976), and Herbert A. Simon, "Making Management Decisions: The Role of Intuition and Emotion," *The Academy of Management Executive*, February 1987, pp. 57–63.

22. Patricia Corner, Angelo Kinicki, and Barbara Keats, "Integrating Organizational and Individual Information Processing Perspectives on Choice," *Organization Science*, August 1994, pp. 294–302.

23. "Unisys: So Far, So Good—But the Real Test Is Yet to Come," *Business Week*, March 2, 1987, pp. 84–86; and "So Far, Married Life Seems to Agree with Unisys," *Business Week*, October 3, 1988, pp. 122–126.

24. Gannes, "America's Fastest-Growing Companies." See also "Can Ms. Fashion Bounce Back?" *Business Week*, January 16, 1989, pp. 64–70.

25. Barry M. Staw and Jerry Ross, "Good Money After Bad," *Psychology Today*, February 1988, pp. 30–33; and D. Ramona Bobocel and John Meyer, "Escalating Commitment to a Failing Course of Action: Separating the Roles of Choice and Justification," *Journal of Applied Psychology*, Vol. 79, no. 3, 1994, pp. 360–363.

26. Stratford Sherman, "Is He Too Cautious to Save IBM?" *Fortune*, October 3, 1994, pp. 78–88.

27. Gannes, "America's Fastest-Growing Companies."

28. Kent D. Miller and Philip Bromley, "Strategic Risk and Corporate Performance: An Analysis of Alternative Risk Measures," *Academy of Management Journal*, December 1990, pp. 756–779; Philip Bromley, "Testing a Causal Model of Corporate Risk Taking and Performance," *Academy of Management Journal*, March 1991, pp. 37–59.

29. Thomas M. Jones, "Ethical Decision Making by Individuals in Organizations: An Issue-Contingent Model," *Academy of Management Review*, April 1988, pp. 366–395.

30. Marvin E. Shaw, *Group Dynamics—The Psychology of Small Group Behavior*, 3rd ed. (New York: McGraw-Hill, 1981); Edwin A. Locke, David M. Schweiger, Gary P. Latham, "Participation in Decision Making: When Should It Be Used?" *Organizational Dynamics*, Winter 1986, pp. 65–79; and Nicholas Baloff and Elizabeth M. Doherty, "Potential Pitfalls in Employee Participation," *Organizational Dynamics*, Winter 1989, pp. 51–62.

31. Andre L. Delbecq, Andrew H. Van de Ven, and David H. Gustafson, *Group Techniques for Program Planning* (Glenview, Ill.: Scott, Foresman, 1975); and Michael J. Prietula and Herbert A. Simon, "The Experts in Your Midst," *Harvard Business Review*, January–February 1989, pp. 120–124.

32. Norman P. R. Maier, "Assets and Liabilities in Group Problem Solving: The Need for an Integrative Function," in J. Richard Hackman, Edward E. Lawler III, and Lyman W. Porter (Eds.), *Perspectives on Business in Organizations*, 2nd ed. (New York: McGraw-Hill, 1983), pp. 385–392.

33. James H. Davis, *Group Performance* (Reading, Mass.: Addison-Wesley, 1969).

34. Richard A. Cosier and Charles R. Schwenk, "Agreement and Thinking Alike: Ingredients for Poor Decisions," *The Academy of Management Executive*, February 1990, pp. 69–78.

35. Irving L. Janis, *Groupthink*, 2nd ed. (Boston: Houghton Mifflin, 1982).

36. Janis, *Groupthink*.

CHAPTER 5

Entrepreneurship and New Venture Management

OBJECTIVES

After studying this chapter, you should be able to:

- *Discuss the nature of entrepreneurship.*
- *Describe the roles of entrepreneurs in society.*
- *Understand the key issues in choosing strategies for small firms.*
- *Discuss the structural challenges unique to entrepreneurial firms.*
- *Understand the determinants of the performance of small firms.*
- *Explain the concept of intrapreneurship and its importance to larger organizations.*

OUTLINE

IN TODAY'S COMPETITIVE business environment, more and more U.S. entrepreneurs are looking to foreign ports-of-call for business opportunities. Indeed, the U.S. Census Bureau estimates that as many as 250,000 U.S. citizens leave the country to live abroad each year, and many of them start their own business when they arrive at their foreign destination.

Michael Giles, a graduate of the Columbia law school, moved to the black township of Soweto, right outside of Johannesburg, South Africa. Giles determined that there were only four laundromats to serve the needs of 4.5 million residents. He arranged for a loan from the U.S. government's Overseas Private Investment Corporation and is today in the midst of launching a chain of 198 coin-operated laundromats throughout many of South Africa's black townships.

Mike DeNoma left a lucrative job at Kentucky Fried Chicken Corp. and launched his own chain of Chinese fast-food restaurants in Hong Kong. Eugene Matthews, another lawyer, shipped 20,000 cows to Vietnam and set up two modern dairy farms in that country. Lisa Frankenberg started her own newspaper in Prague. Robert Brooker and Adam Haven-Weiss are launching a chain of bagel shops in eastern Europe.

"The Iron Curtain's collapse was not just about politics. It was also an unprecedented business opportunity."

Of course, there is no such thing as a sure thing. Many would-be entrepreneurs fail in their quest to launch new enterprises in foreign markets. And many others find success to be not what they had imagined, so they give up and eventually return home. The struggles of opening a business in a foreign country are indeed a challenge. Most emerging markets lack an effective infrastructure, for example, and even getting routine things done can take far longer than one might expect. In many countries, a four-month wait for a telephone hook-up is not uncommon, for example.

People who want to try this route to success need to remember several important things. First, they must tailor their products and services to the local market. Second, they should not expect to get rich, but instead must be willing to work long and hard just to make ends meet. They also need a certain degree of luck, as well as a fair measure of perseverance. And market opportunities are where people find them—many successful entrepreneurs in foreign countries have found their market niche by providing products and services for other entrepreneurs. Still, for those who stick with it the rewards can be enticing.[1]

Source of Quotation: Daniel Arbess, New York attorney now practicing in Prague, quoted in *Fortune*, October 17, 1994, p. 185.

Like Michael Giles, Mike DeNoma, Eugene Matthews, and Lisa Frankenberg, thousands of people all over the world start new businesses each year. And as the opening incident describes, more and more of them are setting up shop in far corners of the world. Many of these people succeed in their enterprise, but many others fail. Some who fail try again, and sometimes it takes two or more failures before a new business gets under way. Henry Ford, for example, went bankrupt twice before succeeding with the Ford Motor Company.

This process of starting a new business, sometimes failing and sometimes succeeding, is part of what is called entrepreneurship, the subject of this chapter. We begin by exploring the nature of entrepreneurship. We then examine the role of entrepreneurship in the business world and discuss strategies for entrepreneurial organizations. We then describe the structure of entrepreneurial organizations. Finally, we discuss the role of entrepreneurship in larger organizations, a process often called intrapreneurship.

THE NATURE OF ENTREPRENEURSHIP

- **entrepreneurship** The process of organizing, operating, and assuming the risk of a business venture
- **entrepreneur** Someone who engages in entrepreneurship

Entrepreneurship is the process of planning, organizing, operating, and assuming the risk of a business venture.[2] An **entrepreneur**, in turn, is someone who engages in entrepreneurship. All of the people highlighted in our opening incident fit this description. They are putting their own resources on the line and taking a personal stake in the success or failure of their budding enterprises. Business owners who hire professional managers to run their businesses and then turn their own attention to other interests are not entrepreneurs. Although they are assuming the risk of the venture, they are not actively involved in organizing or operating it. Likewise, professional managers whose job is running someone else's business are not entrepreneurs, for they assume less-than-total personal risk for the success or failure of the business.

- **small business** A business that is privately owned by one individual, or by a small group of individuals, and has sales and assets that are not large enough to influence its environment

Entrepreneurs start small businesses. We define a **small business** as one that is privately owned by one individual, or by a small group of individuals, and has sales and assets that are not large enough to influence its environment. The U.S. Small Business Administration (SBA), which was created in 1953 by Congress to improve the managerial skills of entrepreneurs and to help them borrow money, has drafted more specific definitions to fit virtually every industry.[3] A partial list appears in Table 5.1. Notice that some definitions go far beyond what many people think of as "small." For example, a petroleum refiner with 1,500 employees probably has sales of several million dollars each year.[4]

THE ROLE OF ENTREPRENEURSHIP IN SOCIETY

The history of entrepreneurship, and of the development of new businesses, is in many ways the history of great wealth and of great failure. Some entrepreneurs have been very successful and have accumulated vast fortunes from their entrepreneurial efforts. For example, when Microsoft

TABLE 5.1 SBA Standards of Size for Selected Industries

Manufacturers	Fewer Employees Than
Petroleum refining	1,500
Electronic computers	1,000
Macaroni and spaghetti	500
Wholesalers	**Fewer Employees Than**
Sporting goods	500
Furniture	500
Paints and varnishes	500
Retailers	**Annual Sales Less Than**
Grocery stores	$13.5 million
Automobile agencies	11.5 million
Restaurants	10.0 million
Services	**Annual Sales Less Than**
Computer-related services	$12.5 million
Accounting services	4.0 million
Television repair	3.5 million

Source: "U.S. Small Business Administration: Small Business Size Standards," *Federal Register,* Vol. 49, No. 28 (Washington D.C.: U.S. Government Printing Office, February 9, 1984), pp. 5024–5048.

The Small Business Administration (SBA) provides different definitions of what constitutes "smallness" for firms in different industries. These differences are presumably associated with relative differences in capital investment, differences in industry structure, and similar factors.

sold its stock to the public in 1986, Bill Gates, then just thirty years old, received $350 million for his share of Microsoft.[5] Today, his holdings—valued at $8 billion—make him one of the richest people in the world. Many more entrepreneurs, however, have lost a great deal of money. Research suggests that the majority of new businesses fail within the first three years of founding.[6] Many that last longer do so only because the entrepreneurs themselves work long hours for very little income.

The experiences of individuals who win (and lose) fortunes as a result of their entrepreneurial activities may make fascinating stories, but the vital role that entrepreneurship plays in our society and our economy is even more telling. More than 99 percent of the nation's 16 million businesses are small. Over 600,000 new businesses are incorporated each year. Their vibrant, almost countless activities influence a number of economic areas, including innovation, job creation, and contributions to large businesses.[7]

Increasingly, small businesses in the United States are being spearheaded by women.[8] There are several reasons for this trend. For one thing, some women, frustrated by what they see as limited promotion opportunities in larger businesses, see starting their own business as the best route to success. Others see owning their own business as a good way to increase their flexibility vis-à-vis child rearing. Many other reasons also account for this trend. Figure 5.1 shows the dramatic increase in women-owned proprietorships in various industries between 1980 and 1990.

The percentage of women-owned businesses in the United States continues to escalate dramatically. Although there are still relatively few women who own businesses in industries such as agriculture or forestry, their presence is quite large in other industries such as wholesaling, retailing, and services.

FIGURE 5.1 Trends in Women-Owned Small Business

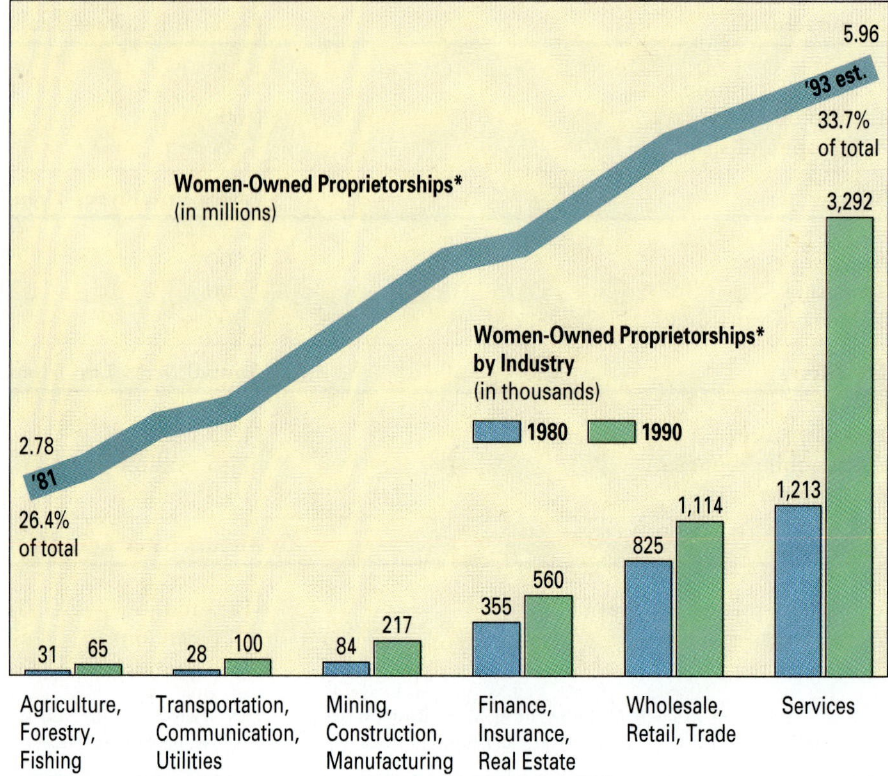

Source: Reprinted from April 18, 1994 issue of *Business Week* by special permission, copyright © 1994 by McGraw-Hill, Inc.

Innovation

The resourcefulness and ingenuity typical of small business have spawned new industries and contributed many innovative ideas and technological breakthroughs to our society. Small businesses or individuals working alone have invented, among other things, the personal computer, the transistor radio, the photocopying machine, the jet engine, and the instant photograph. They also have given us the pocket calculator, power steering, the automatic transmission, air conditioning, and even the nineteen-cent ballpoint pen. There are some scholars who believe that entrepreneurs and small businesses are the driving force behind innovation in a society. As entrepreneurs seek the income and wealth associated with successful innovation, they create new technologies and products that displace older technologies and products.[9]

Job Creation

Small businesses create more new jobs than do larger businesses. One study suggests that small businesses may account for as much as 66 percent of all

new employment in the United States each year. In another study, the U.S. Department of Commerce found that small, young, high-technology businesses created new jobs at a much faster rate than did larger, older businesses.[10]

The new jobs created by small businesses come in small bites. When a new restaurant opens, it may employ fifteen people. When a new retail specialty store opens, it may employ twenty people. However, because so many new businesses are created each year, the cumulative impact on employment can be very significant.

Innovation is often the catalyst for small business. The Internet is providing numerous business opportunities for entrepreneurs innovative enough to capitalize on them. For example, James Clark, deaf since birth, has started ClarkNet, a service firm for hearing-impaired Internet users who cannot use the telephone to call for support. Clark runs his business out of a barn on his father's farm in Maryland.

Contributions to Large Businesses

It is primarily small businesses that supply and distribute the products of large businesses. General Motors, for example, buys materials from over twenty-five thousand suppliers, most of them small businesses. GM also distributes its products through small businesses—independent car dealers. Likewise, an organization such as Sony buys supplies from thousands of small businesses, distributes its electronic products through numerous small distributors and its movies through numerous independent movie theaters, and sells its records through independent record stores.

STRATEGY FOR ENTREPRENEURIAL ORGANIZATIONS

One of the most basic challenges facing an entrepreneurial organization is choosing a strategy. The three strategic challenges facing small firms, in turn, are choosing an industry in which to compete, emphasizing distinctive competencies, and writing a business plan.[11]

Choosing an Industry

Entrepreneurs seeking to begin small-business operations should generally look to industries with favorable industry attributes. Thus, for example, entrepreneurs who start a business based on a technology with few rivals or substitutes and a low threat of entry usually earn higher rates of return than entrepreneurs who start a business without these advantages.

Examples of small businesses that chose a high-potential industry are Microsoft and Lotus, both very successful computer-software companies.[12] These companies have developed personal-computer software that dominates their respective market segments (Microsoft in operating systems, Lotus in spreadsheet software). Because these firms are so dominant in their segments, there is low rivalry in their industries. Because of the skills that computer users have developed in applying these particular software packages, there are few substitutes. And because of the reputation and success of these firms, entry into these software segments is unlikely (although certainly not impossible).

An example of small businesses that begin operations in industries with lower return potential is independent video-rental stores. Because of the large number of video-rental stores, and the fact that all stores carry many of the same videos, rivalry in this industry is intense. Substitutes in the form of cable television, movie theaters, network television, and even books are common. Because the cost of entering this industry is relatively low (the cost of videos plus a lease and computer software), entry into the video-rental business is easy. For these reasons, independent video retail operations are often marginal financial performers, although as members of national chains, video stores can be profitable.[13]

Industries in Which Small Businesses Are Strong Small businesses tend to do well in the service, retail, and wholesale industries. Service organizations are perhaps the most common type of entrepreneurial business because they require a fairly small capital investment to start up. A certified public accountant, for example, can open a business simply by renting an office and hanging out a sign. Small businesses ranging from video-rental shops to hair salons and tax-preparation services have significantly increased in numbers in recent years, all because the costs of the physical assets needed to start these businesses are relatively low.

Entrepreneurs are also effective in the area of specialty retailing. Specialty retailers cater to specific customer groups such as golfers, college students, and people who do their own automobile repairs. Often, the number of these special consumers is relatively small, and thus the dollar size of the market associated with these consumers is small. Although large organizations may be unwilling to enter a business where the market is so small, small businesses may be very successful in these industries.[14]

Wholesalers buy products from large manufacturers and resell them to retailers. Small businesses dominate the wholesale industry because they are often able to develop personal working relationships with several sellers and several buyers. A wholesale supplier of computer equipment may have to develop supply relationships with five or six floppy-disk manufacturers, six or seven hard-disk manufacturers, five or six video-screen manufacturers, and so forth, to have the inventory it needs to respond to the needs of its retail customers. If this wholesaler was not "independent" but instead was part of a larger electronics company, it would have supply relationships with only one supplier of floppy disks, one supplier of hard disks, one maker of video screens, and so forth. As long as end users want more supply options than this, the independent wholesaler can play an important economic role.[15]

Industries in Which Small Businesses Are Weak Small organizations have difficulty succeeding in certain other industries. Industries dominated by large-scale manufacturing are particularly difficult for small organizations. Agriculture is an industry in transition from being dominated by small family farms to being dominated by large corporate farms.

Research has shown that manufacturing costs often fall as the number of units produced by an organization increases. This relationship between cost and production is called an *economy of scale.*[16] Small organizations usually cannot compete effectively on the basis of economies of scale. As depicted in panel (a) of Figure 5.2, organizations with higher levels of production have a significant cost advantage over those with lower levels of production. Given the cost positions of small and large firms when there are strong economies of scale in manufacturing, it is not surprising that small manufacturing organizations generally do not do as well as large ones.

Interestingly, when technology in an industry changes, it often shifts the economies-of-scale curve, thereby creating opportunities for smaller organizations. For example, steel manufacturing was historically dominated by a few large companies that owned several huge facilities. However, with the development of mini-mill technology, it became possible to extract economies of scale at a much smaller level of production. This type of shift is depicted in panel (b) of Figure 5.2. Point A in this panel is the low-cost point with the original economies of scale. Point B is the low-cost point with the economies of scale brought on by the new technology. Notice that the number of units needed for low costs is considerably lower for the new technology. This has allowed the entry of numerous smaller firms into the steel industry. Such entry would not have been possible with the older technology.[17]

Of course, not all manufacturing is capital-intensive. Some manufacturing can be done with minimal plant and equipment. This kind of light industry is typical of some parts of the computer industry and some parts of the plastic fabrication industry, in printing, and elsewhere. Small organizations can excel in these industries.[18]

Agriculture is an industry in transition. Small family farms were among the first small businesses in the world, and until recently they were among the most successful. Economies of scale and high equipment prices, however, have forced many small farmers out of business. Giant agribusiness enterprises and corporate farms are gradually replacing them. These multifarm businesses own and farm million of acres and are large enough to fully exploit economies of scale by purchasing and sharing the most modern farm equipment, applying the latest scientific methods in farming, and even influencing government policy to favor farmers.[19]

FIGURE 5.2 Economies of Scale in Small-Business Organizations

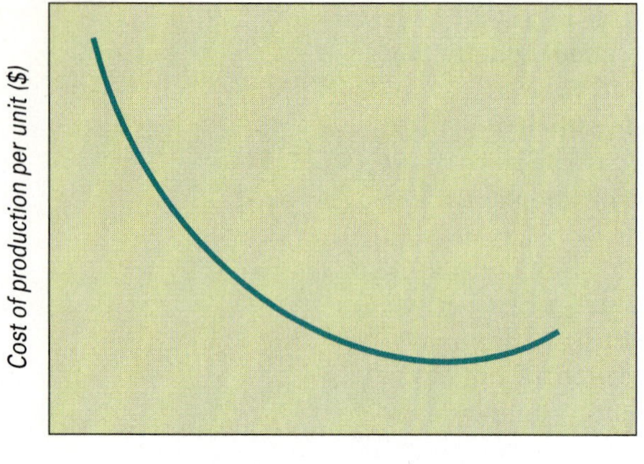

Standard Economies-of-Scale Curve

(a)

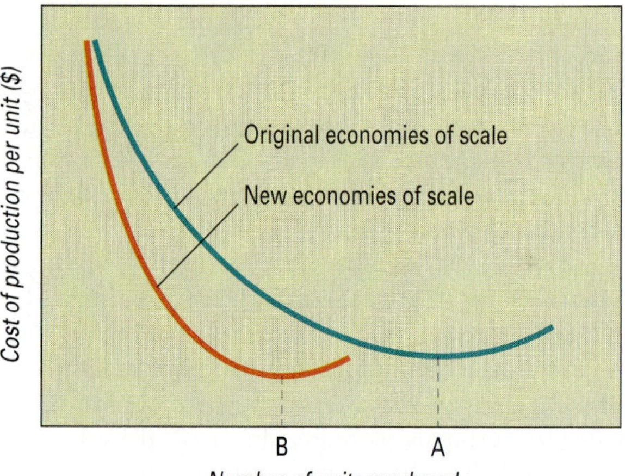

Change in Technology That Shifts Economies of Scale and May Make Small-Business Production Possible

(b)

Small businesses sometimes find it difficult to compete in manufacturing-related industries because of the economies of scale associated with plant, equipment, and technology. As shown (a), firms that produce large number of units (i.e., larger businesses) can do so at a lower per-unit cost. At the same time, however, new forms of technology occasionally cause the economies-of-scale curve to shift, as illustrated in (b). When this happens, smaller firms may be able to compete more effectively with larger ones, because of the drop in per-unit manufacturing cost.

Emphasizing Distinctive Competencies

As discussed in Chapter 3, an organization's distinctive competencies are the aspects of business that the firm performs better than its competitors. The distinctive competencies of small business usually fall into three areas: the ability to identify new niches in established markets, the ability to identify new markets, and the ability to move quickly to take advantage of new opportunities.

• **established market**
One in which several large firms compete according to relatively well-defined criteria

Identifying Niches in Established Markets An **established market** is one in which several large firms compete according to relatively well-defined criteria. For example, throughout the 1970s several well-known computer-manufacturing companies, including IBM, Digital Equipment, and Hewlett-Packard, competed according to three product criteria: computing power, service, and price. Over the years, the computing power and quality of service delivered by these firms continued to improve, while prices (especially relative to computing power) continued to drop.

Enter Apple Computer and the personal computer. For Apple, user-friendliness, not computing power, service, or price, was to be the basis of competition. Apple targeted every manager, every student, and every home. The major entrepreneurial act of Apple was not to invent a new technology (indeed, the first Apple computers used all standard parts) but to recognize a new kind of computer and a new way to compete in the computer industry.[20]

• **niche**
A segment of a market that is not currently being exploited

Apple's approach to competition was to identify a new niche in an established market. A **niche** is simply a segment of a market that is not currently being exploited. In general, small entrepreneurial businesses are better at discovering these niches than are larger organizations. Large organizations usually have so many resources committed to older, established business practices that they may be unaware of new opportunities. Entrepreneurs can see these opportunities and move quickly to take advantage of them.[21]

Identifying New Markets Successful entrepreneurs also excel at discovering whole new markets. Discovery can happen in at least two ways. First, an entrepreneur can transfer a product or service that is well established in one geographic market to a second market. This is what Marcel Bich did with ballpoint pens, which occupied a well-established market in Europe before Bich introduced them to this country. Bich's company, Bic Corp., eventually came to dominate the U.S. market.[22]

Second, entrepreneurs can sometimes create entire industries. Entrepreneurial inventions of the dry paper copying process and the semiconductor have created vast new industries. Not only have the first companies into these markets been very successful (Xerox and National Semiconductor, respectively), but their entrepreneurial activity has spawned the development of hundreds of thousands of other companies and hundreds of thousands of jobs. Again, because entrepreneurs are not encumbered with a history of doing business in a particular way, they are usually better at discovering new markets than are larger, more mature organizations.

First-Mover Advantages A **first-mover advantage** is any advantage that comes to a firm because it exploits an opportunity before any other firm does. Sometimes large firms discover niches within existing markets or new markets at just about the same time as small entrepreneurial firms do but are not able to move as quickly as small companies to take advantage of these opportunities.

• **first-mover advantage** Any advantage that comes to a firm because it exploits an opportunity before any other firm does

There are numerous reasons for this difference. For example, many large organizations make decisions slowly because each of their many layers of hierarchy has to approve an action before it can be implemented. Also, large organizations may sometimes put a great deal of their assets at risk when they take advantage of new opportunities. Every time Boeing decides to build a new model of a commercial jet, it is making a decision that could literally bankrupt the company if it does not turn out well. The size of the risk may make large organizations cautious. The dollar value of the assets at risk in a small organization, in contrast, is quite small. Managers may be willing to "bet the company" when the value of the company is only $100,000. They might be unwilling to "bet the company" when the value of the company is $1 billion.[23]

Writing a Business Plan

Once an entrepreneur has chosen an industry to compete in and determined which distinctive competencies to emphasize, these choices are usually included in a document called a business plan. In a **business plan** the entrepreneur summarizes the business strategy and how that strategy is to be implemented.[24] The very act of preparing a business plan forces prospective entrepreneurs to crystallize their thinking about what they must do to launch their business successfully and obliges them to develop their business on paper before investing time and money in it. The idea of

• **business plan** A document that summarizes the business strategy and structure

a business plan is not new.[25] What is new is the growing use of specialized business plans by entrepreneurs, mostly because creditors and investors demand them for use in deciding whether to help finance a small business.

The plan should describe the match between the entrepreneur's abilities and the requirements for producing and marketing a particular product or service. It should define strategies for production and marketing, legal aspects and organization, and accounting and finance. In particular, it should answer three questions: (1) What are the entrepreneur's goals and objectives? (2) What strategies will the entrepreneur use to obtain these goals and objectives? (3) How will the entrepreneur implement these strategies?

Some idea of the complexity of planning a new business may be gleaned from the PERT diagram shown in Figure 5.3. The diagram shows the key steps in planning the launch of a new business. Notice that the development of a business plan consists of a set of specific activities, perhaps none of which is more pivotal than marketing research—the systematic and intensive study of all the facts, opinions, and judgments that bear on the successful marketing of a product or service.

Business planning involves a number of very specific activities and events, as shown in this PERT diagram. Following a logical and systematic process such as this will enhance the chances for success.

Figure 5.3 also demonstrates the sequential nature of much strategic decision making in small businesses. For example, entrepreneurs cannot forecast sales revenues without first researching markets. The sales forecast itself

FIGURE 5.3 A PERT Diagram for Business Planning

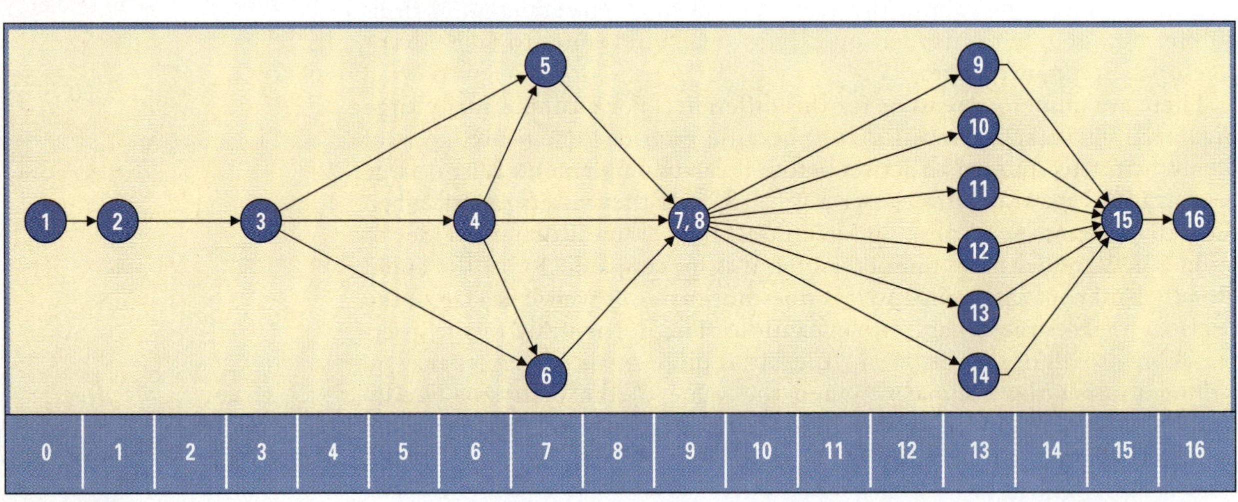

1. Commit yourself
2. Analyze yourself
3. Choose product or service
4. Market research
5. Forecast sales revenues
6. Choose site
7. Develop production plan
8. Develop marketing plan
9. Develop organizational plan
10. Develop legal plan
11. Develop accounting plan
12. Develop insurance plan
13. Develop computer plan
14. Develop total quality management plan
15. Develop financial plan
16. Write cover letter

Source: "A PERT Diagram for Business Planning" from Nicholas C. Siropolis, *Small Business Management,* Sixth Edition. Copyright © 1997 Houghton Mifflin Company. Adapted with permission.

is one of the most important elements in the business plan. Without such forecasts, it is all but impossible to estimate intelligently how large a plant, store, or office should be or to determine how much inventory to carry or how many employees to hire.

Another important activity is financial planning, which translates all other activities into dollars. Generally, the financial plan is made up of a cash budget, an income statement, balance sheets, and a breakeven chart. The most important of these statements is the cash budget because it tells entrepreneurs how much money they need before they open for business and how much money they need to keep the business operating.

STRUCTURE OF ENTREPRENEURIAL ORGANIZATIONS

With a strategy in place and a business plan in hand, the entrepreneur can then proceed to devise a structure that turns the vision of the business plan into a reality. Many of the same concerns in structuring any business, which are described in Part III of this book, are also relevant to small businesses. For example, entrepreneurs need to consider organization design and develop job descriptions, organization charts, management control systems, and so forth. However, small businesses do have some special concerns relating to structure, including the form of ownership and sources of financing, methods for starting the business, and sources of management help.

Forms of Ownership and Sources of Financing

Ownership structure specifies who possesses legal title to all of an organization's assets and who has a claim on any economic profits generated by a firm. Financing a small business involves decisions concerning the sources of capital that will be used to start the business and what claims (if any) these sources have on the organization's profits. There are a number of alternatives for both ownership structure and sources of financing, and each of them has advantages and disadvantages.[26]

Forms of Ownership A popular form of legal ownership for many new businesses is the **sole proprietorship**, in which legal title to all assets and claims on all future economic profits are controlled by a single individual. About 70 percent of all U.S. businesses are sole proprietorships. The major advantages of a sole proprietorship are that the individual entrepreneur has total freedom in conducting business, start-up is simple and inexpensive, and business profits are taxed as ordinary income to the proprietor. The disadvantages are that the proprietor has unlimited liability (his or her personal assets are at risk to cover business debts) and the business ends when the proprietor retires or dies.

Another form of ownership is the **partnership**, in which two or more people agree to be partners in a business, share title in the assets of the firm, be held jointly liable for the firm's debts, and share the firm's profits. The least common form of ownership, partnerships are often used by accounting, legal, and architectural firms. These types of organizations are

• **sole proprietorship**
A form of business ownership in which legal title to all assets and claims on all future economic profits are controlled by a single individual

• **partnership**
A form of business ownership in which two or more people agree to be partners in a business, share title in the assets of the firm, be held jointly liable for the firm's debts, and share in the firm's profits

highly dependent on the professional skills of individuals, and partnerships tend to foster the professional mutual respect that is essential in these business activities. Partnerships provide a larger pool of talent and capital to start a business than do sole proprietorships, but they are just as easy to form and they offer the same tax benefits. They also have similar disadvantages: liability and no legal continuance if the partnership is dissolved. An added difficulty may be conflict or tension between partners.

• **corporation**
A form of business ownership in which a legal entity is created under the law that is independent of any single individual

Most large organizations, and some smaller organizations, use the corporation as the basis for ownership. A **corporation** is a legal entity created under the law that is independent of any single individual. Like an individual, a corporation can borrow money, enter into contracts, own property, sue, and be sued. Its owners are the stockholders. An advantage that distinguishes the corporation from sole proprietorships and partnerships is that it is responsible for its own liabilities, so the owners have limited liability. A corporation continues to exist despite the retirement or death of any of its owners, and it can often borrow money easily. However, corporations have higher start-up costs and are subject to more regulation and to double taxation (the corporation pays taxes on its profits, and then stockholders pay taxes on their dividends).

A few other special forms of ownership exist. Master limited partnerships and sub-chapter S corporations provide many of the advantages of corporations but without double taxation. Cooperatives enable a number of small organizations to pool resources and share markets. Ocean Spray Cranberries is a cooperative that is made up of seven hundred independent cranberry growers and one hundred citrus growers.

Sources of Financing An important issue confronting all entrepreneurs is locating the money necessary to open and operate the business. Personal resources (savings and money borrowed from friends or family) are the most common sources of new-business financing. Personal resources are often the most important source because they reinforce the entrepreneur's personal commitment to the venture.[27] Many entrepreneurs also take advantage of various lending programs and assistance provided by lending institutions and government agencies.[28] Government programs are especially interested in helping women and minority entrepreneurs.

• **venture capitalist**
Someone who actively seeks to invest in new businesses

Another common source of funds is venture capitalists. A **venture capitalist** is someone who actively seeks to invest in new businesses. The advantage of this approach is that it gives entrepreneurs access to a large resource base with fewer restrictions than might be imposed by the government or by banks. In return, however, the entrepreneur must relinquish to the venture capitalist a portion of the profits or share ownership.[29]

Methods for Starting a New Business

Another set of organizational questions that an entrepreneur must address when organizing a business is whether to buy an existing business, start a new one, or seek a franchising agreement.

Buying an Existing Business Buying an existing business offers a strong set of advantages. Because the entrepreneur can examine historical records for the business to determine the pattern of revenue and profit and the type of cash flow, much guesswork about what to expect is eliminated. The entrepreneur also acquires existing supplier, distributor, and customer networks. On the negative side, the entrepreneur inherits whatever problems the business may already have and may be forced to accept existing contractual agreements. As discussed in the opening incident of Chapter 3, Howard Schultz bought Starbucks Corporation when it was a small, struggling outfit and turned it into a big, successful company.

Starting a New Business Starting a new business from scratch allows the owner to avoid the shortcomings of an existing business and to put his or her personal stamp on the enterprise. The entrepreneur also has the opportunity to choose suppliers, bankers, lawyers, and employees without worrying about existing agreements or contractual arrangements. However, there is more uncertainty involved in starting a new business than in taking over an existing one. The entrepreneur starts out with less information about projected revenues and cash flow, has to build a customer base from zero, and may be forced to accept unfavorable credit terms from suppliers. A new business may also have difficulty borrowing money because lenders will not have had any experience with its financial history.

Franchising An alternative to buying an existing business or starting one from scratch is entering into a **franchising agreement.** The entrepreneur pays a parent company (the **franchiser**) a flat fee or a share of the income from the business. In return, the entrepreneur (the **franchisee**) is allowed to use the company's trademarks, products, formulas, and business plan. Industries within which franchising is common include fast foods (e.g., McDonald's), specialty retail-clothing stores (e.g., Benetton Group SPA), personal-computer stores (e.g., ComputerLand), and local automobile dealerships.[30]

• **franchising agreement** A contract between an entrepreneur (the **franchisee**) and a parent company (the **franchiser**); the entrepreneur pays the parent company for the use of the trademarks, products, formulas, and business plans

Franchising may reduce the entrepreneur's financial risk because many parent companies provide advice and assistance. They also provide proven production, sales, and marketing methods; training; financial support; and an established identity and image. Some franchisers also allow successful individual franchisees to grow by opening multiple outlets.

On the negative side, franchises may cost a lot of money. A McDonald's franchise costs several hundred thousand dollars. Also, the parent company often restricts the franchisee to certain types of products. A McDonald's franchisee, for example, cannot change the formula for milkshakes, alter the preparation of Big Macs, or purchase supplies from any other company. Some franchise agreements are difficult to terminate.[31]

Despite the drawbacks, franchising is growing by leaps and bounds. Presently, well over one-third of U.S. retail sales go through franchises, and that figure is expected to climb to one-half by the end of this century.[32] Much of the attraction of franchising is that this approach to starting a new business involves limited risks. At the same time, however, one must also remember that no form of business is completely risk-free.

Sources of Management Help

Since the 1950s, the idea that small businesses benefit from management assistance has grown widely. Many sources of management help are now offered at little or no cost to entrepreneurs, both before and after they embark on a new business. Because of the extent of management sophistication needed to launch a venture such as microcomputer manufacture, special services are available to entrepreneurs who go into a high-technology business.

In addition to numerous federal programs, help is also available from such sources as community colleges and universities, chambers of commerce, and other organizations made up of small businesses. Heading the list is the Small Business Administration (SBA). Many entrepreneurs have the mistaken view that the SBA only lends money or guarantees repayment of loans made by commercial banks. Even more important are SBA efforts to help entrepreneurs manage their businesses effectively and spend their money wisely.

The SBA offers entrepreneurs four major cost-free management-assistance programs: SCORE (Service Corps of Retired Executives), ACE (Active Corps of Executives), SBI (Small Business Institutes), and SBDC (Small Business Development Centers). Under the SCORE and ACE programs, the SBA tries to match an expert to the need. If an entrepreneur needs a marketing plan but does not know how to put one together, the SBA pulls from its list of SCORE or ACE counselors someone with marketing knowledge and experience. SCORE counselors are retired executives. ACE offers the assistance of currently practicing executives. The SBI program taps the talents available at colleges and universities. This program involves not only professors of business administration but also students working for advanced degrees. Under a professor's guidance, such students work with entrepreneurs to help solve their management problems. Finally, the SBDC program brings resources and skills needed by entrepreneurs together at a single location where entrepreneurs can go to receive instruction and training in management and technical skills.

THE PERFORMANCE OF ENTREPRENEURIAL ORGANIZATIONS

The formulation and implementation of an effective strategy plays a major role in determining the overall performance of an entrepreneurial organization.[33] This section examines how entrepreneurial firms evolve over time and details the attributes of these firms that enhance their chance for success.

The Life Cycle of Entrepreneurial Firms

The entrepreneurial life cycle is a series of predictable stages that small businesses pass through. A common pattern of evolution for entrepreneurial organizations is depicted in Figure 5.4.[34] This pattern is similar to the product life cycle discussed in Chapter 3, but it refers specifically to the challenges and changes in small entrepreneurial firms.

First comes the acceptance stage, in which the small business struggles to break even and survive. Entrepreneurial firms are usually small enough at this stage that they can spot obstacles to success and act quickly to re-

FIGURE 5.4 Stages of Evolution for Entrepreneurial Firms

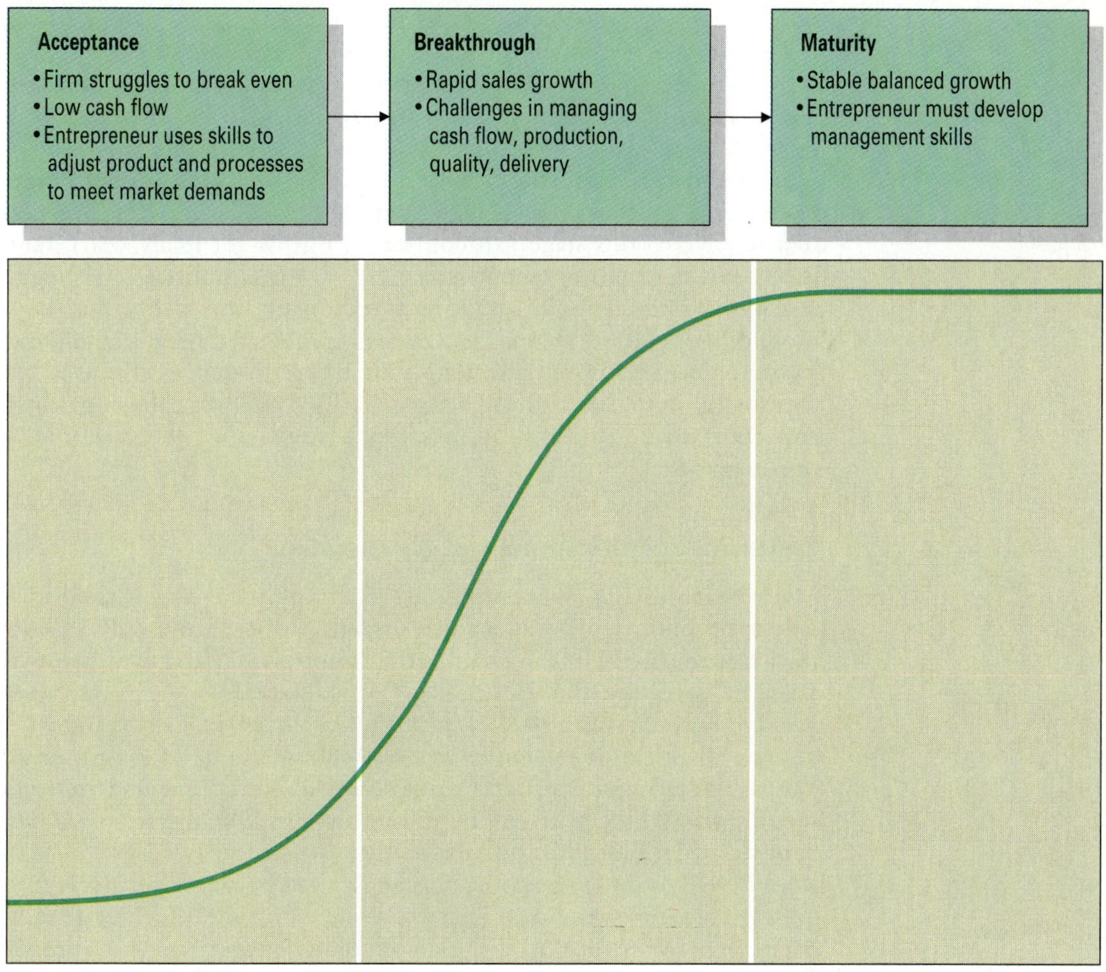

move them. Moreover, entrepreneurs usually have the skills needed to modify their products or services as required by customers during this stage. Such modifications are often necessary for small firms struggling to obtain enough cash from sales and other sources to continue operations. Many small organizations, despite the skill and effort of entrepreneurs, never emerge from the acceptance stage.

Next follows the breakthrough stage. In the preceding stage, the rate of growth is slow—so slow that it is often unnoticed. But in the breakthrough stage, growth is so fast and so unpredictable that many entrepreneurs fail to keep pace with it. Caught unprepared, they blunder. Sales revenues spiral upward as problems begin to surface with cash flow, production, quality, and delivery. At the same time, competition may become more severe.

In the face of these pressures, entrepreneurs may apply hasty, ill-conceived solutions to problems. For example, if sales begin to level off or

Entrepreneurial firms often follow a pattern of evolution that resembles this curve. After an initial period of acceptance, during which the firm struggles and experiences low cash flow, the breakthrough stage is achieved. During this period, the firm experiences rapid sales growth and must focus on managing growth. When the maturity stage is reached, growth becomes more stable and the entrepreneur must begin to focus more attention on the actual management of the enterprise.

slip, they may hire specialists such as an accountant, a quality-control analyst, or a customer services representative to relieve the problem. As a result, costs go up, squeezing profits further.

Perhaps the best way to head off the problems presented by rapid growth is to continue updating the business plan. With a thorough, updated business plan in place, entrepreneurs are less likely to be surprised by breakthroughs.

In the mature stage, the lack of control of the breakthrough stage is replaced by a more stable, balanced period of steady growth. Organizations that survive to this stage can continue to grow for many years. However, in this last stage entrepreneurs often face another challenge. Although they usually have the technical skills required during the acceptance stage, they often do not possess the managerial skills required during the mature stage. Entrepreneurs without these skills either have to develop them or turn the day-to-day operations of their organization over to professional managers and concentrate on new business opportunities or the creation of new organizations.[35]

Reasons for Entrepreneurial Success

Many organizations successfully move through the stages listed in Figure 5.4 to become stable and mature organizations. Many factors contribute to this success. Six of the most common ones are described below.

Hard Work, Drive, and Dedication An individual must have a strong desire to work independently and be willing to put in long hours in order to succeed as an entrepreneur. Successful entrepreneurs tend to be reasonable risk takers, goal setters, and innovators who are self-confident and hard working.[36] In addition, small businesses generally benefit if the owner attends well to detail. Some entrepreneurs fail because they neglect the details of business operations. They may open a business for the glamour and excitement of it, but as the concomitant drudgery of entrepreneurship builds, they may ignore key areas such as inventory control and collections. They may also ignore customer dissatisfaction, worker unrest, or financial difficulties, preferring to think that problems will solve themselves. Over time, though, they rarely do.

Market Demand for Products or Services Provided For any business to succeed, there must be sufficient demand for the product or service it provides. If a college community of 50,000 citizens and 15,000 students has one pizza parlor, there is probably sufficient demand for more. But if fifteen pizza parlors are already in operation, a new one will have to serve especially good pizza or offer something else unique if it is to succeed. Liz Claiborne's clothing business was successful because there was unmet demand for clothing for working women; Apple Computer was successful because there was unmet demand for personal computers.

Managerial Competence It is necessary for the entrepreneur to possess basic managerial competence. He or she needs to know how to select business locations and facilities, how to acquire financing, and how to hire and evaluate employees. The entrepreneur must also be able to manage growth, control costs, negotiate contracts, and make difficult choices and decisions. An entrepreneur who has a product for which there is tremendous demand might be able to survive for a while without managerial skills. Over time, and especially in the mature stage of the life cycle, however, the manager who lacks these skills is unlikely to succeed.

Successful entrepreneurs are always on the alert for new business opportunities, whether at home or abroad. This enterprising person is taking advantage of the growing demand for exotic coffee by delivering it right to Boston commuters stuck in traffic.

Luck Some small businesses succeed purely because of luck. There was an element of luck in Alan McKim's success with Clean Harbors, an environmental cleanup organization based in New England. McKim formed this business just as the federal government committed $1.6 billion to help clean up toxic waste. Although McKim might have succeeded anyway, the extra revenue generated by the government Superfund no doubt contributed to this success.[37]

Strong Control Systems Small businesses, like all organizations, need strong control systems. Small businesses can be ruined by weak control. For example, too many slow-paying customers can reduce a small business's cash flow to a trickle. Excess inventory, employee theft, poor-quality products, plummeting sales, and insufficient profit margins can have equally disastrous effects. If the control system does not alert the entrepreneur to these problems, or alerts the entrepreneur too late, recovery may be difficult or impossible. (Control systems are discussed more fully in Part V of the book.)

Sufficient Capitalization Small businesses need sufficient funds to survive start-up and growth. One rule of thumb is that an entrepreneur should have sufficient personal funds when starting out so as to be able to live with no business income for a year.[38] The entrepreneur needs to be able to maintain his or her personal life, cover all operating expenses, and still have an allowance for unexpected contingencies. An entrepreneur who is planning to pay next month's rent from a new business's profits may be courting disaster.

THE ROLE OF INTRAPRENEURSHIP IN LARGER ORGANIZATIONS

In recent years, many larger businesses have realized that the entrepreneurial spirit that propelled their growth becomes stagnant after they transform themselves from a small but growing concern into a larger one. To help revitalize this spirit, some firms today encourage what they call intrapreneurship. **Intrapreneurs** are similar to entrepreneurs, except that they develop a new business in the context of a larger organization.

intrapreneurs People similar to entrepreneurs, except that they develop a new business in the context of a larger organization

There are three intrapreneurial roles in large organizations.[39] To successfully use intrapreneurship to encourage creativity and innovation, the organization must find one or more individuals to perform these roles. The *inventor* is the person who actually conceives of and develops the new idea, product, or service by means of the creative process.

However, because the inventor may lack the expertise or motivation to oversee the transformation of the product or service from an idea into a marketable entity, a second role comes into play. A *product champion* is usually a middle manager who learns about the project and becomes committed to it. He or she helps overcome organizational resistance and convinces others to take the innovation seriously. The product champion may have only limited understanding of the technological aspects of the innovation. However, product champions are skilled at knowing how the organization works, whose support is needed to push the project forward, and where to go to secure the resources necessary for successful development.

A *sponsor* is a top-level manager who approves of and supports a project. This person may fight for the budget needed to develop an idea, overcome arguments against a project, and use organizational politics to ensure the project's survival. With a sponsor in place, the inventor's idea has a much better chance of being successfully developed.

Several firms have embraced intrapreneurship as a way to encourage creativity and innovation. Colgate-Palmolive has created a separate unit, Colgate Venture Company, staffed with intrapreneurs who develop new products. General Foods developed Culinova Group as a unit to which employees can take their ideas for possible development. S.C. Johnson & Sons, Inc., established a $250,000 fund to support new product ideas, and Texas Instruments refuses to approve a new innovative project unless it has an acknowledged inventor, champion, and sponsor.

SUMMARY OF KEY POINTS

Entrepreneurship is the process of organizing, operating, and assuming the risk of a business venture. An entrepreneur is someone who engages in entrepreneurship. In general, entrepreneurs start small businesses.

Entrepreneurs seeking to start small businesses face the same three challenges as any managers in any organization: choosing a strategy, implementing that strategy through structure, and motivating behavior. In choosing strategies, entrepreneurs have to consider both the characteristics of the industry in which they are going to conduct business and their organization's distinctive competencies.

Small businesses generally have several distinctive competencies that they should exploit in choosing their strategy. Small businesses are usually skilled at identifying niches in established markets, identifying new markets, and acting quickly to obtain first-mover advantages. Small businesses are usually not skilled at exploiting economies of scale.

Once an entrepreneur has chosen a strategy, the strategy is normally written down in a business plan. Writing a business plan forces an entrepreneur to plan very thoroughly and to anticipate problems that might occur.

With a strategy and business plan in place, entrepreneurs must choose a structure to implement them. All the structural issues summarized in Part III of this book are relevant to the entrepreneur. In addition, the entrepreneur has some unique structural choices to make. In determining ownership and financial structure, the entrepreneur can choose between a sole proprietorship, a partnership, a corporation, a master limited partnership, a subchapter S corporation, and a cooperative. In determining financial structure, an entrepreneur has to decide how much personal capital to invest in an organization, how much bank and government support to obtain, and whether to encourage venture capital firms to invest in the firm. Finally, entrepreneurs have to choose among the options of buying an existing business, starting a new business from scratch, or entering into a franchising agreement.

Most small businesses pass through a three-phase life cycle: acceptance, breakthrough, and maturity. There are several reasons why successful small businesses are able to move through all three of these stages of development: hard work, drive, and dedication; market demand for products or services provided; managerial competence; luck; strong control systems; and sufficient capitalization.

Some larger organizations encourage a process they call intrapreneurship, a process similar to entrepreneurship but within the context of a larger business. Inventor, product champion, and sponsor are three key intrapreneurial roles.

QUESTIONS FOR REVIEW

1. How are entrepreneurs and small businesses important to society?
2. In which types of industries do small firms often excel? In which types of industries do small firms often struggle?
3. List the ownership options available to entrepreneurs. What are the advantages and disadvantages of each?
4. What are the elements of success for small businesses?
5. What are the advantages and disadvantages of buying an existing business rather than starting a new one?

QUESTIONS FOR ANALYSIS

1. Entrepreneurs and small businesses play a variety of important roles in society. If these roles are so important, do you think that the government should do more to encourage the development of small business? Why or why not?
2. Franchising agreements seem to be particularly popular ways of starting a new business in industries where retail outlets are geographically widely spread and where the quality of goods or services purchased can be evaluated only after the purchase has occurred. For example, a hamburger may look tasty, but you know for sure that it is well made only after you buy it and eat it. By going to a McDonald's, you know exactly the kind and quality of hamburger you will receive, even before you walk in the door. What is it about franchise arrangements that makes them so popular under these conditions?
3. What special opportunities and challenges would starting a new business in a foreign country pose?
4. If employing family members can cause problems in a small organization, why is this practice so common?
5. What are the basic similarities and differences between entrepreneurship and intrapreneurship?

CASE STUDY

Boston Market

Boston Chicken was founded in Newton, Massachusetts, in 1985 (the chain was renamed Boston Market in 1995). The idea behind Boston Chicken was to serve homestyle meals—rotisserie-roasted chicken along with fresh side dishes—at reasonable prices. It began franchising in 1988 and had three outlets by 1991. Scott Beck, chief operating officer of Blockbuster Entertainment Corp., and two other Blockbuster executives were looking for a business of their own, when in 1991 they found Boston Chicken. Even though it had not yet shown a continuing profit, they took it over and applied the strategy they had learned at Blockbuster—move into markets fast, use the latest technology, and employ the best marketing techniques available. In 1993 Boston Market began not only showing a profit but showing a strong profit. In 1994 the plan was to open almost a store a day; more than three hundred outlets were planned for that year.

As Kentucky Fried Chicken began a major restructuring effort in 1993, many of its executives left the organization. One of those, Kyle Craig, joined Boston Chicken and brought with him an extensive knowledge of and experience in both domestic and international chicken franchise operations. In Boston Market's home office in Naperville, Illinois, executives know that a rapidly expanding business such as this must meet numerous challenges. They must assess their environment, define objectives, develop a clear purpose, employ the right personnel, have effective information, be flexible, and evaluate frequently.

Having effective information is one area in which Boston Market shines. It uses networking computer software with which managers at all levels can collaborate on team projects. Customer complaints are immediately fed into a database that all managers can see and that can be analyzed for patterns. Perhaps this intense use of computer software is a partial reason why one Boston Market area developer formed his own software company, Platinum Technology, which, like Boston Market, is one of the fastest-growing companies in the United States.

Getting the right people is also an area in which Boston Market works very hard. Any prospective franchisee lacking focus or commitment is quickly weeded out. Tests are given to see if people have the excitement needed to feed the energy involved in such a fast-growing business. A careful interview process is used and taken very seriously. Once the right people are located and brought on board, they are given substantial autonomy to help them be creative and to grow in their jobs.

Case Questions

1. What factors have contributed to the success of Boston Market?
2. Why don't more new businesses use the techniques and ideas that have worked so well for Boston Market?
3. What future challenges must Boston Market be prepared to confront if it is to remain successful?

References: Andrew E. Serwer, "Lessons From America's Fastest-Growing Companies," *Fortune,* August 8, 1994, pp. 42–60; Anne Stuart, "Growing Pains and Gains," *CIO,* June 15, 1994, pp. 42–50; Theresa Howard, "Boston Chicken Net Income Soars to 216-Percent Jump," *Nation's Restaurant News,* May 30, 1994, p. 14; Peter Romeo, "The Chicken Wars Are Heading Home," *Restaurant Business,* May 20, 1994, p. 21; and Theresa Howard, "KFC's Craig Flies Coop for Boston Chicken Post," *Nation's Restaurant News,* April 25, 1994, pp. 1, 68.

SKILLS • DEVELOPMENT • PORTFOLIO

BUILDING EFFECTIVE COMMUNICATION SKILLS

Exercise Overview

Communication is important to all organizations. Some entrepreneurs, however, argue that it is even more important in smaller organizations. This exercise will help you understand some of the complexities of communicating in smaller businesses.

Exercise Background

Assume that you are the owner/manager of a small retail chain. Your company sells moderate-priced apparel for professional men and women. You have ten stores located in the Midwest. Each store has a general manager responsible for the overall management of that specific store. Each store also has one assistant manager.

In addition, your corporate office is staffed by a human resource manager, an advertising specialist, and two buyers. In the past, local managers had complete control over their individual stores. As a result, each store had a different layout, a different culture, and different policies and procedures.

You have decided that you want to begin opening more stores at a rapid pace. To expedite this process, however, you also want to standardize your stores. Unfortunately, you realize that many of your current managers will be unhappy with this decision. They will see it as a loss of authority and managerial discretion. Nevertheless, you believe that it is important that you make changes in order to achieve standardization in all areas.

Your plans are to remodel all of your stores to fit a standard layout. You also intend to develop a policy and operations manual for each store. This manual will specify exactly how each store will be managed. You plan to inform your managers of this plan first in a memo and then in a follow-up meeting to discuss questions and concerns.

Exercise Task

Using the background information described above, please do the following:

1. Draft a memo to the store managers that explains your intentions.

2. Make a list of the primary objections you anticipate.

3. Outline an agenda for the meeting in which you plan to address the managers' questions and concerns.

4. Do you personally agree with this communication strategy? Why or why not?

BUILDING EFFECTIVE TECHNICAL SKILLS

Exercise Overview

Technical skills are the skills necessary to accomplish or understand the specific work being done in an organization. This exercise will allow you to gain insights into your own technical skills and understand the relative importance of technical skills in different kinds of organizations.

Exercise Background

Some entrepreneurs have the technical skills that they need to open and run their business successfully. For example, a hair stylist who opens a hair salon, an architect who starts a residential design firm, and a chef who launches a new restaurant all have the technical skills needed to do the work of the organization (hair styling, blueprint rendering, and cooking, respectively).

In other cases, the entrepreneur who starts the organization may have general management skills but essentially may "buy" required technical skills in the labor market. For example, an entrepreneur with no cooking experience could start a new restaurant by hiring a professional chef to run the kitchen.

Exercise Task

Use the background information provided above to do the following:

1. Listed below are examples of ten small businesses that an individual entrepreneur conceivably might launch. Spend a few minutes thinking about each business (hint: think of an existing local business that might fit the general description).

2. Make notes about the specific technical skills required for each business.

3. For each business, decide whether it is especially important that the entrepreneur actually possess the required technical skills or whether it is feasible to consider hiring others who possess the skills instead.

4. What are some major factors that determine the viability of buying technical skills in the labor market?

New Businesses:

1. retail-clothing store
2. computer-clone assembly business
3. tavern
4. sports-card retail store
5. aluminum-recycling operation
6. used compact-disk retail store
7. drop-in healthcare clinic
8. gourmet coffee-bean shop
9. business-services operation
10. appliance-repair shop

YOU MAKE THE CALL

After Cynthia Spenser made the decision to buy The Arbor retail complex, she found it necessary to make a number of other decisions. One important decision involved financing for the purchase. She determined that she had three options. One option was to borrow the funds from a local bank. The second option was to borrow the money from the accumulated capital held by Sunset Landscape Services. The final option was to borrow a portion from the bank and use SLS resources for the remainder.

Discussions with the Spensers' accountant led Cynthia to choose the third option. Although she could borrow the total purchase price from SLS at an attractive interest rate, the loan would essentially reflect negatively on SLS's balance sheet, making it appear to be less solvent and putting more of the

Spensers' personal funds at risk. Thus, she decided to borrow 50 percent of the purchase price from the bank and use personal funds for the remainder. The bank was amenable to this arrangement and agreed to the loan.

A second important decision was how to organize the new business. Mark suggested that they simply fold it into the SLS corporation, making it one more business owned and controlled by the existing company. Cynthia saw some merit to this plan, but she eventually decided to keep it as a separate business. She knew that Mark's real interests were in horticulture, and that he would have no involvement in The Arbor. She also recognized that managing a real-estate investment property was so different from managing a products-and-services retail operation that merging the two simply did not seem as logical as keeping them separate.

The final important decision she had to make involved her own role in Sunset Landscape Services. She was finding that managing the retail nursery was not really a big job because she had a strong staff of sales associates. She also felt that there would not be a great deal of time needed managing The Arbor, at least at first. This was because the retail complex already had a full tenant base and she did not anticipate any major changes, at least at first.

Thus, Cynthia and Mark agreed that she would retain her position as manager of the nursery for the time being. They also agreed that she would promote one of the sales associates to the position of assistant manager and give that person some additional responsibility and authority. If she found it necessary to devote more time to The Arbor, they could always make a management change at the nursery at a later date.

Discussion Questions

1. What decision-making perspectives are reflected in this case?

2. What are the benefits and risks inherent in the plans that Cynthia has made?

3. Do you agree or disagree with Cynthia's decision to keep The Arbor as a separate business?

SKILLS SELF-ASSESSMENT INSTRUMENT

An Entrepreneurial Quiz

Introduction: Entrepreneurs are starting ventures all the time. These new businesses are vital to the economy. The following assessment is designed to help you understand your readiness to start your own business—to be an entrepreneur.

Instructions: Place a checkmark or an X in the box next to the response that best represents your self-evaluation.

1. Are you a self-starter?
- ☐ I do things on my own. Nobody has to tell me to get going.
- ☐ If someone gets me started, I keep going all right.
- ☐ Easy does it. I don't push myself until I have to.

2. How do you feel about other people?
- ☐ I like people. I can get along with just about anybody.
- ☐ I have plenty of friends—I don't need anybody else.
- ☐ Most people irritate me.

3. Can you lead others?
- ☐ I can get most people to go along when I start something.
- ☐ I can give the orders if someone tells me what we should do.
- ☐ I let someone else get things moving. Then I go along if I feel like it.

4. Can you take responsibility?
- ☐ I like to take charge of things and see them through.
- ☐ I'll take over if I have to, but I'd rather let someone else be responsible.
- ☐ There are always eager beavers around wanting to show how smart they are. I let them.

5. How good an organizer are you?
- ☐ I like to have a plan before I start. I'm usually the one to get things lined up when the group wants to do something.
- ☐ I do all right unless things get too confused. Then I quit.
- ☐ You get all set and then something comes along and presents too many problems. So I just take things as they come.

6. How good a worker are you?

- ☐ I can keep going as long as I need to. I don't mind working hard for something I want.
- ☐ I'll work hard for a while, but when I've had enough, that's it.
- ☐ I can't see that hard work gets you anywhere.

7. Can you make decisions?

- ☐ I can make up my mind in a hurry if I have to. It usually turns out okay, too.
- ☐ I can if I have plenty of time. If I have to make up my mind fast, I think later I should have decided the other way.
- ☐ I don't like to be the one who has to decide things.

8. Can people trust what you say?

- ☐ You bet they can. I don't say things I don't mean.
- ☐ I try to be on the level most of the time, but sometimes I just say what's easiest.
- ☐ Why bother if the other person doesn't know the difference?

9. Can you stick with it?

- ☐ If I make up my mind to do something, I don't let *anything* stop me.
- ☐ I usually finish what I start—if it goes well.
- ☐ If it doesn't go well right away, I quit. Why beat your brains out?

10. How good is your health?

- ☐ I *never* run down!
- ☐ I have enough energy for most things I want to do.
- ☐ I run out of energy sooner than most of my friends.

Total the checks or Xs in each column here.

__ __ __

For interpretation, turn to page 447.

Source: From *Business Startup Basics* by Dible, Donald, pp.9–10, © 1978. Adapted by permission of Prentice-Hall, Inc., Upper Saddle River, N.J.

EXPERIENTIAL EXERCISE

Personal Interest and Market Potential in Small-Business Formation

Step One

Assume you have decided to open a small business in the local community when you graduate (the community where you are attending college, not your home). Assume you have funds to start a business without having to find other investors.

Step Two

Without regard to market potential, profitability, or similar considerations, list five businesses that you might want to open and operate based solely on your personal interests. For example, if you enjoy bicycling, you might enjoy opening a cycling shop.

Step Three

Without regard to personal attractiveness or interests, list five businesses that you might want to open and operate based solely on market opportunities.

Step Four

Evaluate the prospects for success of each of the ten businesses.

Step Five

Form a group with three or four classmates and discuss your respective lists. Look for instances where the same type of business appears on either the same or alternative lists. Look for cases where the same business appears with similar or dissimilar prospects for success.

Follow-Up Questions

1. How important is personal interest in small-business success?

2. How important is market potential in small-business success?

CHAPTER NOTES

1. William Echikson, "Young Americans Go Abroad to Strike it Rich," *Fortune,* October 17, 1994, pp. 185–195; Charles Burck, "The Real World of the Entrepreneur," *Fortune,* April 5, 1993, pp. 62–80.
2. Murray B. Low and Ian C. MacMillan, "Entrepreneurship: Past Research and Future Challenges," *Journal of Management,* June 1988, pp. 139–159; Barbara Bird, "Implementing Entrepreneurial Ideas: The Case for Intention," *Academy of Management Review,* July 1988, pp. 442–453.
3. "U.S. Small Business Administration: Small Business Size Standards," *Federal Register,* Vol. 49, No. 28 (Washington, D.C.: Government Printing Office, February 9, 1984), pp. 5024–5048.
4. Brian O'Reilly, "The New Face of Small Business," *Fortune,* May 2, 1994, pp. 82–88.
5. Bro Uttal, "Inside the Deal That Made Bill Gates $350,000,000," *Fortune,* July 21, 1986, pp. 23–33.
6. Low and MacMillan, "Entrepreneurship"; and Arnold C. Cooper and William C. Dunkelberg, "Entrepreneurship and Paths to Business Ownership," *Strategic Management Journal,* January–February 1986, pp. 53–56.
7. See David L. Birch, *The Job Creation Process* (Cambridge, Mass.: MIT Program on Neighborhood and Regional Change, 1979); Nicholas C. Siropolis, *Small Business Management: A Guide to Entrepreneurship,* 5th ed. (Boston: Houghton Mifflin, 1996); and Stuart Gannes, "America's Fastest-Growing Companies," *Fortune,* May 23, 1988, pp. 28–40.
8. "Women Entrepreneurs," *Business Week,* April 18, 1994, pp. 104–110.
9. "Big vs. Small," *Time,* September 5, 1988, pp. 48–50; and J. A. Schumpeter, *Capitalism, Socialism, and Democracy,* 3rd ed. (New York: Harper & Row, 1950).
10. Birch, *The Job Creation Process;* and Siropolis, *Small Business Management.*
11. Amar Bhide, "How Entrepreneurs Craft Strategies That Work," *Harvard Business Review,* March–April 1994, pp. 150–163.
12. Uttal, "Inside the Deal That Made Bill Gates $350,000,000"; and Keith Hammonds, "Spreadsheet Wars: When Will Lotus Do Windows?" *Business Week,* January 14, 1991, p. 42.
13. Erik Calonius, "Meet the King of Video," *Fortune,* June 4, 1990, p. 208.
14. See Faye Brookman, "Specialty Cosmetic Stores: A Hit with Frustrated Consumers," *Advertising Age,* March 4, 1991, p. 32; and Laurie Freeman, "Department Stores in Fight for Their Lives," *Advertising Age,* March 4, 1991, p. 29.
15. See Steve Zurier, "Distribution's Perfect Example," *Industrial Distribution,* April 1991, pp. 18–22; and Donald A. Duscheseneau and William B. Gartner, "A Profile of New Venture Success and Failure in an Emerging Industry," *Journal of Business Venturing,* September 1990, pp. 297–312.
16. F. M. Scherer, *Industrial Market Structure and Economic Performance,* 2nd ed. (Boston: Houghton Mifflin, 1980).
17. Thomas Rohan, "Maverick Remakes Old-Line Steel," *Industry Week,* January 21, 1991, pp. 26–30.
18. "Small Manufacturers Display Nimbleness the Times Require," *The Wall Street Journal,* December 29, 1993, pp. A1, A2.
19. See Kenneth Harling and Phoebe Quail, "Exploring a General Management Approach to Firm Management," *Agribusiness,* September 1990, pp. 425–441; and Charles Silear, "Where Did All the Pigs Go?" *Forbes,* March 19, 1990, pp. 152–156.
20. See Richard Pastore, "Small is Big in PC Land," *Computerworld,* December 24, 1990, pp. 27, 29; and Pat Sweet, "The Evolution of the PC's," *Director,* March 1990, pp. 101–107.
21. The importance of discovering niches is emphasized in Charles Hill and Gareth Jones, *Strategic Management: An Integrated Approach,* 2nd ed. (Boston: Houghton Mifflin, 1992).
22. C. Roland Christensen, Norman A. Berg, and Malcolm Salter, "BIC Pen (A)," *Policy Formulation and Administration,* 8th ed. (Homewood, Ill.: Irwin, 1980), pp. 146–171.
23. See Siropolis, *Small Business Management;* and Richard M. Hodgetts and Donald F. Kuratko, *Effective Small Business Management,* 3rd ed. (Chicago: Harcourt Brace Jovanovich, 1989). The risks run at Boeing are described in "Running Ahead, but Running Scared," *Forbes,* May 13, 1991, pp. 38–40.
24. Siropolis, *Small Business Management.*
25. "Old-Fashioned Ways Still Work," *Forbes,* March 14, 1994, pp. 90–91.
26. See Thomas E. Copeland and J. Fred Weston, *Financial Theory and Corporate Policy,* 2nd ed. (Reading, Mass.: Addison-Wesley, 1983), for a discussion of the different kinds of claims that sources of capital can have on a firm. Eugene Fama and Michael Jensen discuss the advantages and disadvantages of various forms of corporate ownership in E. Fama and M. Jensen, "Agency Problems and Residual Claims," *Journal of Law and Economics,* June 1983, pp. 327–349; and E. Fama and M. Jensen, "Separation of Ownership and Control," *Journal of Law and Economics,* June 1983, pp. 301–325. A more practical guide to choosing ownership structure

is found in Hodgetts and Kuratko, *Effective Small Business Management.*

27. Jay Barney, Lowell Busenitz, James Fiet, and Doug Moesel, "The Structure of Venture Capital Governance," *Academy of Management Proceedings: "Best Papers 1989,"* Meeting of the Academy of Management, Washington, D.C., 1989, pp. 64–68.
28. "Persistence Pays in Search of Funds," *USA Today,* May 11, 1987, p. 3E.
29. Barney et al., "The Structure of Venture Capital Governance."
30. Faye Rice, "How to Succeed at Cloning a Small Business," *Fortune,* October 28, 1985, pp. 60–66; "Franchising Tries to Divvy Up Risk," *USA Today,* May 11, 1987, p. 5E.
31. "Businesses Vie For More Control" *USA Today,* January 5, 1993, pp. 1B, 2B.
32. Rice, "How to Succeed at Cloning a Small Business."
33. Charles Burck, "The Real World of the Entrepreneur."
34. Siropolis, *Small Business Management.*
35. Ibid.
36. Ibid.
37. See Jay Barney, "Strategic Factor Markets: Expectations, Luck, and Business Strategy," *Management Science,* October 1986, pp. 1231–1241.
38. Siropolis, *Small Business Management.*
39. See Gifford Pinchot III, *Intrapreneuring* (New York: Harper and Row, 1985).

As international competition continues to escalate, businesses must constantly adjust their structure to ensure that it is promoting efficiency and effectiveness. Global companies like McDonald's and Philips, for example, must coordinate far-flung operations. At a local level, organizations focus on various training methods to keep everyone working together.

PART

Organizing

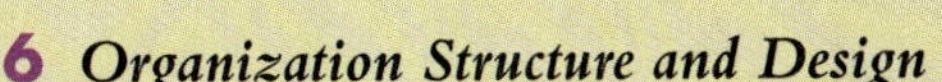

CHAPTER 6

Organization Structure and Design

OBJECTIVES

After studying this chapter, you should be able to:

- *Identify and describe the basic elements of organizations.*
- *Identify and explain the bureaucratic perspective on organization design.*
- *Identify and explain several situational influences on organization design.*
- *Describe the basic forms of organization design that characterize many organizations.*

OUTLINE

OPENING INCIDENT

FOR MUCH OF the 1980s, The Limited was one of the fastest-growing specialty apparel chains in the United States. Essential to its success were staying in touch with consumer trends and tastes, manufacturing and getting new products into stores quickly, and maintaining tight controls over inventory. Although The Limited's total sales exceeded $7 billion in 1994, in recent years Limited has fallen on hard times and is struggling to get itself back on track.

The retail giant is organized around several large divisions. Its cornerstone is The Limited chain, which accounts for almost one-third of the company's total sales. Express is a chain of smaller stores catering to young women. Lerner Stores Corp. focuses on less-expensive fashions for low- to middle-income shoppers. Victoria's Secret specializes in lingerie. Lane Bryant concentrates on larger size clothing. The Limited also owns some smaller chains like Abercrombie & Fitch Co. and Bath & Body Works.

From the beginning, each of the company's divisions has acted autonomously, taking care of activities such as planning its own stores and developing its own marketing campaigns. Each has its own management team, its own buyers, and its own identity. Indeed, chair Leslie Wexner believed that competition among divisions was a healthy stimulus for innovation. He likened each one to a separate business run by its own team of entrepreneurs.

"I believe in entrepreneurship, but we went too far in decentralizing the business. I essentially said to the presidents of the various divisions, 'You'll figure things out.' We didn't give them enough support."

Not surprisingly, however, this arrangement occasionally led to internal conflict, and competition sometimes got out of hand. For example, a Limited and Express store in the same shopping mall commonly carry some of the same products for different prices. In addition, the corporation itself provided little support to the various divisions—each was expected to provide its own services and solve its own problems.

By the mid-1990s, alarm bells started to go off. Other chains, such as The Gap, started making inroads into Limited's market share. And discounters took more and more business away from Lerner New York. Sales leveled off, and profits began to slip. Deliveries were also a problem at some stores; that is, deliveries started to slip, which created inventory problems.

Wexner took notice of these problems, and took major steps to turn things back around. For example, he changed management teams at both The Limited and Lerner New York and put a quality-assurance program in place. Wexner also created more coordination among the various Limited divisions. And he created a corporate staff to help provide basic business services and assistance to the various divisions.[1] ●

Source of Quotation: Leslie Wexner, Limited chair, quoted in *Fortune*, October 17, 1994, p. 162.

Managers at The Limited successfully created a large, national retail chain. The retailer was enormously successful for years, but recently stumbled and is now trying to regain its momentum. One of the key ingredients in managing any business is the creation of a structure to link the various elements that comprise the organization. The Limited's managers have chosen a divisional approach, a design that has both helped and hurt the organization in its quest for effectiveness. The divisional design, moreover, is but one of several different structures managers could have chosen.

This chapter discusses many of the critical elements of organization structure that managers can control and is the first of three devoted to organizing, the second basic managerial function identified in Chapter 1. In Part II, we described managerial planning—deciding what to do. Organizing, the subject of Part III, focuses on how to do it. We first elaborate on the meaning of organization structure. Then, in subsequent sections, we explore the basic elements that managers use to create an organization.

THE NATURE OF ORGANIZING

• **organization structure and design**
The set of building blocks that can be used to configure an organization

Organization structure and design refers to the overall set of structural elements and the relationships among those elements used to manage an organization. This section introduces and describes the critical elements.

Job Specialization

• **job specialization**
The degree to which the overall task of the organization is broken down and divided into smaller component parts

The first element of organization structure is job specialization.[2] **Job specialization** is the degree to which the overall task of the organization is broken down and divided into smaller component parts. Job specialization is a normal extension of organizational growth. For example, when Walt Disney started his company he did everything himself—from writing and drawing cartoons to marketing them to theaters. As the business grew, he eventually hired others to perform many of these same functions. As growth continued, so too did specialization. For example, as animation artists work on Disney movies today, they may specialize in drawing only a single character. And today, The Walt Disney Company has thousands of different specialized jobs. Clearly, no one person could perform them all.

Benefits and Limitations of Specialization One benefit of job specialization is that workers performing small, simple tasks will probably become very proficient at that task.[3] Also, transfer time between tasks may decrease. If employees perform several different tasks, some time may be lost as they stop doing the first task and start doing the next. Further, the more narrowly defined a job is, the easier it may be to develop specialized equipment to assist with that job. Finally, when an employee who performs a highly specialized job is absent or resigns, the manager should be able to train someone new at relatively low cost.

The foremost criticism of job specialization is that workers who perform highly specialized jobs may become bored and dissatisfied. The job may be so specialized that it offers no challenge or stimulation. Boredom and monotony set in, absenteeism rises, and the quality of the work may suffer. Furthermore, the anticipated benefits of specialization do not always occur. For example, a study conducted at Maytag found that the time spent moving work-in-process from one worker to another was greater than the time needed for the same individual to change from job to job.[4] Thus, although some degree of specialization is necessary, it should not be carried to extremes because of the negative consequences that could result. Managers should be sensitive to situations where extreme specialization should be avoided. Several alternative approaches to designing jobs have been developed in recent years.

Alternatives to Specialization To counter the problems associated with specialization, managers have sought other approaches that achieve a better balance between organizational demands for efficiency and productivity and individual needs for creativity and autonomy. Alternative approaches include job rotation, job enlargement, job enrichment, and the job characteristics approach.[5]

Job rotation involves systematically moving employees from one job to another. A worker in a warehouse might unload trucks on Monday, carry incoming inventory to storage on Tuesday, verify invoices on Wednesday, pull outgoing inventory from storage on Thursday, and load trucks on Friday. Thus, the jobs do not change; instead, workers move from job to job. Unfortunately, for this very reason, job rotation has not been very successful in enhancing employee motivation or satisfaction. Jobs that are amenable to rotation tend to be relatively standard and routine. Workers who are rotated to a "new" job may be more satisfied at first, but this satisfaction soon wanes. Although many companies (including Bethlehem Steel, Ford, TRW, and Western Electric) have tried job rotation, it is most often used today as a training device to improve worker skills and flexibility.

• **job rotation**
An alternative to job specialization that involves systematically moving employees from one job to another

Job enlargement was developed to increase the total number of tasks workers perform. As a result, all workers perform a wide variety of tasks, presumably reducing the level of job dissatisfaction. Many organizations have used job enlargement, including IBM, Detroit Edison, AT&T, the U.S. Civil Service, and Maytag.[6] Unfortunately, although job enlargement does have some positive consequences, training costs usually rise, unions sometimes argue that pay should increase because the worker is doing more things, and work often remains boring and routine.

• **job enlargement**
An alternative to job specialization that involves giving the employee more tasks to perform

A more comprehensive approach, **job enrichment**, attempts to increase both the number of tasks a worker does and the control the worker has over the job.[7] To implement job enrichment, managers remove some controls from the job, delegate more authority to employees, and structure the work in complete, natural units. These changes increase the subordinates' sense of responsibility. Another part of job enrichment is to continually assign new and challenging tasks, thereby increasing the employees' opportunity for growth and advancement. Organizations that have tried job enrichment include AT&T, Texas Instruments, IBM, and General Foods. But this approach, too, has its problems. For example, analysis of work systems before enrichment is needed but seldom performed, and managers rarely deal with employee preferences when enriching jobs.

• **job enrichment**
An alternative to job specialization that involves increasing both the number of tasks the worker does and the control the worker has over the job

job characteristics approach An alternative to job specialization that suggests that jobs should be diagnosed and improved along five core dimensions, taking into account both the work system and employee preferences

The **job characteristics approach** is an alternative to job specialization that does take into account the work system and employee preferences.[8] As illustrated in Figure 6.1, the job characteristics approach suggests that jobs should be improved along five core dimensions:

1. *Skill variety*: the number of things a person does in a job
2. *Task identity*: the extent to which the worker does a complete or identifiable portion of the total job
3. *Task significance*: the perceived importance of the task
4. *Autonomy*: the degree of control the worker has over how the work is performed
5. *Feedback*: the extent to which the worker knows how well the job is being performed

Increasing the presence of these dimensions in a job presumably leads to high motivation, high-quality performance, high satisfaction, and low ab-

The job characteristics approach to job design provides a viable alternative to job specialization. Five core job dimensions may lead to critical psychological states that, in turn, may enhance motivation, performance, and satisfaction and reduce absenteeism and turnover.

FIGURE 6.1 The Job Characteristics Approach

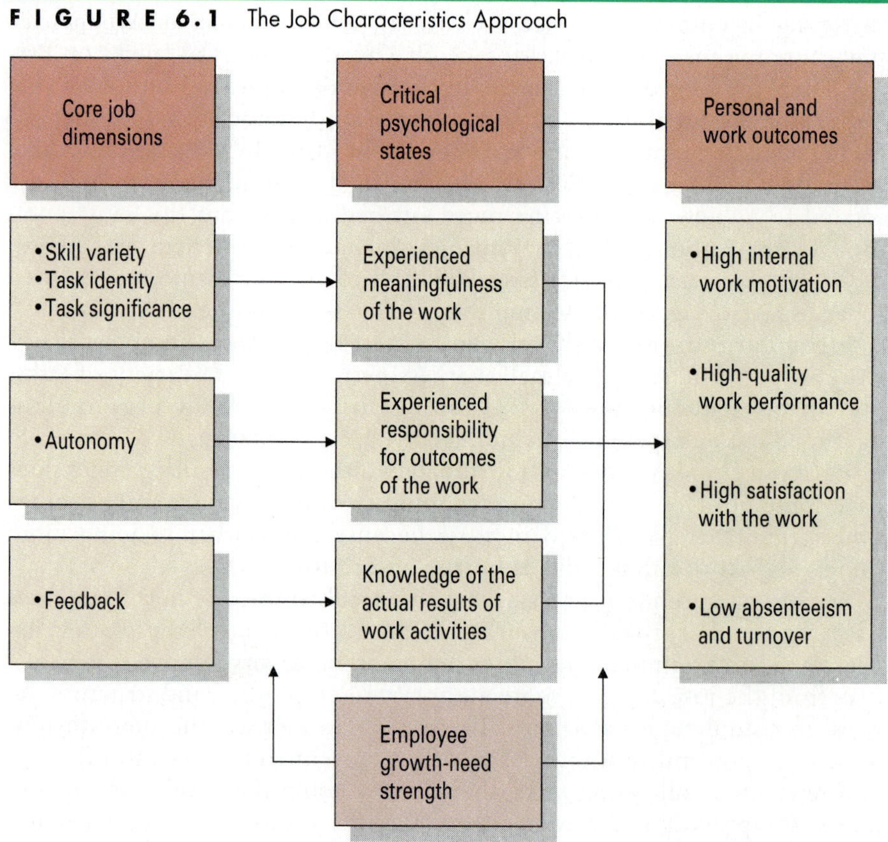

Source: J. R. Hackman and G. R. Oldham, "Motivation Through the Design of Work: Test of a Theory," *Organizational Behavior and Human Performance*, Vol. 16, 1976, pp. 250–279. Copyright © Academic Press, Inc. Reprinted by permission of the publisher.

senteeism and turnover. A large number of studies have been conducted to test the usefulness of the job characteristics approach. Results included moderate declines in turnover and a small but measurable improvement in work quality. Other research findings have not supported this approach as strongly. Thus, although the job characteristics approach is one of the most promising alternatives to job specialization, it is probably not the final answer.[9]

Departmentalization

The second basic element of organization structure is **departmentalization**—the grouping of jobs according to some logical arrangement. When organizations are small, the owner-manager can personally oversee everyone who works there. However, as an organization grows, it becomes more and more difficult for the owner-manager to personally supervise all the employees. Consequently, new managerial positions are created to supervise the work of others. The assignment of employees to particular managers is not done randomly. Rather, jobs are grouped according to some plan. The logic embodied in such a plan is the basis for all departmentalization.[10]

• **departmentalization** Grouping jobs according to some logical arrangement

Functional Departmentalization The most common base for departmentalization, especially among smaller organizations, is by function.[11] **Functional departmentalization** groups together those jobs involving the same or similar activities. This approach has three primary advantages. First, each department can be staffed by experts in that functional area. Marketing experts can be hired to run the marketing function, for example. Second, supervision is facilitated because an individual manager needs to be familiar with only a relatively narrow set of skills. And third, it is easier to coordinate activities inside each department.

• **functional departmentalization** Grouping jobs involving the same or similar activities

On the other hand, as an organization grows, decision making tends to become slower and more bureaucratic. Employees may begin to concentrate too narrowly on their own units and lose sight of the total organizational system. Finally, accountability and performance become increasingly difficult to monitor. For example, it may not be possible to determine whether the failure of a new product is due to production deficiencies or to a poor marketing campaign.

Product Departmentalization **Product departmentalization** involves grouping and arranging activities around products or product groups. Many larger businesses adopt this form of departmentalization for grouping activities at the business or corporate level. There are three major advantages to product departmentalization. First, all activities associated with one product or product group can be easily coordinated. Second, the speed and effectiveness of decision making are enhanced. Third, the performance of individual products or product groups can be assessed more easily and objectively, thereby improving the accountability of departments for the results of their activities.

• **product departmentalization** Grouping activities around products or product groups

On the other hand, managers in each department may focus on their own product or product group to the exclusion of the rest of the organization. That is, a marketing manager may see her primary duty as helping her group, rather than helping the overall organization. Additionally, administrative costs rise because each department must have its own functional specialists for things such as marketing research and financial analysis.

• **customer departmentalization** Grouping activities to respond to and interact with specific customers or customer groups

Customer Departmentalization Under **customer departmentalization**, the organization structures its activities to respond to and interact with specific customers or customer groups. The lending activities in most banks, for example, are usually tailored to meet the needs of different kinds of customers (e.g., business, consumer, mortgage, and agricultural loans). The basic advantage of this approach is that it allows the organization to use skilled specialists to deal with unique customers or customer groups. It takes one set of skills to evaluate a balance sheet and lend a business $100,000 for operating capital and a different set of skills to evaluate an individual's creditworthiness and lend $20,000 for a new car. However, customer departmentalization requires a fairly large administrative staff to integrate the activities of the various departments. In banks, for example, coordination is necessary to make sure the organization does not overcommit itself in any one area and to handle collections on delinquent accounts from a diverse set of customers.

• **location departmentalization** Grouping jobs on the basis of defined geographic sites or areas

Location Departmentalization **Location departmentalization** groups jobs on the basis of defined geographic sites or areas. The defined sites or areas may range in size from a hemisphere to only a few blocks of a large city. Transportation companies, police departments (precincts represent geographic areas of a city), and the Federal Reserve Bank all use location departmentalization. The primary advantage of location departmentalization is that it enables the organization to respond easily to unique customer and environmental characteristics in the various regions. On the negative side, a larger administrative staff may be required if the organization is to keep track of units in scattered locations.

Reporting Relationships

The third basic element of organizing is the establishment of reporting relationships among positions. The purpose of this activity is to clarify the chain of command and the span of management.

• **chain of command** A clear and distinct line of authority among the positions in an organization

The Chain of Command The **chain of command** concept is an old one, first popularized in the early years of this century. Early writers about the chain of command argued that clear and distinct lines of authority need to be established among all positions in the organization. There are actually two components of the chain of command. The first, called *unity of command,* suggests that each person within an organization should have a clear reporting relationship to one and only one boss (as we will see later in this chapter, newer models of organization design successfully violate this premise). The second, called the *scalar principle,* suggests that there should be a clear and unbroken line of authority that extends from the lowest to the highest position in the organization. The popular saying "The buck stops here" is derived from this idea—someone ultimately must be responsible for every decision.

The Span of Management Another part of establishing reporting relationships is determining how many people will report to each manager. This defines the **span of management** (sometimes called the *span of control*). For years managers and researchers sought to determine the optimal span of management. For example, should it be relatively narrow (with few subordinates per manager) or relatively wide (many subordinates)? Although there is no perfect formula, managers can use various situational factors to determine whether the span for a particular situation should be relatively wide or relatively narrow.[12]

• **span of management**
The number of people who report to a particular manager

Tall Versus Flat Organizations The span of management is also a primary determinant of whether the organization is relatively tall or flat. One early study at Sears found that a flat structure led to higher employee morale and productivity.[13] It has also been argued that a tall structure is more expensive (due to the larger number of managers involved) and that it fosters more communication problems (due to the increased number of people through whom information must pass). On the other hand, a wide span of management in a flat organization may result in a manager having more administrative responsibility (because there are fewer managers) and more supervisory responsibility (because there are more subordinates reporting to each manager). If these additional responsibilities become excessive, the flat organization may suffer.[14]

Many experts agree that businesses can function effectively with fewer layers of organization than they currently have. The Franklin Mint, for example, recently reduced its number of management layers from six to four. At the same time, CEO Stewart Resnick increased his span of management from six to twelve. In similar fashion, IBM has recently eliminated several layers of management. One reason for this trend is that improved organizational communication networks allow managers to stay in touch with a larger number of subordinates than was possible even just a few years ago.[15]

Authority

Another important element of organization structure is the determination of how authority is to be distributed among positions. **Authority** is power that has been legitimized by the organization.[16] Two specific issues that managers must address when distributing authority are delegation and decentralization.[17]

• **authority**
Power that has been legitimized by the organization

The Delegation Process Delegation is the establishment of a pattern of authority between a superior and one or more subordinates. Specifically, **delegation** is the process by which managers assign a portion of their total workload to others.[18] The delegation process involves three steps. First, the manager assigns responsibility, or gives the subordinate a job to do. The assignment of responsibility might range from telling a subordinate to prepare a report to placing the person in charge of a task force. Along with the assignment, the individual is also given the authority to do the job. The manager may give the subordinate the power to requisition needed information from confidential files or to direct a group of other

• **delegation**
The process by which a manager assigns a portion of his or her total workload to others

workers. Finally, the manager establishes the subordinate's accountability—that is, the subordinate accepts an obligation to carry out the task assigned by the manager.

Decentralization and Centralization Just as authority can be delegated from one individual to another, organizations also develop patterns of authority across a wide variety of positions and departments; these patterns can be thought of as lying on a continuum. **Decentralization**, at one end, is the process of systematically delegating power and authority throughout the organization to middle and lower-level managers. **Centralization**, at the other end, is the process of systematically retaining power and authority in the hands of higher-level managers. No organization is ever completely decentralized or completely centralized; some firms position themselves toward one end of the continuum, and some lean the other way.[19]

- **decentralization** The process of systematically delegating power and authority throughout the organization to middle and lower-level managers
- **centralization** The process of systematically retaining power and authority in the hands of higher-level managers

What factors determine an organization's position on the decentralization–centralization continuum? One common determinant is the organization's external environment. Usually, the greater the complexity and uncertainty of the environment, the greater is the tendency to decentralize. Another crucial factor is the history of the organization. Firms have a tendency to do what they have done in the past, so there is likely to be some relationship between what an organization did in its early history and what it chooses to do today in terms of centralization or decentralization. The nature of the decisions being made is also considered. The costlier and riskier the decision, the more pressure there is to centralize. Organizations also consider the abilities of lower-level managers. If lower-level managers do not have the ability to make high-quality decisions, there is likely to be a high level of centralization. If lower-level managers are well qualified, top management can take advantage of their talents by decentralizing; in fact, if top management doesn't, talented lower-level managers may leave the organization.[20]

Coordination

- **coordination** The process of linking the activities of the various departments of the organization

A fifth major element of organizing is coordination. **Coordination** is the process of linking the activities of the various departments of the organization. The primary reason for coordination is that departments and work groups are interdependent—they depend on each other for information and resources to perform their respective activities.

The Need for Coordination The greater the interdependence between departments, the more coordination the organization requires if departments are to be able to perform effectively. There are three major forms of interdependence: pooled, sequential, and reciprocal.[21] **Pooled interdependence** represents the lowest level of interdependence. Units with pooled interdependence operate with little interaction—the output of the units is pooled at the organizational level. The Gap clothing stores operate with pooled interdependence. Each has its own operating budget, staff, and so forth. The profits or losses from each store are "added together" at

- **pooled interdependence** A form of interdependence in which unit outputs are pooled at the organizational level

the organizational level. The stores are interdependent to the extent that the final success or failure of one store affects the others, but they do not generally interact on a day-to-day basis.

In **sequential interdependence**, the output of one unit becomes the input for another in a sequential fashion. This creates a moderate level of interdependence. At Nissan, for example, one plant assembles engines and then ships them to a final assembly site at another plant where the cars are completed. The plants are interdependent in that the final assembly plant must have the engines from engine assembly before it can perform its primary function of producing finished automobiles. But the level of interdependence is generally one-way—the engine plant is not necessarily dependent on the final assembly plant.

• **sequential interdependence** A form of interdependence in which the output of one unit becomes the input to another in a sequential fashion

Reciprocal interdependence exists when activities flow both ways between units. This form is clearly the most complex. Within a Marriott Hotel, for example, the reservations department, front-desk check-in, and housekeeping are all reciprocally interdependent. Reservations has to provide front-desk employees with information about how many guests to expect each day, and housekeeping needs to know which rooms require priority cleaning. If any of the three units does not do its job properly, the others will all be affected.

• **reciprocal interdependence** A form of interdependence in which activities flow both ways between units

Structural Coordination Techniques Given the obvious coordination requirements that characterize most organizations, it follows that many techniques for achieving coordination among interdependent units have been developed. Some of the most useful include the managerial hierarchy, rules and procedures, liaison roles, task forces, and integrating departments.[22]

Organizations that use the managerial hierarchy to achieve coordination place one manager in charge of interdependent departments or units. In Kmart distribution centers, major activities include receiving and unloading bulk shipments from railroad cars and loading other shipments onto trucks for distribution to retail outlets. The two groups (receiving and shipping) are interdependent in that they share the loading docks and some equipment. To ensure coordination and to minimize conflict, one manager is in charge of the whole operation.

Routine coordination activities can be handled via rules and standard procedures. In the Kmart distribution center, an outgoing truck shipment has priority over an incoming rail shipment. Thus, when trucks are to be loaded, the shipping unit is given access to all of the center's auxiliary forklifts. This priority is specifically stated in a rule. But, as useful as rules and procedures often are in routine situations, they are not particularly effective when coordination problems are complex or unusual.

Liaisons also serve a coordination function. Managers in liaison roles coordinate interdependent units by acting as a common point of contact. This individual may not have any formal authority over the groups but instead simply facilitates the flow of information between units. Two engineering groups working on component systems for a large project might interact through a liaison. The liaison maintains familiarity with each group as well as with the overall project. She can answer questions and otherwise serve to integrate the activities of all the groups.

A task force may be created when the need for coordination is acute. When interdependence is complex and several units are involved, a single liaison person may not be sufficient. Instead, a task force might be assembled by drawing one representative from each group. The coordination function is thus spread across several individuals, each of whom has special information about one of the groups involved. When the project is completed, task-force members return to their original positions. For example, a college overhauling its degree requirements might establish a task force made up of representatives from each department affected by the change. Each person retains her or his regular departmental affiliation and duties but also serves on the special task force. After the new requirements are agreed upon, the task force is dissolved.

Integrating departments are occasionally used for coordination. These are somewhat similar to task forces but are established on a more permanent basis. An integrating department generally has some permanent members, as well as members who are assigned temporarily from units that are particularly in need of coordination. One study found that successful firms in the plastics industry, which is characterized by complex and dynamic environments, used integrating departments to maintain internal integration and coordination.[23] An integrating department usually has more authority than a task force and may even be given some budgetary control by the organization.

THE BUREAUCRATIC MODEL OF ORGANIZATION DESIGN

In Chapter 1, we made the distinction between contingency and universal approaches to solving management problems. Recall, for example, that universal perspectives try to identify the "one best way" to manage organizations, and contingency perspectives suggest that appropriate managerial behavior in a given situation depends on, or is contingent on, unique elements in that situation. The foundation of contemporary thinking about organization design can be traced back to an important early universal perspective: the bureaucratic model of organization design.

Max Weber, an influential German sociologist, was a pioneer of classical organization theory. At the core of Weber's writings is the bureaucratic model of organizations.[24] The Weberian perspective suggests that a **bureaucracy** is a model of organization design based on a legitimate and formal system of authority. Many people associate bureaucracy with "red tape," rigidity, and passing the buck. For example, how many times have you heard people refer disparagingly to "the federal bureaucracy"?

• **bureaucracy**
A universal model of organization design based on a legitimate and formal system of authority

Weber viewed the bureaucratic form of organization as logical, rational, and efficient. He offered the model as a framework to which all organizations should aspire: the "one best way" of doing things. According to Weber, the ideal bureaucracy exhibits five basic characteristics:

1. The organization should adopt a distinct division of labor, and each position should be filled by an expert.
2. The organization should develop a consistent set of rules to ensure that task performance is uniform.
3. The organization should establish a hierarchy of positions or offices that creates a chain of command from the top of the organization to the bottom.
4. Managers should conduct business in an impersonal way and maintain an appropriate social distance between themselves and their subordinates.
5. Employment and advancement in the organization should be based on technical expertise, and employees should be protected from arbitrary dismissal.

Perhaps the best examples of bureaucracies today are government agencies and universities. Consider, for example, the steps you must go through and the forms you must fill out to apply for admission to college, request housing, register each semester, change majors, submit a degree plan, substitute a course, and file for graduation. The reason these procedures are necessary is that universities deal with large numbers of people who must be treated equally and fairly. Hence rules, regulations, and standard operating procedures are needed. Some bureaucracies, such as the U.S. Postal Service, are trying to become less mechanistic and impersonal. The strategy of the Postal Service is to become more service-oriented as a way to fight back against competitors such as Federal Express and United Parcel Service.

A primary strength of the bureaucratic model is that several of its elements (such as reliance on rules and employment based on expertise) do, in fact, often improve efficiency. Bureaucracies also help prevent favoritism (because everyone must follow the rules) and make procedures and practices very clear to everyone. Unfortunately, this approach also has several disadvantages. One major disadvantage is that the bureaucratic model results in inflexibility and rigidity. Once rules are created and put into place, it is often difficult to make exceptions or to change them. In addition, the bureaucracy often results in the neglect of humanistic issues within the organization.[25]

SITUATIONAL INFLUENCES ON ORGANIZATION DESIGN

The **situational view of organization design** is based on the assumption that the optimal design for any given organization depends on a set of relevant situational factors.[26] That is, situational factors play a role in determining the best organization design for any particular circumstance. Here, we discuss four such factors: technology, environment, size, and organizational life cycle.

situational view of organization design
Based on the assumption that the optimal design for any given organization depends on a set of relevant situational factors

Technology is an important situational determinant of organization design. The Indonesian factory in the left photo is using an assembly-line type, or large-batch, operation to manufacture Barbie Dolls for Mattel. Because of its reliance on this technology, the firm is likely to be relatively bureaucratic. In contrast, the employees in the right photo work for Out on Bale, an Arizona firm that makes straw houses. Because each house is made-to-order, this reflects small-batch technology. Out on Bale has a less bureaucratic organization design.

Core Technology

Technology is the set of conversion processes used to transform inputs (such as materials or information) into outputs (such as products or services). Most organizations use multiple technologies, but an organization's most important one is called its *core technology.* Although most people visualize assembly lines and machinery when they think of technology, the term can also be applied to service organizations. For example, a brokerage firm like Dean Witter uses technology to transform investment dollars into income in much the same way that Union Carbide uses natural resources to manufacture chemical products.

• **technology**
The set of conversion processes used by an organization in transforming inputs (such as materials or information) into outputs (such as products or services)

The link between technology and organization design was first recognized by Joan Woodward.[27] Woodward studied one hundred manufacturing firms in southern England. She collected information about such things as the history of each organization, its manufacturing processes, its forms and procedures, and its financial performance. Woodward expected to find a relationship between the size of an organization and its design, but no such relationship emerged. As a result, she began to seek other explanations for differences. Close scrutiny of the firms in her sample led her to recognize a potential relationship between technology and organization design. This follow-up analysis led Woodward to first classify the organizations according to their technology. Woodward identified three basic forms of technology:

1. *Unit or small-batch technology.* The product is custom-made to customer specifications, or else it is produced in small quantities. Organizations using this form of technology include a tailor shop such as Brooks Brothers (custom suits), a printing shop such as Kinko's (business cards, company stationery), and a photography studio.

2. *Large-batch or mass-production technology.* The product is manufactured in assembly-line fashion by combining component parts into another part or finished product. Examples include automobile manufacturers such as Subaru, washing-machine companies such as Whirlpool Corporation, and electronics firms such as Philips.
3. *Continuous-process technology.* Raw materials are transformed to a finished product by a series of machine or process transformations. The composition of the materials themselves is changed. Examples include petroleum refineries such as Exxon and Shell and chemical refineries such as Dow Chemical and Hoechst Celanese Corporation.

These forms of technology are listed in order of their assumed levels of complexity. That is, unit or small-batch technology is presumed to be the least complex, and continuous-process technology the most complex. Woodward found that different configurations of organization design were associated with each technology.

Woodward found that middle-range organizations (large-batch or mass-production) were much more like bureaucracies, whereas the two extremes (unit or small-batch and continuous-process) tended to be more organic—less rigid and formal. The large-batch and mass-production organizations also had a higher level of specialization.[28] Finally, Woodward found that organizational success was related to the extent to which organizations followed the typical pattern. For example, successful continuous-process organizations tended to be more organic, whereas less successful firms with the same technology were more bureaucratic.

Environment

There are a number of specific linkages between environmental elements and organization design. The first widely recognized analysis of environment–organization design linkages was provided by Tom Burns and G. M. Stalker.[29] Like Woodward, Burns and Stalker worked in England. Their first step was identifying two extreme forms of organizational environment: stable (one that remains relatively constant over time) and unstable (subject to uncertainty and rapid change). Next they studied the designs of organizations in each type of environment. Not surprisingly, they found that organizations in stable environments tended to have a different kind of design from organizations in unstable environments. The two kinds of designs that emerged, summarized in Table 6.1, were called mechanistic and organic organization.

A **mechanistic organization** is most frequently found in stable environments. Free from uncertainty, organizations structure their activities in rather predictable ways by means of rules, specialized jobs, and centralized authority. Mechanistic organizations are also quite similar in nature to bureaucracies. Although no environment is completely stable, Kmart and Wendy's use mechanistic designs. Each Kmart store, for example, has prescribed methods for store design and merchandise-ordering processes. No deviations are allowed from these methods.

• **mechanistic organization**
A rigid and bureaucratic form of design most appropriate for stable environments

TABLE 6.1 Mechanistic and Organic Organizations

Mechanistic	Organic
1. Tasks are highly fractionated and specialized; little regard is paid to clarifying relationship between tasks and organizational objectives.	1. Tasks are more interdependent; emphasis is on relevance of tasks and organizational objectives.
2. Tasks tend to remain rigidly defined unless altered formally by top management.	2. Tasks are continually adjusted and redefined through interaction of organization members.
3. Specific roles are defined (rights, obligations, and technical methods are prescribed for each member).	3. Generalized roles are defined (members accept general responsibility for task accomplishment beyond individual role definition).
4. Structure of control, authority, and communication is hierarchical; sanctions derive from employment contract between employee and organization.	4. Structure of control, authority, and communication is a network; sanctions derive more from community of interest than from contractual relationship.
5. Information relevant to situation and operations of the organization is formally assumed to rest with chief executive.	5. Leader is not assumed to be omniscient; knowledge centers are identified throughout organization.
6. Communication is primarily vertical between superior and subordinate.	6. Communication is both vertical and horizontal, depending on where needed information resides.
7. Communications primarily take the form of instructions and decisions issued by superiors, and of information and requests for decisions supplied by inferiors.	7. Communications primarily take the form of information and advice.
8. Insistence on loyalty to organization and obedience to superiors is present.	8. Commitment to organization's tasks and goals is more highly valued than loyalty or obedience.
9. Importance and prestige are attached to identification with organization and its members.	9. Importance and prestige are attached to affiliations and expertise in external environment.

Source: Adapted from Tom Burns and G. M. Stalker, *The Management of Innovation* (London: Tavistock, 1961), pp. 119–122. Used with permission of Oxford University Press, UK.

organic organization A fluid and flexible design most appropriate for unstable and unpredictable environments

An **organic organization,** on the other hand, is most often found in unstable and unpredictable environments, in which constant change and uncertainty usually dictate a much higher level of fluidity and flexibility. Motorola (facing rapid technological change) and The Limited (facing constant change in consumer tastes) both use organic designs. A manager at Motorola, for example, has considerable discretion over how problems can be solved.

These ideas were extended in the United States by Paul R. Lawrence and Jay W. Lorsch.[30] They agreed that environmental factors influence organization design but believed that this influence varies between different units of the same organization. In fact, they theorized that each organizational unit has its own unique environment and responds by developing unique attributes. Lawrence and Lorsch suggested that organizations could be characterized along two primary dimensions.

One of these dimensions, **differentiation**, is the extent to which the organization is broken down into subunits. A firm with many subunits is highly differentiated; one with few subunits has a low level of differentiation. The second dimension, **integration**, is the degree to which the various units must work together in a coordinated fashion. For example, if each unit competes in a different market and has its own production facilities, little integration may be needed. Lawrence and Lorsch reasoned that the appropriate degree of differentiation and integration depends on the stability of the environments that an organization's subunits face.[31]

differentiation The extent to which the organization is broken down into subunits

integration The extent to which the subunits of an organization must work together in a coordinated fashion

Organizational Size and Life Cycle

The size of an organization is yet another factor that affects its design. **Organizational size** is the total number of full-time or full-time–equivalent employees. A team of researchers at the University of Aston in Birmingham, England, believed that Woodward had failed to find a size–structure relationship (her original expectation) because almost all the organizations she studied were relatively small (three-fourths had fewer than five hundred employees).[32] Thus they decided to undertake a study of a wider array of organizations to determine how size and technology both individually and jointly affect an organization's design.

organizational size The number of full-time or full-time–equivalent employees

Their primary finding was that technology did in fact influence structural variables in small firms, probably because all their activities tended to be centered around their core technology. In large firms, however, the strong technology–design link broke down, most likely because technology is not as central to ongoing activities in large organizations. The Aston studies yielded a number of basic generalizations: when compared to small organizations, large organizations tend to be characterized by higher levels of job specialization, more standard operating procedures, more rules, more regulations, and a greater degree of decentralization.

Of course, size is not constant. As we noted in Chapter 5, for example, some small businesses are formed but soon disappear. Others remain as small, independently operated enterprises as long as their owner-manager lives. A few—such as Compaq Computer, Dell Computer, Liz Claiborne, and Reebok—skyrocket to become organizational giants. And occasionally large organizations reduce their size through layoffs or divestitures. For example, Navistar is today far smaller than was its previous incarnation as International Harvester. Although no clear pattern explains changes in size, many organizations progress through a four-stage **organizational life cycle**.[33]

organizational life cycle A natural sequence of stages most organizations pass through as they grow and mature

The first stage is the *birth* of the organization. At Compaq Computer, this occurred in 1984 when a handful of Texas Instruments engineers resigned, raised some venture capital, and began to design and build portable computers. The second stage, *youth,* is characterized by growth and the expansion of all organizational resources. Compaq passed through the youth stage in 1985 and entered the third stage, *midlife,* around the beginning of

An organization's life cycle plays an important role in its design. Cintas is a rapidly growing business taking full advantage of a booming industry—uniform rental. This employee is overseeing the production of a batch of Cintas uniforms. The firm has been successful in part by attracting new customers—two-thirds of its customers have never rented uniforms before.

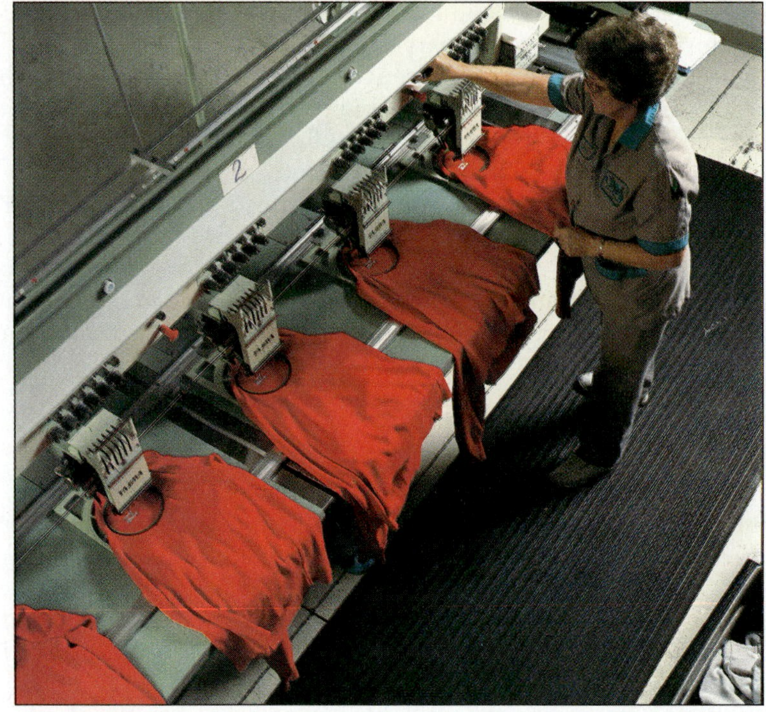

1986. Midlife is a period of growth evolving eventually into stability. The company remains in midlife today, with sales in excess of $9 billion annually. Compaq has not yet reached the final stage of an organization's life cycle, *maturity.* Maturity is a period of stability, perhaps eventually evolving into decline.

Managers must confront a number of organization design issues as the organization progresses through these stages. In general, as an organization passes from one stage to the next, it becomes bigger, more mechanistic, and more decentralized. It also becomes more specialized and devotes more attention to planning. Finally, coordination demands increase, formalization increases, organizational units become geographically more dispersed, and control systems become more extensive. Thus, an organization's size and design are clearly linked—and this link is dynamic because of the organizational life cycle.[34]

BASIC FORMS OF ORGANIZATION DESIGN

Because so many factors can influence organization design, it should come as no surprise that organizations adopt many different kinds of designs. Most designs, however, fall into one of four basic categories. Others are hybrids based on two or more of the basic forms.

Functional (U-Form) Design

The **functional design** is an arrangement based on the functional approach to departmentalization. This design has been termed the **U-form** (for unitary) by the noted economist Oliver E. Williamson.[35] Under this U-form arrangement, the members and units in the organization are grouped into functional departments such as marketing and production. For the organization to operate efficiently in this design, there must be considerable coordination across departments. This integration and coordination are most commonly the responsibility of the CEO and members of senior management. The WD–40 Company, which makes a popular lubricating oil, and the McIlhenny Company, which makes tabasco sauce, are both examples of firms that use the U-form design.

- **functional design (U-form)**
An organization design based on the functional approach to departmentalization

In general, this approach shares the basic advantages and disadvantages of functional departmentalization. Thus, it allows the organization to staff key positions with functional experts and facilitates coordination and integration. On the other hand, it also promotes a functional focus and tends to promote centralization. Functionally-based designs are most commonly used in small organizations because it is fairly easy for an individual CEO to oversee and coordinate the entire organization. As an organization grows, the CEO finds it increasingly difficult to stay on top of all functional areas.

Conglomerate (H-Form) Design

Another common form of organization design is the conglomerate, or **H-form**, approach.[36] The **conglomerate design** is used by an organization made up of a set of unrelated businesses. Thus the H-form design is essentially a holding company that results from unrelated diversification. (The "H" in this term stands for holding.) This approach is based loosely on the product form of departmentalization. Each business or set of businesses is operated by a general manager who is responsible for its profits or losses, and each general manager functions independently of the others. Pearson PLC, a British firm, uses the H-form design. As illustrated in Figure 6.2, Pearson consists of six business groups. Although its periodicals and publishing operations are related to one another, all its other businesses are clearly unrelated. Other firms that use the H-form design include General Electric (aircraft engines, appliances, broadcasting, financial services, lighting products, plastics) and Tenneco (pipelines, auto parts, shipbuilding, financial services).

- **conglomerate design (H-form)**
An organization design used by an organization composed of a set of unrelated businesses

In an H-form organization, a corporate staff usually evaluates the performance of each business, allocates corporate resources across companies, and shapes decisions about buying and selling businesses. The basic shortcoming of the H-form design is the complexity associated with holding diverse and unrelated businesses. Managers usually find it difficult to compare and integrate activities across a large number of diverse operations. Research suggests that many organizations that follow this approach achieve only average-to-weak financial performance.[37] Thus, although some U.S. firms are still using the H-form design, many have abandoned it for other approaches.

FIGURE 6.2 Conglomerate (H-Form) Design at Pearson PLC

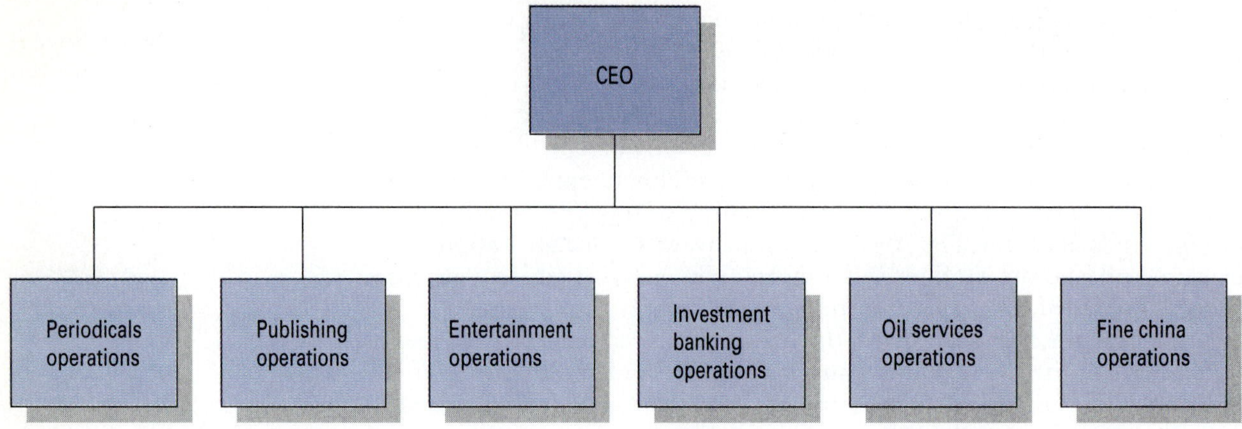

Pearson PLC, a British firm, uses the conglomerate form of organization design. This design, which results from a strategy of unrelated diversification, is a complex one to manage. Managers find that comparing and integrating activities among the dissimilar operations are difficult. Companies may abandon this design for another approach, such as the M-form design.

Divisional (M-Form) Design

In the divisional design, which is becoming increasingly popular, a product form of organization is also used. But, in contrast to the H-form, the divisions are related. Thus the **divisional design**, or **M-form** (for multidivisional), is based on multiple businesses in related areas operating within a larger organizational framework. Some activities are extremely decentralized down to the divisional level; others are centralized at the corporate level.[38] For example, as shown in Figure 6.3, The Limited uses the M-form approach. Each of its divisions is headed by a general manager and operates with reasonable autonomy, but the divisions also coordinate their activities as is appropriate. Other firms that use this approach are Disney (theme parks, movies, and merchandising units, all interrelated) and Hewlett-Packard (computers, printers, scanners, and other electronic instrumentation).

- **divisional design (M-form)** An organization design in which multiple businesses in related areas operate within a large organizational framework based on the product approach to departmentalization

The opportunities for coordination and shared resources represent one of the biggest advantages of the M-form design. The Limited's marketing research and purchasing departments are centralized. Thus a buyer can inspect a manufacturer's entire product line and buy some designs for The Limited chain, others for The Limited Express, and still others for Lerner. The M-form design's basic objective is to optimize internal competition and cooperation. Healthy competition among divisions for resources can enhance effectiveness, but cooperation should also be promoted. Research suggests that the M-form organization that can achieve and maintain this balance will outperform large U-form and all H-form organizations.[39]

Matrix Design

- **matrix design** An organization design wherein a product-based form of departmentalization is superimposed onto an existing functional arrangement

The **matrix design**, another common approach to organization design, is based on two overlapping bases of departmentalization.[40] The foundation of a matrix is a set of functional departments. A set of product groups, or temporary departments, is then superimposed across the functional de-

FIGURE 6.3 Multidivisional (M-Form) Design at The Limited, Inc.

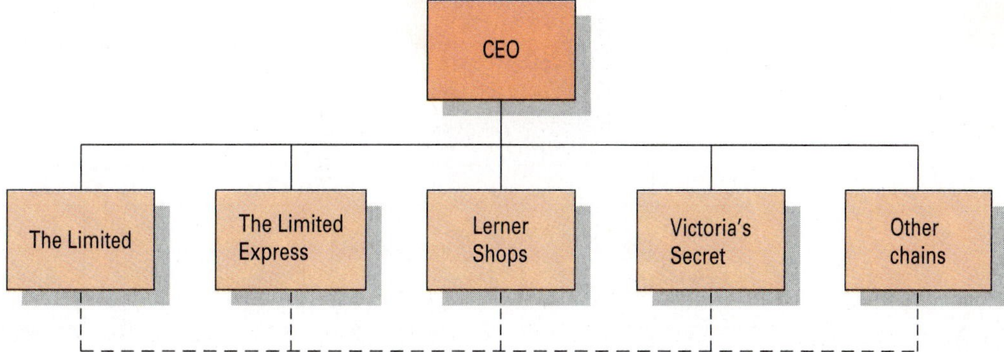

partments. Employees in a matrix are simultaneously members of a functional department (e.g., engineering) and of a project team.

Figure 6.4 shows a basic matrix design. At the top of the organization are functional units headed by vice presidents of engineering, production, finance, and marketing. Each of these managers has several subordinates. Along the side of the organization are a number of positions termed **project manager**. Each project manager heads a project group composed of representatives or workers from the functional departments. Note from the figure that a matrix reflects a **multiple-command structure**—any given individual may report both to a functional superior and to one or more project managers.

The project groups, or teams, are assigned to designated projects or programs. For example, the company might be developing a new product. Representatives are chosen from each functional area to work as a team on the new product. They also retain membership in the original functional group. At any given time, a person may be a member of several teams as well as a member of a functional group. Ford used this approach in creating its popular Taurus automobile. It formed a group called "Team Taurus" made up of designers, engineers, production specialists, marketing specialists, and other experts from different areas of the company. This group facilitated getting a very successful product to the market at least a year earlier than would have been possible using Ford's previous approaches. More recently, the firm used the same approach to create the newest version of the Mustang.

Both advantages and disadvantages are associated with the matrix design. Six primary advantages of the matrix design have been observed. First, it enhances flexibility because teams can be created, redefined, and dissolved as needed. Second, because they assume a major role in decision making, team members are likely to be highly motivated and committed to the organization. Third, employees in a matrix organization have considerable opportunity to learn new skills. A fourth advantage of a matrix design is that it provides an efficient way for the organization to take full advantage of its human resources. Fifth, team members retain membership

The Limited, Inc., uses the multidivisional approach to organization design. Although each of its units operates with relative autonomy, the all function in the same general market. This design resulted from a strategy of related diversification. Other firms that use M-form designs include PepsiCo and Woolworth Corporation.

project manager The head of a project group composed of members from functional departments

multiple-command structure A structure in which an individual reports simultaneously to both a functional superior and one or more project managers

FIGURE 6.4 A Matrix Organization

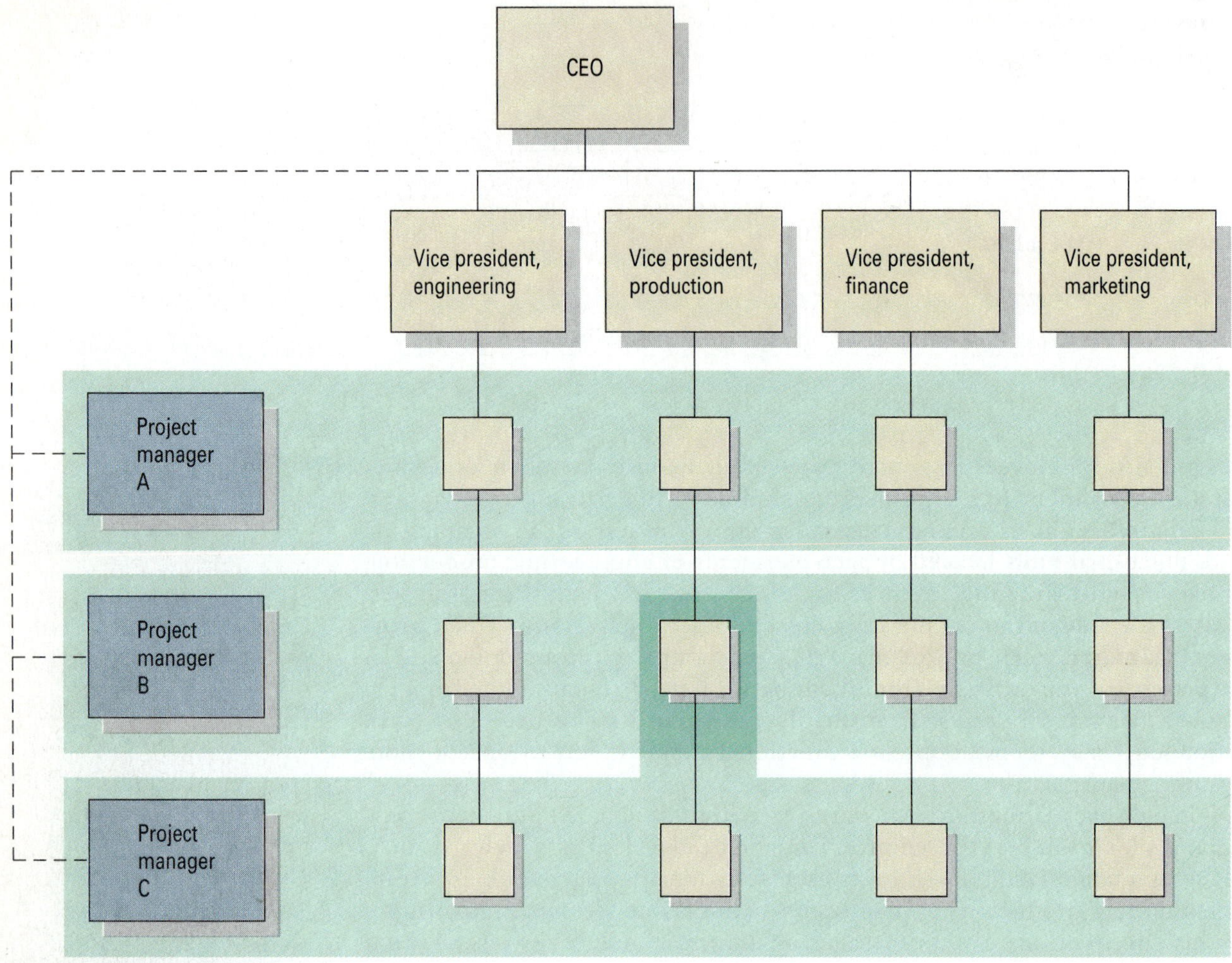

A matrix organization design is created by superimposing a product form of departmentalization onto an existing functional organization. Project managers coordinate teams of employees drawn from different functional departments. Thus a matrix relies on a multiple-command structure.

in their functional unit so they can serve as a bridge between the functional unit and the team, enhancing cooperation. Sixth, the matrix design gives top management a useful vehicle for decentralization. Once the day-to-day operations have been delegated, top management can devote more attention to areas such as long-range planning.

On the other hand, the matrix design also has some major disadvantages. Employees may be uncertain about reporting relationships, especially if they are simultaneously assigned to a functional manager and to several project managers. To complicate matters, some managers see the matrix as a form of anarchy in which they have unlimited freedom. Another set of problems is associated with the dynamics of group behavior. Groups take longer than individuals to make decisions, may be dominated by one individual, and may compromise too much. They may also get bogged down in discussion and not focus on their primary objectives. Finally, in a matrix more time may also be required for coordinating task-related activities.[41]

Hybrid Designs

Some organizations use a design that represents a hybrid of two or more of the common forms of organization design. For example, an organization may have five related divisions and one unrelated division, making its design a cross between an M-form and an H-form. Indeed, few companies use a design in its pure form: Most firms have one basic organization design as a foundation to managing the business but maintain sufficient flexibility so that temporary or permanent modifications can be made for strategic purposes. Ford, for example, used the matrix approach to design the Taurus and the Mustang, but the company is basically a U-form organization showing signs of moving to an M-form design. As noted earlier, any combination of factors may dictate the appropriate form of design for any particular company.

SUMMARY OF KEY POINTS

Organization structure and design are determined by five basic elements. These elements are job specialization, departmentalization, reporting relationships, authority, and coordination.

One early universal model of organization design was the bureaucratic model. This model was based on the need for rational and logical rules, regulations, and procedures.

The situational view of organization design is based on the assumption that the optimal organization design is a function of situational factors. Four important situational factors are technology, environment, size, and organizational life cycle. Each of these factors plays a role in determining how an organization should be designed.

Many organizations today adopt one of four basic organization designs: functional (U-form), conglomerate (H-form), divisional (M-form), or matrix. Other organizations use a hybrid design derived from two or more of these basic designs.

QUESTIONS FOR REVIEW

1. What is job specialization? What are its advantages and disadvantages?
2. What is meant by departmentalization? Why and how is departmentalization carried out?
3. Describe the bureaucratic model of organization design. What are its advantages and disadvantages?
4. What are the basic situational factors that affect an organization's design?
5. Describe the basic forms of organization design. Outline the advantages and disadvantages of each.

QUESTIONS FOR ANALYSIS

1. It is easy to see how specialization can be utilized in manufacturing organizations. How can it be used by other types of organizations such as hospitals, churches, schools, and restaurants? Should those organizations use specialization? Why or why not?
2. Try to develop a different way to departmentalize your college or university, a local fast-food restaurant, a manufacturing firm, or some other organization. What might be the advantages of your form of organization?
3. Can bureaucratic organizations avoid the problems usually associated with bureaucracies? If so, how? If not, why not? Do you think bureaucracies are still necessary? Why or why not? Would it be possible to retain the desirable aspects of bureaucracy and eliminate the undesirable ones? Why or why not?

4. The matrix organization design is complex and difficult to implement successfully. Why then do so many organizations use it?
5. Identify common and unique problems in organization design confronted by international businesses when compared with domestic businesses.

CASE STUDY

Xerox Is No Copy

Xerox Corp. traces its origins to the Haloid Company of Rochester, New York, which began in 1906 to make and sell photographic paper. In 1935 Haloid acquired a photocopier company, Rectigraph. Then in 1947 it acquired the license to a new dry copying process known as electrophotography. At Haloid's request, an Ohio State University Greek scholar came up with the name, xerography, that is used today.

The Haloid company learned early to adapt its organization to meet changing conditions. In 1949 the first copier using the xerographic process was introduced. In 1955 Haloid introduced the Copyflo copier, which became very successful. By 1956 xerographic copiers accounted for nearly half of Haloid's revenues so it reorganized around that product line and changed its name to Haloid Xerox in 1958. Haloid was dropped from the name in 1961.

Xerox began a series of acquisitions during the 1970s, adding printers, plotters, and disk drives. At that same time, however, its core copier business suffered from intense competition from Sharp at the low end and IBM and Eastman Kodak Company at the middle range. In the 1980s it added optical character recognition, scanning, faxing, desktop publishing, and financial services (insurance and investment banking). The organization, however, was becoming cumbersome; to refocus on its core businesses, Xerox sold the insurance and investment banking businesses in the early 1990s.

Xerox reorganized document processing in the early 1990s into three geographical customer units—Desktop Document Systems, Office Document Products, and Personal Document Products—and nine business divisions. These were smaller and more responsive divisions organized around products and customers. Previously it had been organized into huge divisions centered on sales, marketing, manufacturing, service, and engineering.

Downsizing and cost cutting coupled with new products helped Xerox cope with the expenses associated with getting into and out of the financial services business. DocuTech was one of the more innovative and successful new products. It could scan, copy, print, and even collate, bind, and staple small booklets. Coupled with DocuCM (document capturing machine) and DocuSP (document software), printable information from any kind of operating system can be moved, manipulated, and printed, including text, charts, and pictures.

Those new products are developed by microenterprise units—multidisciplinary teams that work in a single process instead of more traditional vertical functions. This approach, known as horizontal organization, is becoming widely used in manufacturing organizations. Xerox and other companies moving toward the horizontal organization employ seven essential elements: (1) the organization is built around processes rather than functions; (2) few levels of management are above the process; (3) multidisciplinary teams are used in the process; (4) customer satisfaction is the driving force for assessing performance; (5) team performance as well as individual performance is rewarded; (6) team members regularly meet with customers and suppliers; and (7) all team members are trained and information is made readily available to them.

If the horizontal organization is a break with the past, so, for Xerox, is working with other companies. Xerox has or is developing partnerships with Sun Microsystems, Novell, Microsoft, and Lotus to bring technology to the market faster. Clearly Xerox is more willing to change than it was twenty years ago.

Case Questions

1. Describe the organization design of Xerox. How does it seem to fit its environment? In what ways does it not seem to fit its environment?
2. What are the advantages and disadvantages to the horizontal organization that Xerox is beginning to adopt? Which are more pertinent to Xerox? Why?
3. Contrast Xerox's new design with the bureaucratic model.

References: "Back in Focus," *Forbes,* June 6, 1994, pp. 72–76; "The Horizontal Corporation," *Business Week,* December 20, 1993, pp. 76–81; and "Can Xerox Duplicate Its Glory Days?" *Business Week,* October 4, 1993, pp. 56–57.

SKILLS • DEVELOPMENT • PORTFOLIO

BUILDING EFFECTIVE TIME-MANAGEMENT SKILLS

Exercise Overview

Time-management skills refer to the manager's ability to prioritize work, to work efficiently, and to delegate appropriately. As noted in this chapter, various situational factors affect the appropriate span of management that is optimal for a particular situation. This exercise relates time-management issues with the appropriate span of management.

Exercise Background

A number of different factors affect the appropriate span of management for a particular situation. The factors that are most often associated with span of management include the following:

1. The competence of the manager and subordinates
2. The physical dispersion of the workstations of subordinates
3. The amount of nonsupervisory responsibilities in the manager's job
4. The degree of required interaction between the manager and subordinates
5. The extent of standardized procedures built into the jobs of subordinates
6. The similarity of the tasks being supervised
7. The frequency with which new job-related questions and problems arise
8. The preferences of the manager and subordinates

For example, if both the manager and his subordinates are all highly competent, it follows logically that the manager can assume responsibility for a greater number of subordinates than would be the case if the competence of the manager or the subordinates was somewhat lower. In general, then, a less-than-optimal span of management is likely to result in an inefficient use of time. If the span is too narrow, the manager may have too little work to do, but if the span is too wide, the manager's other work may get neglected.

Exercise Task

1. Determine the effects of each situational factor noted above on the span of management.
2. Describe how a span inappropriately matched with each factor will result in inefficiencies for both managers and subordinates.
3. If situational factors and the existing span of management are inappropriately matched, it might be possible to change one or the other to achieve a better fit. Examine each factor and decide whether it would be easier to change the factor or the span of management to improve fit.
4. Assume that you are a manager. Assess the relative importance that you would place on each situational factor to define your own span of management.

BUILDING EFFECTIVE CONCEPTUAL SKILLS

Exercise Overview

Conceptual skills are a manager's ability to think in the abstract. This exercise will encourage you to apply your conceptual skills to the concepts associated with the situational influences on organization design.

Exercise Background

As noted in this chapter, several factors affect the appropriate design of an organization. The key factors discussed in the text are core technology, the organization's environment, its size, and its life cycle. The chapter does not provide detail, however, as to how the situational factors working together in different combinations might affect organization design. For example, how might a particular form of technology and certain environmental forces together influence organization design?

The text also notes several basic forms of organization design, such as the functional, conglomerate, divisional, and matrix approaches. Relationships between situational factors and organization design are also shown.

Exercise Task

With these ideas in mind, do the following:

1. Identify four firms that each use a different basic form of organization design. Assess the technology, environment, size, and life cycle of each the four firms.

2. Relate each situational factor to the design used by each firm.

3. Form an opinion as to the actual relationship between each factor and the design used by each firm. That is, do you think that each firm's design is directly determined by its environment, or is the relationship you observe coincidental?

4. Can you prioritize the relative importance of the situational factors across the firms? Does the rank-order importance of the factors vary in any systematic way?

YOU MAKE THE CALL

Within a few months of taking over The Arbor, Cynthia Spenser realized that this was indeed a full-time job. Even though she had an assistant manager to help run the retail nursery operation of Sunset Landscape Services, she felt that she really had no time at all to devote to SLS. To compound the problem, Mark was also having difficulty running SLS's other two operations, landscape services and the lawn-care business, by himself.

Thus, the Spensers decided to expand their organization and create a more distinct and formal organization design. The assistant manager of the retail nursery operation, Susan Turner, was promoted to manager of the business. Mark also promoted the senior and most reliable crew chief from his lawn-care services business, Manuel Hernandez, to manager of that operation. Mark would continue to run the landscape operation, as well as the overall business itself. Susan and Manuel would each report directly to Mark. Cynthia, meanwhile, would devote all of her time and attention to The Arbor.

Susan's total staff consists of six full-time and ten part-time employees. Manuel's staff consists of four lawn crews, each of which is composed of a crew chief and three team members. The landscape operation consists of Mark, an assistant designer, and three installation employees.

Thus, the new organization looks like this:

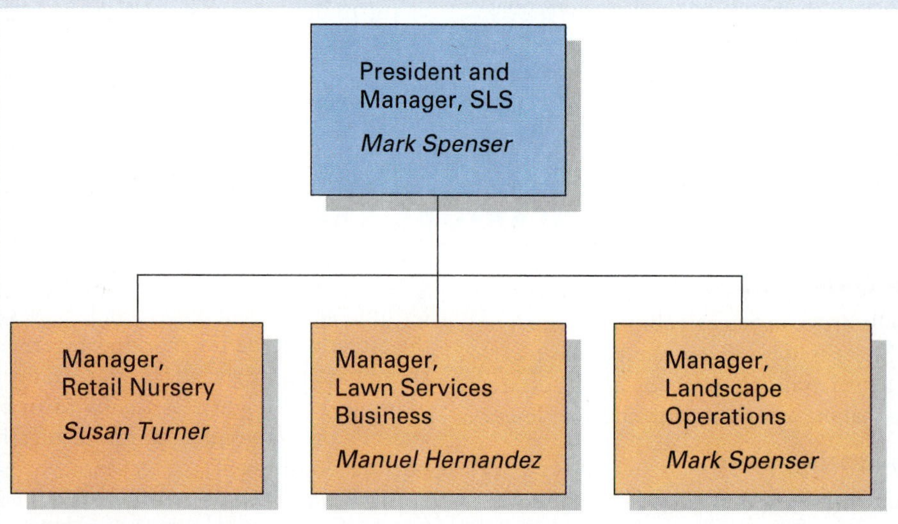

Discussion Questions

1. Characterize SLS in terms of the major dimensions of organization structure.
2. What form of organization design is SLS using?
3. Can you anticipate any problems or weaknesses in the organization design?

SKILLS SELF-ASSESSMENT INSTRUMENT

How Is Your Organization Managed?

Introduction: Organizing is an important function of management. The following assessment helps you define how an organization you are familiar with is organized. With this information, you can determine if this organization's design is consistent with the environmental forces it is facing.

Instructions: For this questionnaire, focus on either an organization for which you are currently working or one for which you have worked in the past. This organization could be a club, sorority or fraternity, or the university you are attending. Please circle the response on the scale indicating the degree to which you agree or disagree with each statement. There is no right or wrong answer. Respond on the following scale to how you see your organization being managed:

Strongly Agree (SA)	Agree (A)	Don't Know (DK)	Disagree (D)	Strongly Disagree (SD)

1. If people believe that they have the right approach to carrying out their job, they can usually go ahead without checking with their superior.	SA	A	DK	D	SD
2. People in this organization don't always have to wait for orders from their superior on important matters.	SA	A	DK	D	SD
3. People in this organization share ideas with their superior.	SA	A	DK	D	SD
4. Different individuals play important roles in making decisions.	SA	A	DK	D	SD
5. People in this organization are likely to express their feelings openly on important matters.	SA	A	DK	D	SD
6. People in this organization are encouraged to speak their minds on important matters, even if it means disagreeing with their superior.	SA	A	DK	D	SD
7. Talking to other people about the problems someone might have in making decisions is an important part of the decision-making process.	SA	A	DK	D	SD
8. Developing employees' talents and abilities is a major concern of this organization.	SA	A	DK	D	SD
9. People are encouraged to make suggestions before decisions are made.	SA	A	DK	D	SD
10. In this organization, most people can have their point of view heard.	SA	A	DK	D	SD
11. Superiors often seek advice from their subordinates before decisions are made.	SA	A	DK	D	SD
12. Subordinates play an active role in running this organization.	SA	A	DK	D	SD
13. For many decisions, the rules and regulations are developed as we go along.	SA	A	DK	D	SD
14. It is not always necessary to go through channels in dealing with important matters.	SA	A	DK	D	SD
15. The same rules and regulations are not consistently followed by employees.	SA	A	DK	D	SD
16. There are few rules and regulations for handling any kind of problem that may arise in making most decisions.	SA	A	DK	D	SD

	Strongly Agree (SA)	Agree (A)	Don't Know (DK)	Disagree (D)	Strongly Disagree (SD)

17. People from different departments are often put together in task forces to solve important problems. **SA A DK D SD**

18. For special problems, we usually set up a temporary task force until we meet our objectives. **SA A DK D SD**

19. Jobs in this organization are not clearly defined. **SA A DK D SD**

20. In this organization, adapting to changes in the environment is important. **SA A DK D SD**

Copy your responses to the following table and then total each column at the bottom. Now add across the "Total Score" row to get an overall score in the lower right-hand corner.

Question	Strongly Agree (SA)		Agree (A)		Don't Know (DK)		Disagree (D)		Strongly Disagree (SD)		
1.	5		4		3		2		1		
2.	5		4		3		2		1		
3.	5		4		3		2		1		
4.	5		4		3		2		1		
5.	5		4		3		2		1		
6.	5		4		3		2		1		
7.	5		4		3		2		1		
8.	5		4		3		2		1		
9.	5		4		3		2		1		
10.	5		4		3		2		1		
11.	5		4		3		2		1		
12.	5		4		3		2		1		
13.	5		4		3		2		1		
14.	5		4		3		2		1		
15.	5		4		3		2		1		
16.	5		4		3		2		1		
17.	5		4		3		2		1		
18.	5		4		3		2		1		
19.	5		4		3		2		1		
20.	5		4		3		2		1		
Total Score:	___	+	___	+	___	+	___	+	___	=	___

For interpretation, turn to page 447.

Source: From *Type of Management System* by Robert T. Keller. Copyright © 1988. Used by permission of the author.

EXPERIENTIAL EXERCISE

Designing a New Organization

Purpose: The purpose of this exercise is to give you insights into some of the management processes and issues associated with questions of organization design.

Introduction: You have decided to open a casual sportswear business in your local community. Your products will be athletic caps, shirts, shorts, and sweats emblazoned with the logos of the local college and high schools. You are a talented designer, and you have developed some ideas that will make your products unique and very popular. You also have inherited enough money to get your business up and running and to cover about one year of living expenses (i.e., you do not need to pay yourself a salary).

You intend to buy sportswear in various sizes and styles from other suppliers. Your firm will then use silkscreen processes to add the logos and other decorative touches to the products. Local clothing store owners have seen samples of your products and have expressed a keen interest in selling them. You know, however, that you will still need to service accounts and keep your customers happy.

At the present time, you are trying to determine how many people you need to get your business going, and how to most effectively group them into an organization. You realize that you can start out quite small, and then expand as sales warrant. But you worry that, if you are continually adding people and rearranging your organization, confusion and inefficiency will result.

Instructions:

Step One: For each of the following three scenarios, decide how to best design your organization. Sketch a basic organization chart to show your thoughts.

Scenario 1: You will sell the products yourself, and you intend to start with a workforce of five people.

Scenario 2: You will oversee production yourself, and you intend to start with a workforce of nine people.

Scenario 3: You do not intend to handle any one function yourself but will instead oversee the entire operation, and you intend to start with a workforce of fifteen people.

Step Two: Form small groups of four to five people each. Compare your various organization charts, focusing on similarities and differences.

Step Three: Working in the same group, assume that five years have passed and your business has become a big success. You have a large plant for making your products, and you are shipping them to fifteen states. You employ almost five hundred people. Create an organization design that you think best fits this organization.

Follow-Up Questions

1. How clear or ambiguous were the decisions about organization design?

2. What are your thoughts about starting out large to maintain stability as opposed to starting small and then growing?

3. What basic factors did you consider in choosing a design for your organization?

CHAPTER NOTES

1. Susan Caminiti, "Can The Limited Fix Itself?" *Fortune,* October 17, 1994, pp. 161–172; "Did Leslie Wexner Take His Eye Off the Ball?" *Business Week,* May 24, 1993, pp. 104–108; Gary Hoover, Alta Campbell, and Patrick J. Spain (Eds.), *Hoover's Handbook of American Business 1995* (Austin, Tex.: The Reference Press, 1994), pp. 690–691; and "The Limited: All Grown Up with Nowhere to Go?" *Business Week,* December 20, 1993, p. 44.
2. Ricky W. Griffin and Gary McMahan, "Motivation Through Job Design," in Jerald Greenberg, *Organizational Behavior: The State of the Science* (Hillsdale, N.J.: Lawrence Erlbaum Associates, 1995), pp. 23–44.
3. Ricky W. Griffin, *Task Design* (Glenview, Ill.: Scott, Foresman, 1982).
4. M. D. Kilbridge, "Reduced Costs Through Job Enlargement: A Case," *Journal of Business,* Vol. 33, 1960, pp. 357–362.

5. Griffin and McMahan, "Motivation Through Job Design."

6. Kilbridge, "Reduced Costs Through Job Enlargement: A Case."

7. Frederick Herzberg, *Work and the Nature of Man* (Cleveland: World Press, 1966).

8. J. Richard Hackman and Greg R. Oldham, *Work Redesign* (Reading, Mass.: Addison-Wesley, 1980).

9. For recent analyses of job design issues, see Ricky W. Griffin, "A Long-Term Investigation of the Effects of Work Redesign on Employee Perceptions, Attitudes, and Behaviors," *Academy of Management Journal,* June 1991, pp. 425–435; and Michael A. Campion, "Interdisciplinary Approaches to Job Design: A Constructive Replication with Extensions," *Journal of Applied Psychology,* August 1988, pp. 467–481.

10. Richard L. Daft, *Organization Theory and Design,* 5th ed. (St. Paul, Minn.: West, 1995).

11. Daniel Twomey, Frederick C. Scherr, and Walter S. Hunt, "Configuration of a Functional Department: A Study of Contextual and Structural Variables," *Journal of Organizational Behavior,* Vol. 9, 1988, pp. 61–75.

12. David Van Fleet, "Span of Management Research and Issues," *Academy of Management Journal,* September 1983, pp. 546–552.

13. James C. Worthy, "Factors Influencing Employee Morale," *Harvard Business Review,* January 1950, pp. 61–73.

14. Dan R. Dalton, William D. Todor, Michael J. Spendolini, Gordon J. Fielding, and Lyman W. Porter, "Organization Structure and Performance: A Critical Review," *Academy of Management Review,* January 1980, pp. 49–64.

15. Brian Dumaine, "The Bureaucracy Busters," *Fortune,* June 17, 1991, pp. 36–50.

16. Daft, *Organization Theory and Design.*

17. William Kahn and Kathy Kram, "Authority at Work: Internal Models and Their Organizational Consequences," *Academy of Management Review,* Vol. 19, No. 1, 1994, pp. 17–50.

18. Carrie R. Leana, "Predictors and Consequences of Delegation," *Academy of Management Journal,* December 1986, pp. 754–774.

19. Daft, *Organization Theory and Design.* See also John Meyer, W. Richard Scott, and David Strang, "Centralization, Fragmentation, and School District Complexity," *Administrative Science Quarterly,* June 1987, pp. 186–201.

20. "Toppling the Pyramids," *Canadian Business,* May 1993, pp. 61–65.

21. James Thompson, *Organizations in Action* (New York: McGraw-Hill, 1967). For a recent discussion, see Bart Victor and Richard S. Blackburn, "Interdependence: An Alternative Conceptualization," *Academy of Management Review,* July 1987, pp. 486–498.

22. Jay R. Galbraith, *Designing Complex Organizations* (Reading, Mass.: Addison-Wesley, 1973); and Jay R. Galbraith, *Organizational Design* (Reading, Mass.: Addison-Wesley, 1977).

23. Paul R. Lawrence and Jay W. Lorsch, "Differentiation and Integration in Complex Organizations," *Administrative Science Quarterly,* March 1967, pp. 1–47.

24. Max Weber, *Theory of Social and Economic Organizations,* trans. T. Parsons (New York: Free Press, 1947).

25. For detailed discussions of the strengths and weaknesses of the bureaucratic model, see James L. Perry and Hal G. Rainey, "The Public-Private Distinction in Organization Theory: A Critique and Research Strategy," *Academy of Management Review,* April 1988, pp. 182–201; and Thomas A. Leitko and David Szczerbacki, "Why Traditional OD Strategies Fail in Professional Bureaucracies," *Organizational Dynamics,* Winter 1987, pp. 52–65.

26. For descriptions of situational factors, see Robert K. Kazanjian and Robert Drazin, "Implementing Internal Diversification: Contingency Factors for Organization Design Choices," *Academy of Management Review,* April 1987, pp. 342–354; Allen Bluedorn, "Pilgrim's Progress: Trends and Convergence in Research on Organizational Size and Environments," *Journal of Management,* Summer 1993, pp. 163–191; and Gareth Jones, *Organization Theory* (Reading, Mass.: Addison-Wesley, 1995).

27. Joan Woodward, *Industrial Organization: Theory and Practice* (London: Oxford University Press, 1965).

28. Joan Woodward, *Management and Technology: Problems of Progress Industry,* No. 3 (London: Her Majesty's Stationery Office, 1958).

29. Tom Burns and G. M. Stalker, *The Management of Innovation* (London: Tavistock, 1961).

30. Paul R. Lawrence and Jay W. Lorsch, *Organization and Environment* (Homewood, Ill.: Irwin, 1967).

31. For detailed discussions of the environment–organization design relationship, see Masoud Yasai-Ardekani, "Structural Adaptations to Environments," *Academy of Management Review,* January 1986, pp. 9–21; Christine S. Koberg and Geraldo R. Ungson, "The Effects of Environmental Uncertainty and Dependence on Organizational Performance: A Comparative Study," *Journal of Management,* Winter 1987, pp. 725–737; and Barbara W. Keats and Michael A. Hitt, "A Causal Model of Linkages Among Environmental Dimensions, Macro Organizational Characteristics, and Performance," *Academy of Management Journal,* September 1988, pp. 570–598.

32. Derek S. Pugh and David J. Hickson, *Organization Structure in Its Context: The Aston Program I* (Lexington, Mass.: D.C. Heath, 1976).

33. Robert H. Miles and Associates, *The Organizational Life Cycle* (San Francisco: Jossey-Bass, 1980). See also "Is Your Company Too Big?" *Business Week,* March 27, 1989, pp. 84–94.

34. Douglas Baker and John Cullen, "Administrative Reorganization and Configurational Context: The Contingent Effects of Age, Size, and Change in Size," *Academy of Management Journal,* Vol. 36, No. 6, 1993, pp. 1251–1277.

35. Oliver E. Williamson, *Markets and Hierarchies* (New York: Free Press, 1975).

36. Ibid.

37. Michael E. Porter, "From Competitive Advantage to Corporate Strategy," *Harvard Business Review,* May–June 1987, pp. 43–59.

38. Williamson, *Markets and Hierarchies.*

39. Jay B. Barney and William G. Ouchi (Eds.), *Organizational Economics* (San Francisco: Jossey-Bass, 1986); and Robert E. Hoskisson, "Multidivisional Structure and Performance: The Contingency of Diversification Strategy," *Academy of Management Journal,* December 1987, pp. 625–644. See also Bruce Lamont, Robert Williams, and James Hoffman, "Performance During 'M-Form' Reorganization and Recovery Time: The Effects of Prior Strategy and Implementation Speed," *Academy of Management Journal,* Vol. 37, No. 1, 1994, pp. 153–166.

40. Stanley M. Davis and Paul R. Lawrence, *Matrix* (Reading, Mass.: Addison-Wesley, 1977).

41. See Lawton Burns and Douglas Wholey, "Adoption and Abandonment of Matrix Management Programs: Effects of Organizational Characteristics and Interorganizational Networks," *Academy of Management Journal,* Vol. 36, No. 1, 1993, pp. 106–138.

CHAPTER

7

Organization Change and Innovation

OBJECTIVES

After studying this chapter, you should be able to:

- *Describe the nature of organization change, including forces for change and planned versus reactive change.*
- *Discuss the steps in organization change, how to manage resistance to change, and major areas of organization change.*
- *Discuss the need for and approaches to organization reengineering.*
- *Discuss the assumptions, techniques, and effectiveness of organization development.*
- *Describe the innovation process, forms of innovation, the failure to innovate, and how organizations can promote innovation.*

OUTLINE

OPENING INCIDENT

A FEW YEARS ago Union Carbide was on the verge of going under. In 1984, the firm weathered the international tragedy at Bhopal, India—a leak at its chemical plant there resulted in the deaths of three thousand people and permanent injuries to fifty thousand more. Then, just a year later, Union Carbide sold its most valuable assets and took on a large debt burden to avoid a hostile takeover by GAF. As major competitors like Dow Chemical and Du Pont diversified out of chemicals, Union Carbide had all the appearances of a slowly sinking ship.

In December 1990, the firm's board of directors appointed Robert Kennedy CEO and charged him with turning things around. Kennedy, in turn, appointed William Joyce to the position of president. One of the first things Kennedy and Joyce did after coming on board was to alter the firm's strategy. They sold unrelated businesses and announced that the firm would concentrate on chemicals and plastics, industrial gases, and carbon products. To successfully implement this strategy, they dictated numerous other changes.

Kennedy and Joyce next changed the firm's organization design. The old structure at Union Carbide was bureaucratic, and work was heavily dependent on hierarchical rules, regulations, and procedures. They scrapped this design in favor of a more organic system that promotes flexibility and delegates decision making to lower levels. They also renewed Union Carbide's investment in technology, in part to keep pace with the industry and in part to lower costs. They automated many of the company's plants and invested heavily in new machinery and equipment. They also overhauled all the firm's administrative systems. Collectively, these measures cut the firm's overall costs almost 20 percent.

"Periodically, Bill Joyce [Union Carbide president] will call me up and say: 'Al, just calling to say hello and check up on you. How are we doing? I don't want to hear the good stuff. I want to hear what we can do better.'"

Next came perhaps the hardest change of all. Kennedy and Joyce realized that if the firm was to maintain its new-found competitiveness, its employees needed to become more customer-oriented and client-driven. Joyce himself set this change in motion by taking a personal interest in the firm's largest customers, frequently calling them himself. Employees also studied firms like Federal Express, L.L. Bean, and Wal-Mart, all renowned for being customer-oriented.

So far, the changes are working out. Union Carbide's sales are once again strong and its costs have dropped substantially. In addition, its employees have embraced the firm's new way of doing business. But Kennedy has warned everyone that the job is not finished. Indeed, he sees change as a way of life from now on.[1]

Source of Quotation: Alfred Dudley, chair of First Brands, Union Carbide's biggest customer, quoted in *Forbes*, March 14, 1994, p. 420.

Managers at Union Carbide have had to grapple with something all managers must eventually confront: the need for change. The firm's environment had changed, but the firm did not. Eventually, however, managers were forced to confront the need for change and to subsequently plan and implement major changes throughout every phase of the firm's business operations. As a result, disaster has been averted and Union Carbide now looks to the future with justifiable optimism.

Understanding when and how to implement change is a vital part of management. This chapter describes how organizations manage change. We first examine the nature of organization change and identify the basic issues of managing change. Next we look at reengineering, a major change program undertaken by many firms recently. We then examine organization development and conclude by discussing a related area, organizational innovation.

THE NATURE OF ORGANIZATION CHANGE

• **organization change** Any substantive modification to some part of the organization

Organization change is any substantive modification to some part of the organization.[2] Thus change can involve virtually any aspect of an organization: work schedules, bases for departmentalization, span of management, machinery, organization design, people themselves, and so on. It is important to keep in mind that any change in an organization may have effects extending beyond the actual area where the change is implemented. For example, when Westinghouse Electric Corp. installed a new computerized production system at one of its plants, employees had to be trained to operate new equipment, the compensation system had to be adjusted to reflect new skill levels, the span of management of supervisors had to be altered, and several related jobs had to be redesigned. Selection criteria for new employees also had to be changed and a new quality control system installed.[3]

Forces for Change

Why do organizations find it necessary to change? The basic reason is that something relevant to the organization either has changed or is going to change. Consequently, the organization has little choice but to change as well. Indeed, a primary reason for the problems that organizations often face is failure to anticipate or respond properly to changing circumstances. Forces for change may be external or internal to the organization.[4]

External Forces External forces for change derive from the organization's general environment. For example, two energy crises, a maturing Japanese automobile industry, floating currency exchange rates, and floating international interest rates have profoundly influenced U.S. automobile companies. New rules of production and competition have necessitated a dramatically altered way of doing business. In the political area, new laws, court decisions, and regulations affect organizations. The technological dimension may yield new production techniques that the organization needs

Organizations today must be prepared to continually confront change. New ways of doing business and new technologies, for example, are fundamentally reshaping how managers do their jobs. One of the most significant forces for change today is the Internet, a computerized information network that has the potential to link every PC in the world. Home pages such as this one provide points of entry and exit on the Internet and serve as conduits for users wanting to communicate with organizations.

to explore. The economic dimension is affected by inflation, the cost of living, and money supplies. The sociocultural dimension, reflecting societal values, determines what kinds of products or services will be accepted in the market.

The task environment is an even more powerful force for change. Competitors influence an organization through their price structures and product lines. When Compaq lowers the prices it charges for computers, Dell and IBM have little choice but to follow suit. Because customers determine product lines and price structures, organizations must be concerned with consumer tastes and preferences. Suppliers affect organizations by raising or lowering prices or changing product lines. Regulators can have dramatic effects on an organization. For example, if OSHA rules that a particular production process is dangerous to workers, it can force a firm to close a plant until higher safety standards are met.

Internal Forces A variety of forces inside the organization may also cause change. If top management revises the firm's strategy, organization change is likely to result. A decision by an electronics company to enter the home computer market or a decision to increase a ten-year product sales goal by 3 percent would occasion many organization changes. Other internal forces for change may be reflections of external forces. As sociocultural values shift, for example, workers' attitudes toward their jobs may also shift—and workers may demand a change in working hours or working conditions. In such a case, even though the force is rooted in the external environment, the organization must respond directly to the internal pressure it generates.

Planned Versus Reactive Change

• **planned change**
Change that is designed and implemented in an orderly and timely fashion in anticipation of future events

• **reactive change**
A piecemeal response to circumstances as they develop

Some change is planned well in advance; other change comes about as a reaction to unexpected events. **Planned change** is change that is designed and implemented in an orderly and timely fashion in anticipation of future events. **Reactive change** is a piecemeal response to events as they occur. Because reactive change may be hurried, the potential for poorly conceived and executed change is increased. Planned change is almost always preferable to reactive change.[5]

Southwestern Bell provides a classic example of how organizations can benefit from planned change. As a result of the deregulation of the telephone industry and the subsequent breakup of AT&T's regional telephone operations, Southwestern Bell had to adapt itself in order to function as an independent corporation. Top managers developed a comprehensive change plan consisting of two thousand major activities needing modification or replacement. The change progressed remarkably well, with only a few slip-ups along the way.[6]

Caterpillar Inc., on the other hand, is a good example of a firm guilty of reactive change. It was caught flat-footed by a worldwide recession in the construction industry, suffered enormous losses, and took several years to recover. Had managers at Caterpillar anticipated the need for change earlier, they might have been able to respond more quickly.

The importance of approaching change from a planned, as opposed to a reactive, perspective is reinforced by the frequency of organization change. Most companies or divisions of large companies implement some form of moderate change at least every year and one or more major changes every four to five years.[7] Managers who sit back and respond only when they have to are likely to spend a lot of time hastily changing and rechanging things. A more effective approach is to anticipate forces urging change and plan ahead to deal with them

MANAGING CHANGE IN ORGANIZATIONS

Organization change is a complex phenomenon. A manager is not a magician who, with the wave of a wand can implement a planned change. Rather, change must be approached systematically and logically to have a realistic opportunity to succeed. To accomplish this, the manager needs to understand the steps of effective change and how to deal with employee resistance to change.

Models of the Change Process

A number of models or frameworks outlining steps for change have been developed over the years. The Lewin model was one of the first, although a more comprehensive approach is usually more useful.

The Lewin Model Kurt Lewin, a noted organizational theorist, suggested that every change requires three steps.[8] The first step is *unfreezing*—individuals who will be affected by the impending change must be led to recognize why the change is necessary. Next the *change itself* is implemented. Finally, *refreezing* involves reinforcing and supporting the change so that it becomes a part of the system. For example, one of the changes Caterpillar faced in response to the recession involved a massive workforce reduction. The first step (unfreezing) was convincing the United Auto Workers to support the reduction because of its importance to long-term effectiveness. After this unfreezing was accomplished, thirty thousand jobs were eliminated (implementation). Then Caterpillar worked to improve its damaged relationship with its workers (refreezing) by guaranteeing future pay hikes and promising no more cutbacks. As interesting as Lewin's model is, it unfortunately lacks operational specificity. Thus, a more comprehensive perspective is often needed.

A Comprehensive Approach to Change The comprehensive approach to change takes a systems view and delineates a series of specific steps that often lead to more successful change. This expanded model is illustrated in Figure 7.1. The first step is recognizing the need for change. Reactive change might be triggered by employee complaints, court injunctions, declines in productivity or turnover, sales slumps, or labor strikes. Recognition may simply be managers' awareness that change in a certain area is inevitable. For example, managers may be aware of the general frequency of organizational change undertaken by most organizations in their

FIGURE 7.1 Steps in the Change Process

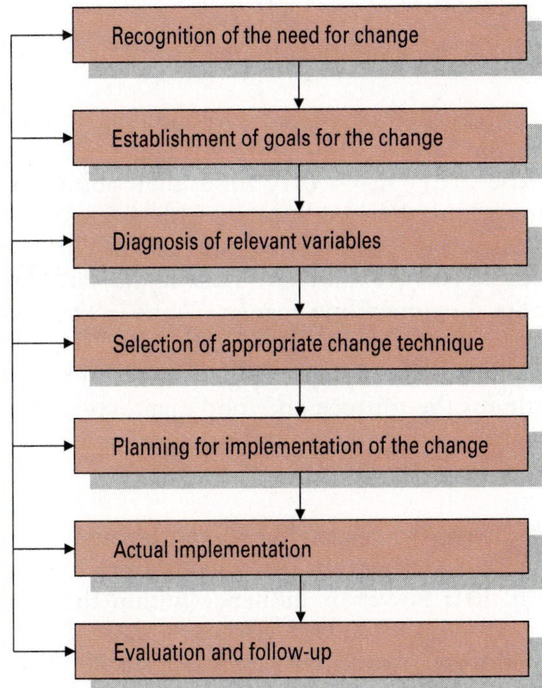

Managers must understand how and why to implement change. A manager who, when implementing change, follows a logical and orderly sequence such as the one shown here is more likely to succeed than is a manager whose change process is haphazard and poorly conceived.

industry and recognize that their organization should probably follow the same pattern. The immediate stimulus might be the result of a new market potential forecast, the accumulation of cash surplus for possible investment, or an opportunity to achieve and capitalize on a key technological breakthrough. Managers might also initiate change because indicators suggest that it will be necessary in the near future anyway.

Managers must then set goals for the change. To increase market share, to enter new markets, to restore employee morale, to settle a strike, to identify investment opportunities—all might be goals for change. Third, managers must diagnose the cause of the need for change. Turnover, for example, might be brought on by low pay, poor working conditions, poor supervisors, or employee dissatisfaction. Thus, although turnover may be the immediate stimulus for change, managers must understand its basic causes to make the right changes.

The next step is to select a change technique to accomplish the intended goals. If turnover is a result of low pay, a new reward system may be needed. If the cause is poor supervision, interpersonal skills training may be called for. (Various change techniques are summarized later in this chapter.) After the appropriate technique has been chosen, its implementation must be planned. Issues to consider include the costs of the change, its effects on other areas of the organization, and the degree of employee participation appropriate for each situation. If the change is implemented as planned, the results should then be evaluated. If the change was intended to reduce turnover, managers must check turnover after the change has been in effect for a while. If turnover is still too high, other changes may be necessary.[9]

Understanding Resistance to Change

Another element in the effective management of change is understanding the resistance that often greets change.[10]

Uncertainty Perhaps the biggest cause of employee resistance to change is uncertainty. In the face of impending change, employees may become anxious and nervous. They may worry about their ability to meet new job demands, they may think their job security is threatened, or they may simply dislike ambiguity. RJR Nabisco, Inc. was recently the target of an extended and confusing takeover battle, and during the entire time employees were nervous about the impending change. *The Wall Street Journal* described them this way: "Many are angry at their leaders and fearful for their jobs. They are swapping rumors and spinning scenarios for the ultimate outcome of the battle for the tobacco and food giant. Headquarters staffers in Atlanta know so little about what's happening in New York that some call their office 'the mushroom complex,' where they are kept in the dark."[11]

Threatened Self-Interests Many impending changes threaten the self-interests of some managers within the organization. A change might potentially diminish their power or influence within the company, so they fight it. Managers at Sears recently developed a plan calling for a new type of store. The new stores would be somewhat smaller than typical Sears stores and would not be located in large shopping malls. Instead, they would be located in smaller strip centers. They would carry clothes and other "soft goods" but not hardware, appliances, furniture, or automotive products. When executives in charge of the excluded product lines heard about the plan, they raised such strong objections that the entire idea was dropped.

Different Perceptions A third reason people resist change is different perceptions. A manager may make a decision and recommend a plan for change on the basis of her own assessment of a situation. Others in the organization may resist the change because they do not agree with the manager's assessment, or they perceive the situation differently. The recent baseball strike provides a good case-in-point. Baseball team owners argued that a salary cap was necessary to control costs, while the players, union believed that such a cap would only serve to lower salaries. As a result of these different perceptions, a lengthy strike occurred, which damaged the credibility of the game.

Feelings of Loss Many changes involve altering work arrangements in ways that disrupt existing social networks. Because social relationships are important, most people resist any change that might adversely affect those relationships. Other intangibles that are threatened by change include power, status, security, familiarity with existing procedures, and self-confidence. For example, Steven Jobs hired John Sculley to bring professional management to Apple. He later found that he did not like Sculley's changes and wanted things as they were before. His own status and self-confidence were being threatened. Jobs tried to oust Sculley, lost a power struggle with the board of directors, and then left himself.

Managing Resistance to Change

Of course, a manager should not give up in the face of resistance to change. Although there are no sure-fire cures, there are several techniques that have the potential to overcome resistance.[12]

Participation Participation is often the most effective technique for overcoming resistance to change. Employees who participate in planning and implementing a change are better able to understand the reasons for the change. Uncertainty is reduced and self-interests and social relationships are less threatened. Having had an opportunity to express their ideas and to assume the perspectives of others, employees are more likely to accept the change gracefully. A classic study of participation monitored the introduction of a change in production methods among four groups in a Virginia pajama factory.[13] The two groups that were allowed to fully participate in planning and implementing the change improved their productivity and satisfaction significantly, relative to the two groups that did not participate. 3M Company recently attributed $10 million in cost savings to employee participation in several organization change activities.[14]

Education and Communication Educating employees about the need for and the expected results of an impending change should reduce their resistance. If open communication is established and maintained during the change process, uncertainty can be minimized. Caterpillar used these methods during many of its cutbacks in order to reduce resistance. First, United Auto Workers (UAW) representatives were educated about the need for and potential value of the planned changes. Then all employees were told what was happening, when it would happen, and how it would affect them individually.

Facilitation Several facilitation procedures are also advisable. For instance, making only necessary changes, announcing those changes well in advance, and allowing time for people to adjust to new ways of doing things can help reduce resistance to change. One manager at a Prudential regional office spent several months systematically planning a change in work procedures and job design. He then became anxious to implement his plan, coming in over the weekend with a work crew and rearranging the office layout. When employees walked in on Monday morning, they were hostile, anxious, and resentful. What had been a promising change became a disaster and the manager was forced to scrap the entire plan.

Force-Field Analysis Although force-field analysis may sound like something from a *Star Trek* movie, it can help overcome resistance to change. In most change situations, there are forces acting for and forces acting against the change. To facilitate the change, managers should start by listing each set of forces and then trying to tip the balance so that the forces facilitating the change outweigh those hindering the change. It is especially important to attempt to remove, or at least minimize, some of the forces acting against the change. Suppose, for example, Chrysler is considering a plant closing as part of a change. As shown in Figure 7.2, three factors are reinforcing the change: Chrysler needs to cut costs, it has excess capacity, and the plant has outmoded production facilities. At the same time, there is resistance from the UAW, concern for workers being put out of their jobs, and a feeling that the plant might be needed again in the future. Chrysler might start by convincing the UAW that the closing is necessary by presenting profit and loss figures. It could then offer relocation and retraining to displaced workers. And it might shut down the plant and put it in "moth balls" so that it could be renovated later. The three major factors hindering the change are thus eliminated or reduced in importance.

A force-field analysis can help a manager facilitate change. A manager able to identify forces acting both for and against a change can see where to focus efforts to remove barriers to change (such as offering training and relocation to displaced workers). By removing the forces against the change, resistance can be at least partially overcome.

FIGURE 7.2 Force-Field Analysis for Plant Closing at Chrysler

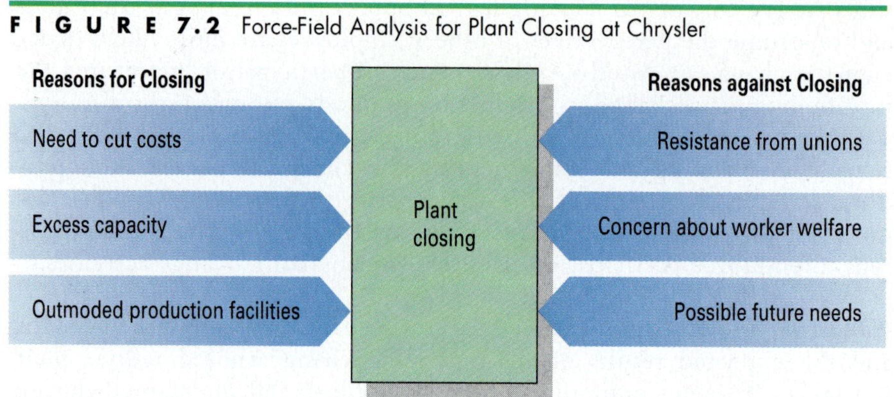

Areas of Organization Change

We note earlier that change can involve virtually any part of an organization. In general, however, most change interventions involve organizational structure and design, technology and operations, or people.

Changing Structure and Design Organization change might be focused on any of the basic components of organization structure or on the organization's overall design. Thus, the organization might change the way it designs its jobs or its bases of departmentalization. Likewise, it might change reporting relationships or the distribution of authority. Coordination mechanisms are also subject to change. On a larger scale, the organization might change its overall design. For example, a growing business could decide to drop its functional design and adopt a divisional design. Or it might transform itself into a matrix. Finally, the organization might change any part of its human resource management system, such as its selection criteria or its compensation package.[15]

Changing Technology and Operations Technology is the conversion process used by an organization to transform inputs into outputs. Technological changes are becoming increasingly important to many organizations. For example, a change in work processes or work activities may be necessary if new equipment is introduced or new products are manufactured. In manufacturing industries, the major reason for changing a work process is to accommodate a change in the materials used to produce a finished product. Work process changes may occur in service organizations as well as in manufacturing firms. As traditional barber shops and beauty parlors are replaced by hair salons catering to both sexes, for example, the hybrid organizations have to develop new methods for handling appointments and setting prices.

Technology is a major area of change for many organizations today. CSX, for example, is collaborating with Buffalo Coal Company in West Virginia to boost productivity for both businesses. CSX railcars are pulled up close to the mines, where Buffalo loads coal directly into them. Buffalo had to change how it transported coal to the surface, while CSX had to change how it distributed railcars. This new technology is helping both companies be more profitable.

A change in work sequence may or may not accompany a change in equipment or a change in work processes. Making a change in work sequence means altering the order or sequence of the workstations involved in a particular manufacturing process. One form of technological change that has been especially important in recent years is change in information systems. It is hard to find a major popular magazine that has not run an article on the computer invasion. Simultaneous advances in personal computers and network tie-in systems have created vast potential for change in most workplaces. The basic goal behind the adoption of computers in offices is the creation of an information-processing station for each employee. The person at each workstation may manipulate ideas and drafts that are still in preliminary form; create, store, and retrieve documents; and distribute final copies.

Changing People A third area of organization change deals with human resources. For example, an organization might decide to change the skill level of its workforce. This change might be prompted by changes in technology or by a general desire to upgrade the quality of the workforce. Thus training programs and new selection criteria might be needed. The organization might also decide to improve its workers' performance level. In this instance, a new incentive system or performance-based training might be in order.

Perceptions and expectations are also a common focus of organization change. Workers in an organization might feel that their wages and benefits are not as high as they should be. Management, however, might have evidence that shows the firm is paying a competitive wage and providing a superior benefit package. The change, then, would be centered on informing and educating the workforce about the comparative value of its compensation package. A common way to do this is to publish a statement that places an actual dollar value on each benefit provided and compares that amount to what other local organizations are providing their workers. Change might also be directed at employee attitudes and values. In many organizations today, managers are trying to eliminate adversarial relationships with workers and adopt a more collaborative relationship. In many ways, changing attitudes and values is perhaps the hardest thing to do.

REENGINEERING IN ORGANIZATIONS

Many organizations today are going through massive and comprehensive change programs involving all aspects of organization design, technology, and people. While various terms are sometimes used, the term currently in vogue for these changes is *reengineering*. Specifically, **reengineering** is the radical redesign of all aspects of a business to achieve major gains in cost, service, or time.[16]

● **reengineering**
The radical redesign of all aspects of a business to achieve major gains in cost, service, or time

The Need for Reengineering

Why are so many organizations finding it necessary to reengineer themselves? We noted in Chapter 1 that all systems, including organizations, are subject to entropy—a normal process leading to system decline. An organization is behaving most typically when it maintains the status quo, doesn't change in sync with its environment, and starts consuming its own resources to survive. In a sense, that is what IBM did. The firm's managers grew complacent assuming that IBM's historic prosperity would continue and that they need not worry about environmental shifts, foreign competition, and so forth—and entropy set in. The key is to recognize the initial decline and to immediately move toward reengineering. Major problems occur when managers either don't recognize the onset of entropy until it is well advanced or else are complacent in taking steps to correct it.

Approaches to Reengineering

The general steps in reengineering are shown in Figure 7.3. The first step is setting goals and developing a strategy for reengineering. The organization must know in advance what reengineering is designed to accomplish and how those accomplishments are intended to be achieved. Next, the reengineering effort must be started and directed by top managers. If a CEO simply announces that reengineering is to occur but does nothing else, the program is unlikely to be successful. But if the CEO is constantly involved in the process, underscoring its importance and taking the lead, reengineering stands a much better chance of success.

Most experts also agree that successful reengineering is usually accompanied by a sense of urgency. People in the organization must see the clear and present need for the changes being implemented and appreciate their importance. In addition, most successful reengineering efforts start with a

FIGURE 7.3 The Reengineering Process

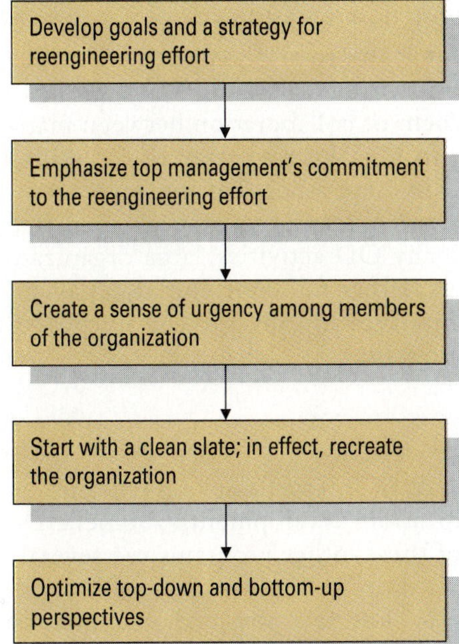

Reengineering is a major redesign of all areas of an organization. To be successful, reengineering requires a systematic and comprehensive assessment of the entire organization. Goals, top management support, and a sense of urgency help the organization re-create itself and blend both top-level and bottom-up perspectives.

new, clean slate. That is, rather than assuming the existing organization is a starting point and then trying to modify it, reengineering usually starts by asking how customers are best served and competitors best neutralized. New approaches and systems are then created and imposed in place of existing ones.

Finally, reengineering requires a careful blend of top-down and bottom-up involvement. On the one hand, strong leadership is necessary, but too much involvement by top management can make the changes seem autocratic. Similarly, employee participation is also important, but too little involvement by leaders can undermine the program's importance and create a sense that top managers don't care. Thus care must be taken to carefully balance these two countervailing forces.

ORGANIZATION DEVELOPMENT

We have noted in several places the importance of people and change. A special area of interest that focuses almost exclusively on people is organization development (OD).

OD Assumptions

• **organization development**
An effort that is planned—organization wide—and managed from the top, intended to increase organization effectiveness and health through planned interventions in the organization's process, using behavioral science knowledge

Organization development is concerned with changing attitudes, perceptions, behaviors, and expectations. More precisely, **organization development** can be defined as "an effort (1) *planned,* (2) *organization wide*, and (3) *managed* from the *top,* to (4) increase *organization effectiveness* and *health* through (5) *planned interventions* in the organization's 'process,' using *behavioral science* knowledge."[17] The theory and practice of OD are based on several very important assumptions. The first is that employees have a desire to grow and develop. Another is that employees have a strong need to be accepted by others within the organization. Still another critical assumption of OD is that the total organization and the way it is designed will influence the behavior of individuals and groups within the organization. Thus, some form of collaboration between managers and their employees is necessary to (1) take advantage of the skills and abilities of the employees and (2) eliminate aspects of the organization that hinder employee growth, development, and group acceptance. Because of the intense personal nature of many OD activities, large organizations rely on one or more OD consultants (either full-time employees assigned to this function or outside experts hired specifically for OD purposes) to implement and manage their OD program.

OD Techniques

There are several kinds of interventions or activities generally considered to be part of organization development.[18] Some OD programs may use only one or a few of these; other programs use several of them at once.

Diagnostic Activities Just as a physician examines patients to diagnose their current condition, an OD diagnosis analyzes the current condition of an organization. To carry out this diagnosis managers use questionnaires, opinion or attitude surveys, interviews, archival data, and meetings to assess various characteristics of the organization. The results from this diagnosis may generate profiles of organizational activities, which can then be used to identify problem areas in need of correction.

Team Building Team-building activities are intended to enhance the effectiveness and satisfaction of individuals who work in groups or teams and to promote overall group effectiveness. Project teams in a matrix organization are good candidates for these activities. An OD consultant might interview team members to determine how they feel about the group; then an off-site meeting could be held to discuss the issues that surfaced and to iron out any problem areas or member concerns. Caterpillar used team building as one method for changing the working relationships between workers and supervisors from confrontational to cooperative.[19]

Survey Feedback In survey feedback, each employee responds to a questionnaire intended to measure perceptions and attitudes (for example, satisfaction and supervisory style). The results of the survey are provided to everyone involved, including the supervisor. This approach usually leads to changing the behavior of supervisors by showing them how they are viewed by their subordinates. After the feedback has been provided, workshops may be conducted to evaluate results and suggest constructive changes.

Third-Party Peacemaking Another approach to OD is through third-party peacemaking. This is most often used when substantial conflict exists within the organization. Third-party peacemaking can be appropriate on the individual, group, or organization level. The third party, usually an OD consultant, uses a variety of mediation or negotiation techniques to resolve any problems or conflicts between individuals or groups.

Team building is an increasingly common organization development technique. These managers are participating in one popular method of team building. As they work together to scale this small cliff, the goal is for them to build trust and to learn how to more effectively work together.

Technostructural Activities Technostructural activities are concerned with the design of the organization, the technology of the organization, and the interrelationship of design and technology with people on the job. A structural change such as an increase in decentralization, a job design change such as an increase in the use of automation, and a technological change involving a modification in work flow would all qualify as technostructural OD activities if their objective is to improve group and interpersonal relationships within the organization.

Process Consultation In process consultation, an OD consultant observes groups in the organization to develop an understanding of their communication patterns, decision-making and leadership processes, and methods of cooperation and conflict resolution. The consultant then provides feedback to the involved parties about the processes he or she has observed. The goal of this form of intervention is to improve the observed processes. A leader who is presented with feedback outlining deficiencies in his or her leadership style, for example, might be expected to change to overcome them.

Coaching and Counseling Coaching and counseling provide nonevaluative feedback to individuals. The purpose is to help people develop a better sense of how others see them and to help people learn behaviors that will assist others in achieving their work-related goals. The focus is not on how the individual is performing today; instead, it is on how the person can perform better in the future.

Planning and Goal Setting More pragmatically oriented than many other interventions are activities designed to help managers improve their planning and goal setting. Emphasis still falls on the individual, however, because the intent is to help individuals and groups integrate themselves into the overall planning process. The OD consultant might use the same approach as in process consultation, but the focus is more technically oriented on the mechanics of planning and goal setting.

The Effectiveness of OD

Given the diversity of activities encompassed by organization development, it is not surprising that managers report mixed results from various OD interventions. Organizations that actively practice some form of OD include American Airlines, Texas Instruments, Procter & Gamble, ITT, Polaroid, and B.F. Goodrich. Goodrich, for example, has trained sixty individuals in OD processes and techniques. These trained experts have subsequently become internal OD consultants to assist other managers in applying the techniques.[20] Many other managers, in contrast, report that they have tried OD but discarded it.[21]

OD will probably remain an important part of management theory and practice. Of course, there are no sure things when dealing with social systems such as organizations, and the effectiveness of many OD techniques is difficult to evaluate. Because all organizations are open systems interacting with their environments, an improvement in an organization after an OD intervention may be attributable to the intervention, but it may also be attributable to changes in economic conditions, luck, or other factors.[22]

ORGANIZATIONAL INNOVATION

A final element of organization change that we address is innovation. **Innovation** is the managed effort of an organization to develop new products or services or new uses for existing products or services. Innovation is clearly important because without new products or services, any organization will lag behind its competition.

innovation
The managed effort of an organization to develop new products or services or new uses for existing products or services

The Innovation Process

The organizational innovation process consists of developing, applying, launching, growing, and managing the maturity and decline of creative ideas.[23] This process is depicted in Figure 7.4.

Innovation Development Innovation development involves the evaluation, modification, and improvement of creative ideas. Innovation development can transform a product or service with only modest potential into a product or service with significant potential. Parker Brothers, for example, decided during innovation development not to market an indoor volleyball game but instead to sell separately the small foam ball designed for the game. The firm will never know how well the volleyball game would have sold, but the Nerf ball and numerous related products have generated millions of dollars in revenues for Parker Brothers.[24]

FIGURE 7.4 The Innovation Process

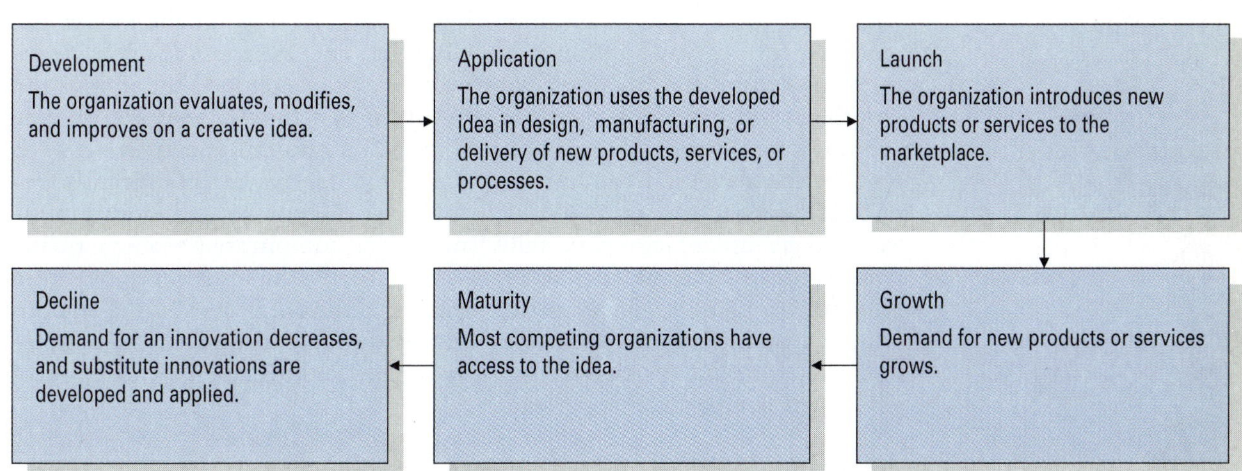

Innovation Application Innovation application is the stage in which an organization takes a developed idea and uses it in the design, manufacturing, or delivery of new products, services, or processes. At this point the innovation emerges from the laboratory and is transformed into tangible goods or services. One example of innovation application is the use of radar-based focusing systems in Polaroid's instant cameras. The idea of using radio waves to discover the location, speed, and direction of moving objects was first applied extensively by Allied forces during World War II. As radar technology developed over the following years, the electrical components needed became smaller and more streamlined. Researchers at Polaroid applied this well-developed technology in a new way.[25]

Application Launch Application launch is the stage in which an organization introduces new products or services to the marketplace. The key question is not "does the innovation work?" but "will customers want to purchase the innovative product or service?" History is full of creative ideas that did not generate enough interest among customers to become successful. Some notable innovation failures include Sony's seat warmer and the Edsel automobile.[26] Thus, despite development and application, it is still possible for new products and services to fail at the application launch phase.

Application Growth Once an innovation has been successfully launched, it then enters the stage of application growth. This is a period of high economic performance for an organization because there is often a greater demand for the product or service than supply. Organizations failing to anticipate this stage may unintentionally limit their growth, as Gillette did by not anticipating demand for its Sensor razor blades. At the same time, overestimating demand for a new product can be just as detrimental to performance. Unsold products can sit in warehouses for years.

Innovation Maturity After a period of growing demand, an innovative product or service often enters a period of maturity. Innovation maturity is the stage in which most organizations in an industry have access to an innovation and are applying it in approximately the same way. The technological application of an innovation during this stage of the innovation process can be very sophisticated. However, because most firms have access to the innovation, either because they have developed the innovation on their own or have copied the innovation of others, it does not provide competitive advantage to any one of them. The time that elapses between innovation development and innovation maturity varies significantly depending on the particular product or service. Whenever an innovation involves the use of complex skills (such as a complicated manufacturing process or highly sophisticated teamwork), it will take longer to move from the growth phase to the maturity phase. In addition, if the skills needed to implement these innovations are rare and difficult to imitate, then strategic imitation may be delayed and the organization may enjoy a period of sustained competitive advantage.

Innovation Decline Every successful innovation bears its own seeds of decline. Innovation decline is the stage during which demand for an innovation decreases and substitute innovations are developed and applied. Since an organization does not gain a competitive advantage from an innovation at maturity, it must encourage its creative scientists, engineers, and managers to begin looking for new innovations. It is this continued search for competitive advantage that usually leads new products and services to move from the creative process through innovation maturity, and finally to innovation decline.

Forms of Innovation

Each creative idea an organization develops poses a different challenge for the innovation process. Innovations can be radical or incremental, technical or managerial, and can involve products or processes.

Radical Versus Incremental Innovations **Radical innovations** are new products or technologies developed by an organization that completely replace the existing products or technologies in an industry. **Incremental innovations** are new products or processes that modify existing ones. Firms that implement radical innovations fundamentally shift the nature of competition and the interaction of firms within their environments. Firms that implement incremental innovations alter, but do not fundamentally change, competitive interaction in an industry.

● **radical innovations** New products, services, or technologies that replace existing ones

● **incremental innovations** New products, services, or technologies that modify existing ones

Many radical innovations have been introduced by organizations over the last several years. For example, compact disk technology has virtually replaced long-playing vinyl records in the recording industry, and high-definition television seems likely to replace regular television technology (both black-and-white and color) in the near future. Whereas radical innovations like these tend to be very visible and public, incremental innovations actually are more numerous. One example is Ford's sports utility vehicle, Explorer. While other companies had similar products, Ford's effective combination of styling and engineering resulted in increased demand for all sports utility vehicles.

Technical Versus Managerial Innovations **Technical innovations** are changes in the physical appearance or performance of a product or service, or the physical processes through which a product or service is manufactured. Many of the most important innovations over the last fifty years have been technical. For example, the serial replacement of the vacuum tube with the transistor, the transistor with the integrated circuit, and the integrated circuit with the microchip has greatly enhanced the power, ease of use, and speed of operation of a wide variety of electronic products.

● **technical innovations** Changes in appearance or performance of products or services or the physical processes through which a product or service passes

Not all innovations developed by organizations are technical, however. **Managerial innovations** are changes in the management process by which products and services are conceived, built, and delivered to customers. Managerial innovations do not necessarily affect the physical appearance or performance of products or services directly. In effect, reengineering, as discussed earlier, represents a managerial innovation.

● **managerial innovations** Changes in the management process in an organization

Product Versus Process Innovations Perhaps the two most important types of technical innovations are product innovations and process innovations. **Product innovations** are changes in the physical characteristics

● **product innovations** Changes in physical characteristics or performance of a product or service or the creation of new ones

process innovations Changes in the way products or services are manufactured, created, or distributed

or performance of existing products or services or the creation of brand new products or services. **Process innovations** are changes in the way products or services are manufactured, created, or distributed. Whereas managerial innovations generally affect the broader context of development, process innovations directly affect the manufacturing process.

Japanese organizations have often excelled at process innovation. The market for 35mm cameras was dominated by German and other European manufacturers when, in the early 1960s, Japanese organizations such as Canon and Nikon began making cameras. Although some of these early Japanese products were not very successful, these companies continued to invest in their process technology eventually increasing quality and decreasing manufacturing costs. Now these Japanese organizations dominate the worldwide market for 35mm cameras, and the German companies, because they were not able to maintain the same pace of process innovation, are struggling to maintain market share and profitability.

The Failure to Innovate

To remain competitive in today's economy, it is essential for organizations to be innovative. And yet, many organizations that should be innovative do not succeed at bringing out new products or services, or do so only after innovations created by others are very mature. There are at least three reasons why organizations may fail to innovate.

Lack of Resources Innovation is expensive in terms of dollars, time, and energy. If a firm does not have sufficient money to fund an innovation program, or does not employ the kinds of employees it needs to be innovative, it may find itself lagging behind in innovation. Even highly innovative organizations cannot become involved in every new product or service its employees think up. For example, numerous other commitments in the electronic instruments and computer industry forestalled Hewlett-Packard from investing in Steve Jobs and Steve Wozniak's idea for a personal computer. With infinite resources of money, time, and technical and managerial expertise, Hewlett-Packard might have entered this market early. However, because the firm did not have this flexibility, it had to make some difficult choices about which innovations to invest in.

Failure to Recognize Opportunities Since firms cannot pursue all innovations, they need to develop the capability to carefully evaluate innovations and to select the ones that hold the greatest potential. To obtain a competitive advantage, an organization usually makes investment decisions before the innovation process reaches the mature stage. However, the earlier the investment, the greater the risk. If organizations lack the skill of recognizing and evaluating opportunities, they may be overly cautious and fail to invest in innovations that turn out later to be successful for other firms.

Resistance to Change As discussed earlier, many organizations tend to resist change. Innovation is giving up old products and ways of doing things in favor of new products and ways of doing things. These kinds of changes can be personally difficult for managers and other members of an organization. Thus, resistance to change can slow the innovation process.

Promoting Innovation in Organizations

A wide variety of ideas for promoting innovation in organizations has been developed over the years. One method, intrapreneurship, was discussed previously in Chapter 5. Two other specific ways for promoting innovation are the reward system and organizational culture.

The Reward System A firm's reward system is the means it uses to encourage and discourage certain behaviors by employees. Key components of the reward system include salaries, bonuses, and perquisites. Using the reward system to promote innovation is a fairly mechanical but nevertheless effective management technique. The goal is to provide financial and nonfinancial rewards to people and groups that develop innovative ideas. Once the members of an organization understand that they will be rewarded for such activities, they are more likely to work creatively. With this end in mind, Monsanto Corporation gives a $50,000 award each year to the scientist or group of scientists that develops the biggest commercial breakthrough.

It is important for organizations to reward creative behavior, but it is vital to avoid punishing creativity when it does not result in highly successful innovations. It is the nature of the creative and innovative processes that many new product ideas will simply not work out in the marketplace. Each process is fraught with too many uncertainties to generate positive results every time. An individual may have prepared herself to be creative, but an insight may not be forthcoming. Or managers may attempt to apply a developed innovation, only to recognize that it does not work. Indeed, some organizations function on the premise that if all their innovative efforts succeed, then they are probably not taking enough risks in research and development. At 3M, nearly 60 percent of the creative ideas suggested each year do not succeed in the marketplace.

Managers need to be very careful in responding to innovative failure. If innovative failure is due to incompetence, systematic errors, or managerial sloppiness, then a firm should respond appropriately, such as by withholding raises or reducing promotion opportunities. However, people who act in good faith to develop an innovation that simply does not work out should not be punished for failure. If they are, they will probably not be creative in the future. A punitive reward system will discourage people from taking risks, and therefore reduce the organization's ability to obtain competitive advantages.

Organizational Culture As we discussed in Chapter 2, an organization's culture is the set of values, beliefs, and symbols that help guide behavior. A strong, appropriately focused organizational culture can be used to support innovative activity. A well-managed culture can communicate a sense that innovation is valued and will be rewarded and that occasional failure in the pursuit of new ideas is not only acceptable but even expected. In addition to reward systems and intrapreneurial activities, firms such as 3M, Corning, Monsanto, Procter & Gamble, Texas Instruments, Johnson & Johnson, and Merck are all known to have strong, innovation-oriented cultures. These cultures value individual creativity, risk taking, and inventiveness.[27]

SUMMARY OF KEY POINTS

Organization change is any substantive modification to some part of the organization. Change may be prompted by forces internal or external to the organization. In general, planned change is preferable to reactive change.

Managing the change process is very important. The Lewin model provides a general perspective on the steps in change, although a more comprehensive model is usually more effective. People tend to resist change because of uncertainty, threatened self-interests, different perceptions, and feelings of loss. Participation, education and communication, facilitation, and force-field analysis are methods for overcoming this resistance. The most common areas of change involve organizational structure and design, technology and operations, or people.

Reengineering is the radical redesign of all aspects of a business to achieve major gains in cost, service, or time. It is occasionally needed to offset entropy. The basic steps are developing goals and strategies, leading from the top, creating a sense of urgency, starting with a clean slate, and balancing top-down and bottom-up perspectives.

Organization development is concerned with changing attitudes, perceptions, behaviors, and expectations. Its effective use relies on an important set of assumptions. There are conflicting opinions about the effectiveness of several OD techniques.

The innovation process has six steps: development, application, launch, growth, maturity, and decline. Basic categories of innovation include radical, incremental, technical, managerial, product, and process innovations. Despite the importance of innovation, many organizations fail to innovate because they lack the required creative individuals, are committed to too many other creative activities, fail to recognize opportunities, or resist the change that innovation may require. Organizations can use a variety of tools to overcome these problems, including the reward system, intrapreneurship, and organizational culture.

QUESTIONS FOR REVIEW

1. What forces or kinds of events lead to organization change? Identify each force or event as planned or reactive change.
2. How is each step in the process of organization change implemented? Are some of the steps likely to meet with more resistance than others? Why or why not?
3. What are the various areas of organization change? In what ways are they similar and in what ways do they differ?
4. What is reengineering? Why has it been so common in recent years?
5. What are the steps in the innovation process?

QUESTIONS FOR ANALYSIS

1. Could reactive change of the type identified in question 1 above have been planned for ahead of time? Why or why not?
2. Should all organization change be planned? Why or why not?
3. A company has recently purchased equipment that, when installed, will do the work of one hundred employees. The workforce of the company is very concerned and is threatening to take some kind of action. If you were the human resource manager, what would you try to do to satisfy all parties concerned? Why?
4. Why might reengineering be resisted by employees? How might that resistance be overcome?
5. Think of several relatively new products or services that you use. What form of innovation was each?

CASE STUDY

Samsung

In 1936 Lee Byung-Chull started a rice mill in Korea. In 1938 he began trading in dried fish and incorporated under the name Samsung. By the end of World War II, Samsung had grown to include transportation and real-estate businesses as well as the fish and rice businesses. Despite scandals in the early 1960s, Samsung continued to diversify and grow. In 1969 it added Samsung Electronics, which grew rapidly by disassembling Western-designed products and producing similar ones cheaper and frequently better. In the 1970s Samsung added industrial companies and it became one of Korea's leading *chaebols* or industrial groups.

In the 1980s Samsung began to export electronic goods under its own name, although all too frequently they ended up at the low end of the consumer market. One reason is name recognition. More than one-third of Samsung's exports have other companies' names on them such as Zenith, Whirlpool, General Electric, JC Penney, and Sears. This has kept Samsung from developing the name recognition and brand loyalty necessary to move into the higher end of the consumer market.

Lee Kun-Hee, son of the founder and chair of the company since 1987, is changing all of that. In June 1993, while on a trip to Frankfurt, he got a consultant's report indicating that the Samsung Design Center was being poorly managed. To make matters worse, management was ignoring the report's recommendations. Lee was furious and issued his Frankfurt Declaration: "Quality first, no matter what."

Lee began bringing executives from Korea to wherever in the world he was for meetings. Twenty to forty at a time in round-the-clock meetings, they met and were chastised for their nonchalance and arrogance. By bringing them to foreign settings, Lee was able to show them how poorly Samsung products were being displayed and how little customers thought of them.

A CEO school was initiated, and all 850 top executives will go through it eventually. It is a six-month process of reeducation, half in Korea and half overseas. While in the school, the executives cannot travel by plane. They must use cars, buses, and trains so that they come in greater contact with the people and their culture. In addition, each year four hundred persons with at least three years with Samsung are sent abroad for a year to learn the language and culture of a foreign country. They are then assigned to that country to sell Samsung products.

One of Lee's more important changes, however, is designed to really break down the Korean culture that had dominated the firm. The Korean work ethic calls for managers to arrive at the office around 9 A.M. and leave at about 8 P.M.; the work day was usually followed by rounds of drinking at restaurants or night clubs. Lee requires everyone to be at work at 7 A.M. and to leave at 4 P.M. This is such a culture shock that it may deliver his message more strongly than anything else he is doing.

Lee predicts that 5 percent of his managers will be unable to make the change at all; they will be let go. Another 25 percent to 30 percent will have a difficult time with the change; they will be demoted to positions that they can handle. Only about 10 percent will actually do so well under the new system that they will be promoted as a result. Changing the organization in this way is necessary, Lee believes, to bring about the creativity and innovativeness he wants Samsung to have.

Case Questions

1. How would you describe the Samsung organizational culture before the Frankfurt Declaration? After?
2. What are the major obstacles Samsung faces in trying to improve quality and establish itself as a high-quality producer of consumer electronic products? How could it overcome those obstacles?
3. If Lee asked you to advise him on how to proceed, what would you recommend? Why?

References: Susumu Awanohara, "Image Is Everything," *Far Eastern Economic Review*, June 23, 1994, pp. 50–52; Jie-Ae Sohn, "Samsung's Grand Ambitions," *Business Korea*, June 1994, pp. 23–25; Louis Kraar, "Korea Goes for Quality," *Fortune*, April 18, 1994, pp. 153–159; and "Samsung's Radical Shakeup," *Business Week*, February 28, 1994, pp. 74–76.

SKILLS • DEVELOPMENT • PORTFOLIO

BUILDING EFFECTIVE INTERPERSONAL SKILLS

Exercise Overview

A manager's interpersonal skills are her or his ability to understand and motivate individuals and groups. These abilities are especially important during a period of change. Thus, this exercise will help you understand how to apply your interpersonal skills to a change situation.

Exercise Background

Assume that you are the manager of a retail store in a local shopping mall. Your staff consists of seven full-time and ten part-time employees. The full-time employees have worked together as a team for three years. The part-timers are all local college students; although a couple of them have worked in the store for more than a year, turnover is high among this group.

Your boss, the regional manager, has just informed you that the national chain that owns your store is planning to open a second store in the same mall. She has also informed you that you must plan and implement the following changes:

1. You will serve as manager of both stores until the sales volume of the new store warrants its own full-time manager.

2. You will designate one of the full-time employees in your present store as the assistant manager to cover the hours you will be out of the store.

3. To have experienced workers in the new store, you will select three of your current full-time employees to move to the new store. One of these employees will be appointed as the assistant manager of that store.

4. You are permitted to hire three new full-time employees to replace those transferred from your present store and three new full-time employees to work at the new store.

5. You may decide for yourself how to deploy your part-timers, but you will need a total of ten in the present store and eight at the new store.

You realize that many of your employees will be unhappy with these changes. They all know each other and work well together. However, the new store will be in a new expansion of the mall and will be a very nice place to work.

Exercise Task

With this background information in mind, do the following:

1. Determine the likely reasons for resistance to this change from your workers.

2. Determine how you will make decisions about promotions and transfers (make whatever assumptions that you think are warranted).

3. Outline how you will inform your employees about what is going to happen.

4. An alternative strategy that could be adopted would involve keeping the existing staff intact and hiring new employees for the new store. Outline a persuasion strategy for convincing your boss that this is what should be done.

BUILDING EFFECTIVE DIAGNOSTIC SKILLS

Exercise Overview

Diagnostic skills help a manager visualize the most appropriate response to a situation. Diagnostic skills are especially important during a period of organization change.

Exercise Background

Assume that you are the general manager of a hotel located on a tropical island. The hotel is situated along a beautiful stretch of beach and is one of six large resorts in the area. The hotel, owned by a group of foreign investors, is one of the oldest on the island. For several years, the hotel has been operated as a franchise unit of a large international hotel chain, as are all of the others on the island.

For the last few years, the hotel's owners have been taking most of the profits earned for themselves, and putting relatively little back into the hotel. They also have informed you that their business is not in good financial health; the money earned from your hotel is being used to offset losses being incurred elsewhere. In contrast, most of the other hotels around you have recently been refurbished, and plans have just been announced to build two new hotels in the near future.

A team of executives from franchise headquarters has just visited your hotel. They expressed considerable disappointment in the property. They feel that it has not kept pace with the other resorts on the island. They also inform you that if the property is not brought up to their standards, the franchise agreement, up for review in a year, will be revoked. You see this as potentially disastrous since you would lose their "brand name" access to their reservation system, and so forth.

Sitting alone in your office, you have identified a variety of alternatives that seem viable:

1. Try to convince the owners to remodel the hotel. You estimate that it will take $5 million to meet the franchisors minimum standards and another $5 million to bring the hotel up to the standards of the top resort on the island.

2. Try to convince the franchisor to give you more time and more options to upgrade the facility.

3. Allow the franchise agreement to terminate and try to succeed as an independent hotel.

4. Assume that the hotel is going to fail and start looking for another job. You have a good reputation, although you might have to start at a lower-level position with another firm (i.e., as an assistant manager).

Exercise Task

With the background information just presented, do the following:

1. Rank-order the four alternatives in terms of their potential success (make assumptions as appropriate).

2. Identify other alternatives not noted above.

3. Can any alternatives be pursued simultaneously?

4. Develop an overall strategy for trying to save the hotel while also protecting your self-interests.

YOU MAKE THE CALL

With their new organization in place, the Spensers believed that their management difficulties were over. They assumed they would each have more time for their own work, and that the organization itself would also function more efficiently. It wasn't long, however, before problems began to arise.

A few weeks after the changes were announced, Manuel Hernandez asked to meet with Mark one day after work. Mark was alarmed to learn that Manuel thought there were some major problems developing in the lawn-care business. Two of the crews, in particular, were of concern. Manuel reported that the two crews were having trouble completing their scheduled lawn work each day. It had been necessary for him to pitch in and help them finish, as well as to authorize overtime pay on a couple of occasions.

Manuel thought that the two crew chiefs might have something to do with the problem. They weren't as friendly toward him as they once had been, and they did not seem to be working as hard as before. Manuel believed that part of the problem was that they resented his promotion. While Manuel had more seniority than either of them, they had nonetheless worked for SLS for several years. Moreover, they and Manuel had been fairly close friends, sharing mutual interests in sports and local politics. Fortunately, the other two crews were functioning fine. One of them had a chief who had been on the job for several months, and the other was the crew formerly led by Manuel. His position had been taken over by one of the team members.

Mark asked Manuel how he wanted to proceed. Manuel indicated that he had already tried talking to his two former friends and had made no headway. After discussing various options, they decided that Mark should talk to the two crew chiefs who were causing problems. First, however, he wanted to discuss the situation with Cynthia. She was often able to come up with other alternatives that Mark had not considered.

In this case she had no other ideas about what to do. She did, however, suggest the cause of the problem. In particular, she pointed out that they had perhaps implemented the changes too quickly. Their strategy had been to do things with as little fuss as possible. They had simply drawn an organization chart, called a staff meeting one day after work, and announced the changes. In retrospect, she wondered if they should have talked to key people in the organization before announcing the changes.

Discussion Questions

1. Describe the change process that the Spensers could have used to plan and implement their changes.

2. Why might workers at SLS have resisted the changes?

3. What could the Spensers have done to overcome the resistance?

SKILLS SELF-ASSESSMENT INSTRUMENT

Innovative Attitude Scale

Introduction: Change and innovation are important to organizations. The following assessment surveys your readiness to accept and participate in innovation.

Instructions: Indicate the extent to which each of the following statements is true of either your *actual* behavior of your *intentions* at work. That is, describe the way you are or the way you intend to be on the job. Use this scale for your responses:

Almost always true	=	**5**
Often true	=	**4**
Not applicable	=	**3**
Seldom true	=	**2**
Almost never true	=	**1**

____ **1.** I openly discuss with my boss how to get ahead.

____ **2.** I try new ideas and approaches to problems.

____ **3.** I take things or situations apart to find out how they work.

____ **4.** I welcome uncertainty and unusual circumstances related to my tasks.

____ **5.** I negotiate my salary openly with my supervisor.

____ **6.** I can be counted on to find a new use for existing methods or equipment.

____ **7.** Among my colleagues and coworkers, I will be the first or nearly the first to try out a new idea or method.

____ **8.** I take the opportunity to translate communications from other departments for my work group.

____ **9.** I demonstrate originality.

____ **10.** I will work on a problem that has caused others great difficulty.

____ **11.** I provide critical input toward a new solution.

____ **12.** I provide written evaluations of proposed ideas.

____ **13.** I develop contacts with experts outside my firm.

____ **14.** I use personal contacts to maneuver myself into choice work assignments.

____ **15.** I make time to pursue my own pet ideas or projects.

____ **16.** I set aside resources for the pursuit of a risky project.

____ **17.** I tolerate people who depart from organizational routine.

____ **18.** I speak out in staff meetings.

____ **19.** I work in teams to try to solve complex problems.

____ **20.** If my coworkers are asked, they will say I am a wit.

For interpretation, turn to page 448.

Source: From J. E. Ettlie and R. D. O'Keefe, "Innovative Attitudes, Values, and Intentions in Organizations," *Journal of Management Studies* 19 (1982), p. 176. Reprinted by permission of Basil Blackwell Ltd.

EXPERIENTIAL EXERCISE

Innovation in Action: Egg Drop

Purpose: Managers are continuously improving on the work flow, the product, and the packaging of products. This is what Total Quality Management is all about. To do this means both thinking creatively and acting innovatively. This skill builder focuses on the *open systems model*. It will help you develop the *innovator role*. One of the skills of the innovator is thinking creatively and acting innovatively.

Introduction: This activity is a practical and entertaining demonstration of creativity and innovation in action. "Egg Drop" provides practice in identifying, defining, or refining a problem or opportunity, developing options and alternatives, choosing the best option or alternative, actually launching the alternative into reality, and verifying the results within a specified time period. Your instructor will provide you with further instructions.

Source: Reproduced with permission from *50 Activities on Creativity and Problem Solving,* by Geof Cox, Chuck DuFault and Walt Hopkins, Gower, Aldershot, 1992.

CHAPTER NOTES

1. "Learning From Winners," *Forbes*, March 14, 1994, pp. 41–43; and Gary Hoover, Alta Campbell, and Patrick J. Spain (Eds.), *Hoover's Handbook of American Business 1995* (Austin, Tex.: The Reference Press, 1994), pp. 1056–1057.
2. For excellent reviews of this area, see Richard W. Woodman, "Organization Change and Development: New Arenas for Inquiry and Action," *Journal of Management*, June 1989, pp. 205–228; and William Pasmore and Mary Fagans, "Participation, Individual Development, and Organizational Change: A Review and Synthesis," *Journal of Management*, June 1992, pp. 375–397.
3. For additional insights into how technological change affects other parts of the organization, see P. Robert Duimering, Frank Safayeni, and Lyn Purdy, "Integrated Manufacturing: Redesign the Organization Before Implementing Flexible Technology," *Sloan Management Review*, Summer 1993, pp. 47–56.
4. Thomas A. Stewart, "How to Lead a Revolution," *Fortune*, November 28, 1994, pp. 48–61.
5. Peter Robertson, Darryl Roberts, and Jerry Porras, "Dynamics of Planned Organizational Change: Assessing Empirical Support for a Theoretical Model," *Academy of Management Journal*, Vol. 36, No. 3, 1993, pp. 619–634.
6. Kenneth Labich, "Was Breaking Up AT&T a Good Idea?" *Fortune*, January 2, 1989, pp. 82–87; and Zane E. Barnes, "Change in the Bell System," *The Academy of Management Executive*, February 1987, pp. 43–46.
7. John P. Kotter and Leonard A. Schlesinger, "Choosing Strategies for Change," *Harvard Business Review*, March–April 1979, p. 106.
8. Kurt Lewin, "Frontiers in Group Dynamics: Concept, Method, and Reality in Social Science," *Human Relations*, June 1947, pp. 5–41.
9. See Connie J. G. Gersick, "Revolutionary Change Theories: A Multilevel Exploration of the Punctuated Equilibrium Paradigm," *Academy of Management Review*, January 1991, pp. 10–36.
10. See Gerald Andrews, "Mistrust, the Hidden Obstacle to Empowerment, *HR Magazine*, November 1994, pp. 66–74, for a good illustration of how resistance emerges.
11. "RJR Employees Fight Distraction Amid Buy-out Talks," *The Wall Street Journal*, November 1, 1988, p. A8.
12. See Paul R. Lawrence, "How to Deal with Resistance to Change," *Harvard Business Review*, January–February 1969, pp. 4–12, 166–176, for a classic discussion.
13. Lester Coch and John R. P. French, Jr., "Overcoming Resistance to Change," *Human Relations*, August 1948, pp. 512–532.
14. Charles K. Day, Jr., "Management's Mindless Mistakes," *Industry Week*, May 29, 1987, p. 42. See also "Inspection from the Plant Floor," *Business Week*, April 10, 1989, pp. 60–61.
15. David A. Nadler, "The Effective Management of Organizational Change," in Jay W. Lorsch (Ed.), *Handbook of Organizational Behavior* (Englewood Cliffs, N.J.: Prentice-Hall, 1987), pp. 358–369.
16. Thomas A. Stewart, "Reengineering—The Hot New Managing Tool," *Fortune*, August 23, 1993, pp. 41–48.
17. Richard Beckhard, *Organization Development: Strategies and Models* (Reading, Mass.: Addison-Wesley, 1969), p. 9. Italics in original.
18. Wendell L. French and Cecil H. Bell, Jr., *Organization Development: Behavioral Science Interventions for Organization Improvement*, 2nd ed. (Englewood Cliffs, N.J.: Prentice-Hall, 1978).
19. William G. Dyer, *Team Building Issues and Alternatives* (Reading, Mass.: Addison-Wesley, 1980).
20. Roger J. Hower, Mark G. Mindell, and Donna L. Simmons, "Introducing Innovation Through OD," *Management Review*, February 1978, pp. 52–56.
21. "Is Organization Development Catching On? A Personnel Symposium," *Personnel*, November–December 1977, pp. 10–22.
22. For a recent discussion on the effectiveness of various OD techniques in different organizations, see John M. Nicholas, "The Comparative Impact of Organization Development Interventions on Hard Criteria Measures," *Academy of Management Review*, October 1982, pp. 531–542.
23. L. B. Mohr, "Determinants of Innovation in Organizations," *American Political Science Review*, 1969, pp. 111–126; G. A. Steiner, *The Creative Organization* (Chicago: University of Chicago Press, 1965); R. Duncan and A. Weiss, "Organizational Learning: Implications for Organizational Design," in B. M. Staw (Ed.), *Research in Organizational Behavior*, Vol. 1 (Greenwich, Conn.: JAI Press, 1979), pp. 75–123; and J. E. Ettlie, "Adequacy of Stage Models for Decisions on Adoption of Innovation," *Psychological Reports*, 1980, pp. 991–995.
24. Beth Wolfensberger, "Trouble in Toyland," *New England Business*, September 1990, pp. 28–36.
25. See Alan Patz, "Managing Innovation in High Technology Industries," *New Management*, September 1986, pp. 54–59.
26. "Flops," *Business Week*, August 16, 1993, pp. 76–82.
27. See Steven P. Feldman, "How Organizational Culture Can Affect Innovation," *Organizational Dynamics*, Summer 1988, pp. 57–68.

CHAPTER

Managing Human Resources

OBJECTIVES

After studying this chapter, you should be able to:

- *Describe the environmental context of human resource management, including its strategic importance and its relationship with legal and social factors.*
- *Discuss how organizations attract human resources, including human resource planning, recruiting, and selecting.*
- *Describe how organizations develop human resources, including training and development, performance appraisal, and performance feedback.*
- *Discuss how organizations maintain human resources, including the determination of compensation and benefits and career planning.*
- *Discuss the nature of diversity, including its meaning, associated trends, dimensions, and impact.*
- *Discuss labor relations, including how employees form unions and the mechanics of collective bargaining.*

OUTLINE

The Environmental Context of Human Resource Management
- The Strategic Importance of HRM
- The Legal Environment of HRM

Attracting Human Resources
- Human Resource Planning
- Recruiting Human Resources
- Selecting Human Resources

Developing Human Resources
- Training and Development
- Performance Appraisal
- Performance Feedback

Maintaining Human Resources
- Determining Compensation
- Determining Benefits

Managing Workforce Diversity
- The Meaning of Diversity
- The Impact of Diversity
- Managing Diversity in Organizations

Managing Labor Relations
- How Employees Form Unions
- Collective Bargaining

OPENING INCIDENT

SATURN HAS BEEN hailed as the future of the U.S. automobile industry. General Motors Corp. first announced plans for its new subsidiary in the early 1980s, and the first automobile rolled out of the new Spring Hill, Tennessee, Saturn factory in 1990. The guiding premise behind Saturn was to model automobile production after successful methods used in Japan—for example, advanced technology, worker participation, and production based on work teams.

Because General Motors itself is unionized, the Saturn operation was launched with the full participation of its unions, especially the United Auto Workers (UAW). When the firm began hiring workers for Spring Hill, the agreement was that any current GM employee belonging to the UAW could apply for a transfer to Saturn. In the beginning, Saturn chose workers from that labor pool who were most attuned to the ideas of cooperation and participation. In addition, all new Saturn workers received up to seven hundred hours of training. This training included not only basic production techniques and methods, but also conflict management and interpersonal relations skills necessary for smoothly functioning work teams. These teams, comprising around fifteen workers each, handle virtually everything from hiring new employees to setting budgets to overseeing operations throughout the Saturn plant.

"These folks are tougher to integrate into Saturn."

The Saturn automobile itself has been a big success. Indeed, it is so successful that the prevailing culture at Spring Hill is threatened. Demand for Saturn automobiles has forced the plant to add shifts and put many of its workers on fifty-hour workweeks. As a result, many of these workers have experienced increased stress, fatigue, and burnout. Management has also been charged by the UAW with exerting more control and pressure to meet new manufacturing projections.

In addition, a new labor contract between the UAW and GM signed in 1990 mandates that Saturn now hire only GM workers who have lost their jobs at other GM plants. As a result, the plant is taking on more and more new workers who are angry at losing their other job and are often prone to distrust management.

General Motors has also cut training programs for new hires. Instead of 700 hours of training, new employees get only 170 hours of training, mostly in job-related skills. Taken together, these changes are seen by some Saturn employees as a sign that traditional GM practices are creeping into the organization. The irony is that Saturn has been the one bright spot in the company for the last few years, and Saturn products are among the highest-rated automobiles in the United States.[1]

Source of Quotation: Timothy Epps, Saturn human resource manager, quoted in *Business Week*, February 8, 1993, p. 122.

Human resources are clearly an integral part of Saturn's success. Saturn was unique in its original approach to selecting and training its employees. Moreover, it used the people hired and trained through its unique approach to launch one of the most successful automobiles in history. Today, however, the company is subtly changing its approach to dealing with human resources. It remains to be seen whether or not it will be able to maintain its success under this new approach.

This chapter is about how organizations manage the people that comprise them. This set of processes is called human resource management, or HRM. We start by describing the environmental context of HRM. We then discuss how organizations attract human resources. Next we describe how organizations seek to develop further the capacities of their human resources. We also examine how high-quality human resources are maintained by organizations. Workforce diversity, an emerging issue in HRM, is then discussed. We conclude by discussing labor relations.

THE ENVIRONMENTAL CONTEXT OF HUMAN RESOURCE MANAGEMENT

• **human resource management (HRM)** The set of organizational activities directed at attracting, developing, and maintaining an effective workforce

Human resource management (HRM) is the set of activities directed at attracting, developing, and maintaining an effective workforce.[2] Human resource management takes place within a complex and ever-changing environmental context.

The Strategic Importance of HRM

Human resources are critical for effective organizational functioning.[3] Most managers realize that the effectiveness of their HR function has a substantial impact on the bottom-line performance of the company. Poor human resource planning can result in spurts of hiring followed by layoffs—costly in terms of unemployment compensation payments, training expenses, and morale. Haphazard compensation systems do not attract, keep, and motivate good employees, and outmoded recruitment practices can expose the company to expensive and embarrassing discrimination lawsuits. Consequently, the chief human resource executive of most large businesses is a vice president directly accountable to the CEO, and many companies are developing strategic HR plans and integrating those plans with other strategic planning activities.[4]

Even relatively small organizations usually have a human resource manager and a human resource department charged with overseeing these activities. Responsibility for HR activities, however, is shared between the HR department and line managers. The HR department may recruit and initially screen candidates, but the final selection is usually made by managers in the department where the new employee will work. Similarly, although the HR department may establish performance appraisal policies and procedures, the actual evaluating and coaching of employees is done by their immediate superiors.

Effective human resource management is of vital strategic importance to an organization. Fruit of the Loom forecast that its sales were about to decline and launched a massive layoff program. When sales ended up increasing, the company had to hire thousands of replacement workers. Thus, the company not only paid out unnecessary severance pay and damaged its public image, but also had to invest more money in hiring and training new employees. Managers estimated that the mistake cost $40 million in lost sales and hiring and training expenses.

The Legal Environment of HRM

A number of laws regulate various aspects of employee-employer relations, especially in the areas of Equal Employment Opportunity, compensation and benefits, labor relations, and occupational safety and health. The major ones are summarized in Table 8.1.

Equal Employment Opportunity **Title VII of the Civil Rights Act of 1964** forbids discrimination on the basis of sex, race, color, religion, or national origin in all areas of the employment relationship, including hiring, compensation, training, promotion, discipline, and discharge. The intent of Title VII is to ensure that employment decisions are made on the basis of an individual's qualifications rather than personal biases. The law has reduced direct forms of discrimination as well as indirect forms of discrimination (using employment tests that whites pass at a higher rate than African Americans). These requirements have an **adverse impact** on minorities and women when such individuals pass the selection standard at a rate less than 80 percent of the pass rate of majority group members. Criteria that have an adverse impact on protected groups can be used only when there is solid evidence that they effectively identify individuals who are better able than others to do the job. The **Equal Employment Opportunity Commission** is charged with enforcing Title VII, as well as several other employment-related laws.

The **Age Discrimination in Employment Act**, passed in 1967, amended in 1978, and amended again in 1986, is an attempt to prevent organizations from discriminating against older workers. In its current form, it outlaws discrimination against people over the age of forty. Both

- **Title VII of the Civil Rights Act of 1964**
Forbids discrimination on the basis of sex, race, color, religion, or national origin in all areas of the employment relationship

- **adverse impact**
When minority group members pass a selection standard at a rate less than 80 percent of the pass rate of majority group members

- **Equal Employment Opportunity Commission**
Charged with enforcing Title VII of the Civil Rights Act of 1964

- **Age Discrimination in Employment Act**
Outlaws discrimination against people over the age of forty; passed in 1967, amended in 1978 and 1986

As much as any area of management, HRM is subject to wide-ranging laws and court decisions. These laws and decisions affect the human resource function in many different areas. For example, AT&T was once fined several million dollars for violating Title VII of the Civil Rights Act of 1964.

TABLE 8.1 The Legal Environment of HRM

Area of Regulation
Equal Employment Opportunity
Title VII of the Civil Rights Act of 1964 (as amended by the *Equal Employment Opportunity Act of 1972*): Forbids discrimination in all areas of the employment relationship
Age Discrimination in Employment Act: Outlaws discrimination against people older than forty years
Americans with Disabilities Act: Specifically outlaws discrimination against disabled persons
Civil Rights Act of 1991: Makes it easier for employees to sue an organization for discrimination, but limits punitive damage awards if they win
Compensation and Benefits
Fair Labor Standards Act: Establishes minimum wage and mandated overtime pay for work in excess of forty hours per week
Equal Pay Act of 1963: Requires that men and women be paid the same amount for doing the same jobs
Employee Retirement Income Security Act of 1974 (ERISA): Regulates how organizations manage their pension funds
Family and Medical Leave Act of 1993: Requires employers to provide up to twelve weeks of unpaid leave for family and medical emergencies
Labor Relations
National Labor Relations Act: Establishes procedures by which employees can establish labor unions and requires organizations to bargain collectively with legally formed unions; also known as the Wagner Act
Labor-Management Relations Act: Limits union power and specifies management rights during a union-organizing campaign; also known as the Taft-Hartley Act
Health and Safety
Occupational Safety and Health Act of 1970: Mandates the provision of safe working conditions

the Age Discrimination in Employment Act and Title VII require passive nondiscrimination, or *equal employment opportunity*. Employers are not required to seek out and hire minorities, but they must treat fairly all who apply.

• **affirmative action** Intentionally seeking and hiring qualified or qualifiable employees from racial, sexual, and ethnic groups that are underrepresented in the organization

Several executive orders, however, require that employers holding government contracts engage in **affirmative action**—intentionally seeking and hiring employees from racial, sexual, and ethnic groups that are underrepresented in the organization. These organizations must have a written affirmative action plan that spells out employment goals for underutilized groups and how those goals will be met.[5] These employers are also required to act affirmatively in hiring Vietnam-era veterans and qualified handicapped individuals.

In 1990, Congress passed the **Americans with Disabilities Act** that forbids discrimination on the basis of disabilities and requires employers to provide reasonable accommodations for disabled employees. More recently, the **Civil Rights Act of 1991** amended the original Civil Rights Act, as well as other related laws, by making it easier to bring discrimination lawsuits while simultaneously limiting the amount of punitive damages that can be awarded in those lawsuits.

Compensation and Benefits The **Fair Labor Standards Act**, passed in 1938 and amended frequently since then, sets a minimum wage and requires the payment of overtime rates for work in excess of forty hours per week. Salaried professional, executive, and administrative employees are exempt from the minimum hourly wage and overtime provisions. The **Equal Pay Act of 1963** requires that men and women be paid the same amount for doing the same jobs. Attempts to circumvent the law by having different job titles and pay rates for men and women who perform the same work are also illegal. However, it is legal to base an employee's pay on seniority or performance, even if it means that a man and woman are paid different amounts for doing the same job.

The provision of benefits is also regulated in some ways by state and federal laws. Certain benefits are mandatory—for example, worker's compensation insurance for employees who are injured on the job. Employers who provide a pension plan for their employees are regulated by the **Employee Retirement Income Security Act of 1974 (ERISA)**. The purpose of this act is to help insure the financial security of pension funds by regulating how they can be invested. The act sets standards for pension plan management and provides federal insurance if pension funds go bankrupt. The **Family and Medical Leave Act of 1993** requires employers to provide up to twelve weeks of unpaid leave for family and medical emergencies.

Labor Relations Union activities and management's behavior toward unions constitute another heavily regulated area. The **National Labor Relations Act** (also known as the *Wagner Act*), passed in 1935, sets up the procedures for employees to vote whether to have a union. If they vote for a union, management is required to bargain collectively with the union. The **National Labor Relations Board** was established by the Wagner Act to enforce its provisions. Following a series of severe strikes in 1946, the **Labor-Management Relations Act** (also known as the *Taft-Hartley Act*) was passed in 1947 to limit union power. The law increases management's rights during an organizing campaign. The Taft-Hartley Act also contains the *National Emergency Strike* provision, which allows the president of the United States to prevent or end a strike that endangers national security. Taken together, those laws balance union and management power. Employees can be represented by a properly constituted union, and management can make nonemployee-related business decisions without interference.

- **Americans with Disabilities Act** Prohibits discrimination against people with disabilities
- **Civil Rights Act of 1991** Amends the original Civil Rights Act, making it easier to bring discrimination lawsuits while also limiting punitive damages
- **Fair Labor Standards Act** Sets a minimum wage and requires overtime pay for work in excess of forty hours per week; passed in 1938 and amended frequently since then
- **Equal Pay Act of 1963** Requires that men and women be paid the same amount for doing the same jobs
- **Employee Retirement Income Security Act of 1974 (ERISA)** Sets standards for pension plan management and provides federal insurance if pension funds go bankrupt
- **Family and Medical Leave Act of 1993** Requires employers to provide twelve weeks of unpaid leave for family and medical emergencies
- **National Labor Relations Act** Passed in 1935 to set up procedures for employees to vote whether to have a union; also known as the Wagner Act
- **National Labor Relations Board** Established by the Wagner Act to enforce its provisions
- **Labor-Management Relations Act** Passed in 1947 to limit union power; also known as the Taft-Hartley Act

Occupational Safety and Health Act of 1970 Directly mandates the provision of safe working conditions

Health and Safety The **Occupational Safety and Health Act of 1970** directly mandates the provision of safe working conditions. It requires that employers (1) provide a place of employment that is free from hazards that may cause death or serious physical harm and (2) obey the safety and health standards established by the Department of Labor. Safety standards are intended to prevent accidents, whereas occupational health standards are concerned with preventing occupational disease. For example, standards limit the concentration of cotton dust in the air because this contaminant has been associated with lung disease in textile workers. The standards are enforced by OSHA inspections, which are conducted when an employee files a complaint of unsafe conditions or when a serious accident occurs. Spot inspections of plants in especially hazardous industries such as mining and chemicals are also made. Employers who fail to meet OSHA standards may be fined.[6]

ATTRACTING HUMAN RESOURCES

With an understanding of the environmental context of human resource management as a foundation, we are now ready to address its first substantive concern—attracting qualified people who are interested in employment with the organization.

Human Resource Planning

The starting point in attracting qualified human resources is planning. HR planning, in turn, involves job analysis and forecasting the demand and supply of labor. This process is depicted in Figure 8.1.

job analysis A systematic analysis of jobs within an organization

Job Analysis **Job analysis** is a systematic analysis of jobs within an organization. A job analysis is made up of two parts. The *job description* lists the duties of a job; the job's working conditions; and the tools, materials, and equipment used to perform it. The *job specification* lists the skills, abilities, and other credentials needed to do the job.

Forecasting Human Resource Demand and Supply After managers fully understand the jobs to be performed within the organization, they can start planning for the organization's future human resource needs. The manager starts by assessing trends in past human resource usage, future organizational plans, and general economic trends. A good sales forecast is often the foundation, especially for smaller organizations. Historical ratios can then be used to predict demand for employees such as operating employees and sales representatives. Large organizations use more complicated models to predict their future human resource needs.

Forecasting the supply of labor is really two tasks: forecasting the internal supply (the number and type of employees who will be in the organization at some future date) and forecasting the external supply (the number and type of people who will be available for hiring in the labor market at

FIGURE 8.1 Human Resource Planning

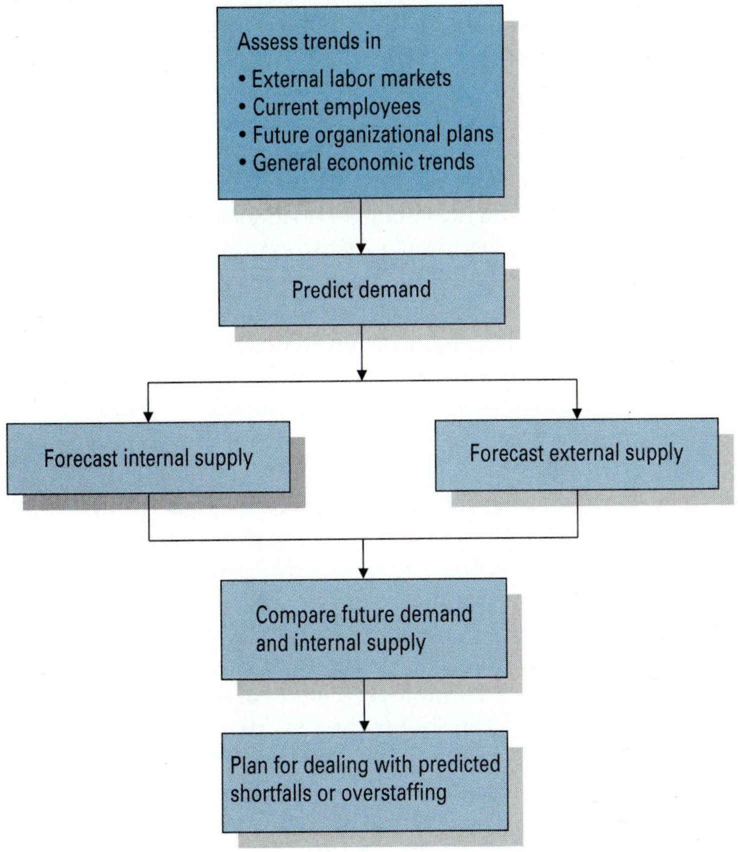

Attracting human resources cannot be left to chance if an organization expects to function at peak efficiency. Human resource planning involves assessing trends, forecasting the supply and demand of labor, and then developing appropriate strategies for addressing any differences.

large). The simplest approach merely adjusts present staffing levels for anticipated turnover and promotions. Larger organizations use more sophisticated models to make these forecasts.

At higher levels of the organization, managers plan for specific people and positions. The technique most commonly used is the **replacement chart**, which lists each important managerial position, who occupies it, how long he or she will probably remain in the position, and who (by name) is now qualified or soon will be qualified to move into the position. This method allows ample time to plan developmental experiences for persons identified as potential successors to critical jobs. Charles Knight, CEO of Emerson Electric, has an entire room dedicated to posting the credentials of his top seven hundred executives.[7]

• **replacement chart** Lists each important managerial position in the organization, who occupies it, how long he or she will probably remain in the position, and who is or will be a qualified replacement

To facilitate both planning and identifying persons for current transfer or promotion, some organizations also have an **employee information system**, or **skills inventory**. Such systems are usually computerized and contain information on each employee's education, skills, work experience, and career aspirations. Such a system can quickly locate all the employees in the organization who are qualified to fill a position.

• **employee information system (skills inventory)** Contains information on each employee's education, skills, experience, and career aspirations; usually computerized

Forecasting the external supply of labor is a different problem altogether. How does a manager, for example, predict how many electrical engineers will be seeking work in Georgia three years from now? To get an idea of the future availability of labor, planners must rely on information from outside sources, such as state employment commissions, government reports, and figures supplied by colleges on the number of students in major fields.

Matching Human Resource Supply and Demand Managers next make plans to deal with predicted shortfalls or overstaffing. If a shortfall is predicted, new employees can be hired, present employees can be retrained and transferred into the understaffed area, individuals approaching retirement can be convinced to stay on, or labor-saving or productivity-enhancing systems can be installed. If the organization needs to hire, the forecast of the external labor supply helps managers plan how to recruit, based on whether the type of person needed is readily available or scarce in the labor market. Temporary workers also help managers in staffing by affording them with extra flexibility. If overstaffing is expected to be a problem, the main options are transferring the extra employees, not replacing individuals who quit, encouraging early retirement, and laying people off.[8]

Recruiting Human Resources

Once an organization has an idea of its future human resource needs, the next phase is recruiting new employees. **Recruiting** is the process of attracting qualified persons to apply for the jobs that are open. Some recruits are found internally; others come from outside of the organization.

- **recruiting** The process of attracting qualified persons to apply for jobs that are open

Internal recruiting means considering present employees as candidates for openings within the organization. Promotion from within can help build morale and keep high-quality employees from leaving the firm. In unionized firms, the procedures for notifying employees of internal job change opportunities are usually spelled out in the union contract. For higher-level positions, a skills inventory system may be used to identify internal candidates, or managers may be asked to recommend individuals who should be considered. One disadvantage of internal recruiting is its "ripple effect." When an employee moves to a different job, someone else must be found to take his or her old job. In one organization, 454 job movements were necessary as a result of filling 195 initial openings![9]

- **internal recruiting** Considering current employees as candidates for openings within the organization

External recruiting involves attracting people from outside the organization to apply for jobs. External recruiting methods include advertising, campus interviews, employment agencies or executive search firms, union hiring halls, referrals by present employees, and hiring "walk-ins" or "gate-hires" (people who show up without being solicited). Of course, a manager must select the most appropriate methods: He or she might use the state employment service to find maintenance workers but not a nuclear physicist. Private employment agencies can be a good source of clerical and technical employees, and executive search firms specialize in locating top management talent. Newspaper ads are often used because they reach a wide audience and thus allow minorities "equal opportunity" to find out about and apply for job openings.

- **external recruiting** Attracting people from outside the organization to apply for jobs

One generally successful method for facilitating a good person-job fit is through the so-called **realistic job preview (RJP)**.[10] As the term suggests, the RJP involves providing the applicant with a real picture of what it would be like to perform the job the organization is trying to fill.

realistic job preview (RJP) Provides the applicant with a real picture of what it would be like to perform the job the organization is trying to fill

Selecting Human Resources

Once the recruiting process has attracted a pool of applicants, the next step is to select whom to hire. The intent of the selection process is to gather from applicants information that will predict their job success and then to hire the candidates likely to be most successful. Of course, the organization can only gather information about factors that are predictive of future performance. The process of determining the predictive value of information is called **validation**.

validation Determining the extent to which a selection device is really predictive of future job performance

Application Blanks The first step in selection is usually asking the candidate to fill out an application blank. Application blanks are an efficient method for gathering information about the applicant's previous work history, educational background, and other job-related demographic data. They should not contain questions about areas not related to the job such as gender, religion, or national origin. Application blank data are generally used informally to decide whether a candidate merits further evaluation, and interviewers use application blanks to familiarize themselves with candidates before interviewing them.

Tests Tests of ability, skill, aptitude, or knowledge that is relevant to the particular job are usually the best predictors of job success, although tests of general intelligence or personality are occasionally useful as well. In addition to being validated, tests should be administered and scored in a consistent fashion. All candidates should be given the same directions, should be allowed the same amount of time, and should experience the same testing environment (temperature, lighting, distractions).[11]

Interviews Although a popular selection device, interviews are sometimes poor predictors of job success. For example, biases inherent in the way people perceive and judge others on first meeting affect subsequent evaluations by the interviewer. Interview validity can be improved by training interviewers to be aware of potential biases and by increasing the structure of the interview. In a structured interview, questions are written in advance and all interviewers follow the same question list with each candidate they interview. This method introduces consistency into the process and allows the company to validate the content of the questions to be asked.[12] For interviewing managerial or professional candidates, a somewhat less-structured approach can be used. Question areas and information-gathering objectives are still planned in advance, but the specific questions vary with the candidates' backgrounds. Trammell Crow Real Estate Investors uses a novel approach in hiring managers. Each applicant is interviewed not only by two or three other managers but also by a secretary or young leasing agent. This format provides information about how the prospective manager relates to nonmanagers.[13]

Assessment Centers Assessment centers are a popular method used to select managers and are particularly good for selecting current employees for promotion. The assessment center is a simulation of key parts of the managerial job. A typical center lasts two to three days, with groups of six to twelve persons participating in a variety of managerial exercises. Centers may also include interviews, public speaking, and ability tests. Candidates are assessed by several trained observers, usually managers several levels above the job for which the candidates are being considered. Assessment centers are quite valid if properly designed and are fair to members of minority groups and women.[14] AT&T pioneered the assessment center concept. For years AT&T has used assessment centers to make virtually all of its selection decisions for management positions.

DEVELOPING HUMAN RESOURCES

Regardless of how effective a selection system is, however, most employees need additional training if they are to grow and develop in their jobs. Evaluating their performance and providing feedback are also necessary.

Training and Development

- **training**
Teaching operational or technical employees how to do the job for which they were hired

- **development**
Teaching managers and professionals the skills needed for both present and future jobs

In HRM, **training** usually refers to teaching operational or technical employees how to do the job for which they were hired. **Development** refers to teaching managers and professionals the skills needed for both present and future jobs. Most organizations provide regular training and development programs for managers and employees.[15] For example, IBM spends more than $700 million annually on programs and has a vice president in charge of employee education. U.S. business spends more than $30 billion annually on training and development programs. And this figure doesn't include wages and benefits paid to employees while they are participating in such programs.[16]

Assessing Training Needs The first step in developing a training plan is to determine what needs exist. For example, if employees do not know how to operate machinery required to do their jobs, a training program on how to operate the machinery is clearly needed. On the other hand, when a group of office workers is performing poorly, training may not be the answer. The problem could be motivation, aging equipment, poor supervision, or a deficiency of skills and knowledge. Only the last can be remedied by training. As training programs are being developed, the manager should set specific and measurable goals specifying what participants are to learn. Plans should also be made to evaluate the training program after it has been completed.

Common Training Methods Many different training and development methods are available. Selection of methods depends on many considerations, but perhaps the most important is training content. When the training content is factual material (such as company rules or explanations of how to fill out forms), assigned reading and lecture methods work well. When the content is interpersonal relations or group decision making, however, companies must use a method that allows interpersonal contact, such as role playing or case discussion groups. When a physical skill must be learned, methods allowing practice and the actual use of tools and material are needed, as in on-the-job training. Interactive video and CD-ROM are also becoming popular. Xerox, Massachusetts Mutual Life Insurance, and Ford have all reported tremendous success with these methods.[17]

Evaluation of Training Training and development programs should always be evaluated. Typical evaluation approaches include measuring one or more relevant criteria (such as attitudes or performance) before and after the training, and determining whether or not the criteria changed. Evaluation measures collected at the end of training are easy to get, but actual performance measures collected when the trainee is on the job are more important. Trainees may say they enjoyed the training and learned a lot, but the true test is whether their job performance improves after their training.

Performance Appraisal

When employees are trained and settled into their jobs, one of the next concerns is performance appraisal. **Performance appraisal** is a formal assessment of how well employees are doing their jobs. Performance should be evaluated regularly for many reasons. One reason is that performance appraisal may be necessary for validating selection devices or assessing the impact of training programs. A second reason is to aid in making decisions about pay raises, promotions, and training. Still another reason is to provide feedback to employees to help them improve their present performance and plan future careers. Because performance evaluations often help determine wages and promotions, they must be fair and nondiscriminatory.[18]

• **performance appraisal** A formal assessment of how well an employee is doing his or her job

Common Appraisal Methods Two basic categories of appraisal methods commonly used in organizations are objective methods and judgmental methods. *Objective measures* of performance include actual output (that is, number of units produced), scrappage rate, and dollar volume of sales. Another type of objective measure, the special performance test, is a method in which each employee is assessed under standardized conditions. This kind of appraisal also eliminates opportunity bias. For example, GTE Southwest Inc. has a series of prerecorded calls that operators in a test booth answer. The operators are graded on speed, accuracy, and courtesy in handling the calls. Performance tests measure ability but do not measure the extent to which one is motivated to use that ability on a daily basis. (A high-ability person may be a lazy performer except when being tested.) Special performance tests must therefore be supplemented by other appraisal methods to provide a complete picture of performance.

Judgmental methods, including ranking and rating techniques, are the most common way to measure performance. Ranking compares employees directly with each other and orders them from best to worst. Rating differs from ranking in that it compares each employee with a fixed standard rather than with other employees. A rating scale provides the standard. Figure 8.2 gives examples of three graphic rating scales for a bank teller. Each consists of a performance dimension to be rated (punctuality, congeniality, and accuracy) followed by a scale on which to make the rating. In constructing graphic rating scales, performance dimensions that are relevant to job performance must be selected. In particular, they should focus on job behaviors and results rather than on personality traits or attitudes.

• Behaviorally Anchored Rating Scale (BARS)
A sophisticated rating method in which supervisors construct a rating scale associated with behavioral anchors

The **Behaviorally Anchored Rating Scale (BARS)** is a sophisticated and useful rating method. Supervisors construct rating scales with associated behavioral anchors. They first identify relevant performance dimensions and then generate anchors—specific, observable behaviors typical of

Graphic rating scales are a very common method for evaluating employee performance. The manager who is doing the rating circles the point on each scale that best reflects her or his assessment of the employee on that scale. Graphic rating scales are widely used for many different kinds of jobs.

FIGURE 8.2 Graphic Rating Scales for a Bank Teller

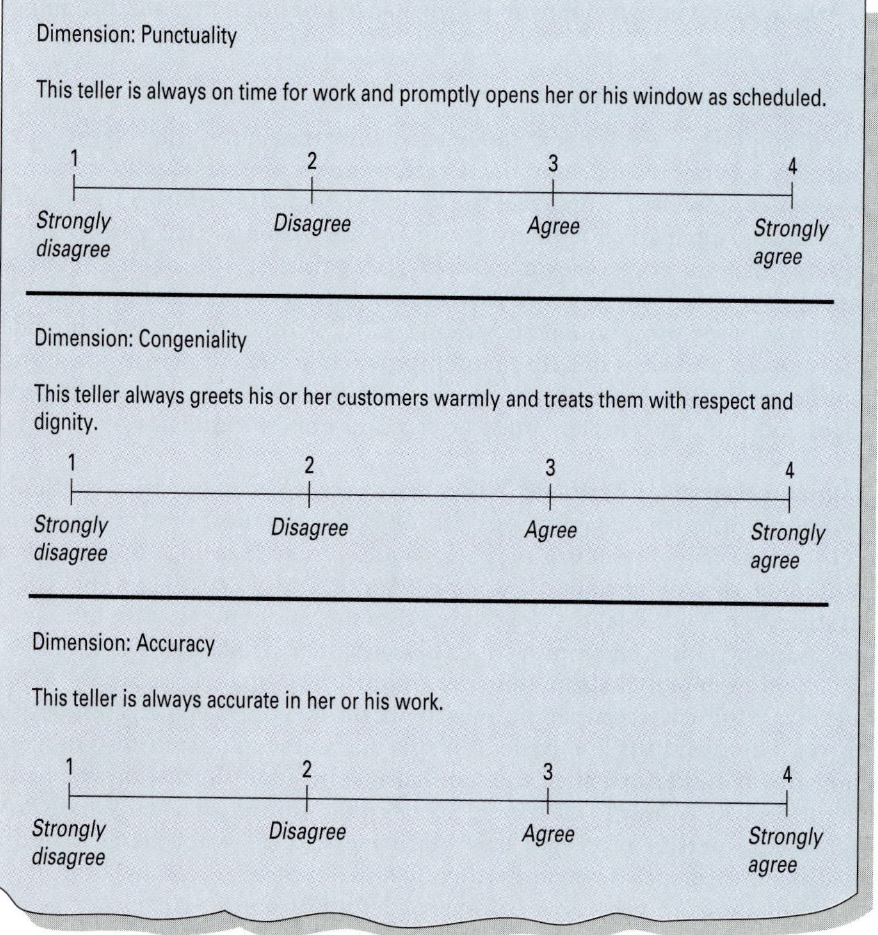

each performance level. An example of a Behaviorally Anchored Rating Scale for the dimension "inventory control" is given in Figure 8.3.

Errors in Performance Appraisal In any kind of rating or ranking system, errors or biases can occur. One common problem is recency error—the tendency to base judgments on the subordinate's most recent performance because it is most easily recalled. Other errors include overuse of one part of the scale by being either too lenient or too severe or giving everyone a rating of "average." Halo error is allowing the assessment of an employee on one dimension to "spread" to ratings of that employee on other dimensions. For instance, if an employee is outstanding on quality of output, a rater might tend to give her or him higher marks than deserved on other dimensions. Errors, either intentional or unintentional, can also occur due to race, sex, or age discrimination. The best way to offset these errors is to ensure that a valid rating system is developed at the outset and then to train managers how to use it.

Performance Feedback

The last step in most performance appraisal systems is giving feedback to subordinates about their performance, usually in a meeting between the person being evaluated and his or her boss. The discussion should be focused on the facts—the assessed level of performance, how and why that assessment was made, and how it can be improved in the future. Feedback

FIGURE 8.3 Behaviorally Anchored Rating Scale

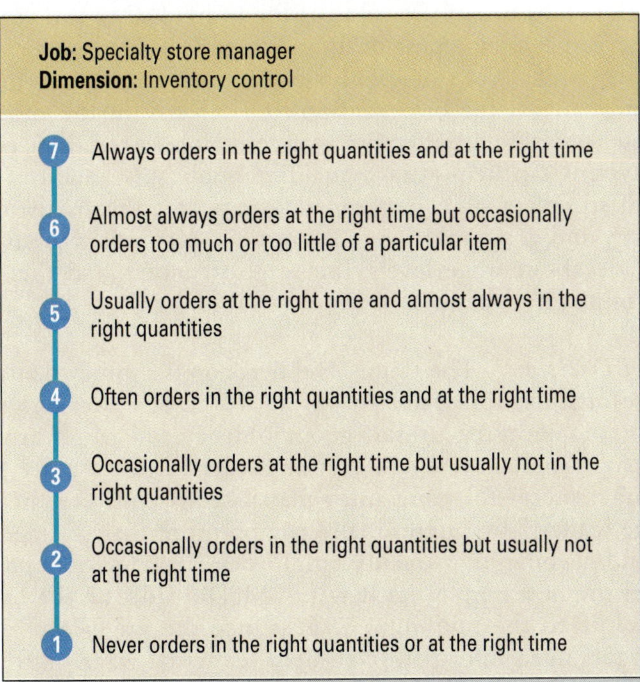

The Behaviorally Anchored Rating Scale helps overcome some of the limitations of standard rating scales. Each point on the scale is accompanied by a behavioral anchor—a summary of an employee behavior that fits that spot on the scale.

interviews are not easy to conduct. Many managers are uncomfortable with the task, especially if feedback is negative and subordinates are disappointed by what they hear. Properly training managers, however, can help them conduct more effective feedback interviews.[19]

A recent innovation in performance appraisal being used in many organizations today is called "360 degree" feedback. The idea is that managers get evaluated by everyone around them—their boss, their peers, and their subordinates. Such a complete and thorough approach provides people with a far richer array of information about their performance than would a conventional appraisal performed just by the boss. Of course, such a system takes considerable time and must be handled so as not to breed fear and mistrust in the workplace.[20]

MAINTAINING HUMAN RESOURCES

After organizations have attracted and developed an effective workforce, they must make every effort to maintain that workforce. To do so requires effective compensation and benefits.

Determining Compensation

• **compensation**
The financial remuneration given by the organization to its employees in exchange for their work

Compensation is the financial remuneration given by the organization to its employees in exchange for their work. Compensation is an important and complex part of the organization-employee relationship. Basic compensation is necessary to provide employees with the means to maintain a reasonable standard of living. Beyond this, however, compensation also provides a tangible measure of the value of the individual to the organization. If they believe that their contributions are undervalued by the organization, employees may leave or exhibit poor work habits, low morale, and little commitment to the organization. It is clearly in the organization's best interests to design an effective compensation system.[21] A good compensation system can help attract qualified applicants, retain present employees, and stimulate high performance at a cost that is reasonable for one's industry and geographic area. To set up a successful system, decisions must be made about wage levels, the wage structure, and the individual wage determination system.

Wage-Level Decision The wage-level decision is a policy decision about whether the organization wants to pay above, at, or below the going rate for labor in the industry or the geographic area.[22] Most organizations choose to pay near the average. Those that cannot afford more pay below average. Large, successful companies may like to cultivate the image of being "wage leaders" by intentionally paying more than average and thus attracting and keeping high-quality employees. IBM, for example, pays top dollar to get the new employees it wants. McDonald's, on the other hand, often pays close to the minimum wage. Once the wage-level decision is made, managers need information to help set actual wage rates. Managers need to know what the maximum, minimum, and average wages are for particular jobs in the appropriate labor market. This information is collected by means of a wage survey. Area wage surveys can be conducted by individual companies or by local HR or business associations. Professional and industry associations often conduct surveys and make the results available to employers.

Wage-Structure Decision Wage structures usually are set up through a procedure called **job evaluation**—an attempt to assess the worth of each job relative to other jobs.[23] At Ben & Jerry's Homemade, company policy dictates that the highest-paid employee in the company cannot make more than seven times what the lowest-paid employee earns. The simplest method for creating a wage structure is to rank jobs from those that should be paid the most (for example, the president) to those that should be paid the least (for example, a mail clerk or a janitor). In a smaller company with few jobs (like Ben & Jerry's), this method is quick and practical, but larger companies with many job titles require more sophisticated methods. The next step is setting actual wage rates on the basis of a combination of survey data and the wage structure that results from job evaluation. Jobs of equal value are often grouped into wage grades for ease of administration.

• **job evaluation**
An attempt to assess the worth of each job relative to other jobs

Individual Wage Decisions After these decisions have been made, the individual wage decision must be addressed. This decision concerns how much to pay each employee in a particular job. Although the easiest decision is to pay a single rate for each job, more typically a range of pay rates is associated with each job. For example, the pay range for an individual job might be \$5.85 to \$6.39 per hour, with different employees earning different rates within the range. A system is then needed for setting individual rates—on the basis of seniority (enter the job at \$5.85, for example, and increase 10 cents per hour every six months on the job), on the basis of initial qualifications (inexperienced people start at \$5.85; more experienced people start at a higher rate), or on the basis of merit (raises above the entering rate are given for good performance). Combinations of these bases may also be used.

Determining Benefits

Benefits are things of value other than compensation provided by the organization to its workers. The average company spends an amount equal to more than one-third of its cash payroll on employee benefits. Thus an average employee who is paid \$18,000 per year averages about \$6,588 more per year in benefits. Benefits come in several forms. Pay for time not worked includes sick leave, vacation, holidays, and unemployment compensation. Insurance benefits often include life and health insurance for employees and their dependents. Worker's compensation is a legally required insurance benefit that provides medical care and disability income for employees injured on the job. Social security is a government pension plan to which both employers and employees contribute. Many employers

• **benefits**
Things of value other than compensation provided by the organization to its workers

also provide a private pension plan to which they and their employees contribute. Employee service benefits include such things as tuition reimbursement and recreational opportunities.

In recent years, companies have started offering even more innovative benefits as a way of accommodating different needs. On-site childcare, cafeteria benefits programs, mortgage assistance, and generous paid leave programs are becoming popular.[24] A good benefits plan may encourage people to join and stay with an organization, but it seldom stimulates high performance because benefits are tied more to membership in the organization than to performance. To manage their benefits programs effectively, companies should shop carefully, avoid redundant coverage, and provide only those benefits that employees want. Benefits programs should be explained to employees in plain English so that they can use the benefits appropriately and appreciate what the company is providing.

MANAGING WORKFORCE DIVERSITY

Workforce diversity has become a very important issue in many organizations. The management of diversity is often seen as a key human resource function today.

The Meaning of Diversity

• **diversity**
Exists in a group or organization when its members differ from one another along one or more important dimensions such as age, gender, or ethnicity

Diversity exists in a group or organization when its members differ from one another along one or more important dimensions such as age, gender, or ethnicity.[25] For example, the average age of the U.S. workforce is gradually increasing and will continue to do so for the next several years. Similarly, as more women have entered the workforce, organizations have experienced changes in the relative proportions of male and female employees. And within the United States, most organizations reflect varying degrees of ethnicity comprised of whites, African Americans, Hispanics, and Asians.[26] Other groups such as single parents, dual-career couples, same-sex couples, and the physically challenged are also important.

The Impact of Diversity

There is no question that organizations are becoming ever more diverse. This diversity provides both opportunities and challenges for organizations.

Diversity as Competitive Advantage Many organizations are finding that diversity can be a source of competitive advantage in the marketplace.[27] For example, businesses that manage diversity effectively will generally have higher levels of productivity and lower levels of turnover and absenteeism, thus lowering costs. Ortho Pharmaceuticals estimates that it has saved $500,000 by lowering turnover among women and ethnic minorities.[28] In addition, organizations that manage diversity effectively will become known among women and minorities as good places to work, thus attracting qualified employees from among these groups. Moreover, organizations with diverse workforces may be better able to understand different market segments than will less diverse organizations. For example, a cosmetics company like Avon that wants to sell its products to women and blacks can understand better how to create such products and to market them effectively if female and black managers are available to provide input into product development, design, packaging, advertising, and so forth.[29] Finally, organizations with diverse workforces will generally be more creative and innovative than will less diverse organizations.

Diversity as a Source of Conflict Unfortunately, diversity can also become a major source of conflict. One potential avenue for conflict is when an individual thinks that someone has been hired, promoted, or fired because of her or his diversity status.[30] Another source of conflict stemming from diversity is through misunderstood, misinterpreted, or inappropriate interactions between people of different groups. Conflict may also arise as a result of fear, distrust, or individual prejudice. Members of the dominant group in an organization may worry that newcomers from other groups pose a personal threat to their own positions in the organization. For example, when U.S. firms have been taken over by Japanese firms, U.S. managers have sometimes been resentful or hostile to Japanese managers assigned to work with them. People may also be unwilling to accept people who are different from themselves. Personal bias and prejudices are still very real among some people today and can lead to potentially harmful conflict.[31]

Managing Diversity in Organizations

Because of the tremendous potential that diversity holds for competitive advantage, as well as the possible consequences of diversity-related conflict,

Individuals and organizations can help deal with diversity by working to understand others. Matsushita, a large Japanese electronics firm, has a major operation in Malaysia. Whereas the Japanese culture is relatively homogeneous, there is much more variation in Malaysia. These Muslim workers at Matsushita's plant in Malaysia are taking time for their midday prayer.

much attention has been focused in recent years on how individuals and organizations can better manage diversity.[32]

Individual Strategies One key element of managing diversity consists of things that individuals themselves can do.[33] Understanding, of course, is the starting point. While people need to be treated fairly and equitably, managers must understand that differences do, in fact, exist among people. People should try to understand the perspective of others. Tolerance is also important. Even though managers may learn to understand diversity, and even though they may try to empathize with others, the fact remains that they may still not accept or enjoy some aspect of behavior on the part of others. Communication is also important. Problems often get magnified over diversity issues because people are afraid or otherwise unwilling to openly discuss issues that relate to diversity. For example, suppose a younger employee has a habit of making jokes about the age of an elderly colleague. Perhaps the younger colleague means no harm and is just engaging in what she sees as good-natured kidding. But the older employee may find the jokes offensive. If there is no communication between the two, the jokes will continue and the resentment will grow. Eventually, what started as a minor problem may erupt into a much bigger one.

Organizational Approaches to Managing Diversity While individuals can play an important role in managing diversity, the organization itself must play a fundamental role.[34] Figure 8.4 summarizes several of the more

As the figure shows, diversity training for managers and communication statements from senior management are currently the most popular initiatives. Several other initiatives are also expected to become more widespread in the future.

F I G U R E 8.4 Corporate Diversity Initiatives

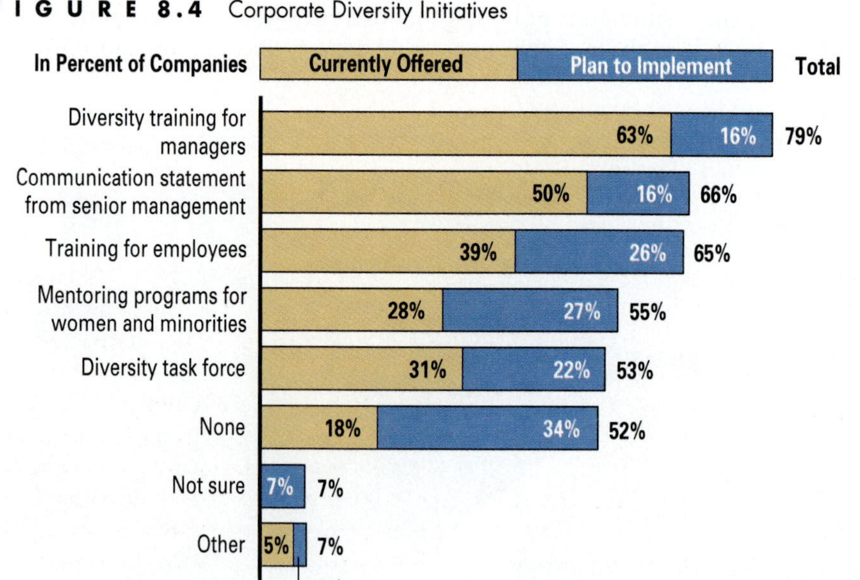

Note: Percentages do not add to 100 because many organizations undertake multiple initiatives at the same time.

Source: "Challenges of Retaining a Diverse Workforce," *Working Together, Boston Globe,* March 7, 1994, p. 15.

common business initiatives regarding diversity. The starting point in managing diversity is the policies that an organization adopts that affect how people are treated. Another aspect of organizational policies that affects diversity is how the organization addresses and responds to problems that arise from diversity. For example, consider a manager charged with sexual harassment. If the organization requires an excessive burden of proof on the individual being harassed and invokes only minor sanctions against the guilty party, it is sending a clear signal about the importance of such matters. But the organization that has a balanced set of policies for addressing questions like sexual harassment sends its employees a different message about the importance of diversity and individual rights and privileges.

Organizations can help manage diversity through a variety of ongoing practices and procedures. Avon has created networks for various groups within the organization. Benefits packages can be structured to better accommodate individual situations. Differences in family arrangements, relig-ious holidays, cultural events, and so forth may each dictate that employees have some degree of flexibility in when they work. Many organizations are finding that diversity training is an effective means for managing diversity and minimizing its associated conflict. **Diversity training** is specifically designed to better enable members of an organization to function in a diverse workplace. The ultimate test of an organization's commitment to managing diversity, however, is its culture.[35] Regardless of what managers say or put in writing, unless there is a basic and fundamental belief that diversity is valued, it cannot ever become truly an integral part of the organization.

• **diversity training** Training that is specifically designed to better enable members of an organization to function in a diverse workplace

MANAGING LABOR RELATIONS

Labor relations is the process of dealing with employees who are represented by a union.[36] Managing labor relations is an important part of HRM.

• **labor relations** The process of dealing with employees who are represented by a union

How Employees Form Unions

For a new local union to be formed, several things must occur. First, employees must become interested in having a union. Nonemployees who are professional organizers employed by a national union (such as the Teamsters or United Auto Workers) may generate interest by making speeches and distributing literature outside the workplace. Inside, employees who want a union try to convince other workers of the benefits of a union.

The second step is to collect signatures of employees on authorization cards. These cards state that the signer wishes to vote to determine if the union will represent him or her. Thirty percent of the employees in the potential bargaining unit must sign these cards to show the National Labor Relations Board (NLRB) that interest is sufficient to justify holding an election. Before an election can be held, however, the bargaining unit must be defined. The bargaining unit consists of all employees who will be eligible to vote in the election and to join and be represented by the union if one is formed.

If employees of an organization want to form a union, the law prescribes a specific set of procedures that both employees and the organization must follow. Assuming that these procedures are followed and the union is approved, the organization must engage in collective bargaining with the new union.

FIGURE 8.5 The Union-Organizing Process

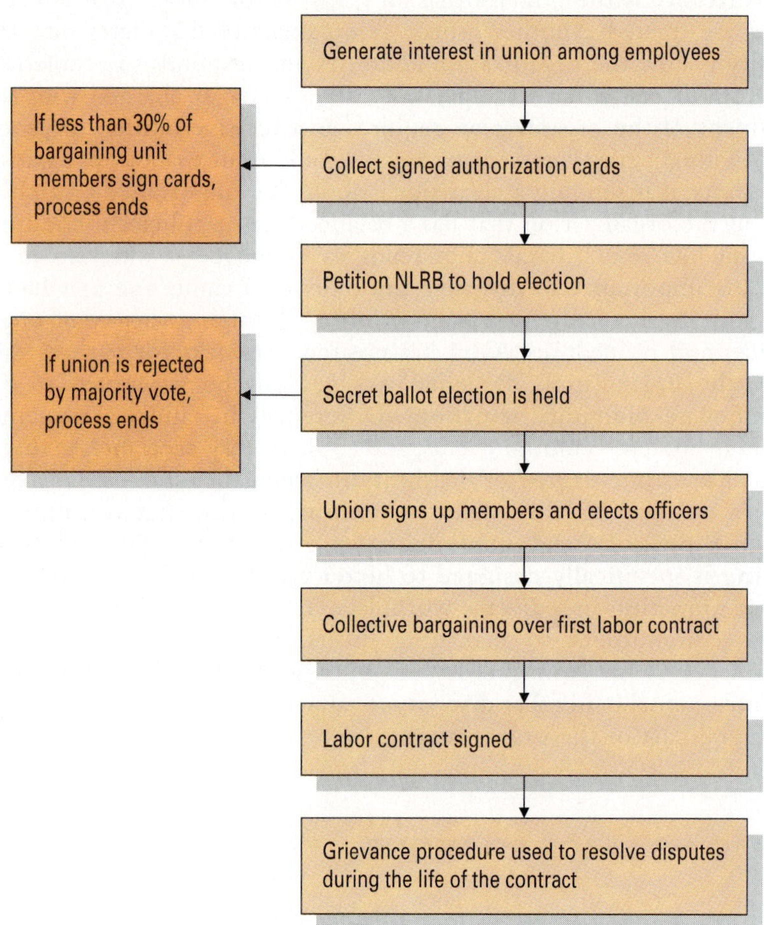

The election is supervised by an NLRB representative (or, if both parties agree, the American Arbitration Association—a professional association of arbitrators) and is conducted by secret ballot. If a simple majority of those voting (not of all those eligible to vote) votes for the union, then the union becomes certified as the official representative of the bargaining unit.[37] The new union then organizes itself by officially signing up members and electing officers; it will soon be ready to negotiate the first contract. This process is diagrammed in Figure 8.5. If workers become disgruntled with their union, or if management presents strong evidence that the union is not representing workers appropriately, the NLRB can arrange a decertification election. The results of such an election determine whether the union remains certified.

Organizations usually prefer that employees not be unionized because unions limit management's freedom in many areas. Management may thus wage its own campaign to convince employees to vote against the union.

Managing labor relations can be a critical concern to an organization. Caterpillar and the United Auto Workers have frequently disagreed over fundamental employment issues. A major strike by the UAW against Caterpillar was called in 1994. These striking workers are heckling other workers who crossed picket lines and went back to work before a settlement could be reached.

It is at this point that "unfair labor practices" are often committed. For instance, it is an unfair labor practice for management to promise to give employees a raise (or any other benefit) if the union is defeated. Experts agree that the best way to avoid unionization is to practice good employee relations all the time—not just when threatened by a union election. Providing absolutely fair treatment with clear standards in the areas of pay, promotion, layoff, and discipline; having a complaint or appeal system for persons who feel unfairly treated; and avoiding any kind of favoritism will help make employees feel that a union is unnecessary.

Collective Bargaining

The intent of **collective bargaining** is to agree on a labor contract between management and the union that is satisfactory to both parties. The contract contains agreements about wages, hours, and other conditions of employment, including promotion, layoff, discipline, benefits, methods of allocating overtime, vacations, rest periods, and the grievance procedure. The process of bargaining may go on for weeks, months, or longer, with representatives of management and the union meeting to make proposals and counterproposals. The resulting agreement must be ratified by the union membership. If it is not approved, the union may strike to put pressure on management, or it may choose not to strike and simply continue negotiating until a more acceptable agreement is reached.

collective bargaining The process of agreeing on a labor contract between management and the union that is satisfactory to both parties

grievance procedures The means by which a labor contract is enforced

The **grievance procedure** is the means by which a labor contract is enforced. Most of what is in a contract concerns how management will treat employees. When employees feel that they have not been treated fairly under the contract, they file a grievance to correct the problem. The first step in a grievance procedure is for the aggrieved employee to discuss the alleged contract violation with her immediate superior. Often the grievance is resolved at this stage. If the employee still believes that she is being mistreated, however, the grievance can be appealed to the next level. A union official may help an aggrieved employee present her case. If the manager's decision is also unsatisfactory to the employee, additional appeals to successively higher levels are made, until finally all in-company steps are exhausted. The final step is to submit the grievance to *binding arbitration*. An arbitrator is a labor-law expert who is paid jointly by the union and management. The arbitrator studies the contract, hears both sides of the case, and renders a decision that must be obeyed by both parties. The grievance system for resolving disputes about contract enforcement prevents any need to strike during the term of the contract.[38]

SUMMARY OF KEY POINTS

Human resource management is concerned with acquiring, developing, and maintaining the human resources an organization needs. Its environmental context consists of its strategic importance and the legal and social environments that affect human resource management.

Attracting human resources is an important part of the HRM function. Human resource planning starts with job analysis and then focuses on forecasting the organization's future need for employees, forecasting the availability of employees both within and outside the organization, and planning programs to ensure that the proper number and type of employees will be available when needed. Recruitment and selection are the processes by which job applicants are attracted, assessed, and hired. Methods for assessing applicants include application blanks, tests, interviews, and assessment centers. Any method used for selection should be properly validated.

Organizations must work to develop their human resources. Training and development enable employees to perform their present jobs well and to prepare for future jobs. Performance appraisals are important for determining training needs, deciding pay raises and promotions, and providing helpful feedback to employees. Both objective and judgmental methods of appraisal can be applied, and a good system usually includes several methods. The validity of appraisal information is always a concern because it is difficult to evaluate accurately the many aspects of a person's job performance.

Maintaining human resources is also important. Compensation rates must be fair compared with rates for other jobs within the organization and with rates for the same or similar jobs in other organizations in the labor market. Properly designed incentive or merit pay systems can encourage high performance, and a good benefits program can help attract and retain employees. Career planning is also a major aspect of human resource management.

Diversity exists in a group or organization when its members differ from one another along one or more important dimensions. Three of the more important dimensions of diversity are age, gender, and ethnicity. Diversity affects organizations in many different ways. Managing diversity in organizations can be done by both individuals and the organization itself.

If a majority of a company's nonmanagement employees so desire, they have the right to be represented by a union. Management must engage in collective bargaining with the union in an effort to agree on a contract. While the contract is in effect, the grievance system is used to settle disputes with management.

QUESTIONS FOR REVIEW

1. Describe recruiting and selection. What are the major sources for recruits? What are the most common selection techniques?
2. What is the role of compensation and benefits in organizations? How should the amount of compensation and benefits be determined?
3. Identify the major dimensions of diversity and discuss recent trends for each.
4. Summarize the basic impact of diversity on organizations.
5. What are the basic steps that employees must follow if they wish to create a union?

QUESTIONS FOR ANALYSIS

1. What are the advantages and disadvantages of internal and external recruiting? Which do you feel is best in the long term? Why? Be sure to think about this issue from the standpoint of both the organization and the individuals (whether inside or outside of the organization) who might be considered for positions.
2. How do you know if a selection device is valid? What are the possible consequences of using an invalid selection method? How can an organization ensure that its selection methods are valid?
3. Are benefits more important than compensation to an organization? To an individual? Why?
4. The text outlines many different advantages of diversity in organizations. What might be some disadvantages?
5. When you finish school and begin your career, what should you be prepared to do in order to succeed in a diverse workplace?

CASE STUDY

Motorola

When Paul Galvin began making car radios in Chicago in 1929, he brought in Daniel Noble, a university professor, to help him with mobile design, and gradually they built and installed the first commercially manufactured car radio. It was named Motorola for *motor* and *victrola*.

In the 1950s Motorola turned to solid-state electronic devices and semiconductors. Later it began manufacturing integrated circuits and microprocessors. By the early 1990s Motorola was either first or second in chips for personal computers and other devices, two-way radios, cellular phones, pagers, and automotive semiconductors. Motorola was the first large company to win the Malcolm Baldrige National Quality Award. It is also frequently referred to as the best managed company in the United States.

One of its keys to success is training. In 1980 Motorola established an education service department with two goals—expand participative management and improve product quality. From 1985 to 1987 Motorola's top executives spent seventeen days each in the classroom, after which the training was moved to lower levels of the organization. During this process Motorola discovered that some of its employees could not read; others could not comprehend basic quality control statistics and computations. Motorola established training to increase literacy and mathematics comprehension levels and changed hiring practices to reduce their occurrences in the future.

Motorola had been spending 4 percent of its payroll for training, but in 1994 the company announced plans to increase that amount dramatically. Every person was expected to undergo forty hours of training each year, and Motorola hoped to quadruple that by the year 2000. Even though promotions are frequently tied to the new skills obtainable through this training, some employees resist it; to get them to go, they are actually threatened with termination. Those who don't seem to learn what is taught may be demoted to jobs requiring fewer new skills.

This level of focus on training is characteristic of what have come to be known as learning organizations. A learning organization facilitates the lifelong learning and personal development of all of its employees while continually transforming itself to respond to changing demands and needs. Learning organizations typically use networking, use individual and group recognition (positive contingent reinforcement in technical terms), have a customer orientation, and train workers to develop people skills. Management styles in those organizations are characterized by openness, communication, self-determination, leadership, and a focus on the organization's strengths.

Motorola's training is highly business-specific. It might set a goal to cut costs in a particular area and then develop a course on how to do that. In addition, the corporate culture is instilled in personnel during the training. That culture is regimented, efficient, and driven.

Sixty-hour workweeks are common, and the pressure to "do it right the first time" can be intense. Motorola suggests that while it allows people to make a mistake and learn from it, it also does not allow them to repeat such mistakes. Developing training to enable its personnel to cope with the stress that arises from such a high-performance environment may be Motorola's next big training challenge.

Case Questions

1. What are the advantages and disadvantages to a learning organization?
2. Should Motorola change its training to make it more general and less geared to specific company problems? Why or why not?
3. There seem to be many contradictions in this description of Motorola—it is described as regimented, efficient, and driven but uses participative management and teams. Are these, in fact, contradictions? Why or why not?

References: Ronald Henkoff, "Keeping Motorola on a Roll," *Fortune,* April 18, 1994, pp. 67–78; "Motorola: Training for the Millennium," *Business Week,* March 28, 1994, pp. 158–162; and William Wiggenhorn, "Motorola U: When Training Becomes an Education," *Harvard Business Review,* July/August 1990, pp. 71–83.

SKILLS • DEVELOPMENT • PORTFOLIO

BUILDING EFFECTIVE TECHNICAL SKILLS

Exercise Overview

Technical skills refer to managers' abilities to accomplish or understand work done in the organization. Many managers must have technical skills in order to hire appropriate people to work in the organization. This exercise will help you use technical skills as part of the selection process.

Exercise Background

Variation 1: If you currently work full-time or have worked full-time in the past, select two jobs with which you have some familiarity. Select one job that is relatively low in skill level, responsibility, required education, and pay and one job that is relatively high in skill level, responsibility, required education, and pay. The exercise will be more useful to you if you choose real jobs that you can relate to at a personal level.

Variation 2: If you have never worked full-time or if you are not personally familiar with an array of jobs, assume that you are a manager for a small manufacturing facility. You need to hire individuals to fill two jobs. One job is for the position of plant custodian. This individual will sweep floors, clean bathrooms, empty trash cans, and so forth. The other job is for an office manager. This individual will supervise a staff of three clerks and secretaries, administer the plant payroll, and coordinate the administrative operations of the plant.

Exercise Task

With the information above as background, do the following:

1. Identify the most basic skills that you think are necessary for someone to perform each job effectively.
2. Identify the general indicators or predictors of whether a given individual can perform each job.
3. Develop a brief set of interview questions that you might use to determine whether an applicant has the qualifications to perform each job.
4. How important is it that a manager hiring employees to perform a job have the technical skills to do that job him- or herself?

BUILDING EFFECTIVE COMMUNICATION SKILLS

Exercise Overview

All managers must be able to communicate effectively with others in the organization. Communication is especially important in the human resource area, since people are the domain of human resource management.

Exercise Background

Many companies provide various benefits to their workers. These benefits may include pay for time not worked, insurance coverage, pension plans, and so forth. These benefits are often very costly to the organization. As noted in the text, for example, benefits often equal around one-third of what employees are paid in wages and salaries.

Yet many employees often fail to appreciate the actual value of the benefits their employers provide to them. For example, they frequently underestimate the dollar value of their benefits. And when comparing their income to that of others or when comparing alternative job offers, many people focus almost entirely on direct compensation—wages and salaries paid directly to the individual.

For example, consider a college graduate who has two offers. One job offer is for $20,000 a year, and the other is for $22,000. The individual is likely to see the second offer as being more attractive, even if the first offer has sufficiently more attractive benefits to make the total compensation packages equivalent to one another.

Exercise Task

With this information as context, respond to the following:

1. Why do you think most people focus on pay when assessing their compensation?

2. If you were the human resource manager for an organization, how would you go about communicating benefit value to your employees?

3. Suppose an employee comes to you and says that he is thinking about leaving for a "better job." You then learn that he is defining "better" only in terms of higher pay. How might you go about helping him compare total compensation (including benefits)?

4. Some companies today are cutting their benefits. How would you go about communicating a benefit cut to your employees?

YOU MAKE THE CALL

Mark Spenser decided that rather than talking to the two crew chiefs together, it might be more productive to meet with them individually. Thus, he asked one of them, Betty Bickham, to come by after work on Tuesday and the other one, Jason Taber, to come by on Wednesday.

His conversation with Betty was a bit tense to begin with. She had been the first woman he had hired for his lawn-care business, and she had worked hard to prove that she could perform the physically challenging work as well as anyone. She had worked hard enough, she believed, that she should have been promoted instead of Manuel Hernandez. Mark assured her that he recognized and appreciated her hard work. He pointed out, however, that Manuel had worked for SLS three years longer than Betty and that he, too, had an exemplary performance record.

Mark also pointed out that because of her strong performance record she was being paid more than any of the other three crew chiefs. He assured her that if she got her crew back on track and kept up her strong performance, she would be next in line for a promotion. After thinking things over for a few minutes, Betty decided that Mark was right. She indicated that she had, indeed, not been working very hard or pushing her crew but that she would turn things around starting the very next day.

On Wednesday, Mark was pleased to see that Betty's crew was the first one finished and back at the warehouse. Jason Taber's crew came in last, but Mark was optimistic that his meeting with Jason would also be productive. Unfortunately, however, Mark's optimism was ill-founded. During their meeting, Mark was both surprised and disappointed to realize that Jason was prejudiced against ethnic minorities. While he had had no trouble working with Manuel when they were both crew chiefs, he indicated that he had trouble taking orders from Manuel and seeing him in a position of authority.

Mark asked Jason point-blank if he could set his prejudices aside and get his performance back to where it needed to be. Jason said that he could not and that he assumed that he would have to resign. Mark indicated that he was sorry that Jason felt as he did but that it would indeed be necessary for Jason to leave.

The next day, Mark and Manuel met and decided to promote one of the regular crew members from Jason's team to the position of crew chief. Manuel placed a "help wanted" ad in the newspaper and called the local office of the Texas Employment Commission to inform them of the new job opening. Within a few days, a new lawn-care team member had been hired and things were under control again.

Discussion Questions

1. Evaluate how Mark handled this situation.

2. If Jason had said that, even though he was prejudiced, he could "hide it" and still work effectively, should Mark still have fired him?

3. What recruiting and selection approaches are most likely to be used in a business like SLS?

SKILLS SELF-ASSESSMENT INSTRUMENT

Diagnosing Poor Performance and Enhancing Motivation

Introduction: Formal performance appraisal and feedback are part of assuring proper performance in an organization. The following assessment is designed to help you understand how to detect poor performance and overcome it.

Instructions: Please respond to the following statements by entering a number from the following rating scale. Your answers should reflect your attitudes and behaviors as they are *now.*

Rating Scale

6 Strongly agree	**3** Slightly disagree
5 Agree	**2** Disagree
4 Slightly agree	**1** Strongly disagree

When another person needs to be motivated,

_____ **1.** I always approach a performance problem by first establishing whether it is caused by a lack of motivation or ability.

_____ **2.** I always establish a clear standard of expected performance.

_____ **3.** I always offer to provide training and information, without offering to do the task myself.

_____ **4.** I am honest and straightforward in providing feedback on performance and assessing advancement opportunities.

_____ **5.** I use a variety of rewards to reinforce exceptional performances.

_____ **6.** When discipline is required, I identify the problem, describe its consequences, and explain how it should be corrected.

_____ **7.** I design task assignments to make them interesting and challenging.

_____ **8.** I determine what rewards are valued by the person and strive to make those available.

_____ **9.** I make sure that the person feels fairly and equitably treated.

_____ **10.** I make sure that the person gets timely feedback from those affected by task performance.

_____ **11.** I carefully diagnose the causes of poor performance before taking any remedial or disciplinary actions.

_____ **12.** I always help the person establish performance goals that are challenging, specific, and time-bound.

_____ **13.** Only as a last resort do I attempt to reassign or release a poorly performing individual.

_____ **14.** Whenever possible I make sure that valued rewards are linked to high performance.

_____ **15.** I consistently discipline when effort is below expectations and capabilities.

_____ **16.** I try to combine or rotate assignments so that the person can use a variety of skills.

_____ **17.** I try to arrange for the person to work with others in a team, for the mutual support of all.

_____ **18.** I make sure that the person is using realistic standards for measuring fairness.

_____ **19.** I provide immediate compliments and other forms of recognition for meaningful accomplishments.

_____ **20.** I always determine if the person has the necessary resources and support to succeed in the task.

For interpretation, turn to page 448.

EXPERIENTIAL EXERCISE

Whom Do You Promote?

Purpose: In this chapter we discuss the importance of staffing to the organization. One method of staffing the organization is through promotion. To staff through promotion requires special skill on the part of the manager. This exercise will help you develop decision-making skills as they relate to staffing issues.

Introduction: Consider, first by yourself and then within a group, which of the following individuals should be promoted. Keep in mind the criteria you are using for making these decisions.

Instructions: Your company recently developed a plan to identify and train top hourly employees for promotion to first-line supervisor. As part of this program, your boss has requested a ranking of the six hourly workers who report to you with respect to their promotion potential. Given their biographical data, rank them in the order in which you would select them for promotion to first-line supervisor; that is, the person ranked number one would be first in line for promotion.

Biographical Data

1. *Sam Nelson:* White male, age forty-five, married, with four children. Sam has been with the company for five years, and his performance evaluations have been average to above average. He is well liked by the other employees in the department. He devotes his spare time to farming and plans to farm after retirement.

2. *Ruth Hornsby:* White female, age thirty-two, married, with no children; husband has a management-level job with the power company. Ruth has been with the company for two years and has received above-average performance evaluations. She is very quiet and keeps to herself at work. She says she is working to save for a down payment on a new house.

3. *Joe Washington:* Black male, age twenty-six, single. Joe has been with the company for three years and has received high performance evaluations. He is always willing to take on new assignments and to work overtime. He is attending college in the evenings and someday wants to start his own business. He is well liked by the other employees in the department.

4. *Ronald Smith:* White male, age thirty-five, recently divorced, with one child, age four. Ronald has received excellent performance evaluations during his two years with the company. He seems to like his present job but has removed himself from the line of progression. He seems to have personality conflicts with some of the employees.

5. *Betty Norris:* Black female, age forty-four, married, with one grown child. Betty has been with the company for ten years and is well liked by fellow employees. Her performance evaluations have been average to below-average, and her advancement has been limited by a lack of formal education. She has participated in a number of technical training programs conducted by the company.

6. *Roy Davis:* White male, age thirty-six, married, with two teenage children. Roy has been with the company for ten years and received excellent performance evaluations until last year. His most recent evaluation was average. He is friendly and well liked by his fellow employees. One of his children has had a serious illness for over a year, resulting in a number of large medical expenses. Roy is working a second job on weekends to help with these expenses. He has expressed a serious interest in promotion to first-line supervisor.

Source: Reproduced from *Supervisory Management: The Art of Working With and Through People,* 2nd ed., by Donald C. Mosley, Leon C. Megginson, and Paul H. Pietri, Jr. with the permission of South-Western Publishing Co. (Cincinnati: South-Western Publishing, 1989).

CHAPTER NOTES

1. "Saturn: Labor's Love Lost?" *Business Week,* February 8, 1993, pp. 122–124; Gary Hoover, Alta Campbell, and Patrick J. Spain (Eds.), *Hoover's Handbook of American Business 1995* (Austin, Tex.: The Reference Press, 1994), pp. 548–549; "New Saturn is Heavy on Outsourcing," *USA Today,* July 5, 1996, p. 1B.
2. For a complete review of human resource management, see Cynthia D. Fisher, Lyle F. Schoenfeldt, and James B. Shaw, *Human Resource Management,* 3rd ed. (Boston: Houghton Mifflin, 1993).
3. David Terpstra and Elizabeth Rozell, "The Relationship of Staffing Practices to Organizational Level Measures of Performance," *Personnel Psychology,* Spring 1993, pp. 27–38.
4. Augustine Lado and Mary Wilson, "Human Resource Systems and Sustained Competitive Advantage: A Competency-Based Perspective," *Academy of Management Review,* 1994, Vol. 19, No. 4, pp. 699–727.
5. Robert Calvert, Jr., *Affirmative Action: A Comprehensive Recruitment Manual* (Garrett Park, Md.: Garrett Park Press, 1979). For recent perspectives on affirmative action, see "Affirmative Action Faces Likely Setback," *The Wall Street Journal,* November 30, 1988, p. B1.
6. "OSHA Awakens from Its Six-Year Slumber," *Business Week,* August 10, 1987, p. 27; and "Workplace Injuries Proliferate as Concerns Push People to Produce," *The Wall Street Journal,* June 16, 1989, pp. A1, A8.
7. "Shades of Geneen at Emerson Electric," *Fortune,* May 22, 1989, p. 39.
8. Leonard Greenhalgh, Anne T. Lawrence, and Robert I. Sutton, "Determinants of Work Force Reduction Strategies in Declining Organizations," *Academy of Management Review,* April 1988, pp. 241–254.
9. Michael R. Carrell and Frank E. Kuzmits, *Personnel: Human Resource Management,* 3rd ed. (New York: Merrill, 1989).
10. Mary K. Suszko and James A. Breaugh, "The Effects of Realistic Job Previews on Applicant Self-Selection and Employee Turnover, Satisfaction, and Coping Ability," *Journal of Management,* Fall 1986, pp. 513–523.
11. Frank L. Schmidt and John E. Hunter, "Employment Testing: Old Theories and New Research Findings," *American Psychologist,* October 1981, pp. 1128–1137; see also "New Test Quantifies the Way We Work," *The Wall Street Journal,* February 7, 1990, p. B1.
12. Robert Liden, Christopher Martin, and Charles Parsons, "Interviewer and Applicant Behaviors in Employment Interviews," *Academy of Management Journal,* June 1993, pp. 372–386.
13. Brian Dumaine, "The New Art of Hiring Smart," *Fortune,* August 17, 1987, pp. 78–81.
14. Paul R. Sackett, "Assessment Centers and Content Validity: Some Neglected Issues," *Personnel Psychology,* 1987, Vol. 40, pp. 13–25.
15. See Bernard Keys and Joseph Wolfe, "Management Education and Development: Current Issues and Emerging Trends," *Journal of Management,* June 1988, pp. 205–229, for a recent review.
16. Michael Brody, "Helping Workers to Work Smarter," *Fortune,* June 8, 1987, pp. 86–88.
17. "Videos Are Starring in More and More Training Programs," *Business Week,* September 7, 1987, pp. 108–110.
18. For recent discussions of why performance appraisal is important, see Walter Kiechel III, "How to Appraise Performance," *Fortune,* October 12, 1987, pp. 239–240; and Donald J. Campbell and Cynthia Lee, "Self-Appraisal in Performance Evaluation: Development Versus Evaluation," *Academy of Management Review,* April 1988, pp. 302–314.
19. Barry R. Nathan, Allan Mohrman, and John Milliman, "Interpersonal Relations as a Context for the Effects of Appraisal Interviews on Performance and Satisfaction: A Longitudinal Study," *Academy of Management Journal,* June 1991, pp. 352–369.
20. Brian O'Reilly, "360 Feedback Can Change Your Life," *Fortune,* October 17, 1994, pp. 93–100.
21. Jaclyn Fierman, "The Perilous New World of Fair Pay," *Fortune,* June 13, 1994, pp. 57–64.
22. Caroline L. Weber and Sara L. Rynes, "Effects of Compensation Strategy on Job Pay Decisions," *Academy of Management Journal,* March 1991, pp. 86–109.
23. Peter Cappelli and Wayne F. Cascio, "Why Some Jobs Command Wage Premiums: A Test of Career Tournament and Internal Labor Market Hypotheses," *Academy of Management Journal,* December 1991, pp. 848–868.
24. "The Future Look of Employee Benefits," *The Wall Street Journal,* September 7, 1988, p. 21.
25. Marlene G. Fine, Fern L. Johnson, and M. Sallyanne Ryan, "Cultural Diversity in the Workplace," *Public Personnel Management,* Fall 1990, pp. 305–319.
26. *Occupational Outlook Handbook* (Washington, D.C.: U.S. Bureau of Labor Statistics, 1990–1991).
27. Based on Taylor H. Cox and Stacy Blake, "Managing Cultural Diversity: Implications for Organizational Competitiveness," *Academy of Management Executive,* August 1991, pp. 45–56.
28. Cox and Taylor, "Managing Cultural Diversity: Implications for Organizational Competitiveness."
29. For an example, see "Get to Know the Ethnic Market," *Marketing,* June 17, 1991, p. 32.

30. "As Population Ages, Older Workers Clash with Younger Bosses," *The Wall Street Journal,* June 13, 1994, pp. A1, A8.

31. Patti Watts, "Bias Busting: Diversity Training in the Workforce," *Management Review,* December 1987, pp. 51–54.

32. See Stephenie Overman, "Managing the Diverse Work Force," *HR Magazine,* April 1991, pp. 32–36.

33. Lennie Copeland, "Making the Most of Cultural Differences at the Workplace," *Personnel,* June 1988, pp. 52–60.

34. Sara Rynes and Benson Rosen, "What Makes Diversity Programs Work?" *HR Magazine,* October 1994, pp. 67–75.

35. Anthony Carneville and Susan Stone, "Diversity—Beyond the Golden Rule," *Training & Development,* October 1994, pp. 22–27.

36. Barbara Presley Nobel, "Reinventing Labor," *Harvard Business Review,* July–August 1993, pp. 115–125.

37. John A. Fossum, "Labor Relations: Research and Practice in Transition," *Journal of Management,* Summer 1987, pp. 281–300.

38. For recent research on collective bargaining, see Wallace N. Davidson III, Dan L. Worrell, and Sharon H. Garrison, "Effect of Strike Activity on Firm Value," *Academy of Management Journal,* June 1988, pp. 387–394; John M. Magenau, James E. Martin, and Melanie M. Peterson, "Dual and Unilateral Commitment Among Stewards and Rank-and-File Union Members," *Academy of Management Journal,* June 1988, pp. 359–376; and Brian E. Becker, "Concession Bargaining: The Meaning of Union Gains," *Academy of Management Journal,* June 1988, pp. 377–387.

Managers today must constantly strive to understand individual behavior and motivate people in an increasingly diverse context. Overseeing a large workforce on a construction project and dealing with individual employees on a one-to-one basis both require leadership skills.

PART

IV

Leading

CHAPTER 9

Managing Individual Behavior

OBJECTIVES

After studying this chapter, you should be able to:

- *Explain the nature of the individual-organization relationship.*
- *Define personality and describe personality attributes that affect behavior in organizations.*
- *Discuss individual attitudes in organizations and how they affect behavior.*
- *Describe basic perceptual processes and the role of attributions in organizations.*
- *Discuss the causes and consequences of stress and describe how it can be managed.*
- *Explain how workplace behaviors can directly or indirectly influence organizational effectiveness.*

OUTLINE

OPENING INCIDENT

THE PRUDENTIAL INSURANCE Co. of America is the largest insurance business in the United States. John Dryden founded the company in 1873, as the Widows and Orphans Friendly Society. Since these early days, Prudential has prided itself on how it treated its employees. Indeed, the company has long been a model for establishing good relations with its employees, and those employees, in turn, have been loyal and dedicated members of the organization.

Recently, however, things have begun to change. Like many other large companies in the United States, Prudential has been going through a painful downsizing process that has cost thousands of people their jobs. In Prudential's case, a series of ill-advised new ventures and legal setbacks cut into the firm's profits. In an effort to restore its profitability, Prudential has eliminated five thousand jobs and scaled back its operations in a number of ways.

> **"The message we're getting now is that the company doesn't owe you anything. . . . [And] I don't owe them anything."**

An unintended side effect of these cutbacks for Prudential has been a decline in employee commitment and lower employee morale. In the past, dedicated and hard-working employees expected to give their all to the company and to work for Prudential for many years. In return, these employees expected the company to provide them with reasonable job security and to treat them like one, big happy family.

Now, however, this "understanding" between the company and its employees has clearly been altered. Company consultants are helping employees redefine their relationship to the company. The new message has been, in the words of one Prudential employee, that the company does not owe its employees emotional support, raises, or job security. Instead, the firm owes its employees an honest and open appraisal of where they stand and how their future with the company is shaping up.

As noted already, however, not all employees have embraced this new relationship and this alternative way of doing business. Many of them feel that the company has betrayed them. Some also report that they enjoy their jobs less today than they did in the past, and that they feel less loyalty and dedication to the firm. Some employees also report that they are feeling more anxiety and stress about their jobs.

A few Prudential managers have left the firm to look for new opportunities elsewhere. Others still with Prudential are looking for new jobs with other companies. One manager noted that the firm was thinking of moving the office where she works to a new city twenty miles away from its present location. She indicates that if she is asked to relocate, she will instead quit and look for a new job closer to home. After all, she argues, she doesn't owe the company anything.[1] ●

Source of Quotation: Anonymous Prudential manager, quoted in *Fortune*, June 13, 1994, pp. 46, 47.

Prudential and its employees are in the process of redefining their relationship with one another. To do so, they must each assess how well their respective needs and capabilities now match each other's. A variety of different and unique characteristics that reside in each and every employee affects how these employees feel about the changes, how they will alter their future attitudes about the company, and how they will perform their jobs. These characteristics reflect the basic elements of individual behavior in organizations.

This chapter describes several of these basic elements and is the first of several chapters designed to develop a more complete perspective on the leading function of management. In the next section we investigate the psychological nature of individuals in organizations. Then we introduce the concept of personality and discuss several important personality attributes that can influence behavior in organizations. We then examine individual attitudes and their role in organizations. The role of stress in the workplace is then discussed. Finally, we describe a number of basic individual behaviors that are important to organizations.

UNDERSTANDING INDIVIDUALS IN ORGANIZATIONS

As a starting point in understanding human behavior in the workplace we must consider the basic nature of the relationship between individuals and organizations. We must also gain an appreciation of the nature of individual differences.

The Psychological Contract

Most people have a basic understanding of a contract. Whenever we buy a car or sell a house, for example, both buyer and seller sign a contract that specifies the terms of the agreement. A psychological contract is similar in some ways to a standard legal contract, but it is less formal and well defined. In particular, a **psychological contract** is the overall set of expectations held by an individual with respect to what he or she will contribute to the organization and what the organization, in return, will provide to the individual.[2] Thus a psychological contract is not written on paper nor are all of its terms explicitly negotiated.

- **psychological contract** The overall set of expectations held by an individual with respect to what he or she will contribute to the organization and what the organization will provide to the individual

The essential nature of a psychological contract is illustrated in Figure 9.1. The individual makes a variety of **contributions** to the organization —such things as effort, skills, ability, time, loyalty, and so forth. These contributions presumably satisfy various needs and requirements of the organization. That is, because the organization may have hired the person because of her skills, it is reasonable for the organization to expect that she will subsequently display those skills in the performance of her job.

- **contributions** What the individual provides to the organization

In return for these contributions, the organization provides **inducements** to the individual. Some inducements, like pay and career opportunities, are tangible rewards. Others, like job security and status, are more

- **inducements** What the organization provides to the individual

FIGURE 9.1 The Psychological Contract

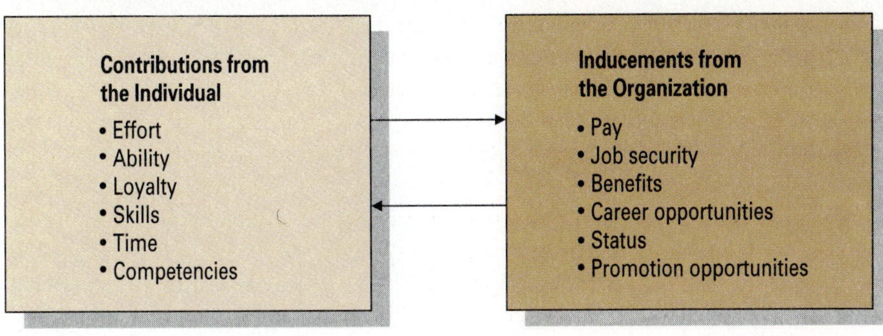

Psychological contracts are the basic assumptions that individuals have about their relationships with their organization. Such contracts are defined in terms of contributions by the individual relative to inducements from the organization.

intangible. Just as the contributions available from the individual must satisfy needs of the organization, the inducements offered by the organization must serve the needs of the individual. That is, if a person accepts employment with an organization because he thinks he will earn an attractive salary and have an opportunity to advance, he will subsequently expect that those rewards will actually be forthcoming.

If both the individual and organization perceive that the psychological contract is fair and equitable, they will be satisfied with the relationship and will likely continue it. On the other hand, if either party sees an imbalance or inequity in the contract, it may initiate a change. For example, the individual may request a pay raise or promotion, decrease her contributed effort, or look for a better job elsewhere. The organization can also initiate change by requesting that the individual improve his skills through training, transfer the person to another job, or terminate the person's employment altogether.

A basic challenge faced by the organization, then, is to manage psychological contracts. The organization must ensure that it is getting value from its employees. At the same time, it must also be sure that it is providing employees with appropriate inducements. If the organization is underpaying its employees for their contributions, for example, they may perform poorly or leave for better jobs elsewhere. If they are being overpaid relative to their contributions, the organization is incurring unnecessary costs.

The Person-Job Fit

One specific aspect of managing psychological contracts is managing the person-job fit. The **person-job fit** is the extent to which the contributions made by the individual match the inducements offered by the organization. In theory, each employee has a specific set of needs that he wants fulfilled and a set of job-related behaviors and abilities to contribute. Thus, if the organization can take perfect advantage of those behaviors and abilities and exactly fulfill his needs, it will have achieved a perfect person-job fit.[3]

• **person-job fit**
The extent to which the contributions made by the individual match the inducements offered by the organization

Of course, such a precise level of person-job fit is seldom achieved. There are several reasons for this. For one thing, organizational selection

Achieving a good person-job fit is an important goal in any organization. For example, it takes someone with special skills and abilities to perform a task like painting San Francisco's Golden Gate Bridge. Bud Wiley has been doing this job for fifteen years. His sense of adventure, dedication to his craft, and love of the outdoors make him an ideal person for this job. On the other hand, a person who is afraid of heights or who prefers to work indoors would not enjoy this job at all.

procedures are imperfect. Organizations can make approximations of employee skill levels when making hiring decisions and can improve them through training. But even simple performance dimensions are hard to measure objectively and validly.

Another reason for imprecise person-job fits is that both people and organizations change. An individual who finds a new job stimulating and exciting may find the same job boring and monotonous after a few years of performing it. And when the organization adopts new technology it has changed the skills it needs from its employees. Still another reason for imprecision in the person-job fit is that each individual is unique. Measuring skills and performance is difficult enough. Assessing needs, attitudes, and personality is far more complex. Each of these individual differences serves to make matching individuals with jobs a difficult and complex process.

The Nature of Individual Differences

● **individual differences** Personal attributes that vary from one person to another

Individual differences are personal attributes that vary from one person to another. Individual differences may be physical, psychological, and emotional. Taken together, all of the individual differences that characterize any specific person serve to make that individual unique from everyone else. Much of the remainder of this chapter is devoted to individual differences. Before proceeding, however, we must also note the importance of the situation in assessing the behavior of individuals.

Are specific differences that characterize a given individual good or bad? Do they contribute to or detract from performance? The answer, of course, is that it depends on the circumstances. One person may be very dissatisfied, withdrawn, and negative in one job setting but very satisfied, outgoing, and positive in another. Working conditions, coworkers, and leadership are all important ingredients. The Prudential manager quoted in our opening incident was apparently quite happy and satisfied in one situation, but her feelings changed as the company altered its practices and, as a result, redefined her situation.

Thus, whenever an organization attempts to assess or account for individual differences among its employees, it must be sure to consider the situation in which behavior occurs. Individuals who are satisfied or productive workers in one context may prove to be dissatisfied or unproductive workers in another context. Attempting to consider both individual differences and contributions in relation to inducements and contexts, then, is a major challenge for organizations as they attempt to establish effective psychological contracts with their employees and achieve optimal fits between people and jobs.

PERSONALITY AND INDIVIDUAL BEHAVIOR

Personality traits represent some of the most fundamental sets of individual differences in organizations today. **Personality** is the relatively permanent set of psychological and behavioral attributes that distinguish one person from another.[4] Understanding basic personality attributes is important because they affect people's behavior in organizational situations and people's perceptions of and attitudes toward the organization. They also play a role in how people handle stress at work.

• **personality**
The relatively permanent set of psychological and behavioral attributes that distinguish one person from another

Personality Formation

The basic personality of a manager or employee is formed before she or he ever becomes a member of an organization. Indeed, personality formation starts at birth and continues throughout adolescence. Hereditary characteristics (e.g., body shape and height) and the social (e.g., family and friends) and cultural (e.g., religion and values) context in which people grow up all interact to shape their basic personalities. As people grow into adulthood, their personalities become very clearly defined and stable.

But a person's personality can still be changed as a result of organizational experiences. For example, suppose a manager is subjected to prolonged periods of stress or conflict at work. As a result, he or she may become withdrawn, anxious, and irritable. While removal of the stressful circumstances may eventually temper these characteristics, the individual's personality may also reflect permanent changes. From a more positive perspective, continued success, accomplishment, and advancement may cause an individual to become increasingly self-confident and outgoing. Situational influences can also affect personality in unexpected ways. For example, an honest employee may be tempted to steal money from the organization if he or she is experiencing severe financial pressures.

These types of extreme examples aside, managers should recognize that they can do little to change the basic personalities of their subordinates. Instead, they should work to understand the basic nature of their subordinates' personalities and how attributes of those personalities affect the subordinates' work behavior.

Personality Attributes in Organizations

Over the past few decades a considerable amount of research has been conducted to identify and further our understanding of personality attributes that are relevant to managers. Several of the more important attributes are discussed here.

● **locus of control**
The degree to which an individual believes that behavior has a direct impact on the consequences of that behavior

Locus of control refers to the degree to which an individual believes that behavior has a direct impact on the consequences of that behavior.[5] Some people, for example, believe that if they work hard they are certain to succeed. They also may believe that people who fail do so simply because they lack ability or motivation. Because these people believe that each person is in control of his or her life, they are said to have an *internal locus of control*. On the other hand, some people think that what happens to them is a result of fate, chance, luck, or the behavior of other people. For example, an employee who fails to get a promotion may attribute that failure to a politically motivated boss or just bad luck, rather than to her own lack of skills or poor performance record. Because these people think that forces beyond their control dictate what happens to them, they are said to have an *external locus of control*.

As a personality attribute, locus of control has clear implications for organizations. For example, individuals with an internal locus of control may have a relatively strong desire to participate in the governance of their organizations and have a voice in how they do their jobs. Thus, they may prefer a decentralized organization and a leader who gives them freedom and autonomy. They may also be more likely to resist control. And they may be most comfortable under a reward system that recognizes individual performance and contributions. People with an external locus of control, on the other hand, are more likely to prefer a more centralized organization where decisions are taken out of their hands. They may gravitate to structured jobs where standard procedures are defined for them. Similarly, they may prefer a leader who makes most of the decisions and could prefer a reward system that puts a premium on seniority.

● **self-efficacy**
An individual's set of beliefs about her or his capabilities to perform a task

A related but subtly different personality trait is self-efficacy. **Self-efficacy** is an individual's set of beliefs about her or his capabilities to perform a task.[6] Individuals with high self-efficacy believe they can perform well on a given task or job. They consequently exhibit high self-confidence and seek out tasks that will challenge them and their abilities. On the other hand, people with low self-efficacy are more prone to doubt their capabilities, will exhibit low self-confidence, and may seek out tasks or jobs that are relatively easy and that present little challenge.

● **authoritarianism**
The extent to which an individual believes that power and status differences are appropriate within hierarchical social systems like organizations

Authoritarianism is the extent to which an individual believes that power and status differences are appropriate within hierarchical social systems like organizations.[7] For example, a person who is highly authoritarian may accept directives or orders from someone with more authority purely because the other person is "the boss." A person who is not highly authoritarian may still carry out appropriate and reasonable directives from the boss but is also more likely to question things, express disagreement with the boss, and even refuse to carry out orders if they are for some reason objectionable. A manager who is highly authoritarian may be relatively autocratic and demanding, and subordinates who are highly authoritarian will be more likely to accept this behavior from their leader. On the other hand, a manager who is less authoritarian may allow subordinates a bigger role in making decisions, and less authoritarian subordinates will respond positively to this behavior.[8]

Dogmatism is the rigidity of a person's beliefs and his or her openness to other viewpoints.[9] The popular terms for dogmatism are *close-minded* and *open-minded*. For example, suppose a manager has such strong beliefs about how certain procedures should be carried out that he is unwilling to even listen to a new idea for doing it more efficiently. We might say this person is close-minded, or highly dogmatic. A manager in the same circumstances that is very receptive to listening to and trying new ideas can be seen as more open-minded, or less dogmatic. Dogmatism can be either beneficial or detrimental to organizations. Given the changing nature of organizations and their environments, individuals who are not dogmatic are more likely to be useful and productive organizational members.

• **dogmatism**
The rigidity of a person's beliefs and his or her openness to other viewpoints

Self-esteem is the extent to which a person believes that he or she is a worthwhile and deserving individual.[10] A person with high self-esteem is more likely to seek high-status jobs, be more confident in his or her ability to achieve higher levels of performance, and derive greater intrinsic satisfaction from his or her accomplishments. In contrast, a person with less self-esteem may be more content to remain in a low-level job, be less confident of his or her ability, and focus more on extrinsic rewards.

• **self-esteem**
The extent to which a person believes that he or she is a worthwhile and deserving individual

Risk propensity is the degree to which an individual is willing to take chances and make risky decisions. A manager with a high risk propensity, for example, might be expected to experiment with new ideas and gamble on new products. She might also lead the organization in new and different directions. This manager might also be a catalyst for innovation. But the same individual might jeopardize the continued well-being of the organization if the risky decisions prove to be bad ones. A manager with low risk propensity might lead to a stagnant and overly conservative organization or help the organization successfully weather turbulent and unpredictable times by maintaining stability and calm. Thus the potential consequences of risk propensity to an organization are heavily dependent on that organization's environment.

• **risk propensity**
The degree to which an individual is willing to take chances and make risky decisions

ATTITUDES AND INDIVIDUAL BEHAVIOR

Another important element of individual behavior in organizations is attitude. An **attitude** is a complex of beliefs and feelings that people have about specific ideas, situations, or other people. Attitudes are important because they are the mechanism through which most people express their feelings. An employee's statement that he feels underpaid by the organization reflects his feelings about his pay. Similarly, when a manager says that she likes the new advertising campaign, she is expressing her feelings about the organization's marketing efforts.

• **attitude**
A complex of beliefs and feelings that people have about specific ideas, situations, or other people

Components of an Attitude

Attitudes have three components. The *affective component* of an attitude reflects feelings and emotions an individual has toward a situation. The *cognitive component* of an attitude is derived from knowledge an individual has about a situation. It is important to note that cognition is subject to individual perceptions (something we discuss more fully later). Thus one person might "know" that a certain political candidate is better than another, while someone else may "know" just the opposite. Finally, the *intentional component* of an attitude reflects how an individual expects to behave toward or in the situation.

To illustrate these three components, consider the case of a manager who places an order for some supplies for his organization from a new office supply firm. Suppose many of the items he orders are out of stock, others are over-priced, and still others arrive damaged. When he calls someone at the supply firm for assistance, he is treated rudely and gets disconnected before his claim is resolved. When asked how he feels about the new office supply firm, he might respond, "I don't like that company (affective component). They are the worst office supply firm I've ever dealt with (cognitive component). I'll never do business with them again (intentional component)."

• cognitive dissonance The conflict an individual may experience among his or her attitudes

People try to maintain consistency among the three components of their attitudes as well as among all their attitudes. Circumstances sometimes arise, however, that lead to conflicts. The conflict individuals may experience among their own attitudes is called **cognitive dissonance**.[11] Say, for example, an individual who has vowed never to work for a big, impersonal corporation intends instead to open her own business and be her own boss. Unfortunately, a series of financial setbacks leads her to having no choice but to take a job with a large company and work for someone else. Thus cognitive dissonance occurs: The affective and cognitive components of the individual's attitude conflict with intended behavior. In order to reduce cognitive dissonance, which is usually an uncomfortable experience for most people, the individual described above might tell herself the situation is only temporary and that she can go back out on her own in the near future. Or she might revise her cognitions and decide that working for a large company is more pleasant than she had ever expected.

Work-Related Attitudes

People in organizations form attitudes about many different things. For example, employees are likely to have attitudes about their salary, promotion possibilities, their boss, employee benefits, the food in the company cafeteria, and even the color of the company softball team uniforms. Of course, some of these attitudes are more important than others. Especially important attitudes are job satisfaction or dissatisfaction, organizational commitment, and job involvement.

• job satisfaction or **dissatisfaction** An attitude that reflects the extent to which an individual is gratified by or fulfilled in his or her work

Job Satisfaction or Dissatisfaction **Job satisfaction** or **dissatisfaction** is an attitude that reflects the extent to which an individual is gratified by or fulfilled in his or her work. Extensive research conducted on job satisfaction has indicated that personal factors such as an individual's needs and aspirations determine this attitude, along with group and organizational factors such as relationships with coworkers and supervisors and working conditions, work policies, and compensation.[12]

A satisfied employee tends to be absent less often, to make positive contributions, and to stay with the organization. In contrast, a dissatisfied employee may be absent more often, may experience stress that disrupts coworkers, and may be continually looking for another job. Contrary to what a lot of managers believe, however, high levels of job satisfaction do not necessarily lead to higher levels of performance. One survey has indicated that contrary to popular opinion, Japanese workers are less satisfied with their jobs than their counterparts in the United States.[13]

Organizational Commitment and Job Involvement Two other important work-related attitudes are organizational commitment and job involvement. **Organizational commitment** is an attitude that reflects an individual's identification with and attachment to the organization itself.[14] A person with a high level of commitment is likely to see herself as a true member of the organization (e.g., referring to the organization in personal terms like "we make high-quality products"), to overlook minor sources of dissatisfaction with the organization, and to see herself remaining a member of the organization. In contrast, a person with less organizational commitment is more likely to see himself as an outsider (e.g., referring to the organization in less personal terms like "they don't pay their employees very well"), to express more dissatisfaction about things, and to not see himself as a long-term member of the organization. Research suggests that Japanese workers may be more committed to their organizations than are American workers.[15]

• **organizational commitment**
An attitude that reflects an individual's identification with and attachment to the organization itself

Job involvement results in an individual's tendency to exceed the normal expectations associated with his or her job. An employee with little job involvement will see it as just something to do in order to earn a living. Thus, all of her motivation is extrinsic and she has little or no interest in learning how to perform the job better. On the other hand, a person with a lot of job involvement will derive intrinsic satisfaction from the job itself and will want to learn about how to perform the job more effectively.

• **job involvement**
Results in an individual's tendency to exceed the normal expectations associated with his or her job

Richard Steers has demonstrated that these two attitudes strengthen with an individual's age, years with the organization, sense of job security, and participation in decision making.[16] Employees who feel committed to an organization and involved with their jobs have highly reliable habits, plan a long tenure with the organization, and muster more effort in performance. While there are few definitive things that organizations can do to promote these attitudes, there are a few specific guidelines available. For one thing, if the organization treats its employees fairly and provides reasonable rewards and job security, those employees more likely will be satisfied and committed. Allowing employees to have a say in how things are done can also promote all three attitudes, and designing jobs so that they are interesting and stimulating can enhance job involvement in particular.

PERCEPTION AND INDIVIDUAL BEHAVIOR

As noted earlier, an important element of an attitude is the individual's perception of the object about which the attitude is formed. Because perception plays a role in a variety of other workplace behaviors, managers need to have a general understanding of basic perceptual processes.[17] The role of attributions is also important.

Basic Perceptual Processes

- **perception**
The set of processes by which an individual becomes aware of and interprets information about the environment

- **selective perception**
The process of screening out information with which we are uncomfortable or that contradicts our beliefs

Perception is the set of processes by which an individual becomes aware of and interprets information about the environment. As shown in Figure 9.2, basic perceptual processes that are particularly relevant to organizations are selective perception and stereotyping.

Selective Perception **Selective perception** is the process of screening out information with which we are uncomfortable or that contradicts our beliefs. For example, suppose a manager is exceptionally fond of a particular worker. The manager has a very positive attitude about the worker and thinks he is a top performer. One day the manager notices that the worker seems to be goofing off. Selective perception may cause the manager to quickly forget what he observed. Similarly, suppose a manager has formed a very negative image of a particular worker. She thinks this worker is a poor performer and never does a good job. When she happens to observe an example of high performance from the worker, she, too, may not remember it for very long. In one sense, selective perception is beneficial because it allows us to disregard minor bits of information. Of course, this holds true only if our basic perception is accurate. If selective perception causes us to ignore important information, however, it can become quite detrimental.

FIGURE 9.2 Perceptual Processes

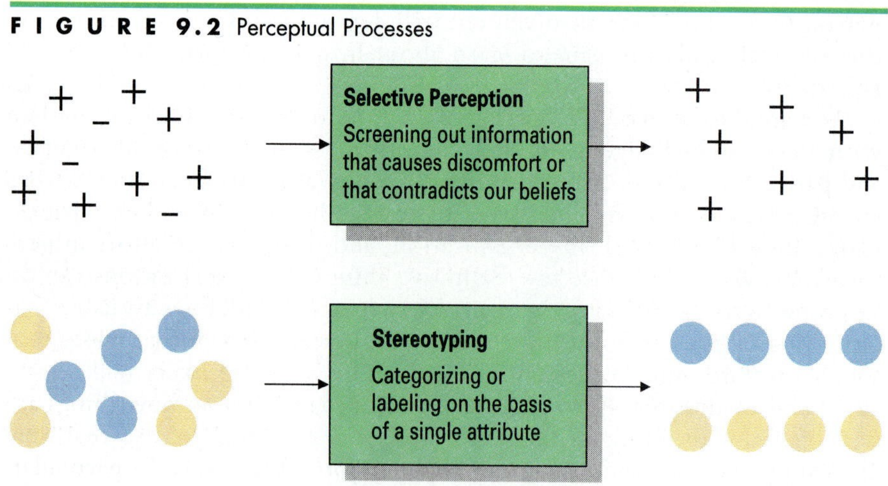

Two of the most basic perceptual processes are selective perception and stereotyping. As shown here, selective perception occurs when we screen out information (represented by the – symbols) that causes us discomfort or that contradicts our beliefs. Stereotyping occurs when we categorize or label people on the basis of a single attribute, illustrated here by color.

Stereotyping **Stereotyping** is the process of categorizing or labeling people on the basis of a single attribute. Common attributes from which people often stereotype are race and sex. Of course, stereotypes along these lines are inaccurate and can be harmful. For example, suppose a manager forms the stereotype that women can perform only certain tasks and that men are best suited for other tasks. To the extent that this stereotype affects the manager's hiring practices, the manager is (1) costing the organization valuable talent for both sets of jobs, (2) violating federal law, and (3) behaving unethically. On the other hand, certain forms of stereotyping can be useful and efficient. Suppose, for example, that a manager believes that communication skills are important for a particular job and that speech communication majors tend to have exceptionally good communication skills. As a result, whenever he interviews candidates for jobs he pays especially close attention to speech communication majors. To the extent that communication skills truly predict job performance and that majoring in speech communication does indeed provide those skills, this form of stereotyping can be beneficial.

• **stereotyping**
The process of categorizing or labeling people on the basis of a single attribute

Perception and Attribution

Perception is also closely linked with another process called attribution. **Attribution** is the process of observing behavior and attributing causes to it.[18] The behavior that is observed may be our own or that of others. For example, suppose someone realizes one day that she is working fewer hours than before, that she talks less about her work, and that she calls in sick more frequently. She concludes that she has become disenchanted with her job and subsequently decides to quit. Thus she observed her own behavior, attributed a cause to it, and developed what she thought was a consistent response. More common is attributing cause to the behavior of others. For example, if the manager of the individual described above had observed the same behavior, he might form exactly the same attribution. On the other hand, he might instead decide that she has a serious illness, that he is driving her too hard, that she is experiencing too much stress, that she has a drug problem, or that she is having family problems.

• **attribution**
The process of observing behavior and attributing causes to it

The basic framework around which we form attributions is *consensus* (the extent to which other people in the same situation behave the same way), *consistency* (the extent to which the same person behaves in the same way at different times), and *distinctiveness* (the extent to which the same person behaves in the same way in other situations). For example, suppose a manager observes that an employee is late for a meeting. The manager might further realize that he is the only one who is late (low consensus), recall that he is often late for other meetings (high consistency), and subsequently realize that the same employee is sometimes late for work and returning from lunch (low distinctiveness). This pattern of attributions might cause the manager to decide that the individual's behavior is something that should be changed. As a result, the manager might meet with the subordinate and establish some punitive consequences for future tardiness.

STRESS AND INDIVIDUAL BEHAVIOR

• **stress**
An individual's response to a strong stimulus called a **stressor**

• **General Adaptation Syndrome**
A cycle that stress generally follows

Another important element of behavior in organizations is stress. **Stress** is an individual's response to a strong stimulus.[19] This stimulus is called a **stressor**. Stress generally follows a cycle referred to as the **General Adaptation Syndrome**, or GAS,[20] shown in Figure 9.3. According to this view, when an individual first encounters a stressor, the GAS is initiated and the first stage, alarm, is activated. He may feel panic, may wonder how to cope, and may feel helpless. For example, suppose a manager is told to prepare a detailed evaluation of a plan by his firm to buy one of its competitors. His first reaction may be, "How will I ever get this done by tomorrow?"

If the stressor is too intense, the individual may feel unable to cope and never really try to respond to its demands. In most cases, however, after a short period of alarm, the individual gathers some strength and starts to resist the negative effects of the stressor. For example, the manager with the evaluation to write may calm down, call home to say he's working late, roll up his sleeves, order out for coffee, and get to work. Thus, at stage 2 of the GAS, the person is resisting the effects of the stressor.

In many cases, the resistance phase may end the GAS. If the manager is able to complete the evaluation earlier than expected, he may drop it in his briefcase, smile to himself, and head home tired but satisfied. On the other hand, prolonged exposure to a stressor without resolution may bring on stage 3 of the GAS—exhaustion. At this stage, the individual literally gives up and can no longer resist the stressor. The manager, for example, might fall asleep at his desk at 3 A.M. and never finish the evaluation.

We should note that stress is not all bad.[21] In the absence of stress, we may experience lethargy and stagnation. An optimal level of stress, on the other hand, can result in motivation and excitement. Too much stress, however, can have negative consequences. It is also important to understand that stress can be caused by "good" as well as "bad" things. Excessive pressure, unreasonable demands on our time, and bad news can all cause stress. But receiving a bonus and then having to decide what to do with the

FIGURE 9.3 The General Adaptation Syndrome

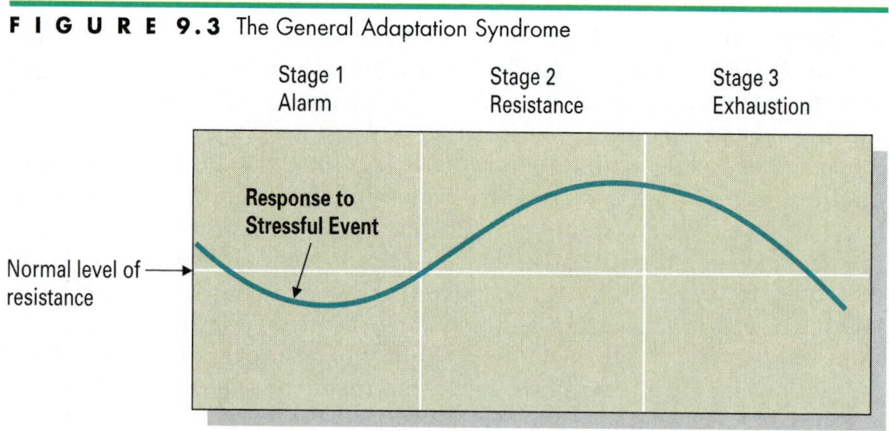

The General Adaptation Syndrome represents the normal process by which we react to stressful events. At stage 1—alarm—we feel panic and alarm and our level of resistance to stress drops. Stage 2—resistance—represents our efforts to confront and control the stressful circumstance. If we fail, we may eventually reach stage 3—exhaustion—and just give up or quit.

money can also be stressful. So, too, can receiving a promotion, gaining recognition, and similar "good" things.

One important line of thinking about stress focuses on **Type A** and **Type B personalities**.[22] Type A individuals are extremely competitive, very devoted to work, and have a strong sense of time urgency. They are likely to be aggressive, impatient, and very work-oriented. They have a lot of drive and want to accomplish as much as possible as quickly as possible. Type B individuals are less competitive, less devoted to work, and have a weaker sense of time urgency. Such individuals are less likely to experience conflict with other people and more likely to have a balanced, relaxed approach to life. They are able to work at a constant pace without time urgency. Type B people are not necessarily more or less successful than are Type A people. But they are less likely to experience stress.

• **Type A personality** A personality type in which individuals are extremely competitive, very devoted to work, and have a strong sense of time urgency

• **Type B personality** A personality type in which individuals are less competitive, less devoted to work, and have a weaker sense of time urgency than are persons with Type A personality

Causes of Stress

Stress is obviously not a simple phenomenon. As noted in Figure 9.4, several different things can cause stress. Note that the figure includes only work-related conditions. We should keep in mind that stress can be the result of personal circumstances as well.[23]

Work-related stressors fall into one of four categories—task, physical, role, and interpersonal demands. *Task demands* are associated with the task itself. Some occupations are inherently more stressful than others. Having to make fast decisions, decisions with less than complete information, or decisions that have relatively serious consequences are some of the things that can make some jobs stressful. The jobs of surgeon, airline pilot, and stock broker are relatively more stressful than the jobs of general practitioner, airplane baggage loader, and office receptionist. While a general practitioner makes important decisions, he is also likely to have time to make a considered diagnosis and fully explore a number of different treatments. But during surgery, the surgeon must make decisions quickly while realizing that the wrong one may endanger her patient's life.

There are several different causes of work stress in organizations. Four general sets of organizational stressors are task demands, physical demands, role demands, and interpersonal demands.

FIGURE 9.4 Causes of Work Stress

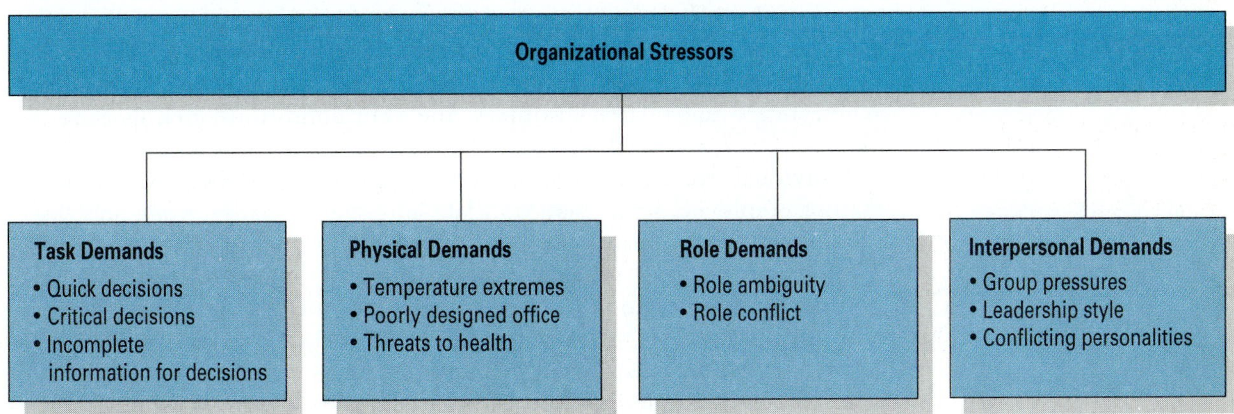

Physical demands are stressors associated with the job setting. Working outdoors in extremely hot or cold temperatures, or even in an improperly heated or cooled office, can lead to stress. A poorly designed office, which makes it difficult for people to have privacy or promotes too little social interaction, can result in stress, as can poor lighting and inadequate work surfaces. Even more severe are actual threats to health. Examples include jobs such as coal mining, poultry processing, and toxic waste handling.

Role demands can also cause stress. A role is a set of expected behaviors associated with a position in a group or organization. Stress can result from either role ambiguity or role conflict that people can experience in groups. For example, an employee who is feeling pressure from her boss to work longer hours while also being asked by her family for more time at home will almost certainly experience stress. Similarly, a new employee experiencing role ambiguity because of poor orientation and training practices by the organization will suffer from stress as well.

Interpersonal demands are stressors associated with relationships that confront people in organizations. For example, group pressures regarding restriction of output and norm conformity can lead to stress. Leadership style may also cause stress. An employee who feels a strong need to participate in decision making may feel stress if his boss refuses to allow participation. And individuals with conflicting personalities may experience stress if required to work too closely together. A person with an internal locus of control might be frustrated when working with someone who prefers to wait and just let things happen.

Consequences of Stress

As noted earlier, the results of stress may be positive or negative. The negative consequences may be behavioral, psychological, or medical. Behaviorally, for example, stress may lead to detrimental or harmful actions, such as smoking, alcoholism, overeating, and drug abuse. Other stress-induced behaviors are accident proneness, violence toward self or others, and appetite disorders.

Psychological consequences of stress interfere with an individual's mental health and well-being. These outcomes include sleep disturbances, depression, family problems, and sexual dysfunction. Managers are especially prone to sleep disturbances when they experience stress at work.[24] Medical consequences of stress affect an individual's physiological well-being. Heart disease and stroke have been linked to stress, as have headaches, backaches, ulcers and related disorders, and skin conditions such as acne and hives.

Individual stress also has direct consequences for businesses. For an operating employee, stress may translate into poor-quality work and lower productivity. For a manager, it may mean faulty decision making and disruptions in working relationships. Withdrawal behaviors can also result from stress. People who are having difficulties with stress in their jobs are more likely to call in sick or to leave the organization. More subtle forms of withdrawal may also occur. A manager may start missing deadlines, for example, or taking longer lunch breaks. Employees may withdraw by developing feelings of indifference. The irritation displayed by people under great stress can make them difficult to get along with. Job satisfaction, morale, and commitment can all suffer as a result of excessive levels of stress. So, too, can motivation to perform.

Another consequence of stress is **burnout**—a feeling of exhaustion that may develop when someone experiences too much stress for an extended period of time. Burnout results in constant fatigue, frustration, and helplessness. Increased rigidity follows, as does a loss of self-confidence and psychological withdrawal. The individual dreads going to work, often puts in longer hours but gets less accomplished than before, and exhibits mental and physical exhaustion. Because of the damaging effects of burnout, some companies are taking steps to help avoid it. For example, British Airways provides all of its employees with training designed to help them recognize the symptoms of burnout and develop strategies to avoid it.

burnout
A feeling of exhaustion that may develop when someone experiences too much stress for an extended period of time

Managing Stress

Given the potential consequences of stress, both people and organizations should be concerned about how to limit its more damaging effects. Numerous ideas and approaches have been developed to help manage stress. Some are strategies for individuals, while others are strategies for organizations.[25]

One way people manage stress is through exercise. People who exercise regularly feel less tension and stress, are more self-confident, and are more optimistic. Their better physical condition also makes them less susceptible to many common illnesses. People who don't exercise regularly, on the other hand, tend to feel more stress and are more likely to be depressed. They are also more likely to have heart attacks. And because of their physical condition, they are more likely to contract illnesses.

Another method people use to manage stress is relaxation. Relaxation allows individuals to adapt to, and therefore better deal with, their stress. Relaxation comes in many forms, such as taking regular vacations. A recent study found that people's attitudes toward a variety of workplace characteristics improved significantly following a vacation. People also can learn to relax while on their jobs. For example, some experts recommend that people take regular rest breaks during their normal workday.

People also can use time management to control stress. The idea behind time management is that many daily pressures can be reduced or eliminated if individuals do a better job of managing time. One approach to time management is to make a list every morning of the things to be done that day. The items on the list are then grouped into three categories: critical activities that must be performed, important activities that should be performed, and optional or trivial things that can be delegated or postponed. The individual performs the items on the list in their order of importance.

Finally, people can manage stress through support groups. A support group can be as simple as a group of family members or friends with whom to enjoy leisure time. Going out after work with a couple of coworkers to a basketball game or a movie, for example, can help relieve stress built up during the day. Family and friends can help people cope with stress on an ongoing basis and during times of crisis. For example, an employee who just learned that she did not get the promotion she had been working toward for months may find it helpful to have a good friend to lean on, to talk to, or to yell at. People also may make use of more elaborate and formal support groups. Community centers or churches, for example, may sponsor support groups for people who have recently gone through a divorce, the death of a loved one, or some other tragedy.

Organizations are beginning to realize that they should be involved in helping employees cope with stress. One argument for this position is that because the business is at least partially responsible for stress, it should also help relieve it. Another is that stress-related insurance claims by employees can cost the organization considerable sums of money. Still another is that workers experiencing lower levels of detrimental stress will be able to function more effectively. AT&T initiated a series of seminars and workshops to help its employees cope with the stress they face in their jobs. The company was prompted to develop these seminars for all three of the reasons noted above.

A wellness stress program is a special part of the organization specifically created to help deal with stress. Organizations have adopted stress management programs, health promotion programs, and other kinds of programs for this purpose. The AT&T seminar program noted earlier is similar to this idea, but true wellness programs are ongoing activities that have a number of different components. They commonly include exercise-related activities as well as classroom instruction programs dealing with smoking cessation, weight reduction, and general stress management.

Some companies develop their own programs or use existing programs of this type. Johns-Manville Corporation, for example, has a gym at its corporate headquarters. Other organizations negotiate discounted health club membership rates with local establishments. For the instructional part of the program, the organization can again either sponsor its own training or perhaps jointly sponsor seminars with a local YMCA, civic organization, or church. Organization-based fitness programs facilitate employee exercise, a very positive consideration, but such programs are also quite costly. Still, more and more companies are developing fitness programs for employees.

TYPES OF WORKPLACE BEHAVIOR

• **workplace behavior** A pattern of action by the members of an organization that directly or indirectly influences organizational effectiveness

Now that we have looked closely at how individual differences can influence behavior in organizations, let's turn our attention to what we mean by workplace behavior. **Workplace behavior** is a pattern of action by the members of an organization that directly or indirectly influences organizational effectiveness. Important workplace behaviors include performance and productivity, absenteeism and turnover, and organizational citizenship.

A vast array of workplace behaviors shape how any individual performs in an organization. Analog Devices recently began offering classes in signing. The idea is that if more people can communicate with hearing-impaired product engineers like Howard Samuels, everyone in the company will be able to perform at a higher level.

Performance Behaviors

Performance behaviors are the total set of work-related behaviors that the organization expects the individual to display. Thus, they derive from the psychological contract. For some jobs, performance behaviors can be narrowly defined and easily measured. For example, an assembly line worker who sits by a moving conveyor and attaches parts to a product as it passes by has relatively few performance behaviors. He or she is expected to remain at the work station and correctly attach the parts. Performance can often be assessed quantitatively by counting the percentage of parts correctly attached.

• **performance behaviors** The total set of work-related behaviors that the organization expects the individual to display

For many other jobs, however, performance behaviors are more diverse and much more difficult to assess. For example, consider the case of a research and development scientist at Merck. The scientist works in a lab trying to find new scientific breakthroughs that have commercial potential. The scientist must apply knowledge learned in graduate school with experience gained from previous research. Intuition and creativity are also important elements. And the desired breakthrough may take months or even years to accomplish. As we discussed in Chapter 8, organizations rely on a number of different methods for evaluating performance. The key, of course, is to match the evaluation mechanism with the job being performed.

Withdrawal Behaviors

Another important type of work-related behavior is that which results in withdrawal—absenteeism and turnover. **Absenteeism** occurs when an individual does not show up for work. The cause may be legitimate (illness, jury duty, death in the family, etc.) or feigned (reported as legitimate but

• **absenteeism** An individual's not showing up for work

actually just an excuse to stay home). When an employee is absent, her or his work does not get done at all or a substitute must be hired to do it. In either case, the quantity or quality of actual output is likely to suffer. Obviously, some absenteeism is expected. The key concern of organizations is to minimize feigned absenteeism and reduce legitimate absences as much as possible. High absenteeism may be a symptom of other problems as well, such as job dissatisfaction and low morale.

• **turnover**
Employees quitting their jobs

Turnover occurs when people quit their jobs. An organization usually incurs costs in replacing individuals who have quit, but if turnover involves especially productive people, it is even more costly. Turnover seems to result from a number of factors including aspects of the job, the organization, the individual, the labor market, and family influences. In general, a poor person-job fit is also a likely cause of turnover.

Efforts to manage turnover directly are frequently fraught with difficulty, even in organizations that concentrate on rewarding good performers. Of course, some turnover is inevitable, and in some cases it may even be desirable. For example, if the organization is trying to cut costs by reducing its staff, having people voluntarily choose to leave is preferable to terminating them. And if the people who choose to leave are low performers or express high levels of job dissatisfaction, the organization may benefit from turnover.

Organizational Citizenship

• **organizational citizenship**
The behavior of individuals that makes a positive overall contribution to the organization

Organizational citizenship refers to the behavior of individuals that makes a positive overall contribution to the organization.[26] Consider, for example, an employee who does work that is acceptable in terms of both quantity and quality. But she refuses to work overtime, she won't help newcomers learn the ropes, and she is generally unwilling to make any contribution to the organization beyond the strict performance of her job. While this person may be seen as a good performer, she is not likely to be seen as a good organizational citizen.

Another employee may exhibit a comparable level of performance. In addition, however, he will always work late when the boss asks him to, he takes time to help newcomers learn their way around, and he is perceived as being helpful and committed to the organization's success. While his level of performance may be seen as equal to that of the first worker, he is likely to be seen as a better organizational citizen.

The determinant of organizational citizenship behaviors is likely to be a complex mosaic of individual, social, and organizational variables. For example, the personality, attitudes, and needs of the individual will have to be consistent with citizenship behaviors. Similarly, the social context, or work group, in which the individual works will need to facilitate and promote such behaviors (we discuss group dynamics in Chapter 13). And the organization itself, especially its culture, must be capable of promoting, recognizing, and rewarding these types of behaviors if they are to be maintained. While the study of organizational citizenship is still in its infancy, preliminary research suggests that it may play a powerful role in organizational effectiveness.[27]

SUMMARY OF KEY POINTS

Understanding individuals in organizations is an important consideration for all managers. A basic framework that can be used to facilitate this understanding is the psychological contract—the set of expectations held by people with respect to what they will contribute to the organization and what they expect to get in return. Organizations strive to achieve an optimal person-job fit, but this process is complicated by the existence of individual differences.

Personality is the relatively stable set of psychological and behavioral attributes that distinguish one person from another. Managers can do little to alter personality. Instead, they should strive to understand the effects of key personality attributes such as locus of control, self-efficacy, authoritarianism, dogmatism, self-esteem, and risk propensity.

Attitudes are based on emotion, knowledge, and intended behavior. Job satisfaction or dissatisfaction, organizational commitment, and job involvement are important work-related attitudes.

Perception is the set of processes by which an individual becomes aware of and interprets information about the environment. Basic perceptual processes include selective perception and stereotyping. Perception and attribution are also closely related.

Stress is an individual's response to a strong stimulus. The General Adaptation Syndrome outlines the basic stress process. Stress can be caused by task, physical, role, and interpersonal demands. Consequences of stress include organizational and individual outcomes, as well as burnout. Several things can be done to manage stress.

Workplace behavior is a pattern of action by the members of an organization that directly or indirectly influences organizational effectiveness. Performance behaviors are the set of work-related behaviors the organization expects the individual to display in order to fulfill the psychological contract. Basic withdrawal behaviors are absenteeism and turnover. Organizational citizenship refers to behavior that makes a positive overall contribution to the organization.

QUESTIONS FOR REVIEW

1. What is a psychological contract? Why is it important?
2. Identify and describe five basic personality attributes.
3. What are the components of an individual's attitude?
4. What are the major factors that cause stress? What are the major consequences of stress?
5. Identify and describe several important workplace behaviors.

QUESTIONS FOR ANALYSIS

1. What is the nature of the psychological contract you have with your college or university? With your instructor in this class?
2. An individual was heard to describe someone else as having "no personality." What is wrong with this statement? What did the individual actually mean?
3. Describe a circumstance in which you formed a new attitude about something.
4. What causes stress for you? How do you deal with it?
5. As a manager, how would you go about trying to make someone a better organizational citizen?

CASE STUDY

Culture Clash

Research and development (R&D) is expensive. In high-technology industries, the cost of R&D is frequently beyond the capability of any one company to fund. As a result, an increasing number of companies are forming joint ventures and strategic alliances to afford the cost. One such joint venture is the Triad.

The Triad consists of about a hundred engineers and technicians who have been assembled to develop a 256-megabyte dynamic random access memory (DRAM) computer chip. Such a chip would have sixteen times more information capacity than current ones. The engineers and technicians were assembled at IBM's Advanced Semiconductor

Technical Center in East Fishkill, New York. Notably, however, they came from three competing companies located in three countries—IBM in the United States, Toshiba in Japan, and Siemens in Germany.

Seemingly these three companies should have been able to develop a successful joint venture far more readily than less-experienced companies. Yet, despite their best intentions and some seemingly solid preparation, the clash of cultures has been obvious and sometimes pronounced.

All participants, about equal numbers from each company, had to be willing to move away from home, adapt to a new work environment, and face some career risks. All three companies provided some preparation for personnel. Of course, the IBM personnel had to adjust to less change because the Triad facility was located in the United States, and so they were provided with less training. Toshiba provided training for its personnel similar to that provided to any employee who goes to work overseas. But it did not provide any special training on working with people from other cultures. Siemens provided some cross-cultural training, but it consisted primarily of explaining the different ways of dealing with criticism. Thus no real cross-training between the three organizations was developed.

Siemens' personnel were stunned when some of the Japanese seemed to doze off during meetings, although that is very common in Japan. IBM people complained that the Germans planned too much and that the Japanese would not make clear decisions. Toshiba staffers disliked the lack of large group meetings and intense, informal communication to which they were accustomed. The Japanese also found communicating orally in English to be very difficult, especially with one another, and so they frequently spoke in their native language.

Even the use of physical space was a problem. The Germans were upset that the offices did not all have windows. The Japanese disliked the small private offices. The offices had doors with narrow windows in them. Both the Germans and Japanese quickly learned to hang their coats over the windows. In addition, IBM's strict no smoking rules became a problem because many of the Germans and Japanese smoked and had to go outdoors to do so.

These cultural clashes have become obstacles instead of opportunities. Each group tends to blame problems on the others, which simply makes cooperation and collaboration more difficult. Because these are competing companies, they all suspect that the others are withholding some information for a competitive advantage. A lack of openness and trust could sabotage the project.

Case Questions

1. What were some of the main cultural differences that clashed in the Triad?
2. What might the three companies have done to reduce the clash of cultures before the start of the project? Afterward?
3. Is there a real danger in such R&D joint ventures of competitors obtaining information that could be used against a company? If so, what could be done to protect the organizations involved?

References: "What's the Word in the Lab? Collaborate," *Business Week,* June 27, 1994, pp. 78–103; "Computer Chip Project Brings Rivals Together but the Cultures Clash," *The Wall Street Journal,* May 3, 1994, pp. A1, A8; Lewis H. Young, "Managing a Three-Country Team Project," *Electronic Business Buyer,* May 1994, pp. 68–69; and "Semiconductors: Talk About Your Dream Team," *Business Week,* July 27, 1994, pp. 59–60.

SKILLS • DEVELOPMENT • PORTFOLIO

BUILDING EFFECTIVE CONCEPTUAL AND DIAGNOSTIC SKILLS

Exercise Overview

Conceptual skills refer to a manager's ability to think in the abstract, while diagnostic skills focus on responses to situations. These skills frequently must be used together to understand better the behavior of others in the organization, as illustrated by this exercise.

Exercise Background

Human behavior is a complex phenomenon in any setting, but especially so in organizations. Understanding how and why people choose particular behaviors can be difficult, frustrating, but quite important. Consider, for example, the following scenario.

Sandra Buckley has worked in your department for several years. Until recently, she has been a "model" employee. She was always on time, or early, for work and stayed late whenever necessary to get her work done. She was upbeat, cheerful, and worked very hard. She frequently said that the company was the best place she had ever worked and that you were the perfect boss.

About six months ago, however, you began to see changes in Sandra's behavior. She began occasionally to come in late, and you cannot remember the last time she agreed to work past 5:00 P.M. She also complains a lot. Other workers have started to avoid her, because she is so negative all the time. You also suspect that she may be looking for a new job.

Exercise Task

Using the scenario described above as background, do the following:

1. Assume that you have done some background work to find out what has happened. Write a brief case with more information that explains why Sandra's behavior has changed (your case might include the fact that you recently promoted someone else when Sandra might have expected to get the job). Make the case as descriptive as possible.

2. Relate elements of your case to the various behavioral concepts discussed in this chapter.

3. Decide whether or not you might be able to resolve things with Sandra in order to overcome the issues you identified in response to question 1 (i.e., if you described her behavior in terms of being passed over for promotion, now describe whether you think you can get past this with Sandra).

4. Which behavioral process or concept discussed in this chapter is easiest to change? Which is the most difficult to change?

BUILDING EFFECTIVE TIME-MANAGEMENT SKILLS

Exercise Overview

Time-management skills help people prioritize work, work more efficiently, and delegate appropriately. Poor time management, in turn, may result in stress. This exercise will help you relate time-management skills to stress reduction.

Exercise Background

Make a list of several of the major things that cause stress for you. Stressors might involve school (hard classes, too many exams, etc.), work (financial pressures, demanding work schedule, etc.), or personal circumstances (friends, romance, family, etc.). Try to be as specific as possible. Try to identify at least ten different stressors.

Exercise Task

Using the list developed above, complete each of the four exercises that follow:

1. Evaluate the extent to which poor time management on your part plays a role in how each stressor affects you. For example, do exams cause stress because you delay studying?

2. Develop a strategy for using time more efficiently in relation to each stressor that relates to time.

3. Note interrelationships among different kinds of stressors and time. For example, financial pressures may cause you to work, but work may interfere with school. Can any of these interrelationships be managed more effectively vis-à-vis time?

4. How do you manage the stress in your life? Is it possible to manage stress in a more time-effective manner?

YOU MAKE THE CALL

The day Susan Turner was promoted to the position of manager of Sunset Landscape Service's retail nursery operation, she felt as though her feet were not touching the ground. She could hardly wait to get home that evening and share her good news with her husband, Will Larson.

As the two of them prepared dinner together that evening and talked about her work, Susan said, "You know, it's really amazing to have just the perfect job. I've always loved watching things grow. Being outside most of the time is just too good to be true. And getting to wear casual clothes at work is also nice. I know that I'm going to be a great manager. I really appreciate Cynthia Spenser giving me this opportunity.

"I also think there are going to be some more opportunities in the future, too. I think the Spensers really know what they're doing. Sunset is already the most successful nursery business in town. I wouldn't be surprised to see them start expanding even more, and maybe even open a new nursery across town."

Will shared his wife's happiness with her work, although he clearly had different preferences. He was a stock broker in the local office of a national firm. He said, "I know what you mean about liking your work. Well, you know how much I've always liked mine. I guess everyone is different, though. While being outside is okay some of the time, I really like my air-conditioned office. The thought of being outside on hot days or when it's raining just doesn't sound good to me. And I guess that I sorta like getting dressed up every morning."

Later that evening, Susan received a telephone call from her sister, Elaine Turner. Elaine had just moved to California for a new job. It was her fourth new job in the past five years. She never seemed to find a job that she really liked. Each new job seemed great at first, but within just a few weeks, Elaine was usually grumbling about something and saying that it didn't suit her in some way or another. And sure enough, after Susan and Elaine had talked for awhile, Elaine said, "I hope that the work gets more exciting soon, though. I thought it was going to be a lot of fun, but so far about the only real fun I'm having is fighting traffic on the way home each evening."

Discussion Questions

1. Describe the elements of person-job fit as they apply to Susan, Will, and Elaine.

2. What inferences about individual differences can be drawn from these people?

3. How do you see the attitudes of Susan, Will, and Elaine affecting their workplace behaviors?

SKILLS SELF-ASSESSMENT INSTRUMENT

Assessing Your Mental Abilities

Introduction: Mental abilities are important to job performance, especially in this information age. The following assessment surveys your judgments about your personal mental abilities.

Instructions: Judge how descriptively accurate each of the following statements is about you. In some cases, making a decision may be difficult, but you should force a choice. Record your answers next to each statement according to the following scale:

Rating Scale

5 Very descriptive of me
4 Fairly descriptive of me
3 Somewhat descriptive of me
2 Not very descriptive of me
1 Not descriptive of me at all

_____ **1.** I am at ease learning visually. I readily take in and hold in mind visual precepts.

_____ **2.** I can produce remotely associated, clever, or uncommon responses to statements or situations.

_____ **3.** I can formulate and test hypotheses directed at finding a principle of relationships among elements of a case or problem.

_____ **4.** I am able to remember bits of unrelated material and can recall parts of such material.

_____ **5.** I can recall perfectly for immediate reproduction a series of items after only one presentation of the series.

_____ **6.** I can manipulate numbers in arithmetical operations rapidly.

_____ **7.** I am fast in finding figures, making comparisons, and carrying out other very simple tasks involving visual perception.

_____ **8.** I can reason from stated premises to their necessary conclusion.

_____ **9.** I can perceive spatial patterns or maintain orientation with respect to objects in space. I can manipulate or transform the image of spatial patterns into other visual arrangements.

_____ **10.** I have a large knowledge of words and their meanings and am able to apply this knowledge in understanding connected discourse.

For interpretation, turn to page 448.

Source: Adapted from M. D. Dunnette, "Aptitudes, Abilities, and Skills," in M. D. Dunnette (Ed.), *Handbook of Industrial and Organizational Psychology* (Chicago: Rand McNally, 1976), pp. 481–483.

EXPERIENTIAL EXERCISE

Assumptions That Color Perceptions

Purpose: Perceptions rule the world. In fact, everything we know or think we know is filtered through our perceptions. Our perceptions are rooted in past experiences and socialization by significant others in our life. This exercise is designed to help you become aware of how much our assumptions influence our perceptions and evaluations of others. It also illustrates how we compare our perceptions with others to find similarities and differences.

Instructions

1. Read the descriptions of the four individuals provided in the personal descriptions below.

2. Decide which occupation is most likely for each person and place the name by the corresponding occupation in the occupations list that follows. Each person is in a different occupation and no two people hold the same one.

Personal Descriptions

R. B. Red is a trim, attractive woman in her early thirties. She holds an undergraduate degree from an eastern woman's college and is active in several professional organizations. She is an officer (on the national level) of Toastmistress International.

Her hobbies include classical music, opera, and jazz. She is an avid traveler, who is planning a sojourn to China next year.

W. C. White is a quiet, meticulous person. W. C. is tall and thin with blond hair and wire-framed glasses. Family, friends, and church are very important and W. C. devotes any free time to community activities.

W. C. is a wizard with figures but can rarely be persuaded to demonstrate this ability to do mental calculations.

G. A. Green grew up on a small farm in rural Indiana. He is an avid hunter and fisherman. In fact, he and his wife joke about their "deer-hunting honeymoon" in Colorado.

One of his primary goals is to "get back to the land" and he hopes to be able to buy a small farm before he is fifty. He drives a pickup truck and owns several dogs.

B. E. Brown is the child of wealthy professionals who reside on Long Island. Mr. Brown, B. E.'s father, is a "self-made" financial analyst who made it a point to stress the importance of financial security as B. E. grew up.

B. E. values the ability to structure one's use of time and can often be found on the golf course on Wednesday afternoons. B. E. dresses in a conservative upper-class manner and professes to be "allergic to polyester."

Occupations

Choose the occupation that seems most appropriate for each person described. Place the name in the spaces next to the corresponding occupations.

________________ Banker

________________ Labor negotiator

________________ Production manager

________________ Travel agent

________________ Accountant

________________ Teacher

________________ Computer operations manager

________________ Clerk

________________ Army general

________________ Salesperson

________________ Physician

________________ Truck driver

________________ Financial analyst

Source: Jerri L. Frantzve, *Behaving in Organizations,* Boston: Allyn & Bacon, 1983, pp. 63–65.

CHAPTER NOTES

1. Brian O'Reilly, "The New Deal," *Fortune,* June 13, 1994, pp. 44–52; Anne Fisher, "Morale Crisis," *Fortune,* November 18, 1991, pp. 70–80; Gary Hoover, Alta Campbell, and Patrick J. Spain (Eds.), *Hoover's Handbook of American Business 1995* (Austin, Tex.: The Reference Press, 1994), pp. 894–895.
2. Lynn McGarlane Shore and Lois Tetrick, "The Psychological Contract as an Explanatory Framework in the Employment Relationship," in C. L. Cooper and D. M. Rousseau (Eds.), *Trends in Organizational Behavior* (London: John Wiley & Sons Ltd., 1994), pp. 58–70.
3. Sandra Robinson, Matthew Kraatz, and Denise Rousseau, "Changing Obligations and the Psychological Contract: A Longitudinal Study," *Academy of Management Journal,* March 1994, pp. 137–152; and Jennifer A. Chatman, "Improving Interactional Organizational Research: A Model of Person-Organization Fit," *Academy of Management Review,* July 1989, pp. 333–349.
4. Lawrence Pervin, "Personality," in Mark Rosenzweig and Lyman Porter (Eds.), *Annual Review of Psychology,* Vol. 36 (Palo Alto, Calif.: Annual Reviews, 1985), pp. 83–114; and S. R. Maddi, *Personality Theories: A Comparative Analysis,* 4th ed. (Homewood, Ill.: Dorsey, 1980).
5. J. B. Rotter, "Generalized Expectancies for Internal vs. External Control of Reinforcement," *Psychological Monographs,* 1966, Vol. 80, pp. 1–28.
6. Cynthia Lee and Philip Bobko, "Self-Efficacy Beliefs: Comparison of Five Measures," *Journal of Applied Psychology,* 1994, Vol. 79, No. 3, pp. 364–369.
7. T. W. Adorno, E. Frenkel-Brunswick, D. J. Levinson, and R. N. Sanford, *The Authoritarian Personality* (New York: Harper & Row, 1950).
8. "Who Becomes an Authoritarian?" *Psychology Today,* March 1989, pp. 66–70.
9. Edward Necka and Malgorzata Kubiak, "The Influence of Training in Metaphorical Thinking on Creativity and Level of Dogmatism," *Polish Psychological Bulletin,* 1989, Vol. 20, pp. 69–78; and A. F. Kostin, "The Truth of History and Stereotypes of Dogmatism," *Soviet Studies in History,* 1988, Vol. 27, pp. 85–96.
10. Barbara Foley Meeker, "Cooperation, Competition, and Self-Esteem: Aspects of Winning and Losing," *Human Relations,* August 1990, Vol. 43, pp. 205–220; and Jon L. Pierce, Donald G. Gardner, and Larry L. Cummings, "Organization-Based Self-Esteem: Construct Definition, Measurement, and Validation," *Academy of Management Journal,* 1989, Vol. 32, pp. 622–648.
11. Leon Festinger, *A Theory of Cognitive Dissonance* (Palo Alto, Calif.: Stanford University Press, 1957).
12. Patricia C. Smith, L. M. Kendall, and Charles Hulin, *The Measurement of Satisfaction in Work and Behavior* (Chicago: Rand-McNally, 1969).
13. James R. Lincoln, "Employee Work Attitudes and Management Practice in the U.S. and Japan: Evidence from a Large Comparative Study," *California Management Review,* Fall 1989, pp. 89–106.
14. Randall Dunham, Jean Grube, and Maria Castaneda, "Organizational Commitment: The Utility of an Integrative Definition," *Journal of Applied Psychology,* 1994, Vol. 79, No. 3, pp. 370–380.

15. Lincoln, "Employee Work Attitudes and Management Practice in the U.S. and Japan: Evidence from a Large Comparative Study."

16. Richard M. Steers, "Antecedents and Outcomes of Organizational Commitment," *Administrative Science Quarterly*, 1977, Vol. 22, pp. 46–56.

17. Kathleen Sutcliffe, "What Executives Notice: Accurate Perceptions in Top Management Teams," *Academy of Management Journal*, November 1994, pp. 1360–1378.

18. See H. H. Kelley, *Attribution in Social Interaction* (Morristown, N.J.: General Learning Press, 1971), for a classic treatment of attribution.

19. For a recent overview of the stress literature, see Frank Landy, James Campbell Quick, and Stanislav Kasl, "Work, Stress, and Well-Being," *International Journal of Stress Management*, 1994, Vol. 1, No. 1, pp. 33–73.

20. Hans Selye, *The Stress of Life* (New York: McGraw-Hill, 1976).

21. Selye, *The Stress of Life*.

22. M. Friedman and R. H. Rosenman, *Type A Behavior and Your Heart* (New York: Alfred A. Knopf, 1974).

23. "Work & Family," *Business Week*, June 28, 1993, pp. 80–88.

24. Anne Fisher, "Welcome to the Age of Overwork," *Fortune*, November 30, 1992, pp. 64–71.

25. Alan Farnham, "Who Beats Stress—And How," *Fortune*, October 7, 1991, pp. 71–86.

26. See Dennis W. Organ, "Personality and Organizational Citizenship Behavior," *Journal of Management*, 1994, Vol. 20, No. 2, pp. 465–478, for recent findings regarding this behavior.

27. Mary Konovsky and S. Douglas Pugh, "Citizenship Behavior and Social Exchange," *Academy of Management Journal*, 1994, Vol. 37, No. 3, pp. 656–669.

CHAPTER 10

Motivating Employee Performance

OBJECTIVES

After studying this chapter, you should be able to:

- *Characterize the nature of motivation, including its importance and basic historical perspectives.*
- *Identify and describe the major content perspectives on motivation.*
- *Identify and describe the major process perspectives on motivation.*
- *Describe reinforcement perspectives on motivation.*
- *Identify and describe other perspectives on motivation, as well as popular motivational strategies.*
- *Describe the role of organizational reward systems in motivation.*

OUTLINE

OPENING INCIDENT

IT'S NO SECRET that International Business Machines Corp., or IBM, is struggling these days. The venerable computer company has recently seen its market share, profitability, and public image all take a pounding. For example, IBM misgauged the personal computer market, was slow to react to the industry shift toward networks, and has been a follower—rather than a leader—in putting more emphasis on customer satisfaction.

To turn things around, the company hired Lou Gerstner to take over as CEO. Gerstner, an outsider to the computer industry, has tried to fundamentally alter everything about the firm. He sold off many of IBM's noncomputer businesses, reduced the firm's workforce, and cut costs. One of his more recent innovations has been to change how the firm compensates and rewards its salesforce. In the past, like most firms, IBM tied its salespeople's pay to the revenues they produced: Salespeople were paid a fixed base salary and, on top of that, a percentage commission.

There are problems with such a system, however. For one, conventional commission systems tend to make salespeople push high-volume, low-profit margin products. Salespeople can also lower selling prices to entice customers to buy more. Third, salespeople may talk customers into buying more than they need, eventually spawning a customer backlash. Fourth, a salesperson has little incentive to maintain good customer relations. Once customers have placed big orders, they usually don't need to buy computer equipment again right away.

"In the old days, we'd give a branch manager a revenue quota, and that would be it. We'd see him at the yearend, and he'd tell us how he did."

Gerstner's new system addresses these shortcomings. A new information system now provides all IBM salespeople with profit margins on all products. They can therefore determine which products produce high profits and which produce lower profits. Sixty percent of their commission is now based on the profits they generate, as opposed to the total revenues used to generate those profits. The remaining 40 percent of the sales commission is based on customer responses to satisfaction surveys. The idea is to get IBM salespeople to stop thinking about sales volume and to think instead about profitability and long-term customer relationships.

Gerstner is also making other changes in his efforts to improve IBM's operations and to enhance the performance of its workforce. For example, IBM has always stressed formal business attire as the company's "uniform." In early 1995, however, Gerstner agreed that employees can dress however they choose. His hope is that a more casual and relaxed atmosphere will spark creativity and motivation.[1]

Source of Quotation: Duke Mitchell, IBM general manager in New Jersey, quoted in *Business Week*, February 7, 1994, p. 110.

It's fairly easy to understand how IBM's new commission system works. More difficult, however, is understanding *why* it works. The answer is rooted in employee motivation. Virtually any organization is capable of having a motivated workforce. The trick is figuring out how to create a system in which employees can receive rewards that they genuinely want by performing in ways that fit the organization's goals and objectives.

In most settings, people can choose how hard they work and how much effort they expend. Thus managers need to understand how and why employees make different choices regarding their own performance. The key ingredient behind this choice is motivation, the subject of this chapter. We first examine the nature of employee motivation and then explore the major perspectives on motivation. Newly emerging approaches are then discussed. We conclude with a description of rewards and their role in motivation.

THE NATURE OF MOTIVATION

• **motivation**
The set of forces that cause people to behave in certain ways

Motivation is the set of forces that cause people to behave in certain ways.[2] On any given day, an employee may choose to work as hard as possible at a job, to work just hard enough to avoid a reprimand, or to do as little as possible. The goal for the manager is to maximize the occurrence of the first incident and minimize the occurrence of the last one. This goal becomes all the more critical when we understand how important motivation is in the workplace.[3]

Individual performance is generally determined by three things: motivation (the desire to do the job), ability (the capability to do the job), and the work environment (the tools, materials, and information needed to do the job). If an employee lacks ability, the manager can provide training or replace the worker. If there is an environmental problem, the manager can also usually make adjustments to promote higher performance. But if motivation is the problem, the task for the manager is more challenging. Individual behavior is a complex phenomenon, and the manager may be hard-pressed to figure out the precise nature of the problem and how to solve it. Thus motivation is important because of its significance as a determinant of performance and because of its intangible character.[4]

The motivation framework in Figure 10.1 is a good starting point for understanding how motivated behavior occurs. The motivation process begins with needs, or a deficiency. For example, because a worker feels that she is underpaid, she experiences a deficiency and a need for more income. In response to this need, the worker searches for ways to satisfy it, such as working harder to try to earn a raise, or seeking a new job. Next, she chooses an option to pursue. After carrying out the chosen option—working harder and putting in more hours for a reasonable period of time, for instance—she then evaluates her success. If her hard work results in a pay raise, she probably feels good about things and will continue to work hard. If no raise is provided, she is likely to try another option.

FIGURE 10.1 The Motivation Framework

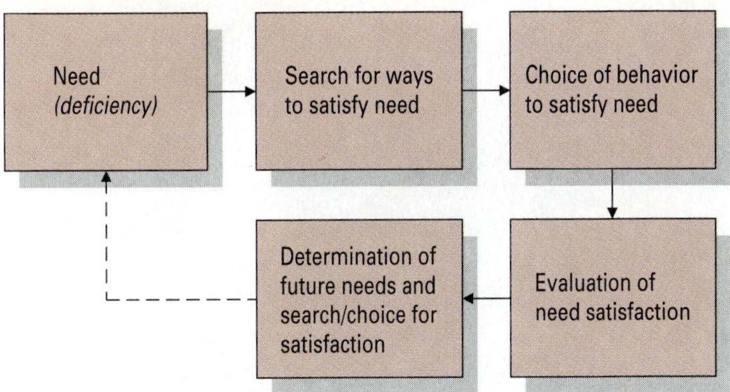

The motivation process progresses through a series of discrete steps. Content, process, and reinforcement perspectives on motivation address different parts of this process.

CONTENT PERSPECTIVES ON MOTIVATION

Content perspectives on motivation deal with the first part of the motivation process—needs and need deficiencies. More specifically, **content perspectives** address the question "What factors in the workplace motivate people?" Labor leaders often argue that workers can be motivated by more pay, shorter working hours, and improved working conditions. Meanwhile, some experts suggest that motivation can be enhanced by providing employees with more autonomy and greater responsibility. Both of these views represent content views of motivation. The former asserts that motivation is a function of pay, working hours, and working conditions; the latter suggests that autonomy and responsibility are the causes of motivation. Two widely known content perspectives on motivation are the need hierarchy and the two-factor theory.

- **content perspectives** Approaches to motivation that try to answer the question "What factor or factors motivate people?"

The Need Hierarchy Approach

The need hierarchy approach has been advanced by many theorists. Need hierarchies assume that people have different needs that can be arranged in a hierarchy of importance. The best known is Maslow's hierarchy of needs.

Abraham Maslow, a human relationist, argued that people are motivated to satisfy five need levels.[5] **Maslow's hierarchy of needs** is shown in Figure 10.2. At the bottom of the hierarchy are the *physiological needs*—such as food, sex, and air—that represent basic issues of survival and biological function. In organizations, these needs are generally satisfied by adequate wages and the work environment itself, which provides restrooms, adequate lighting, comfortable temperatures, and ventilation.

- **Maslow's hierarchy of needs** A theory of motivation that suggests that people must satisfy five groups of needs in order—physiological, security, belongingness, esteem, and self-actualization

Next are the *security needs* for a secure physical and emotional environment. Examples include the desire for housing and clothing and the need to be free from worry about money and job security. These needs can be satisfied in the workplace by job continuity (no layoffs), a grievance system (to protect against arbitrary supervisory actions), and an adequate insurance and retirement benefits package (for security against illness and provision

People must have both the ability and the motivation if they are to perform at a high level. While professional baseball has historically been the province of male athletes, these female athletes are determined to prove that they have both the ability and desire to succeed in a "league of their own." Backed by Coors, the Silver Bullets have already shown that they can compete successfully against all-male top-level minor league teams.

of income in later life). Even today, however, depressed industries and economic decline can put people out of work and restore the primacy of security needs.

Belongingness needs relate to social processes. They include the need for love and affection and the need to be accepted by one's peers. These needs are satisfied for most people by family and community relationships outside of work and friendships on the job. A manager can help satisfy these needs by allowing social interaction and by making employees feel like part of a team or work group.

Esteem needs actually comprise two different sets of needs: the need for a positive self-image and self-respect and the need for recognition and respect from others. A manager can help address these needs by providing a variety of extrinsic symbols of accomplishment, such as job titles, nice offices, and similar rewards as appropriate. At a more intrinsic level, the manager can provide challenging job assignments and opportunities for the employee to feel a sense of accomplishment.

At the top of the hierarchy are the *self-actualization needs*. These involve realizing one's potential for continued growth and individual development. The self-actualization needs are perhaps the most difficult for a manager to address. In fact, it can be argued that these needs must be met entirely from within the individual. But a manager can help by promoting a culture wherein self-actualization is possible. For instance, a manager could give employees a chance to participate in making decisions about their work and the opportunity to learn new things about their jobs and the organization.

Maslow suggests that the five need categories constitute a hierarchy. An individual is motivated first and foremost to satisfy physiological needs. As long as these remain unsatisfied, the individual is motivated only to fulfill

F I G U R E 10.2 Maslow's Hierarchy of Needs

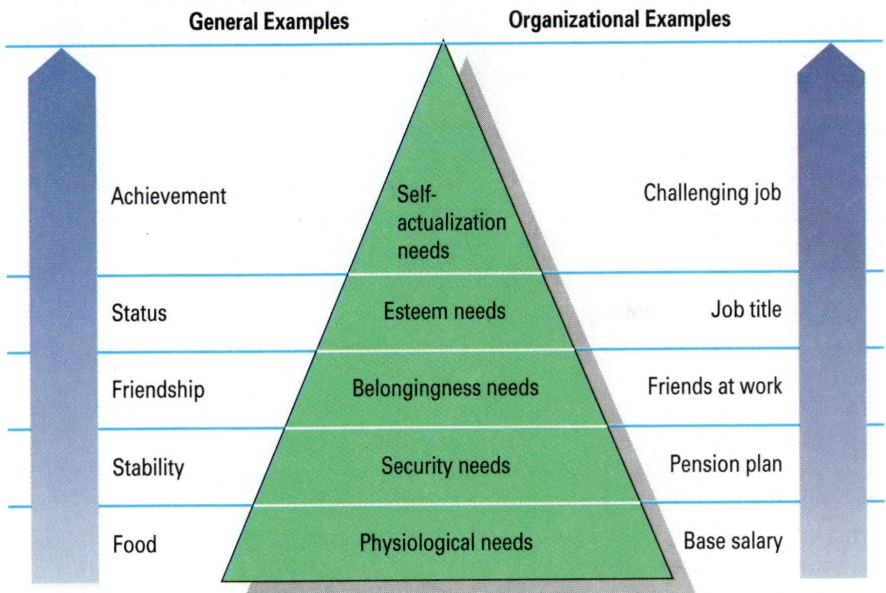

Source: Adapted from Abraham H. Maslow, "A Theory of Human Motivation," *Psychological Review*, Vol. 50, 1943, pp. 370–396.

Maslow's hierarchy suggests that human needs can be classified into five categories and that these categories can be arranged in a hierarchy of importance. A manager should understand that an employee may not be satisfied with only a salary and benefits; he or she may also need challenging job opportunities to experience self-growth and satisfaction.

them. When satisfaction of physiological needs is achieved, they cease to act as primary motivational factors and the individual moves "up" the hierarchy and becomes concerned with security needs. This process continues until the individual reaches the self-actualization level. Maslow's concept of the need hierarchy has a certain intuitive logic and has been accepted by many managers. But research has revealed certain shortcomings and defects in the theory. Some research has found that five levels of need are not always present and that the order of the levels is not always the same as postulated by Maslow.[6] In addition, people from different cultures are likely to have different need categories and hierarchies.

The Two-Factor Theory

Another popular content perspective on motivation is the **two-factor theory**.[7] Frederick Herzberg developed his theory by interviewing two hundred accountants and engineers. He asked them to recall occasions when they had been satisfied with their work and highly motivated and occasions when they had been dissatisfied and unmotivated. Surprisingly, he found that different sets of factors were associated with satisfaction and with dissatisfaction—that is, a person might identify "low pay" as causing dissatisfaction but would not necessarily mention "high pay" as a cause of satisfaction. Instead, different factors—such as recognition or accomplishment—were cited as causing satisfaction.

two-factor theory A theory of motivation that suggests that people's satisfaction and dissatisfaction are influenced by two independent sets of factors—motivation factors and hygiene factors

This finding led Herzberg to conclude that the traditional view of job satisfaction was incomplete. That view assumed that satisfaction and dissatisfaction are at opposite ends of a single continuum. People might be satisfied, dissatisfied, or somewhere in between. But Herzberg's interviews had identified two different dimensions altogether: one ranging from satisfaction to no satisfaction and the other ranging from dissatisfaction to no dissatisfaction.

This perspective, along with several examples of factors that affect each continuum, is shown in Figure 10.3. Note that the factors influencing the satisfaction continuum—called motivation factors—are related specifically to the work content. The factors presumed to cause dissatisfaction—called hygiene factors—are related to the work environment.

Based on these findings, Herzberg argues that there are two stages in the process of motivating employees. First, managers must ensure that the hygiene factors are not deficient. Pay and security must be appropriate, working conditions must be safe, technical supervision must be acceptable, and so on. By providing hygiene factors at an appropriate level, managers do not stimulate motivation but merely ensure that employees are "not dissatisfied." Employees whom managers attempt to "satisfy" through hygiene factors alone will usually do just enough to get by. Thus managers should proceed to stage two—giving employees the opportunity to experience motivation factors such as achievement and recognition. The result is predicted to be a high level of satisfaction and motivation. Herzberg also goes a step further than most theorists and describes

The two-factor theory suggests that job satisfaction has two different dimensions. A manager who tries to motivate an employee using only hygiene factors such as pay and good working conditions will likely not succeed. To motivate employees and produce a high level of satisfaction, managers must also offer factors such as responsibility and the opportunity for advancement (motivation factors).

FIGURE 10.3 The Two-Factor Theory of Motivation

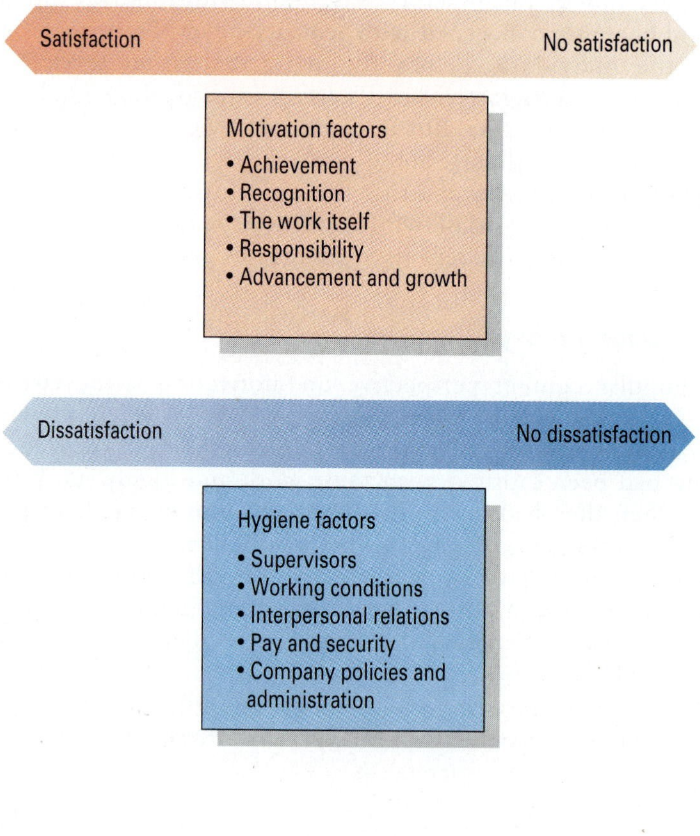

exactly how to use the two-factor theory in the workplace. Specifically, he recommends job enrichment, as discussed in Chapter 6. He argues that jobs should be redesigned to provide higher levels of the motivation factors.

Although widely accepted by many managers, Herzberg's two-factor theory is not without its critics. One criticism is that the findings in Herzberg's initial interviews are subject to different explanations. Another charge is that his sample was not representative of the general population and that subsequent research often failed to uphold the theory.[8] At the present time, Herzberg's theory is not held in high esteem by researchers in the field. The theory has had a major impact on managers, however, and has played a key role in increasing their awareness of motivation and its importance in the workplace.

Individual Human Needs

In addition to these theories, research has also focused on specific individual human needs that are important in organizations. The three most important individual needs are achievement, affiliation, and power.[9]

The **need for achievement**, the best known of the three, is the desire to accomplish a goal or task more effectively than in the past. People with a high need for achievement have a desire to assume personal responsibility, a tendency to set moderately difficult goals, a desire for specific and immediate feedback, and a preoccupation with their task. David C. McClelland, the psychologist who first identified this need, argues that only about 10 percent of the U.S. population has a high need for achievement. In contrast, almost 25 percent of the workers in Japan have a high need for achievement.

• **need for achievement** The desire to accomplish a goal or task more effectively than in the past

The **need for affiliation** is less well understood. Like Maslow's belongingness need, the need for affiliation is a desire for human companionship and acceptance. People with a strong need for affiliation are likely to prefer (and perform better in) a job that entails a lot of social interaction and offers opportunities to make friends.

• **need for affiliation** The desire for human companionship and acceptance

The need for power has also received considerable attention as an important ingredient in managerial success.[10] The **need for power** is the desire to be influential in a group and to control one's environment. Research has shown that people with a strong need for power are likely to be superior performers, have good attendance records, and occupy supervisory positions. One study found that managers as a group tend to have a stronger power motive than the general population and that successful managers tend to have stronger power motives than less successful managers.[11]

• **need for power** The desire to be influential in a group and to control one's environment

In summary, the major content perspectives on motivation focus on individual needs. Maslow's need hierarchy, the two-factor theory, and the needs for achievement, affiliation, and power all provide useful insights into factors that cause motivation. What they do not do is shed much light on the process of motivation. They do not explain why people might be motivated by one factor rather than by another at a given level or how people might go about trying to satisfy the different needs. These questions involve behaviors or actions, goals, and feelings of satisfaction—concepts that are addressed by various process perspectives on motivation.

PROCESS PERSPECTIVES ON MOTIVATION

● **process perspectives** Approaches to motivation that focus on why people choose certain behavioral options to fulfill their needs and how they evaluate their satisfaction after they have attained these goals

Process perspectives are concerned with how motivation occurs. Rather than attempting to identify or list motivational stimuli, **process perspectives** focus on why people choose certain behavioral options to satisfy their needs and how they evaluate their satisfaction after they have attained these goals. Two popular process perspectives on motivation are expectancy theory and equity theory.

Expectancy Theory

● **expectancy theory** Suggests that motivation depends on two things—how much we want something and how likely we think we are to get it

The expectancy theory of motivation has many different forms and labels. We will describe its most basic form. Essentially, **expectancy theory** suggests that motivation depends on two things—how much we want something and how likely we think we are to get it. Assume that you are approaching graduation and looking for a job. You see in the want ads that Exxon is seeking a new vice president with a starting salary of $350,000 per year. Even though you might want the job, you will not apply because you realize that you have little chance of getting it. The next ad you see is for someone to scrape bubble gum from underneath theater seats for a starting salary of $4 an hour. Even though you could probably get this job, you do not apply because you do not want it. Then you see an ad for a management trainee for a big company with a starting salary of $25,000. You will probably apply for this job because you want it and because you think you have a reasonable chance of getting it.[12]

The formal expectancy framework was developed by Victor Vroom.[13] Expectancy theory rests on four basic assumptions. First, it assumes that behavior is determined by a combination of forces in the individual and in the environment. Second, it assumes that people make decisions about their own behavior in organizations. Third, it assumes that different people have different types of needs, desires, and goals. Fourth, it assumes that people make choices from among alternative plans of behavior based on their perceptions of the extent to which a given behavior will lead to desired outcomes.[14]

Figure 10.4 summarizes the basic expectancy model. The model suggests that motivation leads to effort and that effort, combined with employee ability and environmental factors, results in performance. Performance, in turn, leads to various outcomes, each of which has an associated value called its valence. The most important parts of the expectancy model cannot be shown in the figure, however. These are the individual's expectations that effort will lead to high performance, that performance will lead to outcomes, and that each outcome will have some kind of value.

● **effort-to-performance expectancy** The individual's perception of the probability that his or her effort will lead to high performance

Effort-to-Performance Expectancy The **effort-to-performance expectancy** is the individual's perception of the probability that effort will lead to high performance. When the individual believes that effort will lead directly to high performance, expectancy will be quite strong (close to 1.00). The belief that effort is somewhat but not strongly related to performance carries with it a moderate expectancy (somewhere between 0 and 1). When

FIGURE 10.4 The Expectancy Model of Motivation

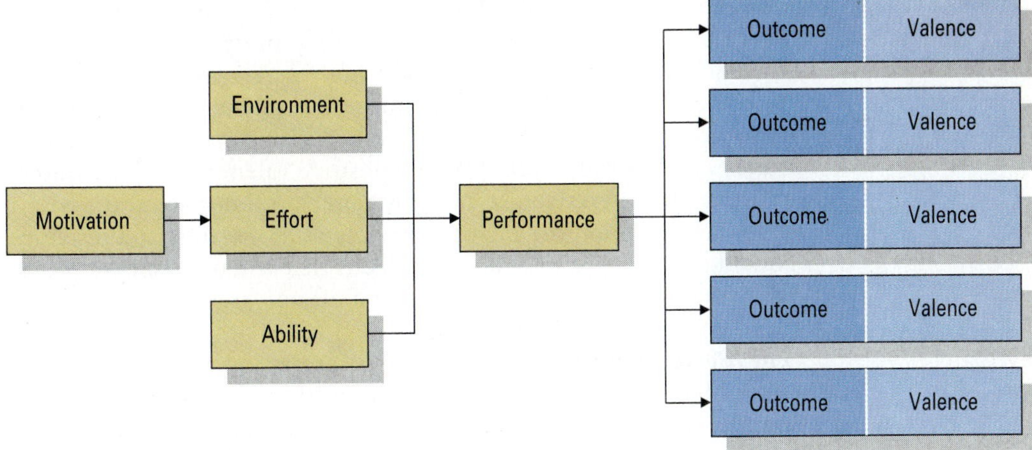

the individual believes that effort and performance are unrelated, the effort-to-performance expectancy is very weak (close to 0).

Performance-to-Outcome Expectancy The **performance-to-outcome expectancy** is the individual's perception that performance will lead to a specific outcome. For example, if the individual believes that high performance will result in a pay raise, the performance-to-outcome expectancy is high (near 1.00). The individual who believes that high performance may lead to a pay raise has a moderate expectancy (between 1.00 and 0). The individual who believes that performance has no relationship with rewards has a low performance-to-outcome expectancy (close to 0).

Outcomes and Valences Expectancy theory recognizes that an individual's behavior results in a variety of **outcomes**, or consequences, in an organizational setting. A high performer, for example, may get bigger pay raises, faster promotions, and more praise from the boss. On the other hand, she may also be subject to more stress and incur resentment from coworkers. Each of these outcomes also has an associated value, or **valence**—an index of how much an individual values a particular outcome. If the individual wants the outcome, its valence is positive; if the individual does not want the outcome, its valence is negative; and if the individual is indifferent to the outcome, its valence is zero.

It is this part of expectancy theory that goes beyond the content perspectives on motivation. Different people have different needs, and they will try to satisfy these needs in different ways. For an employee who has a high need for achievement and a low need for affiliation, the pay raise and promotions cited above as outcomes of high performance might have positive valences, the praise and resentment zero valences, and the stress a negative valence. For a different employee with a low need for achievement and a high need for affiliation, the pay raise, promotions, and praise all might have positive valences, whereas resentment and stress both could have negative valences.

The expectancy theory of motivation is a complex but relatively accurate portrayal of how motivation occurs. According to this model, a manager must understand what employees want (such as pay, promotions, or status) to begin to motivate them.

performance-to-outcome expectancy
The individual's perception that her or his performance will lead to a specific outcome

outcomes
Consequences of behaviors in an organizational setting; usually rewards

valence
An index of how much an individual desires a particular outcome; the attractiveness of the outcome to the individual

For motivated behavior to occur, three conditions must be met. First, the effort-to-performance expectancy must be greater than zero (the individual must believe that if effort is expended, high performance will result). The performance-to-outcome expectancy must also be greater than zero (the individual must believe that if high performance is achieved, certain outcomes will follow). And the sum of the valences for the outcomes must be greater than zero. (One or more outcomes may have negative valences if they are more than offset by the positive valences of other outcomes. For example, the attractiveness of a pay raise, a promotion, and praise from the boss may outweigh the unattractiveness of more stress and resentment from coworkers.) Expectancy theory suggests that when these conditions are met, the individual is motivated to expend effort.

The Porter-Lawler Extension An interesting extension of expectancy theory has been proposed by Porter and Lawler.[15] Recall from Chapter 2 that the human relationists assumed that employee satisfaction causes good performance. We also noted that research has not supported such a relationship. Porter and Lawler suggest that there may indeed be a relationship between satisfaction and performance but that it goes in the opposite direction—that is, high performance may lead to high satisfaction. Figure 10.5 summarizes Porter and Lawler's logic. Performance results in rewards for an individual. Some of these are extrinsic (such as pay and promotions); others are intrinsic (such as self-esteem and accomplishment). The individual evaluates the equity, or fairness, of the rewards relative to the effort expended and the level of performance attained. If the rewards are perceived to be equitable, the individual is satisfied.

Implications for Managers Expectancy theory can be very useful for managers who are trying to improve the motivation of their subordinates.

The Porter-Lawler extension of expectancy theory suggests that if performance results in equitable rewards, people will be more satisfied. Thus performance can lead to satisfaction. Managers must therefore be sure that any system of motivation includes rewards that are fair, or equitable, for all.

FIGURE 10.5 The Porter-Lawler Extension of Expectancy Theory

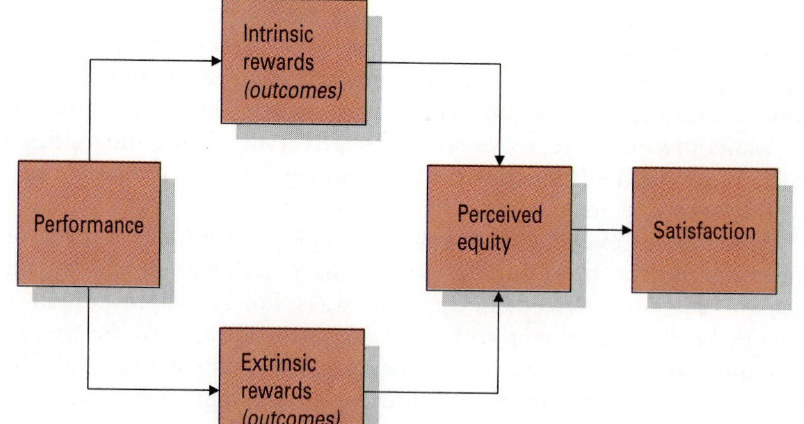

Source: Edward E. Lawler III, and Lyman W. Porter, "The Effect of Performance on Job Satisfaction," *Industrial Relations,* October 1967, p. 23. Permission granted courtesy of Blackwell Publishers, Inc.

Managers can follow a series of steps to implement the basic ideas of the theory. First, figure out the outcomes each employee is likely to want. Second, decide what kinds and levels of performance are needed to meet organizational goals. Then make sure that the desired levels of performance are attainable. Also make sure that desired outcomes and desired performance are linked. Next, analyze the complete situation for conflicting expectancies, and ensure that the rewards are large enough. Finally, make sure the total system is equitable (fair to all).[16] These issues will be explored in more detail later in this chapter when we discuss organizational reward systems.

One firm that has had considerable success with expectancy theory is A & P. At its Philadelphia stores, A & P workers took a 25 percent pay cut, but they can now earn large bonuses by working more efficiently. Each worker knows what needs to be done in order to earn a bonus. Employees are earning more money than before, yet the stores are also achieving higher levels of profitability.[17] IBM's new compensation system is also clearly consistent with expectancy theory. Of course, expectancy theory has its limitations. Although the theory makes sense and has been generally supported by empirical research, it is quite difficult to apply.[18] To really use the complete theory in the workplace, for example, it would be necessary to identify all the potential outcomes for each employee, to determine all relevant expectancies, and then to balance everything somehow to maximize employee motivation.

Equity Theory

After needs have stimulated the motivation process and the individual has chosen an action that is expected to satisfy those needs, the individual assesses the fairness, or equity, of the resultant outcome. Much of our current thinking on equity has been shaped by the **equity theory** of motivation developed by J. Stacy Adams. Adams contends that people are motivated to seek social equity in the rewards they receive for performance.[19] Equity is an individual's belief that the treatment he or she is receiving is fair relative to the treatment received by others.

equity theory Suggests that people are motivated to seek social equity in the rewards they receive for performance

According to equity theory, outcomes from a job include pay, recognition, promotions, social relationships, and intrinsic rewards. To get these rewards, the individual makes inputs to the job, such as time, experience, effort, education, and loyalty. The theory suggests that people view their outcomes and inputs as a ratio and then compare it to the ratio of someone else. This other "person" may be someone in the work group or some sort of group average or composite. The process of comparison looks like this:

$$\frac{\text{Outcomes (self)}}{\text{Inputs (self)}} \stackrel{?}{=} \frac{\text{Outcomes (other)}}{\text{Inputs (other)}}$$

Both the formulation of the ratios and comparisons between them are very subjective and are based on individual perceptions. As a result of comparisons, three conditions may result: The individual may feel equitably rewarded, under-rewarded, or over-rewarded. A feeling of equity will result when the two ratios are equal. This may occur even though the other person's outcomes are greater than the individual's own outcomes—provided that the other's inputs are also proportionately greater. Suppose that Mark has a high school education and earns only $20,000. He may still feel equitably treated relative to Susan, who earns $25,000, because she has a college degree.

People who feel under-rewarded try to reduce the inequity. Such an individual might decrease her inputs by exerting less effort, increase her outcomes by asking for a raise, distort the original ratios by rationalizing, try to get the other person to change her or his outcomes or inputs, leave the situation, or change the object of comparison. An individual may also feel over-rewarded relative to another person. This is not likely to be terribly disturbing to most people, but research suggests that some people who experience inequity under these conditions are somewhat motivated to reduce it.[20] Under such a circumstance, the person might increase his inputs by exerting more effort, reduce his outcomes by producing fewer units (if paid on a per-unit basis), distort the original ratios by rationalizing, or try to reduce the inputs or increase the outcomes of the other person.

Implications for Managers The single most important idea for managers to remember from equity theory is that if rewards are to motivate employees, they must be perceived as being equitable and fair. If a person achieves rewards as a result of performance and regards these rewards as equitable, satisfaction will result. A second implication is that managers need to consider the nature of the "other" to whom the employee is comparing herself or himself. In recent years, for example, the number of dual-career couples has increased dramatically, and husband-and-wife equity comparisons have ruined both marriages and careers.[21] On balance, the research support for equity theory is mixed.[22] The concepts of equity and social comparisons are certainly important for the manager to consider, but it is also apparent that managers should not rely only on this framework in attempting to manage employee motivation.

REINFORCEMENT PERSPECTIVES ON MOTIVATION

A third element of the motivational process addresses why some behaviors are maintained over time and why other behaviors change. As we have seen, content perspectives deal with needs, while process perspectives explain why people choose various behaviors to satisfy needs and how they evaluate the equity of the rewards they get for those behaviors. Reinforcement perspectives explain the role of those rewards as they cause behavior to change or remain the same over time. Specifically, **reinforcement theory** argues that behavior that results in rewarding consequences is likely to be repeated, whereas behavior that results in punishing consequences is less likely to be repeated. This approach to explaining behavior originally was tested on animals, but B. F. Skinner and others have been instrumental in demonstrating how reinforcement theory applies to human behavior as well.[23]

• **reinforcement theory** Approach to motivation that explains the role of rewards as they cause behavior to change or remain the same over time

Kinds of Reinforcement in Organizations

In organizational settings, four basic kinds of reinforcement can result from behavior: positive reinforcement, avoidance, punishment, and extinction.[24] Two kinds of reinforcement strengthen or maintain behavior, and two weaken or decrease behavior. **Positive reinforcement**, a method of strengthening behavior, is a reward or a positive outcome after a desired behavior is performed. When a manager observes an employee doing an especially good job and offers praise, the praise serves to positively reinforce the behavior of good work. Other positive reinforcers in organizations include pay raises, promotions, and awards. Employees who work at General Electric's customer service center receive clothing, sporting goods, and even trips to Disney World as rewards for outstanding performance.[25] The other method of strengthening desired behavior is through **avoidance**. An employee may come to work on time to avoid a reprimand. In this instance, the employee is motivated to perform the behavior of punctuality to avoid an unpleasant consequence that is likely to follow tardiness.

• **positive reinforcement** A method of strengthening behavior with rewards or positive outcomes after a desired behavior is performed

• **avoidance** Used to strengthen behavior by avoiding unpleasant consequences that would result if the behavior were not performed

Punishment is used by some managers to weaken undesired behaviors. When an employee is loafing, coming to work late, doing poor work, or interfering with the work of others, the manager might resort to reprimands, discipline, or fines. The logic is that the unpleasant consequence will reduce the likelihood that the employee will choose that particular behavior again. Given the counterproductive side effects of punishment (such as resentment and hostility), it is often advisable to use the other kinds of reinforcement if at all possible. **Extinction** can also be used to weaken behavior, especially behavior that has previously been rewarded. When an employee tells an off-color joke and the boss laughs, the laughter reinforces the behavior and the employee may continue to tell off-color jokes. By simply ignoring this behavior and not reinforcing it, the boss can cause the behavior to subside and eventually become "extinct."

• **punishment** Used to weaken undesired behaviors by using negative outcomes or unpleasant consequences when the behavior is performed

• **extinction** Used to weaken undesired behaviors by simply ignoring or not reinforcing that behavior

Providing Reinforcement in Organizations

Not only is the kind of reinforcement important, but so is when or how often it occurs. Various strategies are possible for providing reinforcement. The **fixed-interval schedule** provides reinforcement at fixed intervals of time, regardless of behavior. A good example of this schedule is the weekly or monthly paycheck. This method provides the least incentive for good work, because employees know they will be paid regularly regardless of their effort. A **variable-interval schedule** also uses time as the basis for reinforcement, but the time interval varies from one reinforcement to the next. This schedule is appropriate for praise or other rewards based on visits or inspections. When employees do not know when the boss is going to drop by, they tend to maintain a reasonably high level of effort all the time.

• **fixed-interval schedule** Provides reinforcement at fixed intervals of time; for example, a regular weekly paycheck

• **variable-interval schedule** Provides reinforcement at varying intervals of time; for example, occasional visits by the supervisor

A **fixed-ratio schedule** gives reinforcement after a fixed number of behaviors, regardless of the time that elapses between behaviors. This results in an even higher level of effort. For example, when Sears is recruiting new credit-card customers, salespersons get a small bonus for every fifth application returned from their department. Under this arrangement, motivation will be high because each application gets the person closer to the next bonus. The **variable-ratio schedule**, the most powerful schedule in terms of maintaining desired behaviors, varies the number of behaviors needed for each reinforcement. A supervisor who praises an employee for her second order, the seventh order after that, the ninth after that, then the

• **fixed-ratio schedule** Provides reinforcement after a fixed number of behaviors regardless of the time interval involved; for example, a bonus for every fifth sale

• **variable-ratio schedule** Provides reinforcement after varying numbers of behaviors are performed; for example, compliments from a supervisor on an irregular basis

fifth, and then the third is using a variable-ratio schedule. The employee is motivated to increase the frequency of the desired behavior because each performance increases the probability of receiving a reward. Of course, a variable-ratio schedule is difficult (if not impossible) to use for formal rewards such as pay because it would be too complicated to keep track of who was rewarded when.

OTHER PERSPECTIVES ON MOTIVATION

In addition to the established models and theories of motivation, a promising emerging perspective is goal-setting theory. Various motivational strategies are also popular today.

Goal-Setting Theory

Goal-setting theory suggests that managers and subordinates should set goals for the individual on a regular basis.[26] These goals should be moderately difficult and very specific. Moreover, they should be of a type that the employee will accept and commit to accomplishing. Rewards should also be tied directly to reaching the goals. Goal-setting theory helps the manager tailor rewards to individual needs, clarify expectancies, maintain equity, and provide reinforcement on a systematic basis. Thus it provides a comprehensive framework for integrating the other approaches. As illustrated in Figure 10.6, the goal-setting theory of motivation bears close resemblance to both the basic expectancy theory and the Porter-Lawler extension of expectancy discussed earlier.[27]

Popular Motivational Strategies

• **behavior modification** (**OB Mod**; organizational behavior modification) A technique for applying the concepts of reinforcement theory in organizational settings

Managers trying to enhance the motivation of their employees can adopt specific motivational strategies derived from one or more theories discussed in the previous sections. **Behavior modification**, or **OB Mod** (for organizational behavior modification), is a technique for applying the concepts of reinforcement theory in organizational settings.[28] An OB Mod program starts by specifying behaviors that are to be increased (such as producing more units) or decreased (such as coming to work late). These target behaviors are then tied to specific forms or kinds of reinforcement. Although many organizations (such as Procter & Gamble, Warner-Lambert, and Ford) have used OB Mod, the best-known application has been at Emery Worldwide (air freight). Management felt that the containers used to consolidate small shipments into fewer, larger shipments were not being packed efficiently. Through a system of self-monitored feedback and rewards, Emery increased container usage from 45 percent to 95 percent and saved over $3 million during the first three years of the program.[29]

• **modified workweek** A strategy for increasing motivation by helping individuals satisfy higher-order needs through the use of alternative work schedules

Many organizations also use a **modified workweek** for employees as a strategy for increasing motivation. The modified workweek helps individuals satisfy higher-level needs and provides an opportunity to fulfill several needs simultaneously. One alternative is the *compressed workweek*, whereby

F I G U R E 10.6 The Expanded Goal-Setting Theory of Motivation

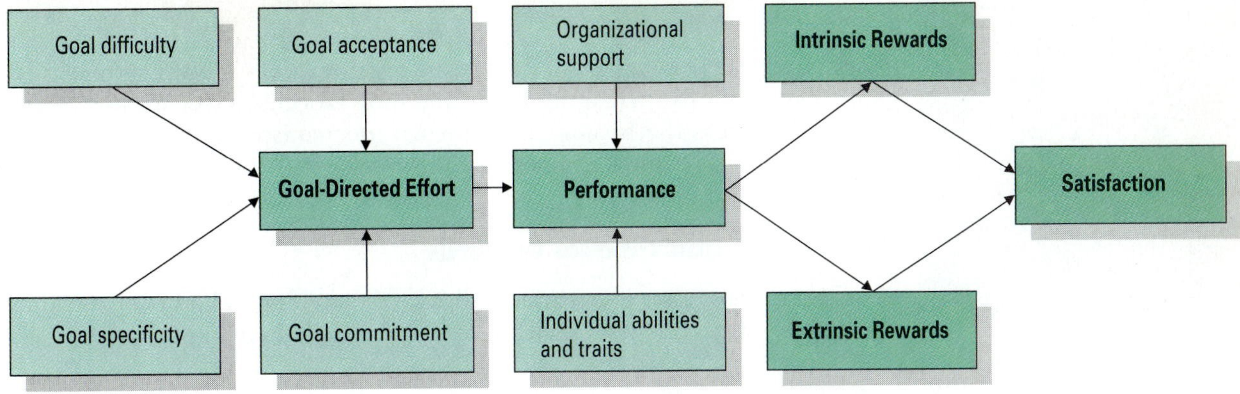

Source: Adapted from "A Motivational Technique That Works" by Gary P. Latham and Edwin A. Locke, reprinted by permission from *Organizational Dynamics,* Autumn 1979, p. 79, © 1979 American Management Association, New York. All rights reserved.

people work forty hours in less than the traditional five full workdays. The most common plan has people work ten hours a day for four days. Another popular plan is the *flexible work schedule.* In this approach, employees are required to work during a certain period called core time and can choose what other hours to work. Thus an individual can come in early and leave early, come in late and leave late, or come in early, take a long lunch, and leave late. Allowing employees to work at home or to share jobs with others is also becoming popular. Working at home is especially useful for writers and others using computers. Job sharing allows two people to work part-time while the organization still gets the benefit of a full-time "worker."[30] Many companies, including John Hancock, ARCO, General Dynamics, Metropolitan Life, and IBM have experimented successfully with one or more of these modifications. By allowing employees some independence in terms of when they come to work and when they leave, managers acknowledge and show "esteem" for the employees' ability to exercise self-control.

One of the most important emerging theories of motivation is goal-setting theory. This theory suggests that goal difficulty, specificity, acceptance, and commitment combine to determine an individual's goal-directed effort. This effort, when complemented by appropriate organizational support and individual abilities and traits, results in performance. Finally, performance is seen as leading to intrinsic and extrinsic rewards which, in turn, result in employee satisfaction.

Changing the nature of the task-related activities of work is also being used more and more as a motivational technique. The idea is that managers can use any of the alternatives to job specialization described in Chapter 6 as a motivational tool. More precisely, job rotation, job enlargement, job enrichment, and the job characteristics approach can all be used as part of a motivational program. A number of studies have shown that improvements in the design of work do often result in higher levels of motivation. One study at Texas Instruments, for example, found that job design resulted in decreased turnover and improved employee motivation.[31]

Finally, many organizations today are using empowerment and participation to boost motivation. The basic idea is that by giving workers more power and allowing them to participate more fully, they will be able to pursue various needs that are important to them as individuals. Likewise, the actual activities themselves will also facilitate the process of motivation. And achieving valued rewards as a result of contributing to the organization will provide positive reinforcement.

Many organizations are finding that empowerment can provide a major boost in employee motivation. Saturn, for example, has empowered everyone in its showrooms to participate in selling new automobiles. When a customer takes delivery of a new Saturn, a team of representatives from sales, service, parts, and reception takes part in a little ceremony—the customer is cheered, has her or his picture taken, and is handed the keys to the car. Saturn ranks relatively high among other car companies in customer satisfaction.

• **reward system**
The formal and informal mechanisms by which employee performance is defined, evaluated, and rewarded

USING REWARD SYSTEMS TO MOTIVATE PERFORMANCE

Aside from these types of strategies, an organization's reward system is its most basic tool for managing employee motivation. An organizational **reward system** is the formal and informal mechanism by which employee performance is defined, evaluated, and rewarded.

Effects of Organizational Rewards

Organizational rewards can affect attitudes, behaviors, and motivation. Thus managers must clearly understand and appreciate their importance.

Effect of Rewards on Attitudes Although employee attitudes such as satisfaction are not a major determinant of job performance, they are nonetheless important. They contribute to (or discourage) absenteeism and affect turnover, and they help establish the culture of the organization. We can draw four major generalizations about employee attitudes and rewards.[32] First, employee satisfaction is influenced by how much is received and how much the individual thinks should be received. Second, employee satisfaction is affected by comparisons with what happens to others. Third, employees often misperceive the rewards of others. When an employee believes that someone else is making more money than that person really makes, the potential for dissatisfaction increases. Fourth, overall job satisfaction is affected by how satisfied employees are with both the extrinsic and the intrinsic rewards tney derive from their jobs. Drawing from the content theories and expectancy theory, this conclusion suggests that a variety of needs may cause behavior and that behavior may be channeled toward a variety of goals.

Effect of Rewards on Behaviors An organization's primary purpose in giving rewards is to influence employee behavior. Extrinsic rewards affect employee satisfaction, which, in turn, plays a major role in determining whether an employee will remain on the job or seek a new job. Reward systems also influence patterns of attendance and absenteeism; if rewards are based on actual performance, employees tend to work harder to earn those rewards.

Effect of Rewards on Motivation Reward systems are clearly related to the expectancy theory of motivation. The effort-to-performance expectancy is strongly influenced by the performance appraisal that is often a part of the reward system. An employee is likely to put forth extra effort if he or she knows that performance will be measured, evaluated, and rewarded. The performance-to-outcome expectancy is affected by the extent to which the employee believes that performance will be followed by rewards. Finally, as expectancy theory predicts, each reward or potential reward has a somewhat different value for each individual. One person may want a promotion more than benefits; someone else may want just the opposite.

Designing Effective Reward Systems

What are the elements of an effective reward system? Experts agree that they have four major characteristics.[33] First, the reward system must meet the needs of the individual for basic necessities. These needs include the physiological and security needs identified by Maslow and the hygiene factors identified by Herzberg. Next, the rewards should compare favorably with those offered by other organizations. Unfavorable comparisons with people in other settings could result in feelings of inequity. Third, the distribution of rewards within the organization must be equitable. When some employees feel underpaid compared with others in the organization, the probable results are low morale and poor performance. (People are more likely to compare their situation with that of others in their own organization than with that of outsiders.) Fourth, the reward system must recognize that different people have different needs and choose different paths to satisfy those needs. Both content theories and expectancy theory contribute to this conclusion. Insofar as possible, a variety of rewards and a variety of methods for achieving them should be made available to employees.

New Approaches to Rewarding Employees

Organizational reward systems traditionally have been one of two kinds: a fixed hourly or monthly rate or an incentive system. Fixed-rate systems are familiar to most people. Hourly employees are paid a specific wage (based on job demands, experience, or other factors) for each hour they work. Salaried employees receive a fixed sum of money on a weekly or monthly basis. Although some reductions may be made for absences, the amount is usually the same regardless of whether the individual works less than or more than a normal amount of time.[34]

From a motivational perspective, such rewards can be tied more directly to performance through merit pay raises. A **merit system** is one whereby people get different pay raises at the end of the year, depending on their overall job performance.[35] When the organization's performance appraisal system is appropriately designed, merit pay is a good system for maintaining long-term performance. Increasingly, however, organizations are experimenting with various kinds of incentive systems. An **incentive system** attempts to reward employees in proportion to what they do. A piece-rate pay plan is a good example of an incentive system. In a factory manufacturing luggage, for example, each worker may be paid 50 cents for each handle and set of locks installed on a piece of luggage. Hence, there is incentive for the employee to work hard: the more units produced, the higher the pay. Four increasingly popular incentive systems are profit sharing, gain sharing, lump-sum bonuses, and pay for knowledge.[36]

- **merit system**
A reward system whereby people get different pay raises at the end of the year depending on their overall job performance

- **incentive system**
A reward system whereby people get different pay amounts at each pay period in proportion to what they do

Profit sharing provides a varying annual bonus to employees based on corporate profits. This system unites workers and management toward the same goal—higher profits. However, there can be equity problems in deciding how to allocate the profits. Ford, USX, and Alcoa all have profit-sharing plans. Gain sharing is a group-based incentive system in which group members all get bonuses when predetermined performance levels are exceeded. This system may facilitate teamwork and trust; on the other hand, it may focus workers too narrowly on attaining the specific goals needed for the bonus while neglecting other parts of their jobs.

Another innovative method for rewarding employees is the lump-sum bonus. This method gives each employee a one-time cash bonus, rather than a base salary increase. The organization can control its fixed costs by not increasing base salaries; however, employees sometimes feel resentful that their increase is contingent on future performance. Aetna Life and Casualty, Timex, and B. F. Goodrich have successfully used this approach. Finally, pay-for-knowledge systems focus on paying the individual rather than the job. Under a traditional arrangement, two workers doing the same job are paid the same rate, regardless of their skills. Under the new arrangement, people are advanced in pay grade for each new skill or set of skills they learn. This approach increases training costs but also results in a more highly skilled workforce. Schoolteachers often receive higher pay for increased training. General Foods and Texas Instruments have also experimented with this method and have had favorable results.

SUMMARY OF KEY POINTS

Motivation is the set of forces that cause people to behave in certain ways. Motivation is an important consideration of managers because it, along with ability and environmental factors, determines individual performance.

Content perspectives on motivation are concerned with what factor or factors cause motivation. Popular content theories include Maslow's need hierarchy and Herzberg's two-factor theory. Other important needs are the needs for achievement, affiliation, and power.

Process perspectives on motivation deal with how motivation occurs. Expectancy theory suggests that people are motivated to perform if they believe that their effort will result in high performance, that this performance will lead to rewards, and that the positive aspects of the outcomes outweigh the negative aspects. Equity theory is based on the premise that people are motivated to achieve and maintain social equity.

The reinforcement perspective focuses on how motivation is maintained. Its basic assumption is that behavior that results in rewarding consequences is likely to be repeated, whereas behavior resulting in negative consequences is less likely to be repeated. Reinforcement contingencies can be arranged in the form of positive reinforcement, avoidance, punishment, and extinction, and they can be provided on fixed-interval, variable-interval, fixed-ratio, or variable-ratio schedules.

A newly emerging approach to employee motivation is goal-setting theory. Managers often adopt behavior modification, modified workweeks, work redesign, and participation programs to enhance motivation.

Organizational reward systems are the primary mechanisms managers have for managing motivation. Properly designed systems can improve attitudes, motivation, and behaviors. Effective reward systems must provide sufficient rewards on an equitable basis at the individual level.

Contemporary reward systems include merit systems and various kinds of incentive systems.

QUESTIONS FOR REVIEW

1. Summarize the basic motivation process.
2. What are the differences between the motivation and hygiene factors in the two-factor theory?
3. Compare and contrast content, process, and reinforcement perspectives on motivation.
4. In what ways is goal-setting theory like expectancy theory? In what ways are they different?
5. What are the similarities and differences between the motivational strategies described in this chapter?

QUESTIONS FOR ANALYSIS

1. Compare the two content theories. Can you think of any ways in which the theories are contradictory?
2. Expectancy theory seems to make a great deal of sense, but it is complicated. Some people argue that its complexity reduces its value to practicing managers. Do you agree or disagree?
3. Under what circumstances might a famous athlete making, say, $3 million a year, feel underpaid? Which theory best explains this phenomenon?
4. Offer examples other than those from this chapter to illustrate positive reinforcement, avoidance, punishment, and extinction.
5. Think about the worst job you have held. What approach to motivation was used in that organization? Now think about the best job you have held. What approach to motivation was used there? Can you base any conclusions on this limited information? If so, what?

CASE STUDY

Lifetime Employment in Japan

One aspect of Japanese management widely misunderstood is lifetime employment. Many Japanese workers legally have never had lifetime employment guarantees. Even among managers, it frequently is not a legal requirement contractually agreed on between companies and their managerial personnel. Thus some non-Japanese observers have argued that it does not play nearly so important a role in Japanese management as is frequently assumed. On the other hand, although lifetime employment is seldom a legal contract, it is a social contract.

Japanese people are expected to be loyal and stay with one employer for life, and that employer is expected to be loyal and to employ them for life. Because of such social contracts, some estimates are that up to two-thirds of Japan's workers expect lifetime employment in some form or another. But just as laws can be rewritten and contracts renegotiated, customs and traditions can change, although they are agonizingly slow to do so.

The worst Japanese economic recession in decades began in the early 1990s. Initially, many companies tried to provide protection for some employees, trimming bonus and overtime compensation rather than personnel. When that proved insufficient, companies such as IBM Japan resorted to early retirement packages to reduce employment and, hence, labor costs. Performance-based compensation and advancement systems are being implemented but their impact will be gradual and long-term. But even these changes may not be sufficient.

Executives of numerous Japanese companies believe that many business institutions are proving to be liabilities instead of assets and will need to change. Those institutions include the *keiretsu* system, seniority-based compensation systems, aspects of management structure such as consensus decision making, and the expectation of lifetime employment. Reengineering that stresses improvement in economic value-added attributes of the production process instead of just reducing numbers of employees is becoming common in Japan, but lifetime employment is being maintained thus far. Indeed, when Pioneer Electric Corporation announced that it planned to lay off thirty-five top-level employees, the outcry was so strong and widespread that it cancelled the layoffs.

Part-time and contract employees are not covered by lifetime employment expectations and so are increasingly being used as yet another way to reduce costs. Those employees frequently work ten hours a day and, hence, actually contribute substantially to the work being performed. Expanding the use of part-time and contract employees, then, could reduce labor costs while continuing the concept of lifetime employment for a core of full-time employees. Other approaches to reduce labor costs include granting leaves of absence to workers while they seek new jobs and reducing new hires. Also, many companies are reducing lower-skilled positions held by women and cutting female career-track positions because women were never expected to have lifetime employment. Indeed, in 1993 at the Nissan Motor Co., 180 persons were hired, only 5 of whom were women.

Case Questions

1. What is the motivational basis for lifetime employment?
2. What long-term effects are expected due to the techniques being used by Japanese

companies to reduce labor costs while maintaining some semblance of lifetime employment?

3. What would be the costs and benefits of lifetime employment to a U.S. company?

References: John Teresko, "Is the Rising Sun Setting?" *Industry Week*, June 6, 1994, pp. 28–30; "New Paradigms in the Japanese Labor Market," *Focus Japan*, April 1994, pp. 1–2; Hiroshi Fukunaga, "The Honeymoon Is Over," *Tokyo Business Today*, April 1994, pp. 14–15; Dave Robson, "The Sun Also Sets," *Work Study*, January/February 1994, pp. 18–19; "Unemployment: Worst Is Yet to Come," *Tokyo Business Today*, January 1994, pp. 24–26; and "Japanese Business Struggles with Its Lifetime Job Ethic," *Boston Globe*, March 14, 1993, pp. A1, A3.

SKILLS • DEVELOPMENT • PORTFOLIO

BUILDING EFFECTIVE INTERPERSONAL SKILLS

Exercise Overview

Interpersonal skills—the ability to understand and motivate individuals and groups—are especially critical when managers attempt to deal with equity and justice issues in the workplace. This exercise will provide you with insights into how these skills may be used.

Exercise Background

You are the manager of a group of professional employees in the electronics industry. One of your employees, David Brown, has asked to meet with you. You think you know what David wants to discuss, and you are unsure as to how to proceed.

You hired David about ten years ago. During his time in your group he has been a solid, but not outstanding, employee. As a result, he has consistently received average performance evaluations, pay increases, and so forth. Indeed, he actually makes somewhat less today than do a couple of people with less tenure in the group but with stronger performance records.

The company has just announced an opening for a team leader position in your group, and you know that David wants the job. He feels that he has earned the opportunity to have the job on the basis of his consistent efforts. Unfortunately, you see things a bit differently. You really want to appoint another individual, Becky Thomas, to the job. Becky has worked for the firm for only six years, but she is your top performer. You want to reward her performance and think that she will do an excellent job. On the other hand, you do not want to lose David, a solid member of the group.

Exercise Task

Using the information above, respond to the following:

1. Using equity theory as a framework, how are David and Becky likely to see the situation?
2. Outline a conversation with David in which you will convey your decision to him.
3. What advice might you offer Becky, in her new job, about interacting with David?
4. What other rewards might you offer David to keep him motivated?

BUILDING EFFECTIVE DECISION-MAKING SKILLS

Exercise Overview

Decision-making skills include the manager's ability to correctly recognize and define situations and to select courses of action. This exercise will allow you to use expectancy theory as part of a hypothetical decision-making situation.

Exercise Background

Assume that you are about to graduate from college and have received three job offers, as summarized below:

1. Offer number one is an entry-level position in a large company. The salary offer is for $22,000, and you will begin work in a very attractive location. However, you also see promotion prospects as being relatively limited, and you know that you are likely to have to move frequently.

2. Offer number two is a position with a new start-up company. The salary offer is $19,000. You know that you will have to work especially long hours. If the company survives for a year, however, opportunities there are unlimited. You may need to move occasionally, but not for a few years.

3. Offer number three is a position in the family business. The salary is $25,000, and you start as a middle manager. You know that you can control your own transfers, but you also know that some people in the company may resent you because of your family ties.

Exercise Task

Using the three job offers as a framework, do the following:

1. Use expectancy theory to assess your own personal valence for each outcome in selecting a job.

2. Evaluate the three jobs in terms of their outcomes and associated valences.

3. Which job would you select from among these three?

4. What other outcomes will be important to you in selecting a job?

YOU MAKE THE CALL

At first, Mark Spenser was at a loss. Michael Chou, his assistant landscape designer, had just given his two-week notice. Mark hated to see Michael leave because he was a good, hard working employee. But even more troubling was that Michael was the third assistant designer to leave in the last two years. During their conversation, Michael had indicated some vague things about wanting to do something different and try some new things in his life. But he had offered nothing concrete in terms of problems or things that were wrong with his job.

Finally, Mark began to understand. It was perhaps a problem of motivation. Perhaps the job of assistant landscape designer wasn't providing the right kinds of rewards. The nursery employees, for example, had a clear incentive system. Each nursery employee received a direct sales commission on her or his monthly sales figures, and all nursery employees shared in another end-of-year bonus that was tied to total nursery sales.

The lawn-care teams also had an incentive system, albeit a different type. Each morning the teams were given a list of jobs to complete that day. While the team members were paid by the hour, they were free to go home if they finished their work early. That is, each day's assignments were developed such that they could be finished in around eight hours, with a one-hour lunch break figured in. If the day's work was not finished, those jobs were either delayed until the next day or else done on an overtime basis. But if the crew finished its jobs early, its members were still paid for eight hours of time.

The job of assistant landscape designer, however, had no incentives. Mark assumed that designers such as himself were motivated more by intrinsic satisfaction than by money. As a result, he paid his assistant a straight monthly salary. But Mark began to realize that, although perhaps his assumptions were partially true, he was guilty of not providing enough sources of intrinsic satisfaction for the individuals he hired. It slowly began to dawn on him that, although he believed them capable of greater responsibility, he treated them like his hourly workers. In particular, he assigned them their jobs, carefully told them how to do it, and often "looked over their shoulder" as they worked.

All of a sudden, he knew that this was indeed the problem. He recognized that he would certainly be frustrated and disappointed in his work if someone else limited him in the same way that he limited his own assistants. He resolved, therefore, to give his next assistant more responsibility. For example, he would let his new assistant do some simple jobs without any supervision at all. And if this worked out, he would let the assistant designer have more and more authority to design projects independently.

Discussion Questions

1. Which motivation theories can you see illustrated in the situation described here?

2. Evaluate the incentives that SLS uses in its retail nursery and lawn-care businesses.

3. Do you agree or disagree with Mark's assessment of motivation for his landscape design assistant?

SKILLS SELF-ASSESSMENT INSTRUMENT

Assessing Your Needs

Introduction: Needs are one factor that influences motivation. The following assessment surveys your judgments about your personal needs that might be partially shaping your motivation.

Instructions: Judge how descriptively accurate each of the following statements is about you. You may find making a decision difficult in some cases, but you should force a choice. Record your answers next to each statement according to the following scale:

Rating Scale

5 Very descriptive of me
4 Fairly descriptive of me
3 Somewhat descriptive of me
2 Not very descriptive of me
1 Not descriptive of me at all

_____ **1.** I aspire to accomplish difficult tasks, maintain high standards, and am willing to work toward distant goals.

_____ **2.** I enjoy being with friends and people in general and accept people readily.

_____ **3.** I am easily annoyed and am sometimes willing to hurt people to get my way.

_____ **4.** I try to break away from restraints or restrictions of any kind.

_____ **5.** I want to be the center of attention and enjoy having an audience.

_____ **6.** I speak freely and tend to act on the "spur of the moment."

_____ **7.** I assist others whenever possible, giving sympathy and comfort to those in need.

_____ **8.** I believe in the saying that "there is a place for everything and everything should be in its place." I dislike clutter.

_____ **9.** I express my opinions forcefully, enjoy the role of leader, and try to control my environment as much as I can.

_____ **10.** I want to understand many areas of knowledge and value synthesizing ideas and generalization.

For interpretation, turn to page 448.

EXPERIENTIAL EXERCISE

An Exercise in Thematic Apperception

Purpose: All people have needs and those needs make people pursue different goals in an effort to satisfy their needs. This exercise introduces you to one of the tools by which managers can identify both their own needs and those of their employees.

Introduction: Over the last thirty years behaviorists have researched the relationship between a person's fantasies and his or her motivation. One popular instrument used to establish this relationship is the Thematic Apperception Test (TAT).

Instructions

Step 1:

1. Examine each picture (provided by your instructor) for about one minute. Then cover the picture.

2. Using the picture as a guide, write a story that could be used in a TV soap opera. Make your story continuous, dramatic, and interesting. Do not just answer the questions. Try to complete the story in less than ten minutes.

3. Do not be concerned about obtaining negative results from this instrument. There are no right or wrong stories.

4. After finishing one story, repeat the same procedure until all six stories are completed.

Step 2: Conduct a story interpretation in groups of three persons each. Taking turns reading one story at a time, each person will read a story out loud to the other two people in the group. Then all three will examine the story for statements that fall into one of the following three categories:

- Category AC—Statements that refer to:
  - High standards of excellence
  - A desire to win, do well, succeed
  - Unique accomplishments
  - Long-term goals
  - Careers
- Category PO—Statements that refer to:
  - Influencing others
  - Controlling others
  - The desire to instruct others
  - The desire to dominate others
  - The concern over weakness, failure, or humiliation
  - Superior-subordinate relationships or status relationship
- Category AF—Statements that refer to:
  - Concern over establishing positive emotional relationships
  - Warm friendships or their loss
  - A desire to be liked
  - One person liking another
  - Parties, reunions, or visits
  - Relaxed small talk
  - Concern for others when not required by social custom

To assist in the interpretation of the test results, assign 10 points to each story. Divide the 10 points among the three categories based on the frequency of statements that refer to AC, PO, and AF behaviors in the story. Once the allocation of the 10 points is determined, record the results in the following scoring table:

Divide 10 points among the following categories:

Number of Story Scored	AC		PO		AF		TOTAL
1	____	+	____	+	____	=	10
2	____	+	____	+	____	=	10
3	____	+	____	+	____	=	10
4	____	+	____	+	____	=	10
5	____	+	____	+	____	=	10
6	____	+	____	+	____	=	10
TOTAL	____	+	____	+	____	=	60
Divide totals by 10 times number of stories scored	____	+	____	+	____		
Category percentages	____	%	____	%	____	%=	100%

Your Thematic Apperception Test values of AC, PO, and AF indicate your mix of needs for achievement (AC), power (PO), and affiliation (AF) respectively. Due to the circumstances under which this exercise was conducted, your values should be considered as only rough estimates. If you feel uncomfortable with your results, it is suggested that you consult with your instructor.

Step 3: In small groups, discuss the following questions:

Do you agree with your TAT results?

Can you cite specific behaviors to substantiate your opinions?

Do other members of your group perceive you as having the needs indicated by your TAT results?

Can they cite specific behaviors to substantiate their opinions?

What interpersonal problems might exist between a manager and an employee who had different need mixes?

In what type of job would you place an employee with a high need for achievement? A high need for power? A high need for affiliation?

Source: *Motives in Fantasy, Action and Society: Method of Assessment and Study.* John W. Atkinson, Ed., (Princeton, N.J.: D.Van Nostrand Co., Inc., 1958). Copyright © 1958. Used with permission of John W. Atkinson, © 1986. (Drawings from Peter P. Dawson, *Fundamentals of Organizational Behavior: An Experimental Approach* (Englewood Cliffs, N.J.: Prentice Hall, 1985), pp. 81–95. Drawings by Della Myers and Doris Weber. Reprinted by permission.)

CHAPTER NOTES

1. "IBM Leans on Its Sales Force," *Business Week*, February 7, 1994, p. 110; and Gary Hoover, Alta Campbell, and Patrick J. Spain (Eds.), *Hoover's Handbook of American Business 1995* (Austin, Tex.: The Reference Press, 1994), pp. 642–643.
2. Richard M. Steers and Lyman W. Porter, *Motivation and Work Behavior*, 5th ed. (New York: McGraw-Hill, 1991).
3. Roland Kidwell and Nathan Bennett, "Employee Propensity to Withhold Effort: A Conceptual Model to Intersect Three Avenues of Research," *Academy of Management Review*, July 1993, pp. 429–456.
4. Jeremiah J. Sullivan, "Three Roles of Language in Motivation Theory," *Academy of Management Review*, January 1988, pp. 104–115.
5. Abraham H. Maslow, "A Theory of Human Motivation," *Psychological Review*, Vol. 50, 1943, pp. 370–396; and Abraham H. Maslow, *Motivation and Personality* (New York: Harper & Row, 1954).
6. For a review, see Craig Pinder, *Work Motivation* (Glenview, Ill.: Scott, Foresman, 1984). See also Steers and Porter, *Motivation and Work Behavior.*
7. Frederick Herzberg, Bernard Mausner, and Barbara Snyderman, *The Motivation to Work* (New York: Wiley, 1959); and Frederick Herzberg, "One More Time: How Do You Motivate Employees?" *Harvard Business Review*, January–February 1987, pp. 109–120.
8. Robert J. House and Lawrence A. Wigdor, "Herzberg's Dual-Factor Theory of Job Satisfaction and Motivation: A Review of the Evidence and a Criticism," *Personnel Psychology*, Winter 1967, pp. 369–389; and Victor H. Vroom, *Work and Motivation* (New York: Wiley, 1964). See also Pinder, *Work Motivation.*
9. David C. McClelland, *The Achieving Society* (Princeton, N.J.: Van Nostrand, 1961); and David C. McClelland, *Power: The Inner Experience* (New York: Irvington, 1975).
10. E. Cornelius and F. Lane, "The Power Motive and Managerial Success in a Professionally Oriented Service Company," *Journal of Applied Psychology*, January 1984, pp. 32–40.
11. David McClelland and David H. Burnham, "Power Is the Great Motivator," *Harvard Business Review*, March–April 1976, pp. 100–110.
12. See Michael Woika, "Pay Plan Based on Performance Motivates Employees," *HRMagazine*, December 1993, pp. 75–82 for an illustration.
13. Vroom, *Work and Motivation.*
14. David A. Nadler and Edward E. Lawler III, "Motivation: A Diagnostic Approach," in J. Richard Hackman, Edward E. Lawler, and Lyman W. Porter (Eds.), *Perspectives on Behavior in Organizations*, 2nd ed. (New York: McGraw-Hill, 1983), pp. 67–78.
15. Lyman W. Porter and Edward E. Lawler III, *Managerial Attitudes and Performance* (Homewood, Ill.: Dorsey Press, 1968).
16. Nadler and Lawler, "Motivation: A Diagnostic Approach."
17. "How A & P Fattens Profits by Sharing Them," *Business Week*, December 22, 1986, p. 44.
18. Terrence Mitchell, "Expectancy Models of Job Satisfaction, Occupation Preference, and Effort: A Theoretical, Methodological, and Empirical Appraisal," *Psychological Bulletin*, December 1974, pp. 1053–1077; and John P. Wanous, Thomas L. Keon, and Jania C. Latack, "Expectancy Theory and Occupational/Organizational Choices: A Review and Test," *Organizational Behavior and Human Performance*, August 1983, pp. 66–86. For recent findings, see also Lynn E. Miller and Joseph E. Grush, "Improving Predictions in Expectancy Theory Research: Effects of Personality, Expectancies, and Norms," *Academy of Management Journal*, March 1988, pp. 107–122.
19. J. Stacy Adams, "Towards an Understanding of Inequity," *Journal of Abnormal and Social Psychology*, November 1963, pp. 422–436; and Richard T. Mowday, "Equity Theory Predictions of Behavior in Organizations," in Steers and Porter, *Motivation and Work Behavior*, pp. 91–113.
20. For a review, see Paul S. Goodman and Abraham Fiedman, "An Examination of Adam's Theory of Inequity," *Administrative Science Quarterly*, September 1971, pp. 271–288.
21. "Pay Problems: How Couples React When Wives Out-Earn Husbands," *The Wall Street Journal*, June 19, 1987, p. 19.
22. Richard A. Cosier and Dan R. Dalton, "Equity Theory and Time: A Reformulation," *Academy of Management Review*, April 1983, pp. 311–319; and Richard C. Huseman, John D. Hatfield, and Edward W. Miles, "A New Perspective on Equity Theory: The Equity Sensitivity Construct," *Academy of Management Review*, April 1987, pp. 222–234.
23. B. F. Skinner, *Beyond Freedom and Dignity* (New York: Knopf, 1971).
24. Fred Luthans and Robert Kreitner, *Organizational Behavior Modification and Beyond: An Operant and Social Learning Approach* (Glenview, Ill.: Scott, Foresman, 1985).
25. Patricia Sellers, "How to Handle Customers' Gripes," *Fortune*, October 24, 1988, pp. 88–100.

26. Edwin Locke, "Toward a Theory of Task Performance and Incentives," *Organizational Behavior and Human Performance*, Vol. 3, 1968, pp. 157–189.

27. For recent developments, see Mark E. Tubbs and Steven E. Ekeberg, "The Role of Intentions in Work Motivation: Implications for Goal-Setting Theory and Research," *Academy of Management Review*, January 1991, pp. 180–199.

28. Luthans and Kreitner, *Organizational Behavior Modification and Beyond*; W. Clay Hamner and Ellen P. Hamner, "Behavior Modification on the Bottom Line," *Organizational Dynamics*, Spring 1976, pp. 2–21.

29. "At Emery Air Freight: Positive Reinforcement Boosts Performance," *Organizational Dynamics*, Winter 1973, pp. 41–50.

30. Allan R. Cohen and Herman Gadon, *Alternative Work Schedules: Integrating Individual and Organizational Needs* (Reading, Mass.: Addison-Wesley, 1978).

31. Earl D. Weed, "Job Environment 'Cleans Up' at Texas Instruments," in J. R. Maher (Ed.), *New Perspectives in Job Enrichment* (New York: Van Nostrand, 1971), pp. 55–77.

32. Edward E. Lawler III, *Pay and Organizational Development* (Reading, Mass.: Addison-Wesley, 1981). See also Edward E. Lawler III, *Pay and Organizational Effectiveness: A Psychological View* (New York: McGraw-Hill, 1971).

33. Lawler, *Pay and Organizational Development.*

34. Bill Leonard, "New Ways to Pay Employees," *HRMagazine*, February 1994, pp. 61–69.

35. "Grading 'Merit Pay,'" *Newsweek*, November 14, 1988, pp. 45–46; and Frederick S. Hills, K. Dow Scott, Steven E. Markham, and Michael J. Vest, "Merit Pay: Just or Unjust Desserts," *Personnel Administrator,* September 1987, pp. 53–59.

36. Perry, "Here Come Richer, Riskier Pay Plans," pp. 50–58.

CHAPTER

Leadership and Influence Processes

OBJECTIVES

After studying this chapter, you should be able to:

- *Describe the nature of leadership and distinguish leadership from management.*
- *Discuss and evaluate the trait approach to leadership.*
- *Discuss and evaluate models of leadership focusing on behaviors.*
- *Identify and describe the major situational approaches to leadership.*
- *Identify and describe three related perspectives on leadership.*
- *Discuss political behavior in organizations and how it can be managed.*

OUTLINE

OPENING INCIDENT

EVEN THOUGH COMPAQ Computer was formed only a little more than a decade ago, the firm seems to have already had two distinct lives. The first started when Rod Canion and two other former Texas Instruments engineers launched the firm in 1982. Led by Canion's rational and deliberate decision-making style, Compaq did all the right things and became the youngest firm to enter the *Fortune* 500 in 1988.

It appeared for a while that the firm's management could do no wrong. But, unfortunately, things have a way of changing in the computer business. Canion's strategy was to sell primarily to big businesses and to be relatively slow and deliberate to avoid making mistakes. When Compaq began to falter in 1991, Canion was at a loss as to how to proceed and was eventually forced out by the firm's board of directors.

To get the firm back on track, the board tapped Eckhard Pfeiffer, a German marketing specialist who had previously headed up Compaq's very successful European operations. Pfeiffer wasted little time in revamping how the firm did business. He mandated that the firm develop and launch dozens of new products, that manufacturing become more efficient so that costs could be lowered, and that the dealer network selling Compaq computers be enlarged. He also announced new initiatives for selling computers to individual consumers and to schools, domains previously controlled by Dell and Apple Computer, respectively.

"He makes it very clear that what he expects is continuous change."

Even the wildest optimist could not have predicted how successful Pfeiffer's approach would be. Since he took over, Compaq has more than doubled its share of the PC market. Moreover, its profits in 1993 exceeded those of IBM and Apple combined. But Pfeiffer does not believe in standing still. Indeed, his ideas and strategies are keeping the firm in a constant state of flux. He continues to push for lower costs, greater productivity, and constant increases in market share, sales, and profits.

How did he do it? His colleagues believe that Pfeiffer has two qualities that enabled him to turn things around at Compaq. The first is that he is able to clearly communicate his vision for the company to each of its managers and employees. The second is that he is able to convey a sense of urgency—a feeling that things have to be done now. This latter characteristic has facilitated the ongoing sense of change that he believes must drive Compaq in the years to come. And he sees plenty of changes on the horizon—lower prices, more powerful machines, and technology unheard of today are all right around the corner. And many experts believe that Pfeiffer will lead Compaq to that corner first.[1]

Source of Quotation: Bob Stearns, Compaq's vice president of corporate development, referring to Eckhard Pfeiffer, Compaq CEO, quoted in *Fortune*, February 21, 1994, p. 90.

Eckhard Pfeiffer has a relatively rare combination of skills that sets him apart from many others: he is both an astute leader and a fine manager, and he recognizes many of the challenges necessary to play both roles. He knows when to make tough decisions, when to lead and encourage his employees, and when to stand back and let them do their jobs. Thus far, Compaq is reaping big payoffs from his efforts.

This chapter examines people like Pfeiffer more carefully—by focusing on leadership and its role in management. We characterize the nature of leadership and trace through the three major approaches to studying leadership—traits, behaviors, and situations. After examining other perspectives on leadership, we conclude by describing another approach to influencing others—political behavior in organizations.

THE NATURE OF LEADERSHIP

In Chapter 10, we described various models and perspectives on employee motivation. From the manager's standpoint, trying to motivate people is an attempt to influence their behavior. In many ways, leadership too is an attempt to influence the behavior of others. In this section, we first define leadership, then differentiate it from management, and conclude by relating it to power.

• **leadership**
As a process, the use of noncoercive influence to shape the group's or organization's goals, motivate behavior toward the achievement of those goals, and help define group or organizational culture; as a property, the set of characteristics attributed to individuals who are perceived to be leaders

The Meaning of Leadership

Leadership is both a process and a property.[2] As a process—focusing on what leaders actually do—leadership is the use of noncoercive influence to shape the group's or organization's goals, motivate behavior toward the

Leadership is both a process and property. Nowhere is this duality illustrated more clearly than by Tommye Jo Daves (shown here on the right). Daves took a job at a Levi Strauss plant in North Carolina in 1959 for 80 cents an hour—because she wanted to buy a new washing machine. Through hard work and dedication—and with the support and backing of her coworkers—she slowly worked her way up the organizational ladder. Today, she is the plant's manager, responsible for 385 workers and the production of three million pairs of jeans each year.

achievement of those goals, and help define group or organizational culture.[3] As a property, leadership is the set of characteristics attributed to individuals who are perceived to be leaders. Thus **leaders** are people who can influence the behaviors of others without having to rely on force; leaders are people whom others accept as leaders.[4]

leaders
People who can influence the behaviors of others without having to rely on force; those accepted by others as leaders

Leadership Versus Management

From these definitions, it should be clear that leadership and management are related, but they are not the same. A person can be a manager, a leader, both, or neither.[5] Some of the basic distinctions between the two are summarized in Table 11.1. On the left side of the table are four elements that differentiate leadership from management. The two columns show how each element differs when considered from a management and a leadership point of view. For example, when executing plans, managers focus on monitoring results, comparing them with goals, and correcting deviations.

TABLE 11.1 Distinctions Between Management and Leadership

Activity	Management	Leadership
Creating an agenda	**Planning and budgeting.** Establishing detailed steps and timetables for achieving needed results; allocating the resources necessary to make those needed results happen	**Establishing direction.** Developing a vision of the future, often the distant future, and strategies for producing the changes needed to achieve that vision
Developing a human network for achieving the agenda	**Organizing and staffing.** Establishing some structure for accomplishing plan requirements, staffing that structure with individuals, delegating responsibility and authority for carrying out the plan, providing policies and procedures to help guide people, and creating methods or systems to monitor implementation	**Aligning people.** Communicating the direction by words and deeds to all those whose cooperation may be needed to influence the creation of teams and coalitions that understand the vision and strategies and accept their validity
Executing plans	**Controlling and problem solving.** Monitoring results versus plan in some detail, identifying deviations, and then planning and organizing to solve these problems	**Motivating and inspiring.** Energizing people to overcome major political, bureaucratic, and resource barriers to change by satisfying very basic, but often unfulfilled, human needs
Outcomes	Produces a degree of predictability and order and has the potential to consistently produce major results expected by various stakeholders (e.g., for customers, always being on time; for stockholders, being on budget)	Produces change, often to a dramatic degree, and has the potential to produce extremely useful change (e.g., new products that customers want, new approaches to labor relations that help make a firm more competitive)

Source: Reprinted with permission of The Free Press, a Division of Simon & Schuster Inc., from *A Force for Change: How Leadership Differs from Management* by John P. Kotter. Copyright © 1990 by John P. Kotter, Inc.

In contrast, the leader focuses on energizing people to overcome bureaucratic hurdles to help reach goals. Thus when Eckhard Pfeiffer monitors the performance of his employees, he is playing the role of manager. When he inspires them to work harder at achieving their goals, he is a leader.

Organizations need both management and leadership if they are to be effective. Leadership is necessary to create change, and management is necessary to achieve orderly results. Management in conjunction with leadership can produce orderly change, and leadership in conjunction with management can keep the organization properly aligned with its environment.

Power and Leadership

• **power**
The ability to affect the behavior of others

To fully understand leadership, it is necessary to understand power. **Power** is the ability to affect the behavior of others. One can have power without actually using it.[6] For example, a football coach has the power to bench a player who is not performing up to par. The coach seldom has to use this power because players recognize that the power exists and work hard to keep their starting positions. In organizational settings, there are usually five kinds of power: legitimate, reward, coercive, referent, and expert power.[7]

• **legitimate power**
Power granted through the organizational hierarchy; it is the power defined by the organization that is to be accorded people occupying particular positions

Legitimate Power **Legitimate power** is power granted through the organizational hierarchy; it is the power accorded people occupying positions as defined by the organization. A manager can assign a subordinate tasks, and a subordinate who refuses to do them can be reprimanded or even fired. Such outcomes stem from the manager's legitimate power as defined and vested in her or him by the organization. Legitimate power, then, is authority. All managers have legitimate power over their subordinates. The mere possession of legitimate power, however, does not by itself make someone a leader. Some subordinates follow only those orders that are strictly within the letter of organizational rules and policies. If asked to do something not in their job description, they refuse or do a poor job. The manager of such employees is exercising authority but not leadership.[8]

• **reward power**
The power to give or withhold rewards, such as salary increases, bonuses, promotions, praise, recognition, and interesting job assignments

Reward Power **Reward power** is the power to give or withhold rewards. Rewards that a manager may control include salary increases, bonuses, promotions, praise, recognition, and interesting job assignments. In general, the greater the number of rewards a manager controls and the more important the rewards are to subordinates, the greater is the manager's reward power. If the subordinate sees as valuable only the formal organizational rewards provided by the manager, then the manager is not a leader. If the subordinate also wants and appreciates the manager's informal rewards like praise, gratitude, and recognition, however, then the manager is exercising leadership.

• **coercive power**
The power to force compliance by means of psychological, emotional, or physical threat

Coercive Power **Coercive power** is the power to force compliance by means of psychological, emotional, or physical threat. In the past, physical coercion in organizations was relatively common. In most organizations today, however, coercion is limited to verbal reprimands, written repri-

Power plays a fundamental role in leadership. When Hewlett-Packard allowed this team of customer service agents to select its own supervisor, it turned to Les Gremett (far right). His experience and close personal relationships with members of the group gave him considerable expert and referent power. These types of power, in turn, made him an easy choice for the group.

mands, disciplinary layoffs, fines, demotions, and terminations. Some managers occasionally go so far as to use verbal abuse, humiliation, and psychological coercion in an attempt to manipulate subordinates. (Of course, most people would agree that these are not appropriate managerial behaviors.) James Dutt, former CEO of Beatrice Company, once told a subordinate that if his wife and family got in the way of his working twenty-four hours a day, seven days a week, he should get rid of them.[9] The more punitive the elements under a manager's control and the more important they are to subordinates, the more coercive power the manager possesses. On the other hand, the more a manager uses coercive power, the more likely he is to provoke resentment and hostility and the less likely he is to be seen as a leader.[10]

Referent Power Compared with legitimate, reward, and coercive power, which are relatively concrete and grounded in objective facets of organizational life, **referent power** is abstract. It is based on identification, imitation, loyalty, or charisma. Followers may react favorably because they identify in some way with a leader, who may be like them in personality, background, or attitudes. In other situations, followers might choose to imitate a leader with referent power by wearing the same kinds of clothes, working the same hours, or espousing the same management philosophy. Referent power may also take the form of charisma, an intangible attribute of the leader that inspires loyalty and enthusiasm. Thus a manager might have referent power, but it is more likely to be associated with leadership.

referent power The personal power that accrues to someone based on identification, imitation, loyalty, or charisma

Expert Power **Expert power** is derived from information or expertise. A manager who knows how to interact with an eccentric but important customer, a scientist who is capable of achieving an important technical

expert power The personal power that accrues to someone based on his or her information or expertise

breakthrough that no other company has dreamed of, and a secretary who knows how to unravel bureaucratic red tape all have expert power over anyone who needs that information. The more important the information and the fewer the people who have access to it, the greater is the degree of expert power possessed by any one individual. In general, people who are both leaders and managers tend to have a lot of expert power.

THE SEARCH FOR LEADERSHIP TRAITS

The first organized approach to studying leadership analyzed the personal, psychological, and physical traits of strong leaders. The trait approach assumed that some basic trait or set of traits existed that differentiated leaders from nonleaders. If those traits could be defined, potential leaders could be identified. Researchers thought that leadership traits might include intelligence, assertiveness, above-average height, good vocabulary, attractiveness, self-confidence, and similar attributes.[11]

During the first several decades of this century, hundreds of studies were conducted in an attempt to identify important leadership traits. For the most part, the results of the studies were disappointing. For every set of leaders who possessed a common trait, a long list of exceptions was also found, and the list of suggested traits soon grew so long that it had little practical value. Alternative explanations usually existed even for relations between traits and leadership that initially appeared valid. For example, it was observed that many leaders have good communication skills and are assertive. Rather than those traits being the cause of leadership, however, successful leaders may begin to display those traits after they have achieved leadership positions.

Although most researchers gave up trying to identify traits as predictors of leadership ability, many people still explicitly or implicitly adopt a trait orientation.[12] For example, politicians are all too often elected on the basis of personal appearance, speaking ability, or an aura of self-confidence.[13]

LEADERSHIP BEHAVIORS

Spurred on by their lack of success in identifying useful leadership traits, researchers soon began to investigate other variables, especially the behaviors or actions of leaders. The new hypothesis was that effective leaders somehow behaved differently than less-effective leaders. Thus the goal was to develop a fuller understanding of leadership behaviors.

Michigan Studies

Researchers at the University of Michigan, led by Rensis Likert, began studying leadership in the late 1940s.[14] Based on extensive interviews with both leaders (managers) and followers (subordinates), this research identified two basic forms of leader behavior: job-centered and employee-centered. Managers using **job-centered leader behavior** pay close attention to subordinates' work, explain work procedures, and are keenly interested in performance. Managers using **employee-centered leader behavior** are interested in developing a cohesive work group and ensuring that employees are satisfied with their jobs. Their primary concern is the welfare of subordinates. The two styles of leader behavior were presumed to be at the ends of a single continuum. Although this presumption suggests that leaders may be extremely job-centered, extremely employee-centered, or somewhere in between, Likert studied only the two end styles for contrast. He argued that employee-centered leader behavior generally tended to be more effective.

• **job-centered leader behavior**
The behavior of leaders who pay close attention to the job and work procedures involved with that job

• **employee-centered leader behavior**
The behavior of leaders who develop cohesive work groups and ensure employee satisfaction

Ohio State Studies

At about the same time that Likert was beginning his leadership studies at the University of Michigan, a group of researchers at Ohio State also began studying leadership.[15] The extensive questionnaire surveys conducted during the Ohio State studies also suggested that there are two basic leader behaviors or styles: initiating-structure behavior and consideration behavior. When using **initiating-structure behavior**, the leader clearly defines the leader-subordinate role so that everyone knows what is expected, establishes formal lines of communication, and determines how tasks will be performed. Leaders using **consideration behavior** show concern for subordinates and attempt to establish a friendly and supportive climate. The behaviors identified at Ohio State are similar to those described at Michigan, but there are important differences. One major difference is that the Ohio State researchers did not interpret leader behavior as being one-dimensional: Each behavior was assumed to be independent of the other. Presumably, then, a leader could exhibit varying levels of initiating structure and at the same time varying levels of consideration.

• **initiating-structure behavior**
The behavior of leaders who define the leader-subordinate role so that everyone knows what is expected, establish formal lines of communication, and determine how tasks will be performed

• **consideration behavior**
The behavior of leaders who are concerned for subordinates and attempt to establish a warm, friendly, and supportive climate

At first, the Ohio State researchers thought that leaders who exhibit high levels of both behaviors would tend to be more effective than other leaders. A study at International Harvester Co. (now Navistar International Corp.), however, suggested a more complicated pattern.[16] The researchers found that employees of supervisors who ranked high on initiating structure were high performers but expressed low levels of satisfaction and had a higher absence rate. Conversely, employees of supervisors who ranked high on consideration had low performance ratings but high levels of satisfaction and few absences from work. Later research isolated other variables that make consistent prediction difficult and determined that situational influences also occurred. (This body of research is discussed in the section on situational approaches to leadership.)

Leadership Grid

Yet another behavioral approach to leadership is the Leadership Grid®.[17] The Leadership Grid® provides a means for evaluating leadership styles and then training managers to move toward an ideal style of behavior. The Leadership Grid® is shown in Figure 11.1. The horizontal axis represents **concern for production** (similar to job-centered and initiating-structure

• **concern for production**
That part of the Leadership Grid® that deals with the job and task aspects of leader behavior

The Leadership Grid® is a method of evaluating leadership styles. The overall objective of an organization using the Grid is to train its managers using OD techniques so that they are concerned for both people and production simultaneously (9,9 style on the grid).

FIGURE 11.1 The Leadership Grid

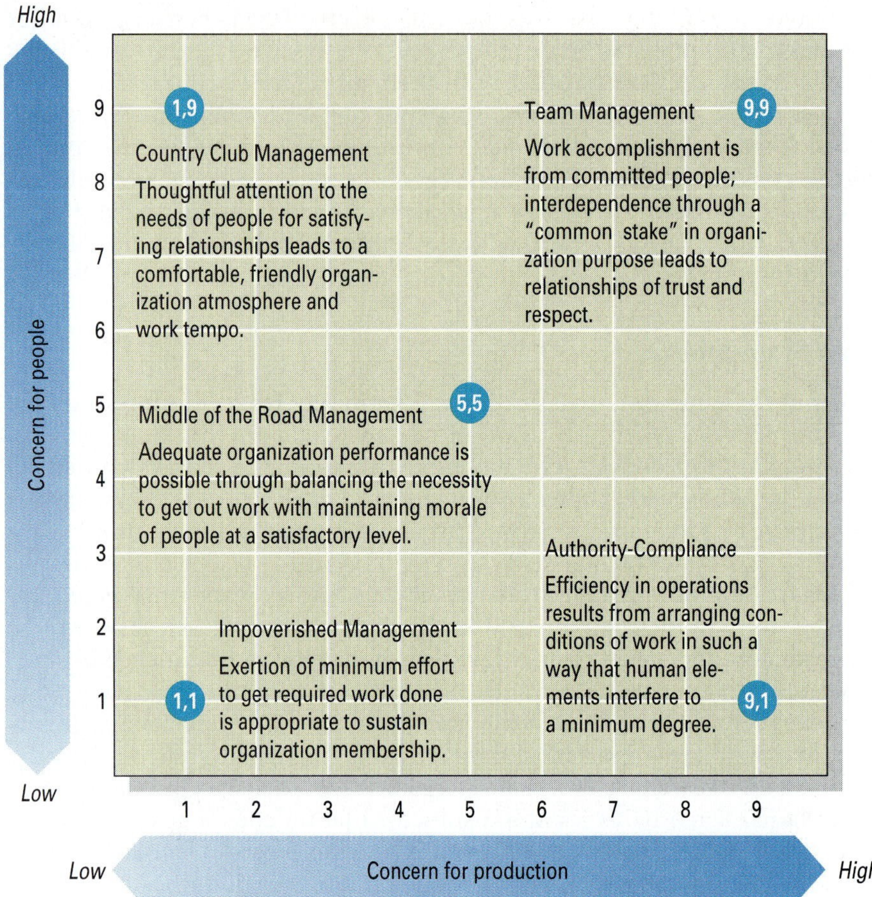

Source: The Leadership Grid® Figure from *Leadership Dilemmas-Grid Solutions,* p. 29, by Robert R. Blake, Ph.D. and Anne Adams McCanse. Copyright © 1991 by Robert R. Blake and the Estate of Jane S. Mouton, Austin, Texas. The Grid® designation is property of Scientific Methods, Inc. Gulf Publishing Company, Houston, Texas. Used with permission. All rights reserved.

• **concern for people** That part of the Leadership Grid® that deals with the human aspects of leader behavior

behaviors), and the vertical axis represents **concern for people** (similar to employee-centered and consideration behavior). Note the five extremes of managerial behavior: the 1,1 manager (impoverished management) who exhibits minimal concern for both production and people; the 9,1 manager (authority-obedience) who is highly concerned about production but exhibits little concern for people; the 1,9 manager (country club management) who has the exact opposite concerns from the 9,1 manager; the 5,5 manager (organization management) who maintains adequate concern for both people and production; and the 9,9 manager (team management) who exhibits maximum concern for both people and production.

According to this approach, the ideal style of managerial behavior is 9,9. Thus there is a six-phase program to assist managers in achieving this style of behavior. A.G. Edwards, Westinghouse, the FAA, Equicor, and other companies have used the Leadership Grid® with reasonable success. Little published scientific evidence regarding its true effectiveness exists, however.

The leader-behavior theories have played an important role in the development of contemporary thinking about leadership. In particular, they urge us not to be preoccupied with what leaders are (the trait approach) but to concentrate on what leaders do (their behaviors). Unfortunately, these theories also make universal prescriptions about what constitutes effective leadership. When dealing with complex social systems composed of complex individuals, few if any relationships are consistently predictable, and certainly no formulas for success are infallible. Yet the behavior theorists tried to identify consistent relationships between leader behaviors and employee responses in the hope of finding a dependable prescription for effective leadership. As one might expect, they often failed. Other approaches to understanding leadership were therefore needed. The catalyst for these new approaches was the realization that, although interpersonal and task-oriented dimensions might be useful to describe the behavior of leaders, they were not useful for predicting or prescribing it. The next step in the evolution of leadership theory was the creation of situational models.[18]

SITUATIONAL APPROACHES TO LEADERSHIP

Situational models assume that appropriate leader behavior varies from one situation to another. The goal of a situational theory, then, is to identify key situational factors and to specify how they interact to determine appropriate leader behavior. In the following sections, we describe the three most important and most widely accepted situational theories of leadership: the LPC theory, the path-goal theory, and the Vroom-Yetton-Jago model.

LPC Theory

The **LPC theory**, developed by Fred Fiedler, was the first true situational theory of leadership.[19] *LPC* stands for *least preferred coworker*. Beginning with a combined trait and behavior approach, Fiedler identified two styles of leadership: task-oriented (analogous to job-centered and initiating-structure behavior) and relationship-oriented (similar to employee-centered and consideration behavior). He went beyond the earlier behavioral approaches by arguing that the style of behavior is a reflection of the leader's personality and that most personalities fall into one of his two categories, task-oriented or relationship-oriented by nature. Fiedler measures leader style by means of a controversial questionnaire called the **least preferred coworker** (**LPC**) measure. To use the measure, a manager or leader is asked to describe the specific person with whom he or she is able to work least well—the LPC—by filling in a set of sixteen scales anchored at each end by a positive or negative adjective. For example, three of the sixteen scales are:

● **LPC theory**
A theory of leadership that suggests that the appropriate style of leadership varies with situational favorableness

● **least preferred coworker (LPC)**
The measuring scale that asks leaders to describe the person with whom he or she is able to work least well

Helpful	8	7	6	5	4	3	2	1	Frustrating
Tense	1	2	3	4	5	6	7	8	Relaxed
Boring	1	2	3	4	5	6	7	8	Interesting

The leader's LPC score is then calculated by adding up the numbers below the line checked on each scale. Note in these three examples that the higher numbers are associated with the positive qualities (helpful, relaxed, and interesting), whereas the negative qualities (frustrating, tense, and boring) have low point values. A high total score is assumed to reflect a relationship orientation and a low score a task orientation on the part of the leader. The LPC measure is controversial because researchers disagree about its validity. Some question exactly what an LPC measure reflects and whether the score is an index of behavior, personality, or some other factor.[20]

Favorableness of the Situation The underlying assumption of situational models of leadership is that appropriate leader behavior varies from one situation to another. According to Fiedler, the key situational factor is the favorableness of the situation from the leader's point of view. This factor is determined by leader-member relations, task structure, and position power. *Leader-member relations* refer to the nature of the relationship between the leader and the work group. If the leader and the group have a high degree of mutual trust, respect, and confidence, and if they like one another, relations are assumed to be good. If there is little trust, respect, or confidence, and if they do not like each other, relations are poor. Naturally, good relations are more favorable.

Task structure is the degree to which the group's task is well defined. The task is structured when it is routine, easily understood, and unambiguous and when the group has standard procedures and precedents to rely on. An unstructured task is nonroutine, ambiguous, complex, with no standard procedures or precedents. You can see that high structure is more favorable for the leader, whereas low structure is less favorable. For example, if the task is unstructured, the group will not know what to do and the leader will have to play a major role in guiding and directing its activities. If the task is structured, the leader will not have to get so involved and can devote time to nonsupervisory activities. *Position power* is the power vested in the leader's position. If the leader has the power to assign work and to reward and punish employees, position power is assumed to be strong. But if the leader must get job assignments approved by someone else and does not administer rewards and punishment, position power is weak and it is more difficult to accomplish goals. From the leader's point of view, strong position power is clearly preferable to weak position power. However, position power is not as important as task structure and leader-member relations.

Favorableness and Leader Style Fiedler and his associates conducted numerous studies linking the favorableness of various situations to leader style and the effectiveness of the group.[21] The results of these studies—and the overall framework of the theory—are shown in Figure 11.2. To interpret the model, look first at the situational factors at the top of the figure: Good or bad leader-member relations, high or low task structure, and strong or weak position power can be combined to yield eight unique situations. For example, good leader-member relations, high task structure, and strong position power (at the far left) are presumed to define the most favorable situation; bad leader-member relations, low task structure, and weak position power (at the far right) are the least favorable. The other combinations reflect intermediate levels of favorableness.

Below each set of situations is shown the degree of favorableness and the form of leader behavior found to be most strongly associated with effective group performance for those situations. When the situation is most and least favorable, Fiedler predicts that a task-oriented leader is most effective. When the situation is only moderately favorable, however, a relationship-oriented leader is predicted to be most effective.

Fiedler's LPC theory of leadership suggests that appropriate leader behavior varies as a function of the favorableness of the situation. Favorableness, in turn, is defined by task structure, leader-member relations, and the leader's position power. According to LPC theory, the most and least favorable situations call for task-oriented leadership, while moderately favorable situations suggest the need for relationship-oriented leadership.

Flexibility of Leader Style Fiedler argued that, for any given individual, leader style is essentially fixed and cannot be changed: leaders cannot change their behavior to fit a particular situation because it is linked to their particular personality traits. Thus when a leader's style and the situation do not match, Fiedler argued that the situation should be changed to fit the leader's style. When leader-member relations are good, task structure is low, and position power is weak, the leader style most likely to be effective is relationship-oriented. If the leader is task-oriented, a mismatch exists. According to Fiedler, the leader can make the elements of the situation

FIGURE 11.2 The Least-Preferred Coworker Theory of Leadership

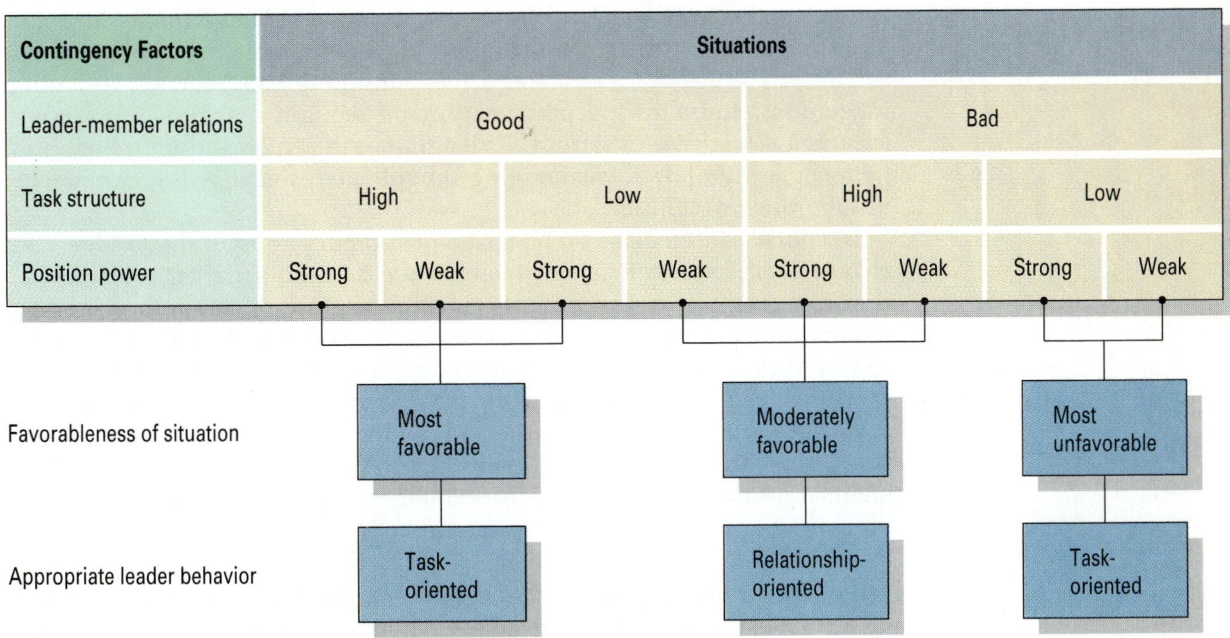

more congruent by structuring the task (by developing guidelines and procedures, for instance) and increasing power (by requesting additional authority or by other means).

Fiedler's contingency theory has been attacked on the grounds that it is not always supported by research, that his findings are subject to other interpretations, that the LPC measure lacks validity, and that his assumptions about the inflexibility of leader behavior are unrealistic.[22] Fiedler's theory, however, was one of the first to adopt a situational perspective on leadership. It has helped many managers recognize the important situational factors they must contend with, and it has fostered additional thinking about the situational nature of leadership. Moreover, in recent years Fiedler has attempted to address some of the concerns about his theory by revising it and adding such additional elements as cognitive resources.

Path-Goal Theory

The path-goal theory of leadership—associated most closely with Martin Evans and Robert House—is a direct extension of the expectancy theory of motivation discussed in Chapter 10.[23] Recall that the primary components of expectancy theory included the likelihood of attaining various outcomes and the value associated with those outcomes. The **path-goal theory** of leadership suggests that the primary functions of a leader are to make valued or desired rewards available in the workplace and to clarify for the subordinate the kinds of behavior that will lead to goal accomplishment and valued rewards—that is, the leader should clarify the paths to goal attainment.

• **path-goal theory**
A theory of leadership suggesting that the primary functions of a leader are to make valued or desired rewards available in the workplace and to clarify for the subordinate the kinds of behavior that will lead to those rewards

Leader Behavior The most fully developed version of path-goal theory identifies four kinds of leader behavior. *Directive leader behavior* is letting subordinates know what is expected of them, giving guidance and direction, and scheduling work. *Supportive leader behavior* is being friendly and approachable, showing concern for subordinate welfare, and treating members as equals. *Participative leader behavior* is consulting subordinates, soliciting suggestions, and allowing participation in decision making. *Achievement-oriented leader behavior* is setting challenging goals, expecting subordinates to perform at high levels, encouraging subordinates, and showing confidence in subordinates' abilities.

In contrast to Fiedler's theory, path-goal theory assumes that leaders can change their style or behavior to meet the demands of a particular situation. For example, when encountering a new group of subordinates and a new project, the leader may be directive in establishing work procedures and in outlining what needs to be done. Next, the leader may adopt supportive behavior to foster group cohesiveness and a positive climate. As the group becomes familiar with the task and as new problems are encountered, the leader may exhibit participative behavior to enhance group members' motivation. Finally, achievement-oriented behavior may be used to encourage continued high performance.

Situational Factors Like other situational theories of leadership, path-goal theory suggests that appropriate leader style depends on situational factors. Path-goal theory focuses on the situational factors of the personal characteristics of subordinates and environmental characteristics of the workplace.

Important personal characteristics include the subordinates' perception of their own ability and their locus of control. If people perceive that they are lacking in ability, they may prefer directive leadership to help them understand path-goal relationships better. If they perceive themselves to have a lot of ability, however, employees may resent directive leadership. Locus of control is a personality trait. People who have an internal locus of control believe that what happens to them is a function of their own efforts and behavior. Those who have an external locus of control assume that fate, luck, or "the system" determines what happens to them. A person with an internal locus of control may prefer participative leadership, whereas a person with an external locus of control may prefer directive leadership. Managers can do little or nothing to influence the personal characteristics of subordinates, but they can shape the environment to take advantage of these personal characteristics by providing rewards and structuring tasks, for example.

Environmental characteristics include factors outside the subordinate's control. Task structure is one such factor. When structure is high, directive leadership is less effective than when structure is low. Subordinates do not usually need their boss to continually tell them how to do an extremely routine job. The formal authority system is another important environmental characteristic. Again, the higher the degree of formality, the less directive is the leader behavior that will be accepted by subordinates. The nature of the work group also affects appropriate leader behavior. When the work group provides the employee with social support and satisfaction, supportive leader behavior is less critical. When social support and satisfaction cannot be derived from the group, the worker may look to the leader for this support.

The path-goal theory of leadership suggests that managers can use four types of leader behavior to clarify subordinates' paths to goal attainment. Personal characteristics of the subordinate and environmental characteristics within the organization both must be taken into account when determining which style of leadership will work best for a particular situation.

The basic path-goal framework as illustrated in Figure 11.3 shows that different leader behaviors affect subordinates' motivation to perform. Personal and environmental characteristics are seen as defining which behaviors lead to which outcomes. The path-goal theory of leadership is a dynamic and incomplete model. The original intent was to state the theory in general terms so that future research could explore a variety of interrelationships and modify the theory. Research suggests that the path-goal theory is a reasonably good description of the leadership process

FIGURE 11.3 The Path-Goal Framework

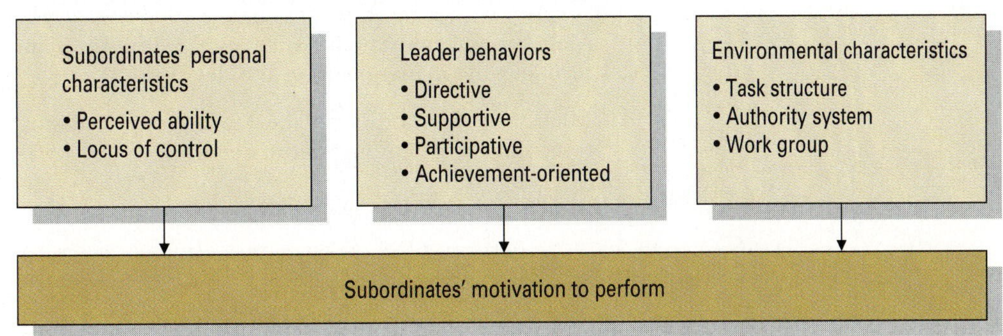

and that future investigations along these lines should enable us to discover more about the link between leadership and motivation.[24]

Vroom-Yetton-Jago Model

• **Vroom-Yetton-Jago (VYJ) model**
Predicts what kinds of situations call for what degrees of group participation

The **Vroom-Yetton-Jago (VYJ) model** predicts what kinds of situations call for what degrees of group participation. The VYJ model, then, sets norms or standards for including subordinates in decision making. The model was first proposed by Victor Vroom and Philip Yetton in 1973 and was revised and expanded in 1988 by Vroom and Arthur G. Jago.[25] The VYJ model is somewhat narrower than the other situational theories in that it focuses on only one part of the leadership process—how much decision-making participation to allow subordinates.

Basic Premises The VYJ model argues that decision effectiveness is best gauged by the quality of the decision and by employee acceptance of the decision. Decision quality is the objective effect of the decision on performance. Decision acceptance is the extent to which employees accept and are committed to the decision. To maximize decision effectiveness, the VYJ model suggests that, depending on the situation, managers adopt one of five decision-making styles. As summarized in Table 11.2, there are two autocratic styles (AI and AII), two consultative styles (CI and CII), and one group style (GII).

The situation that is presumed to dictate an appropriate decision-making style is defined by a series of questions about the characteristics or attributes of the problem under consideration. To address the questions, the

The difference between these decision styles is the degree of participation each provides for subordinates. The extreme forms are purely autocratic (AI) and total participation (GII). The other three styles fall between these extremes.

TABLE 11.2 Decision Styles in the Vroom-Yetton-Jago Model

Decision Style	Definition
AI	Manager makes the decision alone.
AII	Manager asks for information from subordinates but makes the decision alone. Subordinates may or may not be informed about what the situation is.
CI	Manager shares the situation with individual subordinates and asks for information and evaluation. Subordinates do not meet as a group, and the manager alone makes the decision.
CII	Manager and subordinates meet as a group to discuss the situation, but the manager makes the decision.
GII	Manager and subordinates meet as a group to discuss the situation, and the group makes the decision.

A = autocratic; C = consultative; G = group

Source: Reprinted from *Leadership and Decision-Making* by Victor H. Vroom and Philip W. Yetton by permission of the University of Pittsburgh Press. Copyright © 1973 by the University of Pittsburgh Press.

manager uses one of four decision trees. Two of the trees are used when the problem affects the entire group, and the other two are appropriate when the problem relates to an individual. One of each is to be used when the time necessary to reach a decision is important, and the others are to be used when time is less important but the manager wants to develop subordinates' decision-making abilities.

Figure 11.4 shows the tree for time-driven group problems. The problem attributes defining the situation are arranged along the top of the tree and are expressed as questions. To use the tree, the manager starts at the left side of it and asks the first question. Thus the manager first decides whether the problem involves a quality requirement—that is, whether

To use this decision tree, the manager asks a series of questions about the problem situation. The answers to each question lead the manager through the tree. At each endpoint is a recommended decision style (see Table 11.2) that is predicted to enhance decision quality and acceptance.

FIGURE 11.4 Time-Driven Group Problem Decision Tree for VYJ Model

QR Quality requirement: How important is the technical quality of this decision?

CR Commitment requirement: How important is subordinate commitment to the decision?

LI Leader's information: Do you have sufficient information to make a high-quality decision?

ST Problem structure: Is the problem well structured?

CP Commitment probability: If you were to make the decision by yourself, is it reasonably certain that your subordinate(s) would be committed to the decision?

GC Goal congruence: Do subordinates share the organizational goals to be attained in solving this problem?

CO Subordinate conflict: Is conflict among subordinates over preferred solutions likely?

SI Subordinate information: Do subordinates have sufficient information to make a high-quality decision?

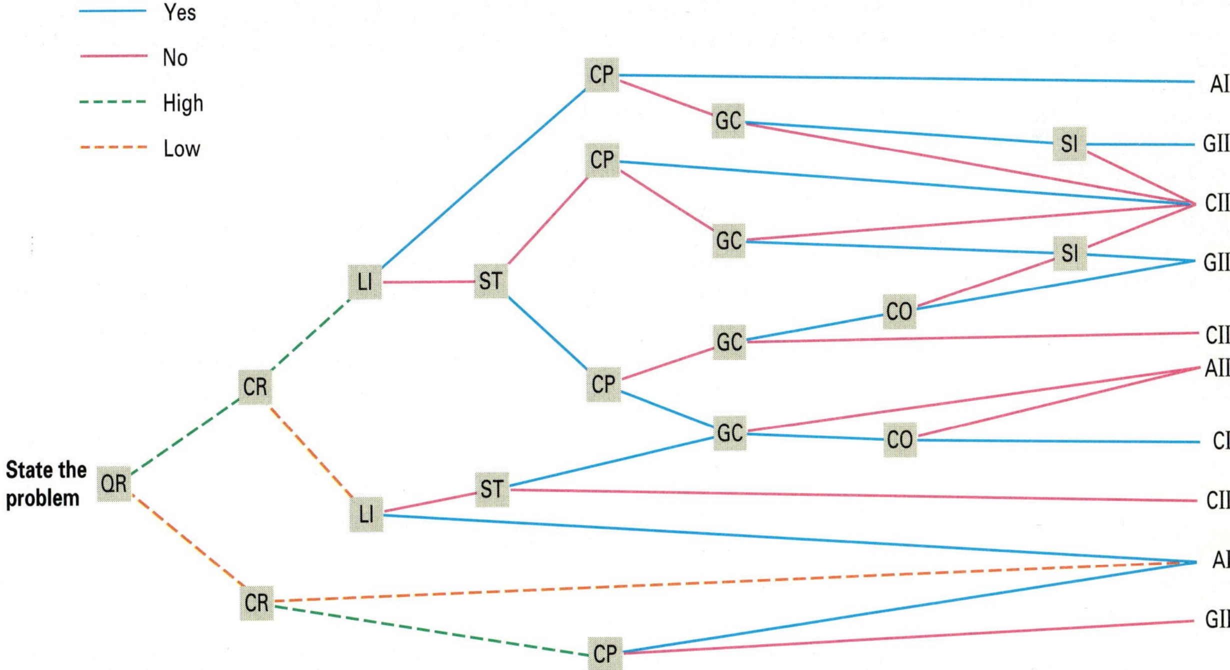

Source: Adapted and reprinted from *Leadership and Decision-Making,* by Victor H. Vroom and Philip W. Yetton, pages 32–34 by permission of the University of Pittsburgh Press. © 1973 by University of Pittsburgh Press.

there are quality differences in the alternatives and if they matter. The answer determines the path to the second node, where the manager asks another question. The manager continues in this fashion until a terminal node is reached and an appropriate decision style is indicated. Each prescribed decision style is designed to protect the original goals of the process (decision quality and subordinate acceptance) within the context of the group versus individual *and* time versus development framework.

Evaluation The original version of the VYJ model has been widely tested. Indeed, one recent review concluded that it had received more scientific support than any other leadership theory.[26] The inherent complexity of the model presents a problem for many managers, however. Even the original version was criticized because of its complexity, and the revised VYJ model is far more complex than the original. To aid managers, computer software has been developed to facilitate their ability to define their situation, answer the questions about problem attributes, and develop a strategy for decision-making participation.[27]

Other Situational Approaches

In addition to the major theories, other situational models have been developed in recent years. We discuss the leader-member exchange model and life cycle theory.

- **leader-member exchange (LMX) model** Stresses that leaders have different kinds of relationships with different subordinates

The Leader-Member Exchange Model The **leader-member exchange (LMX) model** stresses that leaders have different kinds of relationships with different subordinates.[28] Each manager-subordinate relationship represents one vertical dyad. The model suggests that leaders establish special working relationships with a handful of subordinates called the in-group. Other subordinates remain in the out-group. Those in the in-group receive more of the manager's time and attention and tend to be better performers. Early research on this model is quite promising.[29]

- **life cycle theory** A model suggesting that appropriate leader behavior depends on the maturity of the follower

Life Cycle Theory Another well-known situational theory is **life cycle theory**, which suggests that appropriate leader behavior depends on the maturity of the followers.[30] In this context, maturity includes motivation, competence, and experience. The theory suggests that as followers become more mature, the leader needs to move gradually from a high level of task orientation to a low level. Simultaneously, employee-oriented behavior should start low, increase at a moderate rate, and then decline again. This theory is well known among practicing managers, but it has received little scientific support from researchers.[31]

RELATED PERSPECTIVES ON LEADERSHIP

Because of its importance to organizational effectiveness, leadership continues to be the focus of a great deal of research and theory building. New approaches that have attracted much attention are the concepts of substitutes for leadership and transformational leadership.

Substitutes for Leadership

The concept of **substitutes for leadership** was developed because existing leadership models and theories do not account for situations in which leadership is not needed.[32] They simply try to specify what kind of leader behavior is appropriate. The substitute concepts, however, identify situations in which leader behaviors are neutralized or replaced by characteristics of the subordinate, the task, and the organization. For example, when a patient is delivered to a hospital emergency room, the professionals on duty do not wait to be told what to do by a leader. Nurses, doctors, and attendants all go into action without waiting for directive or supportive leader behavior from the emergency-room supervisor.

substitutes for leadership A concept that identifies situations in which leader behaviors are neutralized or replaced by characteristics of subordinates, the task, and the organization

Characteristics of the subordinate that may serve to neutralize leader behavior include ability, experience, need for independence, professional orientation, and indifference toward organizational rewards. For example, employees with a high level of ability and experience may not need to be told what to do. Similarly, a subordinate's strong need for independence may render leader behavior ineffective. Task characteristics that may substitute for leadership include routineness, the availability of feedback, and intrinsic satisfaction. When the job is routine and simple, the subordinate may not need direction. When the task is challenging and intrinsically satisfying, the subordinate may not need or want social support from a leader.

Organizational characteristics that may substitute for leadership include formalization, group cohesion, inflexibility, and a rigid reward structure. Leadership may not be necessary when policies and practices are formal and inflexible, for example. Similarly, a rigid reward system may rob the leader of reward power and thereby decrease the importance of the role. Preliminary research has provided support for the concept of substitutes for leadership.[33]

Charismatic Leadership

The concept of **charismatic leadership**, like trait theories, assumes that charisma is an individual characteristic of the leader. **Charisma** is a form of interpersonal attraction that inspires support and acceptance. All else equal, then, someone with charisma is more likely to be able to influence others than is someone without charisma. For example, a highly charismatic supervisor will be more successful in influencing subordinate behavior than a supervisor who lacks charisma. Thus influence is again a fundamental element of this perspective.

charismatic leadership Assumes that charisma is an individual characteristic of the leader

charisma A form of interpersonal attraction that inspires support and acceptance

Robert House first proposed a theory of charismatic leadership in 1977 based on research findings from a variety of social science disciplines.[34] His theory suggests that charismatic leaders are likely to have a lot of self-confidence, a firm conviction in their beliefs and ideals, and a strong need to influence people. They also tend to communicate high expectations about follower performance and express confidence in followers. Donald Trump is an excellent example of a charismatic leader. Even though he has made his share of mistakes and generally is perceived as only an "average" manager, many people view him as larger than life.[35]

There are three elements of charismatic leadership in organizations that most experts acknowledge today.[36] First, the leader needs to be able to envision the future, to set high expectations, and to model behaviors consistent with meeting those expectations. Next, the charismatic leader must be able to energize others through a demonstration of personal excitement, personal confidence, and patterns of success. Finally, the charismatic leader enables others by supporting them, by empathizing with them, and by expressing confidence in them.[37]

Charismatic leadership ideas are quite popular among managers today and are the subject of numerous books and articles. Unfortunately, few studies have specifically attempted to test the meaning and impact of charismatic leadership. In addition, lingering ethical issues about charismatic leadership trouble some people. For example, critics have warned that charismatic leadership, when used to the extreme, can create such fanatical devotion to the leader by the followers that they may compromise their ability to think for themselves.

Transformational Leadership

• **transformational leadership**
Leadership that goes beyond ordinary expectations by transmitting a sense of mission, stimulating learning experiences, and inspiring new ways of thinking

Another new perspective on leadership has been given a number of different labels: charismatic leadership, inspirational leadership, symbolic leadership, and transformational leadership. We use the term **transformational leadership** and define it as leadership that goes beyond ordinary expectations by transmitting a sense of mission, stimulating learning experiences, and inspiring new ways of thinking.[38] Because of rapid change and turbulent environments, transformational leaders increasingly are seen as vital to the success of business.

A recent popular-press article identified seven keys to successful leadership: trusting one's subordinates, developing a vision, keeping cool, encouraging risk, being an expert, inviting dissent, and simplifying things.[39] Although this list was the result of a simplistic survey of the leadership literature, it is nevertheless consistent with the premises underlying transformational leadership. So, too, are recent examples cited as effective leadership. Take, for example, the case of General Electric Co. When Jack Welch assumed the position of CEO, GE was a lethargic behemoth composed of more than one hundred businesses. Decision making was slow, and bureaucracy stifled individual initiative. Welch stripped away the bureaucracy, streamlined the entire organization, sold dozens of businesses, and bought many new ones. He literally recreated the organization, and today GE is one of the most admired and profitable firms in the world. Transformational leadership was the basis for all of Welch's changes.[40] Other transformational leaders are John Scully at Apple and Lee Iacocca at Chrysler. Given the practical significance of transformational leadership, many managers are beginning to acknowledge this important concept.

• **political behavior**
The activities carried out for the specific purpose of acquiring, developing, and using power and other resources to obtain one's preferred outcomes

POLITICAL BEHAVIOR IN ORGANIZATIONS

Another common influence on behavior is politics and political behavior. **Political behavior** describes activities carried out for the specific purpose of acquiring, developing, and using power and other resources to obtain one's preferred outcomes.[41] Political behavior may be undertaken by managers dealing with their subordinates, subordinates dealing with their managers, and managers and subordinates dealing with others at the same level. In other words, it may be directed upward, downward, or laterally. Decisions ranging from where to locate a manufacturing plant to where to put the company coffeepot are subject to political action. In any situation, individuals may engage in political behavior to further their own ends, to protect themselves from others, to further goals they sincerely believe to be in the organization's best interest, or simply to acquire and exercise power. Power may be sought by individuals, by groups of individuals, or by groups of groups.[42]

Although political behavior is difficult to study because of its sensitive nature, one survey found that many managers believe that politics influence salary and hiring decisions in their organizations. Many also believe that the incidence of political behavior is greater at the upper levels of their organizations and less at the lower levels. More than one-half of the respondents believe that organizational politics is bad, unfair, unhealthy, and irrational but most suggest that successful executives have to be good politicians and be political to "get ahead."[43]

Common Political Behaviors

Research has identified four basic forms of political behavior widely practiced in organizations.[44] One form is *inducement*, which occurs when a manager offers to give something to someone else in return for that individual's support. For example, a product manager might suggest to another product manager that she will put in a good word with his boss if he supports a new marketing plan that she has developed. A second tactic is *persuasion*, which relies on both emotion and logic. An operations manager wanting to construct a new plant on a certain site might persuade others to support his goal on grounds that are objective and logical (e.g., land is less expensive; taxes are lower) as well as subjective and personal.

A third political behavior involves the *creation of an obligation*. For example, one manager might support a recommendation made by another manager for a new advertising campaign. Although he may really have no opinion on the new campaign, he may think that by going along he is incurring a debt from the other manager and will be able to "call in" that debt when he wants to get something done and needs additional support. Finally, *coercion* is the use of force to get one's way. For example, a manager may threaten to withhold support, rewards, or other resources as a way to influence someone else.

Managing Political Behavior

By its very nature, political behavior is tricky to approach in a rational and systematic way. But managers can handle political behavior so that it does not do excessive damage. First, managers should be aware that even if their actions are not politically motivated, others may assume that they are. Second, by providing subordinates with autonomy, responsibility, challenge, and feedback, managers reduce the likelihood of political behavior by subordinates. Third, managers should avoid using power if they want to avoid charges of political motivation. Fourth, managers should get disagreements out in the open so that subordinates will have less opportunity for political behavior, using conflict for their own purposes. Finally, managers should avoid covert activities. Behind-the-scene activities give the impression of political intent even if none really exists.[45] Other guidelines include clearly communicating the bases and processes for performance evaluation, tying rewards directly to performance, and minimizing competition among managers for resources.[46]

Of course, those guidelines are a lot easier to list than they are to implement. The well-informed manager should not assume that political behavior does not exist or, worse yet, attempt to eliminate it by issuing orders or commands. Instead, the manager must recognize that political behavior exists in virtually all organizations and that it cannot be ignored or stamped out. It can, however, be managed in such a way that it will seldom inflict serious damage on the organization. It may even play a useful role in some situations.[47] For example, a manager may be able to use his or her political influence to stimulate a greater sense of social responsibility or to heighten awareness of the ethical implications of a decision.

SUMMARY OF KEY POINTS

As a process, leadership is the use of noncoercive influence to shape the group's or organization's goals, motivate behavior toward the achievement of those goals, and help define group or organizational culture. As a property, leadership is the set of characteristics attributed to those who are perceived to be leaders. Leadership and management are often related but are also different. Managers and leaders use legitimate, reward, coercive, referent, and expert power.

The trait approach to leadership assumes that some basic trait or set of traits differentiates leaders from nonleaders. The leadership-behavior approach to leadership assumes that the behavior of effective leaders is somehow different from the behavior of nonleaders. Research at the University of Michigan and Ohio State identified two basic forms of leadership behavior—one concentrating on work and performance and the other concentrating on employee welfare and support. The Leadership Grid® attempts to train managers to exhibit high levels of both forms of behavior.

Situational approaches to leadership recognize that appropriate forms of leadership behavior are not universally applicable and attempt to specify situations in which various behaviors are appropriate. The LPC theory suggests that a leader's behaviors should be either task-oriented or relationship-oriented depending on the favorableness of the situation. The path-goal theory suggests that directive, supportive, participative, or achievement-oriented leader behaviors may be appropriate, depending on the personal characteristics of subordinates and the environment. The Vroom-Yetton-Jago model maintains that leaders should vary the extent to which they allow subordinates to participate in making decisions as a function of problem attributes. The leader-member exchange model and life cycle theory are two new situational theories.

Related leadership perspectives are the concept of substitutes for leadership, charismatic leadership, and the role of transformational leadership in organizations.

Political behavior is another influence process frequently used in organizations. Managers can take steps to limit the effects of political behavior.

QUESTIONS FOR REVIEW

1. Could someone be a manager but not a leader? A leader but not a manager? Both a leader and a manager? Explain.

_____ **11.** I consult with others before making work-related decisions.

_____ **12.** I delegate responsibility and authority to others and allow them discretion in determining how to do their work.

_____ **13.** I plan in advance how to efficiently organize and schedule the work.

_____ **14.** I look for new opportunities for the group to exploit, propose new undertakings, and offer innovative ideas.

_____ **15.** I take prompt and decisive action to deal with serious work-related problems and disturbances.

_____ **16.** I provide subordinates with supplies, equipment, support services, and other resources necessary to work effectively.

_____ **17.** I keep informed about the activities of the group and check on its performance.

_____ **18.** I keep informed about outside events that have important implications for the group.

_____ **19.** I promote and defend the interests of the group and take appropriate action to obtain necessary resources for the group.

_____ **20.** I emphasize teamwork and try to promote cooperation, cohesiveness, and identification with the group.

_____ **21.** I discourage unnecessary fighting and bickering within the group and help settle conflicts and disagreements in a constructive manner.

_____ **22.** I criticize specific acts that are unacceptable, find positive things to say, and provide an opportunity for people to offer explanations.

_____ **23.** I take appropriate disciplinary action to deal with anyone who violates a rule, disobeys an order, or has consistently poor performance.

For interpretation, turn to page 449.

Source: Adapted from David D. Van Fleet and Gary A. Yukl, *Military Leadership: An Organizational Behavior Perspective*, 1986, pp. 38–39. Copyright 1986 by JAI Press. Used with permission of the publisher.

EXPERIENTIAL EXERCISE

The Leadership/Management Interview Experiment

Purpose: Leadership and management are in some ways the same, but more often they are different. This exercise allows you to develop a conceptual framework for leadership and management.

Introduction: Since most management behaviors and leadership behaviors are a product of individual work experience, each leader/manager tends to have a unique leadership/management style. An analysis of leadership/management styles and a comparison of such styles with different organizational experiences are often rewarding experiences in learning.

Instructions

Fact-Finding and Execution of the Experiment

1. Develop a list of questions relating to issues studied in this chapter that you want to ask a practicing manager and leader during a face-to-face interview. Prior to the actual interview, submit your list of questions to your instructor for approval.

2. Arrange to interview a practicing manager and a practicing leader. For purposes of this assignment, a manager or leader is a person whose job priority involves supervising the work of other people. The leader/manager may work in a business or in a public or private agency.

3. Interview at least one manager and one leader using the interview you have developed. Take good notes on their comments and on your own observations. Do not take more than one hour of each leader/manager's time.

Oral Report

Prepare an oral report using the questions here and your interview information. Complete the following report after the interview. (Attach a copy of your interview questions.)

The Leadership/Management Interview Experiment Report

1. How did you locate the leader/managers you interviewed? Describe your initial contacts.

2. Describe the level and responsibilities of your leader/managers. Do not supply names—their responses should be anonymous.

3. Describe the interview settings. How long did the interview last?

4. In what ways were the leader/managers similar or in agreement about issues?

5. What were some of the major differences between the leader/managers and the ways in which they approached their jobs?

6. In what ways would the managers agree or disagree with ideas presented in this course?

7. Describe and evaluate your own interviewing style and skills.

8. How did your managers feel about having been interviewed? How do you know that?

9. Overall, what were the most important things you learned from this experience?

Source: Adapted from Stephen C. Iman, "The Management Interview Experiment," in *Introducing Organizational Behavior: Exercises and Experiments,* 2nd ed., by Peter P. Dawson and Stephen C. Iman (Lexington, Mass.: Ginn and Company, 1981), pp. 135–138.

CHAPTER NOTES

1. Stephanie Losee, "How Compaq Keeps the Magic Going," *Fortune*, February 21, 1994, pp. 90–92; "The Office That Never Closes," *Forbes*, May 23, 1994, pp. 212–213; David Kirkpatrick, "Fast Times at Compaq," *Fortune*, April 1, 1996, pp. 120–128.
2. Arthur G. Jago, "Leadership: Perspectives in Theory and Research," *Management Science*, March 1982, pp. 315–336.
3. Gary A. Yukl, *Leadership in Organizations*, 3rd ed. (Englewood Cliffs, N.J.: Prentice-Hall, 1995), p. 5.
4. Manfred F. R. Kets de Vries, "The Leadership Mystique," *The Academy of Management Executive*, August 1994, pp. 73–89.
5. See John P. Kotter, "What Leaders Really Do," *Harvard Business Review*, May–June 1990, pp. 103–111.
6. Daniel Brass and Marlene Burkhardt, "Potential Power and Power Use: An Investigation of Structure and Behavior," *Academy of Management Journal*, 1993, Vol. 36, No. 3, pp. 441–470.
7. John R. P. French and Bertram Raven, "The Bases of Social Power," in Dorwin Cartwright (Ed.), *Studies in Social Power* (Ann Arbor, Mich.: University of Michigan Press, 1959), pp. 150–167.
8. William Kahn and Kathy Kram, "Authority at Work: Internal Models and Their Organizational Consequences," *Academy of Management Review*, 1994, Vol. 19, No. 1, pp. 17–50.
9. Hugh D. Menzies, "The Ten Toughest Bosses," *Fortune*, April 21, 1980, pp. 62–73.
10. John Voyer, "Coercive Organizational Politics and Organizational Outcomes: An Interpretive Study," *Organization Science*, February 1994, pp. 72–81.
11. Bernard M. Bass, *Bass & Stogdill's Handbook of Leadership*, 3rd ed. (Riverside, N.J.: Free Press, 1990).
12. Shelley A. Kirkpatrick and Edwin A. Locke, "Leadership: Do Traits Matter?" *The Academy of Management Executive*, May 1991, pp. 48–60.
13. Robert G. Lord, Christy L. De Vader, and George M. Alliger, "A Meta-Analysis of the Relation Between Personality Traits and Leadership Perceptions: An Application of Validity Generalization Procedures," *Journal of Applied Psychology*, August 1986, pp. 402–410.
14. Rensis Likert, *New Patterns of Management* (New York: McGraw-Hill, 1961); Rensis Likert, *The Human Organization* (New York: McGraw-Hill, 1967).
15. The Ohio State studies stimulated many articles, monographs, and books. A good overall reference is Ralph M. Stogdill and A. E. Coons (Eds.), *Leader Behavior: Its Description and Measurement* (Columbus, Ohio: Bureau of Business Research, Ohio State University, 1957).
16. Edwin A. Fleishman, E. F. Harris, and H. E. Burt, *Leadership and Supervision in Industry* (Columbus, Ohio: Bureau of Business Research, Ohio State University, 1955).
17. Robert R. Blake and Jane S. Mouton, *The Managerial Grid* (Houston: Gulf Publishing, 1964); Robert R. Blake and Jane S. Mouton, *The New Managerial Grid* (Houston: Gulf Publishing, 1978); Robert R. Blake and Jane S. Mouton, *The Versatile Manager: A Grid Profile* (Homewood, Ill.: Dow Jones-Irwin, 1981).
18. See Jan P. Muczyk and Bernard C. Reimann, "The Case for Directive Leadership," *The Academy of Management Executive*, November 1987, pp. 301–309, for a recent update.
19. Fred E. Fiedler, *A Theory of Leadership Effectiveness* (New York: McGraw-Hill, 1967).
20. Chester A. Schriesheim, Bennett J. Tepper, and Linda A. Tetrault, "Least Preferred Coworker Score, Situational Control, and Leadership Effectiveness: A Meta-Analysis of Contingency Model Performance Predictions," *Journal of Applied Psychology*, 1994, Vol. 79, No. 4, pp. 561–573.
21. Fiedler, *A Theory of Leadership Effectiveness*; Fred E. Fiedler and M. M. Chemers, *Leadership and Effective Management* (Glenview, Ill.: Scott, Foresman, 1974).
22. For recent reviews and updates, see Lawrence H. Peters, Darrell D. Hartke, and John T. Pohlmann, "Fiedler's Contingency Theory of Leadership: An Application of the Meta-Analysis Procedures of Schmidt

and Hunter," *Psychological Bulletin*, 1992, Vol. 97, pp. 274–285; and Fred E. Fiedler, "When to Lead, When to Stand Back," *Psychology Today*, September 1987, pp. 26–27.

23. Martin G. Evans, "The Effects of Supervisory Behavior on the Path-Goal Relationship," *Organizational Behavior and Human Performance*, May 1970, pp. 277–298; Robert J. House and Terence R. Mitchell, "Path-Goal Theory of Leadership," *Journal of Contemporary Business*, Autumn 1974, pp. 81–98. See also Yukl, *Leadership in Organizations*.
24. For a recent review, see J. C. Wofford and Laurie Z. Liska, "Path-Goal Theories of Leadership: A Meta-Analysis," *Journal of Management*, 1993, Vol. 19, No. 4, pp. 857–876.
25. Victor H. Vroom and Philip H. Yetton, *Leadership and Decision-Making* (Pittsburgh: University of Pittsburgh Press, 1973); and Victor H. Vroom and Arthur G. Jago, *The New Leadership* (Englewood Cliffs, N.J.: Prentice-Hall, 1988).
26. Yukl, *Leadership in Organizations*.
27. Vroom and Jago, *The New Leadership*.
28. Fred Dansereau, George Graen, and W. J. Haga, "A Vertical-Dyad Linkage Approach to Leadership within Formal Organizations: A Longitudinal Investigation of the Role-Make Process," *Organizational Behavior and Human Performance*, 1975, Vol. 15, pp. 46–78; Richard M. Dienesch and Robert C. Liden, "Leader-Member Exchange Model of Leadership: A Critique and Further Development," *Academy of Management Review*, July 1986, pp. 618–634.
29. Antoinette Phillips and Arthur Bedeian, "Leader-Follower Exchange Quality: The Role of Personal and Interpersonal Attributes," *Academy of Management Journal*, 1994, Vol. 37, No. 4, pp. 990–1001.
30. Paul Hersey and Kenneth H. Blanchard, *Management of Organizational Behavior*, 3rd ed. (Englewood Cliffs, N.J.: Prentice-Hall, 1977).
31. Yukl, *Leadership in Organizations*.
32. Steven Kerr and John M. Jermier, "Substitutes for Leadership: Their Meaning and Measurement," *Organizational Behavior and Human Performance*, December 1978, pp. 375–403.
33. See Charles C. Manz and Henry P. Sims, Jr., "Leading Workers to Lead Themselves: The External Leadership of Self-Managing Work Teams," *Administrative Science Quarterly*, March 1987, pp. 106–129.
34. See Robert J. House, "A 1976 Theory of Charismatic Leadership," in J. G. Hunt and L. L. Larson (Eds.), *Leadership: The Cutting Edge* (Carbondale, Ill.: Southern Illinois University Press, 1977), pp. 189–207. See also Jay A. Conger and Rabindra N. Kanungo, "Toward a Behavioral Theory of Charismatic Leadership in Organizational Settings," *Academy of Management Review*, October 1987, pp. 637–647.
35. Stratford P. Sherman, "Donald Trump Just Won't Die," *Fortune*, August 13, 1990, pp. 75–79.
36. David A. Nadler and Michael L. Tushman, "Beyond the Charismatic Leader: Leadership and Organizational Change," *California Management Review*, Winter 1990, pp. 77–97.
37. See Boas Shamir, Robert House, and Michael Arthur, "The Motivational Effects of Charismatic Leadership: A Self-Concept Based Theory," *Organization Science*, November 1993, pp. 577–589; Jay Conger and Rabindra Kanungo, "Charismatic Leadership in Organizations: Perceived Behavioral Attributes and Their Measurement," *Journal of Organizational Behavior*, 1994, Vol. 15, pp. 439–452.
38. James MacGregor Burns, *Leadership* (New York: Harper & Row, 1978). See also John J. Hater and Bernard M. Bass, "Superiors' Evaluations and Subordinates' Perceptions of Transformational and Transactional Leadership," *Journal of Applied Psychology*, November 1988, pp. 695–702; Karl W. Kuhnert and Philip Lewis, "Transactional and Transformational Leadership: A Constructive/Developmental Analysis," *Academy of Management Review*, October 1987, pp. 648–657.
39. Labich, "The Seven Keys to Business Leadership."
40. Thomas A. Stewart, "How to Lead a Revolution," *Fortune*, November 28, 1994, pp. 48–61.
41. Jeffrey Pfeffer, *Power in Organizations* (Marshfield, Mass.: Pitman Publishing, 1981), p. 7.
42. Timothy Judge and Robert Bretz, "Political Influence Behavior and Career Success," *Journal of Management*, 1994, Vol. 20, No. 1, pp. 43–65.
43. Victor Murray and Jeffrey Gandz, "Games Executives Play: Politics at Work," *Business Horizons*, December 1980, pp. 11–13; Jeffrey Gandz and Victor Murray, "The Experience of Workplace Politics," *Academy of Management Journal*, June 1980, pp. 237–251.
44. Don R. Beeman and Thomas W. Sharkey, "The Use and Abuse of Corporate Power," *Business Horizons*, March–April 1987, pp. 26–30.
45. Murray and Gandz, "Games Executives Play."
46. Beeman and Sharkey, "The Use and Abuse of Corporate Power."
47. Stefanie Ann Lenway and Kathleen Rehbein, "Leaders, Followers, and Free Riders: An Empirical Test of Variation in Corporate Political Involvement," *Academy of Management Journal*, December 1991, pp. 893–905.

CHAPTER

12

Communication in Organizations

OBJECTIVES

After studying this chapter, you should be able to:

- *Describe the role and importance of communication in the manager's job.*
- *Identify the basic forms of interpersonal communication and cite advantages and disadvantages of each.*
- *Identify forms of organizational communication and cite characteristics of each.*
- *Discuss information technology and information systems in organizations.*
- *Discuss informal communication, including its various forms and types.*
- *Describe how the communication process can be managed to recognize and overcome barriers.*

OUTLINE

OPENING INCIDENT

TEXAS INSTRUMENTS INCORPORATED has operations around the world. Although the firm's operations are concentrated in the state that is its namesake, TI also has facilities in more than thirty countries scattered across Europe, Asia, and South America. Particularly important in recent years has been a facility in India, created to take advantage of a high-quality but relatively inexpensive labor pool of talented engineers in that country.

TI has long been a leader in integrated global design. Until recently, however, global design teams were relatively inefficient. Days were lost as detailed engineering drawings traveled between countries. Even facsimile technology did not help greatly because images were often blurred and drawings themselves were very large—drawings were sometimes cut into small pieces, each piece was faxed separately, and someone on the other end taped them together.

Eventually the firm began to transmit images and other data electronically through integrated computer information networks linked by satellites. This new technology allowed TI engineers in facilities around the globe to work on the same project simultaneously—to communicate just as easily as if they were sitting in the same room. Almost immediately after implementing this system the time needed to develop a new calculator dropped by 20 percent. Later improvements shaved another 17 percent off development time.

"We're probably 18 to 24 months ahead of the competition, partly as a result of this communications expertise."

One TI group that has taken special advantage of information technology has been the Texas Instruments Registration and Identification System (Tiris) group. This group is managed in England, develops products in the Netherlands and Germany, and produces them in Japan and Malaysia. The TI communication network has made it possible for these engineers to coordinate their efforts. Indeed, Tiris management believes the system has given them a major competitive advantage.

The system has also allowed the firm to expand the boundaries of its workday by taking advantage of different time zones. A U.S. financial exchange recently asked TI for a price quote on some new equipment. A group in Dallas started work late in the afternoon, and at quitting time forwarded the project to their counterparts in Tokyo. Managers there spent their day on it and then passed it on to managers in Nice, France. Managers in Nice finished it and sent the information back to Dallas. Within twenty-four hours of getting the request, TI could show the customer the price quote—and a computer-generated image of what the product would look like.[1]

Source of Quotation: David Slinger, Tiris North American General Manager, quoted in *Fortune*, November 30, 1992, p. 117.

Managers at Texas Instruments face complex problems associated with managing a company with facilities spread throughout the United States, Europe, Asia, and South America. Once relying on traditional mail services, they have progressed through courier service to facsimile technology to today's global communication network. They are now able to compete more effectively and to integrate global resources into one overall organizational effort. Indeed, managers around the world agree that communication is one of their most important tasks. It is important for them to communicate with others in order to convey their vision and goals for the organization, and it is important for others to communicate with them so that they will better understand what's going on in their environment and how they and their organizations can become more effective.

This chapter focuses on communication in organizations. We begin by examining communication in the context of the manager's job. We then identify and discuss forms of interpersonal and organizational communication. Next, we examine information systems and information technology. Informal communication is then discussed. Finally, we describe how organizational communication can be managed effectively.

COMMUNICATION AND THE MANAGER'S JOB

A typical manager's day includes doing desk work, attending scheduled meetings, placing and receiving telephone calls, reading correspondence, answering correspondence, and attending unscheduled meetings.[2] Most of these activities involve communication. In fact, most managers spend over half of their time communicating in some way. On a typical Monday, Nolan Archibald, CEO of Black & Decker, attended five scheduled meetings and two unscheduled meetings; had fifteen telephone conversations; received twenty-nine letters, memos, and reports; and dictated ten letters.[3]

A Definition of Communication

Imagine three managers working in an office building. The first is all alone but is nevertheless yelling for a subordinate to come help. No one appears, but he continues to yell. The second is talking on the telephone to a subordinate, but static on the line causes the subordinate to misunderstand some important numbers being provided by the manager. As a result, the subordinate sends 1,500 crates of eggs to 150 Fifth Street, when he should have sent 150 crates of eggs to 1500 Fifteenth Steet. The third manager is talking in her office with a subordinate who clearly hears and understands what is being said. Each of these managers is attempting to communicate but with different results.

communication
The process of transmitting information from one person to another

Communication is the process of transmitting information from one person to another.[4] Did any of our three managers communicate? The last did and the first did not. How about the second? In fact, she did communicate. She transmitted information and information was received. The problem was that the message transmitted and the message received were not the same. The words spoken by the manager were distorted by static and noise. **Effective communication**, then, is the process of sending a message in such a way that the message received is as close in meaning as possible to the message intended. Although the second manager engaged in communication, it was not effective.

A key element in effective communication is the distinction between data and information. **Data** are raw figures and facts reflecting a single aspect of reality. The facts that a plant has 35 machines, that each machine is capable of producing 1,000 units of output per day, that current and projected future demand for the units is 30,000 per day, and that workers sufficiently skilled to run the machines make $15 an hour are data. **Information** is data presented in a way or form that has meaning. Summarizing the four pieces of data given above provides information—the plant has excess capacity and is therefore incurring unnecessary costs. Information has meaning to a manager and provides a basis for action. The plant manager might use the information and decide to sell four machines (keeping one as a backup) and transfer five operators to other jobs.[5]

- **effective communication** The process of sending a message in such a way that the message received is as close in meaning as possible to the message intended
- **data** Raw figures and facts reflecting a single aspect of reality
- **information** Data presented in a way or form that has meaning

Characteristics of Useful Information

What factors differentiate between information that is useful and information that is not useful? In general, information is useful if it is accurate, timely, complete, and relevant.

Accurate For information to be of real value to a manager, it must be accurate. Accuracy means that the information must provide a valid and reliable reflection of reality. A Japanese construction company once bought information from a consulting firm about a possible building site in London. The Japanese were told that the land, which would be sold in a sealed bid auction, would attract bids of close to $250 million. They were also told that the land currently held an old building that easily could be demolished. Thus the Japanese bid $255 million—which ended up being $90 million more than the next-highest bid. A few days later, the British government declared the building historic, preempting any thought of demolition. Clearly, the Japanese acted on information that was less than accurate.[6]

Timely Information also needs to be timely. Timeliness does not necessarily mean speediness; it means only that information needs to be available in time for appropriate managerial action. What constitutes timeliness is a function of the situation facing the manager. When Marriott was gathering information for its Fairfield Inn project, managers projected a six-month window for data collection. They felt this would give them an opportunity to do a good job of getting the information they needed while not delaying things too much. In contrast, Marriott's computerized reservation and accounting system can provide a manager today with last night's occupancy level at any Marriott facility.[7]

Complete Information must tell a complete story for it to be useful to a manager. If it is less than complete, the manager is likely to get an inaccurate or distorted picture of reality. For example, managers at Kroger used to think that house-brand products were more profitable than national brands because they yielded higher unit profits. On the basis of this information, they gave house brands a lot of shelf space and centered a lot of promotional activities around them. As Kroger's managers became more sophisticated in understanding their information, however, they realized that national brands were actually more profitable over time because they sold many more units than house brands during any given period of time. Hence, while a store might sell 10 cans of Kroger coffee in a day with a profit of 25 cents per can (total profit of $2.50), it would also sell 15 cans of Maxwell House with a profit of 20 cents per can (total profit of $3.00).

Relevant Finally, information must be relevant if it is to be useful to managers. Relevance, like timeliness, is defined according to the needs and circumstances of a particular manager. Operations managers need information on costs and productivity; human resource managers need information on hiring needs and turnover rates; and marketing managers need information on sales projections and advertising rates. As Wal-Mart contemplates countries for possible expansion opportunities, it gathers information about local regulations, customs, and so forth. But the information about any given country isn't really relevant until the decision is made to enter that market.[8]

The Communication Process

Figure 12.1 illustrates how communication generally takes place between people. The process of communication begins when one person (the sender) wants to transmit a fact, idea, opinion, or other information to someone else (the receiver). This fact, idea, or opinion has meaning to the sender, whether it be simple and concrete or complex and abstract. The next step is to encode the meaning into a form appropriate to the situation. The encoding might take the form of words, facial expressions, gestures, or even artistic expressions and physical actions. The encoding process is influenced by the content of the message, the familiarity of sender and receiver, and other situational factors. After the message has been encoded, it is transmitted through the appropriate channel or medium.

The channel by which the present encoded message is being transmitted to you is the printed page. Common channels in organizations include meetings, memos, letters, reports, e-mail, and telephone calls. After the message is received, it is decoded back into a form that has meaning for the receiver. In many cases, the meaning prompts a response, and the cycle is continued when a new message is sent by the same steps back to the original sender.

"Noise" may disrupt communication anywhere along the way. Noise can be the sound of someone coughing, a truck driving by, or two people talking close by. It can also include disruptions such as a letter being lost in the

FIGURE 12.1 The Communication Process

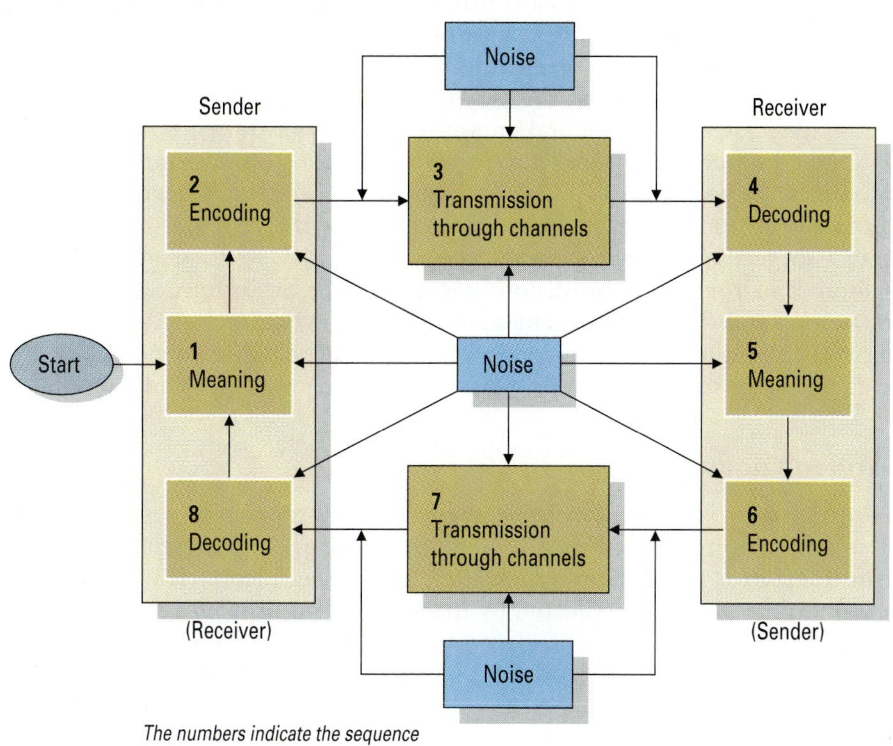

As the figure shows, noise can disrupt the communication process at any step. Managers must therefore understand that a conversation in the next office, a fax machine out of paper, and the receiver's worries may all thwart the manager's best attempts to communicate.

mail, a telephone line going dead, or one of the participants in a conversation being called away before the communication process is completed.

FORMS OF INTERPERSONAL COMMUNICATION

Managers need to understand several kinds of communication. Two forms, oral and written, are primarily interpersonal in nature; we discuss them together here.

Oral Communication

Oral communication takes place in face-to-face conversations, group discussions, telephone calls, and other circumstances in which the spoken word is used to express meaning. Henry Mintzberg demonstrated the importance of oral communication when he found that most managers spend between 50 and 90 percent of their time talking to people.[9] Oral communication is so prevalent for several reasons. The primary advantage of oral communication is that it promotes prompt feedback and interchange in the form of verbal questions or agreement, facial expressions,

• **oral communication** Face-to-face conversations, group discussions, telephone calls, and other circumstances in which the spoken word is used to transmit meaning

and gestures. Oral communication is also easy (all the sender needs to do is talk), and it can be done with little preparation (though careful preparation is advisable in certain situations). The sender does not need pencil and paper, typewriter, or other equipment. In one survey, 55 percent of the executives sampled felt that their own written communication skills were fair or poor, so they chose oral communication to avoid embarrassment![10]

Oral communication does have drawbacks. It may suffer from problems of inaccuracy if the speaker chooses the wrong words to convey meaning or leaves out pertinent details, if noise disrupts the process, or if the receiver forgets part or all of the message. In a two-way discussion, there is seldom time for a thoughtful, considered response or for introducing many new facts, and there is no permanent record of what has been said. In addition, although most managers are comfortable talking to people individually or in small groups, fewer enjoy speaking to larger audiences.[11]

Written Communication

written communication Memos, letters, reports, notes, and other circumstances in which the written word is used to transmit meaning

"Putting it in writing" can solve many of the problems inherent in oral communication. Nevertheless, and perhaps surprisingly, **written communication** is not as common as one might imagine, nor is it a mode of communication much respected by managers. One sample of managers indicated that only 13 percent of the mail they received was of immediate use to them.[12] Over 80 percent of the managers who responded to another survey indicated that the written communication they received was of fair or poor quality.[13]

The biggest single drawback of written communication is that it inhibits feedback and interchange. When one manager sends another manager a letter, it must be written or dictated, typed, mailed, received, routed, opened, and read. If there is a misunderstanding, it may take several days for it to be recognized, let alone rectified. A phone call could settle the whole matter in just a few minutes. Thus written communication often inhibits feedback and interchange and is usually more difficult and time consuming than oral communication.

Of course, written communication offers some advantages. It is often quite accurate and provides a permanent record of the exchange. The sender can take the time to collect and assimilate the information and can draft and revise it before it is transmitted. The receiver can take the time to read it carefully and can refer to it repeatedly, as needed. For these reasons, written communication is generally preferable when important details are involved. At times it is important to one or both parties to have a written record available as evidence of exactly what took place. Moreover, the growth in the use of e-mail by many managers may potentially reduce or eliminate some of the disadvantages noted above.

Choosing the Right Form

Which form of interpersonal communication should the manager use? The best medium will be determined by the situation. Oral communication is often preferred when the message is personal, nonroutine, and brief. Written communication is usually best when the message is more impersonal, routine, and longer.[14] The manager can also combine media to capitalize on the advantages of each. For example, a quick telephone call to set up a meeting is easy and gets an immediate response. Following up the call with a reminder note helps ensure that the recipient will remember the meeting, and it provides a record of the meeting having been called. Recent breakthroughs in electronic communication have facilitated just such actions. As we discuss more fully later, mobile telephones, facsimile machines, and computer networks blur the differences between oral and written communication and help each be more effective.[15]

vertical communication Communication that flows up and down the organization, usually along formal reporting lines; it takes place between managers and their subordinates and may involve several different levels of the organization

FORMS OF ORGANIZATIONAL COMMUNICATION

In addition to the two pure forms of interpersonal communication described above, other varieties of organizational communication are of concern to managers. Each involves oral or written communication, but each also extends to broad patterns of communication across the organization.[16] As shown in Figure 12.2, these forms of communication follow vertical and horizontal linkages in the organization.

Vertical Communication

Vertical communication is communication that flows both up and down the organization, usually along formal reporting lines—that is, it is the communication that takes place between managers and their superiors and

Formal communication in organizations follows official reporting relationships and/or prescribed channels. For example, vertical communication, shown here with dashed lines, flows between levels in the organization and involves subordinates and their managers. Horizontal communication flows between people at the same level and is usually used to facilitate coordination.

FIGURE 12.2 Formal Communication in Organizations

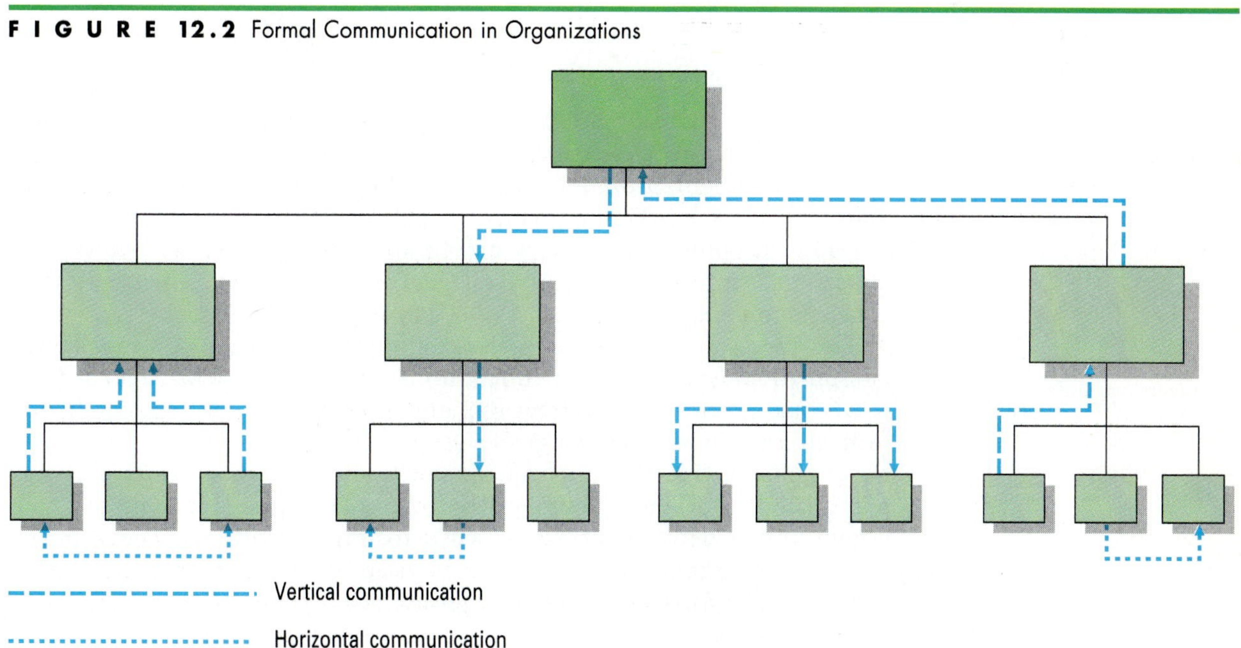

subordinates. Vertical communication may involve only two people, or it may flow through several different organizational levels.

Upward Communication Upward communication consists of messages from subordinates to superiors. This flow is usually from subordinates to their direct superior, then to that person's direct superior, and so on up the hierarchy. Occasionally, a message might bypass a particular superior. The typical content of upward communication is requests, information that the lower-level manager thinks is of importance to the higher-level manager, responses to requests from the higher-level manager, suggestions, complaints, and financial information. Research has shown that upward communication is more subject to distortion than is downward communication. Subordinates are likely to withhold or distort information that makes them look bad. The greater the degree of difference in status between superior and subordinate and the greater the degree of distrust, the more likely the subordinate is to suppress or distort information.[17] For example, when Harold Geneen was CEO of ITT, subordinates routinely withheld information about problems from him if they thought the news would make him angry and if they thought they could solve the problem themselves without his ever knowing about it.[18]

Downward Communication Downward communication occurs when information flows down the hierarchy from superiors to subordinates. The typical content of these messages is directives on how something is to be done, the assignment of new responsibilities, performance feedback, and general information that the higher-level manager thinks will be of value to the lower-level manager. Vertical communication can, and usually should, be two-way in nature. That is, give-and-take communication with active feedback generally is likely to be more effective than one-way communication.[19]

Horizontal Communication

• **horizontal communication** Communication that flows laterally within the organization; it involves colleagues and peers at the same level of the organization and may involve individuals from several different organizational units

Whereas vertical communication involves a superior and a subordinate, **horizontal communication** involves colleagues and peers at the same level of the organization. For example, an operations manager might communicate to a marketing manager that inventory levels are running low and that projected delivery dates should be extended by two weeks. Horizontal communication probably occurs more among managers than among nonmanagers.

This type of communication serves a number of purposes. It facilitates coordination among interdependent units. For example, a manager at Motorola was recently researching the strategies of Japanese semiconductor firms in Europe. He found a great deal of information that was relevant to his assignment. He also uncovered some additional information that was potentially important to another department, so he passed it along to a colleague in that department, who used it to improve his own operations.[20] Horizontal communication can also be used for joint problem solving, as when two plant managers at Westinghouse got together to work out a new method to improve productivity. Finally, horizontal communication plays a major role in work teams with members drawn from several departments.

INFORMATION TECHNOLOGY IN ORGANIZATIONS

Information technology (IT), refers to the resources and systems used by an organization to manage information that it needs to carry out its mission. IT may consist of computers, computer networks, and other pieces of hardware. IT also involves software that facilitates the system's ability to manage information in a way that is useful for managers.

information technology (IT) Refers to the resources used by an organization to manage information that it needs to carry out its mission

The grocery industry uses data, information, and information technology to automate inventory and checkout facilities. The average Kroger store, for example, carries 21,000 items in each of its stores. Computerized scanning machines at checkout counters can provide daily sales figures for any product. These figures alone are data and have little meaning in their pure form. Information is compiled from these data by another computerized system. Using this IT system, managers can identify how any given product or product line is selling in any number of stores over any meaningful period of time.[21]

Information technology is generally of two types—manual or computer-based. All information technology, and the systems that it defines, has five basic parts. The *input medium* is the device that is used to add data and information into the system. For example, the optical scanner at Kroger enters point-of-sale information. Likewise, someone can also enter data through a keyboard. The data that are entered into the system typically flow first to a processor. The *processor* is the part of the system that is capable of organizing, manipulating, sorting, or performing calculations or other transformations with the data. Most systems also have one or more *storage devices*—a place where data can be stored for later use. Floppy disks, hard disks, magnetic tapes, and optical disks are common forms of storage devices. As data are transformed into usable information, the resultant information must be communicated to the appropriate person by means of an *output medium*. Common ways to display output are video displays, printers, other computers, and facsimile machines.

Finally, the entire information technology system is operated by a *control system*—most often software of one form or another. Simple systems in smaller organizations can use off-the-shelf software. Microsoft Windows, DOS, and OS-2 are general operating systems that control ever more specialized types of software. Microsoft Word and WordPerfect are popular systems for word processing. Lotus 1-2-3 and Excel are popular spreadsheet programs, and dBASE III is frequently used for database management. Of course, elaborate systems of the type used by large businesses require a special customized operating system. When organizations start to link computers together into a network, the operating system must be even more complex.

As we noted earlier, information technology systems need not be computerized. Many small organizations still function quite well with a manual system using paper documents, routing slips, paper clips, file folders, file cabinets, and typewriters. Increasingly, however, even small businesses are abandoning their manual systems for computerized ones. As hardware prices continue to drop and software becomes more and more powerful, computerized information systems will likely be within the reach of any business that wants to have one.

Basic Kinds of Information Systems

Organizations that use information systems, especially large organizations, often find that they need several kinds of systems to manage their information effectively. The four most general kinds of information systems are transaction-processing systems, basic management information systems, decision support systems, and executive information systems.[22]

transaction-processing system (TPS)
A system designed to handle routine and recurring transactions within a business

Transaction-Processing Systems A **transaction-processing system (TPS)** is a system designed to handle routine and recurring transactions within a business. Visa uses a TPS to record charges to individual credit accounts, credit payments made on the accounts, and send monthly bills to customers. In general, a TPS is most useful when the organization has a large number of highly similar transactions to process. Thus most forms of customer billings, bank transactions, and point-of-sale records are amenable to this form of information system. A TPS is especially helpful in aggregating large amounts of data into more manageable forms of information summaries. For example, a bank manager probably cares little about any given Visa transaction recorded for any single cardholder. More useful is information about the average number of purchases made by each cardholder, their average daily balances, average monthly finance charges assessed, and so forth.

management information system (MIS)
A system that gathers more comprehensive data, organizes and summarizes it in a form valuable to managers, and provides those managers with the information they need to do their work

Basic Management Information Systems A **management information system (MIS)** is a system that gathers more comprehensive data, organizes and summarizes it in a form that is of value to functional managers, and then provides those same managers with the information they need to do their work. Seminole Manufacturing Co. uses a variation on the standard MIS called an EDE—electronic data exchange. Seminole supplies Wal-Mart with men's pants. The EDE system allows Seminole to tie directly into Wal-Mart's computerized inventory system to check current sales levels and stock on hand. Wal-Mart can then transmit new orders directly into Seminole's system, and managers there are already geared up to start working on it. As a result, delivery times have been cut in half and sales are up 31 percent.[23]

decision support system (DSS)
A system that automatically searches for, manipulates, and summarizes information needed by managers for use in making specific decisions

Decision Support Systems An increasingly common information system is called a **decision support system (DSS)**. A DSS can automatically search for, manipulate, and summarize information needed by managers for specific decisions. A DSS is much more flexible than a traditional MIS and can help cope with nonroutine problems and decisions.[24] Decision support systems are very complex. They take considerable time and resources to develop and more time and resources to maintain and to teach managers how to use them effectively. They also seem to hold considerable potential for improving the quality of information available to managers as they make important decisions. Frito-Lay makes extensive use of decision support systems in the marketing of its various snack food products. As sales data from individual stores are received, managers are cued to what products are selling above and below normal in different markets. They can then take such actions as cutting prices, increasing shipments, or whatever action is suggested by the information flowing into their offices.

Executive Information Systems Executive information systems are the newest form of information system. An **executive information system (EIS)** is a system designed to meet the special information processing needs of top managers. Because many top managers lack basic computer skills and because they need highly specialized information not readily available in conventional systems, many executives were reluctant to use their organizations' information system.

executive information system (EIS)
A system designed to meet the special information processing needs of top managers

An EIS is constructed to be very user-friendly (that is, technical knowledge is not necessary to use it). Instead, such systems generally use icons and symbols and require very few commands. The information they provide allows managers to bypass details and get directly to overall trends and patterns that may affect strategic decision making. It summarizes information for managers, rather than providing specific details. It also tailors the information to the specific needs of the manager.[25]

Recent Advances in Information Technology

Because of the enormous promise of information systems, and despite their occasional limitations, work continues to uncover new approaches to managing information.

Telecommunications One area where great strides have been made is **telecommunications**. Several forms of telecommunications have been or are being developed. Videoconferencing allows people in different locations to see and talk to one another. For example, top managers at Wal-Mart often use teleconferences to talk directly with Wal-Mart employees during their normal Saturday morning meetings.[26] Electronic mail systems allow managers to send messages to one another through computer linkups. People "post" messages on electronic bulletin boards for other interested people to read. Voice messaging allows voice messages to be stored and transferred between computers.

telecommunications
The use of electronic media to communicate over distances; includes the telephone, telegraph, electronic bulletin boards, and facsimile machines

Networks and Expert Systems Networks and expert systems are also becoming more popular. Even computer systems with very different operating systems are increasingly able to communicate with one another. Although there are still a variety of "standard" operating systems, as each is more finely developed it can interface with others more and more effectively.

Expert systems are also becoming more and more practical. An **expert system** is an information system created to duplicate, or at least imitate, the thought processes of a human being.[27] Organizations have developed considerably more complex and useful expert systems. For example,

expert system
An information system created to duplicate or imitate the thought processes of a human expert

Teleconferencing is an increasingly popular form of organizational communication. Teleconferencing is also being used in an ever-greater variety of forms. In the medical profession, for example, teleconferencing can sometimes allow specialists to help patients from rural areas without requiring them to travel long distances just for an examination. Hazel Grier, for example, is shown here having her hand pains diagnosed by a physician who is fifty miles away.

Campbell's developed an expert system to recreate the thought processes of one of its key employees, a manager who was very familiar with operations of the seven-story soup kettles used to cook soup. The manager, Aldo Cimino, knew so much about how the kettles worked that the company feared no one else could learn the job as well as he. So it hired Texas Instruments to study his job, interview him and observe his work, and create an expert system that could mimic his experience. The resultant system, containing over 150 if-then rules, helps operate the kettles today.[28]

information superhighway (Internet) An emerging integrated information system that can be accessed by anyone with a computer and a modem

The Internet The **information superhighway**, or **Internet**, is also an emerging form of information technology that promises to revolutionize communication. The Internet is a vast, integrated information system that is changing the way people communicate. Every day, more and more people tie into the Internet to access information about such wide-ranging things as weather, sports, business, hobbies, and leisure activities.

INFORMAL COMMUNICATION IN ORGANIZATIONS

Organizational communication is often planned and formal. In many cases, however, much of the communication that takes place in an organization transcends formal channels and instead follows any of several informal methods. Common forms of informal communication in organizations include the grapevine, management by wandering around, and nonverbal communication.

The Grapevine

The **grapevine** is an informal communication network that can permeate an entire organization. Grapevines are found in all organizations except the very smallest, but they do not always follow the same patterns as, nor do they necessarily coincide with, formal channels of authority and communication. Research has identified several kinds of grapevines.[29] The two most common are illustrated in Figure 12.3. The *gossip chain* occurs when one person spreads the message to many other people. Each one, in turn, may either keep the information confidential or pass it on to others. The gossip chain is likely to carry personal information. The other common grapevine is the *cluster chain*, in which one person passes the information to a selected few individuals. Some of the receivers pass the information to a few other individuals; the rest keep it to themselves.

grapevine An informal communication network among people in an organization

There is some disagreement about how accurate the information carried by the grapevine is, but research increasingly finds it to be fairly accurate, especially when the information is based on fact rather than speculation. One recent study found that the grapevine may be between 75 percent and 95 percent accurate.[30] That same study also found that informal communication is increasing in many organizations for two basic reasons. One contributing factor is the recent increase in merger, acquisition, and takeover activity. Because such activity can greatly affect the people within an organization, it follows that they may spend more time talking about it.[31] The second contributing factor is that as more and more corporations move facilities from inner cities to suburbs, employees tend to talk less and less to others outside the organization and more and more to each other.

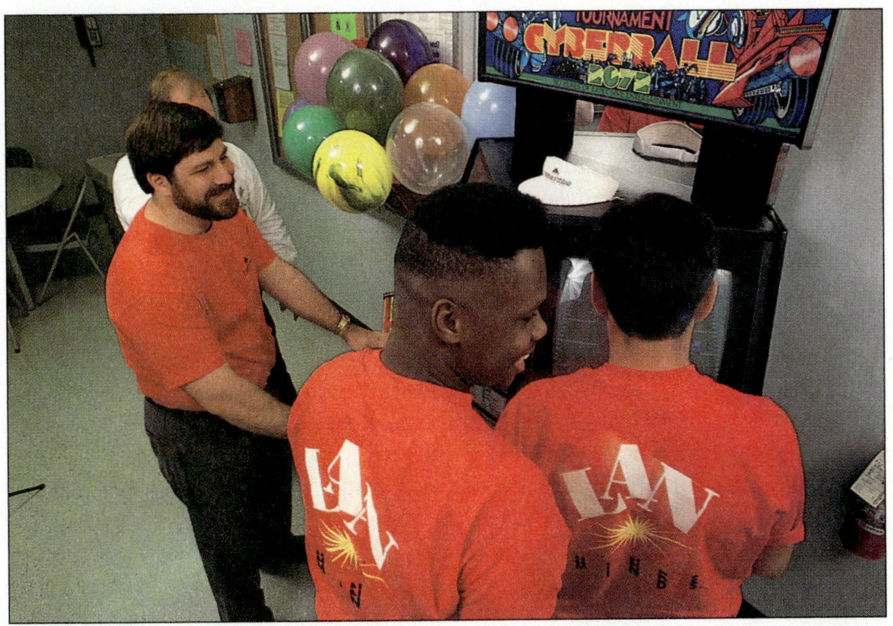

The grapevine is a very powerful form of informal communication in an organization. This firm has established a small game room for its employees to use on breaks and other nonwork time. Its managers can be sure, however, that a fair amount of what their employees talk about in the game room involves some aspect of the organization itself. Thus it will likely play an important role in grapevine communication in the future.

The two most common grapevine chains in organizations are the gossip chain (in which one person communicates messages to many others) and the cluster chain (in which many people pass messages to a few others).

FIGURE 12.3 Common Grapevine Chains Found in Organizations

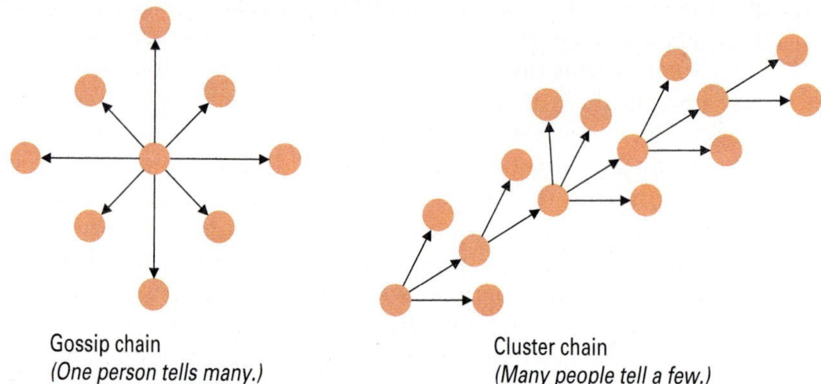

Source: Based on Keith Davis and John W. Newstrom, *Human Behavior at Work: Organizational Behavior,* 8th ed. (New York: McGraw-Hill, 1989). Reproduced with the permission of The McGraw-Hill Companies.

Attempts to eliminate the grapevine are fruitless, but fortunately the manager does have some control over it. By maintaining open channels of communication and responding vigorously to inaccurate information, the manager can minimize the damage the grapevine can do. The grapevine can actually be an asset. By learning who the key people in the grapevine are, for example, the manager can partially control the information they receive and use the grapevine to sound out employee reactions to new ideas such as a change in human resource policies or benefit packages. The manager can also get valuable information from the grapevine and use it to improve decision making.

Management By Wandering Around

• **management by wandering around**
An approach to communication that involves the manager literally wandering around and having spontaneous conversations with others

Another increasingly popular form of informal communication is called **management by wandering around.**[32] The basic idea is that some managers keep in touch with what's going on by wandering around and talking with people—immediate subordinates, subordinates far down the organizational hierarchy, delivery people, customers, or anyone else who is involved with the company in some way. Bill Marriott, for example, frequently visits the kitchens, loading docks, and custodial work areas whenever he tours a Marriott hotel. He claims that by talking with employees throughout the hotel, he gets new ideas and has a better feel for the entire company.

A related form of organizational communication that really has no specific term is the informal interchange that takes place outside the normal work setting. Employees attending the company picnic, playing on the company softball team, or taking fishing trips together will almost always spend part of their time talking about work. For example, Texas Instruments engineers at TI's Lewisville, Texas, facility often frequent a local bar in town after work. On any given evening, they talk about the Dallas Cowboys, the newest government contract received by the company, the weather, their boss, the company's stock price, local politics, and problems at work. There is no set agenda, and the key topics of discussion vary from group to group and from day to day. Still, the social gatherings serve an important role. They promote a strong culture and enhance understanding of how the organization works.

Nonverbal Communication

Nonverbal communication is a communication exchange that does not use words or that uses words to carry more meaning than the strict definition of the words themselves. Nonverbal communication is a powerful but little-understood form of communication in organizations. It often relies on facial expression, body movements, physical contact, and gestures. One study found that as much as 55 percent of the content of a message is transmitted by facial expression and body posture and that another 38 percent derives from inflection and tone. Words themselves account for only 7 percent of the content of the message.[33]

nonverbal communication Any communication exchange that does not use words or that uses words to carry more meaning than the strict definition of the words themselves

Research has identified three kinds of nonverbal communication practiced by managers—images, settings, and body language.[34] In this context, images are the kinds of words people elect to use. "Damn the torpedoes, full speed ahead" and "Even though there are some potential hazards, we should proceed with this course of action" may convey the same meaning. Yet the person who uses the first expression may be perceived as a maverick, a courageous hero, an individualist, or a reckless and foolhardy adventurer. The person who uses the second might be described as aggressive, forceful, diligent, or narrow-minded and resistant to change. In short, our choice of words conveys much more than just the strict meaning of the words themselves.

The setting for communication also plays a major role in nonverbal communication. Boundaries, familiarity, the home turf, and other elements of the setting are all important. Much has been written about the symbols of power in organizations. The size and location of an office, the kinds of furniture in the office, and the accessibility of the person in the office all communicate useful information. For example, H. Ross Perot positions his desk so that it is always between him and a visitor. This keeps him in charge. When he wants a less formal dialogue, he moves around to the front of the desk and sits beside his visitor. Jim Treybig of Tandem Computers has his desk facing a side window so that when he turns around to greet a visitor there is never anything between them.[35]

A third form of nonverbal communication is body language.[36] The distance we stand from someone as we speak has meaning. In the United States, standing very close to someone you are talking to generally signals either familiarity or aggression. The English and Germans stand farther apart than Americans when talking, whereas the Arabs, Japanese, and Mexicans stand closer together.[37] Eye contact is another effective means of nonverbal communication. For example, prolonged eye contact might suggest either hostility or romantic interest. Other kinds of body language include body and arm movement, pauses in speech, and mode of dress.

The manager should be aware of the importance of nonverbal communication and recognize its potential impact. Giving an employee good news about a reward with the wrong nonverbal cues can destroy the reinforcement value of the reward. Likewise, reprimanding an employee but providing inconsistent nonverbal cues can limit the effectiveness of the sanctions. The tone of the message, where and how the message is delivered, facial expressions, and gestures can all amplify, or weaken, the message or change the message altogether.

MANAGING ORGANIZATIONAL COMMUNICATION

In view of the importance and pervasiveness of communication in organizations, it is vital for managers to understand how to manage the communication process.[38] Managers should understand how to maximize the potential benefits of communication and minimize the potential problems. We begin our discussion of communication management by considering the factors that might disrupt effective communication and how to deal with them.

Barriers to Communication

Several factors may disrupt the communication process or serve as barriers to effective communication.[39] As shown in Table 12.1, these may be divided into two classes: individual barriers and organizational barriers.

Individual Barriers Several individual barriers may disrupt effective communication. One common problem is conflicting or inconsistent signals. Another is lack of credibility. A manager is sending conflicting signals when she says on Monday that things should be done one way but then prescribes an entirely different procedure on Wednesday. Inconsistent signals are being sent by a manager who says that he has an "open door" policy and wants his subordinates to drop by but keeps his door closed and becomes irritated whenever someone stops in. Credibility problems arise when the sender is not considered a reliable source of information. He may not be trusted or may not be perceived as knowledgeable about the subject at hand. When a politician is caught withholding information or when

Numerous barriers can disrupt effective communication. Some of these barriers involve individual characteristics and processes. Others are a function of the organizational context in which communication is taking place.

TABLE 12.1 Barriers to Effective Communication

Individual Barriers	Organizational Barriers
Conflicting or inconsistent cues	Semantics
Credibility about the subject	Status or power differences
Reluctance to communicate	Different perceptions
Poor listening skills	Noise
Predispositions about the subject	Overload

a manager makes a series of bad decisions, the extent to which they will be listened to and believed thereafter diminishes. In extreme cases, people may talk about something they obviously know little or nothing about. Some people are simply reluctant to initiate a communication exchange. This reluctance may occur for a variety of reasons. A manager may be reluctant to tell subordinates about an impending budget cut because he knows they will be unhappy about it. Likewise, a subordinate may be reluctant to transmit information upward for fear of reprisal or because it is felt that such an effort would be futile.

Two other individual barriers to effective communication are poor listening habits and predispositions about the subject at hand. Some people are poor listeners. When someone is talking to them, they may be daydreaming, looking around, reading, or listening to another conversation. Because they are not concentrating on what is being said, they may not comprehend part or all of the message. They may even think that they really are paying attention, only to realize later that they cannot remember parts of the conversation. Receivers may also bring certain predispositions to the communication process. They may already have their minds made up, firmly set in a certain way. For example, a manager may have heard that his new boss is unpleasant and hard to work with. When she calls him in for an introductory meeting, he may go into that meeting predisposed to dislike her and discount what she has to say.

Organizational Barriers Other barriers to effective communication involve the organizational context in which the communication occurs. Semantics problems arise when words have different meanings for different people. Words and phrases such as *profit*, *increased output*, and *return on investment* may have positive meanings for managers but less positive meanings for labor. Communication problems may arise when people of different power or status try to communicate with each other. The company president may discount a suggestion from an operating employee, thinking, "How can someone at that level help me run my business?" Or, when the president goes out to inspect a new plant, workers may be reluctant to offer suggestions because of their lower status. The marketing vice president may have more power than the human resource vice president and consequently may not pay much attention to a staffing report submitted by the human resource department. If people perceive a situation differently, they may have difficulty communicating with one another. When two managers observe that a third manager has not spent much time in her office lately, one may believe that she has been to several important meetings while the other may think she is "hiding out." If they need to talk about her in some official capacity, problems may arise because one has a positive impression and the other a negative impression.

Environmental factors may also disrupt effective communication. As mentioned earlier, noise can affect communication in many ways. Similarly, overload may be a problem when the receiver is being sent more information than he or she can effectively handle. When the manager gives a subordinate many jobs on which to work and at the same time the subordinate is being told by family and friends to do other things, overload may result and communication effectiveness diminishes.

Improving Communication Effectiveness

Considering the many factors that can disrupt communication, it is fortunate that managers can resort to several techniques for improving communication effectiveness.[40] As shown in Table 12.2, these techniques include both individual and organizational skills.

Individual Skills The single most important individual skills for improving communication effectiveness is being a good listener. Being a good listener requires that the individual be prepared to listen, not interrupt the speaker, concentrate on both the words and the meaning being conveyed, be patient, and ask questions as appropriate.[41] So important are good listening skills that companies like Delta, IBM, and Unisys conduct programs to train their managers to be better listeners.

In addition to being a good listener, several other individual skills can promote effective communication. Feedback, one of the most important, is facilitated by two-way communication. Two-way communication allows the receiver to ask questions, request clarification, and express opinions that let the sender know whether he or she has been understood. In general, the more complicated the message, the more useful two-way communication is. In addition, the sender should be aware of the meanings that different receivers might attach to various words. For example, when addressing stockholders, a manager might use the word *profits* often. When addressing labor leaders, however, she may choose to use *profits* less often.

Furthermore, the sender should try to maintain credibility. This can be accomplished by not pretending to be an expert when one is not, by "doing one's homework" and checking facts, and by otherwise being as accurate and honest as possible. The sender should also try to be sensitive to the receiver's perspective. A manager who must tell a subordinate that she has not been recommended for a promotion should recognize that the subordinate will be frustrated and unhappy. The content of the message and its method of delivery should be chosen accordingly. The manager should be primed to accept a reasonable degree of hostility and bitterness without getting angry in return.[42] Finally, the receiver should try to be sensitive to the sender's point of view. Suppose that a manager has just received

Because communication is so important, managers have developed a number of methods for overcoming barriers to effective communication. Some of these methods involve individual skills, whereas others are based on organizational skills.

TABLE 12.2 Overcoming Barriers to Communication

Individual Skills	Organizational Skills
Develop good listening skills	Follow up
Encourage two-way communication	Regulate information flows
Be aware of language and meaning	Understand the richness of media
Maintain credibility	
Be sensitive to receiver's perspective	
Be sensitive to sender's perspective	

some bad news—for example, that his position is being eliminated next year. Others should understand that he may be disappointed, angry, or even depressed for a while. Thus they might make a special effort not to take too much offense if he snaps at them, and they might look for signals that he needs someone to talk to.

Organizational Skills Three useful organizational skills can also enhance communication effectiveness for both the sender and the receiver—following up, regulating information flow, and understanding the richness of different media. Following up simply involves checking at a later time to be sure that a message has been received and understood. After a manager mails a report to a colleague, she might call a few days later to make sure the report has arrived. If it has, the manager might ask whether the colleague has any questions about it. Regulating information flow means that the sender or receiver takes steps to ensure that overload does not occur. For the sender, this could mean not passing too much information through the system at one time. For the receiver, it might mean calling attention to the fact that he is being asked to do too many things at once. Many managers limit the influx of information by periodically weeding out the list of journals and routine reports they receive, or they train a secretary to screen phone calls and visitors. Both parties should also understand the richness associated with different media. When a manager is going to lay off a subordinate temporarily, the message should be delivered in person. A face-to-face channel of communication gives the manager an opportunity to explain the situation and answer questions. When the purpose of the message is to grant a pay increase, written communication may be appropriate because it can be more objective and precise. The manager could then follow up the written notice with personal congratulations.

SUMMARY OF KEY POINTS

Communication is the process of transmitting information from one person to another. Effective communication is the process of sending a message in such a way that the message received is as close in meaning as possible to the message intended. Communication is a pervasive and important part of the manager's world. For information to be useful, it must be accurate, timely, complete, and relevant. The communication process consists of a sender encoding meaning and transmitting it to one or more receivers, who receive the message and decode it into meaning. In two-way communication the process continues with the roles reversed. Noise can disrupt any part of the overall process.

Interpersonal communication focuses on communication among a small number of people. Two important forms of interpersonal communication, oral and written, both offer unique advantages and disadvantages. The manager should weigh the pros and cons of each when choosing a medium for communication.

There are a variety of forms of organizational communication. Vertical communication between superiors and subordinates may flow upward or downward. Horizontal communication involves peers and colleagues at the same level in the organization.

Organizations also use information systems to manage communication. Information technology systems contain five basic components: an input medium, a processor, storage, a control system, and an output medium. While the form will vary, both manual and computerized information systems have these components. There are four basic kinds of information systems: transaction-processing systems, basic management information systems, decision support systems, and executive information systems. Electronic communications is likely to have a profound effect on managerial and organizational communication in the years to come.

A great deal of informal communication also occurs in organizations. The grapevine is the informal communication network among people in an organization. Management by wandering around is also a popular informal method of communication. Nonverbal communication includes facial expressions, body movement, physical contact, gestures, and inflection and tone.

Managing the communication process necessitates recognizing the barriers to effective communication and understanding how to overcome them. Barriers can be identified at both the individual and organizational level. Likewise, both individual and organizational skills can be used to overcome these barriers.

QUESTIONS FOR REVIEW

1. Define *communication*. What are the components of the communication process?
2. Which form of interpersonal communication is best for long-term retention? Why? Which form is best for getting across subtle nuances of meaning? Why?
3. What are the informal methods of communication? Identify five examples of nonverbal communication that you have recently observed.
4. What are the characteristics of useful information? How can information management aid in organizational control?
5. What is a management information system? How can such a system be used to benefit an organization?

QUESTIONS FOR ANALYSIS

1. Is it possible for an organization to function without communication? Why or why not?
2. At what points in the communication process can problems occur? Give examples of communication problems, and indicate how they might be prevented or alleviated.
3. Which communication barriers are most likely to affect horizontal communication moreso than vertical communication? Which are most likely to affect vertical communication moreso than horizontal communication? How might a formal information system be designed to reduce such barriers?
4. It has been said that the information revolution now occurring is like the industrial revolution in terms of the magnitude of its impact on organizations and society. What leads to such a view? Why might that view be an overstatement?
5. Characterize your own strengths and weaknesses as a listener. How might you improve?

CASE STUDY

Compagnie des Machines Bull

Compagnie des Machines Bull (usually referred to as Bull or as Groupe Bull) was incorporated in 1933 in Paris. Bull was the first major company to move from electron tubes to germanium diodes in mainframe computers (in 1952). In 1964, however, it appeared that it would go bankrupt because it was unable to repay a $4 million loan associated with that undertaking. General Electric came to the rescue. GE saved Bull by buying a 66 percent share and renaming the company Bull-GE. This was the first of many years of partnerships, which included the French government, Zenith, Honeywell, and Packard Bell, as well as of bailouts.

Despite subsidies from the French government as its owner, Bull continued to lose money. To try to save the company, it began major reorganization, restructuring, and cost-cutting efforts in 1989. In 1991, as a further cost-cutting move, Bull let go of five thousand employees and closed seven of its thirteen plants. Bull's central administration's message was clear: If you can't make your plant profitable, it will be closed. At least one manager got that message loud and clear.

Joel Beck took a job loading trucks at a computer plant in Boston while he attended college at night. He stayed with the computer company and worked his way up to vice president of manufacturing at that plant. Then along came Bull.

Bull bought Beck's plant, and Beck got the message that unprofitable units would be closed. The plant employs about six hundred people and had not made a profit for Bull. To make matters worse, Beck's employees were largely poorly educated immigrants or minority group members who spoke a total of twenty-four different languages.

Although Beck got Bull's message, how was he going to communicate it to his workers and how

5. Lynda M. Applegate, James I. Cash, Jr., and D. Quinn Mills, "Information Technology and Tomorrow's Manager," *Harvard Business Review*, November–December 1988, pp. 128–136.
6. Carla Rapoport, "Great Japanese Mistakes," *Fortune*, February 13, 1989, pp. 108–111.
7. Brian Dumaine, "Corporate Spies Snoop to Conquer," *Fortune*, November 7, 1988, pp. 66–76.
8. John Huey, "Wal-Mart—Will It Take Over the World?" *Fortune*, January 30, 1989, pp. 52–61.
9. Mintzberg, *The Nature of Managerial Work*.
10. Walter Kiechel III, "The Big Presentation," *Fortune*, July 26, 1982, pp. 98–100.
11. "Executives Who Dread Public Speaking Learn to Keep Their Cool in the Spotlight," *The Wall Street Journal*, May 4, 1990, pp. B1, B6.
12. Mintzberg, *The Nature of Managerial Work*.
13. Kiechel, "The Big Presentation."
14. Robert H. Lengel and Richard L. Daft, "The Selection of Communication Media as an Executive Skill," *Academy of Management Executive*, August 1988, pp. 225–232.
15. Janet Fulk, "Social Construction of Communication Technology," *Academy of Management Journal*, 1993, Vol. 36, No. 5, pp. 921–950.
16. Nelson Phillips and John Brown, "Analyzing Communications in and Around Organizations: A Critical Hermeneutic Approach," *Academy of Management Journal*, 1993, Vol. 36, No. 6, pp. 1547–1576.
17. "Walter Kiechel III, "Breaking Bad News to the Boss," *Fortune*, April 9, 1990, pp. 111–112.
18. Myron Magnet, "Is ITT Fighting Shadows—Or Raiders?" *Fortune*, November 11, 1985, pp. 25–28.
19. Mary Young and James Post, "How Leading Companies Communicate with Employees," *Organizational Dynamics*, Summer 1993, pp. 31–43.
20. Brian Dumaine, "Corporate Spies Snoop to Conquer," *Fortune*, November 7, 1988, pp. 68–76.
21. "At Today's Supermarket, the Computer Is Doing It All," *Business Week*, August 11, 1986, pp. 64–66.
22. V. Thomas Dock and James C. Wetherbe, *Computer Information Systems for Business* (St. Paul, Minn.: West, 1988).
23. "An Electronic Pipeline That's Changing the Way America Does Business," *Business Week*, August 3, 1987, pp. 80–82.
24. Applegate, Cash, and Mills, "Information Technology and Tomorrow's Manager."
25. Jeremy Main, "At Last, Software CEOs Can Use," *Fortune*, March 13, 1989, pp. 77–83.
26. Huey, "Wal-Mart—Will It Take Over the World?"
27. Dorothy Leonard-Barton and John J. Sviokla, "Putting Expert Systems to Work," *Harvard Business Review*, March–April 1988, pp. 91–98.
28. "Turning an Expert's Skills into Computer Software," *Business Week*, October 7, 1985, pp. 104–108.
29. Keith Davis, "Management Communication and the Grapevine," *Harvard Business Review*, September–October 1953, pp. 43–49.
30. "Spread the Word: Gossip Is Good," *The Wall Street Journal*, October 4, 1988, p. B1.
31. See David M. Schweiger and Angelo S. DeNisi, "Communication with Employees Following a Merger: A Longitudinal Field Experiment," *Academy of Management Journal*, March 1991, pp. 110–135.
32. See Tom Peters and Nancy Austin, *A Passion for Excellence* (New York: Random House, 1985).
33. Albert Mehrabian, *Non-verbal Communication* (Chicago: Aldine, 1972).
34. Michael B. McCaskey, "The Hidden Messages Managers Send," *Harvard Business Review*, November–December 1979, pp. 135–148.
35. Thomas Moore, "Make-or-Break Time for General Motors," *Fortune*, February 15, 1988, pp. 32–42; Brian O'Reilly, "How Jimmy Treybig Turned Tough," *Fortune*, May 25, 1987, pp. 102–104.
36. David Givens, "What Body Language Can Tell You That Words Cannot," *U.S. News & World Report*, November 19, 1984, p. 100.
37. Edward J. Hall, *The Hidden Dimension* (New York: Doubleday, 1966).
38. For a detailed discussion of improving communication effectiveness, see Courtland L. Bove and John V. Thill, *Business Communication Today*, 3rd ed. (New York: McGraw-Hill, 1992).
39. See Otis W. Baskin and Craig E. Aronoff, *Interpersonal Communication in Organizations* (Glenview, Ill.: Scott, Foresman, 1980).
40. Joseph Allen and Bennett P. Lientz, *Effective Business Communication* (Santa Monica, Calif.: Goodyear, 1979).
41. Walter Kiechel III, "Learn How to Listen," *Fortune*, August 17, 1987, pp. 107–108.
42. For a recent discussion of these and related issues, see Eric M. Eisenberg and Marsha G. Witten, "Reconsidering Openness in Organizational Communication," *Academy of Management Review*, July 1987, pp. 418–426.

CHAPTER

13

Managing Groups and Teams

OBJECTIVES

After studying this chapter, you should be able to:

- *Define and identify types of groups and teams in organizations, discuss reasons people join groups, and define the stages of group development.*
- *Identify and discuss four essential characteristics of teams.*
- *Discuss interpersonal and intergroup conflict in organizations.*
- *Describe how organizations manage conflict.*

OUTLINE

OPENING INCIDENT

SOUTHWEST AIRLINES HAS long been famed for its open, participative culture that fosters involvement, dedication, and commitment. Indeed, that culture is the stuff of business legend. Now, however, one of Southwest's biggest competitors—United Airlines—is taking dead aim at the high-flying regional carrier by trying to copy some of its employment and work practices.

For years United has seen Southwest invade its turf, undercut its prices, and take away vast chunks of its market share. Since Southwest entered the West Coast market in 1989, it has taken more than 44 percent of the market, leaving United with less than 30 percent. Southwest uses its low-cost base to maintain profits while forcing competitors to abandon their routes.

Recently, United decided to fight back. The firm launched what amounts to a new airline called the United Shuttle. The Shuttle will compete head-to-head with Southwest on most of its lucrative West Coast routes. Just as significant as the venture itself, however, is how United planned and implemented its new operation. Specifically, United used teams of workers to plan and design virtually every aspect of the Shuttle.

The company identified one hundred workers for the project, including baggage handlers, reservation clerks, flight attendants, and pilots. These workers were then formed into twenty-two teams that spent six weeks searching for ways to operate the Shuttle more competitively. Their goal was to create a new airline that was more efficient, less expensive, and just as satisfying to customers as Southwest.

> **"If management had made the decisions, they would have been made faster. But they would have been wrong."**

One team studied baggage loading. Previously, all bags on United flights were first unloaded off a plane, and then new bags were put on. For the Shuttle, however, bags are unloaded from one end as new bags are put in the other end. Another team designed a new and more efficient way to seat passengers. All window-seat passengers board first, then middle-seat passengers board, and finally aisle-seat passengers board last. United claims that this system is two minutes faster than the one used by Southwest (boarding the plane in thirds, back to front).

The pilots also came up with some time-saving suggestions of their own. For example, they now have the authority to decide whether some minor nonoperational mechanical problems (such as a broken coffee pot) are sufficient to delay a flight. Similarly, they suggested using their engines to move away from the gate, rather than being towed, to save another three minutes. It is far too early, of course, to know how well the Shuttle will fly. But it looks like a good bet so far.[1]

Source of Quotation: Rono Dutta, United Shuttle Development vice president, quoted in *USA Today*, September 30, 1994, p. 1B.

Managers at United Airlines recognized and took advantage of what many experts are increasingly seeing as a tremendous resource for all organizations—the power of groups and teams. Rather than operate as individual performers reporting to a supervisor, employees at United functioned as members of a team as they sought to design a new product and a new way of doing business.

This chapter is about processes that lead to and follow from activities like those at United. We begin this chapter by introducing basic concepts of group and team dynamics. Subsequent sections explain the characteristics of groups and teams in organizations. We then describe interpersonal and intergroup conflict. Finally, we conclude with a discussion of how conflict can be managed.

GROUPS AND TEAMS IN ORGANIZATIONS

Groups are a ubiquitous part of organizational life. They are the basis for much of the work that gets done, and they evolve both inside and outside the normal structural boundaries of the organization. We will define a **group** as two or more persons who interact regularly to accomplish a common purpose or goal.[2] The purpose of a group or team may range from preparing a new advertising campaign to informally sharing information to making important decisions to fulfilling social needs.[3]

• **group**
Two or more persons who interact regularly to accomplish a common purpose or goal

Types of Groups and Teams

In general, three basic kinds of groups are found in organizations: functional groups, task groups and teams, and informal or interest groups.[4] These are illustrated in Figure 13.1.

• **functional group**
A group created by the organization to accomplish a number of organizational purposes with an indefinite time horizon

Functional Groups A **functional group** is a permanent group created by the organization to accomplish a number of organizational purposes with an unspecified time horizon. The marketing department of Kmart, the management department of the University of North Texas, and the nursing staff of the Mayo Clinic are functional groups. The marketing department at Kmart, for example, seeks to plan effective advertising campaigns, increase sales, run in-store promotions, and develop a unique identity for the company. The functional group remains in existence after it attains its current objectives—those objectives are replaced by new ones.

• **informal group; interest group**
A group created by its members for purposes that may or may not be relevant to the organization's goals

Informal or Interest Groups An **informal** or **interest group** is created by its own members for purposes that may or may not be relevant to organizational goals. A group of employees who lunch together everyday may be discussing how to improve productivity, how to embezzle money, or local politics and sports. As long as the group members enjoy eating together, they will probably continue to do so. When lunches cease to be pleasant, they will seek other company or a different activity. Informal groups can be a powerful force that managers cannot ignore. One writer described how a group of employees at a furniture factory subverted their

FIGURE 13.1 Types of Groups in Organizations

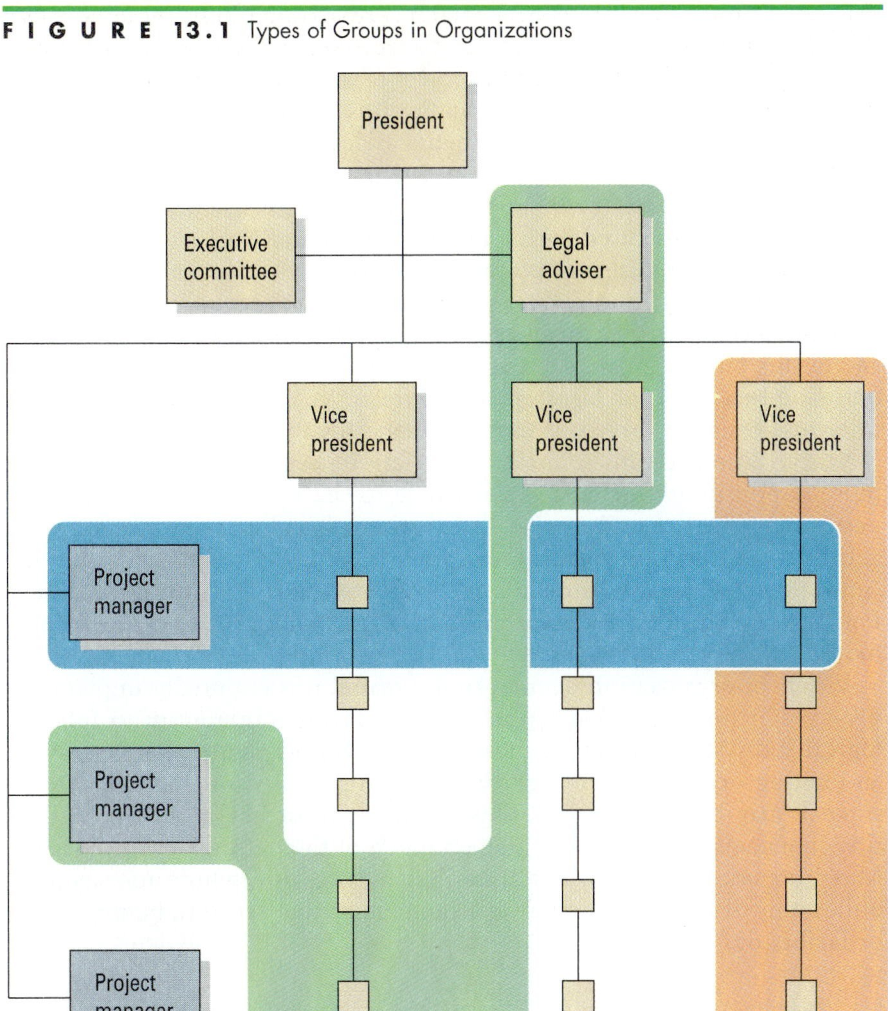

Every organization has many different types of groups. In this hypothetical organization, a functional group is shown within the orange area, a cross-functional group within the blue area, and an informal group within the green area.

boss's efforts to increase production. They tacitly agreed to produce a reasonable amount of work but not to work too hard. One man kept a stockpile of completed work hidden as a backup in case he got too far behind.[5] Of course, informal groups can be a positive force, as demonstrated several years ago when Delta's employees worked together to buy a new plane for the company to show their support.

Task Groups A **task group** is a group created by the organization to accomplish a relatively narrow range of purposes within a stated or implied time horizon. Most committees and task forces are task groups. The organization specifies group membership and assigns a relatively narrow set of goals, such as developing a new product or evaluating a proposed

● **task group**
A group created by the organization to accomplish a relatively narrow range of purposes within a stated or implied time horizon

grievance procedure. The time horizon for accomplishing these purposes is either specified (a committee may be asked to make a recommendation within sixty days) or implied (the project team will disband when the new product is developed). For example, Ford used a task force to design the newest version of the Mustang. When the design was completed, the task force was dissolved.

team
A group of workers that functions as a unit, often with little or no supervision, to carry out organizational functions

Teams are a special form of task group that has become increasingly popular. In the sense used here, a **team** is a group of workers that functions as a unit, often with little or no supervision, to carry out organizational functions. Table 13.1 lists and defines some of the various types of teams that are being used today. Earlier forms of teams included autonomous work groups and quality circles. Today, teams are also sometimes called *self-managed teams*, *cross-functional teams*, or *high-performance teams*. Many companies today routinely use teams to carry out most of their daily operations.[6]

Organizations create teams for a variety of reasons. For one, they give more responsibility for task performance to the workers who are actually performing the tasks. They also empower workers by giving them greater authority and decision-making freedom. In addition, teams allow the organization to capitalize on the knowledge and motivation of its workers. Finally, they enable the organization to shed its bureaucracy and to promote flexibility and responsiveness.[7]

When an organization decides to use teams, it is essentially implementing a major form of organization change. Thus it is important to follow a logical and systematic approach to planning and implementing teams into an existing organization design. It is also important to recognize that resistance may be encountered. This resistance most likely will come from first-line managers who must give up much of their authority to the team. Many organizations find that they must change the whole management philosophy of such managers away from being a supervisor to being a coach or facilitator.[8]

TABLE 13.1 Types of Teams

Problem-solving team Most popular type of team; comprises knowledgeable workers who gather to solve a specific problem and then disband

Management team Consists mainly of managers from various functions like sales and production; coordinates work among other teams

Work team An increasingly popular type of team, work teams are responsible for the daily work of the organization; when empowered, they are self-managed teams

Virtual team A new type of work team that interacts by computer; members enter and leave the network as needed and may take turns serving as leader

Quality circle Declining in popularity, quality circles, comprising workers and supervisors, meet intermittently to discuss workplace problems

Source: "Types of Teams" adapted from Brian Dumaine, "The Trouble with Teams," *Fortune*, September 5, 1994.

After teams are in place, managers should continue to monitor their contributions and how effectively they are functioning. In the best circumstance, teams become very cohesive groups with high performance norms. To achieve this state, the manager can use any or all of the techniques described later in this chapter for enhancing cohesiveness. If implemented properly, and with the support of the workers themselves, performance norms will likely be relatively high. That is, if the change is properly implemented, the team participants will understand the value and potential of teams and the rewards they may expect to get as a result of their contributions. On the other hand, poorly designed and implemented teams will do a less effective job and may detract from organizational effectiveness.[9]

Why People Join Groups and Teams

People join groups for a variety of reasons. They join functional groups simply by virtue of joining organizations. People accept employment to earn money or to practice their chosen profession. Once inside the organization, they are assigned to jobs and roles and thus become members of functional groups. People in existing functional groups are told, are asked, or volunteer to serve on committees, task forces, and teams. People join informal or interest groups for a variety of reasons, most of them quite complex.[10]

Interpersonal Attraction One reason people choose to form informal or interest groups is that they are attracted to each other. Many different factors contribute to interpersonal attraction.[11] When people see a lot of each other, pure proximity increases the likelihood that interpersonal attraction will develop. Attraction is increased when people have similar attitudes, personality, or economic standing.

Group Activities Individuals may also be motivated to join a group because the activities of the group appeal to them. Jogging, playing bridge, bowling, discussing poetry, playing war games, and flying model airplanes are all activities that some people enjoy. Many of them are more enjoyable to participate in as a member of a group, and most require more than one person. Many large firms like Exxon and Microsoft have a league of football, softball, or bowling teams. A person may join a bowling team not because of any noticeable attraction to other group members but simply because being a member of the group allows that person to participate in a pleasant activity. Of course, if the level of interpersonal attraction of the group is very low, a person may choose to forgo the activity rather than join the group.

Group Goals The goals of a group may also motivate people to join. The Sierra Club, which is dedicated to environmental conservation, is a good example of this kind of interest group. Various fundraising groups are another illustration. Members may or may not be personally attracted to the other fundraisers, and they probably do not enjoy the activity of knocking on doors asking for money, but they join the group because they subscribe to its goal. Workers join unions like the United Auto Workers because they support its goals.

Need Satisfaction Still another reason for joining a group is to satisfy the need for affiliation. New residents in a community may join the Newcomers Club partially as a way to meet new people and partially just to be around other people. Likewise, newly divorced individuals often join support groups as a way to have companionship.

Instrumental Benefits A final reason people join groups is that membership is sometimes seen as instrumental in providing other benefits to the individual. For example, it is fairly common for college students entering their senior year to join several professional clubs or associations because listing such memberships on a résumé is thought to enhance the chances of getting a good job. Similarly, a manager might join a certain racquet club not because she is attracted to its members (although she might be) and not because of the opportunity to play tennis (although she may enjoy it). The club's goals are not relevant and her affiliation needs may be satisfied in other ways. She may feel that being a member of this club will lead to important and useful business contacts. The racquet club membership is instrumental in establishing those contacts. Membership in civic groups such as Kiwanis and Rotary may be solicited for similar reasons.

Stages of Group and Team Development

Imagine the differences between a collection of five people who have just been brought together to form a new group or team and a group or team that has functioned like a well-oiled machine for years. Members of a new group or team are unfamiliar with how they will function together and are tentative in their interactions. In a group or team with considerable experience, members are familiar with one another's strengths and weaknesses and are more secure in their role in the group. The former group or team is generally considered to be immature; the latter, mature. To progress from the immature phase to the mature phase, a group or team must go through certain stages of development, as shown in Figure 13.2.[12]

The first stage of development is *forming*. The members of the group or team get acquainted and begin to test which interpersonal behaviors are acceptable and which are unacceptable to the other members. The members are very dependent on others at this point to provide cues about what is acceptable. The basic ground rules for the group or team are established and a tentative group structure may emerge. At Reebok, for example, a merchandising team was created to handle its new sportswear business. The team leader and his members were barely acquainted and had to spend a few weeks getting to know one another.

The second stage of development, often slow to emerge, is *storming*. During this stage there may be a general lack of unity and uneven interaction patterns. At the same time, some members of the group or team may begin to exert themselves to become recognized as the group leader or at least to play a major role in shaping the group's agenda. In Reebok's team, some members advocated a rapid expansion into the marketplace; others argued for a slower entry. The first faction won, with disastrous results. Because of the rush, product quality was poor and deliveries were late. As a result, the team leader was fired and a new manager placed in charge.

FIGURE 13.2 Stages of Group Development

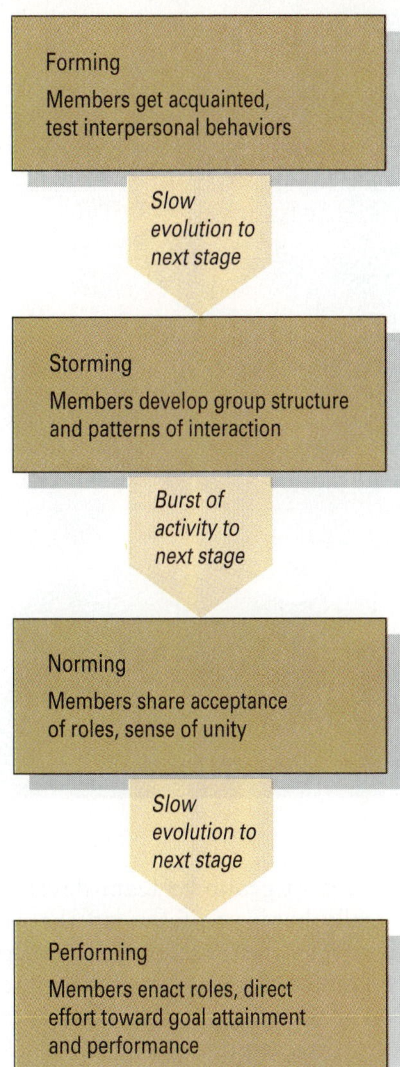

As groups mature, they tend to evolve through four distinct stages of development. Managers must understand that group members need time to become acquainted, accept each other, develop a group structure, and become comfortable with their roles in the group before they can begin to work directly to accomplish goals.

The third stage of development, called *norming*, usually begins with a burst of activity. During this stage each person begins to recognize and accept her or his role and to understand the roles of others. Members also begin to accept one another and to develop a sense of unity. There may also be temporary regressions to the previous stage. For example, the group or team might begin to accept one particular member as the leader. If this person later violates important norms and otherwise jeopardizes his or her claim to leadership, conflict might reemerge as the group rejects this leader and searches for another. Reebok's new leader transferred several people away from the team and set up a new system and structure for managing things. The remaining employees accepted his new approach and settled into doing their jobs.

Groups and teams progress through a series of development stages as they evolve toward "maturity." These managers work for the Bank of Boston. They are a cross-functional team working on problems identified through a recent survey of customer satisfaction. Because they already know each other and appear to be working productively, they have likely reached the performing stage of development and are dedicating all their energies to accomplishing the team's goal.

Performing, the final stage of group or team development, is again slow to develop. The team really begins to focus on the problem at hand. The members enact the roles they have accepted, interaction occurs, and the efforts of the group are directed toward goal attainment. The basic structure of the group or team is no longer an issue but has become a mechanism for accomplishing the purpose of the group. Reebok's sportswear business is now growing consistently and has successfully avoided the problems that plagued it at first.[13]

CHARACTERISTICS OF TEAMS

As groups and teams mature and pass through the four basic stages of development, they begin to take on four important characteristics—a role structure, norms, cohesiveness, and informal leadership.[14]

Role Structures

• **role**
The part an individual plays in a group to help the group reach its goals

Each individual in a team has a part—or **role**—to play in helping the group reach its goals. Some people are leaders, some do the work, some interface with other teams, and so on. Indeed, a person may take on a *task-specialist role* (concentrating on getting the group's task accomplished) or a *socio-emotional role* (providing social and emotional support to others on the team). A few people, usually the leaders, perform both roles; a few others may do neither. The group's **role structure** is the set of defined roles and interrelationships among those roles that the group or team members define and accept. Each of us belongs to many groups and therefore plays multiple roles—in work groups, classes, families, and social organizations.[15]

role structure
The set of defined roles and interrelationships among those roles that the group or team members define and accept

Role structures emerge as a result of role episodes, as shown in Figure 13.3. The process begins with the expected role—what other members of the team expect the individual to do. The expected role gets translated into the sent role—the messages and cues that team members use to communicate the expected role to the individual. The perceived role is what the individual perceives the sent role to mean. Finally, the enacted role is what the individual actually does in the role. The enacted role, in turn, influences future expectations of the team. Of course, role episodes seldom unfold this easily. When major disruptions occur, individuals may experience role ambiguity, conflict, or overload.

Role Ambiguity **Role ambiguity** arises when the sent role is unclear. If your instructor tells you to write a term paper but refuses to provide more information, you probably will experience role ambiguity. You do not know what the topic is, how long the paper should be, what format to use, or when the paper is due. In work settings, role ambiguity can stem from poor job descriptions, vague instructions from a supervisor, or unclear cues from coworkers. The result is likely to be a subordinate who does not know what to do. Role ambiguity can be a significant problem for both the individual who must contend with it and the organization that expects the employee to perform.

role ambiguity
Arises when the sent role is unclear and the individual does not know what is expected of him or her

Role Conflict **Role conflict** occurs when the messages and cues composing the sent role are clear but contradictory or mutually exclusive.[16] One common form is *interrole conflict*—conflict between roles. For example, if a person's boss says that to get ahead one must work evenings and weekends, and the same person's spouse says that more time is needed at home with the family, conflict may result.[17] In a matrix organization, interrole conflict often arises between the roles one plays in different teams as well as between team roles and one's permanent role in a functional group.

role conflict
Occurs when the messages and cues comprising the sent role are clear but contradictory or mutually exclusive

Intrarole conflict may occur when the person gets conflicting demands from different sources within the context of the same role. A manager's

FIGURE 13.3 The Development of a Role

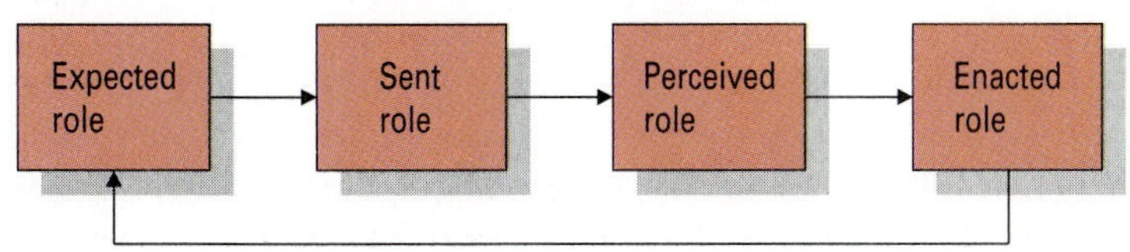

Roles and role structures within a group generally evolve through a series of role episodes. The first two stages of role development are group processes as the group members let individuals know what is expected of them. The other two parts are individual processes as the new group members perceive and enact their roles.

boss may tell her that she needs to put more pressure on subordinates to follow new work rules. At the same time, her subordinates may indicate that they expect her to get the rules changed. Thus the cues are in conflict, and the manager may be unsure about which course to follow. *Intrasender conflict* occurs when a single source sends clear but contradictory messages, such as when the boss says one morning that there can be no more overtime for the next month but after lunch tells someone to work late that same evening. *Person-role conflict* results from a discrepancy between the role requirements and the individual's personal values, attitudes, and needs. If a person is told to do something unethical or illegal, or if the work is distasteful (for example, firing a close friend), person-role conflict is likely. Role conflict of all varieties is of particular concern to managers. Research has shown that conflict may occur in a variety of situations and lead to a variety of adverse consequences, including stress, poor performance, and rapid turnover.[18]

• **role overload**
Occurs when expectations for the role exceed the individual's capabilities to perform

Role Overload A final consequence of a weak role structure is **role overload**, which occurs when expectations for the role exceed the individual's capabilities. When a manager gives an employee several major assignments at once while increasing the person's regular workload, the employee will probably experience role overload. Role overload may also result when an individual takes on too many roles at one time. For example, a person trying to work extra hard at his job, run for election to the school board, serve on a committee in church, coach Little League baseball, maintain an active exercise program, and be a contributing member to his family will probably encounter role overload.

Implications In a functional group or team, the manager can take steps to avoid role ambiguity, conflict, and overload. Having clear and reasonable expectations and sending clear and straightforward cues go a long way toward eliminating role ambiguity. Consistent expectations that take into account the employee's other roles and personal value system may minimize role conflict. Role overload can be avoided simply by recognizing the individual's capabilities and limits. In friendship and interest groups, role structures are likely to be less formal; hence, the possibility of role ambiguity, conflict, or overload may not be so great. However, if one or more of these problems do occur, they may be difficult to handle. Because roles in friendship and interest groups are less likely to be partially defined by a formal authority structure or written job descriptions, the individual cannot turn to these sources to clarify a role.

Behavioral Norms

• **norms**
Standards of behavior that the group accepts and expects of its members

Norms are standards of behavior that the group or team accepts for its members. That is, norms define the boundaries between acceptable and unacceptable behavior.[19] Some groups develop norms that limit the upper bounds of behavior to "make life easier" for the group. In general, these norms are counterproductive—don't ask questions in a committee meeting or don't produce any more than you have to. Other groups may develop norms that limit the lower bounds of behavior. These norms tend to reflect motivation, commitment, and high performance—don't come to meetings unless you've read the reports to be discussed or produce as much as you can. Managers can sometimes use norms for the betterment of the organization. For example, Kodak has successfully used group norms to reduce injuries in some of its plants.[20]

Norm Generalization The norms of one group cannot always be generalized to another group. Some academic departments, for example, have a norm that suggests that faculty members dress up on teaching days. People who fail to observe this norm are "punished" by sarcastic remarks or even formal reprimands. In other departments the norm may be casual clothes, and the person unfortunate enough to wear dress clothes may be punished just as strongly. Even within the same work area, similar groups or teams can develop different norms. One team may strive always to produce above its assigned quota; another may maintain productivity just below its quota. The norm of one team may be to be friendly and cordial to its supervisor; that of another team may be to remain aloof and distant. Some differences are due primarily to the composition of the teams.

Norm Variation In some cases there can be norm variation within a group or team. A common norm is that the least senior member of a group is expected to perform unpleasant or trivial tasks for the rest of the group. These tasks might be to wait on customers who are known to be small tippers (in a restaurant), to deal with complaining customers (in a department store), or to handle the low commission line of merchandise (in a sales department). Another example is when certain individuals, especially informal leaders, violate some norms. If the team is going to meet at 8 o'clock, anyone arriving late will be chastised for holding things up. Occasionally, however, the informal leader may arrive a few minutes late. As long as this does not happen too often, the group will probably not do anything.

Norm Conformity Four sets of factors contribute to norm conformity. First, factors associated with the group are important. For example, some groups or teams may exert more pressure for conformity than others. Second, the initial stimulus that prompts behavior can affect conformity. The more ambiguous the stimulus (for example, news that the team is going to be transferred to a new unit), the more pressure there is to conform. Third, individual traits determine the individual's propensity to conform (for example, more intelligent people are often less susceptible to pressure to conform). Finally, situational factors such as team size and unanimity influence conformity. As an individual learns the group's norms, he can do several different things. The most obvious is to adopt the norms. For example, the new male professor who notices that all the other men in the department dress up to teach can also start wearing a suit. A variation is to try to obey the "spirit" of the norm while retaining individuality. The professor may recognize that the norm is actually to wear a tie; thus he might succeed by wearing a tie with his sport shirt, jeans, and sneakers.

The individual may also ignore the norm. When a person does not conform, several things can happen. At first the group may increase its communication with the deviant individual to try to bring her back in line. If this does not work, communication may decline. Over time, the group may begin to exclude the individual from its activities and, in effect, ostracize the person.

Finally, we need to briefly consider another aspect of norm conformity—socialization. **Socialization** is generalized norm conformity that occurs as a person makes the transition from being an outsider to being an insider. A newcomer to an organization, for example, gradually begins to learn the norms about such things as dress, working hours, and interpersonal relations. As the newcomer adopts these norms, she is being socialized into the organizational culture. Some organizations, like Texas Instruments, work actively to manage the socialization process; others leave it to happenstance.[21]

● **socialization** Generalized norm conformity that occurs as a person makes the transition from being an outsider to being an insider in the organization

Cohesiveness

A third important team characteristic is cohesiveness. **Cohesiveness** is the extent to which members are loyal and committed to the group. In a highly cohesive team, the members work well together, support and trust one another, and are generally effective at achieving their chosen goal. In contrast, a team that lacks cohesiveness is not very coordinated, and its members do not necessarily support one another fully and may have a difficult time reaching goals. Of particular interest are the factors that increase and reduce cohesiveness and the consequences of team cohesiveness; these are listed in Table 13.2.

● **cohesiveness** The extent to which members are loyal and committed to the group; the degree of mutual attractiveness within the group

Factors That Increase Cohesiveness Five factors can increase the level of cohesiveness in a group or team. One of the strongest is intergroup competition. When two or more groups are in direct competition (for example, three sales groups competing for top sales honors or two football teams competing for a conference championship), each group is likely to become more cohesive. Second, just as personal attraction plays a role in causing a group to form, so too does attraction seem to enhance cohesiveness. Third, favorable evaluation of the entire group by outsiders can increase cohesiveness.[22] Thus a group's winning a sales contest or a conference title or receiving recognition and praise from a superior will tend to increase cohesiveness.

TABLE 13.2 Factors That Influence Group Cohesiveness

Factors That Increase Cohesiveness	Factors That Reduce Cohesiveness
Intergroup competition	Group size
Personal attraction	Disagreement on goals
Favorable evaluation	Intragroup competition
Agreement on goals	Domination
Interaction	Unpleasant experiences

Several different factors can potentially influence the cohesiveness of a group. For example, a manager can establish intergroup competition, assign compatible members to the group, create opportunities for success, establish acceptable goals, and foster interaction to increase cohesiveness. Other factors can be used to decrease cohesiveness.

Team cohesiveness is a major contributing factor to the performance and success of any team. These workers are part of a Habitat for Humanity team constructing homes in Atlanta. They share the same goals and recognize the value of working together.

Fourth, if all the members of the group or team agree on their goals, cohesiveness is likely to increase.[23] Finally, the more frequently members of the group interact with each other, the more likely the group is to become cohesive. A manager who wants to foster a high level of cohesiveness in a team might do well to establish some form of intergroup competition, assign members to the group who are likely to be attracted to one another, provide opportunities for success, establish goals that all members are likely to accept, and allow ample opportunity for interaction.

Factors That Reduce Cohesiveness Five factors are also known to reduce team cohesiveness. First, cohesiveness tends to decline as a group increases in size. Second, when members of a team disagree on what the goals of the group should be, cohesiveness may decrease. For example, when some members believe the group should maximize output and others think output should be restricted, cohesiveness declines. Third, intragroup competition reduces cohesiveness. When members are competing among themselves, they focus more on their own actions and behaviors than on those of the group.

Fourth, domination by one or more persons in the group or team may cause overall cohesiveness to decline. Other members may feel that they are not being given an opportunity to interact and contribute, and they may become less attracted to the group as a consequence. Finally, unpleasant experiences that result from group membership may reduce cohesiveness. A sales group that comes in last in a sales contest, an athletic team that sustains a long losing streak, and a work group reprimanded for poor-quality work may all become less cohesive as a result of their unpleasant experiences.

Consequences of Cohesiveness In general, as teams become more cohesive, their members tend to interact more frequently, conform more to norms, and become more satisfied with the team. Although cohesiveness may influence team performance, performance is also influenced by the team's performance norms. Figure 13.4 shows how cohesiveness and performance norms interact to help shape team performance.

When both cohesiveness and performance norms are high, high performance should result because the team wants to perform at a high level (norms) and its members are working together toward that end (cohesiveness). When norms are high and cohesiveness is low, performance will be moderate. Although the team wants to perform at a high level, its members are not necessarily working well together. When norms are low, performance will be low, regardless of whether group cohesiveness is high or low. The least desirable situation occurs when low performance norms are combined with high cohesiveness. In this case, all team members embrace the standard of restricting performance (owing to the low performance norm), and the group is united in its efforts to maintain that standard (owing to the high cohesiveness). If cohesiveness were low, the manager might be able to raise performance norms by establishing high goals and rewarding goal attainment or by bringing in new group members who were high performers. But a highly cohesive group is likely to resist these interventions.[24]

Informal Leadership

Most functional groups and teams have a formal leader—that is, one appointed by the organization or chosen or elected by the members of the group. Because friendship and interest groups are formed by the members themselves, however, any formal leader must be elected or designated by the members. Although some groups do designate such a leader (a softball team may elect a captain, for example), many do not. Moreover, even when a formal leader is designated, the group or team may also look to others

FIGURE 13.4 The Interaction Between Cohesiveness and Performance Norms

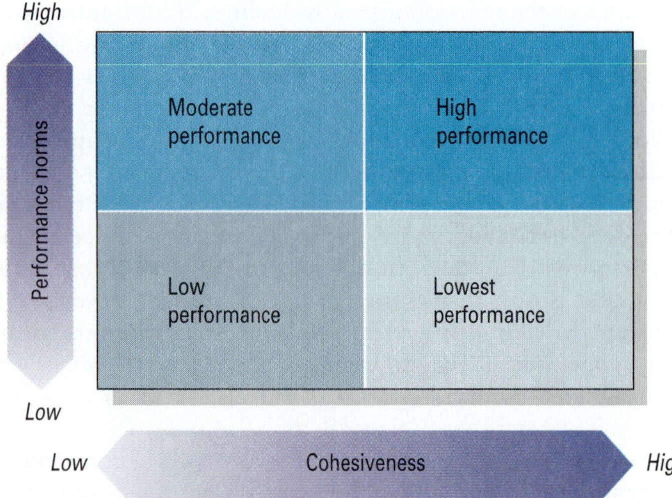

Group cohesiveness and performance norms interact to determine group performance. From the manager's perspective, high cohesiveness combined with high performance norms is the best situation, and high cohesiveness with low performance norms is the worst situation. Managers who can influence the level of cohesiveness and performance norms can greatly improve the effectiveness of a work group.

for leadership. An **informal leader** is a person who engages in leadership activities but whose right to do so has not been formally recognized. The formal and the informal leader in any group or team may be the same person, or they may be different people. An informal leader is likely to be a person capable of carrying out both roles effectively. If the formal leader can fulfill one role but not the other, an informal leader often emerges to supplement the formal leader's functions. If the formal leader cannot fill either role, one or more informal leaders may emerge to carry out both sets of functions.

informal leader
A person who engages in leadership activities but whose right to do so has not been formally recognized by the organization or group

Is informal leadership desirable? In many cases informal leaders are quite powerful because they draw from referent or expert power. When they are working in the best interest of the organization, they can be a tremendous asset. Notable athletes such as David Robinson, Joe Montana, and Nolan Ryan are classic examples of informal leaders. When informal leaders work counter to the goals of the organization, they can cause significant difficulties. Such leaders may lower performance norms, instigate walkouts or wildcat strikes, or otherwise disrupt the organization.

INTERPERSONAL AND INTERGROUP CONFLICT

Of course, when people work together in an organization, things do not always go smoothly. Indeed, conflict is an inevitable element of interpersonal relationships in organizations. In this section we will look at how conflict affects overall performance. We also explore the causes of conflict between individuals, between groups, and between an organization and its environment.

The Nature of Conflict

Conflict is a disagreement among two or more individuals, groups, or organizations. This disagreement may be relatively superficial or very strong. It may be short-lived or exist for months or even years, and it may be work-related or personal. Conflict may manifest itself in a variety of ways. People may compete with one another, glare at one another, shout, or withdraw. Groups may band together to protect popular members or oust unpopular members. Organizations may seek legal remedy.

conflict
A disagreement among two or more individuals, groups, or organizations

Most people assume that conflict is something to be avoided because it connotes antagonism, hostility, unpleasantness, and dissension. Indeed, managers and management theorists have traditionally viewed conflict as a problem to be avoided.[25] In recent years, however, we have come to recognize that although conflict can be a major problem, certain kinds of conflict may be beneficial.[26] For example, when two members of a site selection committee disagree over the best location for a new plant, each may be forced to more thoroughly study and defend his or her preferred alternative. As a result of more systematic analysis and discussion, the committee may make a better decision and be better prepared to justify it to others than if everyone had agreed from the outset and accepted an alternative that was perhaps less well analyzed.

As long as conflict is being handled in a cordial and constructive manner, it is probably serving a useful purpose in the organization. On the other hand, when working relationships are being disrupted and the conflict has reached destructive levels, it has likely become dysfunctional and needs to be addressed.[27] We discuss ways of dealing with such conflict later in this Chapter.

Figure 13.5 depicts the general relationship between conflict and performance for a group or organization. If there is absolutely no conflict in the group or organization, its members may become complacent and apathetic. As a result, group or organizational performance and innovation may subsequently begin to suffer. A moderate level of conflict among group or organizational members, on the other hand, can spark motivation, creativity, innovation, and initiative and raise performance. Too much conflict, though, can produce such undesirable results as hostility and lack of cooperation, which lower performance. The key for managers is to find and maintain the optimal amount of conflict that fosters performance. Of course, what constitutes optimal conflict varies with both the situation and the people involved.[28]

Causes of Conflict

Conflict may arise in both interpersonal and intergroup relationships. Occasionally, conflict between individuals and groups may be caused by

Either too much or too little conflict can be dysfunctional for an organization. In either case performance may be low. An optimal level of conflict that sparks motivation, creativity, innovation, and initiative can result in higher levels of performance. T. J. Rodgers, CEO of Cypress Semiconductor, maintains a moderate level of conflict in his organization as a way of keeping people energized and motivated.

FIGURE 13.5 The Nature of Organizational Conflict

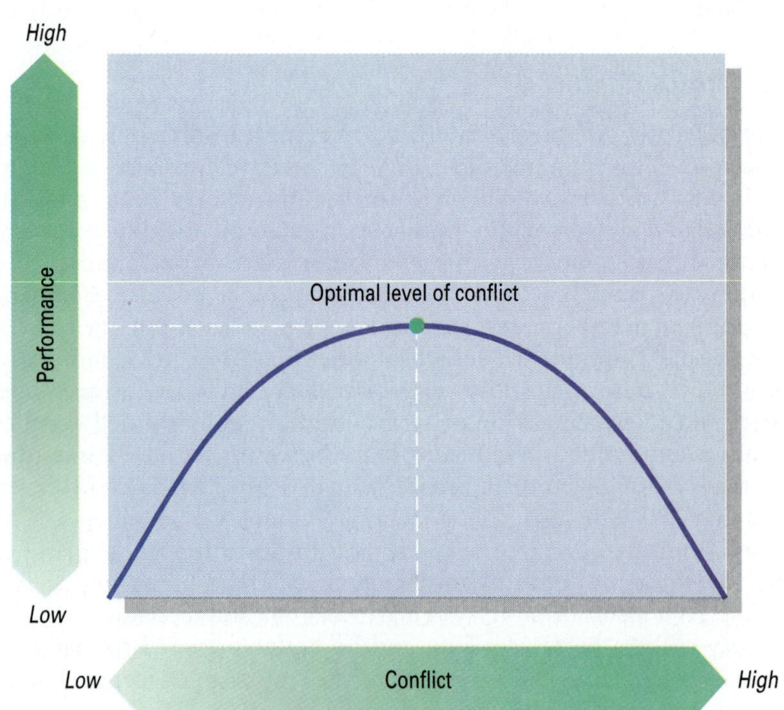

particular organizational strategies and practices. A third arena for conflict is between an organization and its environment.

Interpersonal Conflict Conflict between two or more individuals is almost certain to occur in any organization, given the great variety in perceptions, goals, attitudes, and so forth among its members. William Gates, founder and CEO of Microsoft, and Kazuhiko Nishi, a former business associate from Japan, ended a long-term business relationship because of interpersonal conflict. Nishi accuses Gates of becoming too political, while Gates charges that Nishi became too unpredictable and erratic in his behavior.[29]

A frequent source of interpersonal conflict in organizations is what many people call a personality clash—when two people distrust each others' motives, dislike one another, or for some other reason simply cannot get along. Conflict also may arise between people who have different beliefs or perceptions about some aspect of their work or their organization. For example, one manager may want the organization to require that all employees use IBM personal computers to promote standardization. Another manager may believe that employees should use a variety of equipment to recognize individuality. Similarly, a male manager may disagree with his female colleague over whether the organization is guilty of discriminating against women in promotion decisions.

Conflict also can result from excess competitiveness among individuals. Two people vying for the same job, for instance, may resort to political behavior in an effort to gain an advantage. If either competitor sees the other's behavior as inappropriate, accusations are likely to result. Even after the "winner" of the job is determined, such conflict may continue to undermine interpersonal relationships, especially if the reasons given in selecting one candidate are ambiguous or open to alternative explanation.

Intergroup Conflict Conflict between two or more organizational groups is also quite common. For example, the members of a firm's marketing group may disagree with the production group over product quality and delivery schedules. Two sales groups may disagree over how to meet sales goals, and two groups of managers may have different ideas about how best to allocate organizational resources.

Many intergroup conflicts arise more from organizational causes than interpersonal causes. Just as increased interdependence makes coordination more difficult, it also increases the potential for conflict. For example, in sequential interdependence, work is passed from one unit to another. Intergroup conflict may arise if the first group turns out too much work (the second group will fall behind), too little work (the second group will not meet its own goals), or poor-quality work.

At a JC Penney's department store, conflict arose between stockroom employees and sales associates. The sales associates claimed that the stockroom employees were slow in delivering merchandise to the sales floor so that it could be priced and shelved. The stockroom employees, in turn, claimed that the sales associates were not giving them enough lead time to get the merchandise delivered and failed to understand that they had additional duties besides carrying merchandise to the sales floor.

Just like people, different departments often have different goals. Further, these goals may often be incompatible. A marketing goal of maximizing sales, achieved partially by offering many products in a wide variety of sizes, shapes, colors, and models, probably conflicts with a production goal of minimizing costs, achieved partially by long production runs of a few items. Reebok recently confronted this very situation. One group of managers wanted to introduce a new sportswear line as quickly as possible, while other managers wanted to expand more deliberately and cautiously. Because the two groups were not able to reconcile their differences effectively, conflict between the two factions led to quality problems and delivery delays that plagued the company for months.

Competition for scarce resources can also lead to intergroup conflict. Most organizations—especially universities, hospitals, government agencies, and businesses in depressed industries—do not have unlimited resources. In one New England town, for example, the public works department and the library recently battled over funds from a federal construction grant. The Oldsmobile, Pontiac, and Chevrolet divisions of General Motors fought over the rights to manufacture the company's new futuristic minivan.

Conflict Between Organization and Environment Conflict that arises between one organization and another is called interorganizational conflict. A moderate amount of interorganizational conflict resulting from business competition is, of course, expected, but sometimes conflict becomes more extreme. For example, the owners of Jordache Enterprises Inc. and Guess? Inc. have been battling in court for years over ownership of the Guess label, allegations of design theft, and several other issues.[30] H. Ross Perot and his old friends at EDS are similarly at odds. After Perot sold EDS to General Motors, he resigned and started a new company to compete with his old firm. When he left GM he signed a contract agreeing to not compete for a specified time and in specified areas. He contends that his new company lives up to that agreement, while EDS maintains otherwise. The result of their disagreement has been name-calling, lawsuits, and countersuits—with the end nowhere in sight. The strong personalities of the participants play a major role in their battles.[31]

Conflict can also arise between an organization and other elements of its environment. For example, an organization may conflict with a consumer group over claims it makes about its products. McDonald's faced this problem a few years ago when it published nutritional information about its products that omitted details about fat content. A manufacturer might conflict with a governmental agency such as OSHA. For instance, the firm's management may believe it is in compliance with OSHA regulations, while officials from the agency itself feel that the firm is not in compliance. Or a firm might conflict with a supplier over the quality of raw materials. The firm may think the supplier is providing inferior materials, while the supplier thinks the materials are adequate. Finally, individual managers may have disagreements with groups of workers. For example, a manager may think her workers are doing poor-quality work and that they are unmotivated. The workers, on the other hand, may believe they are doing a good job and that the manager is doing a poor job of leading them.

MANAGING CONFLICT IN ORGANIZATIONS

How do managers cope with all this potential conflict? Fortunately, as Table 13.3 shows, conflict can be stimulated for constructive ends, to control conflict before it gets out of hand, and to resolve it if it does.

Stimulating Conflict

In some situations, an organization may stimulate conflict by placing individual employees or groups in competitive situations. Managers can establish sales contests, incentive plans, bonuses, or other competitive stimuli to spark competition. As long as the ground rules are equitable and all participants perceive the contest as fair, the conflict created by the competition is likely to be constructive because each participant will work hard to win (thereby enhancing some aspect of organizational performance).

Another useful method for stimulating conflict is to bring in one or more outsiders who will shake things up and present a new perspective on organizational practices. Outsiders may be new employees, current employees assigned to an existing work group, or consultants or advisers hired on a temporary basis. Of course, this action can also provoke resentment from insiders who feel they were qualified for the position. The Beecham Group, a British company, hired an American for its CEO position expressly to change how the company did business.[32] His arrival brought with it new ways of doing things and a new enthusiam for competitiveness.

TABLE 13.3 Methods for Managing Conflict

Stimulating conflict

Increase competition among individuals and teams.

Hire outsiders to shake things up.

Change established procedures.

Controlling conflict

Expand resource base.

Enhance coordination of interdependence.

Set supraordinate goals.

Match personalities and work habits of employees.

Resolving and eliminating conflict

Avoid conflict.

Convince conflicting parties to compromise.

Bring conflicting parties together to confront and negotiate conflict.

Conflict is a powerful force in organizations and has both negative and positive consequences. Thus managers can draw on several different techniques to stimulate, control, resolve, or eliminate conflict, depending on their unique circumstance.

Unfortunately, some valued employees also chose to leave Beecham because they resented some of the changes that were made.

Changing established procedures, especially procedures that have outlived their usefulness, can also stimulate conflict. Such actions cause people to reassess how they perform their jobs and whether they perform them correctly. For example, one university president announced that all vacant staff positions could be filled only after written justification had received his approval. Conflict arose between the president and the department heads who felt they were having to do more paperwork than was necessary. Most requests were okayed, but because department heads now had to think through their staffing needs, a few unnecessary positions were appropriately eliminated.

Controlling Conflict

One method of controlling conflict is to expand the resource base. Suppose a top manager receives two budget requests for $100,000 each. If she has only $180,000 to distribute, the stage is set for conflict because each group will feel its proposal is worth funding and will be unhappy if it is not fully funded. If both proposals are indeed worthwhile, it may be possible for her to come up with the extra $20,000 from some other source and thereby avoid difficulty.

If managers use an appropriate technique for enhancing coordination, they can reduce the probability that conflict will arise. Techniques for coordination include making use of the managerial hierarchy, relying on rules and procedures, enlisting liaison persons, forming task forces, and integrating departments. At the JC Penney store mentioned earlier, the conflict was addressed by providing salespeople with clearer forms on which to specify the merchandise they needed and in what sequence. If one coordination technique does not have the desired effect, a manager might shift to another one.

Competing goals can also be a potential source of conflict among individuals and groups. Managers can sometimes focus employee attention on higher-level, or superordinate, goals as a way of eliminating lower-level conflict. When labor unions such as the United Auto Workers make wage concessions to ensure survival of the automobile industry, they are responding to a superordinate goal. Their immediate goal may be higher wages for members, but they realize that without the automobile industry, their members would not even have jobs.

Finally, managers should try to match the personalities and work habits of employees to avoid conflict between individuals. For instance, two valuable subordinates, one a chain smoker and the other a vehement antismoker, should probably not be required to work together in an enclosed space. If conflict does arise between incompatible individuals, a manager might seek an equitable transfer for one or both of them to other units.

Resolving and Eliminating Conflict

Despite everyone's best intentions, conflict will sometimes flare up. If it is disrupting the workplace, creating too much hostility and tension, or otherwise harming the organization, attempts must be made to resolve it.

Some managers who are uncomfortable dealing with conflict choose to avoid the conflict and hope it will go away. Avoidance may sometimes be effective in the short run for some kinds of interpersonal disagreements, but it does little to resolve long-run or chronic conflict. Even more unadvisable, though, is "smoothing"—minimizing the conflict and telling everyone that things will "get better." Often the conflict will only worsen as people continue to brood over it.

Compromise is striking a middle-range position between two extremes. This approach can work if it is used with care, but in most compromise situations someone wins and someone loses. Budget problems are one of the few areas amenable to compromise because of their objective nature. Assume, for example, that additional resources are not available to the manager mentioned earlier. She has $180,000 to divide, and each of two groups claims to need $100,000. If the manager believes that both projects warrant funding, she can allocate $90,000 to each. The fact that the two groups have at least been treated equally may minimize the potential conflict.[33]

The confrontation approach to conflict resolution—also called interpersonal problem solving—consists of bringing the parties together to confront the conflict. The parties discuss the nature of their conflict and attempt to reach an agreement or a solution. Confrontation requires a reasonable degree of maturity on the part of the participants, and the manager must structure the situation carefully. If handled well, this approach can be an effective means of resolving conflict.[34]

Regardless of the approach, organizations and their managers must realize that conflict must be addressed if it is to serve constructive purposes and be prevented from bringing about destructive consequences. Conflict is inevitable in organizations, but its effects can be constrained with proper attention. For example, Union Carbide once sent two hundred of its managers to a three-day workshop on conflict management. The managers engaged in a variety of exercises and discussions to learn with whom they were most likely to come into conflict and how they should try to resolve it. As a result, managers at the company later reported that hostility and resentment in the organization had been greatly diminished and that employees reported more pleasant working relationships.[35]

SUMMARY OF KEY POINTS

A group is two or more persons who interact regularly to accomplish a common purpose or goal. General kinds of groups in organizations are functional groups, task groups and teams, and informal or interest groups. A team is a group of workers that functions as a unit, often with little or no supervision, to carry out organizational functions.

People join functional groups and teams to pursue a career. Their reasons for joining informal or interest groups include interpersonal attraction, group activities, group goals, need satisfaction, and potential instrumental benefits. The stages of team development include testing and dependence, intragroup conflict and hostility, development of group cohesion, and focusing on the problem at hand.

Four important characteristics of teams are role structures, behavioral norms, cohesiveness, and informal leadership. Role structures define task and socioemotional specialists. Role structures may be victimized by role ambiguity, role conflict, or role overload. Norms are standards of behavior for group members. Cohesiveness is the extent to which members are loyal and committed to the team and to one another. Several factors can increase or reduce team cohesiveness. The relationship between performance norms and cohesiveness is especially important. Informal leaders are those leaders whom the group members themselves choose to follow.

Conflict is a disagreement between two or more people, groups, or organizations. Too little or too much conflict may hurt performance, but an optimal level of conflict may improve performance. Interpersonal and intergroup conflict in organizations may be caused by personality differences or by particular organizational strategies and practices.

Organizations may encounter conflict with one another and with various elements of the environment. Three methods of managing conflict are to stimulate it, control it, or resolve and eliminate it.

QUESTIONS FOR REVIEW

1. What is a group? Describe the several different types of groups and indicate the similarities and differences between them.
2. Why do people join groups? Do all teams develop through all of the stages discussed in this chapter? Why or why not?
3. Describe the characteristics of teams. How might the management of a mature team differ from the management of teams that are not yet mature?
4. Identify and summarize the causes and consequences of group cohesiveness.
5. Describe the nature and causes of conflict in organizations. Is conflict always bad? Why or why not?

QUESTIONS FOR ANALYSIS

1. Is it possible for a group to be of more than one type at the same time? If so, under what circumstances? If not, why not?
2. Think of several groups of which you have been a member. Why did you join each? Did each group progress through the stages of development discussed in this chapter? If not, why not?
3. Do you think teams are a valuable new management technique that will endure, or are they just a fad that will be replaced with something else in the near future?
4. Suppose you were the manager of a highly cohesive group with low performance norms. What would you do?
5. Would a manager ever want to stimulate conflict in his or her organization? Why or why not?

CASE STUDY

Boeing Is Trying

Since The Boeing Co. was forced to focus exclusively on manufacturing when the government ordered it to sell its airline operations, United Airlines, it has come to dominate the manufacture of commercial aircraft. In an effort to smooth out fluctuations in sales and earnings that frequently occur in commercial aviation, Boeing moved into computer services in 1970, artificial intelligence in aviation in 1984, and defense electronics in 1987.

In 1988, CEO Frank Shrontz became chair of Boeing. He felt that the strong hierarchy and the long, complicated approval system that were traditional at Boeing needed to be changed. Slowly, change is taking place. One manifestation of that change is a weekly meeting of Boeing's four top executives. They meet every Tuesday at 7:00 A.M. to talk about the company's future. They have no agenda, make no reports, and have no audiovisual equipment present; they just talk.

The group is led by Philip M. Condit, president, whose philosophy seems to be "working together." Under his quiet, soft-spoken guidance, the group has developed an informal camaraderie that is gradually setting the stage for change in the corporate culture. Each member of the group is acquiring a unique way of informally communicating with his part of the organization. One makes spontaneous visits to plants every week, another has potluck lunches with employees, and yet another meets with randomly selected groups over coffee and doughnuts.

Boeing has begun to experiment with other ways of worker participation. In 1989, at a highly automated sheet metal facility in Auburn, Washington, it implemented a participant approach between management and labor. An outside consultant coordinated team-building sessions for six months. After that a steering committee composed of management, employees, and labor leaders was formed to oversee the activities of twelve employee focus groups. These focus groups made recommendations to the steering committee about how to set up and operate the facility. The experiment at the Auburn plant proved successful, and so Boeing is slowly using the team approach elsewhere.

The use of teams and informal approaches has percolated downward in the organization. Boeing's newest transport jet, the 777, was developed in direct response to customer needs for a plane with larger carrying capacity for long distances. More than two hundred "design and build" teams worked to define every part of the 777. The overwhelming success of the 777 has led Boeing to use the teamwork approach on the 737X, which is scheduled to begin production in 1997, and on the F-22 fighter for the Air Force, due in 2003.

Today Boeing's teams include customers and suppliers, as well as all of the functional areas within the company—finance, operations, engineering design, manufacturing, and customer support. Boeing has long had a customer focus, so including customers in its new team efforts has been relatively easy. With the new emphasis on improved communication, requests for changes in airplanes that once took weeks to get answers now take three days.

Clearly Boeing's corporate culture is changing. Whether it can change enough to prevent irreparable damage as the company is forced to undergo severe cutbacks in employment remains to be seen. But Boeing is trying.

Case Questions

1. Describe Boeing's corporate culture as it relates to the use of teams and participation.
2. Is Boeing's corporate culture conducive to the use of teams? Why or why not?
3. Is the use of groups and teams in an organization whose dominant customer is the military a good idea? Why or why not?

References: James P. Woolsey and J. A. Donoghue, "Egalitarian Roll-out," *Air Transport World*, May 1994, pp. 51–54; "When the Going Gets Tough, Boeing Gets Touchy-Feely," *Business Week*, January 17, 1994, pp. 65–67; Shawn Tully, "Can Boeing Reinvent Itself?" *Fortune*, March 8, 1993, pp. 66–73; and "Boeing, Unions Plan New Plant," *Industry Week*, April 3, 1989, p. 27.

SKILLS • DEVELOPMENT • PORTFOLIO

BUILDING EFFECTIVE INTERPERSONAL SKILLS

Exercise Overview

A manager's interpersonal skills refer to her or his ability to understand what motivates individuals and groups. Clearly, interpersonal skills play a major role in determining how well a manager can interact with others in a group setting. This exercise will allow you to practice your interpersonal skills in relation to just such a setting.

Exercise Background

You have just been transferred to a new position supervising a group of five employees. The business you work for is fairly small and has few rules and regulations. Unfortunately, the lack of rules and regulations is creating a problem that you must now address.

Specifically, two of the group members are nonsmokers. They are becoming increasingly vocal about the fact that two other group members smoke at work. These two workers feel that the secondary smoke in the workplace is endangering their health and want to establish a nonsmoking policy like that of many large businesses today.

The two smokers, however, argue that since the company did not have such a policy when they started working there, it would be unfair to impose such a policy on them now. One of them, in particular, says that he turned down an attractive job with another company because he wanted to work in a place where he could smoke.

The fifth worker is also a nonsmoker but says that she doesn't care if others smoke. Her husband smokes at home anyway, and she is used to being around smokers. You suspect that if the two vocal nonsmokers are not appeased, they may leave. You also think that the two smokers will leave if you mandate a no-smoking policy. All five workers do good work, and you do not want any of them to leave.

Exercise Task

With the above information as context, do the following:

1. Explain the nature of the conflict that exists in this work group.
2. Develop a course of action for dealing with the situation.

BUILDING EFFECTIVE CONCEPTUAL SKILLS

Exercise Overview

Groups and teams are becoming ever more important in organizations. This exercise will allow you to practice your conceptual skills as they apply to work teams in organizations.

Exercise Background

A variety of highly effective groups exists outside the boundaries of typical business organizations. For example, each of the following represents a team:

1. A basketball team
2. An elite military squadron
3. A government policy group such as the presidential cabinet
4. A student planning committee

Exercise Task

1. Identify an example of a real team, such as one of the above. Choose one that is not part of a normal business and that you can argue is highly effective.
2. Determine the reasons for the team's effectiveness.
3. Determine how a manager can learn from this particular team and use its success determinants in a business setting.

YOU MAKE THE CALL

One day Mark Spenser and Manuel Hernandez decided to see if they could improve the work performance of Sunset Landscape Service's lawn-care operation. Under the current arrangement, each of the four lawn-care teams, consisting of a crew chief and three team members, is given a set of lawns to work on a daily basis. The assignments are chosen so that the crew should have no trouble completing the work in eight hours. If a crew finishes early, however, its members are free to leave while still getting paid for a full day.

Mark and Manuel noticed, however, that the crews seldom finished very early, because, in part, they were given enough work to take most of the day. Getting done in much less than eight hours was not easy.

Mark and Manuel decided to hold a contest to see which crew could finish its work the fastest. The contest called for each team to log the exact time it worked each day for a three-month period. To ensure equity, various lawn assignments would be rotated across the teams. The winning team members would receive an extra week of paid vacation as their prize.

Within a couple of weeks, Mark and Manuel began to notice some interesting things. First, one group began showing up in matching T-shirts. Next, another group also got matching T-shirts, but with a team name printed on the back. Soon, each team had its own team name, logo, and set of T-shirts to wear.

They also noticed that absenteeism was down. If a team member did not work one day, the remaining team members still had to do the same amount of work. And, of course, it took them somewhat longer to complete their work. Now, employees were taking a day off only when it was absolutely necessary.

When the contest was over, Mark and Manuel felt so good about how it had worked that they gave the three losing teams each one extra day off with pay. Within a matter of days, employees began asking if the contest was going to be repeated.

Discussion Questions

1. Explain what happened in terms of group/team characteristics.

2. Should Mark and Manuel run the same contest again? Why or why not?

3. What risks did they run with the contest?

SKILLS SELF-ASSESSMENT INSTRUMENT

Using Teams

Introduction: The use of groups and teams is becoming more common in organizations throughout the world. The following assessment surveys your beliefs about the effective use of teams in work organizations.

Instructions: You will agree with some of the statements and disagree with others. In some cases, you may find making a decision difficult, but you should force a choice. Record your answers next to each statement according to the following scale:

Rating Scale

4 Strongly agree	**2** Somewhat disagree
3 Somewhat agree	**1** Strongly disagree

_____ **1.** Each individual in a work team should have a clear assignment so that individual accountability can be maintained.

_____ **2.** For a team to function effectively, the team must be given complete authority over all aspects of the task.

_____ **3.** One way to get teams to work is to simply assemble a group of people, tell them in general what needs to be done, and let them work out the details.

_____ **4.** Once a team "gets going," management can turn its attention to other matters.

_____ **5.** To ensure that a team develops into a cohesive working unit, managers should be especially careful not to intervene in any way during the initial start-up period.

_____ **6.** Training is not critical to a team because the team will develop any needed skills on its own.

_____ **7.** It's easy to provide teams with the support they need because they are basically self-motivating.

_____ **8.** Teams need little or no structure to function effectively.

_____ **9.** Teams should set their own direction with managers determining the means to the selected end.

_____**10.** Teams can be used in any organization.

For interpretation, turn to page 450.

Source: Adapted from J. Richard Hackman (Ed.), *Groups That Work (and Those That Don't)* (San Francisco: Jossey-Bass Publishers, 1990), pp. 493–504.

EXPERIENTIAL EXERCISE

Individual Versus Group Performance

Purpose: This exercise demonstrates the benefits a group can bring to accomplishing a task.

Introduction: You will be asked to do the same task both individually and as part of a group.

Instructions

Part 1: You will need a pen or pencil and an 8½″ × 11″ sheet of paper. Working alone, do the following:

1. Write the letters of the alphabet in a vertical column down the lefthand side of the paper: A–Z.

2. Your instructor will randomly select a sentence from any written document and read out loud the first twenty-six letters in that sentence. Write these letters in a vertical column immediately to the right of the alphabet column. Everyone should have identical sets of 26 two-letter combinations.

3. Working alone, think of a famous person whose initials correspond to each pair of letters, and write the name next to the letters, for example, "MT Mark Twain." You will have ten minutes. Only one name per set is allowed. One point is awarded for each legitimate name, so the maximum score is 26 points.

4. After time expires, exchange your paper with another member of the class and score each other's work. Disputes about the legitimacy of names will be settled by the instructor. Keep your score for use later in the exercise.

Part 2: Your instructor will divide the class into groups of five to ten. All groups should have approximately the same number of members. Each group now follows the procedure given in part 1. Again write the letters of the alphabet down the lefthand side of the sheet of paper, this time in reverse order: Z–A. Your instructor will dictate a new set of letters for the second column. The time limit and scoring procedure are the same. The only difference is that the groups will generate the names.

Part 3: Each team identifies the group member who came up with the most names. The instructor places these "best" students into one group. Then all groups repeat part 2, but this time the letters from the reading will be in the first column and the alphabet letters will be in the second column.

Part 4: Each team calculates the average individual score of its members on part 1 and compares it with the team score from parts 2 and 3. Your instructor will put the average individual score and team scores for each group on the board.

Follow-Up Questions

1. Do the average individual scores and the team scores differ? What are the reasons for the difference, if any?

2. Although the team scores in this exercise usually are higher than the average individual scores, under what conditions might individual averages exceed group scores?

Source: Adapted from John E. Jones and J. William Pfeiffer (Eds.), *The 1979 Annual Handbook for Group Facilitators* (San Diego, Calif.: University Associates, 1979), pp. 19–20. Copyright © 1979 by Pfeiffer, an imprint of Jossey-Bass Inc., Publishers, San Francisco, CA.

CHAPTER NOTES

1. "United Shuttle Puts New Spin on Fare Wars," *USA Today*, September 30, 1994, pp. 1B, 2B; "Flying High," *Business Week*, February 27, 1995, pp. 90–91; and "United's 'Dumb' Idea," *Business Week*, February 20, 1995, pp. 42–43.
2. See Gregory Moorhead and Ricky W. Griffin, *Organizational Behavior*, 4th ed. (Boston: Houghton Mifflin, 1995), for a review of definitions of groups.
3. Marilyn E. Gist, Edwin A. Locke, and M. Susan Taylor, "Organizational Behavior: Group Structure, Process, and Effectiveness," *Journal of Management*, Summer 1987, pp. 237–257.
4. Dorwin Cartwright and Alvin Zander (Eds.), *Group Dynamics: Research and Theory*, 3rd ed. (New York: Harper & Row, 1968).
5. Robert Schrank, *Ten Thousand Working Days* (Cambridge, Mass.: MIT Press, 1978); Bill Watson, "Counter Planning on the Shop Floor," in Peter Frost, Vance Mitchell, and Walter Nord (Eds.), *Organizational Reality*, 2nd ed. (Glenview, Ill.: Scott, Foresman, 1982), pp. 286–294.
6. Brian Dumaine, "Payoff from the New Management," *Fortune*, December 13, 1993, pp. 103–110.
7. Glenn Parker, "Cross-Functional Collaboration," *Training & Development*, October 1994, pp. 49–58.
8. Michael Stevens and Michael Campion, "The Knowledge, Skill, and Ability Requirements for Teamwork: Implications for Human Resource Management," *Journal of Management*, 1994, Vol. 20, No. 2, pp. 503–530.
9. Brian Dumaine, "The Trouble with Teams," *Fortune*, September 5, 1994, pp. 86–92.
10. Marvin E. Shaw, *Group Dynamics—The Psychology of Small Group Behavior*, 4th ed. (New York: McGraw-Hill, 1985).
11. Rupert Brown and Jennifer Williams, "Group Identification: The Same Thing to All People?" *Human Relations*, July 1984, pp. 547–560.
12. See Connie Gersick, "Marking Time: Predictable Transitions in Task Groups," *Academy of Management Journal*, June 1989, pp. 274–309.
13. Stuart Gannes, "America's Fastest-Growing Companies," *Fortune*, May 23, 1988, pp. 28–40.
14. See Michael Campion, Gina Medsker, and A. Catherine Higgs, "Relations Between Work Group Characteristics and Effectiveness: Implications for Designing

Effective Work Groups," *Personnel Psychology*, Winter 1993, pp. 823–850, for a review of other team characteristics.

15. David Katz and Robert L. Kahn, *The Social Psychology of Organizations*, 2nd ed. (New York: Wiley, 1978), pp. 187–221.

16. Robert L. Kahn, D. M. Wolfe, R. P. Quinn, J. D. Snoek, and R. A. Rosenthal, *Organizational Stress: Studies in Role Conflict and Role Ambiguity* (New York: Wiley, 1964).

17. For recent research in this area, see Donna L. Wiley, "The Relationship Between Work/Nonwork Role Conflict and Job-Related Outcomes: Some Unanticipated Findings," *Journal of Management*, Winter 1987, pp. 467–472; and Arthur G. Bedeian, Beverly G. Burke, and Richard G. Moffett, "Outcomes of Work-Family Conflict Among Married Male and Female Professionals," *Journal of Management*, September 1988, pp. 475–485.

18. See Donna M. Randall, "Multiple Roles and Organizational Commitment," *Journal of Organizational Behavior*, Vol. 9, 1988, pp. 309–317.

19. Daniel C. Feldman, "The Development and Enforcement of Group Norms," *Academy of Management Review*, January 1984, pp. 47–53. See also Monika Henderson and Michael Argyle, "The Informal Rules of Working Relationships," *Journal of Organizational Behavior*, Vol. 7, 1986, pp. 259–275.

20. "Companies Turn to Peer Pressure to Cut Injuries as Psychologists Join the Battle," *The Wall Street Journal*, March 29, 1991, pp. B1, B3.

21. Walter Kiechel III, "Love, Don't Lose, the Newly Hired," *Fortune*, June 6, 1988, pp. 271–274.

22. Matt Riggs and Patrick Knight, "The Impact of Perceived Group Success-Failure on Motivational Beliefs and Attitudes: A Causal Model," *Journal of Applied Psychology*, 1994, Vol. 79, No. 5, pp. 755–766.

23. Anne O'Leary-Kelly, Joseph Martocchio, and Dwight Frink, "A Review of the Influence of Group Goals on Group Performance," *Academy of Management Journal*, 1994, Vol. 37, No. 5, pp. 1285–1301.

24. For an example of how to increase cohesiveness, see Paul F. Buller and Cecil H. Bell, Jr., "Effects of Team Building and Goal Setting on Productivity: A Field Experiment," *Academy of Management Journal*, June 1986, pp. 305–328.

25. Clayton P. Alderfer, "An Intergroup Perspective on Group Dynamics," in Jay W. Lorsch (Ed.), *Handbook of Organizational Behavior* (Englewood Cliffs, N.J.: Prentice-Hall, 1987), pp. 190–222. See also Eugene Owens and E. Leroy Plumlee, "Intraorganizational Competition and Interorganizational Conflict: More Than a Matter of Semantics," *Business Review*, Winter 1988, pp. 28–32.

26. Catherine Alter, "An Exploratory Study of Conflict and Coordination in Interorganizational Service Delivery Systems," *Academy of Management Journal*, September 1990, pp. 478–502.

27. Thomas Bergmann and Roger Volkema, "Issues, Behavioral Responses and Consequences in Interpersonal Conflicts," *Journal of Organizational Behavior*, 1994, Vol. 15, pp. 467–471.

28. Robin Pinkley and Gregory Northcraft, "Conflict Frames of Reference: Implications for Dispute Processes and Outcomes," *Academy of Management Journal*, 1994, Vol. 37, No. 1, pp. 193–205.

29. "How 2 Computer Nuts Transformed Industry Before Messy Breakup," *The Wall Street Journal*, August 27, 1986, pp. 1, 10.

30. "A Blood War in the Jeans Trade," *Business Week*, November 13, 1989, pp. 74–81.

31. "Perot War with EDS Pits Former Friends in High-Stakes Affair," *The Wall Street Journal*, October 6, 1988, pp. A1, A12.

32. "Beecham's Chief Imports His American Ways," *The Wall Street Journal*, October 27, 1988, p. B9.

33. Todd Carver and Albert Vondra, "Alternative Dispute Resolution: Why It Doesn't Work and Why It Does," *Harvard Business Review*, May–June 1994, pp. 120–131.

34. "Battling Executives Seek out Therapists," *The Wall Street Journal*, November 7, 1988, p. B1.

35. "Teaching How to Cope with Workplace Conflicts," *Business Week*, February 18, 1980, pp. 136, 139.

Control and total quality management are important considerations for all managers. Checking the colors of silk cloth to ensure that they are exactly right is an ancient ritual. Quality control teams in modern textile mills serve the same purpose.

PART

V

Controlling

CHAPTER 14

Managing the Control Process

OBJECTIVES

After studying this chapter, you should be able to:

- *Explain the purpose of control, identify different types of control, and describe the steps in the control process.*
- *Identify and explain the three forms of operations control.*
- *Describe budgets and other tools of financial control.*
- *Identify and distinguish between two opposing forms of structural control.*
- *Identify characteristics of effective control, why people resist control, and how managers can overcome this resistance.*

OUTLINE

OPENING INCIDENT

CONAGRA IS NOT exactly a household word. But given that the firm is the second-largest food company in the United States and controls brand names such as Armour, Chun King, Decker, Healthy Choice, Orville Redenbacher, Peter Pan, and Wesson, most households are quite likely stocked with ConAgra products. Charles Harper took over ConAgra in the mid-1970s when it was just a poorly performing collection of flour mills. He continually added new companies and brand names until he had built a huge, multiproduct food-processing firm with total annual revenues of more than $21 billion.

Harper structured the firm as a loose confederation of enterprises, allowing each to pursue its own goals, objectives, and market opportunities. The idea was that each unit would then be able to more quickly respond to competition and to changing consumer tastes. One manager who excelled in this low-key, decentralized system was Philip Fletcher, who ran Banquet Foods Corp.

"He's making more money than I did with the company."

In 1993, Harper stepped down and Fletcher took over. Unfortunately, the timing for Fletcher and ConAgra could not have been worse. High commodity prices had just wounded the firm's meat-processing businesses, and a vicious frozen-food price war had cut ConAgra's profits to a razor-thin margin. In addition, new competition was making business more complicated than ever. ConAgra's operating profits were also an anemic 3.9 percent, and it had taken on too much debt as a result of a large acquisition of Beatrice Company.

Fletcher knew he had to increase control while simultaneously maintaining the entrepreneurial spirit that was so integral to ConAgra's success. His solution was to create executive councils comprising division heads. These councils meet regularly to discuss how they can pool resources and activities. Each is still free to operate autonomously, but the idea is that they can share ideas and try to learn how others are saving money and cutting costs. Fletcher also mandated tight cost control systems, implemented from the top down. More approvals are now needed to spend money. Each unit also has targets for cost cuts, and 25 percent of division heads' pay has been tied to meeting savings targets.

So far, things are paying off for ConAgra: Profit margins have increased to 4.7 percent, and long-term debt has been cut to 30 percent of capital, down from 40 percent just a couple of years ago. Market shares are also increasing, and sales growth has escalated. Fletcher seems to have taken the formula pioneered by his predecessor and improved it.[1] ●

Source of Quotation: Former ConAgra CEO Charles Harper, referring to his successor Philip Fletcher, quoted in *Business Week*, July 25, 1994, p. 73.

Philip Fletcher relied on one of the four fundamental functions of management to jump-start ConAgra—control. He decided where he wanted the business to go, pointed it in that direction, and created systems to keep it on track. Any business can enhance its financial health by taking the same steps, although each organization must work with its own particular configuration of revenues and costs. The general framework for achieving and maintaining financial health is control.

As we discuss in Chapter 1, control is one of the four basic managerial functions that provide the organizing framework for this book. In the first section of this chapter we explain the purpose of control. We then look at types of control and the steps in the control process. The rest of the chapter examines the three levels of control most organizations must employ to remain effective: operations, financial, and structural control. We conclude by discussing the characteristics of effective control, noting why some people resist control, and describing what organizations can do to overcome this resistance.

THE NATURE OF CONTROL IN ORGANIZATIONS

• **control**
The regulation of organizational activities so that some targeted element of performance remains within acceptable limits

Control is the regulation of organizational activities so that some targeted element of performance remains within acceptable limits.[2] Without this regulation, organizations have no indication of how well they perform in relation to their goals. Control keeps the organization moving in the proper direction. At any point in time, it compares where the organization is to where it is supposed to be. Like a rudder, control provides an organization with a mechanism for adjusting its course if performance falls outside of acceptable boundaries. For example, FedEx has a performance goal of delivering 99 percent of its packages on time. If on-time deliveries fall to 97 percent, control systems signal the problem to managers so they can make necessary adjustments in operations to regain the target level of performance.

The Purpose of Control

As Figure 14.1 illustrates, control provides an organization with ways to adapt to environmental change, to limit the accumulation of error, to cope with organizational complexity, and to minimize costs.

Adapting to Environmental Change In today's turbulent business environment, all organizations must contend with change.[3] If managers could establish goals and achieve them instantaneously, control would not be needed. But between the time a goal is established and the time it is reached, many things can happen in the organization and its environment to disrupt movement toward the goal—or even to change the goal itself. A properly designed control system can help managers anticipate, monitor, and respond to changing circumstances.[4] In contrast, an improperly designed system can result in organizational performance that falls far below acceptable levels.

FIGURE 14.1 The Purpose of Control

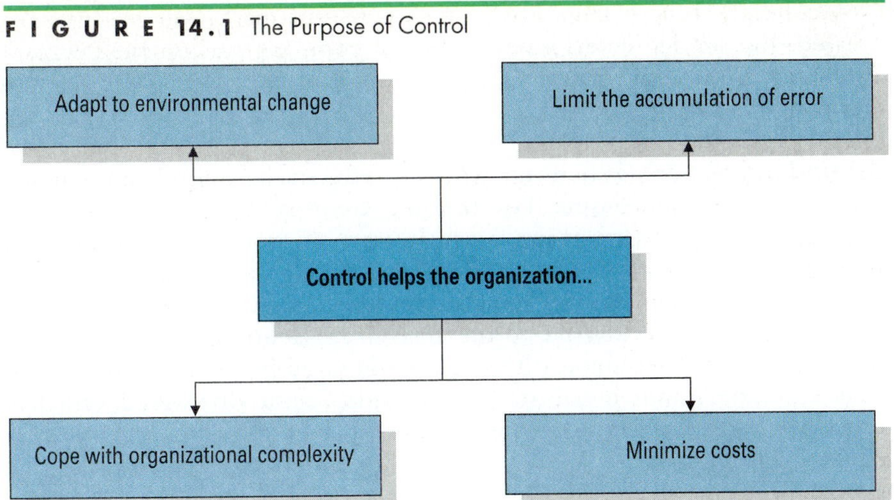

Control is one of the four basic management functions in organizations. The control function, in turn, has four basic purposes. Properly designed control systems are able to fulfill each of these purposes.

Michigan-based Metalloy, a metal casting company, signed a contract to make engine-seal castings for NOK, a big Japanese auto parts maker. Metalloy was satisfied when its first 5,000-unit production run yielded 4,985 acceptable castings and only 15 defective ones. NOK, however, was quite unhappy with this performance and insisted that Metalloy raise its standards. In short, global quality standards had shifted so dramatically that managers at Metalloy had lost touch with how high their own standards had to be in order to remain competitive.[5]

Limiting the Accumulation of Error Small mistakes and errors do not often seriously damage the financial health of an organization. Over time, however, small errors may accumulate and become very serious. For example, Whistler Corporation, a large radar detector manufacturer, was once faced with such rapidly escalating demand that it essentially stopped worrying about quality. The defect rate rose from 4 percent to 9 percent to 15 percent and eventually reached 25 percent. One day, a manager realized that 100 of the company's 250 employees were spending all their time fixing defective units and that $2 million worth of inventory was awaiting repair. Had the company adequately controlled quality as it responded to increased demand, the problem never would have reached such proportions.[6]

Coping with Organizational Complexity When a company purchases only one raw material, produces one product, has a simple organization design, and enjoys constant demand for its product, its managers can maintain control with a very basic and simple system. But a business that produces many products from myriad raw materials and has a large market area, a complicated organization design, and many competitors needs a sophisticated system to maintain adequate control. Emery Worldwide (air freight) was quite profitable until it bought Purolator Courier Corporation. The new Emery that resulted from the acquisition was much bigger and more complex, but no new controls were added to operations.

Consequently, Emery began to lose money and market share, costs increased, and service deteriorated until the company was on the verge of bankruptcy. Only when more elaborate controls were developed did the company turn itself around.

Minimizing Costs When it is practiced effectively, control can help reduce costs and boost output. For example, Georgia-Pacific Corporation, a large wood products company, recently learned of a new technology to make thinner blades for its saws. The company's control system was used to calculate the amount of wood that could be saved from each cut made by the thinner blades relative to the costs of replacing the existing blades. The results have been impressive—the wood saved by the new blades each year fills eight hundred railcars.[7] As Georgia-Pacific discovered, effective control systems can eliminate waste, lower labor costs, and improve output per unit of input.

Types of Control

The examples of control thus far have illustrated the regulation of several organizational activities, from producing quality products to coordinating complex organizations. Organizations practice control in a number of different areas and at different levels, and the responsibility for managing control is widespread.

Areas of Control Control can focus on any area of an organization. Most organizations define areas of control in terms of the four basic types of resources they use: physical, human, information, and financial resources. Control of physical resources includes inventory management (stocking neither too few nor too many units in inventory), quality control (maintaining appropriate levels of output quality), and equipment control (supplying the necessary facilities and machinery). Control of human resources includes selection and placement, training and development, performance appraisal, and compensation. Control of information resources includes sales and marketing forecasting, environmental analysis, public relations, production scheduling, and economic forecasting. Financial control involves managing the organization's debt so that it does not become excessive, ensuring that the organization always has enough cash on hand to meet its obligations but that it does not have excess cash in a checking account, and that receivables are collected and bills paid on a timely basis.

In many ways, the control of financial resources is the most important area because financial resources are related to the control of all the other resources in an organization. Too much inventory leads to storage costs; poor selection of personnel leads to termination and rehiring expenses; inaccurate sales forecasts lead to disruptions in cash flows and other financial effects. Financial issues tend to pervade most control-related activities. Indeed, financial issues are the basic problem faced by Emery Worldwide (air freight). Various inefficiencies and operating blunders put the company in a position where it lacked the money to service its debt (make interest payments on loans), had little working capital (cash to cover daily operating expenses), and was too heavily leveraged (excessive debt) to borrow more money.

Levels of Control Control generally takes place at three different levels in an organization. **Operations control** focuses on the processes the organization uses to transform resources into products or services (quality control is one type of operations control).[8] **Financial control** is concerned with the organization's financial resources (monitoring receivables to make sure customers are paying their bills on time is an example of financial control). **Structural control** is concerned with how the elements of the organization's structure are serving their intended purposes (monitoring the administrative ratio to make sure staff expenses do not become excessive is an example of structural control).

- **operations control** Focuses on the processes the organization uses to transform resources into products or services
- **financial control** Concerned with the organization's financial resources
- **structural control** Concerned with how the elements of the organization's structure are serving their intended purpose

Responsibilities for Control Traditionally, managers have been responsible for overseeing the wide array of control systems and concerns in organizations. They decide which types of control the organization will use, and they implement control systems and take actions based on the information provided by control systems. Thus ultimate responsibility for control rests with all managers throughout an organization. Most larger organizations also have one or more specialized managerial positions called controller. A **controller** is responsible for helping line managers with their control activities, for coordinating the organization's overall control system, and for gathering and assimilating relevant information. Many businesses that use an H-form or M-form organization design have several controllers: one for the corporation and one for each division. The job of controller is especially important in organizations where control systems are complex.[9]

- **controller** A position in organizations that helps line managers with their control activities

In addition, many organizations are beginning to use operating employees to help maintain effective control. Indeed, employee participation is often used as a vehicle for giving operating employees an opportunity to help facilitate organizational effectiveness. For example, Whistler Corporation increased employee participation in an effort to turn its quality problems around. As a starting point, the quality control unit, formerly responsible for checking product quality at the end of the assembly process, was eliminated. Next, all operating employees were encouraged to check their own work and told that they would be responsible for correcting their own errors. As a result, Whistler has eliminated its quality problems and is highly profitable once again.

Steps in the Control Process

Regardless of the types or levels of control systems an organization needs, any control process has four fundamental steps.[10] These are illustrated in Figure 14.2.[11]

Establish Standards The first step in the control process is to establish standards. A **control standard** is a target against which subsequent performance is to be compared. Employees at Taco Bell, a fast-food restaurant, for example, work toward the following service standards:

- **control standard** A target against which subsequent performance is to be compared

1. A minimum of 95 percent of all customers will be greeted within three minutes of their arrival.

FIGURE 14.2 Steps in the Control Process

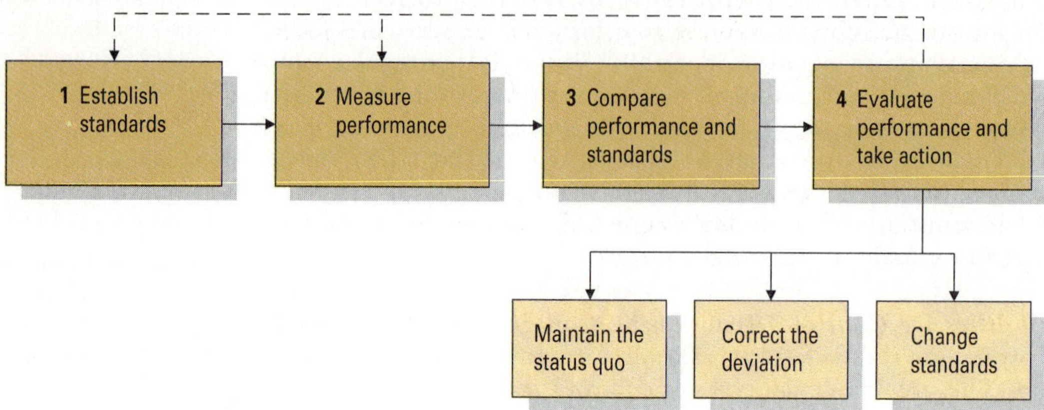

Having an effective control system can help ensure that an organization achieves its goals. Implementing a control system, however, is a systematic process that generally proceeds through four interrelated steps.

2. Preheated tortilla chips will not sit in the warmer more than thirty minutes before they are served to customers.
3. Empty tables will be cleaned within five minutes after being vacated.

Standards established for control purposes should be expressed in measurable terms. Note that standard 1 has a time limit of three minutes and an objective target of 95 percent of all customers. In standard 3, the objective target is implied: "all" empty tables.

Control standards should be consistent with the organization's goals. Taco Bell has organizational goals involving customer service, food quality, and restaurant cleanliness. A control standard for a retailer like Home Depot should be consistent with its goal of increasing its annual sales volume by 25 percent within five years. A hospital trying to shorten the average hospital stay by a patient will have control standards that reflect current averages. A university reaffirming its commitment to academics might adopt a standard of graduating 80 percent of its student athletes within five years of their enrollment. Control standards can be as narrow or as broad as the level of activity to which they apply and must follow logically from organizational goals and objectives.

A final aspect of establishing standards is to identify performance indicators. Performance indicators are measures of performance that provide information directly relevant to what is being controlled. For example, suppose an organization is following a tight schedule in building a new plant. Relevant performance indicators could be buying a site, selecting a building contractor, and ordering equipment. Monthly sales increases are not, however, directly relevant. On the other hand, if control is being focused on revenue, monthly sales increases are relevant, and buying land for a new plant is less relevant.

Measure Performance The second step in the control process is to measure performance. Performance measurement is a constant, ongoing activity for most organizations. For control to be effective, performance measures must be valid. Daily, weekly, and monthly sales figures measure sales performance, and production performance may be expressed in terms of unit cost, product quality, or volume produced. Employee performance is often measured in terms of quality or quantity of output, but for many jobs measuring performance is not so straightforward.

A research and development scientist at Merck, for instance, may spend years working on a single project before achieving a breakthrough. A manager who takes over a business on the brink of failure may need months or even years to turn things around. Valid performance measurement, however difficult to obtain, is nevertheless vital in maintaining effective control, and performance indicators usually can be developed. The scientist's progress, for example, may be partially assessed by peer review, and the manager's success may be evaluated by her ability to convince creditors that she eventually will be able to restore profitability.

Compare Performance Against Standards The third step in the control process is to compare measured performance against established standards. Performance may be higher than, lower than, or identical to the standard. In some cases, comparison is easy. The goal of each product manager at General Electric is to make the product either number one or number two (on the basis of total sales) in its market. Since this standard is clear and total sales are easy to calculate, it is relatively simple to determine whether the standard has been met. Sometimes, however, comparisons are less clear-cut. If performance is lower than expected, the question is how much deviation from standard to allow before taking remedial action. For example, is increasing sales by 7.9 percent when the standard was 8 percent close enough?

The timetable for comparing performance to standards depends on a variety of factors, including the importance and complexity of what is being controlled. For longer-run and higher-level standards, annual comparisons may be appropriate. In other circumstances, more frequent comparisons are necessary. For instance, a business with a cash shortage may need to monitor its on-hand cash reserves daily. We noted earlier the cash-flow problems Emery Worldwide faced after it purchased Purolator Courier. As part of their efforts to improve the company's control, Emery's managers eventually started monitoring their cash reserves weekly.

Evaluate Performance and Take Action The final step in the control process is to evaluate performance and take action. Decisions regarding corrective actions draw heavily on a manager's analytic and diagnostic skills. After comparing performance against control standards, one of three actions is appropriate: maintain the status quo (do nothing); correct the deviation; or change the standard. Maintaining the status quo is preferable when performance essentially matches the standard, but it is more likely that some action will be needed to correct a deviation from the standard.

Sometimes performance that is higher than expected may also cause problems for organizations. For example, when Toyota introduced its new mini sports utility vehicle into the U.S. market in early 1996, demand was so strong that waiting lists developed, with many customers willing to pay more than the suggested retail price to obtain a vehicle. The company was unable to ship more units to the United States because of import quotas.

At the same time, however, it did not want to alienate potential customers. Consequently, Toyota decided to simply reduce its advertising, curtailing demand a bit and limiting customer frustration.

Changing an established standard usually is necessary if it was set too high or too low at the outset. This is apparent if large numbers of employees routinely beat the standard by a wide margin or if no employees ever meet the standard. Standards that seemed perfectly appropriate when first established may need to be adjusted when circumstances change.

OPERATIONS CONTROL

One of the three levels of control practiced by most organizations, **operations control**, is concerned with the processes the organization uses to transform resources into products or services. As Figure 14.3 shows, the three forms of operations control—preliminary, screening, and postaction—occur at different points in relation to the transformation processes used by the organization.

Preliminary Control

preliminary control Attempts to monitor the quality or quantity of financial, physical, human, and information resources before they actually become part of the system

Preliminary control concentrates on the resources—financial, material, human, and information—the organization brings in from the environment. Preliminary control attempts to monitor the quality or quantity of these resources before they enter the organization. Organizations like PepsiCo and General Mills hire only college graduates for their management training programs, and even then only after applicants satisfy several interviewers and selection criteria. In this way, they control the quality of the human resources entering the organization. When Sears orders mer-

Most organizations develop multiple control systems that incorporate all three basic forms of control. For example, the publishing company that produced this book screens inputs by hiring only qualified editors, typesetters, and printers (preliminary control). In addition, quality is checked during the transformation process such as after the manuscript is typeset (screening control), and the outputs—printed and bound books—are checked before they are shipped from the bindery (postaction control).

FIGURE 14.3 Forms of Operations Control

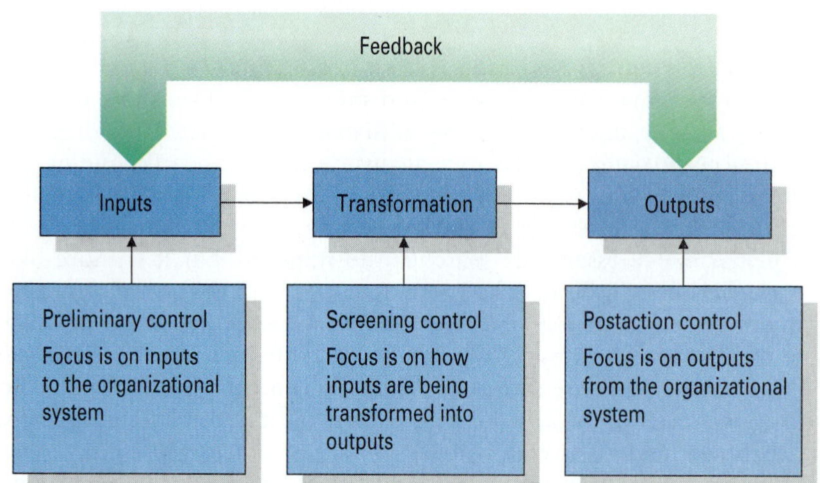

Operations control is concerned with the processes used by an organization to transform resources into products or services. Shaw Industries in Georgia uses this yarn to manufacture carpet. Its managers must make sure that the yarn is available in the right quantities, colors, and textures—and at the right times—so that carpet production runs can be most efficiently scheduled. Operations control helps facilitate this process.

chandise to be manufactured under its own brand name, it specifies rigid standards of quality, thereby controlling physical inputs. Organizations also control financial and information resources. For example, privately held companies like UPS and Mars limit the extent to which outsiders can buy their stock, and television networks verify the accuracy of news stories before they are broadcast.

Screening Control

Screening control focuses on meeting standards for product and service quality or quantity during the actual transformation process. Screening control relies heavily on feedback processes. For instance, in a Compaq Computer factory, computer system components are checked periodically as each unit is being assembled to ensure that all the components that have been assembled up to that point are working properly. The periodic quality checks provide feedback to workers so they know what, if any, corrective actions to take. Because they are useful in identifying the cause of problems, screening controls tend to be used more often than other forms of control.

• **screening control** Focuses on meeting standards for products and service quality or quantity during the actual transformation process; relies heavily on feedback processes during the transformation process

More and more companies are adopting screening controls because they are an effective way to promote employee participation and to catch problems early in the overall transformation process. For example, Corning recently adopted screening controls for use in manufacturing television glass. In the past, finished television screens were inspected only after they were finished. Unfortunately, over 4 percent of them were later returned by customers because of defects. Now the glass screens are inspected at each step in the production process rather than at the end, and the return rate from customers has dropped to .03 percent.[12]

Postaction Control

• **postaction control** Monitors the outputs or results of the organization after the transformation process is complete

Postaction control focuses on the outputs of the organization after the transformation process is complete. Corning's old system was postaction control—final inspection after the product is completed. Although Corning abandoned its postaction control system, this control method still may be effective, primarily if a product can be manufactured in only one or two steps or if the service is fairly simple and routine. Although postaction control alone may not be as effective as preliminary or screening control, it can provide management with information for future planning. For example, if a quality check of finished goods indicates an unacceptably high defect rate, the production manager knows that he or she must identify the causes and take steps to eliminate them. Postaction control also provides a basis for rewarding employees. Recognizing that an employee has exceeded personal sales goals by a wide margin, for instance, may alert the manager that a bonus or promotion is in order.[13]

Most organizations use more than one form of operations control. For example, Honda's preliminary control includes hiring only qualified employees and specifying strict quality standards when ordering parts from other manufacturers. Honda uses numerous screening controls in checking the quality of components during the assembly of cars. A final inspection and test drive as each car rolls off the assembly line is part of the company's postaction control. Organizations employ a wide variety of techniques to facilitate operations control.

FINANCIAL CONTROL

• **financial control** Concerned with the organization's financial resources

Financial control is the control of financial resources as they flow into the organization (i.e., revenues, shareholder investments), are held by the organization (i.e., working capital, retained earnings), and flow out of the organization (i.e., pay expenses). Businesses must manage their finances so that revenues are sufficient to cover costs and still return a profit to the company's owners. Not-for-profit organizations such as universities have the same concerns: their revenues (from tax dollars or tuition) must cover operating expenses and overhead. A complete discussion of financial management is beyond the scope of this book, but we will examine the control provided by budgets and other financial control tools.

Budgetary Control

• **budget** A plan expressed in numerical terms

A **budget** is a plan expressed in numerical terms.[14] Organizations establish budgets for work groups, departments, divisions, and the whole organization. The usual time period for a budget is one year, although breakdowns of budgets by the quarter or month are also common. Budgets are generally expressed in financial terms, but they occasionally may be expressed in units of output, time, or other quantifiable factors. Because of their quantitative nature, budgets provide yardsticks for measuring performance and facilitate comparisons across departments, between levels in the organization, and from one time period to another.

Budgets serve four primary purposes: (1) they help managers coordinate resources and projects (because they use a common denominator, usually dollars), (2) they help define the established standards for control, (3) they provide guidelines about the organization's resources and expectations, and (4) they enable the organization to evaluate the performance of managers and organizational units.

Types of Budgets Most organizations develop and make use of three different kinds of budgets: financial, operating, and nonmonetary. Table 14.1 summarizes the characteristics of each.

TABLE 14.1 Types of Budgets

Type of Budget	What Budget Shows
Financial budget	**Sources and uses of cash**
Cash-flow or cash budget	All sources of cash income and cash expenditures in monthly, weekly, or daily periods
Capital expenditures budget	Costs of major assets such as a new plant, machinery, or land
Balance sheet budget	Forecast of the organization's assets and liabilities in the event all other budgets are met
Operating budget	**Planned operations in financial terms**
Sales or revenue budget	Income the organization expects to receive from normal operations
Expense budget	Anticipated expenses for the organization during the coming time period
Profit budget	Anticipated differences between sales or revenues and expenses
Nonmonetary budget	**Planned operations in nonfinancial terms**
Labor budget	Hours of direct labor available for use
Space budget	Square feet or meters of space available for various functions
Production budget	Number of units to be produced during the coming time period

Organizations use many types of budgets to help manage their control function. The three major categories of budgets are financial, operating, and nonmonetary budgets. There are several different types of budgets in each category. Each budget must be carefully matched with the specific function being controlled in order to be most effective.

A financial budget indicates where the organization expects to get its cash for the coming time period and how it plans to use it. Since financial resources are critically important, the organization needs to know from where those resources will be coming and how they are to be used. The financial budget provides answers to both these questions. Usual sources of cash include sales revenue, short- and long-term loans, the sale of assets, and the issuance of new stock. Several years ago, MCA realized that revenues from its Universal Studios theme park in Florida were going to be significantly lower than expected. As a result, it moved quickly to modify its financial budget to reflect lower revenues. Common uses of cash are operating expenses, debt repayment, purchase of new assets, retained earnings, and stock dividends. Heavily leveraged companies such as Continental Airlines must commit much of their cash to debt repayment. MCA revised its financial budget by cutting back on planned expansion activities.

An operating budget is concerned with planned operations within the organization. It outlines what quantities of products and services the organization intends to create and what resources will be used to create them. IBM creates an operating budget that specifies how many of each model of its personal computers will be produced each quarter.

A nonmonetary budget is simply a budget expressed in nonfinancial terms, such as units of output, hours of direct labor, machine hours, or square-foot allocations. Nonmonetary budgets are most commonly used by managers at the lower levels of an organization. For example, a plant manager can schedule work more effectively knowing that he or she has 8,000 labor hours to allocate in a week, rather than trying to determine how to best spend $76,451 in wages in a week.

Developing Budgets Traditionally, budgets were developed by top management and the controller and then imposed on lower-level managers. Although some organizations still follow this pattern, many contemporary organizations now allow all managers to participate in the budget process. As a starting point, top management generally issues a call for budget requests, accompanied by an indication of overall patterns the budgets may take. For example, if sales are expected to drop in the next year, managers may be told up front to prepare for cuts in operating budgets.

The heads of each operating unit typically submit budget requests to the head of their division. An operating unit head might be a department manager in a manufacturing or wholesaling company or a program director in a social service agency. A division head might include a plant manager, a regional sales manager, or a college dean. The division head integrates and consolidates the budget requests from operating unit heads into one overall division budget request. A great deal of interaction among managers usually takes place at this stage, as the division head coordinates the budgetary needs of the various departments.

Division budget requests are then forwarded to a budget committee. The budget committee is usually composed of top managers. The committee reviews budget requests from several divisions, and, once again, duplications and inconsistencies are corrected. Finally, the budget committee, the controller, and the CEO review and agree on the overall budget for the organization as well as specific budgets for each operating unit. These decisions are then communicated back to each manager.

Strengths and Weaknesses of Budgeting Budgets offer a number of advantages, but they have weaknesses as well. On the plus side, budgets facilitate effective control. Placing dollar values on operations enables managers to monitor operations better and pinpoint problem areas. Budgets also facilitate coordination and communication between departments because they express diverse activities in a common denominator (dollars). Budgets help maintain records of organizational performance and are a logical complement to planning. That is, as managers develop plans, they should simultaneously consider control measures to accompany them. Organizations can use budgets to link plans and control by first developing budgets as part of the plan and then using those budgets as part of control.

On the other hand, some managers apply budgets too rigidly. Budgets are intended to serve as frameworks, but managers sometimes fail to recognize that changing circumstances may warrant budget adjustments. The process of developing budgets can also be very time consuming. Finally, budgets may limit innovation and change. When all available funds are allocated to specific operating budgets, it may be impossible to procure additional funds to take advantage of an unexpected opportunity.[15]

Indeed, for these very reasons, some organizations are working to scale back their budgeting system. While most organizations are likely to continue to use budgets, the goal is to make them less confining and rigid. For example, Xerox, 3M, and Digital Equipment have all cut back on their budgeting systems by reducing the number of budgets they generate and by injecting more flexibility into the budgeting process.[16]

Other Tools of Financial Control

Although budgets are the most common means of financial control, other useful tools are financial statements, ratio analysis, and financial audits.

Financial Statements A **financial statement** is a profile of some aspect of an organization's financial circumstances. Financial statements are prepared and presented in commonly accepted and required ways.[17] The two most basic financial statements prepared and used by virtually all organizations are a balance sheet and an income statement.

• **financial statement**
A profile of some aspect of an organization's financial circumstances

The **balance sheet** lists the organization's assets and liabilities at a specific point in time, usually the last day of an organization's fiscal year. For example, the balance sheet may summarize the financial condition of an organization on December 31, 1997. Most balance sheets are divided into current assets (assets that are relatively liquid, or easily convertible into cash), fixed assets (assets that are longer-term in nature and less liquid), current liabilities (debts and other obligations that must be paid in the near future), long-term liabilities (payable over an extended period of time), and stockholders' equity (the owners' claim against the assets).

• **balance sheet**
A list of an organization's assets and liabilities at a specific point in time

Whereas the balance sheet reflects a snapshot profile of an organization's financial position at a single point in time, the **income statement** summarizes financial performance over a period of time, usually one year. For example, the income statement might be for the period January 1, 1997, through December 31, 1997. The income statement adds up all income to the organization and then subtracts all expenses, debts, and liabilities. The "bottom line" of the statement represents net income, or profit. Information

• **income statement**
A summary of financial performance over a period of time

from the balance sheet and income statement is used in computing important financial ratios.

ratio analysis The calculation of one or more financial ratios to assess some aspect of the organization's financial health

Ratio Analysis Financial ratios compare different elements of a balance sheet and income statement to one another. **Ratio analysis** is the calculation of one or more financial ratios to assess some aspect of the financial health of an organization. Organizations use a variety of different financial ratios as part of financial control. For example, *liquidity ratios* indicate how liquid (easily converted into cash) an organization's assets are. *Debt ratios* reflect the ability to meet long-term financial obligations. *Return ratios* show managers and investors how much return the organization is generating relative to its assets. *Coverage ratios* help estimate the organization's ability to cover interest expenses on borrowed capital. *Operating ratios* indicate the effectiveness of specific functional areas rather than of the total organization.

audits An independent appraisal of an organization's accounting, financial, and operational systems

Financial Audits **Audits** are independent appraisals of an organization's accounting, financial, and operational systems. The two major types of financial audit are the external audit and the internal audit.

External audits are financial appraisals conducted by experts who are not employees of the organization.[18] External audits are typically concerned with determining that the organization's accounting procedures and financial statements are compiled in an objective and verifiable fashion. The organization contracts with certified public accountants (CPAs) for this service. The CPA's main objective is to verify for stockholders, the IRS, and other interested parties that the methods by which the organization's financial managers and accountants prepare documents and reports are legal and proper. External audits are so important that publicly held corporations are required by law to have external audits regularly, as assurance to investors that the financial reports are reliable. An external audit at U.S. Shoe Corporation once discovered some significant accounting irregularities in one of the organization's divisions. As a result, the company was fined and had to revamp its entire accounting system.[19]

Some organizations are also starting to employ external auditors to review other aspects of their financial operations. For instance, some auditing firms now specialize in checking corporate legal bills. An auditor for the Fireman's Fund Insurance Corporation uncovered several thousands of dollars in legal fee errors. Other auditors specialize in real estate, employee benefits, and pension plan investments.[20]

Whereas external audits are conducted by external accountants, an *internal audit* is handled by employees of the organization. Its objective is the same as that of an external audit—to verify the accuracy of financial and accounting procedures used by the organization. Internal audits also examine the efficiency and appropriateness of financial and accounting procedures. Because the staff members who conduct them are a permanent part of the organization, internal audits tend to be more expensive than external audits. But employees, who are more familiar with the organization's practices, may point out significant aspects of the accounting system besides its technical correctness. Large organizations such as Dresser Industries and Ford have internal auditing staffs that spend all their time conducting audits of different divisions and functional areas of the organization. Smaller organizations may assign accountants to an internal audit group on a temporary or rotating basis.

STRUCTURAL CONTROL

Organizations can create designs for themselves that result in very different approaches to control. Two major forms of structural control—bureaucratic control and clan control—represent opposite ends of a continuum, as shown in Figure 14.4.[21] The six dimensions shown in the figure represent perspectives adopted by the two extreme types of structural control. That is, they have different goals, degrees of formality, performance focus, organization designs, reward systems, and levels of participation. Although a few organizations fall precisely at one extreme or the other, most tend toward one end but may have specific characteristics of either.

Bureaucratic Control

bureaucratic control A form of organizational control characterized by formal and mechanistic structural arrangements

Bureaucratic control is an approach to organization design characterized by formal and mechanistic structural arrangements. The goal of bureaucratic control is employee compliance. Organizations that use it rely on strict

FIGURE 14.4 Organizational Control

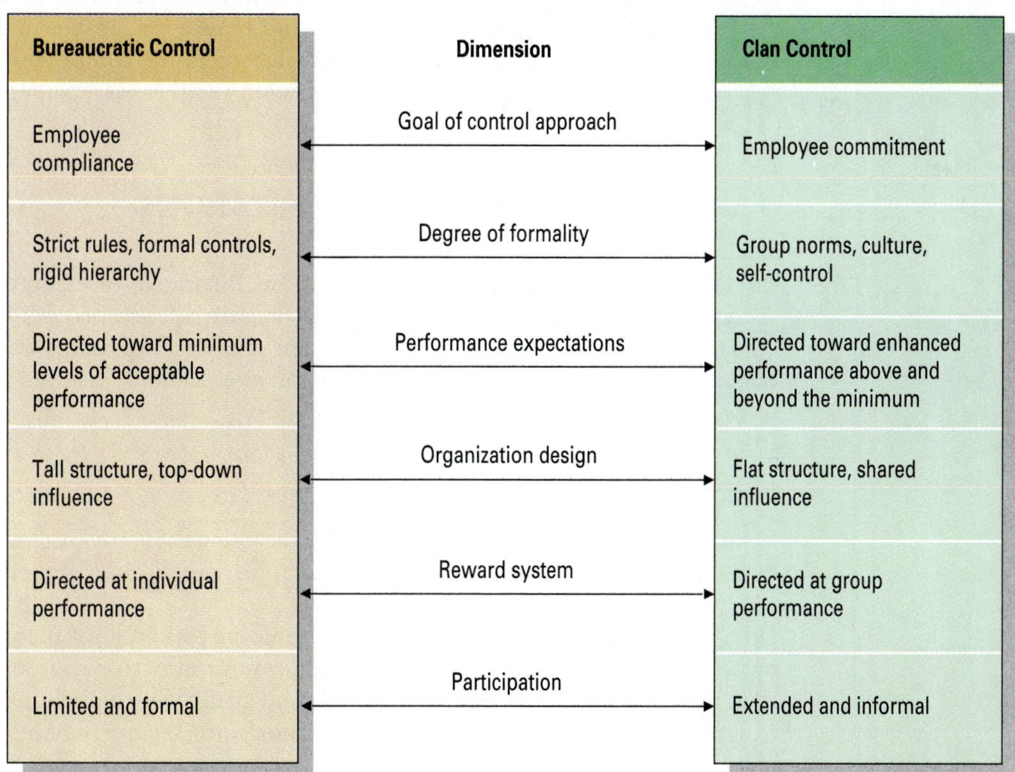

rules and a rigid hierarchy, insist that employees meet minimally acceptable levels of performance, and often have a tall structure. They focus their rewards on individual performance and allow only limited and formal employee participation.

NBC television applies structural controls that reflect many elements of bureaucracy. The organization relies on numerous rules to regulate employee travel, expense accounts, and other expenses. A new performance appraisal system precisely specifies minimally acceptable levels of performance for everyone. The organization's structure is considerably taller than those of the other major networks, and rewards are based on individual contributions. Perhaps most significantly, many NBC employees have argued that they have too small a voice in how the organization is managed.

Clan Control

• **clan control**
An approach to organizational control based on informal and organic structural arrangements

Clan control, in contrast, is an approach to organization design characterized by informal and organic structural arrangements. As Figure 14.4 shows, its goal is employee commitment to the organization. Accordingly, it relies heavily on group norms and a strong corporate culture, and it gives employees the responsibility for controlling themselves. Employees are encouraged to perform beyond minimally acceptable levels. Organizations using this approach are usually relatively flat. They direct rewards at group performance and favor widespread employee participation.

Levi Strauss practices clan control. The company's managers use groups as the basis for work and have created a culture wherein group norms help facilitate high performance. Rewards are subsequently provided to the higher performing groups and teams. The company's culture also reinforces contributions to the overall team effort, and employees have a strong sense of loyalty to the organization. Levi's has a flat structure, and power is widely shared. Employee participation is encouraged in all areas of operation.

MANAGING CONTROL IN ORGANIZATIONS

Effective control, whether at the operations, financial, or structural level, successfully regulates and monitors organizational activities. To use the control process, managers must recognize the characteristics of effective control and understand how to identify and overcome occasional resistance to control.[22]

Characteristics of Effective Control

Control systems tend to be most effective when they are integrated with planning and when they are flexible, accurate, timely, and objective.

Integration with Planning Control should be linked with planning. The more explicit and precise this linkage, the more effective the control system. The best way to integrate planning and control is to account for control as plans develop. In other words, as goals are set during the planning process, attention should be paid to developing standards that will reflect how well the plan is realized. Managers at Champion Spark Plug Company decided to broaden their product line to include a full range of automotive accessories—a total of twenty-one new products. As part of this plan, managers decided in advance what level of sales they wanted to realize from each product for each of the next five years. They established these sales goals as standards against which actual sales would be compared. Thus, by accounting for their control system as they developed their plan, managers at Champion did an excellent job of integrating planning and control.

Flexibility The control system itself must be flexible enough to accommodate change. The alternative—designing and implementing a new control system—is an avoidable expense. Champion's control system includes a mechanism that automatically ships products to major customers to keep their inventory at predetermined levels. The company had to adjust this system when one of its biggest customers, Montgomery Ward & Company, decided not to stock the full line of Champion products. Because its control system was flexible, modifying it for Montgomery Ward was relatively simple.

Accuracy Managers make a surprisingly large number of decisions based on inaccurate information. Field representatives may hedge their sales estimates to make themselves look better. Production managers may hide costs to meet their targets. Human resource managers may overestimate their minority recruiting prospects to meet affirmative action goals. In each case, the information other managers receive is inaccurate, and the results of inaccurate information may be quite dramatic. If sales projections are inflated, a manager might cut advertising (thinking it is no longer needed)

Effective control doesn't just happen—it has to be carefully managed. Effective control usually is based on flexibility. These archeologists are working at an ancient burial site in Russia. Their work must be carefully planned and needs to remain accurate, timely, and objective. But since they often don't know what they will find at a particular site as it is excavated, they also must remain flexible in terms of their schedules, procedures, and operations.

or increase advertising (to further build momentum). Similarly, a production manager unaware of hidden costs may quote a sales price much lower than desirable. Or a human resource manager may speak out publicly on the effectiveness of the company's minority recruiting, only to find out later that these prospects have been overestimated. In each case, the result of inaccurate information is inappropriate managerial action.

Timeliness Timeliness does not necessarily mean quickness. Rather, it describes a control system that provides information as often as is necessary. Since Champion has a wealth of historical data on its sparkplug sales, it does not need information on sparkplugs as frequently as it needs sales feedback for its newer products. Retail organizations usually need sales results daily to manage cash flow and adjust advertising and promotion. In contrast, they may require information about physical inventory only quarterly or annually. In general, the more uncertain and unstable the circumstances, the more frequently measurement is needed.

Objectivity The control system should provide information that is as objective as possible. To appreciate this, imagine the task of a manager responsible for control of his organization's human resources. He asks two plant managers to submit reports. One manager notes that morale at his plant is "okay," that grievances are "about where they should be," and that turnover is "under control." The other reports that absenteeism at her plant is running at 4 percent, that sixteen grievances have been filed this year (compared with twenty-four last year), and that turnover is 12 percent. The second report will almost always be more useful than the first. Of course, managers also need to look beyond the numbers when assessing performance. For example, a plant manager may be boosting productivity and profit margins by putting too much pressure on workers and using poor-quality materials. As a result, impressive short-run gains may be overshadowed by longer-run increases in employee turnover and customer complaints.

Resistance to Control

Managers may sometimes make the mistake of assuming that the value of an effective control system is self-evident to employees. For a variety of reasons, however, employees may resist control.

Overcontrol Occasionally, organizations try to control too many things. This becomes especially problematic when the control directly affects employee behavior. An organization that instructs its employees when to come to work, where to park, when to have morning coffee, and when to leave for the day exerts considerable control over people's daily activities. Yet many organizations attempt to control not only these but other aspects of work behavior. Troubles arise when employees perceive these attempts to limit their behavior as being unreasonable. A company that tells its employees how to dress, how to arrange their desks, and how to wear their hair may meet with more resistance. Employees at Chrysler complained when they were forced to park in a distant parking lot if they drove a non-

Chrysler vehicle. People felt that these efforts to control their personal behavior (i.e., what kind of car to drive) were excessive. Managers eventually removed these controls and now allow open parking.

Inappropriate Focus The control system may be too narrow or it may focus too much on quantifiable variables and leave no room for analysis or interpretation. A sales standard that encourages high-pressure tactics to maximize short-run sales may do so at the expense of goodwill from long-term customers. Such a standard is too narrow. A university reward system that encourages faculty members to publish large numbers of articles but fails to consider the quality of the work is also inappropriately focused. Employees resist the intent of the control system by focusing their efforts only at the performance indicators being used.

Rewards for Inefficiency Imagine two operating departments that are approaching the end of the fiscal year. Department 1 expects to have $5,000 of its budget left over; department 2 is already $3,000 in the red. As a result, department 1 is likely to have its budget cut for the next year ("They had money left, so they obviously got too much to begin with") and department 2 is likely to get a budget increase ("They obviously haven't been getting enough money"). Thus, department 1 is punished for being efficient and department 2 is rewarded for being inefficient. As with inappropriate focus, people resist the intent of this control and behave in ways that run counter to the organization's intent.

Too Much Accountability Effective controls allow managers to determine whether or not employees successfully discharge their responsibilities. If standards are properly set and performance accurately measured, managers know when problems arise and which departments and individuals are responsible. People who do not want to be answerable for their mistakes or who do not want to work as hard as their boss might like therefore resist control. For example, American Express has a system that provides daily information on how many calls each of its operators handles. If one operator has typically worked at a slower pace and handled fewer calls than other operators, that individual's deficient performance can now be easily pinpointed.

Overcoming Resistance to Control

Perhaps the best way to overcome resistance to control is to create effective control to begin with. Two other ways to overcome resistance are to encourage participation and to develop verification procedures.

Encourage Employee Participation Chapter 7 notes that participation can help overcome resistance to change. By the same token, when employees are involved with planning and implementing the control system, they are less likely to resist it. For instance, employee participation in planning, decision making, and quality control at the Chevrolet Gear Axle plant in Detroit has resulted in increased employee concern for quality and a greater commitment to meeting standards.

Develop Verification Procedures Multiple standards and information systems provide checks and balances in control and allow the organization to verify the accuracy of performance indicators. Suppose a production manager argues that she failed to meet a certain cost standard because of increased prices of raw materials. A properly designed inventory control system will either support or contradict her explanation. Suppose that an employee who was fired for excessive absences argues that he was not absent "for a long time." An effective human resource control system should have records that support the termination. Resistance to control declines because these verification procedures protect both employees and management. If the production manager's claim about the rising cost of raw materials is supported by the inventory control records, she will not be held solely accountable for failing to meet the cost standard, and some action may be taken to lower the cost of raw materials.

SUMMARY OF KEY POINTS

Control is the regulation of organizational activities so that some targeted element of performance remains within acceptable limits. Control provides ways to adapt to environmental change, to limit the accumulation of errors, to cope with organizational complexity, and to minimize costs. Control can focus on financial, physical, information, and human resources and includes operations, financial, and structural levels. Control is the function of managers, the controller, and, increasingly, operating employees.

Steps in the control process are (1) establish standards of expected performance, (2) measure actual performance, (3) compare performance against the standards, and (4) evaluate the performance and take appropriate action.

Operations control focuses on the processes the organization uses to transform resources into products or services. Preliminary control is concerned with the resources that serve as inputs to the system. Screening control is concerned with the transformation processes used by the organization. Postaction control is concerned with the outputs of the organization. Most organizations need multiple control systems because no one system alone can provide adequate control.

Financial control focuses on controlling the organization's financial resources. The foundation of financial control is budgets, plans expressed in numerical terms. Most organizations rely on financial, operating, and nonmonetary budgets. Financial statements, various kinds of ratios, and external and internal audits are also important tools organizations use as part of financial control.

Structural control addresses how well an organization's structural elements serve their intended purpose. Two basic forms of structural control are bureaucratic and clan control. Bureaucratic control is relatively formal and mechanistic, whereas clan control is informal and organic. Most organizations use a form of organizational control somewhere in between these two extremes.

One way to increase the effectiveness of control is to fully integrate planning and control. The control system should be flexible, accurate, timely, and as objective as possible. Employees may resist organizational controls because of overcontrol, inappropriate focus, rewards for inefficiency, and a desire to avoid accountability. Managers can overcome this resistance by improving the effectiveness of controls and by allowing employee participation and developing verification procedures.

QUESTIONS FOR REVIEW

1. What is the purpose of organizational control? Why is it important?
2. What are the steps in the control process? Which step is likely to be the most difficult to perform? Why?

3. What are the similarities and differences between the various forms of operations control? What are the costs and benefits of each form?
4. What are the basic differences between bureaucratic control and clan control?
5. How can a manager understand and overcome resistance and make control effective?

QUESTIONS FOR ANALYSIS

1. How is the control process related to the functions of planning, organizing, and leading?
2. Are the differences in bureaucratic control and clan control related to differences in organization structure? If so, how? If not, why not?
3. Do you use a budget for your personal finances? Relate your experiences with budgeting to the discussion in the chapter.
4. Have you ever resisted control? Why?
5. Why might control in an international business be more complex and difficult than control in a domestic business?

CASE STUDY

Sherwin-Williams

Sherwin-Williams and Company has been an industry leader since it was founded in 1871. In an effort to boost earnings and draw more customers into its stores, the company diversified during the 1970s by adding carpeting, draperies, and other decorating products to its lines. That effort proved to be a bad decision: in 1977, Sherwin-Williams lost more than $8 million. Something had to be done.

In 1979 the board hired John (Jack) Gerald Breen, a Cleveland executive. Breen moved immediately to gain better control of costs. He got rid of more than half of the company's top management positions and closed inefficient production facilities. Breen also took action to get better control over the marketing functions. He focused the retail product lines on paint and wallpaper. In addition, he acquired Dutch Boy to strengthen the paint line. Sherwin-Williams became profitable again and has remained so ever since. To expand its markets, in 1990 it began to market the Dutch Boy brand through Sears and the Kem-Tone label through Wal-Mart. To expand its product offerings, it acquired two aerosol paint businesses and four special coatings businesses.

Breen argues that attention to detail is what counts in the paint business. Because the key elements to success are brand, price, distribution, and quality, Breen positioned each of Sherwin-Williams four main brands so that they had a focused distribution system. Its retail outlets sell only the Sherwin-Williams brand, mass merchandisers sell the Dutch Boy brand, independent paint and hardware stores sell Martin-Senour, and discount stores sell Kem-Tone. Sherwin-Williams also makes many private-label paints such as those for Sears. This multiple distribution system is one key to its success because it enables the company to have a strong presence in a variety of markets.

In a move to control costs, Sherwin-Williams has reduced travel costs by consolidating the purchase of travel from more than seventy agencies to just one. In addition, it has installed an executive information system for its 110 district managers. The computerized system enables it to track sales of its brands, colors, and products across stores and regions to take better advantage of differing consumption patterns so that inventory does not build up in any one location.

The use of high-technology information systems also is apparent in its warehousing. Sherwin-Williams hired a software designer to help develop an automated control system for its warehouses. Workers get orders electronically through handheld devices that are combinations of radios, scanners, and a computer terminal. The orders are prioritized and recalculated every time an order is filled. At each stop, everything is updated and new tasks assigned. Thus when an operator drives a forklift to a spot in the warehouse to pick up an order, he or she enters that location into the computer, and it determines where the forklift should go next. Mistakes are reduced and warehouse space is used far more effectively with the system than it had been in the past.

Breen's attention to detail in costs, marketing, distribution, warehousing, information processing, and other areas clearly contributes to an effective control system. The system has also shown itself to be flexible so that the company is not constrained or limited by an overuse of rules and regulations.

Case Questions

1. Would the attention to detail described here be appropriate to all organizations? Why or why not?
2. What forms of control are evident at Sherwin-Williams? Cite specific examples of each.
3. Given that Sherwin-Williams has developed such excellent computerized information and warehouse operations systems, why doesn't it move to use them in businesses other than the slow-growing paint business? Would you diversify if you were Breen? Why or why not?

References: "The House That Jack Rebuilt," *Forbes*, April 25, 1994, pp. 91–93; Ellis Booker, "Pushing Decision Support Beyond Executive Suite," *Computerworld*, December 20, 1993, p. 65; Nancy A. Lang, "Business Travel on a Shoestring," *Management Review*, January 1992, pp. 30–32; and Larry Stevens, "Painting Itself out of a Corner," *Manufacturing Systems*, August 1990, pp. 34–37.

SKILLS • DEVELOPMENT • PORTFOLIO

BUILDING EFFECTIVE TIME-MANAGEMENT SKILLS

Exercise Overview

Time-management skills—a manager's abilities to prioritize work, to work efficiently, and to delegate appropriately—play a major role in the control function. That is, a manager can use time-management skills to control his or her own work more effectively. This exercise will help demonstrate the relationship between time-management skills and control.

Exercise Task

You are a middle manager in a small manufacturing plant. Today is Monday and you have just returned from a one-week vacation. The first thing you discover is that your secretary will not be in today. His aunt died, and he is out of town at the funeral. He did, however, leave you the following note:

Dear Boss:
Sorry about not being here today. I will be back tomorrow. In the meantime, here are some things you need to know about:

1. Ms. Glinski [your boss] wants to see you today at 4:00.
2. The shop steward wants to see you ASAP about a labor problem.
3. Mr. Bateman [one of your big customers] has a complaint about a recent shipment.
4. Ms. Ferris [one of your major suppliers] wants to discuss a change in the delivery schedule.
5. Mr. Prescott from the Chamber of Commerce wants you to attend a breakfast meeting on Wednesday and discuss our expansion plans.
6. The legal office wants to discuss our upcoming OSHA inspection.
7. Human resources wants to know when you can interview someone for the new supervisor's position.
8. Mr. Williams, the machinist you fired last month, has been hanging around the parking lot.

Exercise Task

With the information above as a framework, do the following:

1. Prioritize into three categories—very timely, moderately timely, and less timely—the work that needs to be done to address the issues above.
2. Are importance and timeliness the same thing?
3. What additional information do you need to acquire before you can really begin to prioritize this work?
4. How would your approach differ if your secretary was in today?

BUILDING EFFECTIVE DIAGNOSTIC SKILLS

Exercise Overview

Diagnostic skills enable managers to visualize responses to situations. Diagnostic skills are clearly important to the determination of what activities should be regulated, how to best assess activities, and how to respond to deviations observed during the control process. This exercise helps demonstrate the role of diagnostic skills in control.

Exercise Background

You are the manager of a popular, locally owned restaurant. Your restaurant competes with such chains as Chili's, Bennegan's, and Applebee's. You have been able to maintain your market share in light of increased competition from these outlets by concentrating on providing exceptional service.

Recently, you have become aware of three trends that concern you. First, your costs are increasing. Monthly charges for food purchases seem to be growing at an exceptionally rapid pace. Second, customer complaints are increasing. While the actual number of complaints is still quite small, complaints nevertheless are increasing. Finally, turnover among your employees is increasing. While turnover in the restaurant business is almost always very high, the recent increase is in marked contrast to your historical turnover pattern.

Exercise Task

Using the information presented above, do the following:

1. Identify as many potential causes as possible for each of the three problem areas.

2. Group each cause into one of two categories: "more likely" and "less likely."

3. Develop at least one potential action that you might take to address each cause.

YOU MAKE THE CALL

As Cynthia Spenser began to devote all of her time to managing The Arbor, she was dismayed to find what she believed to be a fairly haphazard management system. While the developer of the retail complex was clearly an astute entrepreneur, she began to feel that he had not paid enough attention to detail in the course of day-to-day operating procedures.

She and Mark had learned a lot about management from their experience with SLS. Mark, for example, had found that the most effective way of running the business involved buying only from reputable suppliers, keeping all plants well fertilized and pruned while they were in inventory, and checking with customers after landscape jobs had been completed to ensure that they were satisfied.

When she bought The Arbor, Cynthia talked with a friend who managed a store at the regional shopping mall in town. Her friend explained how the mall development company had elaborate rules and procedures for its tenants. These rules and procedures dictated store hours, appearance standards, lease terms, promotional and advertising policies, and just about everything else imaginable.

The Arbor, however, was a different story. There were no written policies for tenants. As a result, there was considerable variation in how they were managed. Some stores opened on Sunday or in the evening, for example, while others did not; some tenants had long-term leases while others had no current lease at all.

To address these and other issues, Cynthia called a meeting of all the tenants and expressed her concerns. To her surprise, she found that they already were aware of each of her issues, as well as some others that she had not yet had time to consider. They argued, however, that the current system was really best for The Arbor. As a smaller operation, each tenant knew all the others, and they worked together to keep things in good order. They thought it was fine that they kept different hours—few customers came to The Arbor just to walk around and shop. Customers usually came to visit specific stores and were aware of that store's hours. The tenants even thought the lease situation was fine. Some wanted the security afforded by a lease, while others preferred the flexibility of no lease.

Discussion Questions

1. What kinds of control examples are illustrated in this situation?

2. What kinds of control systems might be most useful for retailers?

3. What does this situation illustrate regarding the situational nature of control?

SKILLS SELF-ASSESSMENT INSTRUMENT

Understanding Control

Introduction: Control systems must be carefully constructed for all organizations regardless of their goals. The following assessment surveys your ideas about and approaches to control.

Instructions: You will agree with some of the statements and disagree with others. In some cases, making a decision may be difficult, but you should force a choice. Record your answers next to each statement according to the following scale:

Rating Scale

4 Strongly agree	**2** Somewhat disagree
3 Somewhat agree	**1** Strongly disagree

_____ **1.** Effective controls must be unbending if they are to be used consistently.

_____ **2.** The most objective form of control is one that uses measures such as stock prices and rate of return on investment (ROI).

_____ **3.** Control is restrictive and should be avoided if at all possible.

_____ **4.** Controlling through rules, procedures, and budgets should not be used unless measurable standards are difficult or expensive to develop.

_____ **5.** Overreliance on measurable control standards is seldom a problem for business organizations.

_____ **6.** Organizations should encourage the development of individual self-control.

_____ **7.** Organizations tend to try to establish behavioral controls as the first type of control to be used.

_____ **8.** The easiest and least costly form of control is output or quantity control.

_____ **9.** Short-run efficiency and long-run effectiveness result from the use of similar control standards.

_____ **10.** Rate of return on investment (ROI) and stock prices are ways of ensuring that a business organization is responding to its external market.

_____ **11.** Self-control should be relied on to replace other forms of control.

_____ **12.** Controls such as rate of return on investment (ROI) are more appropriate for corporations and business units than they are for small groups or individuals.

_____ **13.** Control is unnecessary in a well-managed organization.

_____ **14.** The use of output or quantity controls can lead to unintended or unfortunate consequences.

_____ **15.** Standards of control do not depend on which constituency is being considered.

_____ **16.** Controlling through the use of rules, procedures, and budgets can lead to rigidity and a loss of creativity in an organization.

_____ **17.** Different forms of control cannot be used at the same time. An organization must decide how it is going to control and just do it.

_____ **18.** Setting across-the-board output or quantity targets for divisions within a company can lead to destructive results.

_____ **19.** Control through rules, procedures, and budgets are generally not very costly.

_____ **20.** Individual self-control can lead to integration and communication problems.

For interpretation, turn to page 451.

Source: Adapted from Chapter 9 (especially pp. 262–279) in Charles W. L. Hill and Gareth R. Jones, *Strategic Management*.

EXPERIENTIAL EXERCISE

Learning About "Real" Control

Purpose: The purpose of this exercise is to give you additional insights into how organizations deal with fundamental control issues.

Instructions

Step One

Working individually, interview a manager, owner, or employee of an organization. The individual can be a local entrepreneur, a manager in a larger company, or an administrator in your college or university, among other choices. If you currently work, interviewing your boss would be excellent.

Using your own words, ask these general questions:

1. In your organization, what are the most important resources to control?

2. Who is primarily responsible for control?

3. Which level of control is most important to your organization? [Briefly describe the three levels of operations control.]

4. Do you use budgets? If so, what kinds and in what ways?

5. Which of these types of control does your organization most typically use? [Briefly describe bureaucratic and clan control.]

6. Have you had any instances in which employees resisted control? Can you explain why and what you did about it?

Step Two

Form small groups of four or five. Then do the following:

1. Each member should describe the organization and manager interviewed and the interview findings.

2. Identify as many commonalities across findings as possible.

3. Summarize all of the differences you found.

4. Select one group member to report your group's experiences to the rest of the class.

CHAPTER NOTES

1. "How a New Boss Got ConAgra Cooking Again," *Business Week*, July 25, 1994, pp. 72–73; Gary Hoover, Alta Campbell, and Patrick J. Spain (Eds.), *Hoover's Handbook of American Business 1995* (Austin, Tex.: The Reference Press, 1994), pp. 380–381.
2. Anne Tsui and Susan Ashford, "Adaptive Self-Regulation: A Process View of Managerial Effectiveness," *Journal of Management*, 1994, Vol. 20, No. 1, pp. 93–121.
3. Thomas A. Stewart, "Welcome to the Revolution," *Fortune*, December 13, 1993, pp. 66–77.
4. William Taylor, "Control in an Age of Chaos," *Harvard Business Review*, November–December 1994, pp. 64–70.
5. Joel Dreyfuss, "Victories in the Quality Crusade," *Fortune*, October 10, 1988, pp. 80–88.
6. Dreyfuss, "Victories in the Quality Crusade."
7. "America's Leanest and Meanest," *Business Week*, October 5, 1987, pp. 78–84.
8. Sim Sitkin, Kathleen Sutcliffe, and Roger Schroeder, "Distinguishing Control from Learning in Total Quality Management: A Contingency Perspective," *Academy of Management Review*, 1994, Vol. 19, No. 3, pp. 537–564.
9. Robert Lusch and Michael Harvey, "The Case for an Off-Balance-Sheet Controller," *Sloan Management Review*, Winter 1994, pp. 101–110.
10. Edward E. Lawler III and John G. Rhode, *Information and Control in Organizations* (Pacific Palisades, Calif.: Goodyear, 1976).
11. Robert N. Anthony, *The Management Control Function* (Boston, Mass.: Harvard Business School Press, 1988).
12. Dreyfuss, "Victories in the Quality Crusade."
13. Anthony, *The Management Control Function.*
14. See Belverd E. Needles, Jr., Henry R. Anderson, and James C. Caldwell, *Principles of Accounting*, 5th ed. (Boston: Houghton Mifflin, 1993).
15. Christopher K. Bart, "Budgeting Gamesmanship," *Academy of Management Executive*, November 1988, pp. 285–294.
16. Thomas A. Stewart, "Why Budgets Are Bad for Business," *Fortune*, June 4, 1990, pp. 179–190.
17. Needles, Anderson, and Caldwell, *Principles of Accounting.*
18. Needles, Anderson, and Caldwell, *Principles of Accounting.*
19. "Questions About U.S. Shoe Corp. Continue to Mount," *The Wall Street Journal*, April 5, 1990, p. A4.
20. "Auditors of Corporate Legal Bills Thrive," *Wall Street Journal*, February 13, 1991, p. B1.
21. William G. Ouchi, "The Transmission of Control Through Organizational Hierarchy," *Academy of Management Journal*, June 1978, pp. 173–192; Richard E. Walton, "From Control to Commitment in the Workplace," *Harvard Business Review*, March–April 1985, pp. 76–84.
22. See Diana Robertson and Erin Anderson, "Control System and Task Environment Effects on Ethical Judgment: An Exploratory Study of Industrial Salespeople," *Organization Science*, November 1993, pp. 617–629, for a recent study of effective control.

CHAPTER

15

Managing for Total Quality

OBJECTIVES

After studying this chapter, you should be able to:

- *Explain the meaning of quality and the importance of total quality management.*
- *Explain the meaning and importance of managing productivity, productivity trends, and ways to improve productivity.*
- *Explain the nature of operations management and its role in managing quality.*
- *Identify and discuss the components involved in using operations systems for quality.*

OUTLINE

OPENING INCIDENT

AS THE 1970s drew to a close, Chrysler Corp., the number-three automobile company in the United States, teetered on the brink of bankruptcy. Supported by government-backed loans and the pure strength of will shown by CEO Lee Iacocca, Chrysler gradually righted itself and returned to profitability. New products like the K-cars and the minivan and the acquisition of American Motors (and its popular Jeep) provided new avenues for growth and profitability.

Iacocca resigned in 1992 and was replaced by Robert Eaton, previously head of Chrysler's European operations. One of the first things Eaton recognized was that even though Chrysler was profitable, Chrysler automobiles were still near the bottom of most lists of high-quality automobiles. Eaton pinned the firm's hopes on several new products such as the Chrysler Cirrus and the Dodge Neon.

Eaton's first step was to change how Chrysler made cars. He implemented a team approach throughout the organization and continually stressed the importance of quality. He also stretched the time the firm would devote to development to avoid hurrying and to provide more time to correct defects. Eaton also created a new executive position called Vice President for Customer Satisfaction and Vehicle Quality. In addition, he changed the way that defects were counted to provide more useful information to everyone in the company.

"We've talked about quality for ten years. The difference this time is, we're actually doing it."

The Neon was the first of the three new products Chrysler launched, appearing in mid-1994. During development of the Neon, Chrysler paid more attention to quality than ever before in its history. Every supplier, for example, was forced to explain in writing how it would ensure delivery of flawless parts. Unfortunately, when the Neon was first launched, a few things had been overlooked. For example, after the production of ten thousand cars Chrysler discovered a leaky seal that could cause a loss of braking power. In addition, it found that plastic radiator supports had to be replaced with metal ones. Although the Neon proved to be better than other Chrysler products, it was not nearly as good as the firm had hoped.

Next came the Cirrus. Eaton himself took a very personal interest in this new model. For example, when the first prototype was assembled in early 1994, he spent two days driving it. He was so disappointed in the car that he delayed its launch six months so that numerous defects and shortcomings could be corrected. Fortunately, the extra time was worthwhile: Shortly after the car was unveiled in fall 1994, it was awarded the prestigious *Motor Trend Car of the Year* award.[1]

Source of Quotation: Chrysler engineer John Fernandez, quoted in *Business Week*, August 22, 1994, p. 26.

Managers at Chrysler have learned two valuable lessons in recent times. First, quality is a critically important factor in today's competitive business environment. Second, achieving higher levels of quality is not an easy accomplishment. Simply ordering that quality be improved is about as effective as waving a magic wand.[2]

In this chapter we explore quality and its role in business today. We first discuss managing total quality. We then discuss productivity, which is closely related to quality. Next we introduce operations management and its role in improving quality. The remaining section of the chapter discusses using operations systems for quality.

MANAGING TOTAL QUALITY

As noted above, quality has become a central issue in managing organizations today.[3] The catalyst for its emergence as a mainstream management concern was foreign business, especially Japanese. And nowhere was it more visible than in the auto industry. During the energy crisis of the late 1970s, many people bought Toyotas, Hondas, and Nissans because they were more fuel efficient than U.S. cars. Consumers soon found, however, that the Japanese cars not only were more fuel efficient, they were also of higher quality than U.S. cars. Parts fit together better, the trim work was neater, and the cars were more reliable. Thus, after the energy crisis subsided, Japanese cars remained formidable competitors because of their reputation for quality.

The Meaning of Quality

• **quality**
The totality of features and characteristics of a product or service that bears on its ability to satisfy stated or implied needs

The American Society for Quality Control defines **quality** as the totality of features and characteristics of a product or service that bear on its ability to satisfy stated or implied needs.[4] Quality has several different attributes. Table 15.1 lists eight dimensions that determine the quality of a particular product or service. For example, a product that is durable and reliable is of higher quality than a product with less durability and reliability.

Quality is also relative. For example, a Lincoln Continental is a higher-grade car than a Ford Taurus, which, in turn, is a higher-grade car than a Ford Escort. The difference in quality stems from differences in design and other features. The Escort, however, is considered a high-quality car relative to its engineering specifications and price. Likewise, the Taurus and Continental may also be high-quality cars, given their standards and prices. Thus quality is both an absolute and a relative concept.

Quality is relevant for both products and services. While its importance for products like cars and computers was perhaps recognized first, quality is also a vitally important determinant of the success or failure of service firms, ranging from airlines to restaurants. Service quality, as we will discuss later in this chapter, has become a major competitive issue in U.S. industry today.

TABLE 15.1 Eight Dimensions of Quality

1. **Performance.** A product's primary operating characteristic. Examples are automobile acceleration and a television set's picture clarity.
2. **Features.** Supplements to a product's basic functioning characteristics, such as power windows on a car.
3. **Reliability.** A probability of not malfunctioning during a specified period.
4. **Conformance.** The degree to which a product's design and operating characteristics meet established standards.
5. **Durability.** A measure of product life.
6. **Serviceability.** The speed and ease of repair.
7. **Aesthetics.** How a product looks, feels, tastes, and smells.
8. **Perceived quality.** As seen by a customer.

Source: Adapted and reprinted by permission of *Harvard Business Review.* From "Competing on the Eight Dimensions of Quality," by David A. Garvin, November/December 1987.

These eight dimensions generally capture the meaning of quality, which is a critically important ingredient to organizational success today. Understanding the basic meaning of quality is a good first step to managing it more effectively.

The Importance of Quality

To help underscore the importance of quality, the U.S. government created the **Malcolm Baldrige Award**, named after the former Secretary of Commerce who championed quality in U.S. industry. The award, administered by an agency of the Commerce Department, is given annually to companies that achieve major improvements in the quality of their products or services. That is, the award is based on changes in quality, as opposed to absolute quality.

Malcolm Baldrige Award Named after a former Secretary of Commerce, this prestigious award is given to companies that achieve major quality improvements

Recent winners of the Baldrige Award include Motorola; the Cadillac Division of General Motors; and divisions of Texas Instruments, AT&T, Xerox, and Westinghouse. In addition, numerous other quality awards have been created. For example, the Rochester Institute of Technology and *USA Today* award their Quality Cup award not to entire organizations but to individual teams of workers within organizations. Quality is also an important concern for individual managers and organizations for three very specific reasons: competition, productivity, and costs.[5]

Competition Quality has become one of the most competitive points in business today. Among Ford, Chrysler, and General Motors, each argues, for example, that its cars are higher in quality than the cars of the others. IBM, Apple Computer, and Digital Equipment stress the quality of their products as well. And America, United, and Delta airlines each argues that it provides the best and most reliable service. Indeed, it seems that virtually every U.S. business has adopted quality as a major point of competition. Thus a business that fails to keep pace may find itself falling behind not only foreign competition but also other U.S. firms.[6]

Productivity Managers have come to recognize that quality and productivity are related. In the past, many managers thought that they could increase output (productivity) only by decreasing quality. Managers today have learned the hard way that such an assumption is almost always wrong. If a company installs a meaningful quality enhancement program, three things are likely to result. First, the number of defects is likely to decrease, causing fewer returns from customers. Second, because the number of defects goes down, resources (materials and people) dedicated to reworking flawed output will decrease. Third, because making employees responsible for quality reduces the need for quality inspectors, the organization is able to produce more units with fewer resources.

Costs Improved quality also lowers costs. Poor quality results in higher returns from customers, high warranty costs, and lawsuits from customers injured by faulty products. Future sales are lost because of disgruntled customers. An organization with quality problems often has to increase inspection expenses just to catch defective products. We noted in Chapter 14, for example, how Whistler Corporation was using one hundred of its 250 employees just to fix poorly assembled radar detectors.[7]

Total Quality Management

• total quality management (TQM) A strategic commitment by top management to change its whole approach to business to make quality a guiding factor in everything it does

Once an organization makes a decision to enhance the quality of its products and services, it must decide how to implement this decision. The most pervasive approach to managing quality has been called **total quality management (TQM)**—a real and meaningful effort by an organization to change its whole approach to business to make quality a guiding factor in everything the organization does.[8] Figure 15.1 highlights the major ingredients of TQM.

Strategic Commitment The starting point for TQM is a strategic commitment by top management. Such commitment is important for several reasons. First, the organizational culture must change to recognize that quality is not just an ideal but is instead an objective goal that must be pursued.[9] The fact that Robert Eaton at Chrysler took two days out of his schedule to test drive the Cirrus helped alter the company's culture regarding quality. Second, a decision to pursue the goal of quality carries with it some real costs—for expenditures such as new equipment and

FIGURE 15.1 Total Quality Management

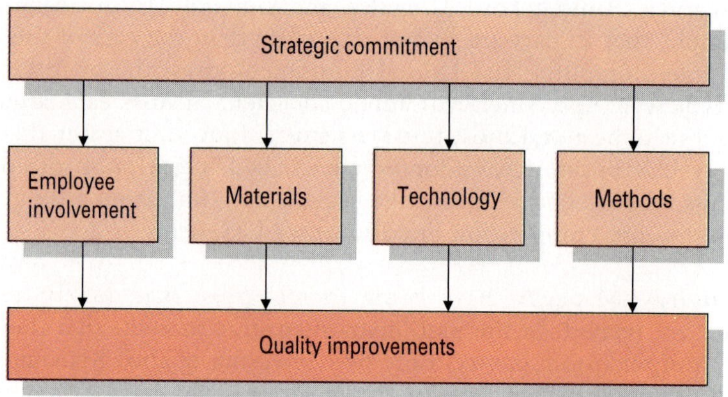

Quality is one of the most important issues facing organizations today. Total quality management, or TQM, is a comprehensive effort to enhance an organization's product or service quality. TQM involves the five basic dimensions shown here. Each is important and must be addressed effectively if the organization truly expects to increase quality.

facilities. Again, Eaton's decision to delay the Cirrus cost the company money, at least in the short run. Without a commitment from top management, quality improvement will prove to be just a slogan or gimmick, with little or no real impact.

Employee Involvement Employee involvement is another critical ingredient in TQM. Virtually all successful quality enhancement programs involve making the person responsible for doing the job also responsible for making sure it is done right.[10] By definition, then, employee involvement is a critical component in improving quality. Work teams, discussed in Chapter 13, are common vehicles for increasing employee involvement.

Technology New forms of technology are also useful in TQM programs. Automation and robots, for example, can often make products with higher precision and better consistency than can people. Investing in higher-grade machines capable of doing jobs more precisely and reliably often improves quality. For example, AT&T achieved notable improvements in product quality by replacing many of its machines with new equipment. Similarly, most U.S. auto and electronics firms have all made significant investments in technology to help boost quality.

Materials Another important part of TQM is improving the quality of the materials that organizations use. Suppose that a company that assembles stereos buys chips and circuits from another company. If the chips have a high failure rate, consumers will return defective stereos to the company whose nameplate appears on them, not to the company that made the chips. The stereo company then loses in two ways: refunds back to customers and a damaged reputation. As a result, many companies have increased the quality requirements they impose on their suppliers as a way of improving the quality of their own products. Chrysler has raised its standards regarding the quality of parts and materials it will buy from others.

Methods Improved methods can improve product and service quality. Methods are operating systems used by the organization during the actual transformation process. American Express, for example, has found ways to cut its approval time for new credit cards from twenty-two to only eleven days. This results in improved service quality.[11]

TQM Tools and Techniques

Beyond the strategic context of quality, managers can rely on several specific tools and techniques for improving quality. Among the most popular today are benchmarking, outsourcing, speed, ISO 9000, and statistical quality control.

Benchmarking **Benchmarking** is the process of learning how other organizations do things in an exceptionally high-quality manner. Some approaches to benchmarking are simple and straightforward. For example, Xerox routinely buys copiers made by other companies and takes them apart to see how they work, enabling it to stay abreast of improvements

• **benchmarking** The process of learning how other organizations do things in an exceptionally high-quality manner

and changes its competitors are using. When Ford was planning the Taurus, it identified the four hundred features customers identified as being most important to them. It then found the competing cars that did the best job on each feature. Ford's goal was to equal or surpass each of its competitors on those four hundred features. Other benchmarking strategies are more indirect. For example, many companies study how L.L. Bean manages its mail-order business and how FedEx tracks packages for applications they can employ in their own businesses.[12]

● **outsourcing**
Subcontracting services and operations to other companies that can perform them cheaper or better

Outsourcing Another innovation for improving quality is outsourcing. **Outsourcing** is the process of subcontracting services and operations to other companies that can perform them cheaper or better. If a business performs each and every one of its own administrative and business services and operations, it is almost certain to be doing at least some of them in an inefficient or low-quality manner. If those areas can be identified and outsourced, the company will save money and realize a higher-quality service or operation. For example, until recently Eastman Kodak handled all of its own computing operations. Recently, however, those operations were subcontracted to IBM, which now handles all of Kodak's computing. The result is higher-quality computing systems and operations at Kodak for less money than it was spending before.[13]

● **speed**
The time needed by the organization to get its activities, including developing, producing, and distributing products or services, accomplished

Speed A third popular TQM technique is speed. **Speed** is the time needed by the organization to get something accomplished, and it can be emphasized in any area, including developing, making, and distributing products or services.[14] One recent survey identified speed as the number-

Outsourcing is becoming an increasingly important tool in total quality management. One of the hottest new food products in recent years has been Trix yogurt for kids. General Mills got the product to market quickly by outsourcing its production to Dairyman's, a company in Tular, California. General Mills dictates the quality standards it expects, and Dairyman's complies in order to maintain the account.

one strategic issue confronting managers in the 1990s.[15] A good illustration of the power of speed comes from General Electric. At one point GE needed six plants and three weeks to produce and deliver custom-made industrial circuit-breaker boxes. By emphasizing speed, the same product can now be delivered in three days, and only a single plant is involved. Table 15.2 identifies a number of basic suggestions that have helped companies increase the speed of their operations. For example, GE found it better to start from scratch with a remodeled plant. GE also wiped out the need for approvals by eliminating most managerial positions and set up teams as a basis for organizing work. Stressing the importance of the schedule helped Motorola build a new plant and start production of a new product in only eighteen months.

ISO 9000 Still another useful technique for improving quality is ISO 9000. **ISO 9000** refers to a set of quality standards created by the International Organization for Standardization. There are five such standards, covering such areas as product testing, employee training, recordkeeping, supplier relations, and repair policies and procedures. Companies that want to meet these standards apply for certification and are audited by a firm chosen by the organization's domestic affiliate (in the United States, this is the American National Standards Institute). These auditors review every aspect of the company's business operations in relation to the standards. Many companies report that merely preparing for an ISO 9000 audit has been helpful. Many organizations today, including General Electric, Du Pont, Eastman Kodak, British Telecom, and Philips Electronics, are urging—and in some cases requiring—that their suppliers achieve ISO 9000 certification.[16]

• **ISO 9000**
A set of quality standards created by the International Organization for Standardization

Statistical Quality Control A final quality control technique is **statistical quality control (SQC)**. As the term suggests, SQC is primarily concerned with managing quality. Moreover, it is a set of specific statistical techniques that can be used to monitor quality. *Acceptance sampling*

• **statistical quality control (SQC)**
A set of specific statistical techniques that can be used to monitor quality; includes acceptance sampling and in-process sampling

TABLE 15.2 Guidelines for Increasing the Speed of Operations

1. Start from scratch (it's usually easier than trying to do what the organization does now faster).
2. Minimize the number of approvals needed to do something (the fewer people who have to approve something, the faster it will get done).
3. Use work teams as a basis for organization (teamwork and cooperation work better than individual effort and conflict).
4. Develop and adhere to a schedule (a properly designed schedule can greatly increase speed).
5. Don't ignore distribution (making something faster is only part of the battle).
6. Integrate speed into the organization's culture (if everyone understands the importance of speed, things will naturally get done quicker).

Source: Adapted from Brian Dumaine, "How Managers Can Succeed Through Speed," *Fortune*, February 13, 1989, pp. 54–59.

Many organizations today are using speed for competitive advantage. These are six common guidelines that organizations follow when they want to shorten the time they need to get things accomplished. Although not every manager can do each of these things, most managers can do at least some of them. Increasing speed will give organizations a strategic advantage and help them compete more effectively.

involves sampling finished goods to ensure that quality standards have been met. Acceptance sampling is effective only when the correct percentage of products that should be tested (for example, 2, 5, or 25 percent) is determined. This decision is especially important when the test renders the product useless. Flash cubes, wine, and collapsible steering wheels, for example, are consumed or destroyed during testing. Another SQC method is *in-process sampling*. In-process sampling involves evaluating products during production so that needed changes can be made. The painting department of a furniture company might periodically check the tint of the paint it is using. The company can then adjust the color as necessary to conform to customer standards. The advantage of in-process sampling is that it allows problems to be detected before they accumulate.

MANAGING PRODUCTIVITY

Although the current focus on quality by U.S. companies is a relatively recent phenomenon, managers have been aware of the importance of productivity for several years. The stimulus for this attention was a recognition that the gap between productivity in the United States and productivity in other industrialized countries was narrowing. In this section we describe the meaning of productivity and underscore its importance. After summarizing recent productivity trends, we suggest ways that organizations can increase their productivity.

The Meaning of Productivity

• **productivity**
An economic measure of efficiency that summarizes the value of outputs relative to the value of the inputs used to create them

In a general sense, **productivity** is an economic measure of efficiency that summarizes the value of outputs relative to the value of the inputs used to create them.[17] Productivity can be and often is assessed at different levels of analysis and in different forms.

Levels of Productivity By level of productivity we mean the units of analysis used to calculate or define productivity. For example, aggregate productivity is the total level of productivity achieved by a country. Industry productivity is the total productivity achieved by all the companies in a particular industry. Company productivity is the level of productivity achieved by an individual company. Unit and individual productivity refer to the productivity achieved by a unit or department within an organization and the level of productivity attained by a single person.

Forms of Productivity Productivity takes many different forms. Total factor productivity is defined by the following formula:

$$\text{Productivity} = \frac{\text{Outputs}}{\text{Inputs}}$$

Total factor productivity is an overall indicator of how well an organization uses all of its resources, such as labor, capital, materials, and energy, to create all of its products and services. The biggest problem with total factor productivity is that all the ingredients must be expressed in the same terms—dollars (it is difficult to add hours of labor to number of units of a raw material in a meaningful way). Total factor productivity also gives little insight into how things can be changed to improve productivity.

Consequently, most organizations find it more useful to calculate a partial productivity ratio. Such a ratio uses only one category of resource. For example, labor productivity could be calculated by this simple formula:

$$\text{Labor Productivity} = \frac{\text{Outputs}}{\text{Direct Labor}}$$

This method has two advantages. First, it is not necessary to transform the units of input into some other unit. Second, this method provides managers with specific insights into how changing different resource inputs affects productivity. Suppose that an organization can manufacture one hundred units of a particular product with twenty hours of direct labor. The organization's labor productivity index is 5 (or five units per labor hour). Now suppose that worker efficiency is increased so that the same twenty hours of labor results in the manufacture of 120 units of the product. The labor productivity index increases to 6 (six units per labor hour), and the company can see the direct results of a specific managerial action.

The Importance of Productivity

Managers consider it important that their companies maintain high levels of productivity for a variety of reasons. Productivity is a primary determinant of an organization's level of profitability and, ultimately, its ability to survive. If one organization is more productive than another, it will have more products to sell at lower prices and have more profits to reinvest in other areas. Productivity also partially determines people's standards of living within a particular country. At an economic level, businesses consume resources and produce goods and services. The goods and services created within a country can be used by that country's own citizens or exported for sale in other countries. The more goods and services the businesses within a country can produce, the more goods and services the country's citizens will have. Even goods that are exported result in financial resources flowing back into the home country. Thus the citizens of a highly productive country are likely to have notably higher standards of living than are the citizens of a country with low productivity.

Productivity Trends

The United States has the highest level of productivity in the world. For example, Japanese workers produce only about 76 percent as much as U.S. workers, while German workers produce about 84 percent as much.[18] An alarming trend began in the 1960s, however, and continued into the 1980s. During this time, the rate of productivity growth in the United States slowed, especially in comparison to the rates in other industrialized countries. That is, while U.S. workers continued to be the most productive workers in the world, their counterparts in Japan, Germany, and similar countries began to close the gap.

This trend was a primary factor in the decisions made by U.S. businesses to retrench, retool, and become more competitive in the world marketplace. For example, General Electric's dishwasher plant in Louisville has cut its inventory requirements by 50 percent, reduced labor costs from 15 percent to only 10 percent of total manufacturing costs, and cut product development time in half. As a result of these kinds of efforts, productivity trends have now leveled out and U.S. workers are generally maintaining their lead in most industries.

Several factors have been cited to account for the productivity slowdowns recorded during the 1960s and 1970s. First, the composition of the U.S. workforce underwent major changes. After World War II, more and more of the general population went to college. Thus postwar gains in productivity were at least partially attributable to higher levels of education. Later, as the proportion of workers with higher education leveled off, productivity gains tended to level off. Another factor is that the workforce absorbed many new and inexperienced employees during that period as more and more women and younger workers joined the workforce.

A second contributing factor was a decline in the quality of U.S. production facilities relative to facilities in the rest of the world. Generally, existing factories continued to operate as they had in years past, while companies in other countries were investing heavily in new and highly efficient facilities. For example, the average U.S. plant is over eighteen years old. Its counterpart in Japan is around twelve years old.

A final contributor was the tremendous growth of the service sector in the United States. While this sector grew, its productivity levels did not. One part of this problem relates to measurement. For example, it is fairly easy to calculate the number of tons of steel produced at a Bethlehem Steel mill and divide it by the number of labor hours used; it is more difficult to determine the output of an attorney or a certified public accountant. Still, virtually everyone agrees that improving service-sector productivity is the next major hurdle facing U.S. business.

Figure 15.2 illustrates recent trends in productivity growth for the total U.S. economy, broken down into manufacturing and service (agricultural productivity is not included). As you can see, manufacturing productivity had stalled out from the mid-1970s into the early 1980s but has been increasing since that time. Service-sector productivity, meanwhile, has remained relatively stable. Total productivity, therefore, has been increasing, but only at a modest pace.

Improving Productivity

How does a business or industry improve its productivity? Numerous specific suggestions made by experts generally fall into two broad categories: improving operations and increasing employee involvement.

Improving Operations One way that companies can improve operations is by spending more on research and development (R&D). R&D spending helps identify new products, new uses for existing products, and new

F I G U R E 15.2 Manufacturing and Service Productivity Growth Trends (1970–1993)

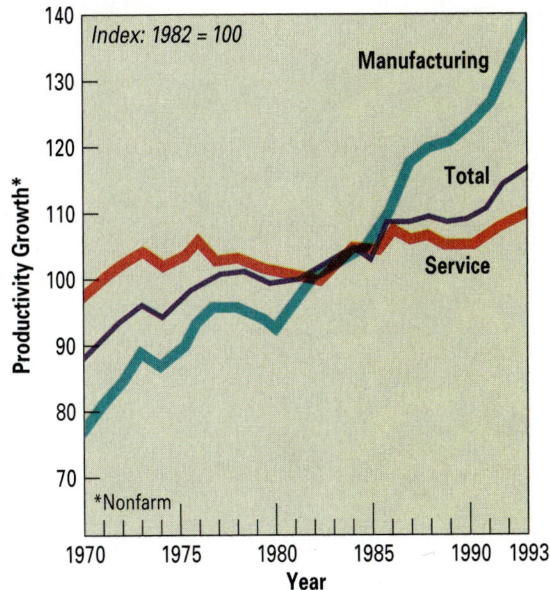

Source: Graph "Productivity Growth" from Myron Magnet, "The Productivity Payoff Arrives," *Fortune*, June 27, 1994, p. 79.

Both manufacturing productivity and service productivity in the United States continue to grow, although manufacturing productivity is growing at a faster pace. Total productivity, therefore, also continues to grow.

methods for making products. Each of these contributes to productivity. For example, Bausch & Lomb almost missed the boat on extended-wear contact lenses because the company had neglected R&D. When it became apparent that major competitors were almost a year ahead of Bausch & Lomb in developing the new lenses, management made R&D a top-priority concern. As a result, the company made several scientific breakthroughs, shortened the time needed to introduce new products, and greatly enhanced both total sales and profits—and all with a smaller workforce than the company used to employ. Even though other countries are greatly increasing their R&D spending, the United States continues to be the world leader in this area.

Another way companies can boost productivity through operations is by reassessing and revamping their transformation facilities. Just building a new factory is no guarantee of success, but IBM, Ford, Allen-Bradley, Caterpillar, and many other businesses have achieved dramatic productivity gains by revamping their production facilities. Facility refinements are not limited to manufacturers. In recent years, many McDonald's restaurants have added drive-through windows, and many are moving soft-drink dispensers out to the restaurant floor so that customers can get their own drinks. Each of these moves is an attempt to increase the speed with which customers can be served and thus to increase productivity.

Increasing Employee Involvement The other major thrust in productivity enhancement has been toward employee involvement. We noted earlier

Managing productivity is a critical part of total quality management. Organizations are always on the alert, therefore, for ways to boost productivity. Managers at Sky Chefs have increased productivity by decreasing worker injuries. Stretching sessions such as this one have helped the company improve the health of its workers while simultaneously decreasing injuries.

that participation can enhance quality. So, too, can it boost productivity. Examples of this involvement are an individual worker being given a bigger voice in how she does her job, a formal agreement of cooperation between management and labor, and total involvement throughout the organization.[19] GE eliminated most of the supervisors at its one new circuit-breaker plant and put control in the hands of workers.

Another method popular in the United States is increasing the flexibility of an organization's workforce by training employees to perform a number of different jobs. Such cross-training allows the company to function with fewer workers because workers can be transferred easily to areas where they are most needed. For example, the Lechmere department store in Sarasota, Florida, encourages workers to learn numerous jobs within the store. One person in the store can operate a forklift in the stockroom, serve as a cashier, or provide customer service on the sales floor. At a Motorola plant, 397 of 400 employees have learned at least two skills under a similar program.

Rewards are essential to making employee involvement work. Organizations must reward people for learning new skills and using them proficiently. At Motorola, for example, workers who master a new skill are assigned for five days to a job requiring them to use that skill. If they perform with no defects, they are moved to a higher pay grade, and then they move back and forth between jobs as they are needed. If there is a performance problem, they receive more training and practice. This approach is fairly new, but preliminary indicators suggest that it can increase productivity significantly. Many unions resist such programs because they threaten job security and reduce a person's identification with one skill or craft.

MANAGING QUALITY THROUGH OPERATIONS MANAGEMENT

We noted earlier that both quality and productivity can be enhanced through various elements of operations. But what exactly are operations? And how are they managed? **Operations management** is the set of managerial activities used by an organization to transform resource inputs into products, services, or both. When IBM buys electronic components, assembles them into computers, and then ships them to customers, it is relying on operations management. When a Pizza Hut employee orders food and paper products and then combines dough, cheese, and tomato paste to create a pizza, he or she is using operations management.

• **operations management** The set of managerial activities used by an organization to transform resource inputs into products, services, or both

Operations mangement is an important functional concern for organizations because efficient and effective management of operations goes a long way toward ensuring quality and productivity. Inefficient or ineffective operations management, on the other hand, will almost inevitably lead to lower levels of both quality and productivity. In an economic sense, operations management provides utility, or value, of one type or another, depending on the nature of the company's products or services. If the product is a physical good, such as a Yamaha motorcycle, operations management provides form utility by combining many dissimilar inputs (sheet metal, rubber, paint, combustion engines, and human craftsmanship) to produce the desired output. The inputs are converted from their incoming forms into a new physical form. This conversion is typical of manufacturing operations and essentially reflects the organization's technology.

In contrast, the operations activities of American Airlines provide time and place utility through its services. The airline transports passengers and freight according to agreed-on departure and arrival places and times. Other service operations, such as an Adolph Coors beer distributorship or The Gap retail chain, provide place and possession utility by bringing the customer and products made by others together. Although the organizations in these examples produce different kinds of products or services, their operations processes share many important features.[20]

It should be clear that operations management is very important to organizations. Beyond its direct impact on quality and productivity, it directly influences the organization's overall level of effectiveness. For example, the deceptively simple strategic decision of whether to stress high quality regardless of cost, lowest possible cost regardless of quality, or some combination of the two, has numerous important implications. A highest-possible-quality strategy will dictate state-of-the-art technology and rigorous control of product design and materials specifications. A combination strategy might call for lower-grade technology and less concern about product design and materials specifications. Just as strategy affects operations management, so too does operations management affect strategy. Suppose that an organization decides to upgrade the quality of its products or services. The organization's ability to implement the decision is dependent in part on current production capabilities and other resources. If existing technology will not permit higher-quality work and if the organization lacks the resources to replace its technology, increasing quality to the desired new standards will be difficult.

Manufacturing and Production

• manufacturing
A form of business that combines and transforms resources into tangible outcomes

Because manufacturing once dominated U.S. industry, the entire area of operations management used to be called production management. **Manufacturing** is a form of business that combines and transforms resources into tangible outcomes that are then sold to others. The Goodyear Tire & Rubber Company is a manufacturer because it combines rubber and chemical compounds and uses blending equipment and molding machines to ultimately create tires. Broyhill is a manufacturer because it buys wood and metal components, pads, and fabric and then combines them into furniture.

During the 1970s, manufacturing entered a long period of decline in the United States, primarily because of foreign competition. U.S. firms had grown lax and sluggish, and new foreign competitors came onto the scene with new equipment and much higher levels of efficiency. For example, steel companies in the Far East were able to produce high-quality steel for much lower prices than were U.S. companies like Bethlehem Steel and U.S. Steel (now USX Corporation). Faced with a battle for survival, many companies underwent a long and difficult period of change by eliminating waste and transforming themselves into leaner, more efficient, and more responsive entities. They reduced their workforces dramatically, closed antiquated or unnecessary plants, and modernized their remaining plants. In recent years, their efforts have started to pay dividends as U.S. business has regained its competitive position in many different industries. Although manufacturers from other parts of the world are still formidable competitors and U.S. companies may never again be competitive in some markets, the overall picture is much better than it was just a few years ago. And prospects continue to look bright.

Manufacturing Technology

Numerous forms of manufacturing technology are used in organizations. Two forms of technology especially pertinent to quality and productivity are automation and robotics.

• automation
The process of designing work so that it can be completely or almost completely performed by machines

Automation **Automation** is the process of designing work so that it can be completely or almost completely performed by machines. Because automated machines operate quickly and make few errors, they increase the amount of work that can be done. Thus automation helps to improve products and services, and it fosters innovation. Automation is the most recent step in the development of machines and machine-controlling devices. Machine-controlling devices have been around since the 1700s. James Watt, a Scottish engineer, invented a mechanical speed control to regulate the speed of steam engines in 1787. The Jacquard loom, developed by a French inventor, was controlled by paper cards with holes punched in them. Early accounting and computing equipment was controlled by similar punched cards.

Automation relies on feedback, information, sensors, and a control mechanism. Feedback is the flow of information from the machine back to the sensor. Sensors are the parts of the system that gather information and compare it to some preset standards. The control mechanism is the device that sends instructions to the automatic machine. Early automatic machines were primitive, and the use of automation was relatively slow to develop. These elements are illustrated by the example in Figure 15.3. A thermostat has sensors that monitor air temperature and compare it to a preset low value. If the air temperature falls below the preset value, the thermostat sends an electrical signal to the furnace, turning it on. The furnace heats the air. When the sensors detect that the air temperature has reached a value higher than the preset low value, the thermostat stops the furnace. The last step (shutting off the furnace) is known as feedback, a critical component of any automated operation.

The big move to automate factories began during World War II. The shortage of skilled workers and the development of high-speed computers combined to bring about a tremendous interest in automation. Programmable automation (the use of computers to control machines) was introduced during this era, far outstripping conventional automation (the use of mechanical or electromechanical devices to control machines).[21] The automobile industry began to use automatic machines for a variety of jobs. In fact, the term *automation* came into use in the 1950s in the automobile industry. The chemical and oil-refining industries also began to use computers to regulate production. This computerized, or programmable, automation presents the greatest opportunities and challenges for management today.

The impact of automation on people in the workplace is complex. In the short term, people whose jobs are automated find themselves without jobs. In the long term, however, more jobs are created than are lost. Nevertheless, not all companies are able to help displaced workers find new jobs, so the human costs are sometimes high. In the coal industry, for instance, automation has been used primarily in mining. The output per miner has risen dramatically from the 1950s. The demand for coal,

FIGURE 15.3 A Simple Automatic Control Mechanism

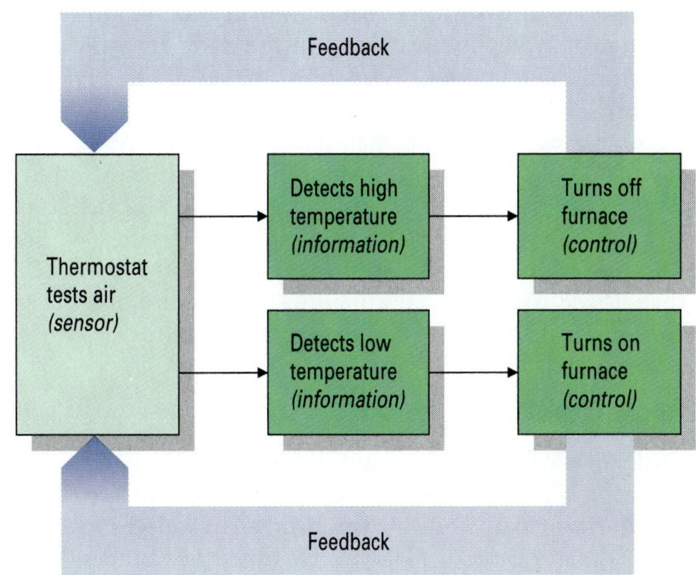

All automation includes feedback, information, sensors, and a control mechanism. A simple thermostat is an example of automation. Another example is Benetton Group SPA's distribution center in Italy. Orders are received, items are pulled from stock and packaged for shipment, and invoices are prepared and transmitted with no human intervention.

however, has decreased; and productivity gains resulting from automation have lessened the need for miners. Consequently, a lot of workers have lost their jobs, and the industry has not been able to absorb them. In contrast, in the electronics industry, the rising demand for products has led to increasing employment opportunities despite the use of automation.

• **robot**
Any artificial device that is able to perform functions ordinarily thought to be appropriate for human beings

Robotics One of the newest trends in manufacturing technology is robotics. A **robot** is any artificial device that is able to perform functions ordinarily thought to be appropriate for human beings. Robotics refers to the science and technology of the construction, maintenance, and use of robots. The use of industrial robots has increased steadily since 1980 and is expected to continue to increase slowly as more companies recognize the benefits that accrue to users of industrial robots.

Welding was one of the first applications for robots, and it continues to be the area of most applications. In second place and close behind is materials handling. Other applications include machine loading and unloading, painting and finishing, assembly, casting, and machining applications such as cutting, grinding, polishing, drilling, sanding, buffing, and deburring. Chrysler, for instance, replaced about two hundred welders with fifty robots on an assembly line and increased productivity about 20 percent.[22] The use of robots in inspection work is increasing. They can check for cracks and holes, and they can be equipped with vision systems to perform visual inspections.

Robots are beginning to move from the factory floor to all other applications. The Dallas police used a robot to apprehend a suspect who had barricaded himself in an apartment building. The robot smashed a window and reached with its mechanical arm into the building. The suspect panicked and ran outside. At the Long Beach Memorial Hospital in California, brain surgeons are assisted by a robot arm that drills into the patient's skull with excellent precision.[23] Some newer applications involve remote work. For example, the use of submergible robots controlled from the surface can help divers in remote locations. Surveillance robots fitted with microwave sensors can do things that a human guard cannot do, such as "seeing" through nonmetallic walls and in the dark. In other applications, automated farming (agrimation) uses robot harvesters to pick fruit from a variety of trees.[24]

Robots are also used by small manufacturers. One robot slices carpeting to fit the inside of custom vans in an upholstery shop. Another stretches balloons flat so that they can be spray-painted with slogans at a novelties company. At a jewelry company, a robot holds class rings while they are engraved by a laser. These robots are lighter, faster, stronger, and more intelligent than those used in heavy manufacturing and are the types that more and more organizations will be using in the future.[25]

Service Operations

• **service organization**
An organization that transforms resources into intangible outputs and creates time or place utility for its customers

During the decline of the manufacturing sector, a tremendous growth in the service sector kept the U.S. economy from declining at the same rate. A **service organization** is one that transforms resources into an intangible output and creates time or place utility for its customers. For example,

Merrill Lynch & Co. makes stock transactions for its customers, Avis leases cars to its customers, and your local hairdresser cuts your hair. In 1947, the service sector was responsible for less than half of the U.S. gross national product (GNP). By 1975, however, this figure reached 65 percent, and by 1991 it approached 73 percent. The service sector was responsible for almost 90 percent of all new jobs created in the United States during the 1980s and has surpassed that same figure each year so far in the 1990s.

Managers have come to see that many of the tools, techniques, and methods that are used in a factory are also useful to a service firm. For example, managers of automobile plants and hair salons must decide how to design their facilities, identify the best locations for them, determine optimal capacities, make decisions about inventory storage, set procedures for purchasing raw materials, and set standards for productivity and quality.

Service Technology

Service technology is also changing rapidly. It, too, is moving more and more toward automated systems and procedures. In banking, for example, new technological breakthroughs have led to automated teller machines and have made it much easier to move funds between accounts or between different banks. Some people now have their paychecks deposited directly into a checking account from which many of their bills are then automatically paid. Credit card transactions by Visa customers are recorded and billed electronically.

Hotels use increasingly sophisticated technology to accept and record room reservations. Universities use new technologies to electronically store and provide access to all manner of books, scientific journals, government reports, and articles. Hospitals and other health care organizations use new forms of service technology to manage patient records, dispatch ambulances, and monitor vital signs. Restaurants use technology to record and fill customer orders, order food and supplies, and prepare food. Given the increased role that service organizations are playing in today's economy, even more technological innovations are likely to be developed in the years to come.[26]

USING OPERATIONS SYSTEMS FOR QUALITY

After operations systems have been properly designed, they must be put into use by the organization. Their basic functional purpose is to control transformation processes to ensure that relevant goals are achieved in areas such as quality and costs. Operations has a number of special purposes within this control framework, including purchasing and inventory management.

Operations Management as Control

One way of using operations management as control is to coordinate it with other functions. Monsanto Company, for example, established a consumer products division that produces and distributes fertilizers and lawn chemicals. To facilitate control, the operations function was organized as an autonomous profit center. Monsanto finds this effective because its manufacturing division is given the authority to determine not only the costs of creating the product but also the product price and the marketing programs.

In terms of overall organizational control, a division like the one used by Monsanto should be held accountable only for the activities over which it has decision-making authority. It would be inappropriate, of course, to make operations accountable for profitability in an organization that stresses sales and market share over quality and productivity. Misplaced accountability results in ineffective organizational control, to say nothing of hostility and conflict. Depending on the strategic role of operations, then, operations managers are accountable for different kinds of results. For example, in an organization using bureaucratic control, accountability will be spelled out in rules and regulations. In a clan system, it is likely to be understood and accepted by everyone.

Within operations, managerial control ensures that resources and activities achieve primary goals such as a high percentage of on-time deliveries, low unit-production cost, or high product reliability. Any control system should focus on the elements that are most crucial to goal attainment. For example, firms in which product quality is a major concern (as it is at Rolex), might adopt a screening control system to monitor the product as it is being created. If quantity is a pressing issue (as it is at Timex), a postaction system might be used to identify defects at the end of the system without disrupting the manufacturing process itself.

Purchasing Management

• **purchasing management** Buying the materials and resources needed to create products and services

Purchasing management is concerned with buying the materials and resources needed to create products and services. Thus the purchasing manager for a retailer like Sears is responsible for buying the merchandise the store will sell. The purchasing manager for a manufacturer buys raw materials, parts, and machines needed by the organization. Large companies like GE, IBM, and Westinghouse have large purchasing departments. The manager responsible for purchasing must balance a number of constraints. Buying too much ties up capital and increases storage costs. Buying too little might lead to shortages and high reordering costs. The manager must ensure that the quality of what is purchased meets the organization's needs, that the supplier is reliable, and that the best financial terms are negotiated.

Many organizations have recently changed their approach to purchasing as a means to lower costs and improve quality and productivity. In particular, rather than relying on hundreds or even thousands of suppliers, many companies are reducing the number of suppliers and negotiating special production-delivery arrangements. For example, the Honda plant in Marysville, Ohio, found a local business owner looking for a new opportunity. They negotiated an agreement whereby he would start a new company to mount car stereo speakers into plastic moldings. He delivers finished goods to the plant three times a day, and Honda buys all he can manufacture. Thus he has a stable sales base, Honda has a local and reliable supplier, and both companies benefit.

Inventory Management

Inventory control, also called *materials control,* is essential for effective operations management. The four basic kinds of inventories are *raw materials*, *work-in-process*, *finished-goods*, and products *in-transit*. As shown in Table 15.3, the sources of control over these inventories are as different as their purposes. Work-in-process inventories, for example, are made up of partially completed products that need further processing; they are controlled by the shop-floor system. In contrast, the quantities and costs of finished-goods inventories are under the control of the overall production scheduling system, which is determined by high-level planning decisions. In-transit inventories are controlled by the transportation and distribution systems.

• **inventory control**
Managing the organization's raw materials, work-in-process, finished-goods, and products in-transit

Like most other areas of operations management, inventory management has changed notably in recent years. One particularly important breakthrough is the **just-in-time (JIT) method**. First popularized by the Japanese, JIT reduces the organization's investment in storage space for raw materials and in the materials themselves. Historically, manufacturers built large storage areas and filled them with materials, parts, and supplies that would be needed days, weeks, and even months in the future. A manager using the JIT approach orders materials and parts more often and in smaller quantities, thereby reducing investment in both storage space and actual inventory. The ideal arrangement is for materials to arrive just as they are needed—or just in time.

• **just-in-time (JIT) method**
An inventory system in which necessary materials arrive as soon as they are needed (just in time) so that the production process is not interrupted

TABLE 15.3 Inventory Types, Purposes, and Sources of Control

Type	Purpose	Source of Control
Raw materials	Provide the materials needed to make the product	Purchasing models and systems
Work-in-process	Enables overall production to be divided into stages of manageable size	Shop-floor control systems
Finished-goods	Provide ready supply of products on customer demand and enable long, efficient production runs	High-level production scheduling systems in conjunction with marketing
In-transit (pipeline)	Distributes products to customers	Transportation and distribution control systems

Most organizations maintain four types of inventory, each serving its own unique purpose. Different sources of control are used to manage each type of inventory.

Johnson Controls makes automobile seats for Chrysler and ships them by small truckloads to a Chrysler plant seventy-five miles away. Each shipment is scheduled to arrive two hours before it is needed. Clearly, the JIT approach requires high levels of coordination and cooperation between the company and its suppliers. If shipments arrive too early, Chrysler has no place to store them. If they arrive too late, the entire assembly line may have to be shut down, resulting in enormous expense. When properly designed and used, the JIT method controls inventory very effectively.

SUMMARY OF KEY POINTS

Quality is a major consideration for all managers today. Quality is important because it affects competition, productivity, and costs. Total quality management is a comprehensive, organization-wide effort to enhance quality through a variety of avenues.

Productivity is also a major concern to managers. Productivity is a measure of how efficiently an organization is using its resources to create products or services. The United States still leads the world in individual productivity, but other industrialized nations are catching up.

Quality and productivity are often addressed via operations management, the set of managerial activities that organizations use in creating their products and services. Operations management is important to both manufacturing and service organizations. It plays an important role in an organization's strategy.

Technology also plays an important role in quality. Automation is especially important today. Robotics is also a growing area. Technology is as relevant to service organizations as it is to manufacturing organizations.

After an operations system has been designed and put into place, it serves a critical role in quality control. Major areas of interest during the use of operations systems are purchasing and inventory management.

QUESTIONS FOR REVIEW

1. What is quality? Why is it so important today?
2. How can an organization go about trying to increase the speed of its operations?
3. What are some of the basic TQM tools and techniques that managers can use to improve quality?
4. What is productivity? How can it be increased?
5. What is the relationship of operations management to overall organizational strategy? Where do productivity and quality fit into that relationship?

QUESTIONS FOR ANALYSIS

1. How might the management functions of planning, organizing, and leading relate to the management of quality and productivity?
2. Some people argue that quality and productivity are inversely related; as one goes up, the other goes down. How can that argument be refuted?
3. Is operations management most closely linked to corporate-level, business-level, or functional strategies? Why and in what way?
4. Consider your college or university as an organization. How might it go about developing a TQM program?
5. Think of a product or service you purchased recently that subsequently failed to meet your expectations regarding quality. What about that product or service specifically could have been improved to make it of higher quality?

CASE STUDY

Puttin' On the Ritz

The Ritz Carlton Hotel Co. manages twenty-five luxury hotels. Those hotels target industry executives, meeting and corporate travel planners, and affluent travelers. Because the Ritz targets such a relatively small market, critical to its success is that customers be satisfied and return again and again. Accordingly, Ritz Carlton has developed a strong quality management program.

Horst Schulze, president and CEO of Ritz Carlton Hotel Co., stresses that, in the hospitality field, a focus on quality is essential for any organization that wants to remain in business for long. In the fall of 1992, the Ritz Carlton became the first hotel company to win the Malcolm Baldrige Award. That award was the culmination of a three-year effort that began when Ritz Carlton created the position of corporate director of quality to coordinate and spearhead its total quality management (TQM) program. Hallmarks of its program include participatory executive leadership, information gathering, coordinated planning and execution, and a workforce empowered to go to great lengths to satisfy customers.

Ritz Carlton's approach to service is built on the concept that service can be accomplished only by people. All employees are therefore trained in the three steps of service that the company uses to guarantee that every guest has a "memorable experience." The three steps of service are (1) warmly greeting every guest by name; (2) anticipating and complying with every guest's needs; and (3) bidding every guest a warm farewell, again using the guest's name.

A statistical study indicated that customer satisfaction was causally related to employee satisfaction, so Ritz Carlton managers spend a lot of time listening to employees and responding to their concerns. Given this, Ritz Carlton places a lot of importance on people. Not surprisingly, then, it has identified a fourfold approach to customer satisfaction that is based on its people. First, the right people must be hired within each hotel, so considerable effort is made to recruit and select people who have the set of characteristics Ritz Carlton values. After the right people are hired, they receive an orientation to the Ritz Carlton TQM philosophy. Then, once on the job, regular training ensures that they have and maintain the right mix of skills necessary to do their jobs well and to be able to move to other jobs as the need arises. Finally, all personnel are taught what Ritz Carlton regards as appropriate behavior for each of its jobs. Each employee gets at least one hundred hours of training a year to ensure that these concepts are carried out.

Team building has been another important part of the Ritz Carlton's quality management effort. At each level of the company, teams are charged with setting objectives and devising action plans that are reviewed by a corporate steering committee. Daily production reports derived from data submitted from each of the 720 work areas in the hotel system are monitored so that problems can be identified early and corrected before any major difficulties occur.

Since adopting this TQM program, Ritz Carlton has seen several positive benefits. Operation costs have dropped, turnover has fallen from 100 percent to 30 percent, and profit has risen dramatically even in the face of strong competition and rough economic times.

Case Questions

1. What are the major characteristics of the quality management program at Ritz Carlton? Because this is a service organization, are they different from what you might expect at a manufacturing firm?
2. What role does Horst Schulze play in the quality management program at Ritz Carlton?
3. Would the Ritz Carlton approach to quality management be appropriate for a hotel company with a very different target audience? Why or why not?

References: Alan Salomon, "Schulze: Focus on Quality or Fail," *Hotel and Motel Management*, July 25, 1994, pp. 3, 9; Horst Schulze, "What Makes the Ritz the Ritz?" *Across the Board*, May 1994, p. 58; Echo Montgomery Garrett, "Putting on the Ritz," *World Trade*, April 1994, pp. 52–56; and Cheri Henderson, "Tuning into Ritz Philosophy," *Managing Service Quality*, November 1992, pp. 385–389.

SKILLS • DEVELOPMENT • PORTFOLIO

BUILDING EFFECTIVE CONCEPTUAL SKILLS

Exercise Overview

A manager's conceptual skills are her or his ability to think in the abstract. As this exercise will demonstrate, there is often a relationship between conceptual skills of key managers in an organization and that organization's ability to implement total quality initiatives.

Exercise Background

Conceptual skills may be useful in helping managers see opportunities for learning how to improve some aspect of their own operations from observations or experiences gleaned from dealings with other organizations.

To begin this exercise, carefully recall the last time you ate in a restaurant that involved some degree of self-service. Examples might include a fast-food restaurant like McDonald's, a cafeteria, or even a traditional restaurant with a salad bar. Recall as much about the experience as possible, and develop some ideas as to why the restaurant is organized and laid out as it is.

Now carefully recall the last time you purchased something in a retail outlet. Examples might include the purchase of an article of clothing from a specialty store, a book from a bookstore, or some software from a computer store. Again recall as much about the experience as possible, and develop some ideas as to why the store is organized and laid out as it is.

Exercise Task

Using the two examples you developed above, do the following:

1. Identify three or four elements of the service received at each location that you think most directly influenced—either positively or negatively—the quality and efficiency of the experience there.

2. Analyze the service elements from one organization and see if they can somehow be used by the other.

3. Repeat the process for the second organization.

BUILDING EFFECTIVE DIAGNOSTIC SKILLS

Exercise Overview

As noted in this chapter, the quality of a product or service is relative to price and expectations. A manager's diagnostic skills—the ability to visualize responses to a situation—can be useful in helping to position quality relative to price and expectations most effectively.

Exercise Background

Think of a recent occasion in which you purchased a tangible product that you subsequently came to view as of especially high quality. For example, think about clothing, electronic equipment, luggage, or professional supplies. Now recall another product that you evaluated as having appropriate or adequate quality. Recall a third product that you felt had low or poor quality.

Next, recall three parallel experiences—high quality, adaquate quality, and poor quality—involving purchases of services. Examples might include an airline, train, or bus trip; a meal in a restaurant; a haircut; or an oil change for your car.

Finally, recall three experiences in which both products and services were involved. Examples might include having questions answered by someone about a product you were buying or returning a defective or broken product for a refund or warranty repair. Try to recall instances in which there was an apparent disparity between product and service quality (i.e., a poor-quality product accompanied by outstanding service or a high-quality product with mediocre service).

Exercise Task

Using the nine examples identified above, do the following:

1. Assess the extent to which the quality you associated with each was a function of price and your expectations.

2. Could the quality of each be improved without greatly affecting price? If so, how?

3. Can high-quality service offset only adequate or even poor product quality? Can outstanding product quality offset only adequate or even poor service?

YOU MAKE THE CALL

Mark Spenser could hardly wait to get home. He had just attended a regional convention of nursery operators. During the convention, he attended a workshop on total quality management and was excited about using some of the methods at Sunset Landscape Services.

For example, one thing he planned to start was a benchmarking program. He had not visited Lion Gardens, a competitor, in over a year and he had no idea how much the local Wal-Mart was charging for fertilizer or mulch. He had long ago decided to focus on service and quality rather than the competition; he realized, nonetheless, that he should know more about his competitors.

Mark also thought that perhaps he should outsource some of his operations. For example, he did his own payroll each week and managed his own employee benefits program. He was aware, however, that many other small businesses in town outsourced these human resource services to other firms. He decided to investigate this idea very soon.

Mark thought that applying what he had learned about speed might also help his operation. At present, for example, his customers were waiting at least a few days, and sometimes up to a week, for home delivery. He wondered if he could start promising same-day delivery and, if so, how this service might affect his business. He also wondered if he could get his suppliers to service his own purchases faster. It did seem to take longer than necessary to get his orders in. And while he was not a huge customer, he felt that he had sufficient clout with them to at least get them to try.

Discussion Questions

1. How do you think Mark's efforts will affect his business?

2. Do you see any areas for concern in his plans?

3. Do you agree or disagree with his assumption that he should be more knowledgeable about his competitors even if he is not going to emulate them?

SKILLS SELF-ASSESSMENT INSTRUMENT

Defining Quality and Productivity

Introduction: Quality is a complex term whose meaning has no doubt changed over time. The following assessment surveys your ideas about and approaches to quality.

Instructions: You will agree with some of the statements and disagree with others. In some cases, making a decision may be difficult, but you should force a choice. Record your answers next to each statement according to the following scale:

Rating Scale

4 Strongly agree | **2** Somewhat disagree
3 Somewhat agree | **1** Strongly disagree

_____ **1.** Quality refers to a product's or service's ability to fulfill its primary operating characteristics such as providing a sharp picture for a television set.

_____ **2.** Quality is an absolute, measurable aspect of a product or service.

_____ **3.** The concept of quality includes supplemental aspects of a product or service such as the remote control for a television set.

____ **4.** Productivity and quality are inversely related so that to get one you must sacrifice the other.

____ **5.** The concept of quality refers to the extent to which a product's design and operating characteristics conform to certain set standards.

____ **6.** Productivity refers to what is created relative to what it takes to create it.

____ **7.** Quality means that a product will not malfunction during a specified period of time.

____ **8.** Quality refers only to products; it is immeasurable for services.

____ **9.** The length of time that a product or service will function is what is known as quality.

____ **10.** Everyone uses exactly the same definition of quality.

____ **11.** Quality refers to the repair ease and speed of a product or service.

____ **12.** Being treated courteously has nothing to do with the quality of anything.

____ **13.** How a product looks, feels, tastes, or smells is what is meant by quality.

____ **14.** Price, not quality, is what determines the ultimate value of service.

____ **15.** Quality refers to what customers think of a product or service.

____ **16.** Productivity and quality cannot both increase at the same time.

For interpretation, turn to page 451.

Source: Adapted from Chapter 21, especially pp. 473–474, in David D. Van Fleet and Tim O. Peterson, *Contemporary Management.*

EXPERIENTIAL EXERCISE

Preparing the Fishbone Chart

Purpose: The fishbone chart is an excellent procedure for indentifying possible causes of a problem. It provides you with knowledge that you can use to improve the operations of any organization. This skill exercise focuses on the *administrative management model.* It will help you develop the *monitor role* of the administrative management model. One of the skills of the monitor is the ability to analyze problems.

Introduction: Japanese quality circles often use the fishbone "cause and effect" graphic technique to initiate the resolution of a group work problem. Quite often the causes are clustered in categories such as materials, methods, people, and machines. The fishbone technique is usually accomplished in the following six steps.

1. Write the problem in the "head" of the fish (the large block).

2. Brainstorm the major causes of the problem and list them on the fish "bones."

3. Analyze each main cause, and write in minor subcauses on bone subbranches.

4. Reach consensus on one or two of the major causes of the problem.

5. Explore ways to correct or remove the major cause(s).

6. Prepare a report or presentation explaining the proposed change.

Instructions: Your instructor will provide you with further instructions.

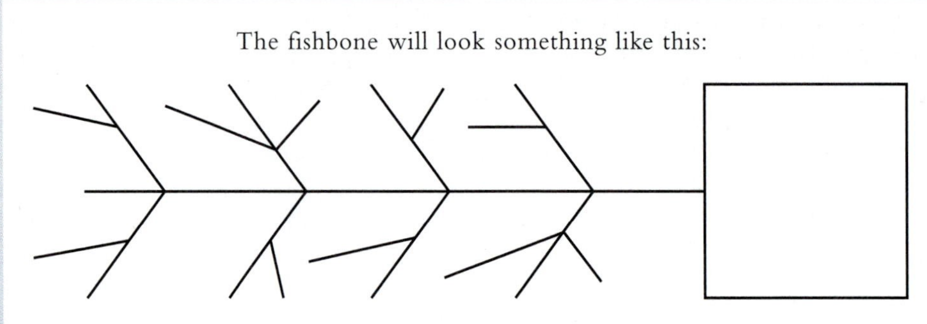

Source: Adapted from *Exercises in Management* by Gene E. Burton. Copyright © 1996 by Houghton Mifflin Company. Reprinted by permission of the publisher.

CHAPTER NOTES

1. "Chrysler Mounts Campaign to Cut Defects," *The Wall Street Journal*, January 27, 1994, pp. B1, B6; "Bug Control at Chrysler," *Business Week*, August 22, 1994; p. 26; Gary Hoover, Alta Campbell, and Patrick J. Spain (Eds.), *Hoover's Handbook of American Business 1995* (Austin, Tex.: The Reference Press, 1994), pp. 350–351.
2. Rhonda Reger, Loren Gustafson, Samuel DeMarie, and John Mullane, "Reframing the Organization: Why Implementing Total Quality Is Easier Said Than Done," *Academy of Management Review*, 1994, Vol. 19, No. 3, pp. 565–584.
3. "Quality—How to Make It Pay," *Business Week*, August 8, 1994, pp. 54–59.
4. Ross Johnson and William O. Winchell, *Management and Quality* (Milwaukee: American Society for Quality Control, 1989). See also Carol Reeves and David Bednar, "Defining Quality: Alternatives and Implications," *Academy of Management Review*, 1994, Vol. 19, No. 3, pp. 419–445.
5. W. Edwards Deming, *Out of the Crisis* (Cambridge, Mass.: MIT Press, 1986).
6. David Waldman, "The Contributions of Total Quality Management to a Theory of Work Performance," *Academy of Management Review*, 1994, Vol. 19, No. 3, pp. 510–536.
7. Joel Dreyfuss, "Victories in the Quality Crusade," *Fortune*, October 10, 1988, pp. 80–88.
8. Barbara Spencer, "Models of Organization and Total Quality Management: A Comparison and Critical Evaluation," *Academy of Management Review*, 1994, Vol. 19, No. 3, pp. 446–471.
9. James Dean and David Bowen, "Management Theory and Total Quality: Improving Research and Practice Through Theory Development," *Academy of Management Review*, 1994, Vol. 19, No. 3, pp. 392–418.
10. Edward E. Lawler, "Total Quality Management and Employee Involvement: Are They Compatible?" *Academy of Management Executive*, 1994, Vol. 8, No. 1, pp. 68–76.
11. "Quality Is Becoming Job One in the Office, Too," *Business Week*, April 29, 1991, pp. 52–56.
12. Jeremy Main, "How to Steal the Best Ideas Around," *Fortune*, October 19, 1992, pp. 102–106.
13. James Brian Quinn and Frederick Hilmer, "Strategic Outsourcing," *Sloan Management Review*, Summer 1994, pp. 43–52.
14. Thomas Robertson, "How to Reduce Market Penetration Cycle Times," *Sloan Management Review*, Fall 1993, pp. 87–95.
15. Brian Dumaine, "How Managers Can Succeed Through Speed," *Fortune*, February 13, 1989, pp. 54–59.
16. Ronald Henkoff, "The Hot New Seal of Quality," *Fortune*, June 28, 1993, pp. 116–120.
17. John W. Kendrick, *Understanding Productivity: An Introduction to the Dynamics of Productivity Change* (Baltimore, Md.: Johns Hopkins, 1977).
18. "The Productivity Payoff Arrives," *Fortune*, June 27, 1994, pp. 79–84.
19. David Wright and Paul Brauchle, "Teaming up for Quality," *Training & Development*, September 1994, pp. 67–75.
20. Paul M. Swamidass, "Empirical Science: New Frontier in Operations Management Research," *Academy of Management Review*, October 1991, pp. 793–814.
21. Paul D. Collins, Jerald Hage, and Frank M. Hull, "Organizational and Technological Predictors of Change in Automaticity," *Academy of Management Journal*, September 1988, pp. 512–543.
22. Otto Friedrich, "The Robot Revolution," *Time*, December 8, 1980, pp. 72–83.
23. Gene Bylinsky, "Invasion of the Service Robots," *Fortune*, September 14, 1987, pp. 81–88.
24. "Robots Head for the Farm," *Business Week*, September 8, 1986, pp. 66–67.
25. Boldly Going Where No Robot Has Gone Before," *Business Week*, December 22, 1986, p. 45.
26. James Brian Quinn and Martin Neil Baily, "Information Technology: Increasing Productivity in Services," *Academy of Management Executive*, 1994, Vol. 8, No. 3, pp. 28–38.

APPENDIX

Managerial Careers

OUTLINE

When you graduate from college and receive your degree, you will likely have a number of options to pursue: take a job with a big company, start your own company, go to work in a family-owned business, enter graduate school, or join the military. But which- ever option you take, the chances are very good that it will not be where you end up. Indeed, you are likely to change jobs—and companies—many times during your work life. This overall set of work-related experiences you accumulate will comprise your career. This appendix provides some insight into managerial careers.

THE NATURE OF MANAGERIAL CAREERS

A person's **career** is the set of work-related experiences, behaviors, and attitudes encountered throughout his or her working life. One person may spend his entire career doing the same kind of work for the same company. Another may work for a number of different companies in a number of different jobs. Still another may open her own business and never work for someone else. Each of these patterns represents a career in its fullest sense.[1] This contrasts sharply with the notion of a job—a single work assignment performed for an organization.

- **career**
A set of work-related experiences, behaviors, and attitudes encountered throughout working life

Perhaps the key distinction between a job and a career is the level of psychological involvement by the employee. When employees think of their work only in terms of what they have to do between 8 and 5 every day and how much they are paid for doing it, and they do not consider what they will be doing next year or the year after or how important the work itself is to them, they are viewing their work as simply a job. When individuals view their work in the context of a career, however, they are much more involved with what they do. They view the career with a long-term outlook and recognize that it is made up of a sequence of steps that, taken together, will engage their entire working lives. And although money is important, it is only one of many things (including promotion opportunities, recognition, and personal satisfaction) that influence their behavior.

Figure A1.1 illustrates the general stages people go through in their careers. The first stage, which usually occurs during the first few years of the individual's adult life, is called **exploration**. Through a long period of self-examination (based on observations of others, part-time jobs, talking to other people, and educational coursework), the person gradually decides that she may want to be an engineer, a doctor, a manager, or an artist and begins to prepare. The exploration stage continues even after the person finishes school and takes her first job. The chosen career may not live up to her expectations, or she may decide to work a few years and then return to graduate, medical, or law school.

- **exploration**
The first stage of one's career; usually occurs during the first few years of an individual's adult life

Most people eventually settle on a career and then proceed into the **establishment** stage. During this phase, the individual is likely to receive occasional promotions and reassignments. Although changes may still occur, at this stage the person generally knows what she or he is interested

- **establishment**
Second stage of one's career during which an individual is likely to receive occasional promotions and reassignments

FIGURE A1.1 Common Career Stages

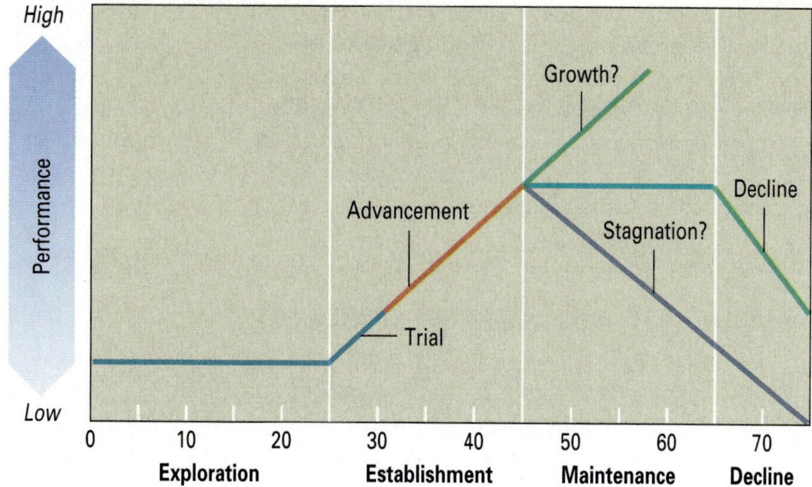

Source: Adapted from *Careers in Organizations,* by Douglas T. Hall. Copyright © 1976 by Scott, Foresman and Co. Reprinted by permission of Douglas T. Hall and Lyman Porter.

in and starts to establish an occupational identity.[2] Thus a person is somewhat likely to work in a number of jobs, but they may all be in computer firms, in food-processing companies, or in retailers. Few people spend their whole careers with the same organization.

• **maintenance**
The midcareer stage during which some people continue on an upward career track, and others reach a plateau

The next phase, which starts around the age of forty-five for the average person, is called the **maintenance**, or midcareer, stage. During this time, several things are possible. Some people continue on an upward track toward an upper-level management position. Others reach a plateau—a position where they are likely to remain.[3] Still others begin to stagnate and decline. Managers in the first position are likely to be groomed for specific openings at the highest levels of the organization. Managers on a plateau often find themselves serving as mentors for younger managers. Those in the last group find themselves increasingly less valued by the organization and may be subject to demotion, termination, or early retirement.

• **decline**
The disengagement stage during which a person begins to plan for retirement and gradually starts to withdraw psychologically from an organization

The final career stage for most people is **decline** or disengagement. During this stage, the person can look ahead and see the end of her or his career. She or he begins to plan for retirement and gradually starts psychologically withdrawing from the organization. Many top executives stay on for a while after their formal retirement, however, to work as advisers and to help train their replacements. And more and more "retired" managers, not content to relax at home, are starting new careers late in life. For example, when he retired at the age of sixty-three after thirty years as an insurance agent, Thomas S. Duck founded the Ugly Duckling Rent-a-Car company in Tucson. Now he has over six hundred outlets and annual revenues of $85 million.[4]

CAREER MANAGEMENT

Given this basic understanding of how careers unfold, and given the importance of a career to the person involved, you should not be surprised to learn that managing career dynamics is important both to individuals and to organizations.

Individual Career Planning

Career planning must start with the individual.[5] After all, only the individual can truly know what he or she wants from life and work. However, people must avoid overplanning. For example, some people set specific goals as to when they want to be promoted, and they identify specific jobs they want to have as they progress up the organizational ladder. Such rigidity promises disappointment if the promotion is delayed and may cause the person to miss an opportunity to have an exciting new job. Walter Wriston, former CEO of Citibank, held several jobs on his way to the top spot—and not one of them had even existed when he joined the bank! Thus, it is important to achieve a balance between knowing generally what you want and how to go about getting it and being rigidly fixed on a specific goal with an inflexible timetable and agenda. Two important tools for achieving this balance are personal assessment and mentor relationships.

Personal Assessment Personal assessment is learning about yourself—your aspirations, strengths, and weaknesses—and about career opportunities. Many people argue that it is important that you choose a career in an area you enjoy. For example, Debbi Fields enjoyed baking cookies more than anything else. After several years of frustration while searching for a career, she decided to open a store and sell her cookies. Today, Mrs. Fields Inc. is a multi-million-dollar business with hundreds of stores around the world. The starting point in individual career management is learning about oneself. This inner exploration can be achieved through analysis of the kinds of part-time work you have enjoyed, the courses you have enjoyed, and an honest assessment of what you want from life. University counseling centers offer tests and aptitude profiles that can provide useful insights.

Coupled with this kind of assessment is determining what kind of organization you want to be a part of. Some people want to work for a large company like Xerox or Digital Equipment because it provides security and prestige. Others want to work in a smaller organization. Others want to start their own business in order to be independent. And, of course, preferences and options often change over the course of a career. It may be necessary to work for a big company at first in order to save enough money to launch your own business later.

You should try to be realistic about your options. If you are a small adult with limited athletic skills, you are not likely to succeed as a professional football player. You might, however, be successful as a coach or trainer. If your grades are mediocre and you have no aptitude for science, you are unlikely to gain admittance to medical school and should therefore not be too committed to a career as a doctor. But you might succeed as a medical administrator.

Another important element of personal assessment is learning about opportunities. A field that is growing and expanding provides more opportunities than one that is shrinking. Some fields are more difficult to break into than are others. Consider, for example, the hundreds of young people who trek to Hollywood to become movie stars. Only a few succeed. Many fields, such as medicine, university teaching, and law, require extra years of formal education. You must decide what is best for you, what sacrifices you are willing to make to reach your goals, and then, with realistic expectations, set out to reach them.

Mentor Relationships Another useful tool for managing one's career is mentor relationships. A mentor is a senior manager who acts as a sponsor, advocate, and teacher for a younger and less experienced new manager, sometimes called a protégé.[6] Mentors are usually in the maintenance stage of their own careers. The mentor-protégé relationship is usually informal and can be initiated by either party. The younger manager may ask the mentor for advice or assistance, or the senior manager may recognize special traits in the younger manager and start taking special interest in his or her performance. At various times during the mentor-protégé relationship, the mentor teaches and counsels the protégé about performance-related issues, organizational politics, and other important matters. If the mentor thinks it appropriate, he or she also helps advance the protégé's career by telling others how good the protégé's work is, recommending her or him for new job assignments, and so forth.[7]

Johnson & Johnson, Jewel Food Stores, Federal Express, AT&T Bell Laboratories, Colgate-Palmolive, and other organizations have formal mentor programs. Colgate-Palmolive CEO Reuben Marks is a firm believer in the importance of mentor relationships. Besides taking part in the formal program within his company, Marks also participates in another program where he serves as a mentor to disadvantaged minority youths.[8]

Organizational Career Planning

Mentoring can be either an individual or an organizational approach to career planning. Other techniques are more purely organizational. Table A1.1 summarizes several career-planning programs used by U.S. companies.[9] AT&T, Bank of America, General Electric, General Foods, and Sears all have formal career management programs for employees. Each attempts to help employees understand career options and limits within the company, identify their individual priorities and potential, and develop general strategies for achieving a good match between what the organization and the individual want and need.[10]

Increasingly, organizations are also confronting the interrelationships of career management and the globalization of the business world. Nestlé and other organizations have a cadre of international managers who have been trained to accept work assignments anywhere in the world. Because of both the costs of overseas assignments and the important role that such assign-

TABLE A1.1 Organizational Career Planning Techniques

Technique	Description
Career management program	Formal and comprehensive program to help organizations and individuals understand career dynamics within the organization
Career counseling	Formal method for providing employees with counseling and advice about their careers
Career-pathing	Identification of logical and coherent progressions of jobs that individuals might choose to pursue
Career resources planning	Application of planning methods to help people and organizations understand and predict when specific jobs might be open and when specific individuals might be prepared to fill them
Career information systems	Formal information system that makes some or all of the information from the above-mentioned techniques highly accessible to employees

ments can play in a person's career, organizations are paying increased attention to incorporating foreign experiences into key managers' careers.[11]

SPECIAL ISSUES IN CAREERS

Recent years have seen the advent of new career issues for managers to contend with. These issues include opportunities for women and minorities, dual-career couples, and career transitions.

Women and Minorities

Most people are generally aware of the dramatic changes in recent years in the number of women and minorities pursuing professional careers of all types, but especially as managers. In 1972, only 4 percent of those receiving MBA degrees were women, and women held only 20 percent of U.S. management and administrative positions. By 1987, those figures increased to 33 and 37 percent, respectively. And by 1992, the figures had climbed higher still, to 41 and 44 percent, respectively.[12]

Nevertheless, women still experience various forms of discrimination, often subtle; and although some have made it to the upper echelons, there are still few women in the top-management ranks of large U.S. companies. Many of those companies, however, recognize the importance of women managers to organizational success and are actively working to help them attain top positions.[13]

The situation of minorities is less positive. Even though many organizations have hired large numbers of black managers, for example, few have moved into meaningful top-management positions.[14] And there are very few Hispanic managers in American business. Still, progress is being made, and the minority communities have success stories they can be proud of. Reginald F. Lewis, for example, is a successful black entrepreneur. His TLC Group is one of the largest investment companies on Wall Street. Its biggest deal to date was purchasing Beatrice International Foods for $985 million in the late 1980s.[15]

Dual-Career Couples

The entry of more and more women into the workplace has created an issue that organizations must increasingly confront—the dual-career couple. A dual-career couple exists when both partners in a relationship are pursuing careers. The tensions and problems caused by two careers range from the mundane to the traumatic. For example, with both partners working, there are relatively simple problems of coordination, such as buying groceries and scheduling vacations. More significant, however, are questions about who will stay home with a sick child (especially if the illness is long-term) and what will happen if one partner is transferred to another city.[16] Some couples decide that one partner's career will take precedence over the other's; some couples manage with a "commuter" marriage.

Some organizations are becoming sensitive to the needs and problems faced by dual-career couples. General Motors provides counseling and referral services for the spouse of a transferred employee. IBM provides childcare assistance and provides all employees with up to a year of unpaid leave for childcare at home. Merck provides childcare, flexible working hours, and work-at-home options to dual-career couples. Still, most businesses are just beginning to address the problem.[17]

Career Transitions

A final area of concern and interest involves career transitions. Most people go through a series of stages in the course of their careers. Transitions through these stages may be either planned or unplanned.

Planned Transition A planned transition occurs when the individual or the organization knows about a change in advance and can plan for it. Candidates for top-management positions often know about new job assignments several months in advance, for example, and can carefully plan things associated with the new assignment. Even middle and lower-level managers often have some advance word about transfers or promotions. More problematic, but no less important, is an employee who has reached a career plateau. Some people in this circumstance are no longer valued by the organization and may be targeted for early retirement or termination. Many others, though, are quite valuable in their current positions, and both the manager and the organization must work together to preserve a valuable working relationship.[18]

Unplanned Transition Unplanned transitions occur when the individual or the organization has little or no advance warning about a career change. For example, a death or unexpected resignation can prompt a promotion with no advance warning. Corporate restructurings, unexpected layoffs and terminations, mergers, acquisitions, and takeovers can create circumstances in which managers previously secure in their jobs find themselves out of work.[19] Some organizations do little to help in these circumstances, but more and more firms provide outplacement assistance to terminated employees. Outplacement assistance, usually administered by a specialized service firm, helps the employee cope with the problem and locate new employment. Such services are likely to become increasingly common.[20]

APPENDIX NOTES

1. For reviews of the careers literature, see Edgar H. Schein, "Individuals and Careers," in Jay W. Lorsch (Ed.), *Handbook of Organizational Behavior* (Englewood Cliffs, N.J.: Prentice-Hall, 1987), pp. 155–171; and Douglas T. Hall and Associates, *Career Development in Organizations* (San Francisco: Jossey-Bass, 1986).
2. Mary Pat McEnrue, "Length of Experience and the Performance of Managers in the Establishment Phase of Their Careers," *Academy of Management Journal*, March 1988, pp. 175–185.
3. Gregory Stephens, "Crossing Internal Career Boundaries: The State of Research on Subjective Career Transitions," *Journal of Management*, 1994, Vol. 20, No. 2, pp. 479–501.
4. Faye Rice, "Lessons from Late Bloomers," *Fortune*, August 31, 1987, pp. 87–91.
5. Kenneth Labich, "Take Control of Your Career," *Fortune*, November 18, 1991, pp. 87–96.
6. Raymond A. Noe, "Women and Mentoring: A Review and Research Agenda," *Academy of Management Review*, January 1988, pp. 65–78; Charles D. Orth, Harry E. Wilkinson, and Robert C. Benfari, "The Manager's Role as Coach and Mentor," *Organizational Dynamics*, Spring 1987, pp. 66–74; and Kathy E. Kram, *Mentoring at Work: Developmental Relationships in Organizational Life* (Glenview, Ill.: Scott, Foresman, 1985).
7. William Whitely, Thomas Dougherty, and George Dreher, "Relationship of Career Mentoring and Socioeconomic Origin to Managers' and Professionals' Early Career Progress," *Academy of Management Journal*, June 1991, pp. 331–351.
8. Dan Hurley, "The Mentor Mystique," *Psychology Today*, May 1988, pp. 38–43.
9. See Cherlyn Skromme Granrose and James D. Portwood, "Matching Individual Career Plans and Organizational Career Management," *Academy of Management Journal*, December 1987, pp. 699–720; and Douglas T. Hall, "Careers and Socialization," *Journal of Management*, Summer 1987, pp. 301–321.
10. Beverly Kaye and Zandy Leibowitz, "Career Development," *HR Magazine*, September 1994, pp. 78–86.
11. "As Costs of Overseas Assignments Climb, Firms Select Expatriates More Carefully," *The Wall Street Journal*, January 9, 1992, pp. B1, B2.
12. "Corporate Women," *Business Week*, August 21, 1994, pp. 56–59.
13. Mariann Jelinek and Nancy J. Adler, "Women: World-Class Managers for Global Competition," *The Academy of Management Executive*, February 1988, pp. 11–19; and Jan Grant, "Women as Managers: What They Can Offer to Organizations," *Organizational Dynamics*, Winter 1988, pp. 56–63.
14. "Many Hurdles, Old and New, Keep Black Managers Out of Top Jobs," *The Wall Street Journal*, July 10, 1986, p. 25.
15. "Beatrice Deal a Landmark for Black Business," *USA Today*, August 11, 1987, p. 2B.
16. "Paternal, Managerial Roles Often Clash," *The Wall Street Journal*, September 12, 1991, pp. B1, B4.
17. "Best Employers for Women and Parents," *The Wall Street Journal*, November 30, 1987, p. 21.
18. Priscilla M. Elsass and David A. Ralston, "Individual Responses to the Stress of Career Plateauing," *Journal of Management*, March 1989, pp. 35–47.
19. John Huey, "Where Managers Will Go," *Fortune*, January 27, 1992, pp. 50–60.
20. "The Do's and Don'ts of Outplacement," *Psychology Today*, May 1988, p. 26.

APPENDIX

Tools for Planning and Decision Making

OUTLINE

This appendix discusses a number of the basic tools and techniques that managers can use to enhance the efficiency and effectiveness of planning and decision making. We first describe forecasting, an extremely important tool, and then discuss several other planning techniques. Next we discuss several other tools that relate more to decision making. We conclude by assessing the strengths and weaknesses of the various tools and techniques.[1]

FORECASTING

To plan, managers must make assumptions about future events. But unlike wizards of old, planners cannot simply look into a crystal ball. Instead, they must develop forecasts of probable future circumstances. **Forecasting** is the process of developing assumptions or premises about the future that managers can use in planning or decision making.[2]

- **forecasting** The process of developing assumptions or premises about the future that managers can use in planning or decision making

Sales and Revenue Forecasting

As the term implies, **sales forecasting** is concerned with predicting future sales. Because monetary resources (derived mainly from sales) are necessary to finance both current and future operations, knowledge of future sales is of vital importance. Sales forecasting is something that every business, from Exxon to a neighborhood pizza parlor, must do. Consider, for example, the following questions that a manager might need to answer:

- **sales forecasting** The prediction of future sales

1. How much of each of our products should we produce next week, next month, and next year?
2. How much money will we have available to spend on research and development and on new-product test marketing?
3. When and to what degree will we need to expand our existing production facilities?
4. How should we respond to union demands for a 15 percent pay increase?
5. If we borrow money for expansion, can we pay it back?

None of these questions can be adequately answered without some notion of what future revenues are likely to be. Thus sales forecasting is generally one of the first steps in planning.

Unfortunately, the term sales forecasting suggests that this form of forecasting is appropriate only for organizations that have something to sell. But other kinds of organizations also depend on financial resources, and so they also must forecast. The University of South Carolina, for example, must forecast future state aid before planning course offerings, staff size, and so on. Hospitals must forecast their future income from patient fees, insurance payments, and other sources to assess their ability to expand. Although we will continue to use the conventional term, keep in mind that what is really at issue is **revenue forecasting**.

- **revenue forecasting** The prediction of future revenues from all sources

Several sources of information are used to develop a sales forecast. Previous sales figures and any obvious trends, such as the company's growth or stability, usually serve as the base. General economic indicators, technological improvements, new marketing strategies, and the competition's behavior all may be added together to ensure an accurate forecast. Once projected, the sales (or revenues) forecast becomes a guiding framework for a variety of other activities. Raw-material expenditures, advertising budgets, sales-commission structures, and similar operating costs are all based on projected sales figures.

Organizations often forecast sales across several time horizons. The longer-run forecasts may then be updated and refined as various shorter-run cycles are completed. For obvious reasons, a forecast should be as accurate as possible, and the accuracy of sales forecasting tends to increase as organizations learn from their previous forecasting experience. But the more uncertain and complex future conditions are likely to be, the more difficult it is to develop accurate forecasts. To partially offset these problems, forecasts are more useful to managers if they are expressed as a range rather than as an absolute index or number. If projected sales increases are expected to be in the range of 10 to 12 percent, a manager can consider all the implications for the entire range. A 10 percent increase could dictate one set of activities; a 12 percent increase could call for a different set of activities.

Technological Forecasting

• **technological forecasting** The prediction of what future technologies are likely to emerge and when they are likely to be economically feasible

Technological forecasting is another type of forecasting used by many organizations. It focuses on predicting what future technologies are likely to emerge and when they are likely to be economically feasible.[3] In an era when technological breakthrough and innovation have become the rule rather than the exception, it is important that managers be able to anticipate new developments. If a manager invests heavily in existing technology (such as production processes, equipment, and computer systems) and the technology becomes obsolete in the near future, the company has wasted its resources.

The most striking technological innovations in recent years have been in electronics, especially semiconductors. Home computers, electronic games, and sophisticated communications equipment are all evidence of the electronics explosion. Given the increasing importance of technology and the rapid pace of technological innovation, it follows that managers will grow increasingly concerned with technological forecasting in the years to come.

Other Types of Forecasting

Other types of forecasting are also important to many organizations. Resource forecasting projects the organization's future needs for and availability of human resources, raw materials, and other resources. General economic conditions are the subject of economic forecasts. For example, some organizations undertake population or market-size forecasting. Some

FIGURE A2.1 An Example of Time-Series Analysis

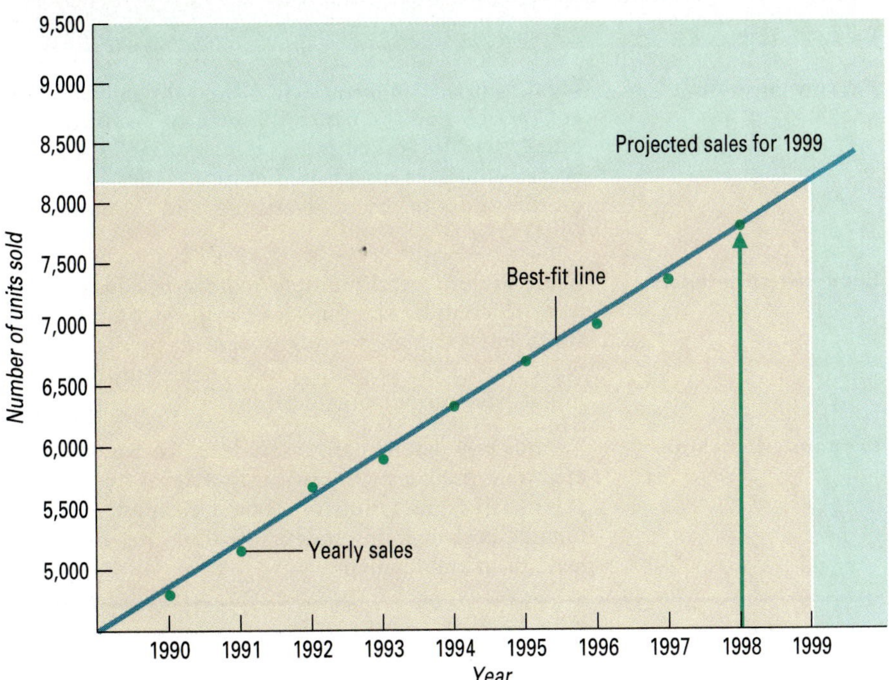

Because time-series analysis assumes that the past is a good predictor of the future, it is most useful when historical data are available, trends are stable, and patterns are apparent. For example, it can be used for projecting estimated sales for products such as shampoo, pens, and automobile tires.

organizations also attempt to forecast future government fiscal policy and various government regulations that might be put into practice. Indeed, virtually any component in an organization's environment may be an appropriate area for forecasting.

Forecasting Techniques

To carry out the various kinds of forecasting we have identified, managers use several different techniques. Time-series analysis and causal modeling are two common quantitative techniques.

Time-Series Analysis The underlying assumption of **time-series analysis** is that the past is a good predictor of the future. This technique is most useful when the manager has a lot of historical data available and when stable trends and patterns are apparent. In a time-series analysis, the variable under consideration (such as sales or enrollment) is plotted across time, and a "best-fit" line is identified.[4] Figure A2.1 shows how a time-series analysis might look. The dots represent the number of units sold for each year from 1990 through 1998. The "best-fit" line has also been drawn in. This is the line around which the dots cluster with the least variability. A manager who wants to know what sales to expect in 1999 simply extends the line. In this case, the projection would be around 8,200 units.

● **time-series analysis** A forecasting technique that extends past information into the future through the calculation of a best-fit line

Managers use several different types of causal models in planning and decision making. Three popular models are regression models, econometric models, and economic indicators.

TABLE A2.1 Summary of Causal Modeling Forecasting Techniques

Regression models	Used to predict one variable (called the dependent variable) on the basis of known or assumed other variables (called independent variables). For example, we might predict future sales based on the values of price, advertising, and economic levels.
Econometric models	Make use of several multiple-regression equations to consider the impact of major economic shifts. For example, we might want to predict what impact the migration toward the Sun Belt might have on our organization.
Economic indicators	Various population statistics, indexes, or parameters that predict organizationally relevant variables such as discretionary income. Examples include cost-of-living index, inflation rate, and level of unemployment.

It is important to recognize that real time-series analysis involves much more than simply plotting sales data and then using a ruler and a pencil to draw and extend the line. Sophisticated mathematical procedures, among other things, are necessary to account for seasonal and cyclical fluctuations and to identify the true "best-fit" line. In real situations, data seldom follow the neat pattern found in Figure A2.1. Indeed, the data points may be so widely dispersed that they mask meaningful trends from all but painstaking, computer-assisted inspection.

- **causal modeling** A group of different techniques that determine causal relationships between different variables
- **regression models** Equations that use one set of variables to predict another variable

Causal Modeling Another useful forecasting technique is **causal modeling**. Actually, the term causal modeling represents a group of several different techniques.[5] Table A2.1 summarizes three of the most useful approaches. **Regression models** are equations created to predict a variable (such as sales volume) that depends on a number of other variables (such as price and advertising). The variable being predicted is called the dependent variable; the variables used to make the prediction are called independent variables. A typical regression equation used by a small business might take this form:

$$y = ax_1 + bx_2 + cx_3 + d$$

where

y = the dependent variable (sales, in this case)

x_1, x_2, and x_3 = independent variables (advertising budget, price, and commissions)

a, b, and c = weights for the independent variables calculated during development of the regression model

d = a constant

To use the model, a manager can insert various alternatives for advertising budget, price, and commissions into the equation and then compute y. The calculated value of y represents the forecasted level of sales, given various levels of advertising, price, and commissions.[6]

Econometric models employ regression techniques at a much more complex level. **Econometric models** attempt to predict major economic shifts and the potential impact of those shifts on the organization. They might be used to predict various age, ethnic, and economic groups that will characterize different regions of the United States in the year 2000 and to further predict the kinds of products and services these groups may want. A complete econometric model may consist of hundreds or even thousands of equations. Computers are almost always necessary to apply them. Given the complexities involved in developing econometric models, many firms that decide to use them rely on outside consultants specializing in this approach.

• **econometric models**
Causal models that predict major economic shifts and their impact on the organization

Economic indicators, another form of causal model, are population statistics or indexes that reflect the economic well-being of a population. Examples of widely used economic indicators include the current rates of national productivity, inflation, and unemployment. In using such indicators, the manager draws on past experiences that have revealed a relationship between a certain indicator and some facet of the company's operations. Pitney Bowes' Data Documents Division, for example, can predict future sales of its business forms largely on the basis of current GNP estimates and other economic growth indexes.

• **economic indicators**
Key population statistics or indexes that reflect the economic well-being of a population

Qualitative Forecasting Techniques There are also several qualitative techniques that organizations use to develop forecasts. A **qualitative forecasting technique** is one that relies more on individual or group judgment or opinion than on sophisticated mathematical analyses. The Delphi procedure, described in Chapter 4 as a mechanism for managing group decision-making activities, can also be used to develop forecasts. A variation of it—the *jury-of-expert-opinion* approach—involves using the basic Delphi process with members of top management. In this instance, top management serves as a collection of experts asked to make a prediction about something—competitive behavior, trends in product demand, and so forth. Either a pure Delphi or a jury-of-expert-opinion approach might be useful in technological forecasting.

• **qualitative forecasting technique**
One of several techniques that rely on individual or group judgment rather than on mathematical analyses

The *sales-force-composition* method of sales forecasting is a pooling of the predictions and opinions of experienced salespeople. Because of their experience, these individuals are often able to forecast quite accurately what various customers will do. Management takes these forecasts and combines and interprets the data in order to create plans. Textbook publishers use this procedure to project how many copies of a new title they might sell. The *customer evaluation* technique goes beyond an organization's sales force and collects data from customers of the organization. The customers provide estimates of their own future needs for the goods and services that the organization supplies. Managers must combine, interpret, and act on this information. It is important to recognize that there are two major limitations to this approach. Customers may be less interested in taking time to develop accurate predictions than are members of the organization itself, and the method makes no provision for including any new customers that the organization may acquire. Wal-Mart helps its suppliers use this approach by providing them with detailed projections regarding what it intends to buy several months in advance.

Selecting an appropriate forecasting technique can be as important as applying it correctly. Some techniques are appropriate only for specific circumstances. For example, the sales-force-composition technique is good only for sales forecasting. Other techniques, such as the Delphi method, are useful in a variety of situations. Some techniques, such as the econometric models, require extensive use of computers, whereas others, such as customer evaluation models, can be used with little mathematical expertise. For the most part, selection of a particular technique depends on the nature of the problem, the experience and preferences of the manager, and available resources.[7]

OTHER PLANNING TECHNIQUES

Of course, planning involves more than just forecasting. Other tools and techniques that are of help for a variety of planning purposes include linear programming, breakeven analysis, simulations, and PERT.

Linear Programming

• **linear programming** A planning technique that determines the optimal combination of resources and activities

One of the most widely used quantitative tools for planning, **linear programming** is a procedure for calculating the optimal combination of resources and activities. It is appropriate when there is some objective to be met (such as a sales quota or a certain production level) within a set of constraints (such as a limited advertising budget or limited production capabilities).

To illustrate how linear programming can be used, assume that a small electronics company produces two basic products—a high-quality cable television tuner and a high-quality receiver for picking up television audio and playing it through a stereo amplifier. Both products go through the same two departments, first production and then inspection and testing. Each product has a known profit margin and a high level of demand. The production manager's job is to produce the optimal combination of tuners *(T)* and receivers *(R)* in order to maximize profits and use the time in production (PR) and in inspection and testing (IT) most efficiently. Table A2.2 gives the information needed for using linear programming to solve this problem.

The *objective function* is an equation that represents what we want to achieve. In technical terms, it is a mathematical representation of the de-

TABLE A2.2 Production Data for Tuners and Receivers

Department	Number of Hours Required per Unit: Tuners (*T*)	Number of Hours Required per Unit: Receivers (*R*)	Production Capacity for Day (in Hours)
Production (PR)	10	6	150
Inspection and testing (IT)	4	4	80
Profit margin	$30	$20	

Linear programming can be used to determine the optimal number of tuners and receivers an organization might make. Essential information needed to perform this analysis includes the number of hours each product spends in each department, the production capacity for each department, and the profit margin for each product.

sirability of the consequences of a particular decision. In our example, the objective function can be represented as follows:

$$\text{Maximize profit} = \$30X_T + \$20X_R$$

where

R = the number of receivers to be produced

T = the number of tuners to be produced

The $30 and $20 figures are the respective profit margins of the tuner and receiver, as noted in Table A2.2. The objective, then, is to maximize profits.

However, this objective must be accomplished within a specific set of constraints. In our example, the constraints are the time required to produce each product in each department and the total amount of time available. These data are also found in Table A2.2, and can be used to construct the relevant constraint equations:

$$10T + 6R \leq 150$$
$$4T + 4R \leq 80$$

(that is, we cannot use more capacity than is available), and, of course,

$$T \geq 0$$
$$R \geq 0$$

The set of equations consisting of the objective function and constraints can be solved graphically. To start, we first assume that production of each product is maximized when production of the other is at zero. The resultant solutions are then plotted on a coordinate axis. In the PR department, if $T = 0$ then:

$$10T + 6R \leq 150$$
$$10(0) + 6R \leq 150$$
$$R \leq 25$$

In the same department, if $R = 0$ then:

$$10T + 6R \leq 150$$
$$10T + 6(0) \leq 150$$
$$T \leq 15$$

Similarly, in the IT department, if no tuners are produced,

$$4T + 4R \leq 80$$
$$4(0) + 4R \leq 80$$
$$R \leq 20$$

and, if no receivers are produced,

$$4T + 4R \leq 80$$
$$4T + 4(0) \leq 80$$
$$T \leq 20$$

The four resulting inequalities are graphed in Figure A2.2. The shaded region represents the feasibility space, or production combinations that do not exceed the capacity of either department. The optimal number of products will be defined at one of the four corners of the shaded area—that is,

Finding the solution to a linear programming problem graphically is useful when only two alternatives are being considered. When problems are more complex, computers that can execute hundreds of equations and variables are necessary. Virtually all large firms, such as General Motors, Texaco, and Sears, use linear programming.

FIGURE A2.2 The Graphical Solution of a Linear Programming Problem

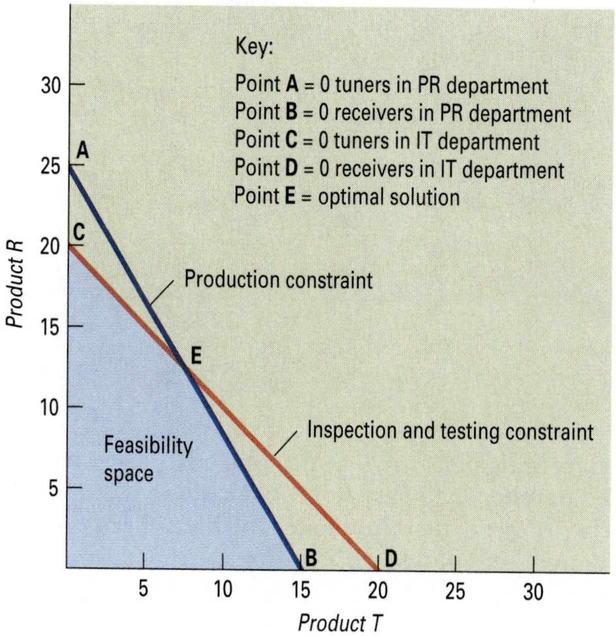

the firm should produce 20 receivers only (point **C**), 15 tuners only (point **B**), 13 receivers and 7 tuners (point **E**), or no products at all. With the constraint that production of both tuners and receivers must be greater than zero, it follows that point **E** is the optimal solution. That combination requires 148 hours in PR and 80 hours in IT and yields $470 in profit. (Note that if only receivers were produced, the profit would be $400; producing only tuners would mean $450 in profit.)

Unfortunately, only two alternatives can be handled by the graphical method, and our example was extremely simple. When there are other alternatives, a complex algebraic method must be employed. Many real-world problems may require several hundred equations and variables. Clearly, computers are necessary to execute such sophisticated analyses. Linear programming is a powerful technique, playing a key role in both planning and decision making. It can be used to schedule production, select an optimal portfolio of investments, allocate sales representatives to territories, or produce an item at some minimum cost.[8]

Breakeven Analysis

Linear programming is called a *normative procedure* because it prescribes the optimal solution to a problem. Breakeven analysis is a *descriptive procedure* because it simply describes relationships among variables; then it is up to the manager to make decisions. We can define **breakeven analysis** as a procedure for identifying the point at which revenues start covering their associated costs. It might be used to analyze the effects on profits of different price and output combinations or various levels of output.

breakeven analysis A procedure for identifying the point at which revenues start covering costs

Figure A2.3 represents the key cost variables in breakeven analysis. Creating most products or services includes three types of costs: fixed costs, variable costs, and total costs. Fixed costs are costs that are incurred regardless of what volume of output is being generated. They include rent or mortgage payments on the building, managerial salaries, and depreciation of plant and equipment. Variable costs are those that vary with the

FIGURE A2.3 An Example of Cost Factors for Breakeven Analysis

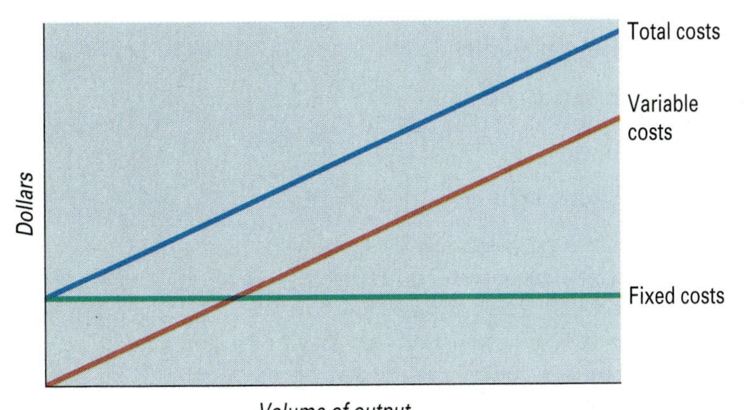

To determine the breakeven point for profit on sales for a product or service, the manager first must determine both fixed and variable costs. These costs are then combined to show total costs.

After total costs are determined and graphed, the manager then graphs the total revenues that will be earned on different levels of sales. The regions defined by the intersection of the two graphs show loss and profit areas. The intersection itself shows the breakeven point—the level of sales at which all costs are covered but no profits are earned.

FIGURE A2.4 Breakeven Analysis

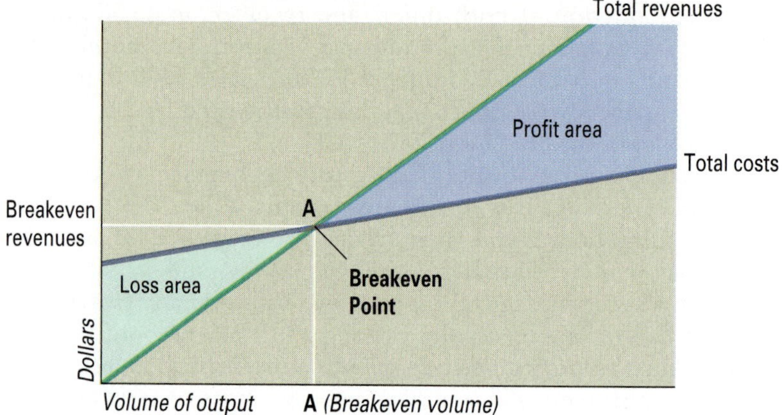

number of units produced, such as the cost of raw materials and direct labor used to make each unit. Total costs are fixed costs plus variable costs. Note that because of fixed costs, the line for total costs never begins at zero.

Other important factors in breakeven analysis are revenue and profit. Revenue, the total dollar amount of sales, is computed by multiplying the number of units sold by the sales price of each unit. Profit is then determined by subtracting total costs from total revenues. When revenues and total costs are plotted on the same axes, the breakeven graph shown in Figure A2.4 emerges. The point at which the lines representing total costs and total revenues cross is the breakeven point. If the company represented in Figure A2.4 sells more units than are represented by point **A**, it will realize a profit; selling below that level will result in a loss.

Mathematically, the breakeven point (expressed as units of production or volume) is shown by the formula

$$BP = \frac{TFC}{P - VC}$$

where

BP = breakeven point

TFC = total fixed costs

P = price per unit

VC = variable cost per unit

Assume that you are considering the production of a new garden hoe with a curved handle. You have determined that an acceptable selling price will be \$20. You have also determined that the variable costs per hoe will be \$15, and you have total fixed costs of \$400,000 per year. The question is how many hoes must you sell each year to break even. Using the breakeven model, you find that:

$$BP = \frac{TFC}{P - VC}$$

$$BP = \frac{400{,}000}{20 - 15}$$

$$BP = 80{,}000 \text{ units}$$

Thus, you must sell 80,000 hoes to break even. Further analysis would also show that if you could raise your price to $25 per hoe, you would need to sell only 40,000 to break even, and so on.

The state of New York used a breakeven analysis to evaluate seven different variations of prior approvals for its Medicaid service. Comparisons were conducted of the costs involved in each variation against savings gained from efficiency and improved quality of service. The state found that only three of the variations were cost-effective.[9]

Breakeven analysis is a popular and important planning technique, but it also has noteworthy weaknesses.[10] It considers revenues only up to the breakeven point, and it makes no allowance for the time value of money. For example, because the funds used to cover fixed and variable costs could be used for other purposes (such as investment), the organization is losing interest income by tying up its money prior to reaching the breakeven point. Thus managers often use breakeven analysis as only the first step in planning. After the preliminary analysis has been completed, more sophisticated techniques (such as rate-of-return analysis or discounted-present-value analysis) are used. Those techniques can help the manager decide whether to proceed or to divert resources into other areas.

Simulations

Another useful planning device is simulation. The word *simulate* means to copy or to represent. An **organizational simulation** is a model of a real-world situation that can be manipulated to discover how it functions. Simulation is a descriptive rather than a prescriptive technique. Northern Research & Engineering Corporation is an engineering consulting firm that helps clients plan new factories. By using a sophisticated factory simulation model, the firm recently helped a client cut several machines and operations from a new plant and save over $750,000.

organizational simulation
A model of a real-world situation that can be manipulated to discover how it functions

To consider another example, suppose the city of Denver were going to build a new airport. Issues to be addressed might include the number of runways, the direction of those runways, the number of terminals and gates, the allocation of various carriers among the terminals and gates, and the technology and human resources needed to achieve a target frequency of takeoffs and landings. (Of course, actually planning such an airport would involve many more variables than these.) A model could be constructed to simulate these factors, as well as their interrelationships. The planner could then insert several different values for each factor and observe the probable results.

Simulation problems are in some ways similar to those addressed by linear programming, but simulation is more useful in very complex situations characterized by diverse constraints and opportunities. The development of sophisticated simulation models may require the expertise of outside specialists or consultants, and the complexity of simulation almost always necessitates the use of a computer. For these reasons, simulation is most likely to be used as a technique for planning in large organizations that have the required resources.

PERT

• **PERT**
A planning tool that uses a network to plan projects involving numerous activities and their interrelationships

A final planning tool we will discuss is PERT. **PERT**, an acronym for Program Evaluation and Review Technique, was developed by the U.S. Navy to help coordinate the activities of three thousand contractors during the development of the Polaris nuclear submarine, and it was credited with saving two years of work on the project.[11] It has subsequently been used by most large companies in a variety of ways. The purpose of PERT is to develop a network of activities and their interrelationships so as to highlight critical time intervals that affect the overall project. There are six basic steps in PERT:

1. Identify the activities to be performed and the events that will mark their completion.
2. Develop a network showing the relationships among the activities and events.
3. Calculate the time needed for each event and the time necessary to get from each event to the next.
4. Identify within the network the longest path that leads to completion of the project. This path is called the critical path.
5. Refine the network.
6. Use the network to control the project.

Suppose that a marketing manager wants to use PERT to plan the test marketing and nationwide introduction of a new product. Table A2.3 identifies the basic steps involved in carrying out this project. The activities are then arranged in a network like the one shown in Figure A2.5. In the

FIGURE A2.5 A PERT Network for Introducing a New Product

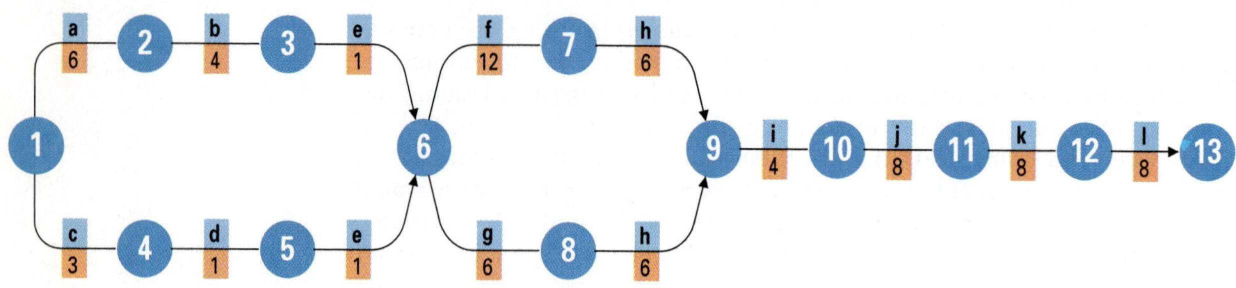

The blue numbers and letters correspond to the numbers and letters used in Table A2.3.

The orange numbers refer to the expected number of weeks for each activity.

PERT is used to plan schedules for projects and it is particularly useful when many activities with critical time intervals must be coordinated. Besides launching a new product, PERT is useful for projects like constructing a new factory or building, remodeling an office, or opening a new store.

TABLE A2.3 Activities and Events for Introducing a New Product

Activities	Events
a Produce limited quantity for test marketing.	1 Origin of project.
	2 Completion of production for test marketing.
b Design preliminary package.	3 Completion of design for preliminary package.
c Locate test market.	4 Test market located.
d Obtain local merchant cooperation.	5 Local merchant cooperation obtained.
e Ship product to selected retail outlets.	6 Product for test marketing shipped to retail outlets.
f Monitor sales and customer reactions.	7 Sales and customer reactions monitored.
g Survey customers in test-market area.	8 Customers in test-market area surveyed.
h Make needed product changes.	9 Product changes made.
i Make needed package changes.	10 Package changes made.
j Mass produce the product.	11 Product mass produced.
k Begin national advertising.	12 National advertising carried out.
l Begin national distribution.	13 National distribution completed.

figure, each completed event is represented by a number in a circle. The activities are indicated by letters on the lines connecting the events. Notice that some activities are performed independently of one another and others must be performed in sequence. For example, test production (activity a) and test site location (activity c) can be done at the same time, but test site location has to be done before actual testing (activities f and g) can be done.

The time needed to get from one activity to another is then determined. The normal way to calculate the time between each activity is to average the most optimistic, most pessimistic, and most likely times, with the most likely time weighted by 4. Time is usually calculated with the following formula:

$$\text{Expected time} = \frac{a + 4b + c}{6}$$

where

a = optimistic time

b = most likely time

c = pessimistic time

• **critical path**
The longest path through a PERT network

The expected number of weeks for each activity in our example is shown by the orange numbers along each path in Figure A2.5. The **critical path**—or the longest path through the network—is then identified. This path is considered critical because it shows the shortest time that the project can be completed in. In our example, the critical path is 1-2-3-6-7-9-10-11-12-13, totaling 57 weeks. PERT thus tells the manager that the project will take 57 weeks to complete.

The first network may be refined. If 57 weeks to completion is too long a time, the manager might decide to begin preliminary package design before the test products are finished. Or the manager might decide that 10 weeks rather than 12 is a sufficient time period to monitor sales. The idea is that if the critical path can be shortened, so too can the overall duration of the project. The PERT network serves as an ongoing framework for both planning and control throughout the project. For example, the manager can use it to monitor where the project is relative to where it needs to be. Thus if an activity on the critical path takes longer than planned, the manager needs to make up the time elsewhere or live with the fact that the entire project will be late.

DECISION-MAKING TOOLS

Managers can also use a number of tools that relate more specifically to decision making than to planning. Two commonly used tools and procedures are payoff matrices and decision trees.

The Payoff Matrix

• **payoff matrix**
A decision-making tool that specifies the probable value of different alternatives depending on different possible outcomes associated with each

• **probability**
The likelihood, expressed as a percentage, that a particular event will or will not occur

A **payoff matrix** specifies the probable value of different alternatives, depending on different possible outcomes associated with each. The use of a payoff matrix requires that several alternatives be available, that several different events could occur, and that the consequences depend on which alternative is selected and on which event or set of events occurs. An important concept in understanding the payoff matrix, then, is probability. A **probability** is the likelihood, expressed as a percentage, that a particular event will or will not occur. If we believe that a particular event will occur 75 times out of 100, we can say that the probability of its occurring is 75 percent, or .75. Probabilities range in value from 0 (no chance of occurrence) to 1.00 (certain occurrence—also referred to as 100 percent). In the business world, there are few probabilities of either 0 or 1.00. Most probabilities that managers use are based on subjective judgment, intuition, and historical data.

The **expected value** of an alternative course of action is the sum of all possible values of outcomes due to that action multiplied by their respective probabilities. Suppose, for example, that a venture capitalist is considering investing in a new company. If he believes there is a .40 probability of making $100,000, a .30 probability of making $30,000, and a .30 probability of losing $20,000, the expected value *(EV)* of this alternative is:

expected value When applied to alternative courses of action, the sum of all possible values of outcomes from that action multiplied by their respective probabilities

$$EV = .40(100{,}000) + .30(30{,}000) + .30(-20{,}000)$$
$$EV = 40{,}000 + 9{,}000 - 6{,}000$$
$$EV = \$43{,}000$$

The investor can then weigh the expected value of this investment against the expected values of other available alternatives. The highest *EV* signals the investment that should most likely be selected.

For example, suppose another venture capitalist is looking to invest $20,000 in a new business. She has identified three possible alternatives: a leisure products company, an energy enhancement company, and a food-processing company. Because the expected value of each alternative depends on short-run changes in the economy, especially inflation, she decides to develop a payoff matrix. She estimates that the probability of high inflation is .30 and the probability of low inflation is .70. She then estimates the probable returns for each investment in the event of both high and low inflation. Figure A2.6 shows what the payoff matrix might look like (a minus sign indicates a loss). The expected value of investing in the leisure products company is:

$$EV = .30(-10{,}000) + .70(50{,}000)$$
$$EV = -3{,}000 + 35{,}000$$
$$EV = \$32{,}000$$

Similarly, the expected value of investing in the energy enhancement company is:

$$EV = .30(90{,}000) + .70(-15{,}000)$$
$$EV = 27{,}000 + (-10{,}500)$$
$$EV = \$16{,}500$$

And, finally, the expected value of investing in the food-processing company is:

$$EV = .30(30{,}000) + .70(25{,}000)$$
$$EV = 9{,}000 + 17{,}500$$
$$EV = \$26{,}500$$

Investing in the leisure products company, then, has the highest expected value.

A payoff matrix helps the manager determine the expected value of different alternatives. A payoff matrix is effective only if the manager ensures that probability estimates are as accurate as possible.

FIGURE A2.6 An Example of a Payoff Matrix

		High inflation *(Probability of .30)*	Low inflation *(Probability of .70)*
Investment alternative 1	Leisure products company	−$10,000	+$50,000
Investment alternative 2	Energy enhancement company	+$90,000	−$15,000
Investment alternative 3	Food-processing company	+$30,000	+$25,000

Other potential uses for payoff matrices include determining optimal order quantities, deciding whether to repair or replace broken machinery, and deciding which of several new products to introduce. Of course, the real key to effectively using payoff matrices is making accurate estimates of the relevant probabilities.

Decision Trees

decision trees Planning tools that extend the concept of a payoff matrix through a sequence of decisions

Decision trees are like payoff matrices in that they enhance a manager's ability to evaluate alternatives by making use of expected values. However, they are most appropriate when there are a number of decisions to be made in sequence.[12]

Figure A2.7 illustrates a hypothetical decision tree. The firm represented wants to begin exporting its products to a foreign market, but limited capacity restricts it to only one market at first. Managers feel that either France or China would be the best alternative to start with. Whichever alternative is selected, sales for the product in that country may turn out to be high or low. In France, there is a .80 chance of high sales and a .20 chance of low sales. The anticipated payoffs in these situations are predicted to be $20 million and $3 million, respectively. In China, the probabilities of high versus low sales are .60 and .40 respectively, and the associated payoffs are presumed to be $25 million and $6 million. As shown in the figure, the expected value of shipping to France is $16,600,000, whereas the expected value of shipping to China is $17,400,000.

The astute reader will note that this part of the decision could have been set up as a payoff matrix. However, the value of decision trees is that we can extend the model to include subsequent decisions. Assume, for example, that the company begins shipping to China. If high sales do in fact materialize, the company will soon reach another decision situation. It might use the extra revenues to (1) increase shipments to China, (2) build a plant close to China in order to cut shipping costs, or (3) begin shipping to France. Various outcomes are possible for each decision, and each out-

F I G U R E A2.7 An Example of a Decision Tree

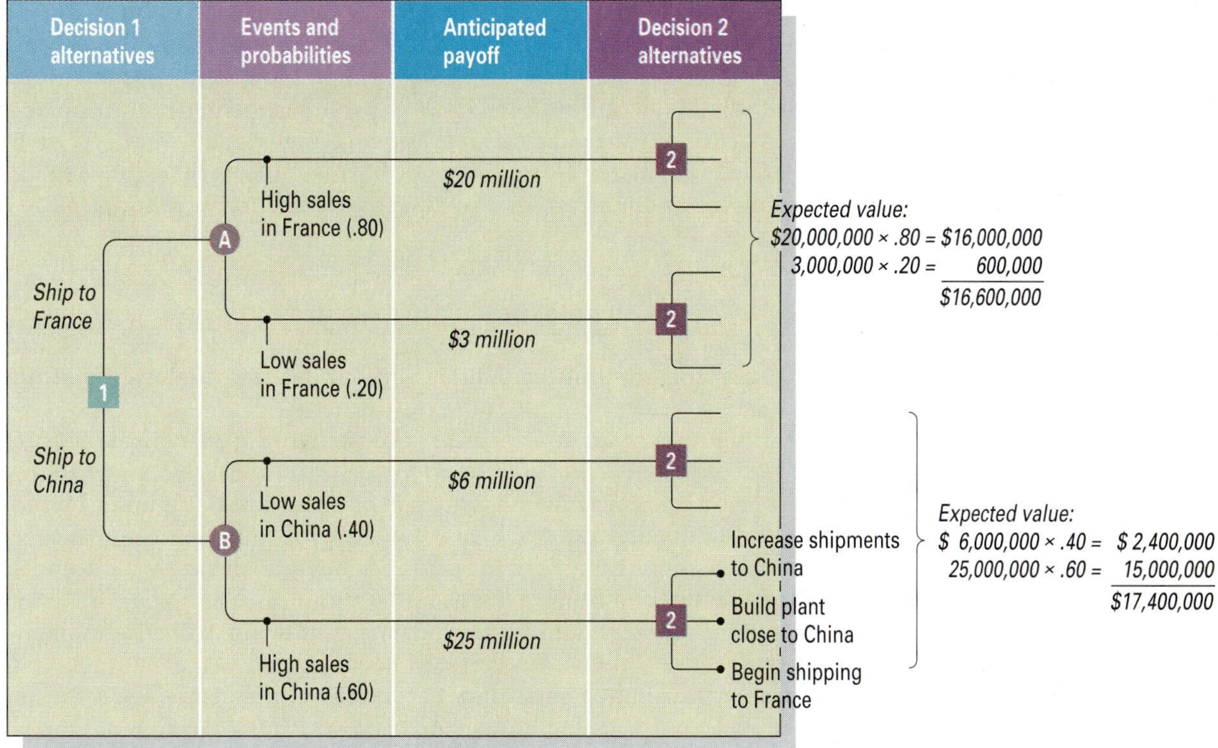

A decision tree extends the basic concepts of a payoff matrix through multiple decisions. This tree shows the possible outcomes of two levels of decisions. The first decision is whether to expand to China or France. The second decision, assuming that the company expands to China, is whether to increase shipments to China, build a plant close to China, or initiate shipping to France.

come will also have both a probability and an anticipated payoff. It is therefore possible to compute expected values back through several tiers of decisions all the way to the initial one. As it is with payoff matrices, determining probabilities accurately is the crucial element in the process. Properly used, however, decision trees can provide managers with a useful road map through complex decision situations.

Other Techniques

In addition to payoff matrices and decision trees, a number of other quantitative methods are also available to facilitate decision making.[13]

Inventory Models **Inventory models** are techniques that help the manager decide how much inventory to maintain. Chains such as Target use inventory models to help determine how much merchandise to order, when to order it, and so forth. Inventory consists of both raw materials (inputs) and finished goods (outputs). Polaroid, for example, maintains a supply of the chemicals it uses to make film, the cartons it packs film in, and packaged film ready to be shipped. For finished goods, both extremes are bad: excess inventory ties up capital, whereas a small inventory may result in shortages and customer dissatisfaction. The same holds for raw materials: too much inventory ties up capital, but if a company runs

inventory model A technique that helps managers decide how much inventory to maintain

out of resources, work stoppages may occur. Finally, because the process of placing an order for raw materials and supplies has associated costs (such as clerical time, shipping expenses, and higher unit costs for small quantities), it is important to minimize the frequency of ordering. Inventory models help the manager make decisions in such a way as to optimize the size of inventory. New innovations in inventory management such as **just-in-time**, or **JIT**, rely heavily on decision-making models. A JIT system involves scheduling materials to arrive in short batches as they are needed, thereby eliminating the need for a big reserve inventory, warehouse space, and so forth.[14]

- **just-in-time (JIT)** An inventory management technique in which materials are scheduled to arrive in small batches as they are needed, eliminating the need for resources such as big reserves and warehouse space

- **queuing model** A model used to optimize waiting lines in organizations

Queuing Models **Queuing models** are intended to help organizations manage waiting lines. We are all familiar with such situations: shoppers waiting to pay for groceries at Kroger, drivers waiting to buy gas at an Exxon station, travelers calling American Airlines for reservations, and customers waiting for a teller at Citibank. Take the Kroger example. If a store manager has only one checkout stand in operation, the store's cost for checkout personnel is very low; however, many customers are upset by the long line that frequently develops. To solve the problem, the store manager could decide to keep twenty checkout stands open at all times. Customers would like the short waiting period, but personnel costs would be very high. A queuing model would be appropriate in this case to help the manager determine the optimal number of checkout stands: the number that would balance personnel costs and customer waiting time. Target uses queuing models to determine how many checkout lanes to put in its stores.

Distribution Models A decision facing many marketing managers relates to the distribution of the organization's products. Specifically, the manager must decide where the products should go and how to transport them. Railroads, trucking, and air freight all have associated shipping costs, and all follow different schedules and routes. The problem is to identify the combination of routes that optimizes distribution effectiveness and distribution costs. **Distribution models** help managers determine this optimal pattern of distribution.

- **distribution model** A model used to determine the optimal pattern of distribution across different carriers and routes

- **game theory** A planning tool used to predict how competitors will respond to different actions the organization might take

Game Theory **Game theory** was originally developed to predict the effect of one company's decisions on competitors. Models developed from game theory are intended to predict how a competitor will react to various activities that an organization might undertake, such as price changes, promotional changes, and the introduction of new products.[15] If Bank of America were considering raising its prime lending rate by 1 percent, it might use a game theory model to predict whether Citicorp would follow suit. If the model revealed that Citicorp would, Bank of America would probably proceed; otherwise, it would probably maintain the current interest rates. Unfortunately, game theory has not yet proved as useful as it was originally expected to be. The complexities of the real world combined with the limitation of the technique itself restrict its applicability. Game theory, however, does provide a useful conceptual framework for analyzing competitive behavior, and its usefulness may be improved in the future.

Artificial Intelligence A fairly new addition to the manager's quantitative tool kit is **artificial intelligence (AI)**. The most useful form of AI is the expert system.[16] An expert system is essentially a computer program that tries to duplicate the thought processes of experienced decision makers. For example, Digital Equipment has developed an expert system that checks sales orders for new computer systems and then designs preliminary layouts for those new systems. Digital can now ship the computer to a customer in components for final assembly on site. This has enabled the company to cut back on its own final assembly facilities.

• **artificial intelligence (AI)**
A computer program that attempts to duplicate the thought processes of experienced decision makers

STRENGTHS AND WEAKNESSES OF PLANNING TOOLS

Like all issues confronting management, planning tools of the type described here have a number of strengths and weaknesses.

Weaknesses and Problems

One weakness of the planning and decision-making tools discussed in this appendix is that they may not always adequately reflect reality. Even with the most sophisticated and powerful computer-assisted technique, reality must often be simplified. Many problems are also not amenable to quantitative analysis because important elements of them are intangible or nonquantifiable. Employee morale or satisfaction, for example, is often a major factor in managerial decisions.

The use of these tools and techniques may also be quite costly. For example, only larger companies can afford to develop their own econometric models. Even though the computer explosion has increased the availability of quantitative aids, there is still some expense involved, and it will take time for many of these techniques to become widely used. Resistance to change also limits the use of planning tools in some settings. If a manager for a retail chain has always based decisions for new locations on personal visits, observations, and intuition, she or he may be less than eager to begin using a computer-based model for evaluating and selecting sites. Finally, problems may arise when managers have to rely on technical specialists to use sophisticated models. Experts trained in the use of complex mathematical procedures may not understand or appreciate other aspects of management.

Strengths and Advantages

On the plus side, planning and decision-making tools offer many advantages. For situations that are amenable to quantification, they can bring sophisticated mathematical processes to bear on planning and decision making. Properly designed models and formulas also help decision makers "see reason." For example, a manager might not be inclined to introduce a new product line simply because she or he doesn't think it will be profitable. After seeing a forecast predicting first-year sales of 100,000 units coupled with a breakeven analysis showing profitability after only 20,000, however, the manager will probably change her or his mind. Thus, rational planning tools and techniques force the manager to look beyond personal prejudices and predispositions. Finally, the computer explosion is rapidly making sophisticated planning techniques available in a wider range of settings than ever.

The crucial point to remember is that planning tools and techniques are a means to an end, not an end in themselves. Just as a carpenter uses a handsaw in some situations and an electric saw in others, a manager must recognize that a particular model may be useful in some situations but not in others. Knowing the difference is one mark of a good manager.

APPENDIX NOTES

1. Anirudh Dhebar, "Managing the Quality of Quantitative Analysis," *Sloan Management Review,* Winter 1993, pp. 69–79.
2. See Wayne W. Daniel, *Essentials of Business Statistics,* 2nd ed. (Boston: Houghton Mifflin, 1988), for an overview of basic forecasting methods.
3. R. Balachandra, "Technological Forecasting: Who Does It and How Useful Is It?" *Technological Forecasting and Social Change,* January 1980, pp. 75–85.
4. Charles Ostrom, *Time-Series Analysis: Regression Techniques* (Beverly Hills, Calif.: Sage Publications, 1980).
5. See John C. Chambers, S. K. Mullick, and D. Smith, "How to Choose the Right Forecasting Technique," *Harvard Business Review,* July–August 1971, pp. 45–74, for a classic review.
6. Fred Kerlinger and Elazar Pedhazur, *Multiple Regression in Behavioral Research* (New York: Holt, 1973).
7. Chambers, Mullick, and Smith, "How to Choose the Right Forecasting Technique"; see also J. Scott Armstrong, *Long-Range Forecasting: From Crystal Ball to Computers* (New York: Wiley, 1978).
8. Nicholas A. Glaskowsky and Donald R. Hudson, *Business Logistics,* 3rd ed. (Fort Worth, Tex.: Harcourt Brace Jovanovich, 1992).
9. Edward Hannan, Linda Ryan, and Richard Van Orden, "A Cost-Benefit Analysis of Prior Approvals for Medicaid Services in New York State," *Socio-Economic Planning Sciences,* 1984, Vol. 18, pp. 1–14.
10. Glaskowsky and Hudson, *Business Logistics.*
11. Everett Adam, Jr., and Ronald J. Ebert, *Production and Operations Management,* 5th ed. (Englewood Cliffs, N.J.: Prentice Hall, 1992).
12. Robert E. Markland, *Topics in Management Science,* 4th ed. (New York; Wiley, 1993).
13. Adam and Ebert, *Production and Operations Management.*
14. Ramon L. Alonso and Cline W. Fraser, "JIT Hits Home: A Case Study in Reducing Management Delays," *Sloan Management Review,* Summer 1991, pp. 59–68.
15. "Businessman's Dilemma," *Forbes,* October 11, 1993, pp. 107–109.
16. Beau Sheil, "Thinking About Artificial Intelligence," *Harvard Business Review,* July–August 1987, pp. 91–97; and Dorothy Leonard-Barton and John J. Sviokla, "Putting Expert Systems to Work," *Harvard Business Review,* March–April 1988, pp. 91–98.

Interpretations of Skills Self-Assessment Instruments

Chapter 1: Self-Awareness

Total your scores for each of the two skill areas.

Skill Area	Items	Score
Self-disclosure and openness to feedback from others	1, 2, 3, 9, 11	_____
Awareness of own values, cognitive style, change orientation, and interpersonal orientation	4, 5, 6, 7, 8, 10	_____
Now total your score:		_____

To assess how well you scored on this instrument, compare your scores to three comparison standards. (1) Compare your scores with the maximum possible (66). (2) Compare your scores with the scores of other students in your class. (3) Compare your scores to a norm group consisting of 500 business school students. In comparison to the norm group, if you scored

55 or above, you are in the top quartile.
52 to 54, you are in the second quartile.
48 to 51, you are in the third quartile.
47 or below, you are in the bottom quartile.

Chapter 2: Global Awareness

All of the statements are true. Thus your score should be close to 40. The closer your score is to 40, the more you understand the global context of organizational environments. The closer your score is to 10, the less you understand the global context. For developmental purposes, you should note any particular items for which you had a low score and concentrate on improving your knowledge of those areas.

Chapter 3: Are You a Good Planner?

According to the author of this questionnaire, the "perfect" planner would have answered: (1) Yes, (2) No, (3) Yes, (4) Yes, (5) Yes, (6) Yes, (7) Yes, and (8) No.

Chapter 4: Decision-Making Styles

Generally there are three decision-making styles: reflexive, consistent, and reflective. To determine your style, add up your score by totaling the numbers assigned to each response. The total will be between 10 and 30. A score of between 10 and 16 indicates a reflexive style, 17 to 23 indicates a consistent style, and 24 to 30 indicates a reflective style.

Reflexive Style: A reflexive decision maker likes to make quick decisions (to shoot from the hip) without taking the time to get all the information that may be needed, and without considering all alternatives. On the positive side, reflexive decision makers are decisive; they do not procrastinate. On the negative side, making quick decisions can lead to waste and duplication when the best possible alternative is overlooked. Employees may see a decision maker as a poor supervisor if he or she consistently makes bad decisions. If you use a reflexive style, you may want to slow down and spend more time gathering information and analyzing alternatives.

Reflective Style: A reflective decision maker likes to take plenty of time to make decisions, gathering considerable information and analyzing several alternatives. On the positive side, the reflective type does not make hasty decisions. On the negative side, he or she may procrastinate and waste valuable time and other resources. The reflective decision maker may be viewed as wishy-washy and indecisive. If you use a reflective style, you may want to speed up your decision making. As Andrew Jackson once said, "Take time to deliberate; but when the time for action arrives, stop thinking and go on."

Consistent Style: Consistent decision makers tend to make decisions without rushing or wasting time. They know when they have enough information and alternatives to make a sound decision. Consistent decision makers tend to have the best record for making good decisions.

Chapter 5: An Entrepreneurial Quiz

If most of your marks are in the first column, you probably have what it takes to run a business. If not, you are likely to have more trouble than you can handle by yourself. You should look for a partner who is strong on the points on which you are weak. If most marks are in the third column, not even a good partner will be able to shore you up. Now go back and answer the first question on the self-assessment.

Chapter 6: How Is Your Organization Managed?

Score	System
0–9 **10–19** **20–29** **30–39**	Bureaucratic System 1
40–49 **50–59** **60–69** **70–79**	Mixed Systems 2 and 3

80–89 **90–100**	Organic System 4

High scores indicate a highly organic and participatively managed organization. Low scores are associated with a mechanistic or a bureaucratically managed organization.

Chapter 7: Innovative Attitude Scale

To determine your score, simply add the numbers associated with your responses to the twenty items. The higher your score, the more receptive to innovation you are. You can compare your score with that of others to see if you seem to be more or less receptive to innovation than a comparable group of business students.

Score	Percentile*
39	5
53	16
62	33
71	50
80	68
89	86
97	95

*Percentile indicates the percentage of the people who are expected to score below you.

Chapter 8: Diagnosing Poor Performance and Enhancing Motivation

Skill Area	**Item**	**Rating**
Diagnosing performance problems	1	_____
	11	_____
Establishing expectations and setting goals	2	_____
	12	_____
Facilitating performance (enhancing ability)	3	_____
	13	_____
	20	_____
Linking performance to rewards and discipline	5	_____
	14	_____
	6	_____
	15	_____
Using salient internal and external incentives	7	_____
	16	_____
	8	_____
	17	_____
Distributing rewards equitably	9	_____
	18	_____
Providing timely and straightforward performance feedback	4	_____
	10	_____
	19	_____
Total score:		_____

To assess how well you scored, compare your score to three comparison standards: (1) Compare your score with the maximum possible (120). (2) Compare your score with the scores of other students in your class. (3) Compare your score to a norm group consisting of 500 business school students. In comparison to the norm group, if you scored

101 or above, you are in the top quartile.
94 to 100, you are in the second quartile.
85 to 93, you are in the third quartile.
84 or below, you are in the bottom quartile.

The higher your score, the better you are at identifying performance problems and the more skillful you are at taking steps to correct them. You can compare your score with that of others to see if you seem to be more or less skillful than a comparable group of business students.

Chapter 9: Assessing Your Mental Abilities

Research spanning fifty years has identified ten primary mental abilities. The higher your score on each statement, the more you see yourself as having the corresponding mental ability. The mental abilities associated with each statement are as follows:

1. Flexibility and speed of closure
2. Originality/fluency
3. Inductive reasoning
4. Associative memory
5. Span memory
6. Number facility
7. Perceptual speed
8. Deductive reasoning
9. Spatial orientation and visualization
10. Verbal comprehension

Chapter 10: Assessing Your Needs

This set of needs was developed by H. A. Murray, a psychologist in 1938, and operationalized by another psychologist, J. W. Atkinson. These needs correspond one-to-one to the items on the assessment questionnaire. Known as Murray's Manifest Needs because they are visible through behavior, they are:

1. Achievement
2. Affiliation
3. Aggression
4. Autonomy
5. Exhibition
6. Impulsivity
7. Nurturance
8. Order
9. Power
10. Understanding

Although little research has evaluated Murray's theory, the different needs have been researched. People seem to have a different profile of needs underlying their motivations at different ages. The more any one or more are descriptive of you, the more you see yourself as having that particular need active in your motivational makeup. For more information, see H. A. Murray, *Explorations in Personality* (New York: Oxford University Press, 1938), and J. W. Atkinson, *An Introduction to Motivation* (Princeton, N.J.: Van Nostrand, 1964).

Chapter 11: Managerial Leader Behavior Questionnaire

These statements represent twenty-three behavior categories identified by research as descriptive of managerial leadership. Not all twenty-three are important in any given situation. Typically less than half of these behaviors are associated with effective performance in particular situations; thus there is no "right" or "wrong" set of responses on this questionnaire. The behavior categories are

1. Emphasizing performance
2. Showing consideration
3. Career counseling
4. Inspiring subordinates
5. Providing praise and recognition
6. Structuring reward contingencies
7. Clarifying work roles
8. Goal setting
9. Training-coaching
10. Disseminating information
11. Encouraging decision participation
12. Delegating
13. Planning
14. Innovating
15. Problem solving
16. Facilitating the work
17. Monitoring operations
18. Monitoring the environment
19. Representing the unit
20. Facilitating cooperation and teamwork
21. Managing conflict
22. Criticism
23. Administering discipline

In military organizations at war, inspiring subordinates, emphasizing performance, clarifying work roles, problem solving, and planning seem most important. In military organizations during peacetime, inspiring subordinates, emphasizing performance, clarifying work roles, showing consideration, criticism, and administering discipline seem most important. In business organizations, emphasizing performance, monitoring the environment, clarifying work roles, goal setting, and sometimes innovating seem to be most important. In each of these instances, however, the level of organization, type of technology, environmental conditions, and objectives sought all help determine the exact mix of behaviors that will lead to effectiveness. You should analyze your particular situation to determine which subset of these behavior categories is most likely to be important and then strive to develop that subset.

Chapter 12: Sex Talk Quiz

1. False—According to studies there is no truth to the myth that women are more intuitive than men. However, research has shown that women pay greater attention to "detail." Linguist Robin Lakoff in her classic book, *Language and Woman's Place* (Harper Colophon, 1975), confirms this and states that women tend to use finer descriptions of colors.

2. True—Men are listened to more often than women. In "Sex Differences in Listening Comprehension," Kenneth Gruber and Jacqueline Gaehelein (*Sex Roles,* Vol. 5, 1979) found that both male and female audiences tended to listen more attentively to male speakers than to female speakers.

3. False—Contrary to popular stereotype it is men—not women—who talk more. Studies like the one done by linguist Lynnette Hirshman showed that men far outtalk women ("Analysis of Supportive and Assertive Behavior in Conversations." Paper presented at the Linguists Society of America, July 1974).

4. False—Although several studies show that women talk more rapidly than men, women don't necessarily talk extremely fast.

5. False—Numerous studies show that women, not men, tend to maintain more eye contact and facial pleasantries. Dr. Nancy Henley in her chapter "Power, Sex, and Non-Verbal Communication" in *Language and Sex: Difference and Dominance* (Newbury House Publishers, 1975), shows that women exhibit more friendly behavior such as smiles, facial pleasantries, and head nods than men.

6. True—Studies show that women are more open in their praise and give more "nods of approval" than men. They also use more complimentary terms throughout their speech according to Peter Falk, in his book *Word-Play: What Happens When People Talk* (Knopf, 1973).

7. True—Donald Zimmerman and Candace West showed that 75 percent to 93 percent of the interruptions were made by men. ("Sex Roles, Interruptions and Silences in Conversation," in *Language and Sex: Difference and Dominance,* edited by B. Thorne and N. Henley, Newbury House Publishers, 1975.)

8. False—Men use more command terms or imperatives, which makes them sound more demanding. In essence, several researchers have concluded that women tend to be more polite in their speech.

9. False—Men and women definitely differ in their sense of humor. Women are more likely to tell jokes when there is a small, non-mixed sex group, and men were even more likely to tell jokes in a larger, mixed sex group.

10. False—In a survey conducted for the Playboy Channel, people were asked what they wanted to hear when making love. In general, women wanted to be told they were beautiful and loved, and men wanted to hear how good they were in bed and how they pleased their woman.

11. True—Deborah Tannen in her book, *You Just Don't Understand: Women and Men in Conversation* (William Morrow, 1990), found that men usually will not ask for help by asking for directions while women will.

12. False—Several surveys and numerous psychotherapists' observations have indicated that women tend to be more self-critical and more apt to blame themselves than men. Deborah Tannen's findings confirm this as she states that women also tend to use more "apologetic phrases" in their conversations such as, "I'm sorry," "I didn't mean to," or "Excuse me."

13. True—Naturalist Charles Darwin stated that making oneself appear smaller by bowing the head to take up less space can inhibit human aggression. Other researchers found that women tend to inhibit themselves by crossing their legs at the ankles or knees or keeping their elbows to their sides.

14. False—As mentioned earlier, women tend to be more detailed and more descriptive than men in what they say and in how they explain things. As Robin Lakoff's research shows (see Item 1), women tend to use more description in word choices.

15. False—Men tend to touch more than females. According to several researchers, women are more likely to be physically touched by men who guide them through the door, assist them with jackets and coats, and help them into cars.

16. False—Women, not men, appear to be more attentive when listening. Studies consistently show that women exhibit greater eye contact and express approval by smiling and head-nodding as a form of attentiveness and agreement.

17. True—Men and women are equally emotional when they speak. However, women appear to sound more emotional according to researchers such as Robin Lakoff (see Item 1) because they use more psychological-state verbs: I *feel,* I *hope,* and I *wish.*

18. False—In general, men tend to bring up less personal topics than women. Women tend to discuss people, relationships, children, self-improvement, and how certain experiences have affected them. Men, on the other hand, tend to be more "outer directed" as they originate discussions about events, news, sports-related issues, and topics related to more concrete physical tasks.

19. False—Even though men do not bring up as many subjects of conversation as women, men interrupt more which ultimately gives them control of the topics that are raised by women.

20. False—Even though there are many progressive and socially enlightened parents in the modern world, parents still treat their male children differently than their female children. They tend to communicate differently to their children according to their sex, which in turn, induces sex-stereotyped behaviors.

21. True—Even though men make more direct statements, a recent survey indicated that women tend to confront and bring up a problem more often than men. Even though women bring up a problem more often, they tend to be more indirect and polite, as Deborah Tannen relates in her book.

22. False—In several studies, it was determined that women are more animated and livelier speakers than men. Studies also show that women make more eye contact, use more body movement, use more intonation, have a more varied pitch range, and use more emotionally laden words and phrases than men.

23. False—Just as women bring up more topics of conversation, they also ask more questions. According to researchers, this is usually done to facilitate the conversation.

24. False—Men and women usually talk about different things. Studies indicate that women enjoy talking about diet, personal relationships, personal appearance, clothes, self-improvement, children, marriages, personalities of others, actions of others, relationships at work, and emotionally charged issues that have a personal component. Men, on the other hand, enjoy discussing sports, what they did at work, where they went, news events, mechanical gadgets, latest technology, cars, vehicles, and music.

25. True—A recent Gallup poll survey commissioned for Lillian Glass, *He Says, She Says,* found that women rather than men were more likely to introduce the topics of AIDS testing and safe sex.

Chapter 13: Using Teams

Based on research conducted by J. Richard Hackman and others, all of the statements are false.

1. An emphasis on individual accountability essentially undermines any effort to develop a team.

2. Complete authority is likely to lead to anarchy. Limits should be set.

3. Teams should be kept small, have clear boundaries, and have an enabling structure that ensures member motivation.

4. Teams need coaching, counseling, and support at certain intervals during their functioning.

5. The start-up period is critical, which is why managers must spend time and energy coaching and counseling the team during this period. Once the team gets going, the manager should pull back until it reaches a natural break or completes a performance cycle.

6. Training is absolutely critical and should be done before the team is assembled or shortly thereafter. If the needed skills and knowledge change, management should be ready to assist in training to help the team quickly learn the new skills and knowledge.

7. Providing support for teams is difficult. A reward system must recognize and reinforce team performance, an educational system must provide needed skills and knowledge, an information system must provide necessary information, and physical and fiscal resources must be available as needed.

8. Teams need some structure to work effectively.

9. The opposite is true. Managers should set the direction and establish wide limits on constraints with the means to the end determined by the team.

10. Teams cannot effectively be used in organizations that have strong individualistic cultures.

Chapter 14: Understanding Control

The odd-numbered items are all false, and the even-numbered ones are all true. Thus you should have positive responses for the even-numbered items and negative responses for the odd-numbered ones. If you agreed strongly with all of the even ones and disagreed strongly with all of the odd ones, your total score would be zero.

Examine your responses to see which items you responded to incorrectly. Focus your attention on learning why the answers are what they are.

Chapter 15: Defining Quality and Productivity

The odd-numbered items are all true; they refer to eight dimensions of quality (see Table 15.1). Those eight dimensions are performance, features, conformance, reliability, durability, serviceability, aesthetics, and perceived quality. The even-numbered statements are all false. Thus you should have positive responses for the odd-numbered items and negative responses for the even-numbered ones. If you agree strongly with all of the odd-numbered ones and disagree strongly with all of the even-numbered ones, your total score is zero.

Examine your responses to see which items you responded to incorrectly. Focus your attention on learning why the answers are what they are. Remember that the American Society for Quality Control defines quality as the *total* set of features and characteristics of a product or service that bears on its ability to satisfy stated or implied needs of customers.

PHOTO CREDITS

continued from p. iv

Chapter 3

p. 65: Louise Gubb/The Image Works, Inc. p. 68: Forrest Anderson/ Gamma Liaison.

Chapter 4

p. 93: Darryl Estrine; p. 103: Jan-Peter Boning/Zenit.

Chapter 5

p. 119: Chris Buck; p. 131: Joel Sartore, © National Geographic Society.

Chapter 6

p. 154 (left): Robin Moyer/ *Time* Magazine; p. 154 (right): Phil Schermeister, © National Geographic Image Collection; p. 158: Dan Dry.

Chapter 7

p. 175: John Harrington Photography; p. 181: Nina Barnett; p. 185: Tom Stewart.

Chapter 8

p. 201: Greg Kinney; p. 215: Alan Levenson; p. 219: Jeffrey Scott/ Impact Visuals.

Chapter 9

p. 234: Galen Rowell/Mountain Light Photography; p. 247: Tom Herde/*The Boston Globe.*

Chapter 10

p. 260: Ken Jarecke/Contact Press Images; p. 272: David Graham.

Chapter 11

p. 284: Michael A. Schwarz; p. 287: Andy Freeberg.

Chapter 12

p. 322: Ann States/SABA; p. 323: Bob Daemmrich.

Chapter 13

p. 344: Photo courtesy of Bank of Boston; p. 349: Rob Nelson for Time/Black Star.

Chapter 14

p. 375: Jeff Smith; p. 383: Charles O'Rear/Westlight.

Chapter 15

p. 398: Mark Richards; p. 404: Don Gletzer.

NAME INDEX

ORGANIZATION INDEX

SUBJECT INDEX